T0178074

Lecture Notes in Artificial Intelligence   **13442**

Subseries of Lecture Notes in Computer Science

More information about this subseries at https://link.springer.com/bookseries/1244

Dorothea Baumeister · Jörg Rothe (Eds.)

Multi-Agent Systems

19th European Conference, EUMAS 2022
Düsseldorf, Germany, September 14–16, 2022
Proceedings

 Springer

Editors
Dorothea Baumeister ⓘ
University of Düsseldorf
Düsseldorf, Germany

Jörg Rothe ⓘ
University of Düsseldorf
Düsseldorf, Germany

ISSN 0302-9743   ISSN 1611-3349 (electronic)
Lecture Notes in Artificial Intelligence
ISBN 978-3-031-20613-9   ISBN 978-3-031-20614-6 (eBook)
https://doi.org/10.1007/978-3-031-20614-6

LNCS Sublibrary: SL7 – Artificial Intelligence

This Springer imprint is published by the registered company Springer Nature Switzerland AG
The registered company address is: Gewerbestrasse 11, 6330 Cham, Switzerland

Preface

This volume constitutes the proceedings of the 19th European Conference on Multi-Agent Systems (EUMAS 2022), held in September 2022 in Düsseldorf, Germany. In the past two decades, we have seen an enormous increase of interest in agent-based computing and multi-agent systems (MAS). This field is set to become one of the key intelligent systems technologies in the 21st century. The EUMAS conference series aims to provide the main forum for academics and practitioners in Europe to discuss current MAS research and applications.

EUMAS 2022 followed the tradition of previous editions: Oxford 2003, Barcelona 2004, Brussels 2005, Lisbon 2006, Hammamet 2007, Bath 2008, Agia Napa 2009, Paris 2010, Maastricht 2011, Dublin 2012, Toulouse 2013, Prague 2014, Athens 2015, Valencia 2016, Evry 2017, Bergen 2018, Thessaloniki 2020 (virtual), and 2021 in Israel again virtually. Like them, EUMAS 2022 aimed to provide—in academic and industrial efforts—the prime European forum for presenting, encouraging, supporting, and discussing activity in the research and development of multi-agent systems as the annual designated event of the European Association for Multi-Agent Systems (EURAMAS). We are grateful for the guidance provided by the EURAMAS Board, and especially so for the great help and ongoing support of Georgios Chalkiadakis and Davide Grossi.

The peer-review process carried out by the 37 Program Committee (PC) members put great emphasis on ensuring the high quality of accepted contributions. These papers were presented at EUMAS 2022 and are contained in this volume. Each submission to EUMAS 2022 was peer reviewed by at least three PC members in a double-blind fashion. Out of 36 submissions, the PC decided to accept 23 papers for oral presentation. In addition, EUMAS 2022 was preceded by a Doctoral Consortium (PhD Day) at which eight talks were given by PhD students who presented their previous results, ongoing work, and future research plans. Six short papers summarizing such contributions to the PhD Day are also contained in this volume. We thank our PhD students, Linus Boes and Christian Laußmann, for organizing the PhD Day, sifting through the submissions, and selecting them for presentation. We also thank Linus and Christian for designing and running the EUMAS 2022 website (https://ccc.cs.hhu.de/eumas2022/) as well as Ariel Rosenfeld and Nimrod Talmon, who organized EUMAS 2021 last year in Israel (online), for sharing their conference websites with us.

In addition to the papers contained in this volume, the EUMAS 2022 program was highlighted by two great keynote talks given by Carles Sierra (Artificial Intelligence Research Institute, IIIA-CSIC, Barcelona) and Marija Slavkovik (University of Bergen), and Piotr Faliszewski (AGH University of Science and Technology, Kraków) gave a great keynote talk at the PhD Day.

Among the accepted papers, we chose the best ones based on their review scores, and then the reviewers of these papers and the two program chairs held a Borda election to determine the winners of the Best Paper Award ("Maximin Shares under Cardinality Constraints" by Halvard Hummel and Magnus Lie Hetland) and of the Best Paper Runner-Up Award ("Preserving Consistency for Liquid Knapsack Voting" by Pallavi

Jain, Krzysztof Sornat, and Nimrod Talmon). The award recipients were invited to submit an extended version of their outstanding papers for fast-track publication in the Journal of Autonomous Agents and Multi-Agent Systems (JAAMAS). In addition, selected authors were invited to extend their contribution for a special issue of SN Computer Science.

We thank the authors for submitting their work to EUMAS 2022; the PC members of EUMAS 2022 as well as the additional reviewers for reviewing the submissions; the participants for traveling to Düsseldorf, listening to and giving great talks, and making this conference a wonderful event; the invited speakers for their excellent talks; the editors of JAAMAS for inviting the award recipients to extend their papers and enjoy a fast-track publication process; the editors of SN Computer Science for supporting a special issue of extended selected papers; our sponsors: Gesellschaft von Freunden und Förderern der HHU Düsseldorf for supporting our invited speakers and Springer for sponsoring the Best Paper Award; once more Georgios Chalkiadakis and Davide Grossi for their invaluable help in the background; and Linus Boes, Christian Laußmann, and our entire team here in Düsseldorf for their great support and efforts in the local organization.

September 2022

Dorothea Baumeister
Jörg Rothe

Organization

Program Committee Chairs

Dorothea Baumeister   Heinrich-Heine-Universität Düsseldorf, Germany
Jörg Rothe   Heinrich-Heine-Universität Düsseldorf, Germany

Program Committee

Natasha Alechina	Utrecht University, The Netherlands
Ana L. C. Bazzan	Universidade Federal do Rio Grande do Sul, Brazil
Linus Boes	Heinrich-Heine-Universität Düsseldorf, Germany
Sylvain Bouveret	Université Grenoble Alpes, France
Robert Bredereck	TU Clausthal, Germany
Georgios Chalkiadakis	University of Crete, Greece
Sylvie Doutre	University of Toulouse 1 – IRIT, France
Edith Elkind	University of Oxford, UK
Piotr Faliszewski	AGH University of Science and Technology, Poland
Nicoletta Fornara	Università della Svizzera italiana, Switzerland
Malvin Gattinger	University of Amsterdam, The Netherlands
Judy Goldsmith	University of Kentucky, USA
Gianluigi Greco	University of Calabria, Italy
Nathan Griffiths	University of Warwick, UK
Davide Grossi	University of Groningen, The Netherlands
Tatiana V. Guy	Czech Academy of Sciences, Czech Republic
Anna M. Kerkmann	Heinrich-Heine-Universität Düsseldorf, Germany
Franziska Klügl	Örebro University, Sweden
Dušan Knop	Czech Technical University in Prague, Czech Republic
Martin Lackner	TU Wien, Austria
Jérôme Lang	Université Paris-Dauphine, France
Nicolas Maudet	Sorbonne Université, France
Stefano Moretti	Université Paris-Dauphine, France
Jörg P. Müller	TU Clausthal, Germany
Ariel Rosenfeld	Bar-Ilan University, Israel
Ildikó Schlotter	Budapest University of Technology and Economics, Hungary
Heiner Stuckenschmidt	University of Mannheim, Germany
Nimrod Talmon	Ben-Gurion University of the Negev, Israel

Zoi Terzopoulou	University of Amsterdam, The Netherlands
Paolo Turrini	University of Warwick, UK
Onuralp Ulusoy	Utrecht University, The Netherlands
Leon van der Torre	University of Luxembourg, Luxembourg
Angelina Vidali	De Montfort University, UK
Gerhard Weiss	Maastricht University, The Netherlands
Anaëlle Wilczynski	Université Paris-Saclay, France

Organizers of the PhD Day

Linus Boes	Heinrich-Heine-Universität Düsseldorf, Germany
Christian Laußmann	Heinrich-Heine-Universität Düsseldorf, Germany

Local Organizing Committee

Dorothea Baumeister	Heinrich-Heine-Universität Düsseldorf, Germany
Linus Boes	Heinrich-Heine-Universität Düsseldorf, Germany
Claudia Forstinger	Heinrich-Heine-Universität Düsseldorf, Germany
Christian Laußmann	Heinrich-Heine-Universität Düsseldorf, Germany
Jörg Rothe	Heinrich-Heine-Universität Düsseldorf, Germany

Additional Reviewers

Rachael Colley	Rutvik Page
Fatema Tuj Johora	Sören Schleibaum
Gil Leibiker	Cory Siler
Maaike Los	Errikos Streviniotis
Michael Oesterle	Yuzhe Zhang

Sponsors

GESELLSCHAFT VON
FREUNDEN UND FÖRDERERN
DER HHU DÜSSELDORF

SPRINGER NATURE

Invited Talks

Map of Elections: The Story So Far

Piotr Faliszewski

AGH University, Krakow, Poland
faliszew@agh.edu.pl

Overview

The concept of a map of elections was introduced by Szufa et al. [4] and Boehmer et al. [1] as a way to visually present multiple elections, so that the relations among them would be clearly visible and one could present experimental results in a nonaggregate way. To obtain a map of elections, one first collects a dataset where each election has the same number of candidates and the same number of voters, then one computes some distance between each two of them, and finally presents them on a 2D plane as points, so that the Euclidean distances between the points are as close to the distances between the elections that they represent as possible.

In this talk, I will present the main idea of the map, discuss the distances between elections that we use (with a focus on justifying why the positionwise distance is appealing but not perfect [3]), show relations between various statistical cultures [2] and real-life data [1], and argue how the map is useful for presenting the results of experiments in computational social choice. Finally, I will show some open questions regarding the map framework.

Acknowledgments. This project has received funding from the European Research Council (ERC) under the European Union's Horizon 2020 research and innovation programme (grant agreement No. 101002854).

References

1. Boehmer, N., Bredereck, R., Faliszewski, P., Niedermeier, R., Szufa, S.: Putting a compass on the map of elections. In: Proceedings of IJCAI-2021, pp. 59–65 (2021). ijcai.org
2. Boehmer, N., Bredereck, R., Elkind, E., Faliszewski, P., Szufa, S.: Expected frequency matrices of elections: Computation, geometry, and preference learning. Technical report, May 2022. arXiv.2205.07831
3. Boehmer, N., Faliszewski, P., Niedermeier, R., Szufa, S., Was, T.: Understanding distance measures among elections. In: Proceedings of IJCAI-2022, pp. 102–108 (2022). ijcai.org
4. Szufa, S., Faliszewski, P., Skowron, P., Slinko, A., Talmon, N.: Drawing a map of elections in the space of statistical cultures. In: Proceedings of AAMAS-2020, pp. 1341–1349. IFAAMAS (2020)

Biology Bit My Finger or Why AI Ethics Needs Us to Not Forget the Agent

Marija Slavkovik🄳

University of Bergen, Norway
marija.slavkovik@uib.no

Abstract. In the narrative of the latest AI success story, there are no agents. For those who do not conflate AI and data science, the absence of agents is suspicious. For all of us who are interested in ensuring socially responsible AI, the absence of agents is dangerous.

Keywords: AI ethics · Computational agency

There are many ways to define what artificial intelligence is [4, p. 19], but all revolve around computationally recreating some behaviour that we associate with human intelligence. Within the scientific community artificial intelligence is a scientific discipline studying problems of computationally recreating intelligent behaviour. In engineering and the tech business, the focus is not on the problems but the entity itself that exhibits this intelligent behaviour. Here, artificial intelligence is seen as "a 'special form' of ICTs, capable of displaying intelligent behaviour and completing tasks normally said to require human intelligence" [1]. Going further down in "simplifying the message" most press has dispelled even with the 'technology' and simply makes claims such as "AI that recommends diets based on the microbiome relieves constipation", or "New AI Can Automatically Detect a Serious Heart Condition". This is akin to saying things like "biology bit my finger!", "physics fell on my head" or "astronomy made this crater". The computational entity that exhibits some form of intelligent behaviour is well defined in AI – we call it an artificial agent!

Artificial agents are defined very undemandingly as anything that can perceive an environment and act upon that environment. They are studied in two fields: multi-agent systems (MAS) and agent-based modelling (ABM). MAS is concerned with solving reasoning and other operation problems that involve interaction. ABM is concerned with capturing the dynamics of a system that is affected by interaction. Dignum [2] argued that these two main agent approaches, multi-agent systems (MAS) and agent-based modelling (ABM), have largely developed on two separate tracks omitting to observe that the agent paradigm has a crucial role to play in artificial intelligence.

Very basically, there can be no intelligent behaviour without an entity that behaves. Very generally, a large part of intelligent behaviour hinges on adequate management

---

A longer version of this abstract can be found at https://drops.dagstuhl.de/opus/volltexte/2022/16004/.

of relationships with other agents [3]. Without understanding and computationally handling interactions, how close can we get to intelligent behaviour? The agent should be unavoidable in AI, but somehow we continue to manage avoiding them. Yet understanding the responsibility of using AI research and technology and its ethical impact demands facing, naming and shaming the agent.

The more we develop the practical applications of artificial intelligence and use them to automate tasks in our lives and society, the more we are faced with the fact that the people who did those tasks were not only task performers but also parts of a social system. When I make a decision I rarely do so without consideration for others. Any automation that replaces me must do the same. When we say the decision was made by AI we obfuscate all the complex agent interactions that were involved.

AI ethics is an umbrella of research in algorithmic accountability, privacy, transparency, trust, explainability, fairness [5]. The talk addresses the socio-technical system nature of the applications of AI that exist today and why that system needs the tools, insights and new research from the agent communities to be responsibly governed.

References

1. European Commission, Joint Research Centre, Misuraca, G., Noordt, C.: AI watch, artificial intelligence in public services: overview of the use and impact of AI in public services in the EU. Publications Office, Luxembourg (2020). https://doi.org/10.2760/039619
2. Dignum, V.: Social agents: Bridging simulation and engineering. Commun. ACM **60**(11), 32–34 (2017). https://doi.org/10.1145/3148265
3. Dignum, V., Dignum, F.: Agents are dead. long live agents! In: Proceedings of the 19th International Conference on Autonomous Agents and MultiAgent Systems, AAMAS 2020, pp. 1701–1705, Richland, SC, 2020. International Foundation for Autonomous Agents and Multiagent Systems (2020)
4. Russell, S., Norvig, P.: Artificial Intelligence: A Modern Approach, 4th edn. Pearson Education (2021)
5. Slavkovik, M.: Artificial intelligence: is the power matched with responsibility? In: Saeverot, H. (ed.) Meeting the Challenges of Existential Threats Through Educational Innovation: A Proposal for an Expanded Curriculum, Chapter 12, Routledge, UK, 1 November 2021. https://www.taylorfrancis.com/chapters/edit/10.4324/9781003019480-12/artificial-intelligence-marija-slavkovik

Contents

EUMAS 2022 Papers

Iterative Goal-Based Approval Voting 3
    Leyla Ade and Arianna Novaro

Mind the Gap! Runtime Verification of Partially Observable MASs
with Probabilistic Trace Expressions 22
    Davide Ancona, Angelo Ferrando, and Viviana Mascardi

Advising Agent for Service-Providing Live-Chat Operators 41
    Aviram Aviv, Yaniv Oshrat, Samuel Assefa, Toby Mustapha,
    Daniel Borrajo, Manuela Veloso, and Sarit Kraus

Initial Conditions Sensitivity Analysis of a Two-Species Butterfly-Effect
Agent-Based Model 60
    Cristian Berceanu and Monica Patrascu

Proxy Manipulation for Better Outcomes 79
    Gili Bielous and Reshef Meir

The Spread of Opinions via Boolean Networks 96
    Rachael Colley and Umberto Grandi

Robustness of Greedy Approval Rules 116
    Piotr Faliszewski, Grzegorz Gawron, and Bartosz Kusek

Using Multiwinner Voting to Search for Movies 134
    Grzegorz Gawron and Piotr Faliszewski

Allocating Teams to Tasks: An Anytime Heuristic Competence-Based
Approach 152
    Athina Georgara, Juan A. Rodríguez-Aguilar, and Carles Sierra

Collaborative Decision Making for Lane-Free Autonomous Driving
in the Presence of Uncertainty 171
    Pavlos Geronymakis, Dimitrios Troullinos, Georgios Chalkiadakis,
    and Markos Papageorgiou

Maximin Shares Under Cardinality Constraints 188
    Halvard Hummel and Magnus Lie Hetland

Welfare Effects of Strategic Voting Under Scoring Rules 207
  Egor Ianovski, Daria Teplova, and Valeriia Kuka

Preserving Consistency for Liquid Knapsack Voting 221
  Pallavi Jain, Krzysztof Sornat, and Nimrod Talmon

Strategic Nominee Selection in Tournament Solutions 239
  Grzegorz Lisowski

Sybil-Resilient Social Choice with Low Voter Turnout 257
  Reshef Meir, Nimrod Talmon, Gal Shahaf, and Ehud Shapiro

A Survey of Ad Hoc Teamwork Research 275
  *Reuth Mirsky, Ignacio Carlucho, Arrasy Rahman, Elliot Fosong,
  William Macke, Mohan Sridharan, Peter Stone, and Stefano V. Albrecht*

Combining Theory of Mind and Abduction for Cooperation Under
Imperfect Information 294
  Nieves Montes, Nardine Osman, and Carles Sierra

A Modular Architecture for Integrating Normative Advisors in MAS 312
  *Mostafa Mohajeri Parizi, L. Thomas van Binsbergen, Giovanni Sileno,
  and Tom van Engers*

Participatory Budgeting with Multiple Resources 330
  Nima Motamed, Arie Soeteman, Simon Rey, and Ulle Endriss

A Methodology for Formalizing Different Types of Norms 348
  Soheil Roshankish and Nicoletta Fornara

Explainability in Mechanism Design: Recent Advances and the Road Ahead ... 364
  Sharadhi Alape Suryanarayana, David Sarne, and Sarit Kraus

Integrating Quantitative and Qualitative Reasoning for Value Alignment 383
  Jazon Szabo, Jose M. Such, Natalia Criado, and Sanjay Modgil

Resource Allocation to Agents with Restrictions: Maximizing Likelihood
with Minimum Compromise 403
  Yohai Trabelsi, Abhijin Adiga, Sarit Kraus, and S. S. Ravi

PhD Day Short Papers

Proactivity in Intelligent Personal Assistants: A Simulation-Based
Approach 423
  Awais Akbar

Stability, Fairness, and Altruism in Coalition Formation 427
  Anna Maria Kerkmann

Engineering Pro-social Values in Autonomous Agents – Collective
and Individual Perspectives 431
  Nieves Montes

Axiomatic and Algorithmic Study on Different Areas of Collective
Decision Making 435
  Tessa Seeger

Participatory Budgeting: Fairness and Welfare Maximization 439
  Gogulapati Sreedurga

Human Consideration in Analysis and Algorithms for Mechanism Design 444
  Sharadhi Alape Suryanarayana

Author Index 449

EUMAS 2022 Papers

Iterative Goal-Based Approval Voting

Leyla Ade[1] and Arianna Novaro[2(✉)]

[1] Institut für Philosphie, Universität Bayreuth, Bayreuth, Germany
leyla.ade@uni-bayreuth.de
[2] Centre d'Economie de la Sorbonne, Université Paris 1 Panthéon-Sorbonne,
Paris, France
arianna.novaro@univ-paris1.fr

Abstract. In iterative voting, a group of agents who has to take a collective decision has the possibility to individually and sequentially alter their vote, to improve the outcome for themselves. In this paper, we extend with an iterative component the recent framework of goal-based voting, where agents submit compactly expressed individual goals. For the aggregation, we focus on an adaptation of the classical Approval rule to this setting, and we model agents having optimistic or pessimistic satisfaction functions based on the Hamming distance. The results of our analysis are twofold: first, we provide conditions under which the application of the Approval rule is guaranteed to converge to a stable outcome; second, we study the quality of the social welfare yielded by the iteration process.

Keywords: Iterative voting · Preference extensions · Social choice theory

1 Introduction

Iterative voting [23] has been introduced as a framework to model situations where groups of agents are asked to report their preferences about a collective issue, having the option to change their vote based on the current outcome. A classical example is that of a group of colleagues having to choose a time-slot for a meeting by using an online platform that automatically highlights the current most popular options. Compared to classical 'one-shot' voting, the agents thus have the possibility to improve their individual satisfaction about the outcome, and they can do so multiple times.

The result of such a voting procedure thus highly depends, among other things, on the choices for the type of ballots the agents submit, on which kind of preferences they hold, and on which aggregation rule is used to compute the outcome.

In this paper, we extend a recently introduced framework for collective decision-making, where agents can submit complex ballots, by adding an iterative component to it. In *goal-based voting* [26], the agents can submit individual goals over a set of binary issues (compactly expressed as formulas of propositional logic). Although the choice of representation for the agents' input is of course crucial from a computational point of view, for the kind of results presented here we can equivalently think of the input as the agents voting in favour of a set of options (i.e., the models of their goal).

© The Author(s), under exclusive license to Springer Nature Switzerland AG 2022
D. Baumeister and J. Rothe (Eds.): EUMAS 2022, LNAI 13442, pp. 3–21, 2022.
https://doi.org/10.1007/978-3-031-20614-6_1

The following example illustrates the kind of situations we model in this paper.

Example 1. Four agents have to decide together which of three items ($\{a, b, c\}$) to include in a goodies bag for a conference. They each write down their preferred compositions of the bag, by marking with a checkmark ($\checkmark$) the items that should be included, and by a cross ($\times$) those to be left out. Then, the combinations of items approved most often are selected. The table below represents the situation schematically.

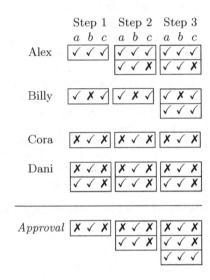

At the first step, the vote of Alex means that all goodies should be included, while according to Dani the bag may or may not include item a, should include b, and should not include c (i.e., Dani equally supports both bag options). By using the *Approval* rule, the bag option where only item b is included will be chosen, since it is approved by two agents (Cora and Dani), while all other options are approved by only one agent.

Since Alex would like more items to be included in the bag, she realizes that by supporting the option without item c, the outcome will change in her favor (by including a preferred option)—she changes her vote accordingly at the second step. Then, Billy decides to support the option which includes all three items, since this differs from their truthful preference in just one item, unlike the current options in the outcome.

We can see how, in Example 1, beyond the choice of the aggregation rule, the behaviour of the agents is determined by how their preferences over outcomes are defined. For instance, the four agents there were concerned with adding preferable options to the outcome, but they could have focused on withdrawing less desirable options instead. Moreover, since in their vote they can support multiple options, and the outcome itself may not return a unique option, we need to consider complex preferences over sets.

In order to handle these kind of situations, we introduce a framework for iterated goal-based voting and we study it for (an adaption to this setting of) the *Approval* rule. We consider agents having two types of satisfaction functions based on the Hamming distance—as well as two classes of functions generalizing these. In addition to the novelty of extending with an iterative component the existing model of goal-based voting, our contribution is twofold: first, we provide simple conditions under which we can *guarantee that the iterative process will terminate*. Second, we analyze the *quality yielded by the iteration process*, according to three classical notions of social welfare (i.e., the utilitarian, Nash, and egalitarian welfare notions).

Related Work. Iterative voting has been a popular research direction in recent years within the field of computational social choice—cf. Meir's work for an overview [23,24]. The approach is often game-theoretic, focusing for instance on modeling the strategic behaviour of agents participating in Doodle polls [35], or agents having to reach a consensus under a deadline [3]. The type of problems we study in this paper fall in the stream of literature analyzing the conditions for convergence of an iterative process [21,22,25,28] and of the quality of its final outcome [7,32], for different rules and settings. Particularly relevant is the study of iterative judgment aggregation by Terzopoulou and Endriss [34], who analyzed the iteration of the premise-based and the plurality rules—where the latter corresponds to a resolute version of our *Approval* rule.

Judgment (or binary) aggregation [11,14,16] can be seen as a special case of goal-based voting, where the agents are only allowed to submit one choice of acceptance or rejection decision for each of the issues at stake (i.e., giving support for just one bag option in the situation described in Example 1). By contrast, the recently introduced framework of goal-based voting [26] that we extend here, allows the agents to submit more complex goals which can be made true by multiple complete choices of values for the binary issues (as they are expressed in the language of propositional logic).

A framework which is also closely related is that of belief merging, where propositional formulas representing beliefs are aggregated. In particular, the Δ_μ^{Σ, d_H}-rule [19] in belief merging coincides with the *Approval* rule in goal-based voting. Although the two frameworks are technically similar, their approaches and studied problems are rather different. For example, Delgrande et al. [9] define a framework for iterated belief revision which differs from our approach in one key aspect: while we assume agents to keep a truthful goal during the iteration process, and to modify their votes according to it, in iterated belief revision the agents change their beliefs, knowledge or opinions through the iteration. More recently, Schwind and Konieczny [33] have proposed an incremental belief merging approach for iterated belief revision. However, to the best of our knowledge, ours is the first study of iterative voting for this kind of complex input.

While our definitions for the iteration process are general, in this paper we focus on the *Approval* rule, which is an adaptation to goal-based voting of the classical approval rule in voting, that has received undying attention by researchers due to its simplicity and versatility (see, e.g., the handbook by Laslier and Sanver [20]). The plurality rule [25] and positional scoring rules [15] have been studied as well in the literature on iterative voting, while the majority rule was studied in the context of a slightly different framework of iterative proposal, comparison and choice of collective options [2].

Finally, a key component of the iteration dynamics is the choice of the satisfaction function held by the agents to evaluate the current outcome with respect to their truthful goal. Previous work in strategic goal-based voting [27] and belief merging [12] has focused on a simple notion of dichotomous preferences (separating between the models and the non-models of the agents' goals). By contrast, we follow here a preference extension approach [5,13,18,30], and in particular the classical work by Packard [29], by which we define satisfaction functions based on the Hamming distance.

Paper Structure. We recall the general setting of goal-based voting and its *Approval* rule in Sect. 2.1. Then, we define the agents' satisfaction functions in Sect. 2.2 and we introduce the key notion of iterated goal-based voting in Sect. 2.3. We present the main termination results in Sect. 3. The definition and the analysis of social welfare for the iterated *Approval* rule can be found in Sect. 4. We conclude in Sect. 5.

2   Preliminaries

In this section we recall the main definitions of goal-based voting, and in particular of the *Approval* rule. Then, we show how to model the agents' preferences with respect to potential outcomes by using a pessimistic and optimistic definition based on the Hamming distance. Finally, we define the iteration process for goal-based voting.

2.1   Goal-Based Voting

In goal-based voting, a finite set of *agents*, or *voters*, $\mathcal{N} = \{1, \ldots, n\}$, takes a collective decision on a finite set of binary issues $\mathcal{I} = \{1, \ldots, m\}$. In the domain $\{0, 1\}$ of the issues, a 1 denotes acceptance and a 0 denotes rejection.

The *goal* of agent i is expressed as a consistent propositional formula γ_i, whose language $\mathcal{L}$ is built from the variables in $\mathcal{I}$ and the classical propositional connectives. The set of *models* of a goal γ_i, denoted by $Mod(\gamma_i)$, consists of all those interpretations that make the formula γ_i true. Namely, each $v \in Mod(\gamma_i)$ is a function $v : \mathcal{I} \to \{0, 1\}$ which assigns truth-value false (0) or true (1) to each variable in $\mathcal{I}$. We interchangeably represent a model v as a vector $(v(1), \ldots, v(m))$. A *profile* is a vector collecting the goals for all agents in $\mathcal{N}$ over the issues in $\mathcal{I}$, and we denote it by $\boldsymbol{\Gamma} = (\gamma_1, \ldots, \gamma_n)$.[1]

---

[1] Observe that, as mentioned in the introduction, while the choice of representation of the agents' input—i.e., goals expressed compactly as propositional formulas, or explicitly as the set of their models—has immediate consequences on the computational complexity of some related problems [26], since these fall outside of the scope of this paper we will often represent the corresponding set of models for ease of illustration.

The agents take a collective decision by means of a *voting rule*. For $\mathcal{L}$ the set of all possible goals (i.e., all propositional formulas on the variables in $\mathcal{I}$), a voting rule F is a function mapping profiles with any number of agents and issues (n and m) to a non-empty subset of all interpretations, i.e., we have $F : (\mathcal{L})^n \rightarrow \mathcal{P}(\{0, 1\}^m) \setminus \{\emptyset\}$. The co-domain of F is the power-set of all vectors to allow for *irresolute* rules, i.e., rules that on some profiles may return multiple interpretations as the outcome.

Given a profile $\boldsymbol{\Gamma}$ for n agents and m issues, and an interpretation $v \in \{0, 1\}^m$, the *support of v in $\boldsymbol{\Gamma}$*, denoted by $supp_{\boldsymbol{\Gamma}}(v)$, is the number of agents in $\boldsymbol{\Gamma}$ having v as one model of their goal, i.e., $supp_{\boldsymbol{\Gamma}}(v) := |\{i \in \mathcal{N} \mid v \in Mod(\gamma_i)\}|$.

Many rules have been defined to aggregate the goals submitted by the agents [26]; we focus here on an adaptation to goal-based voting of the well-known approval rule, which returns all those interpretations that received the most support from the agents (i.e., that are models of the most goals in the profile).

Definition 1. *For any profile $\boldsymbol{\Gamma}$ of n agents and m issues, the* Approval *rule returns:*

$$Approval(\boldsymbol{\Gamma}) = \operatorname{argmax}_{v \in \cup_{i \in \mathcal{N}} Mod(\gamma_i)} supp_{\boldsymbol{\Gamma}}(v).$$

Although the irresoluteness of this rule can be considered a drawback, the *Approval* rule also satisfies many desirable properties. Among them, we can mention a form of *consensus* identification: that is, the rule is guaranteed to return the set of interpretations which models all of the agents' goals, if such set is non-empty. This is not a trivial requirement, as *independent* rules (such as some issue-wise majority rules that have been proposed for goal-based voting [26]) may fail to do so.

2.2 Satisfaction Functions

In this section we present functions that can be used to model the agents' preferences over outcomes. In fact, an agent will want to alter their vote depending on how much they like the current outcome, and on whether they can make it better for themselves.

A *satisfaction function* $sat : \mathcal{L} \times \mathcal{P}(\{0, 1\}^m) \rightarrow \mathbb{R}$ is a function which takes as input an agent's goal and a possible outcome, and it returns a real number, where a higher value indicates a greater satisfaction. For simplicity, we will consider situations where all the agents are assumed to have the same type of satisfaction function.

We say that an agent i with satisfaction function sat (weakly) prefers an outcome $F(\boldsymbol{\Gamma})$ to an outcome $F(\boldsymbol{\Gamma}')$, given her goal γ_i, when her satisfaction for $F(\boldsymbol{\Gamma})$ is at least as high as her satisfaction for $F(\boldsymbol{\Gamma}')$. Formally, we have:

$$F(\boldsymbol{\Gamma}) \succeq_i F(\boldsymbol{\Gamma}') \text{ if and only if } sat(\gamma_i, F(\boldsymbol{\Gamma})) \geq sat(\gamma_i, F(\boldsymbol{\Gamma}')).$$

Hence, the satisfaction function, in combination with an agent's goal, yields a preference ordering over the possible outcomes of a rule. The strict part of the ordering is induced by a strictly higher satisfaction.

Among the simplest satisfaction functions we find those based on a *dichotomous* view of agents' preferences, where an agent is equally satisfied by any model of their goal, and equally dissatisfied by any non-model. Three such functions have been studied in the context of strategy-proof belief merging for the Δ_μ^{Σ,d_H}-rule [12], which is equivalent to our *Approval* rule. For these functions, the rule has been shown to be strategy-proof, which means that no agent can improve her satisfaction by altering her vote, and thus it always (trivially) terminates.

While appealing in reason of their simplicity, dichotomous satisfaction functions lack nuance by definition: e.g., an agent whose goal has $Mod(\gamma) = \{(000)\}$ is equally dissatisfied by $F(\boldsymbol{\Gamma}) = \{(111)\}$ and by $F(\boldsymbol{\Gamma}) = \{(001)\}$, while arguably the latter is 'closer' to the agent's goal than the former. Therefore, we now move to consider a more sophisticated view of agents' preferences based on the Hamming distance.

Given vectors $v, w \in \{0,1\}^m$, the *Hamming distance between* v *and* w corresponds to the number of entries on which they differ, i.e., $H(v,w) = |\{j \mid v(j) \neq w(j)\}|$. Since the *Approval* rule is irresolute, in order to define agents' preferences we need to compare a *set* of vectors (i.e., the models of an agent's goal) with another *set* of vectors (i.e., the interpretations in the outcome). We thus need to extend preferences over vectors to preferences over sets of vectors.

The *lowest Hamming distance between a vector* w *and a set of vectors* W is the minimal Hamming distance that w has to any element of W: given a vector $w \in \{0,1\}^m$ and a set of vectors $W \in \mathcal{P}(\{0,1\}^m)$, we let $lowH(w,W) = \min_{v \in W} H(w,v)$. For ease of notation, we also write $lowH(v,\gamma)$ instead of $lowH(v, Mod(\gamma))$.

We can now define two satisfaction functions, for *H-optimist* and *H-pessimist* agents:

Definition 2. *Given a profile* $\boldsymbol{\Gamma} = (\gamma_1, \ldots \gamma_n)$ *for* m *issues, and a rule* F, *let*

$$d_{optH}(\gamma_i, F(\boldsymbol{\Gamma})) = \min_{w \in F(\boldsymbol{\Gamma})} lowH(w, Mod(\gamma_i))$$

$$d_{pessH}(\gamma_i, F(\boldsymbol{\Gamma})) = \max_{w \in F(\boldsymbol{\Gamma})} lowH(w, Mod(\gamma_i))$$

be the H-optimist and H-pessimist distances. Then, the optH and pessH satisfaction functions are defined as $sat(\gamma_i, F(\boldsymbol{\Gamma})) = m - d_{sat}(\gamma_i, F(\boldsymbol{\Gamma}))$ *for* $sat \in \{optH, pessH\}$.

Both functions range between 0 and m, where a higher value expresses a greater satisfaction. Given a set of interpretations in an outcome, an H-optimist's and H-pessimist's satisfaction is only based on the best or worst interpretation in this set, respectively, according to the agent's truthful goal. Observe, in particular, that the preference ordering over outcomes for an H-pessimist will have as its top element the set of models of their goal plus any of its subsets (and nothing else), while the H-optimist will also include at the top any of its supersets. The two function are different, and can thus yield different preference orderings over outcomes. For instance, for $Mod(\gamma) = \{(0000), (1000)\}$ and outcomes $A = \{(0110)\}$ and $B = \{(0111), (0100)\}$, we get that $A \succ B$ for *pessH*, while

$B \succ A$ for $optH$, since we have $lowH((0110), \gamma) = 2$, $lowH((0111), \gamma) = 3$ and $lowH((0100), \gamma) = 1$. However, the two functions coincide when $|F(\boldsymbol{\Gamma})| = 1$.

We conclude this section by observing that the $optH$ and $pessH$ satisfaction functions are instances of the $maxi\text{-}max$ and $maxi\text{-}min$ preference extensions (respectively) that Packard characterized [29]. In addition to connectedness and transitivity, the $maxi\text{-}max$ extension is the only extension satisfying what Packard calls the $(c.3)$ and $(f.1)$ properties, while $maxi\text{-}min$ is the only extension satisfying the $(d.3)$ and $(e.1)$ properties. While properties $(e.1)$ and $(f.1)$ compare preferences over three sets, properties $(c.3)$ and $(d.3)$ only compare two sets A and B. We report here the latter two properties, as some of our results in Sect. 3 generalize to the class of functions satisfying them (as well as connectedness and transitivity):

(c.3) $A \cup B \succeq B$,
(d.3) $A \succeq A \cup B$.

Property $(c.3)$ states that a set (of interpretations over the issues, in our case) is always considered at least as good as any of its subsets. Conversely, property $(d.3)$ states that a set is always considered at least as good as any of its supersets. Since our optimist (respectively, pessimist) agents only judge an outcome based on the best (respectively, worst) of the included interpretations, according to their individual goals, it is easy to see why indeed for them a superset (respectively, a subset) may be preferred.

2.3 The Iteration Process

The iteration process is based on the idea that agents may realize that by voting differently, they can get a better outcome (with respect to their truthful goal).[2]

For a profile $\boldsymbol{\Gamma}$ and an agent $i \in \mathcal{N}$, let $(\boldsymbol{\Gamma}_{-i}, \gamma'_i)$ be the profile $\boldsymbol{\Gamma}$ where only agent i changes her goal from γ_i to γ'_i. We say that agent i with satisfaction sat has an *incentive to alter* her goal γ_i to goal γ'_i at profile $\boldsymbol{\Gamma}$ under rule F if we have that $F(\boldsymbol{\Gamma}_{-i}, \gamma'_i) \succ_i F(\boldsymbol{\Gamma})$. Given a rule F, a satisfaction function sat and a profile $\boldsymbol{\Gamma}$, we consider iterations over profiles where $\boldsymbol{\Gamma}^0 = \boldsymbol{\Gamma}$ is the initial (truthful) profile and for each stage of the iteration $t \geq 0$ we have $\boldsymbol{\Gamma}^{t+1} = (\boldsymbol{\Gamma}^t_{-i}, \gamma'_i)$ for some agent $i \in \mathcal{N}$ such that $sat(\gamma^0_i, F(\boldsymbol{\Gamma}^t)) < sat(\gamma^0_i, F(\boldsymbol{\Gamma}^{t+1}))$, i.e., an agent who has an incentive to alter at $\boldsymbol{\Gamma}^t$. Note that outcomes are always compared to the initial (truthful) goal γ^0_i.

The agents act according to a *best response dynamics*, i.e., if agent i has an incentive to alter her vote, then a goal γ' is a *best response* at step t, if for any other goal γ it is the case that $sat(\gamma^0_i, F(\boldsymbol{\Gamma}^t_{-i}, \gamma)) \leq sat(\gamma^0_i, F(\boldsymbol{\Gamma}^t_{-i}, \gamma'))$. This means that an agent does not choose just any alternative goal which improves the outcome for her, but the best possible alteration. At any stage t of the iteration,

---

[2] In the case of strategy-proofness this action is called a *manipulation*; we prefer to avoid this negative connotation for iterative voting and we simply say that agents *alter* their vote.

there could be multiple agents having an incentive to alter, each having multiple possible best responses. If this is the case, one agent is chosen randomly, as there is only one alteration at each step. Thus, in principle, multiple different iteration dynamics are possible from one initial profile.

We say that an iteration process *terminates*, or *converges*, if after a finite number of steps no agent has an incentive to alter her vote. In case for some stage $t > 0$ and $s < t$ it is the case that $\boldsymbol{\Gamma}^t = \boldsymbol{\Gamma}^s$, the iteration process does not terminate (i.e., it is *circular*).

In line with previous work on iterative voting [23], our agents are assumed to be *myopic*, i.e., they select their best response by only considering the next step of the iteration process and do not predict future steps; *improvement-driven*, i.e., an agent always chooses to alter her vote if this increases her satisfaction (hence, at each step, some agent among those who could alter their vote actually does it); and *fully informed* [34], i.e., they know the other agents' votes and which voting rule is being used.

3   Termination Results for the Approval Rule

In this section we study the dynamics of iteration for the *Approval* rule, considering different satisfaction functions for the agents. As mentioned in Sect. 2.2, agents with dichotomous satisfaction functions do not have any incentive to alter their vote under the *Approval* rule, but they do if their satisfaction functions are based on the Hamming distance (as hinted in Example 1).

Our first result shows that the iteration of goal-based voting under the *Approval* rule for H-pessimist agents always terminates. We start by proving the following Lemma, which shows that the *support* of the winning alternatives at stage t (i.e., for any of the interpretations in the outcome at t, the number of agents whose current goal has it as a model), defined as $k_t = |\{i \in \mathcal{N} \mid v \in Mod(\gamma_i^t)$ for $v \in Approval(\boldsymbol{\Gamma}^t)\}|$, always increases in the iteration of *Approval* for H-pessimist agents.

Lemma 1. *If every agent* $i \in \mathcal{N}$ *is a H-pessimist, then every alteration of an agent's goal from stage t to $t+1$ will result in* $k_{t+1} > k_t$ *under the* Approval *rule.*

Proof. Let $\mathcal{N}$ be the set of H-pessimist voters, $\mathcal{I}$ the set of issues, and $\boldsymbol{\Gamma}^0$ the initial (truthful) voting profile. First, observe that no H-pessimist would prefer an outcome $Approval(\boldsymbol{\Gamma}^{t+1})$ that is a superset of the current $Approval(\boldsymbol{\Gamma}^t)$. In fact, for any sets $X' \subseteq X$ we have $d_{pessH}(\gamma_i, X) \geq d_{pessH}(\gamma_i, X')$ by definition, and since an alteration which results in a lower support $k_{t+1} < k_t$ would lead to $Approval(\boldsymbol{\Gamma}^t) \subset Approval(\boldsymbol{\Gamma}^{t+1})$, no agent i would alter their γ_i^t in such a way. Hence, the support from stage t to stage $t+1$ can either stay the same or increase.

Take t to be the first stage at which, by an alteration of some agent i, we have $k_{t+1} = k_t$. By the reasoning above, we get that for any stage $r < t$:

$$k_{r+1} > k_r, \quad \text{and} \tag{1}$$

$$Approval(\boldsymbol{\Gamma}^{r+1}) \subseteq Approval(\boldsymbol{\Gamma}^r) \subseteq Approval(\boldsymbol{\Gamma}^0). \tag{2}$$

The only way an agent i can improve her satisfaction by keeping the support constant is by withdrawing her support from the least preferred interpretations in the current outcome. Take $W = \{w_0, \ldots, w_l\} \subseteq Approval(\boldsymbol{\Gamma}^t)$ to be these interpretations, i.e., each w_j is such that $lowH(w_j, \gamma_i) = d_{pessH}(\gamma_i, Approval(\boldsymbol{\Gamma}^t))$ and for all $v \in Approval(\boldsymbol{\Gamma}^t) \setminus W$ we have $lowH(v, \gamma_i) < lowH(w_j, \gamma_i)$. Hence, $lowH(w_j, \gamma_i) \neq 0$ and thus $w_j \notin Mod(\gamma_i)$ for all $w_j \in W$.

We now distinguish two cases on how agent i could alter at stage t:

(a) The agent withdraws support from the interpretations in the outcome which are the most distant to her goal, i.e., $Approval(\boldsymbol{\Gamma}^{t+1}) = Approval(\boldsymbol{\Gamma}^t) \setminus W$. Since these interpretations w_j are not models of her goal and yet they are in $Mod(\gamma_i^t)$, agent i must have altered her vote at some stage $r_j < t$ for every such $w_j \in W$. But by (1), we know that agent i added support to all the interpretations in $Approval(\boldsymbol{\Gamma}^{r_j})$ and thus by (2) she supports all those in $Approval(\boldsymbol{\Gamma}^t)$. Hence, the possibility to improve at t contradicts the fact that the alteration at stage r_j was a best response.

(b) The agents withdraws support from the interpretations in W and also adds support for some 'better' interpretations, i.e., $Approval(\boldsymbol{\Gamma}^{t+1}) = Approval(\boldsymbol{\Gamma}^t) \setminus W \cup V$ for some set V such that for all $v \in V$ we have $lowH(v, \gamma_i) < lowH(w_j, \gamma_i)$. Observe that for this alteration to be effective, it must be that all $v \in V$ are only lacking the support of 1 agent to be added in the outcome, i.e. $supp_{\boldsymbol{\Gamma}^t}(v) = k_t - 1$. But by (1) and the fact that each model can only gain the support of 1 more agent per alteration, we know that at stage r_j—as defined at point (a) of this proof—either:

(b.1) Agent i supported some $v \in V$. Then, the current alteration is not possible.

(b.2) Agent i did not support the elements in V. But then, every $v \in V$ was in $Approval(\boldsymbol{\Gamma}^{r_j})$ and so the alteration at stage r_j was not a best response.

In conclusion, there will never be such an alteration at stage t by an H-pessimist. $\qquad\square$

Thanks to Lemma 1 we can now prove our first main theorem, which shows that the iteration of goal-based voting under the *Approval* rule is guaranteed to terminate for H-pessimist agents, assuming no restrictions on the alterations available to them.[3]

Theorem 1. *If every agent is a H-pessimist, then iterated* Approval *voting terminates after at most* $|\mathcal{N}| - k_0$ *steps.*

---

[3] Note that this does not hold for arbitrary weak preferences over sets of interpretations w_j. Let the best outcomes for agent 1 be $\mathcal{P}(\{w_1, w_3, w_5\}) \cup \mathcal{P}(\{w_2, w_4\})$; those of agent 2 be $\mathcal{P}(\{w_2, w_4, w_5\}) \cup \mathcal{P}(\{w_1, w_3\})$; and that of agent 3 be $\{w_5\}$. Initially, agent 1 submits $\{w_2, w_4\}$, agent 2 sends $\{w_1, w_3\}$ and agent 3 sends $\{w_5\}$. Then, agent 1 alters to $\{w_1, w_2, w_5\}$, while agent 2 alters to $\{w_2, w_3\}$ next. Not only we have $k_1 = k_2$, but we can construct a circular iteration following a similar structure to that of the example in Table 2.

Proof. Let $\boldsymbol{\Gamma}^0$ be the initial (truthful) profile. By Lemma 1, any alteration of an H-pessimist from stage t to $t+1$ leads to $k_{t+1} > k_t$. Thus, an agent can only add support to interpretations already in the outcome. Since any interpretation can only receive at most $|\mathcal{N}|$ units of support and any $v \in Approval(\boldsymbol{\Gamma}^0)$ has support k_0, there can be at most $|\mathcal{N}| - k_0$ many alterations. Thus, the iteration stops in at most $|\mathcal{N}| - k_0$ steps. □

Given the result of Theorem 1 for H-pessimist agents, we may wonder if the same holds for H-optimist agents. Unfortunately, Table 1 gives us a negative answer, as it shows an example of an initial profile which leads to a circular iteration for H-optimist agents for the given alteration choices. In fact, for this initial profile $\boldsymbol{\Gamma}^0$ over five agents and six issues, the iteration leads to profile $\boldsymbol{\Gamma}^6$ which is identical to profile $\boldsymbol{\Gamma}^2$.

Table 1. A non-terminating iteration under the *Approval* rule for H-optimist agents.

	Γ^0	Γ^1	Γ^2	Γ^3	Γ^4	Γ^5	Γ^6
$Mod(\gamma_1)$	(000000)	**(000000)**	(000000)	**(000000)**	(000000)	**(000000)**	(000000)
		(110000)	(110000)	**(100000)**	(100000)	**(110000)**	(110000)
				(111110)	(111110)		
$Mod(\gamma_2)$	(111111)	(111111)	**(111111)**	(111111)	**(111111)**	(111111)	**(111111)**
			(111100)	(111100)	**(111110)**	(111110)	**(111100)**
			(100000)	(100000)			**(100000)**
$Mod(\gamma_3)$	(111000)	(111000)	(111000)	(111000)	(111000)	(111000)	(111000)
	(100000)	(100000)	(100000)	(100000)	(100000)	(100000)	(100000)
	(110000)	(110000)	(110000)	(110000)	(110000)	(110000)	(110000)
$Mod(\gamma_4)$	(111000)	(111000)	(111000)	(111000)	(111000)	(111000)	(111000)
	(110000)	(110000)	(110000)	(110000)	(110000)	(110000)	(110000)
	(111100)	(111100)	(111100)	(111100)	(111100)	(111100)	(111100)
$Mod(\gamma_5)$	(111000)	(111000)	(111000)	(111000)	(111000)	(111000)	(111000)
	(111100)	(111100)	(111100)	(111100)	(111100)	(111100)	(111100)
	(111110)	(111110)	(111110)	(111110)	(111110)	(111110)	(111110)
Approval	(111000)	(111000)	(111000)	(111000)	(111000)	(111000)	(111000)
	(110000)	(110000)	(110000)	(100000)	(111110)	(110000)	(110000)
			(111100)	(111100)			(111100)

In Theorem 2 we show a result which generalizes the situation in Table 1. In fact, not only the result of Theorem 1 for H-pessimists does not hold for H-optimists, but termination cannot be analogously guaranteed for their respective generalizations to the classes of satisfaction functions defined by the $(c.3)$ and $(d.3)$ properties (as well as connectedness and transitivity) presented in Sect. 2.2.

Theorem 2. *Iterated* Approval *voting might not terminate for the classes of agents' satisfaction functions defined by the $(c.3)$ or $(d.3)$ properties.*

Proof. We give two examples of initial profiles and satisfaction functions—belonging, respectively, to the class of functions defined by the $(c.3)$ or $(d.3)$ properties—which lead to a circular iteration according to our iteration process.

For the class of functions defined by the $(c.3)$ property, it suffices to consider the Example given in Table 1, since the $optH$ function is an instance of this class.

For the class by the $(d.3)$ property, consider the Example given in Table 2: starting from the initial profile Γ^0, we get by a sequence of alterations to profile Γ^6 which is identical to Γ^2. For a function satisfying property $(d.3)$ to lead to the alterations in the Example, we should have $\{(111)\} \succ_1 \{(110), (000), (111), (011)\}$, $\{(011)\} \succ_1 \{(110)\}$ and $\{(111)\} \succ_1 \{(000)\}$ for agent 1. For agent 2, the satisfaction function should be such that $\{(110)\} \succ_2 \{(111)\}$ and $\{(000)\} \succ_2 \{(011)\}$.

A function which satisfies these constraints, as well as property $(d.3)$, could be one where the agents prefer singletons over bigger sets, and they prefer to get an outcome which satisfies the other agent's goal rather than their own: i.e., agents who are decisive (preferring singletons) and altruistic (prioritizing the satisfaction of the other agents).

Table 2. A non-terminating iteration of *Approval* for a satisfaction function in the $(d.3)$-class.

	Γ^0	Γ^1	Γ^2	Γ^3	Γ^4	Γ^5	Γ^6
$Mod(\gamma_1)$	(110)	**(111)**	(111)	**(011)**	(011)	**(111)**	(111)
	(000)	**(110)**	(110)	**(000)**	(000)	**(110)**	(110)
$Mod(\gamma_2)$	(111)	(111)	**(110)**	(110)	**(000)**	(000)	**(110)**
	(011)	(011)	**(011)**	(011)	**(111)**	(111)	**(011)**
Approval	(110)	(111)	(110)	(011)	(000)	(111)	(110)
	(000)						
	(111)						
	(011)						

Therefore, the iteration for the classes of satisfaction functions defined by the $(c.3)$ and $(d.3)$ properties is not guaranteed to terminate under the *Approval* rule. ☐

Theorem 2 is related to a result by Terzopoulou and Endriss [34], who proved that the plurality rule with lexicographic tie-breaking (which is a resolute version of *Approval*) may not converge for *truth-biased* agents[4] with Hamming-distance preferences.

In order to guarantee termination for the *Approval* rule in these general cases, and thus also for H-optimist agents, we need to introduce a restriction on the type of alterations that the agents are allowed to make. In particular, we consider a restriction whereby agents are only allowed to alter their vote by either adding or subtracting models from their current goal's set of models, but not mix these two actions.

---

[4] A *truth-biased* agent has an incentive to alter to her truthful goal when the corresponding outcome which will be obtained by this alteration is at least as satisfying as the current outcome.

Definition 3. *Given a profile Γ and a set $V \subseteq \{0,1\}^m$, an agent i with an incentive to alter her vote does a minimal alteration from stage t to stage $t+1$ if $Mod(\gamma_i^{t+1})$ is equal to either:*

(i) $Mod(\gamma_i^t) \cup V$, or
(ii) $Mod(\gamma_i^t) \setminus V$.

Under a minimal alteration, an agent can thus only submit a goal at step $t+1$ whose models are a superset or a subset of their goal at step t, but not a goal whose models include only some of the old models plus some new ones: intuitively, we can see this alteration as an agent wanting to appear either more decisive (i.e., by refining their goal) or more open to compromise (i.e., by making their goal more easily satisfied).[5]

The following two results show that minimal alterations are enough to ensure termination, when considering agents whose satisfaction functions are in the classes defined by the $(c.3)$ and $(d.3)$ properties, respectively.

Theorem 3. *Iterated Approval voting with agents whose satisfaction function has property $(c.3)$, using minimal alterations only, always terminates. The iteration takes at most $|\{w \in \{0,1\}^m \mid supp_{\Gamma^0}(w) < k_0\}|$ steps.*

Proof. Let $\mathcal{N}$ be a set of voters, $\mathcal{I}$ a set of issues and Γ^0 the initial (truthful) profile. For a stage t, let C and B be two elements of $\mathcal{P}(\{0,1\}^m)$ such that $C \cap A = \emptyset$ and $B \subset A$ for $A = Approval(\Gamma^t)$ the current outcome.

From stage t to stage $t+1$ of the iteration, the current outcome A can only change according to one of the following four cases:

(1) $Approval(\Gamma^{t+1}) = A \cup C$,
(2) $Approval(\Gamma^{t+1}) = A \setminus B$,
(3) $Approval(\Gamma^{t+1}) = A \setminus B \cup C$,
(4) $Approval(\Gamma^{t+1}) = C$.

The four cases above describe all possible ways the outcome could change through an alteration, for some choices of C and B. However, in order to reach case (3) or (4) an agent would have to alter in a non-minimal way, i.e. using an alteration that does not fall under Definition 3. In fact, for case (3), the altering agent would have to lower the support of all models in B (hence, removing them from the models of her current goal) while raising it for all models in C (hence, adding them to the models of her goal), resulting in a combination of dilatation *and* erosion. Analogously for case (4), where the agent would have to lower the support for all interpretations in the current outcome.

An alteration resulting in case (2) will never be performed by an agent whose satisfaction function has property $(c.3)$, since $A \cup B \succeq A$ directly implies that $A \cup B \succeq A \setminus B$.

---

[5] Alterations (i) and (ii) from Definition 3 correspond to *dilatation* and *erosion* manipulation, respectively, in the literature on strategic goal-based voting [27] and belief merging [12].

Hence, such an agent would only alter to reach a new outcome as in case (1). This implies that the outcome strictly increases in size at each step, since $|A| < |A \cup C|$.

Therefore, the iteration will terminate after at most as many steps as there are interpretations not in the outcome of $\boldsymbol{\Gamma}^0$, i.e., $|\{w \in \{0,1\}^m \mid supp_{\boldsymbol{\Gamma}^0}(w) < k_0\}|$. $\qquad\square$

Theorem 3 yields us two immediate corollaries. First of all, since $optH$ is a satisfaction function which satisfies the $(c.3)$ property, the result applies to H-optimist agents.

Corollary 1. *Iterated* Approval *voting with H-optimists, using minimal alterations, always terminates. The iteration takes at most* $|\{w \in \{0,1\}^m \mid supp_{\boldsymbol{\Gamma}^0}(w) < k_0\}|$ *steps.*

Moreover, the proof of Theorem 3 implies that the outcome at step $t+1$ is always a superset of the outcome at step t—and in particular, of the outcome of $\boldsymbol{\Gamma}^0$.

Corollary 2. *For H-optimists agents restricted to minimal alterations, we have that $Approval(\boldsymbol{\Gamma}^0) \subseteq Approval(\boldsymbol{\Gamma}^t)$ for any stage t.*

We can now prove an analogous result of Theorem 3 for the $(d.3)$ property.

Theorem 4. *Iterated* Approval *voting with agents whose satisfaction function has property $(d.3)$, using minimal alterations only, always terminates and the iteration takes at most $|Approval(\boldsymbol{\Gamma}^0)| - 1$ steps.*

Proof. Let $\mathcal{N}$ be a set of voters, $\mathcal{I}$ a set of issues and $\boldsymbol{\Gamma}^0$ the initial profile. For any stage t, let C and B be two elements of $\mathcal{P}(\{0,1\}^m)$ such that $C \cap A = \emptyset$ and $B \subset A$ for $A = Approval(\boldsymbol{\Gamma}^t)$. We distinguish the same cases as in the proof of Theorem 3.

Cases (3) and (4) are still non-minimal alterations and can therefore be discarded. Assume an alteration leads to a change as per case (1); by property $(d.3)$ we know that no superset is preferred, i.e., $A \succeq A \cup C$. Hence, the only change an agent with a satisfaction function with property $(d.3)$ will consider is of kind (2). These changes, however, will lead to a strict decrease in the size of the outcome from each step t to $t+1$. Hence, the iteration will terminate at the latest when there is only one model left in the outcome, i.e., after at most $|Approval(\boldsymbol{\Gamma}^0)| - 1$ many steps. $\qquad\square$

We have thus established conditions which ensure termination results for our choices of optimist and pessimist satisfaction functions based on the Hamming distance. In the next section we will analyze the impact that the iteration has on the social welfare.

4 Social Welfare in Iteration with the Approval Rule

In the previous section we have studied the conditions that yield termination of iterative goal-based voting for the *Approval* rule. We now focus on analyzing the *quality* of such iterations, from the point of view of a possible increase in social welfare.

We study three classical notions of social welfare: utilitarian (additive), which was also studied by Caragiannis and Procaccia for classical voting [8] and by Barrot et al. for Hamming-based approval voting [4]; Nash (multiplicative), as studied in voting [10,17]; and lastly, egalitarian (max-min) welfare as introduced by Rawls [31] and studied by Botan et al. [6] for the judgment aggregation framework.

Definition 4. *For a set of agents $\mathcal{N}$ and a set of issues $\mathcal{I}$, the utilitarian (utw), Nash product (npw) and egalitarian (egw) welfare for a satisfaction function sat, a truthful profile $\boldsymbol{\Gamma} = (\gamma_1, \ldots, \gamma_n)$ and the outcome of rule F under a profile $\boldsymbol{\Gamma}'$ are defined as:*

$$utw(F(\boldsymbol{\Gamma}'), \boldsymbol{\Gamma}) = \sum_{i\in\mathcal{N}} sat(\gamma_i, F(\boldsymbol{\Gamma}')),$$
$$npw(F(\boldsymbol{\Gamma}'), \boldsymbol{\Gamma}) = \Pi_{i\in\mathcal{N}} sat(\gamma_i, F(\boldsymbol{\Gamma}')),$$
$$egw(F(\boldsymbol{\Gamma}'), \boldsymbol{\Gamma}) = \min_{i\in\mathcal{N}} sat(\gamma_i, F(\boldsymbol{\Gamma}')).$$

Intuitively, the utilitarian welfare only considers the sum of individual satisfactions of the agents, while the Nash welfare penalizes profiles in which some agents are completely dissatisfied, and the egalitarian welfare focuses on the least satisfied agent.

We call an alteration from profile $\boldsymbol{\Gamma}^t$ to $\boldsymbol{\Gamma}^{t+1}$ a *Pareto improvement* if for none of the agents the satisfaction in $\boldsymbol{\Gamma}^{t+1}$ decreased from the satisfaction in $\boldsymbol{\Gamma}^t$, and for at least one agent their satisfaction strictly increased: namely, for all agents $i \in \mathcal{N}$, we have $sat(\gamma_i, F(\boldsymbol{\Gamma}^{t+1})) \geq sat(\gamma_i, F(\boldsymbol{\Gamma}^t))$ and there is at least one agent $k \in \mathcal{N}$ such that $sat(\gamma_k, F(\boldsymbol{\Gamma}^{t+1})) > sat(\gamma_k, F(\boldsymbol{\Gamma}^t))$.

Our first result establishes that iteration under the *Approval* rule for H-pessimist agents is never detrimental to the social welfare.

Theorem 5. *If the iteration of the* Approval *rule with H-pessimist agents has at least one step, the utilitarian and Nash social welfare always increase, while the egalitarian welfare does not decrease.*

Proof. We prove the first part of the theorem by showing that any iteration step is a Pareto improvement: this suffices since a sum increases if at least one term increases (and all others stay constant), and analogously for a product and its factors.

Let $\mathcal{N}$ be the voters, $\mathcal{I}$ the issues and $\boldsymbol{\Gamma}^0$ the initial profile. By Lemma 1, for any step t with H-pessimists we have $k_{t+1} > k_t$ and hence $Approval(\boldsymbol{\Gamma}^{t+1}) \subseteq Approval(\boldsymbol{\Gamma}^t)$. Hence, the interpretations with the maximal lowest Hamming distance $(lowH)$ to the goal of any agent i are either still in the new outcome, or the distance decreased. Thus $d_{pessH}(\gamma_i, Approval(\boldsymbol{\Gamma}^{t+1})) \leq d_{pessH}(\gamma_i, Approval(\boldsymbol{\Gamma}^t))$. In fact, suppose that for some agent i the distance increased; then, since $Appoval(\boldsymbol{\Gamma}^{t+1}) \subseteq Approval(\boldsymbol{\Gamma}^t)$ the interpretation with the lowest distance $d_{pessH}(\gamma_i, Approval(\boldsymbol{\Gamma}^{t+1}))$ must have been in $Approval(\boldsymbol{\Gamma}^t)$, and therefore $d_{pessH}(\gamma_i, Approval(\boldsymbol{\Gamma}^t))$ was not the maximal distance, which contradicts the definition of $pessH$.

Additionally, the altering agent j changes her goal such that her satisfaction strictly increases, i.e., $d_{pessH}(\gamma_j, Approval(\boldsymbol{\Gamma}^{t+1})) < d_{pessH}(\gamma_j, Approval(\boldsymbol{\Gamma}^t))$. Hence, any step is a Pareto improvement. Since by Theorem 1 the iteration with H-pessimists always terminates, the final stage will yield an outcome that has a higher utilitarian and Nash social welfare than the outcome under the initial profile.

For the egalitarian welfare, the worst-off agent could keep the same satisfaction throughout, and thus the welfare would not increase (but still never decrease). □

In order to establish an analogous result to Theorem 5 for H-optimists as well, we first need to prove the following Lemma, which extends the result of Corollary 2 to general iteration (i.e., not limited to minimal alterations).

Lemma 2. *For iterated* Approval *voting with H-optimists, it is always the case that* $Approval(\boldsymbol{\Gamma}^0) \subseteq Approval(\boldsymbol{\Gamma}^t)$ *for any stage t.*

Proof. Let $\mathcal{N}$ be a set of voters, $\mathcal{I}$ a set of issues and $\boldsymbol{\Gamma}^0$ the initial profile, whose outcome is $Approval(\boldsymbol{\Gamma}^0)$. Observe that any agent i who includes a winning interpretation in her current goal at step t, which also models her truthful goal, has no incentive to alter. In fact, H-optimists only consider the minimal $lowH$, which in this case is 0 and hence cannot be decreased. The support of these interpretations will thus not decrease, i.e., $supp_{\Gamma^t}(v) \geq supp_{\Gamma^0}(v)$ for any stage t and all interpretations $v \in Approval(\boldsymbol{\Gamma}^0)$.

Further, note that the support of the winning interpretations from one stage t to the next will not increase, i.e., $k_{t+1} \leq k_t$. In fact, if this was not the case, there would be an iteration step t where $k_{t+1} > k_t$. Since support of interpretations can only be raised by 1 per step we have $k_{t+1} = k_t + 1$. Hence, the new outcome must be a subset of the previous one $Approval(\boldsymbol{\Gamma}^{t+1}) \subseteq Approval(\boldsymbol{\Gamma}^t)$. We would have $optH(\gamma_i, Approval(\boldsymbol{\Gamma}^{t+1})) \leq optH(\gamma_i, Approval(\boldsymbol{\Gamma}^t))$ and no H-optimist has an incentive to induce such a change, because one of their closest interpretations is either still in the outcome, which makes no difference to them, or now a worse interpretation is their closest, which would make them worse off. Therefore, the support of the winning interpretations from one stage t to the next will not increase, i.e., $k_{t+1} \leq k_t$.

In conclusion, the initial winning interpretations will have a stable support of k_0 and the support of the winning interpretations does not increase during the iteration, i.e., $k_t = k_0$ for all stages t. Therefore, the interpretations $v \in Approval(\boldsymbol{\Gamma}^0)$ will always hold the maximal support. Hence $Approval(\boldsymbol{\Gamma}^0) \subseteq Approval(\boldsymbol{\Gamma}^t)$. □

We can now show that for H-optimists as well the social welfare is guaranteed to always improve or stay constant after the iteration process has terminated.

Theorem 6. *In case the iteration of the* Approval *rule with H-optimists has at least one step and terminates, the utilitarian and Nash social welfare always increase, while the egalitarian welfare does not decrease.*

Proof. Let $\mathcal{N}$ be a set of voters, $\mathcal{I}$ a set of issues and Γ^0 the initial profile. By Lemma 2 we know that for H-optimists at any stage t we have $Approval(\Gamma^0) \subseteq Approval(\Gamma^t)$. Hence, at any stage t and for any agent i their satisfaction never drops below the one for the initial profile $optH(\gamma_i, Approval(\Gamma^0))$. In fact, their preferred interpretation in the initial outcome is guaranteed to be included in any subsequent outcome as well.

Therefore, $d_{optH}(\gamma_i, Approval(\Gamma^t)) \leq d_{optH}(\gamma_i, Approval(\Gamma^0))$ for any agent i and any stage t. Additionally, at each step t there is some agent j strictly improving her satisfaction, i.e., whose distance strictly decreases with respect to the initial outcome $d_{optH}(\gamma_j, Approval(\Gamma^t)) < d_{optH}(\gamma_j, Approval(\Gamma^0))$. Hence, any step t is a Pareto improvement compared to the initial profile, and by the argument in the proof of Theorem 5, the utilitarian welfare and the Nash welfare always increase, while for the egalitarian welfare the worst-off agent could keep the same satisfaction throughout the iteration (and thus it could not increase, though never decrease). □

Given the conditions found in Sect. 3 to guarantee termination of the iterated *Approval* rule for H-optimists, we can derive the following corollary of Theorem 6.

Corollary 3. *The iterated* Approval *rule with H-optimists, using minimal alterations, always yields an increase in utilitarian and Nash social welfare.*

Table 3. The change in outcome from Γ^2 to Γ^3 in this iteration with H-optimists under the *Approval* rule is not a Pareto improvement for the utilitarian and Nash social welfare; however, $Approval(\Gamma^3)$ still yields an increase in social welfare compared to $Approval(\Gamma^0)$.

	Γ^0	Γ^1	Γ^2	Γ^3
$Mod(\gamma_1)$	(010)	(010)	**(001)**	(001)
			(000)	(000)
$Mod(\gamma_2)$	(001)	**(101)**	(101)	**(001)**
		(000)	(000)	
$Mod(\gamma_3)$	(100)	(100)	(100)	(100)
$Mod(\gamma_4)$	(100)	(100)	(100)	(100)
	(101)	(101)	(101)	(101)
$Approval$	(100)	(100)	(100)	(100)
		(101)	(101)	(001)
			(000)	

Note that the Pareto improvement in the proof of Theorem 6 is global and not local: every stage is a Pareto improvement with respect to the initial stage, but not necessarily to the previous stage. It thus is weaker than the proof for Theorem 5, which guarantees an improvement across every stage. This is related to the corresponding termination result, as an iteration consisting of only Pareto improvements can only have a finite number of steps, since the satisfaction has an upper bound. Table 3 gives an example of an iteration with H-optimists in which some steps are not Pareto improvements.

5 Conclusions

In this paper, we have extended the framework of goal-based voting by giving the agents the possibility to revise their vote based on the current outcome, if by doing so they can improve their satisfaction. In particular, we have focused on the well-known *Approval* rule and two notions of optimist and pessimist agents, whose satisfaction functions $optH$ and $pessH$ are based on the Hamming distance.

Our results have focused on analyzing *termination* and *quality* for the iterative process. We proved in Theorem 1 that for the H-pessimists, the iteration is guaranteed to always terminate, while the same does not hold for the H-optimists, as well as for the general classes of satisfaction functions having the properties $(c.3)$ and $(d.3)$ by Packard [29], as shown in Theorem 2. Nevertheless, we were able to establish termination results for these general classes of satisfaction functions in Theorems 3 and 4, which required restrictions on the type of alterations the agents are allowed to make. We also gave upper bounds on the number of steps necessary to reach convergence.

Regarding the quality of iteration, we analyzed its variation according to three classical notions of social welfare brought by the iterative process. For both H-pessimists and H-optimists we showed that the utilitarian and Nash welfare always increase, while the egalitarian welfare never decreases, as per Theorems 5 and 6, respectively.

Therefore, we have shown that under none or small restrictions, the iteration of the *Approval* rule for H-pessimists and H-optimists is well-behaved from both points of view of convergence and social welfare.

Natural avenues for future work include the study of convergence for other goal-based voting rules. For instance, some issue-wise generalizations of majority have been proven to be susceptible to manipulation for dichotomous satisfaction functions [27]: it would be interesting to study under which conditions they can be ensured to converge to a stable outcome under the more sophisticated Hamming-based preferences.

Moreover, we could consider groups of agents coordinating their alterations to satisfy a shared goal; we could also add restrictions on the information available to the agents (cf. the relevant work in judgment aggregation [34]) or on the type of goals that they are allowed to submit (as it has been done for strategy-proof majoritarian goal-based voting [27]), or more general classes of preferences over outcomes.

Finally, although one example suffices to show circularity of iteration, it would be interesting to perform a thorough analysis via simulations of how often such cases are likely to occur in practice. Some preliminary work in these directions and related results on iterative goal-based voting can be found in the Master thesis of the first author [1].

Acknowledgements. We would like to thank the reviewers for their detailed and valuable comments. We also thank the *actions transversales du Centre d'Economie de la Sorbonne* for funding Leyla Ade's research visit to work on the results presented here.

References

1. Ade, L.: Iterative goal-based voting. Master's thesis, University of Amsterdam (2021)
2. Airiau, S., Endriss, U.: Iterated majority voting. In: International Conference on Algorithmic Decision Theory (ADT 2009) (2009)
3. Bannikova, M., Dery, L., Obraztsova, S., Rabinovich, Z., Rosenschein, J.S.: Reaching consensus under a deadline. Auton. Agent. Multi-Agent Syst. **35**(9), 1–42 (2021)
4. Barrot, N., Lang, J., Yokoo, M.: Manipulation of Hamming-based approval voting for multiple referenda and committee elections. In: Proceedings of the 16th Conference on Autonomous Agents and Multiagent Systems (AAMAS 2017) (2017)
5. Bossert, W., Pattanaik, P.K., Xu, Y.: Choice under complete uncertainty: axiomatic characterizations of some decision rules. Econ. Theor. **16**(2), 295–312 (2000)
6. Botan, S., de Haan, R., Slavkovik, M., Terzopoulou, Z.: Egalitarian judgment aggregation. In: Proceedings of the 20th International Conference on Autonomous Agents and Multiagent Systems (AAMAS 2021) (2021)
7. Brânzei, S., Caragiannis, I., Morgenstern, J., Procaccia, A.: How bad is selfish voting? In: Proceedings of the 27th Conference on Artificial Intelligence (AAAI 2013) (2013)
8. Caragiannis, I., Procaccia, A.D.: Voting almost maximizes social welfare despite limited communication. Artif. Intell. **175**(9–10), 1655–1671 (2011)
9. Delgrande, J.P., Dubois, D., Lang, J.: Iterated revision as prioritized merging. In: Proceedings of the 15th International Conference on Principles of Knowledge Representation and Reasoning (KR 2006) (2006)
10. DeMeyer, F., Plott, C.R.: A welfare function using "relative intensity" of preference. Q. J. Econ. **85**(1), 179–186 (1971)
11. Endriss, U.: Judgment aggregation. In: Brandt, F., Conitzer, V., Endriss, U., Lang, J., Procaccia, A.D. (eds.) Handbook of Computational Social Choice, chap. 17. Cambridge University Press, Cambridge (2016)
12. Everaere, P., Konieczny, S., Marquis, P.: The strategy-proofness landscape of merging. J. Artif. Intell. Res. **28**, 49–105 (2007)
13. Fishburn, P.C.: Even-chance lotteries in social choice theory. Theor. Decis. **3**(1), 18–40 (1972)
14. Grandi, U., Endriss, U.: Binary aggregation with integrity constraints. In: Proceedings of the 22nd International Joint Conference on Artificial Intelligence (IJCAI 2011) (2011)

15. Grandi, U., Loreggia, A., Rossi, F., Venable, K.B., Walsh, T.: Restricted manipulation in iterative voting: Condorcet efficiency and Borda score. In: International Conference on Algorithmic Decision Theory (ADT 2013) (2013)
16. Grossi, D., Pigozzi, G.: Judgment Aggregation: A Primer. Synthesis Lectures on Artificial Intelligence and Machine Learning. Morgan & Claypool Publishers, San Rafael (2014)
17. Kaneko, M., Nakamura, K.: The Nash social welfare function. Econometrica Soc. **47**(2), 423–435 (1979)
18. Kelly, J.S.: Strategy-proofness and social choice functions without singlevaluedness. Econom. J. Econom. Soc. **45**(2), 439–446 (1977)
19. Konieczny, S., Pérez, R.P.: Logic based merging. J. Philos. Log. **40**(2), 239–270 (2011)
20. Laslier, J.F., Sanver, M.R.: Handbook on Approval Voting. Studies in Choice and Welfare. Springer, Heidelberg (2010). https://doi.org/10.1007/978-3-642-02839-7
21. Lev, O., Rosenschein, J.S.: Convergence of iterative voting. In: Proceedings of the 11th International Conference on Autonomous Agents and Multiagent Systems (AAMAS 2012) (2012)
22. Lev, O., Rosenschein, J.S.: Convergence of iterative scoring rules. J. Artif. Intell. Res. **57**, 573–591 (2016)
23. Meir, R.: Iterative voting. In: Trends in Computational Social Choice, pp. 69–86 (2017)
24. Meir, R.: Strategic voting. Synth. Lect. Artif. Intell. Mach. Learn. **13**(1), 1–167 (2018)
25. Meir, R., Polukarov, M., Rosenschein, J.S., Jennings, N.R.: Iterative voting and acyclic games. Artif. Intell. **252**, 100–122 (2017)
26. Novaro, A., Grandi, U., Longin, D., Lorini, E.: Goal-based collective decisions: axiomatics and computational complexity. In: Proceedings of the 27th International Joint Conference on Artificial Intelligence (IJCAI 2018) (2018)
27. Novaro, A., Grandi, U., Longin, D., Lorini, E.: Strategic majoritarian voting with propositional goals. In: Proceedings of the 18th International Conference on Autonomous Agents and Multiagent Systems (AAMAS 2019) (2019)
28. Obraztsova, S., Markakis, E., Polukarov, M., Rabinovich, Z., Jennings, N.: On the convergence of iterative voting: how restrictive should restricted dynamics be? In: Proceedings of the 29th AAAI Conference on Artificial Intelligence (AAAI 2015) (2015)
29. Packard, D.J.: Preference relations. J. Math. Psychol. **19**(3), 295–306 (1979)
30. Pattanaik, P.K., Peleg, B.: An axiomatic characterization of the lexicographic maximin extension of an ordering over a set to the power set. Soc. Choice Welfare **1**(2), 113–122 (1984)
31. Rawls, J.: A Theory of Justice. Harvard University Press, Cambridge (1971)
32. Reyhani, R., Wilson, M.: Best-reply dynamics for scoring rules. In: Proceedings of the 20th European Conference on Artificial Intelligence (ECAI 2012) (2012)
33. Schwind, N., Konieczny, S.: Non-prioritized iterated revision: improvement via incremental belief merging. In: Proceedings of the 17th International Conference on Principles of Knowledge Representation and Reasoning (KR 2020) (2020)
34. Terzopoulou, Z., Endriss, U.: Modelling iterative judgment aggregation. In: Proceedings of the 32nd AAAI Conference on Artificial Intelligence (AAAI 2018) (2018)
35. Zou, J., Meir, R., Parkes, D.: Strategic voting behavior in Doodle polls. In: Proceedings of the 18th ACM Conference on Computer Supported Cooperative Work & Social Computing (2015)

Mind the Gap! Runtime Verification of Partially Observable MASs with Probabilistic Trace Expressions

Davide Ancona, Angelo Ferrando, and Viviana Mascardi[✉]

University of Genova, Via Dodecaneso 35, 16146 Genova, Italy
{davide.ancona,angelo.ferrando,viviana.mascardi}@unige.it

Abstract. In this paper we present the theory behind Probabilistic Trace Expressions (PTEs), an extension of Trace Expressions where types of events that can be observed by a monitor are associated with an observation probability. PTEs can be exploited for monitoring that agents in a MAS interact in compliance with an Agent Interaction Protocol (AIP) modeled as a PTE, even when the monitor realizes that an interaction took place in the MAS, but it was not correctly observed ("observation gap"). To this aim, we adapt an existing approach for runtime verification with state estimation, we present a semantics for PTEs that allows for the estimation of the probability to reach a given state, given a sequence of observations which may include observation gaps, we present a centralized implemented algorithm to dynamically verify the behavior of the MAS under monitoring and we discuss its potential and limitations.

Keywords: Probabilistic Trace Expressions · Partial observability · State estimation · Multiagent systems · Agent interaction protocols

1 Introduction

Runtime verification of complex, distributed systems under ideal conditions (perfect observability of all the relevant events, no leaky communication channels, etc.) is an hard task to perform, and has been addressed by many scientific works including surveys and introductory papers [14,24,27], books [13], seminars [18,23], and conferences[1]. When the conditions are not ideal and some relevant events cannot be observed by the monitor, generating a *gap* in the event trace, the problem becomes even harder [11,15,22,25,31]. A gap represents the absence of information in the analyzed trace and corresponds to an execution point – or to a time slot – where the monitor does not know what the system did. Gaps may be due to the process of sampling observed events to reduce monitoring overhead, but also to events that are partially observable or not observable at all by the monitor: the monitor might be aware that an event took place, but does not know which. We say that the monitor "observes a gap" to describe this

---

[1] http://www.runtime-verification.org/.

D. Baumeister and J. Rothe (Eds.): EUMAS 2022, LNAI 13442, pp. 22–40, 2022.
https://doi.org/10.1007/978-3-031-20614-6_2

situation. The introduction of gaps raises problems in checking that a temporal property is verified by the system, given that a trace of events (which may include gaps) has been observed. If the monitor does not know which event has been observed, it cannot know whether the temporal property is satisfied or not.

In [32], each time a gap in observed a Hidden Markov Model (HMM) of the system is queried to know which events could be observed in the current state of the system, and with which probability. This allows the authors to estimate the probability to reach some state s_i after observing $obs = O_1, O_2, ..., O_t$ events, and – by generating a monitor that combines the system HMM and the temporal property ϕ into a single integrated model – to estimate the probability that ϕ is satisfied after observing $obs = O_1, O_2, ..., O_t$ events.

In this paper, we take [32] as our starting point, and we combine the approach presented therein with the adoption of an existing expressive formalism to model systems and properties, Trace Expressions [1, 2, 5, 6, 10].

After an overview of the background in Sect. 2, we present Probabilistic Trace Expressions (PTEs) which extend Trace Expressions with probabilities associated with event types (Sect. 3). PTEs are more expressive than HMM, deterministic finite state machines and linear time temporal logic (LTL [28]), being able to model more than context free languages. In Sect. 4 (1) we use PTEs to model the probabilistic behaviour of the system under observation, possibly starting from an HMM and then refining or extending it; (2) we show how – by applying the rules defining the operational semantics of PTEs – we obtain the same results of the forward algorithm presented in [32]; (3) we present the *Probabilize* algorithm for transforming Trace Expressions corresponding to LTL properties into PTEs; (4) by joining the two representations obtained in steps 1 and 3 above using the $\wedge$ conjunction operator natively provided by PTEs, we obtain for free a way to verify satisfaction of LTL properties in presence of observation gaps. Section 5 discusses the implementation of a centralized algorithm for Runtime Verification of partially observable MASs and suggests that a decentralized approach may solve some of its limitations, at the expense of communication overhead among the monitors. Future directions of our research are addressed in Sect. 6.

2   Background

Hidden Markov Models. A Hidden Markov Model (HMM [16, 30]) is a statistical Markov model where the system being modeled is assumed to be a Markov process with hidden states. It can be modeled as a quintuple $H = \langle S, A, V, B, \Pi \rangle$ where

- $S = \{s_1, ..., s_{N_s}\}$ is the set of states;
- A is the $N_s \times N_s$ transition probability matrix: $A_{i,j} = \Pr(\text{state is } s_j \text{ at time } t + 1 \mid \text{state is } s_i \text{ at time } t)$;
- $V = \{v_1, ..., v_{N_v}\}$ is the set of observation symbols;
- B is the $N_s \times N_v$ observation probability matrix: $B_{i,j}$, also denoted with $b_i(v_j)$ for clarity, is $\Pr(v_j \text{ is observed at time } t \mid \text{state is } s_i \text{ at time } t)$;

– $\Pi = \{\pi_1, ..., \pi_{N_s}\}$ is the initial state distribution: π_i is the probability that the initial state is s_i.

We use as our running example the one presented in [32], where a model of a planetary rover mission is modeled. The rover hosts two generic instruments, A and B, and all the events generated by the rover are recorded on a log file. We consider four different kinds of events, inspired by Barringer et al. [12]:

– *command* (cmd in the HMM figure), the command submitted to the rover;
– *dispatch* (disp), the dispatch of the command from the rover to the instrument;
– *success* (succ), the success of the command on the instrument;
– *fail* (fail), the failure of the command on the instrument.

All these events are characterized by three parameters: the instrument id (a or b), the issued command (*start* or *reset*), and a time stamp indicating when the event occurred. When the rover receives a command, it reports the information to the logger and sends the command to the relevant instrument. Once received the command, the instrument issues a dispatch event to the logger and then executes the command. If the execution is successful (resp. fails), a corresponding success (resp. failure) event is reported to the logger. It is also possible that the command is simply lost for some reason and neither a success nor a fail occurs. Events have some probability to be observed, and the chance to move from one state to another is also modeled by a probability.

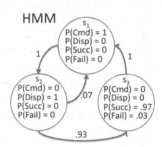

Fig. 1. An example of HMM (from [32]).

Figure 1 represents an HMM inspired to the rover example, where

– $S = \{s_1, s_2, s_3\}$;
– $A_{1,1} = A_{1,3} = 0; A_{1,2} = 1; A_{2,1} = 0.07; A_{2,2} = 0; A_{2,3} = 0.93;$
  $A_{3,1} = 1; A_{3,2} = A_{3,3} = 0;$
– $V = \{C, D, S, F\}$ (C stands for cmd, D for disp, etc.);
– $b_1(C) = 1; b_1(D) = b_1(S) = b_1(F) = 0; b_2(D) = 1; b_2(C) = b_2(S) = b_2(F) = 0; b_3(C) = b_3(D) = 0; b_3(S) = 0.97; b_3(F) = 0.03;$
– $\pi_1 = 1, \pi_2 = \pi_3 = 0$ (not shown in the figure).

To compute the probability that an HMM H ends in a specific state given an observation sequence $O = \langle O_1, O_2, ..., O_T \rangle$, the forward algorithm can be used [29]. Let $Q = \langle q_1, q_2, ..., q_T \rangle$ denote the (unknown) state sequence that the system passed through, i.e., q_t denotes the state of the system when observation O_t is made. Let $\alpha_t(i) = Pr(O_1, O_2, ..., O_t, q_t = s_i|H)$, i.e., the probability that the first t observations yield $O_1, O_2, ..., O_t$ and that q_t is s_i, given the model H. The base case is:

$$\alpha_1(j) = \pi_j b_j(O_1) \text{ for } 1 \leq j \leq N_s$$

whereas the recursive case is:

$$\alpha_{t+1}(j) = (\Sigma_{i=1..N_s} \alpha_t(i) A_{i,j}) b_j(O_{t+1}) \text{ for } 1 \leq t \leq T - 1 \text{ and } 1 \leq j \leq N_s$$

Trace Expressions. Trace expressions are based on the notions of *event* and *event type*. $\mathcal{E}$ denotes the fixed universe of events subject to monitoring. An event trace over $\mathcal{E}$ is a possibly infinite sequence of events in $\mathcal{E}$, and a Trace Expression over $\mathcal{E}$ denotes a set of event traces over $\mathcal{E}$. Trace expressions are built on top of event types (chosen from a set $\mathcal{ET}$), each specifying a subset of events in $\mathcal{E}$. A Trace Expression $\tau \in \mathcal{T}$ represents a set of possibly infinite event traces, and is defined on top of the following operators:

- ϵ (empty trace), denoting the singleton set $\{\epsilon\}$ containing the empty event trace ϵ.
- $\vartheta{:}\tau$ (*prefix*), denoting the set of all traces whose first event e matches the event type ϑ, and the remaining part is a trace of τ.
- $\tau_1 \cdot \tau_2$ (*concatenation*), denoting the set of all traces obtained by concatenating the traces of τ_1 with those of τ_2.
- $\tau_1 \wedge \tau_2$ (*intersection*), denoting the intersection of the traces of τ_1 and τ_2.
- $\tau_1 \vee \tau_2$ (*union*), denoting the union of the traces of τ_1 and τ_2.
- $\tau_1|\tau_2$ (*shuffle*), denoting the set obtained by shuffling the traces of τ_1 with the traces of τ_2.

The derived constant Trace Expression 1 is equivalent to the expression $\tau = \epsilon \vee everyEvent{:}\tau$, where $everyEvent = \mathcal{E}$. Trace expressions support recursion through cyclic terms expressed by finite sets of recursive syntactic equations, as supported by modern Prolog systems. The semantics of Trace Expressions is specified by a transition relation $\delta \subseteq \mathcal{T} \times \mathcal{E} \times \mathcal{T}$, where $\mathcal{T}$ and $\mathcal{E}$ denote the set of Trace Expressions and of events, respectively. $\tau_1 \overset{e}{\rightarrow} \tau_2$ means $(\tau_1, e, \tau_2) \in \delta$; the transition $\tau_1 \overset{e}{\rightarrow} \tau_2$ expresses the property that the system under monitoring can safely move from the state specified by τ_1 into the state specified by τ_2 when event e is observed. A Trace Expression models the current state of a protocol. Protocol state transitions are ruled by the transition system shown in Fig. 2, which define δ.

Runtime Verification with State Estimation. Given a trace (possibly with gaps), in [32] Stoller et al. propose an approach to compute the probability that a LTL temporal property ϕ is satisfied by a system modeled by an HMM H, given that $obs = O_1, O_2, ..., O_t$ have been observed. More formally, they evaluate $Pr(\phi| obs, H)$ by applying the following steps:

$$(\text{prefix})\frac{}{\vartheta{:}\tau \xrightarrow{e} \tau}\ e{\in}\vartheta \qquad (\text{or-l})\frac{\tau_1 \xrightarrow{e} \tau_1'}{\tau_1 \vee \tau_2 \xrightarrow{e} \tau_1'} \qquad (\text{or-r})\frac{\tau_2 \xrightarrow{e} \tau_2'}{\tau_1 \vee \tau_2 \xrightarrow{e} \tau_2'}$$

$$(\text{and})\frac{\tau_1 \xrightarrow{e} \tau_1' \quad \tau_2 \xrightarrow{e} \tau_2'}{\tau_1 \wedge \tau_2 \xrightarrow{e} \tau_1' \wedge \tau_2'} \qquad (\text{shuffle-l})\frac{\tau_1 \xrightarrow{e} \tau_1'}{\tau_1 | \tau_2 \xrightarrow{e} \tau_1' | \tau_2} \qquad (\text{shuffle-r})\frac{\tau_2 \xrightarrow{e} \tau_2'}{\tau_1 | \tau_2 \xrightarrow{e} \tau_1 | \tau_2'}$$

$$(\text{cat-l})\frac{\tau_1 \xrightarrow{e} \tau_1'}{\tau_1 \cdot \tau_2 \xrightarrow{e} \tau_1' \cdot \tau_2} \qquad (\text{cat-r})\frac{\tau_2 \xrightarrow{e} \tau_2'}{\tau_1 \cdot \tau_2 \xrightarrow{e} \tau_2'}\ \epsilon(\tau_1)$$

$$(\epsilon\text{-empty})\frac{}{\epsilon(\epsilon)} \qquad (\epsilon\text{-or-l})\frac{\epsilon(\tau_1)}{\epsilon(\tau_1 \vee \tau_2)} \qquad (\epsilon\text{-or-r})\frac{\epsilon(\tau_2)}{\epsilon(\tau_1 \vee \tau_2)} \qquad (\epsilon\text{-others})\frac{\epsilon(\tau_1) \quad \epsilon(\tau_2)}{\epsilon(\tau_1 \, op \, \tau_2)}\ op{\in}\{|,\cdot,\wedge\}$$

Fig. 2. Transition system for trace expressions.

1. learn the HMM H from a given set of traces without gaps, using standard HMM learning algorithm;
2. generate the deterministic finite state machine (DFSM) corresponding to ϕ;
3. generate a monitor combining H and the DFSM to check the sequence *obs*.

Step 1 falls outside the boundaries of their investigation, and in the sequel we will disregard how the HMM has been created as well.

3 Probabilistic Trace Expressions

A probabilistic Trace Expression (PTE) is a Trace Expression where occurrences of event types in the expression have a probability associated with them. The probability is written after the occurrence of the event type, in square brackets. From a syntactic point of view, this extension is the only difference w.r.t. "normal" Trace Expressions introduced in Sect. 2.

Example. We present the PTE corresponding to the rover example. Event type *cmd* is { command(Inst, Comm, TS) such that Inst $\in$ {a, b}, Comm $\in$ {start, reset}, TS a time stamp in the range 0...3 }; event type *disp* is { dispatch(Inst, Comm, TS) }, *succ* = { success(Inst, Comm, TS) } and *fail* is { fail(Inst, Comm, TS) }. The resulting Trace Expression can be written in two equivalent (from the PTE semantics viewpoint) ways:

$$\tau_{s_1} = cmd[1]{:}\tau_{s_2}$$

$$\tau_{s_2} = disp[0.07]{:}\tau_{s_1} \vee disp[0.93]{:}\tau_{s_3}$$

$$\tau_{s_3} = succ[0.97]{:}\tau_{s_1} \vee fail[0.03]{:}\tau_{s_1}$$

(note the *disp* occurrence in both branches of τ_{s_2} definition, with different probabilities and different Trace Expressions after the ":" operator) and

$$\tau'_{init} = cmd[1]{:}\tau'_{s_2}$$

$$\tau'_{s_1} = cmd[0.07]{:}\tau'_{s_2}$$

$$\tau'_{s_2} = disp[1]{:}(\tau'_{s_1} \vee \tau'_{s_3})$$

$$\tau'_{s_3} = succ[0.9021]{:}\tau'_{s_1} \vee fail[0.0279]{:}\tau'_{s_1}$$

The Trace Expression in the first form tells us, for example, that the probability of the protocol to reach τ_{s_1} starting from τ_{s_2} and having observed $disp$ is 0.07 while the probability to reach τ_{s_3} starting from τ_{s_2} and having observed $disp$ is 0.93 (second equation of the first formulation). To make this information explicit, the transition from state s_2 to states s_1 and s_3 in the HMM has been modeled by $\tau_{s_2} = disp[0.07]{:}\tau_{s_1} \vee disp[0.93]{:}\tau_{s_3}$, introducing non-determinism due to the occurrence of the same event type $disp$ in both branches of the "or" operator. While in a non probabilistic setting $\tau_{s_2} = disp{:}\tau_{s_1} \vee disp{:}\tau_{s_3}$ would be equivalent to $\tau_{s_2} = disp{:}(\tau_{s_1} \vee \tau_{s_3})$ and the second version would be definitely preferred, as – besides being more readable and compact – is deterministic, in a probabilistic setting this simplification would cause us to lose precious information on the probability to move to some state S, given some observed event O.

The second version overcomes this problem by propagating – via multiplication – the different probabilities associated with $disp$ in s_2' to the states s_1' and s_3' that can be reached from s_2' (second and fourth equation of the second formulation). With this second form, we gain determinism at the price of adding an initial state τ_{init} for each state whose initial probability is not zero, and of losing the one-to-one clear correspondence with the HMM. As an example, in the fourth equation, understanding that $succ[0.9021]$ comes from the probability 0.97 associated with observing $succ$ in state s_3' multiplied by the probability 0.93 of having reached s_3' from s_2' is far from intuitive.

Given that a structure-driven transformation from the first form to the second can be implemented in time linear with the Trace Expression length, we adopt the first form for presentation purposes, since it is closer to the HMM, but we use the second one in the implementation, since it is more efficient.

Like a "normal" Trace Expression, a PTE τ can be seen as the current state of a protocol that started in some initial state τ_{init} and reached τ after n events $O_1...O_n$ took place, that moved τ_{init} to τ through intermediate states $\tau_{q1}, \tau_{q2},$ ... , $\tau_{qn} = \tau$. If we denote with $\tau \xrightarrow{O} \tau'$ the transition from state τ to state τ' due to the event O taking place and being observed, we may write $\tau_{init} \xrightarrow{O_1} \tau_{q1} \xrightarrow{O_2} \tau_{q2} \xrightarrow{O_3} \tau_{q3}... \xrightarrow{O_n} \tau_{qn}$, where $\tau_{qn} = \tau$.

In order to properly manage probabilities, it is convenient to associate with τ – in an explicit and easily computable way – the probability of the protocol to have reached τ starting from τ_{init} and having observed $O_1...O_n$.

We define a "PTE state" (simply "state" from now on) the triple consisting of a Trace Expression τ, a sequence of events $O_1...O_n$ observed before reaching τ, and the probability π_τ that the protocol reached τ. We represent the state with the notation $\langle \tau, \pi_\tau, O_1...O_n \rangle$.

In this work, we are interested in analyzing the protocol evolution in presence of observation gaps: in a state τ_c (for $\tau_{current}$), the monitor driven by a PTE may either observe an event O, and then its behaviour is the same as in the non-probabilistic setting – it moves to the next state τ, if $\tau_c \xrightarrow{O} \tau$ is an allowed move –, or "observe a gap". Observing, or perceiving, a gap means that the monitor is aware that some event took place and hence the protocol must move one step forward, but it is also aware that the event has not been correctly observed. The monitor cannot commit to the $\tau_c \xrightarrow{O} \tau$ move in this case, but it must remember that many moves were possible, one for each of the events that could have taken place in τ, and that could have filled the perceived gap: $\tau_c \xrightarrow{gap} \tau$ (if the event were O, modeled by $gap(O)$ in the sequence of observed events), $\tau_c \xrightarrow{gap} \tau'$ (if the event were O', modeled by $gap(O')$), $\tau_c \xrightarrow{gap} \tau''$ (if the event were O'', modeled by $gap(O'')$), etc.

$$(\text{prefix}) \frac{}{\langle \vartheta[\pi_e]{:}\tau, \pi_{tr}, obs \rangle \xrightarrow{any} \langle \tau, \pi_e * \pi_{tr}, obs\ any(e) \rangle} \ e \in \vartheta$$

$$(\text{or-l}) \frac{\langle \tau_1, \pi_{tr}, obs \rangle \xrightarrow{any} \langle \tau_1', \pi_{tr}', obs\ any(e) \rangle}{\langle \tau_1 \vee \tau_2, \pi_{tr}, obs \rangle \xrightarrow{any} \langle \tau_1', \pi_{tr}', obs\ any(e) \rangle}$$

$$(\text{or-r}) \frac{\langle \tau_2, \pi_{tr}, obs \rangle \xrightarrow{any} \langle \tau_2', \pi_{tr2}, obs\ any(e) \rangle}{\langle \tau_1 \vee \tau_2, \pi_{tr}, obs \rangle \xrightarrow{any} \langle \tau_2', \pi_{tr2}, obs\ any(e) \rangle}$$

$$(\text{and}) \frac{\langle \tau_1, \pi_{tr}, obs \rangle \xrightarrow{any} \langle \tau_1', \pi_{t1}, obs\ any(e) \rangle \ \langle \tau_2, \pi_{tr}, obs \rangle \xrightarrow{any} \langle \tau_2', \pi_{t2}, obs\ any(e) \rangle}{\langle \tau_1 \wedge \tau_2, \pi_{tr}, obs \rangle \xrightarrow{any} \langle \tau_1' \wedge \tau_2', \pi_{tr}', obs\ any(e) \rangle} \ \pi_{tr}' = f(\pi_{t1}, \pi_{t2})$$

$$(\text{shuffle-l}) \frac{\langle \tau_1, \pi_{tr}, obs \rangle \xrightarrow{any} \langle \tau_1', \pi_{tr}', obs\ any(e) \rangle}{\langle \tau_1 | \tau_2, \pi_{tr}, obs \rangle \xrightarrow{any} \langle \tau_1' | \tau_2, \pi_{tr}', obs\ any(e) \rangle}$$

$$(\text{shuffle-r}) \frac{\langle \tau_2, \pi_{tr}, obs \rangle \xrightarrow{any} \langle \tau_2', \pi_{tr}', obs\ any(e) \rangle}{\langle \tau_1 | \tau_2, \pi_{tr}, obs \rangle \xrightarrow{any} \langle \tau_1 | \tau_2', \pi_{tr}', obs\ any(e) \rangle}$$

$$(\text{cat-l}) \frac{\langle \tau_1, \pi_{tr}, obs \rangle \xrightarrow{any} \langle \tau_1', \pi_{tr}', obs \rangle}{\langle \tau_1 \cdot \tau_2, \pi_{tr}, obs \rangle \xrightarrow{any} \langle \tau_1' \cdot \tau_2, \pi_{tr}', obs\ any(e) \rangle}$$

$$(\text{cat-r}) \frac{\langle \tau_2, \pi_{tr}, obs \rangle \xrightarrow{any} \langle \tau_2', \pi_{tr}', obs\ any(e) \rangle}{\langle \tau_1 \cdot \tau_2, \pi_{tr}, obs \rangle \xrightarrow{any} \langle \tau_2', \pi_{tr}', obs\ any(e) \rangle} \ \epsilon(\tau_1)$$

Fig. 3. Transition system for probabilistic trace expressions states.

The transition rules between states are shown in Fig. 3 and follow the pattern of the rules defined for Trace Expressions, with modifications for taking care of the probability propagation and of observed events including gaps. The rules for ϵ are the same as for normal Trace Expressions. Appendix A of the longer version of this paper available as a DIBRIS technical report provides a deep explanation of each of them [8].

In Fig. 3 the use of *any* and *any(e)* allows us to model the transition in the case that an event has been observed and in the case an observation gap took place, using the same rule. In fact, $any \in \{e, gap\}$ and if $any == e$ then $any(e) == e$; if $any == gap$ then $any(e) == gap(e)$.

If $any == e$, then e has been observed, the arrow modeling the state transition function $\overset{any}{\rightarrow}$ is actually labeled with e, and e is concatenated with the previously observed events, *obs*; if $any == gap$, then a gap took place, the arrow $\overset{any}{\rightarrow}$ is labeled with *gap*, and *gap(e)*, meaning that a gap took place, and that it could be filled with event e, is concatenated with the previously observed events.

Nondeterminism in State Transitions. The state transition function $\overset{any}{\rightarrow}$ is nondeterministic: one state can move into more than one state for many different reasons. Let us consider the *cmd* event type introduced at the beginning of this section. The transitions below can take place starting from the state $\langle cmd[0.3]{:}\tau, 0.2, obs \rangle$ when an observation gap occurs.

- $\langle cmd[0.3]{:}\tau, 0.2, obs \rangle \overset{gap}{\rightarrow} \langle \tau, 0.06, obs\ gap(command(a, start, 0)) \rangle$
- $\langle cmd[0.3]{:}\tau, 0.2, obs \rangle \overset{gap}{\rightarrow} \langle \tau, 0.06, obs\ gap(command(b, start, 0)) \rangle$
- ... plus 14 more transitions.

As another example, let us consider again the event type *cmd* defined above and the state $\langle cmd[0.75]{:}\tau_1 \vee cmd[0.25]{:}\tau_2, 0.4, obs \rangle$. If $command(a, start, 3)$ (abbreviated in $c(a, s, 3)$ for presentation purposes) is observed, both branches of the choice in $cmd[0.75]{:}\tau_1 \vee cmd[0.25]{:}\tau_2$ are valid, leading to the two transitions below.

- $\langle cmd[0.75]{:}\tau_1 \vee cmd[0.25]{:}\tau_2, 0.4, obs \rangle \overset{c(a,s,3)}{\rightarrow} \langle \tau_1, 0.3, obs\ c(a, s, 3) \rangle$
- $\langle cmd[0.75]{:}\tau_1 \vee cmd[0.25]{:}\tau_2, 0.4, obs \rangle \overset{c(a,s,3)}{\rightarrow} \langle \tau_2, 0.1, obs\ c(a, s, 3) \rangle$

If, starting from $\langle cmd[0.75]{:}\tau_1 \vee cmd[0.25]{:}\tau_2, 0.4, obs \rangle$, a gap is observed, the two sources of nondeterminism (the first due to the gap that can be filled with many events matching the expected event type, and the second due to the nondeterministic choice in the Trace Expression) combine together, generating 32 possible transitions. Other sources of nondeterminism in the Trace Expression are due to the shuffle and the concatenation operators, defined by two transitions rules each. Figure 4 presents the rules for dealing with nondeterminism and for introducing the notion of transitive closure of transitions:

(state-to-set) The function represented by $\rightarrow_\gamma$ takes one PTE state γ, one observed event or gap *any*, and returns the set of all the PTE states that γ can reach via $\overset{any}{\rightarrow}$.

(set-to-set) The function represented by $\twoheadrightarrow$ takes one set of PTE states $\{\gamma_1, \gamma_2, ..., \gamma_n\}$, one observed event or gap *any*, and returns the union of the sets of PTE states that each $\gamma_i \in \{\gamma_1, \gamma_2, ..., \gamma_n\}$ can reach via $\overset{any}{\rightarrow}_\gamma$.

$$(\text{state-to-set}) \dfrac{\gamma \overset{any}{\rightarrow} \gamma_1 \quad \gamma \overset{any}{\rightarrow} \gamma_2 \quad ... \quad \gamma \overset{any}{\rightarrow} \gamma_n}{\gamma \overset{any}{\rightarrow_\gamma} \{\gamma_1, \gamma_2, ..., \gamma_n\}}$$

$$(\text{set-to-set}) \dfrac{\gamma_1 \overset{any}{\rightarrow_\gamma} \Gamma_1 \quad \gamma_M \overset{any}{\rightarrow_\gamma} \Gamma_2 \quad ... \quad \gamma_n \overset{any}{\rightarrow_\gamma} \Gamma_n}{\{\gamma_1, \gamma_2, ..., \gamma_n\} \overset{any}{\twoheadrightarrow} \Gamma_1 \cup \Gamma_2 \cup ... \cup \Gamma_1}$$

$$(\text{closure}) \dfrac{\Gamma_0 \overset{O_1}{\twoheadrightarrow} \Gamma_1 \overset{O_2}{\twoheadrightarrow} \quad ... \quad \Gamma_{n-1} \overset{O_n}{\twoheadrightarrow} \Gamma_n}{\Gamma_0 \overset{O_1...O_n}{\twoheadrightarrow} \Gamma_n}$$

$$(\text{closure-init}) \dfrac{\{\langle \tau, 1, \sigma \rangle\} \overset{O_1...O_n}{\twoheadrightarrow} \Gamma_n}{\tau \overset{O_1...O_n}{\twoheadrightarrow} \Gamma_n} \quad \sigma = \text{empty sequence}$$

Fig. 4. Rules for nondeterminism and transitive closure.

(closure) We use $\twoheadrightarrow$ to denote the transitive closure of $\twoheadrightarrow$ by putting the sequence of observed events on top of the arrow.

(closure-init) Finally, a PTE τ can evolve into any state $\gamma \in \Gamma_n$ after observation of $O_1...O_n$, if the PTE state $\langle \tau, 1, \sigma \rangle$ can, where σ is the empty sequence.

Example. Starting from the PTE τ_{s_1} used as running example, we have:

$$\tau_{s_1} \overset{cmd\ disp\ gap}{\twoheadrightarrow} \{\langle \tau_{s_2}, 0.07, cmd\ disp\ gap(cmd) \rangle,$$

$$\langle \tau_{s_1}, 0.9021, cmd\ disp\ gap(succ) \rangle, \langle \tau_{s_1}, 0.0279, cmd\ disp\ gap(fail) \rangle\}$$

because

$$\{\langle \tau_{s_1}, 1, \sigma \rangle\} \overset{cmd}{\twoheadrightarrow} \{\langle \tau_{s_2}, 1, cmd \rangle\} \overset{disp}{\twoheadrightarrow} \{\langle \tau_{s_1}, 0.07, cmd\ disp \rangle, \langle \tau_{s_3}, 0.93, cmd\ disp \rangle\} \overset{gap}{\twoheadrightarrow}$$

$$\{\langle \tau_{s_2}, 0.07, cmd\ disp\ gap(cmd) \rangle, \langle \tau_{s_1}, 0.9021, cmd\ disp\ gap(succ) \rangle,$$

$$\langle \tau_{s_1}, 0.0279, cmd\ disp\ gap(fail) \rangle\}$$

4   From HMMs to PTEs

A PTE where probabilities associated with event types are consistent with their intended meaning and with the probability properties might be complex when written from scratch. Besides needing a deep knowledge of the modeled system, the developer would also need a means to ensure that, for example, a PTE like $cmd[0.9] : \tau_{s_1} \lor disp[0.8] : \tau_{s_2}$ is recognized as wrong, since there are two mutually exclusive branches and the sum of their probabilities is greater than one. While this error is trivial and can be easily catched and corrected, if the PTE grows in size and complexity a manual development becomes more and more error-prone.

A good practice in engineering new software applications is to reuse well established approaches as much as possible. Even if we want to model probabilistic systems using an extension of Trace Expressions, which is more expressive than HMM and deterministic finite state machines, this does not prevent us from starting from a less expressive but widely used formalism like HMM in order to create a simple, but correct, PTE modeling the system, and extend/refine the PTE if necessary.

If an HMM representing the behaviour of the modeled system exists, for example because it has been learned using existing algorithms, we can indeed use it to generate the corresponding PTE in an automatic way. Once such PTE has been obtained, we can modify it in order to model those features of the actual system that could not be directly represented with an HMM. Ensuring consistency of the modifications is up to the developer.

The HMM2PTE Algorithm. Given an HMM $H = \langle S, A, V, B, \Pi \rangle$, the algorithm to construct an equivalent PTE is the following:

1. for each observation symbol $v_k \in V$, generate the corresponding singleton event type $\beta_k = \{v_k\}$ (recall that Trace Expressions are defined on top of event types and not of events);
2. for each $i = 1..N_s$, for each $j = 1..N_s$, for each $k = 1..N_v$, if $A_{i,j} \neq 0$ then $\tau_{s_i} = \bigvee_{j=1..N_s, k=1..N_v} \beta_k[A_{i,j} * b_i(v_k)]{:}\tau_{s_j}{}^2$. If, for some given i, there exists only one j such that $A_{i,j}$ is different from 0, then $\tau_{s_i} = \beta_k[A_{i,j} * b_{i,k}]{:}\tau_{s_j}$. If, for some given i, all $A_{i,j}$ are equal to 0, then $\tau_{s_i} = \epsilon$.

As an example, the HMM2PTE algorithm translates the HMM presented in Sect. 2 into the PTE τ'_{init} presented in Sect. 3.

Forward Algorithm for Probabilistic Trace Expressions. Let us consider the set of PTEs states $\Gamma_0 = \{\langle \tau_{s_1}, \pi_{s_1}, \sigma \rangle, \langle \tau_{s_2}, \pi_{s_2}, \sigma \rangle, ..., \langle \tau_{s_N}, \pi_{s_N}, \sigma \rangle\}$, where each τ_{s_i} corresponds to a state s_i in the HMM H and has been obtained applying the HMM2PTE translation algorithm to H. π_{s_i} is the initial probability of s_i, according to H. If $\pi_{s_i} = 0$, the corresponding state $\langle \tau_{s_i}, \pi_{s_i}, \sigma \rangle$ is not included in Γ_0.

If $\Gamma_0 \overset{O_1...O_{t-1}}{\twoheadrightarrow} \Gamma_{t-1}$, all the states in Γ_{t-1} must have the form $\langle \tau_{s_x}, \pi, O_1...O_{t-1} \rangle$ for some x: they are the states where τ_{s_x} can be reached from one of the states in Γ_0, upon observing $O_1...O_{t-1}$. Given i_1 and i_2 two indexes, we denote with $\Gamma_{i_1}(\tau_{i_2}) = \{\langle \tau_{s_{i_2}}, \pi, O_1...O_{i_1-1} \rangle \in \Gamma_{i_1}\}$.

Theorem 1. *If* $\Gamma_0 \overset{O_1...O_{t-1}}{\twoheadrightarrow} \Gamma_{t-1}$ *and* $\Gamma_{t-1}(\tau_{s_t}) \overset{O_t}{\twoheadrightarrow} \Gamma_t$, *then* $\alpha_t(j) = \Sigma_{\langle \tau_{s_j}, \pi_j, O_1...O_t \rangle \in \Gamma_t} \pi_j$.

We give the intuition behind the theorem by means of our running example. Let us suppose that we want to compute the probability that, after observing

---

2 By $\bigvee_{h=1..m} \tau_h$ we mean the conjunction via the $\vee$ operator of the Trace Expressions $\tau_1, ..., \tau_m$. The notation can only be used if $m \geq 2$.

command(a, start, 0) (C in the sequel), dispatch(a, start, 1) (D in the sequel), fail(a, start, 2) (F in the sequel), the system is in state s_3.

Step 1: computation of $\Gamma_0 \overset{O_1...O_{t-1}}{\twoheadrightarrow} \Gamma_{t-1}$.
In our example, the first step amounts to computing $\Gamma_0 \overset{CD}{\twoheadrightarrow} \Gamma_2$.

$$\Gamma_0 = \{\langle \tau_{s_1}, 1, \sigma \rangle\} \overset{C}{\twoheadrightarrow} \Gamma_1 = \{\langle \tau_{s_2}, 1, C \rangle\} \overset{D}{\twoheadrightarrow} \Gamma_2 = \{\langle \tau_{s_1}, 0.07, CD \rangle, \langle \tau_{s_3}, 0.93, CD \rangle\}$$

Step 2: computation of $\Gamma_{t-1}(\tau_{s_t}) \overset{O_t}{\twoheadrightarrow} \Gamma_t$.
In our example, this step amounts to computing $\Gamma_2(\tau_{s_3}) \overset{F}{\twoheadrightarrow} \Gamma_3$.
Once reached $\Gamma_2 = \{\langle \tau_{s_1}, 0.07, CD \rangle, \langle \tau_{s_3}, 0.93, CD \rangle\}$ we have to limit the last transition, tagged with F, to those states whose Trace Expression corresponds to s_3, namely τ_{s_3}. We have

$$\Gamma_2(\tau_{s_3}) = \{\langle \tau_{s_3}, 0.93, CD \rangle\} \overset{F}{\twoheadrightarrow} \Gamma_3 = \{\langle \tau_{s_1}, 0.0279, CDF \rangle\}$$

Step 3: computation of $\Sigma_{\langle \tau_{s_j}, \pi_j, O_1...O_t \rangle \in \Gamma_t} \pi_j$
In the last step, we have to sum all the probabilities of the states in Γ_t, namely Γ_3 in our example. There is only one state in Γ_3, with probability 0.0279. It turns out that $\Sigma_{\langle \tau_{s_j}, \pi_j, O_1...O_t \rangle \in \Gamma_3} \pi_j = \pi_3 = 0.0279$.

Step 4: computation of $\alpha_t(j)$ as defined in the forward algorithm [29] and summarized in Sect. 2.
In our example, $\alpha_t(j)$ is $\alpha_3(3)$, namely the probability to observe CDF, with F observed in state s_3. We use the sequence of events as subscript for α instead of their indexes for sake of clarity.
The base case leads to the following computation:

$$\alpha_C(1) = \pi_1 * b_1(C) = 1 * 1 = 1$$
$$\alpha_C(2) = \pi_2 * b_2(C) = 0 * 0 = 0$$
$$\alpha_C(3) = \pi_3 * b_3(C) = 0 * 0 = 0$$

The first recursive step leads to the following computation (we omit some details and keep the result)

$$\alpha_{CD}(1) = (\Sigma_{i=1..N_s} \alpha_C(i) A_{i,1}) b_1(D) = 0$$
$$\alpha_{CD}(2) = (\Sigma_{i=1..N_s} \alpha_C(i) A_{i,2}) b_2(D) = 1 * A_{1,2} * b_2(D) = 1 * 1 * 1 = 1$$
$$\alpha_{CD}(3) = (\Sigma_{i=1..N_s} \alpha_C(i) A_{i,3}) b_3(D) = 0$$

and the second recursive step leads to

$$\alpha_{CDF}(1) = (\Sigma_{i=1..N_s} \alpha_{CD}(i) A_{i,1}) b_1(F) = 0$$

$$\alpha_{CDF}(2) = (\Sigma_{i=1..N_s}\alpha_{CD}(i)A_{i,2})b_2(F) = 0$$
$$\alpha_{CDF}(3) = (\Sigma_{i=1..N_s}\alpha_{CD}(i)A_{i,3})b_3(F) = \alpha_{CD}(2)*A_{2,3}*b_3(F) = 1*0.97*0.03 = 0.0279$$

Step 5: check that $\alpha_t(j)$ and $\Sigma_{\langle\tau_{s_j},\pi_j,O_1...O_t\rangle\in\Gamma_t}\pi_j$ are equal.
From Steps 3 and 4 above, we obtain $\Sigma_{\langle\tau_{s_3},\pi_3,CDF\rangle\in\Gamma_{CDF}}\pi_3 = 0.0279$ and $\alpha_{CDF}(3) = 0.0279$: for this example the theorem is satisfied.

Proof: the proof of Theorem 1 is reported in Appendix B of the extended version of this paper [8].

Satisfying LTL Properties when Gaps Are Observed. In order to verify whether a LTL property ϕ is verified by a PTE τ, also in presence of observation gaps, we need to specify ϕ into the same formalism in which τ has been modelled, namely PTEs.

The pipeline for implementing the translation from ϕ into an equivalent PTE $\tau(\phi)$ is the following:

1. translate ϕ into a non probabilistic Trace Expression $\tau_{np}(\phi)$ using the implemented algorithm presented in [5];
2. translate the non probabilistic Trace Expression $\tau_{np}(\phi)$ into a probabilistic Trace Expression $\tau(\phi)$ using the "Probabilize" implemented algorithm presented below.

The first step above returns by construction a Trace Expression $\tau_{np}(\phi)$ modeled as a set of equations $\tau_{np}(\phi)_1, ..., \tau_{np}(\phi)_K$, where $\tau_{np}(\phi) = \tau_{np}(\phi)_1$ and each $\tau_{np}(\phi)_i$ has the following form: $\tau_{np}(\phi)_i = \vartheta_{i1}{:}X_{i1} \vee \vartheta_{i2}{:}X_{i2} \vee ... \vee \vartheta_{iK}{:}X_{iK}$.

X_{iK} can in turn be one of the $\tau_{np}(\phi)$ variables, or the constant Trace Expression 1 defined in Sect. 2.

Probabilize correctly terminates on Trace Expressions of this form. If run on Trace Expressions which contain "$\wedge$", "$|$" and "$\cdot$" operators, or that just do not meet the structure above, *Probabilize* fails.

Given a non probabilistic Trace Expression $\tau_{np}(\phi)$, we can obtain its corresponding probabilistic version $Probabilize(\tau_{np}(\phi))$ by adding probability parameters to all the event types that appear in the disjuncts of $\tau_{np}(\phi)$. To achieve this result, we have to define an algorithm that operates on τ_{np} following its structure and that, when there are more than one possible moves from the current state to the next ones due to observability of different event types, shares the probability among these event types following some probability distribution, the uniform one in the simplest case. For instance, if the algorithm is currently analyzing the state $cmd : \tau_{s_1}\vee disp : \tau_{s_2}$ and if it is using a uniform distribution probability,

$$Probabilize(cmd : \tau_{s_1} \vee disp : \tau_{s_2}) = cmd[0.5] : \tau_{s_1} \vee disp[0.5] : \tau_{s_2}$$

If uniform distribution probability is adopted, the structure-driven definition of *Probabilize* is the following:

$$Probabilize(\vartheta_{i1}{:}X_{i1} \vee \vartheta_{i2}{:}X_{i2} \vee ... \vee \vartheta_{iK}{:}X_{iK}) =$$

$$\vartheta_{i1}[1/K]\!:\!Pr(X_{i1}) \lor \vartheta_{i2}[1/K]\!:\!Pr(X_{i2}) \lor ... \lor \vartheta_{iK}[1/K]\!:\!Pr(X_{iK})$$

where $Pr(X_{ij}) = X_{ij}$ if $X_{ij} \neq 1$, and $Pr(X_{ij}) = \epsilon \lor everyEvent[1]\!:\!X_{ij}$ otherwhise. Because of the special form of $\tau_{np}(\phi)$, and the absence of operators besides ":" and "$\lor$" therein, the simple rule above is the only one we need for defining *Probabilize*.

Given these ingredients, satisfaction of LTL properties in presence of observation gaps can be verified in a natural and straightforward way thanks to

- the possibility to represent a LTL property as a standard Trace Expression,
- the possibility to transform such a Trace Expression into a probabilistic one thanks to the *Probabilize* algorithm, and
- the "and" operator, $\land$, modeling the fact that the (probabilistic) Trace Expressions in the two branches must perform the same transitions. From an set-theoretic viewpoint, $\land$ models the intersection of the event traces represented by the two branches it joins.

Let us identify with τ_{HMM} the PTE representing an HMM, and with $\tau_{np}(\phi)$ the standard Trace Expression representing the temporal property ϕ to be verified.

The PTE $\tau_{HMM} \land Probabilize(\tau_{np}(\phi))$ models the intersection of traces of events consistent with the HMM and traces of events that satisfy ϕ: by making the intersection of the states in τ_{HMM} with those in $Probabilize(\tau_{np}(\phi))$ we automatically constrain the evaluation process to those traces produced by the HMM that respect ϕ.

5   Minding Gaps in a Centralized Setting

All the algorithms presented in the previous sections have been implemented using SWI-Prolog[3]. The code and the examples used for our experiments can be downloaded from https://vivianamascardi.github.io/Software/PTE.pl.

PTEs can be modelled as Prolog terms; by exploiting syntactic equations where the same variable appears both to the left and to the right of the "=" syntactic equality symbol, recursive PTEs can be easily defined. This feature is supported by most Prolog implementations, including SWI-Prolog, and allows us to define the PTEs shown in the examples provided so far, with almost the same syntax used in the paper. The adoption of Prolog is a winning choice not only for representing PTEs, but also for implementing their semantics and for manipulating them. Thanks to Prolog's rule-based, declarative interpretation, the rules defining PTE operational semantics have a one-to-one correspondence with Prolog clauses: backtracking and "all-solutions" predicates are powerful tools to deal with the generation of multiple PTE states, when gaps introduce nondeterminism (*set-to-set* rule). A SWI-Prolog PTE-driven monitor observing events taking place in the system under verification, and checking whether they

---

[3] http://swi-prolog.org/.

comply with the PTE or not, can be automatically generated from the PTE Prolog representation. Connectors with such SWI-Prolog PTE-driven monitors exist both for MASs [2,20,21] and for other systems, including Internet of Things [9,26] and object oriented applications [3]. So far, the algorithms for RV of partially observable MASs have been tested in a simulated environment, namely, with no real connection with implemented systems.

Events can be observed as an online stream while they are generated by the system (*online RV*), or can be recorded on a log file and then inspected (*offline RV*). In both scenarios there may be gaps, due to different reasons. In offline RV, gaps might be caused by event sampling, as usually done to reduce the monitor workload. In online RV, a gap indicates lack of information (a lost message, event or perception); in this case, the absence of information may be due to technical constraints of the system or of the monitor observation capabilities rather than to optimization purposes.

The *set-to-set* semantic rule generates a set of states each time it is applied. The states are maintained by SWI-Prolog in its local knowledge base, to allow the monitor to retrieve the current set of states, query each of them, and update the knowledge base with newly generated states. Unfortunately, a rule like *set-to-set* suffers from state space explosion, in particular when there are many sources of nondeterminism. Each time a gap takes place, the monitor must make guesses on the possible actual events that the gap represents and save all the states generated by these guesses. A possibly huge logical tree-like structure with states as nodes, and moves from states to states as edges, represents these open possibilities. If RV takes place online, the exploration of this logical structure must follow a breadth-first strategy (more space needed but possibly less time required to recognize that the trace is not compliant with the expected behaviour), as the final trace of events is unknown and the levels of the structure are generated and explored at the same time. When, instead, a log file is analyzed offline, the trace in the log is already complete and the logical tree-like structure can be explored, looking for violations, following a depth-first search (less space needed, but the violation could be discovered after exploring all the structure).

Online RV is definitely more challenging: if the log file is analyzed offline, after the system has completed its execution, discovering a violation with some (further) delay is not an issue. But if RV takes place online, it must be performed as efficiently as possible, and in such a way that violations are discovered as soon as possible, to take actions including repairing the system if possible or even stopping its execution, to avoid more serious consequences. This paves the way to two more scenarios: centralized online RV, discusses in this paper, and decentralized online RV, discussed in the companion paper presented at CILC 2022 [7]. In this section we present the reader with an example to understand how a centralized PTE-driven monitor works, and what the state explosion problem means in practice.

Let us consider a MAS involving four agents: $\{alice, bob, charlie, dave\}$. The set of events of our interest in this scenario is the set of messages $Msgs$ that these agents can use to communicate with each other. Such events can be represented as $a_1 \overset{c}{\Longrightarrow} a_2$, meaning that agent a_1 sends a message to a_2 with content c. Since messages are composed by (at least) three mandatory components, sender, receiver and content, besides the totally uninstantiated gap where nothing is known, there may be many partially instantiated gaps such as:

- $gap(a_1 \Longrightarrow a_2)$, where the content of the message is unknown;
- $gap(\_ \overset{m}{\Longrightarrow} a_2)$, where the sender is unknown;
- $gap(a_1 \overset{m}{\Longrightarrow} \_)$, where the receiver is unknown.

In order to make the presentation easier to read we consider event types containing only one message (singleton): instead of writing for example $\vartheta{:}\tau$ where $[\![\vartheta]\!] = \{alice \overset{m_1}{\Longrightarrow} bob\}$ (event type representing the message from $alice$ to bob with content m_1), we directly write $alice \overset{m_1}{\Longrightarrow} bob{:}\tau$. Given the PTE

$$\tau = \tau_1 \vee \tau_2$$

$$\tau_1 = alice \overset{msg_1}{\Longrightarrow} bob[0.7] : (bob \overset{msg_2}{\Longrightarrow} charlie[0.6] : \tau_1 \mid bob \overset{msg_3}{\Longrightarrow} dave[0.4] : \epsilon)$$

$$\tau_2 = alice \overset{msg_4}{\Longrightarrow} dave[0.3] : (charlie \overset{msg_5}{\Longrightarrow} dave[0.3] : \epsilon \mid bob \overset{msg_3}{\Longrightarrow} dave[0.7] : \tau_2)$$

and initial probability of τ equal to 1, a centralized monitor M_c observing all the interactions among the agents starting from the state τ would behave in the following way. Let us identify with $M_{0,c}$ where c stands for "centralized", the initial state of M_c. $M_{0,c} = \langle \tau, 1, \sigma \rangle$. We highlight that τ contains the shuffle operator $\mid$ and hence cannot be the output of the HMM2PTE algorithm. It has been designed "by hand", to show that PTEs can be also designed and developed from scratch, besides being automatically generated from a HMM. Being very simple, we can easily check that it is consistent w.r.t. the properties that probability of events must ensure. In the general case, a manual consistency check may be hard to carry out, and its automation is out of the scope of this paper. Let us suppose that the first observed event is a totally uninstantiated gap. Starting from τ, the only two possible evolutions of the protocol are those where either $alice$ sends msg_1 to bob ($alice \overset{msg_1}{\Longrightarrow} bob$) or $alice$ sends msg_4 to $dave$ ($alice \overset{msg_4}{\Longrightarrow} dave$). These evolutions may be formalized as (we use ch instead of $charlie$ for space constraints)

$$M_{0,c} \overset{gap}{\rightharpoonup} M_{1,c} = \{\langle (bob \overset{msg_2}{\Longrightarrow} ch[0.6] : \tau_1 \mid bob \overset{msg_3}{\Longrightarrow} dave[0.4] : \epsilon, 0.7, gap(alice \overset{msg_1}{\Longrightarrow} bob)\rangle,$$

$$\langle ch \overset{msg_5}{\Longrightarrow} dave[0.3] : \epsilon \mid bob \overset{msg_3}{\Longrightarrow} dave[0.7] : \tau_2, 0.3, gap(alice \overset{msg_4}{\Longrightarrow} dave)\rangle\}$$

If another totally uninstantiated gap is observed, each state in $M_{1,c}$ can evolve in two different ways because of the shuffle, leading to

$$M_{1,c} \overset{gap}{\rightharpoonup} M_{2,c} = \{\langle \tau_1 \mid bob \overset{msg_3}{\Longrightarrow} dave[0.4] : \epsilon, 0.42, gap(alice \overset{msg_1}{\Longrightarrow} bob) \ gap(bob \overset{msg_2}{\Longrightarrow} ch)\rangle,$$

$$\langle bob \overset{msg_2}{\Longrightarrow} ch[0.6] : \tau_1, 0.28, gap(alice \overset{msg_1}{\Longrightarrow} bob) \ gap(bob \overset{msg_3}{\Longrightarrow} dave)\rangle,$$

$\langle bob \overset{msg3}{\Longrightarrow} dave[0.7] : \tau_2, 0.09, gap(alice \overset{msg4}{\Longrightarrow} dave) \ gap(ch \overset{msg5}{\Longrightarrow} dave)\rangle$

$\langle ch \overset{msg5}{\Longrightarrow} dave[0.3] : \epsilon \mid \tau_2, 0.21, gap(alice \overset{msg4}{\Longrightarrow} dave) \ gap(bob \overset{msg3}{\Longrightarrow} dave)\rangle\}$

It is easy to see that the number of states can rapidly grow, because one single monitor is in charge for the RV of all the MAS and takes care of all the possibilities that open up when gaps are observed, that is the main limitation and bottleneck of the approach implemented so far. One approach to cope with state space explosion is to split the centralized monitor into a set of decentralized ones, each observing a portion of the MAS. Since each decentralized monitor has to make its guesses about gaps, when a gap is observed there may be different opinions about its possible values. With respect to a centralized approach, different perspectives due to decentralization need to be managed through synchronization between the monitors, which generates some communication overhead. The algorithm for "minding gaps in a decentralized way" is presented in [7]. The experiments presented in that paper show that, despite the communication overhead due to synchronization, decentralization reduces the search space, in particular when the number of components that generate observable events in the system, be them agents, actors, artefacts, sensors, increases.

6   Conclusions and Future Work

In this paper, we addressed the presence of gaps in observed traces and the need to estimate the probability that the (incomplete) traces satisfy some LTL properties, when the system is modelled by a PTE.

Differently from the work by Stoller at al. we took inspiration from [32], to perform runtime verification using PTEs, we need that each gap represents one single unobserved event: if we have a sequence of three unobserved events, we must have three different gaps in the observed trace. If, in the real system, this one event-one gap correspondence cannot be achieved, we should estimate the number of unobserved events that took place in a time slot T by computing the average rate of the event generation G, and inserting $T * G$ gaps in the event trace. As an example, if the monitor pauses for 3 s and the average events generation rate is 4 events for second, the trace should have 12 consecutive gaps corresponding to what happened in the time slot T.

Although PTEs have a higher potential expressive power than HMM and LTL, being able to express traces like $a^n b^n c^n$, in this work we start from an HMM of the real system and generate an equivalent PTE from it, which of course is as expressive as the HMM it originates from. This is a safe approach to generate a PTE consistent with the known probability distribution of events, which can then be refined in such a way that its expressivennes is fully exploited. Providing guidelines and automatic tools to support the developer in this refinement step is part of our future investigations: we plan to extend RIVERtools [4] towards this direction. More urgent, both the centralized and the decentralized versions of the algorithm have been experimented in a simulated setting; implementing them on top of a real MAS framework like JADE [17] or Jason [19] is the first item in our agenda.

References

1. Ancona, D., Briola, D., Ferrando, A., Mascardi, V.: Global protocols as first class entities for self-adaptive agents. In: AAMAS, pp. 1019–1029. ACM (2015)
2. Ancona, D., Drossopoulou, S., Mascardi, V.: Automatic generation of self-monitoring MASs from multiparty global session types in Jason. In: Declarative Agent Languages and Technologies X - 10th International Workshop, DALT 2012, Valencia, Spain, 4 June 2012, Revised Selected Papers, pp. 76–95 (2012)
3. Ancona, D., Ferrando, A., Franceschini, L., Mascardi, V.: Parametric trace expressions for runtime verification of Java-like programs. In: FTfJP@ECOOP, pp. 10:1–10:6. ACM (2017)
4. Ancona, D., Ferrando, A., Franceschini, L., Mascardi, V.: Managing bad AIPs with RIVERtools. In: Demazeau, Y., An, B., Bajo, J., Fernández-Caballero, A. (eds.) PAAMS 2018. LNCS (LNAI), vol. 10978, pp. 296–300. Springer, Cham (2018). https://doi.org/10.1007/978-3-319-94580-4_24
5. Ancona, D., Ferrando, A., Mascardi, V.: Comparing trace expressions and linear temporal logic for runtime verification. In: Ábrahám, E., Bonsangue, M., Johnsen, E.B. (eds.) Theory and Practice of Formal Methods. LNCS, vol. 9660, pp. 47–64. Springer, Cham (2016). https://doi.org/10.1007/978-3-319-30734-3_6
6. Ancona, D., Ferrando, A., Mascardi, V.: Parametric runtime verification of multi-agent systems. In: AAMAS, pp. 1457–1459. ACM (2017)
7. Ancona, D., Ferrando, A., Mascardi, V.: Exploiting probabilistic trace expressions for decentralized runtime verification with gaps. In: The 37th Italian Conference on Computational Logic, CILC 2022, CEUR Workshop Proceedings. CEUR-WS.org (2022)
8. Ancona, D., Ferrando, A., Mascardi, V.: Mind the gap! Runtime verification of partially observable MASs with probabilistic trace expressions - extended version. Technical report, University of Genova, DIBRIS (2022). This technical report extends the contents of this EUMAS 2022 paper with two appendices. https://vivianamascardi.github.io/Documents/technical-report-EUMAS2022.pdf
9. Ancona, D., Franceschini, L., Delzanno, G., Leotta, M., Ribaudo, M., Ricca, F.: Towards runtime monitoring of Node.js and its application to the Internet of Things. In: ALP4IoT@iFM. EPTCS, vol. 264, pp. 27–42 (2017)
10. Ancona, D., Franceschini, L., Ferrando, A., Mascardi, V.: RML: theory and practice of a domain specific language for runtime verification. Sci. Comput. Program. **205**, 102610 (2021)
11. Babaee, R., Gurfinkel, A., Fischmeister, S.: *Prevent*: a predictive run-time verification framework using statistical learning. In: Johnsen, E.B., Schaefer, I. (eds.) SEFM 2018. LNCS, vol. 10886, pp. 205–220. Springer, Cham (2018). https://doi.org/10.1007/978-3-319-92970-5_13
12. Barringer, H., Groce, A., Havelund, K., Smith, M.H.: Formal analysis of log files. JACIC **7**(11), 365–390 (2010)
13. Bartocci, E., Falcone, Y. (eds.): Lectures on Runtime Verification - Introductory and Advanced Topics. LNCS, vol. 10457. Springer, Cham (2018). https://doi.org/10.1007/978-3-319-75632-5
14. Bartocci, E., Falcone, Y., Francalanza, A., Reger, G.: Introduction to runtime verification. In: Bartocci, E., Falcone, Y. (eds.) Lectures on Runtime Verification. LNCS, vol. 10457, pp. 1–33. Springer, Cham (2018). https://doi.org/10.1007/978-3-319-75632-5_1

15. Bartocci, E., Grosu, R., Katsaros, P., Ramakrishnan, C.R., Smolka, S.A.: Model repair for probabilistic systems. In: Abdulla, P.A., Leino, K.R.M. (eds.) TACAS 2011. LNCS, vol. 6605, pp. 326–340. Springer, Heidelberg (2011). https://doi.org/10.1007/978-3-642-19835-9_30
16. Baum, L.E., Petrie, T.: Statistical inference for probabilistic functions of finite state Markov chains. Ann. Math. Statist. **37**(6), 1554–1563 (1966)
17. Bellifemine, F., Caire, G., Greenwood, D.: Developing Multi-Agent Systems with JADE. Wiley, Hoboken (2007)
18. Bonakdarpour, B., Fraigniaud, P., Rajsbaum, S., Travers, C. (eds.) Bertinoro Seminar on Distributed Runtime Verification, May 2016 (2016). http://www.labri.fr/perso/travers/DRV2016/
19. Bordini, R.H., Hübner, J.F., Wooldridge, M.: Programming Multi-Agent Systems in AgentSpeak using Jason. Wiley, Hoboken (2007)
20. Briola, D., Mascardi, V., Ancona, D.: Distributed runtime verification of JADE and Jason multiagent systems with Prolog. In: CILC. CEUR Workshop Proceedings, vol. 1195, pp. 319–323. CEUR-WS.org (2014)
21. Briola, D., Mascardi, V., Ancona, D.: Distributed runtime verification of JADE multiagent systems. In: Camacho, D., Braubach, L., Venticinque, S., Badica, C. (eds.) Intelligent Distributed Computing VIII. SCI, vol. 570, pp. 81–91. Springer, Cham (2015). https://doi.org/10.1007/978-3-319-10422-5_10
22. Cairoli, F., Bortolussi, L., Paoletti, N.: Neural predictive monitoring under partial observability. In: Feng, L., Fisman, D. (eds.) RV 2021. LNCS, vol. 12974, pp. 121–141. Springer, Cham (2021). https://doi.org/10.1007/978-3-030-88494-9_7
23. Havelund, K., Leucker, M., Sachenbacher, M., Sokolsky, O., Williams, B.C. (eds.) Runtime Verification, Diagnosis, Planning and Control for Autonomous Systems, 07.11. - 12.11.2010. Dagstuhl Seminar Proceedings, vol. 10451. Schloss Dagstuhl - Leibniz-Zentrum für Informatik, Germany (2010)
24. Havelund, K., Reger, G., Rosu, G.: Runtime verification - past experiences and future projections. In: Special Issue in Celebration of Issue Number 10,000 of Lecture Notes in Computer Science. LNCS, vol. 10000 (2018)
25. Joshi, Y., Tchamgoue, G.M., Fischmeister, S.: Runtime verification of LTL on lossy traces. In: SAC, pp. 1379–1386. ACM (2017)
26. Leotta, M., Ancona, D., Franceschini, L., Olianas, D., Ribaudo, M., Ricca, F.: Towards a runtime verification approach for internet of things systems. In: Pautasso, C., Sánchez-Figueroa, F., Systä, K., Murillo Rodríguez, J.M. (eds.) ICWE 2018. LNCS, vol. 11153, pp. 83–96. Springer, Cham (2018). https://doi.org/10.1007/978-3-030-03056-8_8
27. Leucker, M., Schallhart, C.: A brief account of runtime verification. J. Log. Algebr. Program. **78**(5), 293–303 (2009)
28. Pnueli, A.: The temporal logic of programs. In: 18th Annual Symposium on Foundations of Computer Science, Providence, Rhode Island, USA, 31 October–1 November 1977, pp. 46–57. IEEE Computer Society (1977)
29. Rabiner, L.R.: A tutorial on hidden Markov models and selected applications in speech recognition. In: Waibel, A., Lee, K.-F. (eds.) Readings in Speech Recognition, pp. 267–296. Morgan Kaufmann Publishers Inc., San Francisco (1990)
30. Rabiner, L.R., Juang, B.-H.: An introduction to hidden Markov models. IEEE ASSP Mag. 4–16 (1986)
31. Sánchez, C., et al.: A survey of challenges for runtime verification from advanced application domains (beyond software). Formal Methods Syst. Des. **54**(3), 279–335 (2019)

32. Stoller, S.D., et al.: Runtime verification with state estimation. In: Khurshid, S., Sen, K. (eds.) RV 2011. LNCS, vol. 7186, pp. 193–207. Springer, Heidelberg (2012). https://doi.org/10.1007/978-3-642-29860-8_15

Advising Agent for Service-Providing Live-Chat Operators

Aviram Aviv[1], Yaniv Oshrat[1(✉)], Samuel Assefa[2], Toby Mustapha[3],
Daniel Borrajo[4], Manuela Veloso[3], and Sarit Kraus[1]

[1] Bar-Ilan University, Ramat-Gan, Israel
`oshblo@zahav.net.il, sarit@cs.biu.ac.il`
[2] US Bank AI Innovation, Minneapolis, USA
[3] JP Morgan AI Research, New York, USA
`manuela.veloso@jpmorgan.com`
[4] University Carlos III of Madrid, Madrid, Spain
`dborrajo@ia.uc3m.es`

Abstract. Call centers, in which human operators attend clients using textual chat, are very common in modern e-commerce. Training enough skilled operators who are able to provide good service is a challenge. We propose a methodology for the development of an assisting agent that provides online advice to operators while they attend clients. The agent is easy-to-build and can be introduced to new domains without major effort in design, training and organizing sknowledge of the professional discipline. We demonstrate the applicability of the system in an experiment that realizes its full life-cycle on a specific domain, and analyze its capabilities.

Keywords: Human study · Advising agent · Human-agent interaction · Call center

1 Introduction

In modern e-commerce, many business services are provided via the Internet. Not only do new web-oriented enterprises use this option, but traditional ones as well have moved relevant services to the digital medium. For example, banks are increasingly closing their physical branches and moving services, formerly provided only face-to-face, to the internet [42]. There are many actions that customers can perform by themselves via the Internet, without human intervention, either by a self-service application or using a conversational chatbot. However, when customers want to perform actions that do not yet have an online solution, or when they fail to do it by themselves, they still need to approach the bank's customer service and seek human help.

There are several communication channels between the customers and the call center employees (operators). The first method is a telephone call. This method gives the customer the full attention of someone capable of helping, but at the same time it forces the operator to wait for the customer's reactions. In many of these calls, the customers need to perform actions with which they are not familiar, making the operator wait idly for the customers to finish. Since the operator can attend only one customer at a time, this approach wastes time that could be better utilized. With the rise of the Internet, another approach for call centers emerged, using a text-based chat service. This method obviates the constraint of giving one customer the full attention of the operator, as it parallels the service. Instead of talking with one customer at a time, the operator interacts textually with 2–4 customers in parallel, switching between customers instead of waiting for the customer's reactions.

While this approach has its advantages, it also raises some challenges for the human operator to deal with. As the number of tasks that the operators have to perform simultaneously grows, so may their stress. Operators also need to prioritize the tasks, keep track of each individual's information while assisting different clients, and provide help without making any client wait too long.

We propose to mitigate these challenges by assisting the human operator in creating an **advising agent**. This kind of agent works alongside the operator during the chat session, and suggests on-line advice to help the operator deal with a given situation. To the best of our knowledge, we are the first to use an advising agent to cope with these challenges. However, building an advising agent and training it to the specific service domain can be a long and expensive process that requires both domain expertise and system engineering knowledge.

In this work we present a design for an automated agent that assists the operator during textual chat interactions with customers in real-time, by providing the operator with advice about possible actions and relevant information. Our design combines standard ML methods with domain-expert annotations, and tries to predict the actions and suggestions of the expert. The novelty of our method is twofold: First, the assistance of the agent is not focused on providing answers to customers' questions (as in former works, e.g. [11,20]), but rather in guiding the operator as to what questions she should ask in order to get the required information to provide service. Second, the process of training the agent to a new domain is short and does not require many resources or domain knowledge from outer sources. Finally, we field-test our design on a specific domain and present our findings.

2   Related Work

2.1   Call Centers

Many research fields look at call centers as a source of interesting problems to study. Some of them analyze the call center as a business to be run, trying to improve the total income and customer satisfaction [24], predict customer abandonment [23], or predict attrition rates [12]. Other fields examine the effect of working in call centers on the human employees [29]. However, when looking at call centers from the computer science point of view, most of the research is focused on solving problems like staffing, customer queuing or scheduling processes [1,30,31,34,51].

In recent years, many companies have started to develop chatbots for the task of customer service [45]. There is much work regarding the design and deployment of such bots in various domains [46]. It is evident that currently chatbots cannot fully replace human workers, and when a bot detects that it cannot help the customer, it refers the customer to human help. Li *et al.* [36] and Liu *et al.* [37] explore the challenge of detecting this kind of situation in various domains.

Lee *et al.* [33] show that chatbots can reduce the human workload, but the change is almost imperceptible (less than 5% improvement). The vast majority of the problems found refer to parts of the call center that have little to no effect on the human workers. To the best of our knowledge, this is the first research study that tries to help the human worker directly by providing advice.

2.2   Agents that Support Human Actions

Intelligent agents that support humans in their complex activities need to be able to predict the user's behavior and decisions [4,32,48,49]. This is a difficult task because of an extensive set of factors that influence human decision-making and behavior [15], such as experience [26], decision complexity [19] and emotions [7]. These factors also include inherent differences between individuals and groups of individuals [9], which make the prediction of an individual's decisions and behavior even more challenging [44].

There are several previous methods for prediction of human behavior and decisions in agent-human interactions. Azaria *et al.* [6] developed CARE (automobile Climate control Advisor for Reducing Energy consumption) – an agent that uses two models: one for predicting the influence a certain climate has on the human driver, and one for estimating the energy consumption of a particular setting. The agent finds a compromise between them and offers it to the driver, who chooses whether or not to accept it. Rosenfeld *et al.* [47] developed automated agents that can assist a single operator to better manage a group of robots in a search task and a warehouse operation task, showing that an agent can significantly improve the performance of a team comprised of an operator and ten low-cost mobile robots. The agent uses the world state to determine which human actions are urgent and which actions can wait for later. This work also compared two approaches of advice: one looks for the advice that will have the best impact on the current situation, and the other searches for advice that will lead to better results in the near future (2 or 3 actions ahead). In both domains, the agent gave the operator advice about what should be done next, depending on the world state at every moment.

2.3   Method of Advice Provision

When it comes to advising in repeated human interaction environments, several methods have been used in the literature. Rosenfeld *et al.* [47] directly estimated the reward for every possible piece of advice and recommended a piece of advice that maximizes the reward that the user will get if the provided advice is chosen. Elmalech *et al.* [16] suggested that the agent will try to find a compromise between maximizing rewards and user acceptance, and Azaria *et al.* [5] used human models inspired by behavioral economic theories for advice provision. The common ground of these advising agents is that they all advise in order to maximize a certain reward function. The drawback of this kind of advising mechanism is that it tends to recommend non-intuitive advice that the operators often reject, making it ineffective [10].

2.4   Learning How to Provide Advice

In recent years, companies began keeping records of their workers' actions and their interactions with the customers due to low digital storage costs [27]. This accumulation of information was mostly used for basic performance analysis, but with the improvement of machine learning capabilities this abundance called for new uses [17].

Using human actions and decisions as the base of the learning process has many names in the literature such as learning from observation, learning by demonstration, or mimic agent, among others. Argall *et al.* [2] united many of these names under "learning from demonstration" (LfD), and mentioned that LfD does not require expert knowledge of the domain dynamics, an essential notion for our research as we use demonstrations from people with little to no experience in the field. The LfD approach is used in a large variety of fields (e.g., [18,54]). In our context, Levy and Sarne [35] combined LfD and advice provision as they created an agent that used the way people act in a specific scenario in order to guess what they would do in similar situations.

Even though there are many examples in the literature of ways to generate conversational data [13,38,39], we focus on using human-human conversations for the learning process of the agent because they better reflect the real-life scenario [53] and hopefully help in generating more intuitive advice.

3   Modus Operandi and Life-Cycle of the Agent

Our research goal is to develop an easy-to-build, data-driven method for an automated system that will assist in the operators' training process and daily activities, will help new and experienced operators, and will advise the operators about possible actions and relevant information during textual chat interactions with customers in real-time. Implementing the automated system (i.e., the agent) in a call center has the potential to reduce the daily workload and improve interaction with the customers from the human operator's point of view. It will improve the system's service efficiency and reduce the time needed to help each customer.

3.1   Agent's Life-Cycle

The process of building an advising-agent for a new domain is performed in three phases, as follows:

1. **The Apprentice Phase (Phase 1)** – experienced human operators serve human customers regarding the new domain of service. The operators tag the information they find important in the chat conversation: They may do it in real-time, as the chat goes on, or afterwards. The collected data is fed to the learning process (as detailed in Sect. 3.2). This phase exists only for the sake of collecting information for the next phases, and does not include any agent assistance. Section 4.2 elaborates about the experimentation of this phase.

2. **The Novice-Advisor Phase (Phase 2)** – this phase contains both data collection (for the improvement of the agent's capabilities) and service to clients: the agent works alongside a non-experienced human operator who attends clients, and it simultaneously advises and learns. For advising the human operator, the agent uses the tagging from the chat conversation to predict messages that the operator should send or actions it should perform, and offers them to the operator. The operator may use this advice or not, as suits her.

   In addition, the data collected in this phase may be fed into the agent's machine learning model in order to improve its tagging and advising capabilities. This feeding may be performed daily, weekly, monthly or in any batch form that is suitable to the managers of the service. Additional details regarding this phase are presented in Sect. 4.3.

3. **The Expert-Advisor Phase (Phase 3)** – The agent works alongside a non-experienced human operator and provides advice based on former tags and a learned model. The agent is not engaged in further learning, since its capabilities have already reached an adequate level. This phase is the final and steady state of the agent in the current domain.

A rollback from Phase 3 to previous phases may be performed if needed (as elaborated on in Sect. 4.4). The system can be returned to Phase 1 or to Phase 2 (according to the managers' preferences), collect additional data (i.e. tagged chat conversations) and feed them to the machine learning model. Upon reaching the desired level of advice, the agent may be advanced again to Phase 3, and so forth.

The 3-Phase life-cycle was chosen because it enables the adjustment of the phase to the opportunities and the needs of the users: It uses the knowledge of experienced operators in Phase 1, it combines exploration and exploitation in Phase 2, and enables steady production in Phase 3. As pointed out in the previous paragraph, the system may be switched between phases according to the needs of the users and other circumstances.

This model suggests a method to implement an assisting agent in a new domain with a relatively small effort: The needed knowledge is derived from authentic dialogues with clients, that is to say it uses the resources that are already invested to build the domain knowledge. The specific agent that is built is suited to the specific domain, but the method is domain-independent, and it may be applied to a wide variety of domains.

3.2   The Learning Process

In order to provide advice, the agent relies on a predictive model learned from observations of the domain: Operators conduct chat sessions with clients and attend to their needs. During the chat sessions, the operators tag the vital information items they used to reach the satisfactory outcomes. An information item may include a single word or a phrase (a few words), and it depends on the specific domain in which the service is provided. All the tagging is done during the chat conversation or after it; there is no tagging in advance.

A tag contains **a label**, which is the category of the tag, and **information**, which cites the specific knowledge of the tag. For example, if an operator asks clients about their occupation, then the label of the tag will be "occupation", and possible information can be "engineer", "marketing manager", "driver", "none", etc. Figure 1 presents several examples of tags from various domains.

<vehicle><Ford Explorer>	<occupation><none>
<vehicle><Toyota Avensis>	<occupation><cost analyst>
<education><PhD>	<occupation><bus driver>
<education><BSc>	<occupation><accountant>
<education><MA>	<university><ucla>
<military service><yes>	<university><stanford>
<military service<no>	<university><cmu>

Fig. 1. Examples of tags. In this structure, the first item is the label of the tag and the second one is the information.

Each session's tag-list is turned into an **information vector**. Each time a new tag is added, the vector's current version is saved to be used later in the learning process as an information vector.

Building the Information Vector. We build the information vector as follows: First, we take the n most common labels that operators marked in the data and sort them in alphabetical order (the label list).

Notation remark: We write X_t as the information vector after t pieces of information (that is, X at time t), and $X[t]$ for the value of X at index t. Whenever we mention tag i, we refer to the value of the tag list at index i.

We define two vectors of size n. The first one is:

$$V[i] := \begin{cases} item, & \text{if a known item was tagged as label i} \\ \text{"unknown"}, & \text{if an unknown item was tagged as label i} \\ \text{" -- "}, & \text{if no input was tagged as label i} \end{cases}$$

A known item is an item that was already tagged (in previous chat conversations or previously in the current conversation). An unknown item is an item that has not yet been tagged.

The second vector is:

$$W[i] := \begin{cases} 1, & \text{if there is an input tagged as label i} \\ 0, & \text{otherwise} \end{cases}$$

We define $X[i] = (V[i], W[i])$ (that is, the vector X is made of (V, W) tuples). Figure 2 demonstrates the building of the information vector.

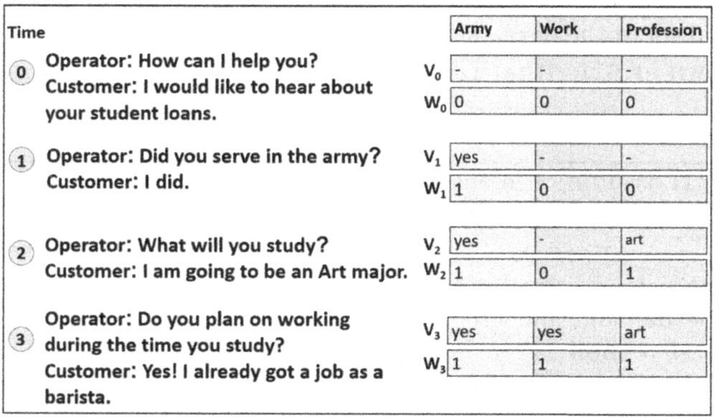

Time		Army	Work	Profession
(0) Operator: How can I help you? Customer: I would like to hear about your student loans.	V_0	-	-	-
	W_0	0	0	0
(1) Operator: Did you serve in the army? Customer: I did.	V_1	yes	-	-
	W_1	1	0	0
(2) Operator: What will you study? Customer: I am going to be an Art major.	V_2	yes	-	art
	W_2	1	0	1
(3) Operator: Do you plan on working during the time you study? Customer: Yes! I already got a job as a barista.	V_3	yes	yes	art
	W_3	1	1	1

Fig. 2. The process of building an information vector as the chat between an operator and a client proceeds.

Advice Types. There are three types of advice that we wish to provide: (1) Topic acquisition – questions the operator should ask the client in order to acquire information she needs in order to help him; (2) Resolution – data the operator should provide to the client as a response to his query; and (3) Useful information – data the operator may need in order to provide answers, such as relevant websites, calculations, etc.

Advice Providing Process. During the chat conversation with the customer, whenever the operator uses a website operation or finds out new information about the customer, useful information is marked under a suitable label, and the customer information vector X is updated accordingly.

For each advice type i of the three mentioned above, advice is provided by taking the label vector X_t and inserting it into a machine learning module F_i that tries to find the best set of advice A for the current situation (A_t). The module uses k pairs $D_1 \dots D_k$ of past experiences $D_j = (X_j, A_j)$, where X_j is an information vector at time j and A_j is the respective set of advice, in order to find a set that maximizes the chance to be the most used set of advice in the past similar situations: $P(A_t = A | X_t, D_1, ..., D_k)$.

For the learning algorithm, we wanted to find an algorithm with the ability to work efficiently on several domains and handle messy and conflicting data. The first model that came to mind was Random Forest [8], a model that works well but cannot fully utilize the vast amount of data usually available in such domains. To deal with this problem, we thought of using neural networks. That idea was relatively successful, but an architecture that works on one domain might fail to learn on another. With all that in mind, we decided to combine them as an ensemble method of neural networks [21] where each network takes the information known about a customer at a certain time and outputs the recommended set of advice for the situation. Each network in the ensemble was trained on a subset of the data and had a random number of layers of an arbitrary length, as shown in Algorithm 1.

Algorithm 1: Training the ensemble:

Result: a list of trained neural networks
1 nets=∅
2 **while** *length(nets) <ensembleSize* **do**
3   num=GetRandomNumber()
4   **if** *num >0.5* **then**
5 | trainSet=getRandomSubSet(trainData)
6   **else**
7 | trainSet=getBalancedSubSet(trainData)
8   **end**
9   net=GenerateRandomNeuralNetwork()
10   train(net,trainSet)
11   P_{net}=accuracy(net,testData)
   if $P_{net} >P_{threshold}$ **then**
12 | nets $\xleftarrow{add}$ net
13   **end**
14 **end**

The final set of advice was chosen using a majority voting variation (as shown in Algorithm 2). We also tested the ensemble method of neural networks against other variations of Random Forest (LGBM [28] and regular Random Forest) and other crowd related algorithms (SVM and KNN). This method outperformed the others in an 80:20 cross-validation where the target label needed to be in the top 2 recommendations (the ensemble reached 87% accuracy, regular and gradient boosted Random Forests with 84%, KNN with 83%, neural network with 77% and SVM with 70%). We chose this metric because there can be a large variation based on the operator's preferences, even with a small amount of data.

Algorithm 2: Using the ensemble:

Result: Final recommendations
1 results=∅
2 X=getData()
3 **for** *net in ensemble* **do**
4 | results$\xleftarrow{\text{add}}$ prediction(X)
5 **end**
6 bestOptions=twoMostCommonOptions(results)
7 finalRecommendations=∅
8 **if** *rankOf(bestOptions[0]) >firstOptionThreshold* **then**
9 | finalRecommendations $\xleftarrow{\text{add}}$ bestOptions[0]
10 **end**
11 **if** *rankOf(bestOptions[1]) >secondaryOptionThreshold* **then**
12 | finalRecommendations $\xleftarrow{\text{add}}$ bestOptions[1]
13 **end**
14 return finalRecommendations

As can be seen in Algorithm 2, the agent can recommend one set, recommend a combination of two sets, or remain silent (when ∅ is chosen or when finalRecommendations is empty).

4   Experiment

Our experiment was designed to test whether working with the suggested assisting agent improves operators' performance. For this purpose we chose a domain, set up a working environment and recruited participants to play the roles of operators and clients in various configurations. At the end of each session, the operators filled out questionnaires to quantify their opinions regarding different aspects of the performance. We analyzed the results, learned some lessons and made amendments to the model. We will now describe the setup and course of the experiments. The results will be presented in Sect. 5.

4.1   Experiment Domain - Student Loans

The domain on which we chose to perform our experiment is student loans in the US. Customers who are interested in understanding their options in getting such loans, either for themselves or for their relatives (usually a son or a daughter), call the information center and chat with the operator. In some cases, the customers know what the relevant data is, and they can provide it to the operator right away. Nevertheless, in many cases the customers are not familiar with the parameters that define their entitlement to a loan, and they should be guided. For example, in the US men are required to register in the Selective Service System in order to be entitled to a federal loan. Many applicants are not aware of this requirement, and informing them of it, or of other parameters that might affect their ability to get a loan of the sum they need, is very beneficial. Good service by the operator should clarify these issues in order to enable the customer to exhaust his rights. Hence, there is much room for accurate advice to the operator in this process. Since Phase 3 in our model is the steady state working mode, we performed our field experience on phases 1 and 2 which implement the building of the model.

4.2 Phase 1 – The Apprentice Phase

As mentioned above, the goal of this phase is to provide the agent with labeled data regarding our domain by listening to sessions in which experienced human operators chat with clients. This phase was implemented in our experiment by recruits that played the operators and the customers. The operators were thoroughly briefed and trained about the domain and the service they should provide to customers. At the end of this preparation stage, it was assumed that the recruits were at the level of a practised operator in the domain of student loans. The customer received storyboards, each with character information (profession, university, savings, financial status etc.) and objectives to achieve (loan options, pre-specified information about the loans etc.).

The chat between the customers and the operators was performed using a textual chat application. We used "WhatsApp" as a basis for our interface, as this application is commonly used by businesses for communications with customers (e.g. [25,41,43]). The operators used a computer where half of the screen is a "WhatsApp web" interface with a special browser extension that knows when the operator switches between two conversations (as a single operator attended 2–3 customers simultaneously), and allows the operator to mark words. The other half of the screen shows a website which presents information and enables the operator to perform common calculations by clicking on pre-defined buttons.

The subjects played multiple client-operator sessions. In these sessions there was no participation of an assisting agent, and only the human operators and the human clients took part. During the sessions, in addition to collecting relevant information from the clients and answering clients' questions, the operators also tagged phrases in the chat. They were asked to tag (by marking words on the screen) any information that they considered relevant to the loan issue. Each tag contained a label (e.g. university name) and information for that label (e.g. UCLA, MIT, Columbia University). Operators were neither told nor limited regarding what labels of tags they could mark. They saw what labels were tagged and used before, but did not see their information. They could add additional tags as needed.

In this phase of experiment, 4 subjects took part as operators and one subject played the clients. Note that this subject played 2–3 clients simultaneously, but since the work of the operator is more complicated than the work of the clients, and since the experimenter who played the clients was practiced and followed pre-prepared scenarios, he was able to play more than one client simultaneously without causing a delay to the work of the operator. In total there were 76 sessions, and in each of them a single operator attended 2–3 simulated clients.

4.3   Phase 2 – The Novice-Advisor Phase

The goal of the Novice-Advisor Phase is twofold: To assist operators in their work, as well as to collect additional data for the improvement of the agent. In the experiment, our main goal was to evaluate the helpfulness of the agent we built in Phase 1.

In our experiment this phase was implemented using recruits from the AI course for undergraduate students in Bar-Ilan University as clients, and paid recruits from the general population as operators or clients. Each operator played two sessions: one with an agent's assistance and the other without it. Half of the operators played the assisted session first and the unassisted session second, and the other half vice versa. Each client played a single session, in which they received two different storyboards and played them with the operator.

At the end of each session, we asked the participants who played the operators to fill out a NASA-TLX questionnaire [22], which is an assessment tool for comparing the workload of different tasks (a summary of the NASA-TLX questionnaire can be found in Appendix A in [3]). These opinions were analyzed in order to evaluate the performance of the agent and its contribution to the performance of the operators. The findings of the analysis are presented in Sect. 5.

At this point we had 23 operators who played 46 sessions: 15 of the 23 operators attended 2 clients simultaneously and the remaining 8 operators attended 3 clients simultaneously. The tagging of the text was done manually by the operators during the sessions.

The Tagging Problem. The tagging of the chat conversations is essential for the agent in order to follow the line of conversation and provide proper advice. Our preliminary design was to tag the chat by the human operator, in real-time, during the session. Unfortunately, we found out that the operators of Phase 2 managed to perform the tagging well while attending 2 clients simultaneously, but when they needed to attend 3 clients simultaneously the workload was too heavy, and they could not tag the conversation properly; as the session proceeded, there was much less tagging or none at all. As a result, the ability of the agent to provide advice weakened. This situation called for a change.

In order to perform good tagging even in stressed sessions, we introduced an automated tagging mechanism. We took the raw data in real-time and made the agent use it directly, a common notion in goal-oriented dialogue systems, and chatbots in general [50]. We used a machine learning module that follows the messages in real-time and outputs annotations for the advising agent. The module that we chose is a combination of two sub-models, as follows: We denote a network consisting of a BERT [14] embedding layer with a linear layer on top as a **BERTLL**. At first, a BERTLL predicts what labels the message may contain. For each label that the first model predicted, another BERTLL predicted what information the message may contain (again, see Fig. 1 for the tag structure). We chose to use this combination after it reached a maximum F_1 score of 0.72 and was seen to generalize well in practice. It also outperformed a gradient boosted

Random Forest (that reached an F_1 score of 0.7), a single BERTLL for all the labels (that reached a maximum F_1 score of 0.5) and a large variety of neural network-based models that were far from reaching a 0.5 F_1 score. Implementing the automated tagging mechanism relieves the operator from the tagging task, and enables her to concentrate on the sole task of attending the clients.

Another improvement in the experiment method (relative to the original design) was the introducing of bots as clients in this phase: Instead of human subjects playing the role of clients, we deployed bots that were built using a combination of two strategies: a rule-based approach, and a learning approach. The first approach followed the spirit of early chatbots, such as Eliza [52]. Based on the previous interaction with the operator, the bot would randomly generate answers to operator's questions, or questions to ask of the operator. The second approach used BERT to learn how to perform the interaction. We found out that these two models (knowledge-based and learning-based) complemented each other quite well in overcoming their respective disadvantages. This change was made because the use of bots instead of human subjects made the experiment much easier to perform, since we needed to recruit and to brief only the operators, and the influence of the agent on the clients was not examined in this study.

A third change was to introduce a level test to the recruits who were to play the role of operators, after their briefing and training. In order to verify that the recruits are indeed trained and to an appropriate professional level, each of them took a short test with questions regarding the domain and the service. Only after successfully completing the test with high grades were the recruits allowed to move on to the experiment.

After implementing the aforementioned changes, we performed the experiment of Phase 3, this time with each operator attending 3 clients simultaneously. In this improved design we did not encounter an excessive load on the operators, since the tagging was done automatically by the agent. We had 14 operators playing two sessions each (again, half of the operators played the assisted session first and the unassisted session second, and the other half vice versa). Together with the 15 operators who attended 2 clients simultaneously, we had 29 operators, and each of them played 2 sessions.

The experiments were performed according to the institution's guidelines regarding experimenting with humans, and permission to perform the experiments was accepted from the institution IRB prior to the experiments. The demographic data regarding the subjects in the experiments is presented in Appendix B in [3].

4.4   Phase 3 – The Expert-Advisor Phase

As explained above, the goal of Phase 2 is to help operators while they serve clients, and at the same time to improve the capabilities of the agent to provide good advise in the domain. The system works in Phase 2 (i.e., new data is fed to the machine learning model) as long as managers feel the agent needs improvement and the performance of it indeed improves with the additional data. At a certain point there is no further need for improvement, and the system can be turned to Phase 3 - the Expert-Advisor Phase. The machine learning model is stabilized, and the collection of data is stopped. The agent works alongside the operators and provides advice according to the data that was collected in the previous phases. Therefore, there was no need to perform experiments on Phase 3.

Nevertheless, the experiment domain may illustrate the possibility of phase rollback described above (Sect. 3.1). In our experiment domain of student loans, if, for example, new terms of loans are available in the market, the steady-state agent will not know how to advise operators regarding them. In order to teach the agent about the new terms, the system should be returned to Phase 1 or to Phase 2, collect data (i.e. tagged chat conversations) and feed them to the machine learning model. When reaching the desired level of advice again, the agent may be advanced again to Phase 3, and so forth.

5 Results

5.1 Operators' Opinions

The participants who played the role of operators filled out NASA-TLX questionnaires. The goal of this process is to compare the grades regarding sessions that were played with the agent's assistance to the grades regarding sessions that were played without the agent's assistance, in order to learn about the operator's experience with the advising agent. The results of these questionnaires are presented in Figs. 3 and 4: Fig. 3 presents the data of the experiment in which a human subject played the role of clients (two clients simultaneously). Figure 4 presents the data of the experiment in which bots were deployed as clients (three clients simultaneously). In both cases, human subjects played the role of the operators. We present the total TLX grade, which sums the six categories of the questionnaire (as elaborated on in the Appendix A). In addition, we present the grade of the Temporal Demand category, since this category is of special concern in our model.

As we described in Sect. 4.3, each operator played two sessions. Therefore, the data in Figs. 3 and 4 is presented in two views:

1. First Session - counts only the first session of every operator (whether with the assisting agent or without it).
2. Total Sessions - counts all of the sessions (both the first and the second) of all of the operators.

It can be seen that both total workload (Total TLX) and temporal demand **decreased in all cases** when having the agent working alongside the operator as compared to not having the agent. All data presented in Figs. 3 and 4 are statistically significant ($p < 0.05$).

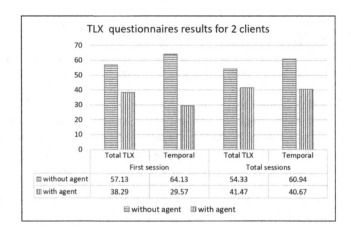

Fig. 3. NASA-TLX questionnaires' data of Phase 2 (lower is better). The experiment with 2 simultaneous clients was conducted using human subjects as clients.

5.2 Time Performance

We presumed that a good performance of the agent would be manifested in providing the service in less time, and with less idle time during the session. Figure 5 presents the time performance data of the operators in three categories:

1. Total session time - the average length of a full session, including clients' time, operator's time and idle time.
2. Maximal waiting time - the maximal time a client had to wait for an operator's response.
3. Total waiting time - the average total time a client spent waiting for an operator's responses during a session.

In all categories the times are shorter when the agent assisted the operator than when it did not, and in most of the categories the reduction is greater than 10%. It implies that the use of an agent alongside the operator reduces the time needed for the session in general as well as the time spent by the client idly waiting for the operator to respond. Nevertheless, the data was not found to be statistically significant in most of the categories.

5.3 Learning Effectiveness of Phase 2

The Apprentice Phase (Phase 1) is, naturally, crucial to the building of the preliminary knowledge base of the agent. Nevertheless, we wondered whether Phase 2 actually improves the capabilities of the agent, or if it is superfluous and we may skip it and go straight to the final stage (Phase 3). In order to answer this question we compared the performance of the tagging model in two configurations: The first one was based on data collected in Phase 1 only, while the second one was based on data collected in both Phase 1 and Phase 2. We found that

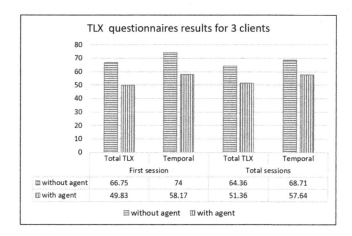

Fig. 4. NASA-TLX questionnaires' data of Phase 2 (lower is better). The experiment with 3 simultaneous clients deployed bots as clients.

Time Performance (in minutes)				
Category	parameter	without agent	with agent	reduction
First session	total session time	40.86	34.29	16.1%
	maximal waiting time	4.69	4.57	2.6%
	total waiting time	22.63	19.38	14.4%
Second session	total session time	37.43	34.63	7.5%
	maximal waiting time	5.57	3.81	31.6%
	total waiting time	20	15.56	22.2%
Total sessions	total session time	39.27	34.47	12.2%
	maximal waiting time	5.1	4.17	18.2%
	total waiting time	21.4	17.33	19.0%
First with agent	total session time	37.43	34.29	8.4%
	maximal waiting time	5.57	4.57	18.0%
	total waiting time	20	19.36	3.2%
First without agent	total session time	40.86	34.63	15.2%
	maximal waiting time	4.69	3.81	18.8%
	total waiting time	22.63	15.56	31.2%

Fig. 5. Time performance data (in minutes, decimal notation).

the performance of the second model (precision – 78%, recall – 75%, F_1-score – 72%) was better than the performance of the first model (precision – 65%, recall – 60%, F_1-score – 58%). This result indicates that although the data of Phase 1 alone suffices to provide basic assistance to human operators, expanding it with the data of Phase 2 significantly improves the tagging capability and, as a result, the quality of the agent's performance.

6   Conclusions, Discussion and Future Work

In this paper we introduced an algorithm and a method to implement an advising agent that assists operators who attend clients in a call center using chat conversations. The main advantage of this method is its adaptability – the agent can be fitted to a new domain with relatively little effort and little time. Training the agent does not require prolonged design, domain analysis or rule-definition. In an existing human call center, the agent only needs tagged conversations of experienced human operators with clients in order to build all the required knowledge. Having said that, we still think that additional experimenting is needed in order to conclude that this method is domain-independent, and specifically it should be tested in other domains.

Integrating the results of the role-playing experiment, we see that operators who were assisted by the agent enjoyed a lower cognitive load in attending their clients, with less effort and less time-pressure. Time is used more efficiently, as sessions are shorter and less time is spent on idle waiting. This trend is evident both in the objective measure of time to perform a mission (Sect. 5.2) and in the subjective views of the participants who played the operators (Sect. 5.1).

There are several issues that still need to be examined. One such issue is optimization of the process of adjusting the agent to a new domain. We found that the Novice-Advisor Phase (Phase 2) indeed improves the performance of the agent, and therefore the 3-stage process that was suggested is justified. However, the optimal conditions for switching from Phase 2 to Phase 3 still need to be determined. Another issue is the possibility that an operator attend to a larger number of clients simultaneously when having the agent's assistance. We performed experiments when attending 2 and 3 clients because this was seen to be a reasonable number (several views on this issue are presented in [40]). However, an operator might be able to attend more than 3 clients simultaneously by having an agent working alongside her. The feasibility of this option should be tested as well.

Note that this research study was designed to examine the effects of the assisting agent on the assisted operators. A differently designed experiment may explore the influence of the agent on the service from the clients' perspective.

Disclaimer. This paper was prepared for informational purposes by the Artificial Intelligence Research group of JPMorgan Chase & Coånd its affiliates ("JP Morgan"), and is not a product of the Research Department of JP Morgan. JP Morgan makes no representation and warranty whatsoever and disclaims all liability, for the completeness, accuracy or reliability of the information contained herein. This document is not intended as investment research or investment advice, or a recommendation, offer or solicitation for the purchase or sale of any security, financial instrument, financial product or service, or to be used in any way for evaluating the merits of participating in any transaction, and shall not constitute a solicitation under any jurisdiction or to any person, if such solicitation under such jurisdiction or to such person would be unlawful.

References

1. Aktekin, T., Ekin, T.: Stochastic call center staffing with uncertain arrival, service and abandonment rates: a Bayesian perspective. Nav. Res. Logist. (NRL) **63**(6), 460–478 (2016)
2. Argall, B.D., Chernova, S., Veloso, M., Browning, B.: A survey of robot learning from demonstration. Robot. Auton. Syst. **57**(5), 469–483 (2009)
3. Aviv, A., et al.: Advising agent for service-providing live-chat operators. arXiv preprint arXiv:2105.03986 (2021)
4. Azaria, A., Gal, Y., Kraus, S., Goldman, C.V.: Strategic advice provision in repeated human-agent interactions. Auton. Agent. Multi-Agent Syst. **30**(1), 4–29 (2016)
5. Azaria, A., Rabinovich, Z., Kraus, S., Goldman, C.V., Gal, Y.: Strategic advice provision in repeated human-agent interactions. In: Twenty-Sixth AAAI Conference on Artificial Intelligence (2012)
6. Azaria, A., Rosenfeld, A., Kraus, S., Goldman, C.V., Tsimhoni, O.: Advice provision for energy saving in automobile climate-control system. AI Mag. **36**(3), 61–72 (2015)
7. Bechara, A., Damasio, H., Damasio, A.R.: Emotion, decision making and the orbitofrontal cortex. Cereb. Cortex **10**(3), 295–307 (2000)
8. Breiman, L.: Random forests. Mach. Learn. **45**(1), 5–32 (2001)
9. Bruine de Bruin, W., Parker, A.M., Fischhoff, B.: Individual differences in adult decision-making competence. J. Pers. Soc. Psychol. **92**(5), 938 (2007)
10. Carroll, J.S., Bazerman, M.H., Maury, R.: Negotiator cognitions: a descriptive approach to negotiators' understanding of their opponents. Organ. Behav. Hum. Decis. Process. **41**(3), 352–370 (1988)
11. Cheetham, W.: Lessons learned using CBR for customer support. In: FLAIRS Conference, pp. 114–118 (2003)
12. Coussement, K., Van den Poel, D.: Improving customer attrition prediction by integrating emotions from client/company interaction emails and evaluating multiple classifiers. Expert Syst. Appl. **36**(3), 6127–6134 (2009)
13. Crook, P.A., Marin, A.: Sequence to sequence modeling for user simulation in dialog systems. In: INTERSPEECH, pp. 1706–1710 (2017)
14. Devlin, J., Chang, M.W., Lee, K., Toutanova, K.: Bert: pre-training of deep bidirectional transformers for language understanding (2019)
15. Dietrich, C.: Decision making: factors that influence decision making, heuristics used, and decision outcomes. Inquiries J. **2**(02) (2010)
16. Elmalech, A., Sarne, D., Grosz, B.J.: Problem restructuring for better decision making in recurring decision situations. Auton. Agent. Multi-Agent Syst. **29**(1), 1–39 (2015)
17. Esposito, C., Ficco, M., Palmieri, F., Castiglione, A.: A knowledge-based platform for big data analytics based on publish/subscribe services and stream processing. Knowl.-Based Syst. **79**, 3–17 (2015)
18. Floyd, M.W., Turner, J., Aha, D.W.: Using deep learning to automate feature modeling in learning by observation: a preliminary study. In: 2017 AAAI Spring Symposium Series (2017)
19. Ford, J.K., Schmitt, N., Schechtman, S.L., Hults, B.M., Doherty, M.L.: Process tracing methods: contributions, problems, and neglected research questions. Organ. Behav. Hum. Decis. Process. **43**(1), 75–117 (1989)

20. Graef, R., Klier, M., Kluge, K., Zolitschka, J.F.: Human-machine collaboration in online customer service-a long-term feedback-based approach. Electron. Mark. **31**, 1–23 (2020). https://doi.org/10.1007/s12525-020-00420-9

21. Hansen, L.K., Salamon, P.: Neural network ensembles. IEEE Trans. Pattern Anal. Mach. Intell. **12**(10), 993–1001 (1990)

22. Hart, S.G., Staveland, L.E., et al.: Development of NASA-TLX (task load index): results of empirical and theoretical research, vol. 52, pp. 139–183 (1988)

23. Hathaway, B.: Data-driven studies of caller behavior under call center innovations (2019). https://doi.org/10.17615/7ckx-xq92s

24. Holman, D., Batt, R., Holtgrewe, U.: The global call center report: international perspectives on management and employment (2007). http://ecommons.cornell.edu/handle/1813/74325

25. Jitesh: Whatsapp customer support (2020). www.wati.io/whatsapp-as-a-customer-support-channel/. Accessed 04 July 2021

26. Juliusson, E.Á., Karlsson, N., Gärling, T.: Weighing the past and the future in decision making. Eur. J. Cogn. Psychol. **17**(4), 561–575 (2005)

27. Katal, A., Wazid, M., Goudar, R.H.: Big data: issues, challenges, tools and good practices. In: 2013 Sixth International Conference on Contemporary Computing (IC3), pp. 404–409. IEEE (2013)

28. Ke, G., et al.: LightGBM: a highly efficient gradient boosting decision tree. In: Advances in neural Information Processing Systems, pp. 3146–3154 (2017)

29. Kenda, I.: Assessment of cognitive impairment generated by job strain. CAS of call center teleoperators in kinshasales (2017)

30. Koçağa, Y.L., Armony, M., Ward, A.R.: Staffing call centers with uncertain arrival rates and co-sourcing. Prod. Oper. Manag. **24**(7), 1101–1117 (2015)

31. Koole, G., Mandelbaum, A.: Queueing models of call centers: an introduction. Ann. Oper. Res. **113**(1–4), 41–59 (2002)

32. Kraus, S.: Human-agent decision-making: Combining theory and practice. arXiv preprint arXiv:1606.07514 (2016)

33. Lee, K., Jo, J., Kim, J., Kang, Y.: Can chatbots help reduce the workload of administrative officers? - Implementing and deploying FAQ chatbot service in a university. In: Stephanidis, C. (ed.) HCII 2019. CCIS, vol. 1032, pp. 348–354. Springer, Cham (2019). https://doi.org/10.1007/978-3-030-23522-2_45

34. Legros, B., Jouini, O.: On the scheduling of operations in a chat contact center. Eur. J. Oper. Res. **274**(1), 303–316 (2019)

35. Levy, P., Sarne, D.: Intelligent advice provisioning for repeated interaction. In: Thirtieth AAAI Conference on Artificial Intelligence (2016)

36. Li, C.H., Yeh, S.F., Chang, T.J., Tsai, M.H., Chen, K., Chang, Y.J.: A conversation analysis of non-progress and coping strategies with a banking task-oriented chatbot. In: Proceedings of the 2020 CHI Conference on Human Factors in Computing Systems, pp. 1–12 (2020)

37. Liu, J., et al.: Time to transfer: predicting and evaluating machine-human chatting handoff. arXiv preprint arXiv:2012.07610 (2020)

38. Madotto, A., et al.: Learning knowledge bases with parameters for task-oriented dialogue systems. arXiv preprint arXiv:2009.13656 (2020)

39. Majumdar, S., Tekiroglu, S.S., Guerini, M.: Generating challenge datasets for task-oriented conversational agents through self-play. arXiv preprint arXiv:1910.07357 (2019)

40. Mashburn, J., Rogers, A., Rogers, I., Cheung, A., Wallace, J.: how many customers can an agent handle? (2021). www.quora.com/During-a-customer-live-chat-about-how-many-customers-on-average-can-a-single-agent-handle-concurrently. Accessed 03 Oct 2021
41. Modak, A., Mupepi, M.G.: Dancing with whatsapp: small businesses pirouetting with social media. In: Conference Proceedings by Track, vol. 51 (2017)
42. Nam, K., Lee, Z., Lee, B.G.: How internet has reshaped the user experience of banking service? KSII Trans. Internet Inf. Syst. **10**(2), 684–702 (2016)
43. Naneetha, R.: A new paradigm shift on how whatsapp empower small business to develop customer relationship and it becomes an integral part of business. Res. J. Humanit. Soc. Sci. **9**(1), 119–124 (2018)
44. Nguyen, T.H., Yang, R., Azaria, A., Kraus, S., Tambe, M.: Analyzing the effectiveness of adversary modeling in security games. In: Twenty-Seventh AAAI Conference on Artificial Intelligence (2013)
45. Nuruzzaman, M., Hussain, O.K.: A survey on chatbot implementation in customer service industry through deep neural networks. In: 2018 IEEE 15th International Conference on e-Business Engineering (ICEBE), pp. 54–61. IEEE (2018)
46. Okuda, T., Shoda, S.: Ai-based chatbot service for financial industry. Fujitsu Sci. Tech. J. **54**(2), 4–8 (2018)
47. Rosenfeld, A., Agmon, N., Maksimov, O., Kraus, S.: Intelligent agent supporting human-multi-robot team collaboration. Artif. Intell. **252**, 211–231 (2017)
48. Rosenfeld, A., Keshet, J., Goldman, C.V., Kraus, S.: Online prediction of exponential decay time series with human-agent application. In: Proceedings of the Twenty-second European Conference on Artificial Intelligence, pp. 595–603. IOS Press (2016)
49. Rosenfeld, A., Kraus, S.: Predicting human decision-making: from prediction to action. Synth. Lect. Artif. Intell. Mach. Learn. **12**(1), 1–150 (2018)
50. Serban, I.V., Lowe, R., Henderson, P., Charlin, L., Pineau, J.: A survey of available corpora for building data-driven dialogue systems. arXiv preprint arXiv:1512.05742 (2015)
51. Ta, T., l'Ecuyer, P., Bastin, F.: Staffing optimization with chance constraints for emergency call centers. In: MOSIM 2016–11th International Conference on Modeling, Optimization and Simulation, Aug 2016, Montréal, Canada. hal-01399507f (2016)
52. Weizenbaum, J.: Eliza-a computer program for the study of natural language communication between man and machine. Commun. ACM **9**(1), 36–45. (1966). https://doi.org/10.1145/365153.365168
53. Williams, J.D., Young, S.: Partially observable Markov decision processes for spoken dialog systems. Comput. Speech Lang. **21**(2), 393–422 (2007)
54. Wong, J., Hastings, L., Negy, K., Gonzalez, A.J., Ontañón, S., Lee, Y.C.: Machine learning from observation to detect abnormal driving behavior in humans. In: The Thirty-First International Flairs Conference (2018)

Initial Conditions Sensitivity Analysis of a Two-Species Butterfly-Effect Agent-Based Model

Cristian Berceanu[1] and Monica Patrascu[1,2]([✉])

[1] Complex Systems Laboratory, University Politehnica of Bucharest, Bucharest, Romania
cristian.berceanu@stud.acs.upb.ro
[2] Department of Global Public Health and Primary Care, Centre for Elderly and Nursing Home Medicine, University of Bergen, Bergen, Norway
monica.patrascu@uib.no

Abstract. Agent-based models are powerful tools for understanding complex systems. Their accuracy and capacity for prediction, however, are dependent on the initial conditions of the model during simulation. Current agent-based modeling endeavors show a lack of systematic analysis of sensitivity to initial conditions, and renewed interest is given to this issue. In this paper, we hypothesize that we can analyze the effect of initial conditions in agent-based models through the positive and negative feedback behaviors of individual agents. For this, we present a systems theory interpretation of local agent behaviors based on closed loops. Our approach illustrates how the initial conditions (of the whole model or of individual agents) determine the presence of positive or negative feedback agents in the agent-based model, and that their numbers influence the steady state of the model. We perform a proof-of-concept analysis on a two-species butterfly-effect agent-based model.

Keywords: Agent-based model · Initial conditions · Sensitivity analysis

1 Introduction

Agent-based modeling [38] is a valuable tool for understanding complex systems [4], facilitating the study of nonlinear interactions, stochastic processes and heterogeneous spatial structures [11]. Agents of an agent-based model (ABM) are autonomous representations of entities that interact with the environment and with other agents based on the rules of the model [12]. ABMs can generate emergent patterns, often in unexpected ways, resulting from the interactions between agents and overlapping latent feedback effects [9,18].

One of the open issues of agent-based modeling is the systematic analysis of sensitivity to initial conditions in ABMs [3]. This affects the model reliability measures regarding predictive power and accuracy [28]. The challenge to find alternative means of investigating initial conditions sensitivity was raised by [7].

D. Baumeister and J. Rothe (Eds.): EUMAS 2022, LNAI 13442, pp. 60–78, 2022.
https://doi.org/10.1007/978-3-031-20614-6_4

Complex systems often display behaviors in which small disturbances or inputs generate wide-scale outcomes, known as the butterfly effect [15]. One example of such phenomena is the propagating spread of infection or misinformation from a singular source [22], and while ABMs are useful, their validation is difficult due to uncertainties caused by unknown parameter correlations [23]. Chaotic systems are common in nature, deterministic, and sensitive to initial conditions [10]. The butterfly effect was popularized by Lorentz in 1972 [16] and is "a well-known metaphor for the idea that complex, dynamic, nonlinear systems produce unpredictable effects due to the profound influence of tiny variations" [20].

The butterfly effect is a famous instance of positive feedback in systems, which is characterized by the accumulation of energy in such a way that the system can no longer reach an equilibrium state described by finite parameters [24]. When two stable behaviors (i.e., that can reach and maintain finite equilibrium or steady states) are connected through positive feedback, the closed loop becomes unstable [5]. In a network, this instability propagates until observable at network level, which suggest the presence of the butterfly effect in the system as a whole. As a complex network, which has irregular topology, clusters and cycles, etc. [6], an ABM is not easily formalized to uncover positive feedback at whole system level. We must therefore look at local agent behavior.

Our hypothesis is that we can analyze the effect of initial conditions in ABMs through the positive and negative feedback behaviors of individual agents. In this study, we perform the first proof-of-concept analysis of our hypothesis on the two-species butterfly-effect agent-based model described in Sect. 3.1, for which we adopt a generative experiment approach [8]. Thus, we aim to study the effect of initial conditions on ABM states, and not to calibrate the ABM to reach desired states (the demonstrative experiment).

Two-species models [13,14,33,34] are common in multi-agent systems research, with the predator-prey model [31,39] as one of the most studied [21]. Disease spread models [32] are another popular topic in multi-agent systems research. Although there are certain disease spread models available on the NetLogo Community Models website [1], few of them are documented. To study the sensitivity to initial conditions under our hypothesis, we have combined the two concepts and created a new model where one of the species is the infected variant of the main agent species that feed on the agents of the main species.

The paper is organized as follows. Section 3.1 describes the two-species NetLogo ABM, while Sect. 3 covers the initial conditions analysis concept based on feedback loops. Section 4 contains the results and discussion. The paper finishes with conclusions in Sect. 6.

2   Concept

In this study, we use positive and negative feedback loops to model the behavior of agents. Figure 1 illustrates the two types of systems: $D(s)$ is the operational domain representation of the direct open loop transfer, while $F(s)$ is the feedback transfer. Here, by transfer, we understand a system that processes energy,

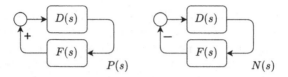

Fig. 1. Positive and negative feedback loops

information or matter from input to output. Systems $P(s)$ and $N(s)$ represent the positive and negative feedback loops. In what follows, we often omit the complex variable s for brevity. Thus:

$$P = \frac{D}{1 - DF} \text{ and } N = \frac{D}{1 + DF}. \tag{1}$$

For D and F rational, linear, and stable, i.e., with all poles $p_i^{D,F} \in \mathbb{C}^-$ (the roots of the denominator polynomial) and all zeroes $z_i^{D,F} \in \mathbb{C}^-$ (the roots of the numerator), the closed loop with negative feedback transfer N has all poles $p_i^N \in \mathbb{C}^-$ (stable), while the closed loop with positive feedback P has at least one pole $p_i^P \in \mathbb{C}^+$ (unstable) [5]. The addition of the feedback F influences the stability and behavior of the system D. Of note here is that we can rewrite a negative feedback as positive by changing the signs of the poles in (1).

When systems are neither stable, nor unstable, they are at limit, which is a state with different interpretations depending on the type of stability [5]; most commonly, limit behavior is cyclic and often encountered in biological systems, revealing a sort of oscillating response around various equilibrium points. All systems can be classified based on these three behaviors. Some (e.g., nonlinear, biosystems) may exhibit all behaviors at different times or operating points, regardless of how simple or complex their dynamics might be.

Hypothesis. Let a complex system formed of n agents $A_i \in \{A_1, ..., A_n\}$ with behaviors described by (1), and I_{ij} the interaction between agents i and j. Let the equilibrium state of agent i be described by $y_i(\infty) = \lim_{t \to \infty} \mathcal{L}^{-1}\{A_i(s)\}$ and the equilibrium state of the interaction be $\psi_{ij}(\infty) = \lim_{t \to \infty} I_{ij}(t)$. For $x(t)$ the state of the complex system formed of all observable agent and interaction outputs $y_i(t)$ and $\psi_{ij}(t)$, the equation for heterogeneous consensus (i.e., system equilibrium state formed of nonhomogeneous local equilibria) is:

$$\lim_{t \to \infty} x(t) = \Gamma(\{y_i(\infty), \psi_{ij}(\infty) \mid i, j = 1..n\}, t) = \sum_{i=1}^{n} \sum_{j=1}^{n} (y_i(t) * \psi_{ij}(t)), \tag{2}$$

where Γ is the result of the convolution $*$ between agents and interactions. It follows that the equilibrium state of the system, $x(\infty)$, will be determined by the ratio of positive vs. negative feedback agents and interactions.

This hypothesis investigates the manner in which initial conditions (of the ABM or of individual agents) determine the number of positive and negative feedback agents, and how the ratio of positive vs. negative feedback agents in

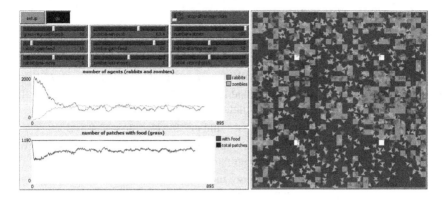

Fig. 2. NetLogo model user interface

the ABM influence the steady state of the ABM. In Sects. 3 and 4, we test this hypothesis on a butterfly-effect ABM and numerical simulation results.

3   Initial Conditions Sensitivity Analysis

3.1   A Two-Species Butterfly-Effect Agent-Based Model

In this paper we illustrate our feedback-based analysis concept on a two-species butterfly-effect ABM, implemented in NetLogo [37]. This model has been developed by our team at the Complex Systems Laboratory. Its purpose is to emulate the spread of misinformation or disease in social networks [35,36], with special focus on the butterfly effect, which is often present in complex systems [30]. To disambiguate the two behaviors (infected/misinformed or not), we consider the infected agents as a separate species.

The ABM adjustable parameters (Table 1) are accessible through the NetLogo user interface (Fig. 2). In this model, a species of *rabbits* (gray turtles) exists in a world where they move around and reproduce (by hatching a new *rabbit*). In NetLogo, the world is comprised of static agents named patches [2]. The *rabbit* agents' food source is grass (green patches) that can be consumed and grow back. Some grass locations are infected (red patches), which when consumed cause the *rabbit* to become a *zombie* (crimson turtles). The food source for *zombies* are the *rabbit* agents. An encounter between two agents of different species results in one of them surviving, based on a probability operator. *Zombies* do not reproduce. The infected grass is assigned to 4 patches in the entire world, one in each quadrant, with an option to enable or disable them. The butterfly effect models the spread of infection throughout the *rabbit* population. The two species achieve co-evolving balance under certain conditions.

Table 1. NetLogo experiment parameters

Parameter	Range	Description
grass-regrowth-prob	[0,100]	The probability (in percentages) that an empty patch will turn green (grow grass) on the next tick
zombie-win-prob	[0,100]	The probability (in percentages) that a *zombie* will win the fight with a rabbit on the next tick
number-rabbits	[0,100]	The initial number of *rabbits* in a simulation
rabbit-gain-feed	[0,100]	The energy increase after a *rabbit* consumes the grass on a green patch
zombie-gain-feed	[0,100]	The energy increase after a *zombie* wins the fight with a *rabbit*
rabbit-staring-energy	[0,100]	The initial *rabbit* energy level
rabbit-loss-move	[0,10]	The energy decrease after a *rabbit* moves
zombie-loss-move	[0,10]	The energy decrease after a *zombie* moves
rabbit-reprod-prob	[0,100]	The probability (in percentages) that a *rabbit* will hatch a new *rabbit* on the next tick

The ABM world is defined as a plane of 33×33 patches with different types of grass. Let $\mathbf{P}$ be the set of all patches on the plane so that:

$$\mathbf{P} = \mathbf{P}_{green} \cup \mathbf{P}_{empty} \cup \mathbf{P}_{contaminated} \qquad (3)$$

where $\mathbf{P}_{green}$ is the set of patches with grass (green), $\mathbf{P}_{empty}$ is the set of empty patches (brown), and $\mathbf{P}_{contaminated}$ is the set of patches with contaminated grass (red). The contaminated patches are selected at the beginning of the simulation and do not change their status during the experiments. The green and empty patches change their color as described in Algorithms 1 and 3.

Let $\mathbf{A}$ be the set of all agents in the environment so that $\mathbf{A} = \mathbf{R} \cup \mathbf{Z}$, where $\mathbf{R}$ is the set of *rabbit* agents and $\mathbf{Z}$ is the set of *zombie* agents. Both *rabbits* and *zombies* require energy to survive. Each of their food sources increases the energy of the agents, while moving around and reproducing decrease the energy levels. Each agent has an energy between 0 and 100; at 0, the agent is considered dead and is removed from the environment. *Rabbits* gain energy by eating grass (Algorithm 1, lines 5–7), while *zombies* gain energy by eating *rabbits* (Algorithm 2, lines 5–13). *Rabbits* can only feed on green or red grass. When green grass is consumed, the respective patch becomes empty, changing color to brown (Algorithm 1, line 7). Red grass is never exhausted by consumption and always exists on its assigned patch. Green grass regrows over time and empty patches become green again (Algorithm 3, lines 1–5). When *zombies* feed on *rabbits*, the *rabbits* become *zombies* and their current energy level becomes the initial energy in their life as a *zombie* (Algorithm 2, lines 7–9). The logic of the algorithms is executed at every simulation tick and for each agent or patch in the environment. The

---

Algorithm 1: Rabbit Behavior

Data: $rabbit_i \in \mathbf{R}$, $N = card(\mathbf{R})$, $grass_i \in \mathbf{P}$

1 **for** $i \leftarrow 1$ **to** N **do**

  // $heading_i$ is the direction where $rabbit_i$ is heading

2    $heading_i \leftarrow random\_direction(360)$;

3    $move\_forward(rabbit_i)$;

  // $energy_i$ is the energy of $rabbit_i$

4    $energy_i \leftarrow energy_i -$ rabbit-loss-move;

5   **if** $grass_i \in \mathbf{P_{green}}$ **then**

6     $energy_i \leftarrow energy_i +$ rabbit-gain-feed;

7     $grass_i \leftarrow empty$;   // $grass_i$ becomes empty

8   **else if** $grass_i \in \mathbf{P_{contaminated}}$ **then**

9     $breed_i \leftarrow zombie$;   // $rabbit_i$ becomes zombie

10   **end**

11   **if** $random(100) <$ rabbit-reprod-prob **then**

12     $hatch\_rabbit()$;

13   **end**

14 **end**

ABM allows for a stop condition based on a maximum number of ticks, e.g. 1000 ticks, which can be toggled on and off (Fig. 2).

Algorithm 1 describes the behavior of the *rabbit* agents. A *rabbit* agent moves in a random direction with variable $heading_i \in [0, 360) \cap \mathbb{N}$ (in degrees) while losing energy (Algorithm 1 lines 2–4) and consumes grass if available on the current patch (Algorithm 1 lines 5–7). The $random\_direction(360)$ function generates a random $heading_i$ and the $move\_forward(rabbit_i)$ function moves the agent 1 patch forward with $heading_i$. If the grass of the current patch is contaminated, then the *rabbit* becomes a *zombie* agent (Algorithm 1 lines 8–9). The $hatch\_rabbit()$ function creates a new *rabbit* at the current location and halves the energy of the parent (Algorithm 1 lines 11–12), with a probability given by rabbit-reprod-prob (Table 1).

The *zombie* agents behaviour is described by Algorithm 2. A *zombie* moves with a random variable $heading_i \in [0, 360)$ (in degrees) while losing energy (Algorithm 2 lines 2–4) and tries to fight with and feed on *rabbits* if there are any nearby (Algorithm 1 lines 5–9). If the *zombie* wins the encounter, the *rabbit* becomes a *zombie* and the *zombie* gains energy (Algorithm 1 lines 6–9). If the *zombie* loses, it dies (Algorithm 1 lines 10–11). The $here(zombie_i)$ function return the patch location of current agent and the $count(rabbits, location)$ function counts the rabbits at current patch location. The $die(zombie_i)$ function removes the agent from the simulation.

Algorithm 3 describes the other behaviors in the ABM. At every simulation tick and for each empty patch, there is a probability that the grass will regrow and become green (Algorithm 3 lines 1–3). Also, at every tick, the simulation engine checks if there are agents that have reached zero energy (or less) and removes them from the simulation (Algorithm 3 lines 6–8).

Algorithm 2: Zombie Behavior

Data: $zombie_i \in \mathbf{Z}$, $N = card(\mathbf{Z})$, $rabbit_j \in \mathbf{R}$

1 **for** $i \leftarrow 1$ **to** N **do**
    // $heading_i$ is the direction where $zombie_i$ is heading
2     $heading_i \leftarrow random\_direction(360)$;
3     $move\_forward(zombie_i)$;
    // $energy_i$ is the energy of $zombie_i$
4     $energy_i \leftarrow energy_i -$ zombie-loss-move;
    // count the number of rabbits with the same patch as $zombie_i$
5   **if** $count(rabbits, here(zombie_i)) > 0$ **then**
6   **if** $random(100) <$ zombie-win-prob **then**
            // $rabbit_j$ is a rabbit with same patch as $zombie_i$
7             $rabbit_j \leftarrow find\_rabbit(here(zombie_i))$;
8             $breed_j \leftarrow zombie$;   // $rabbit_j$ becomes zombie
9             $energy_i \leftarrow energy_i +$ zombie-gain-feed;
10   **else**
11             $die(zombie_i)$;   // $zombie_i$ dies
12   **end**
13   **end**
14 **end**

3.2 Feedback Systems Interpretation of Agent Behaviors

We look at the *rabbit* and *zombie* agents through their energy. At each tick, the agents gain energy from their food source and lose energy during movement. For *rabbits*, energy is lost to procreation. Let k be the current tick, $e^{R,Z}$ the energy of a *rabbit* or a *zombie*, $feed^{R,Z} > 0$ the energy gained by feeding, and $move^{R,Z} > 0$ and $breed^R \in (0, 1]$ (1 for no reproduction, probabilistic) the energy lost:

$$\begin{cases} e_{k+1}^R = (e_k^R + feed_k^R - move_k^R) \cdot breed_k^R \\ e_{k+1}^Z = e_k^Z + feed_k^Z - move_k^Z \end{cases} . \tag{4}$$

Algorithm 3: Other Behaviors

Data: $grass_i \in \mathbf{P_{empty}}$, $agent_i \in \mathbf{R} \cup \mathbf{Z}$

1 **for** $grass_i \in \mathbf{P_{empty}}$ **do**
2   **if** $random(100) <$ grass-regrowth-prob **then**
3         $grass_i \leftarrow green$;   // $grass_i$ becomes green
4   **end**
5 **end**
6 **for** $agent_i \in \mathbf{R} \cup \mathbf{Z}$ **do**
7   **if** $energy_i \leq 0$ **then**
8         $die(agent_i)$;   // $agent_i$ dies
9   **end**
10 **end**

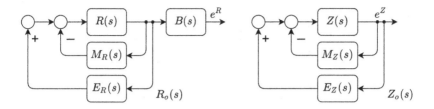

Fig. 3. Agents represented with positive and negative feedback loops

The components of (4) are outputs of their respective processes. We now assign dynamic models to each process of gaining and losing energy. Let $R(s)$ be the *rabbit* base process of storing energy, $M_R(s)$ the movement process, $B(s)$ reproduction, and $E_R(s)$ feeding. Similarly, let $Z(s)$ be the *zombie* base process of storing energy, $M_Z(s)$ the movement process, and $E_Z(s)$ feeding. Figure 3 shows the system representation of the two agents.

Thus, the closed loops of the *rabbit* (R_o) and *zombie* (Z_o) agents are:

$$R_o = \frac{RB}{1 + R(M_R - E_R)}, \tag{5}$$

$$Z_o = \frac{Z}{1 + Z(M_Z - E_Z)}. \tag{6}$$

In this paper we choose the simplest representation for the two agents: the base system for energy storage behaves like a capacitor, while the processes of gaining and losing energy are constant gains. Thus:

$$\begin{cases} R(s) = \dfrac{K_R}{T_R s + 1} \\ E_R(s) = K_{RE} > 0 \text{ and } M_R(s) = K_{RM} > 0 \\ B(s) = K_B \in (0,1) \text{ for reproduction and } K_B = 1 \text{ otherwise} . \\ Z(s) = \dfrac{K_Z}{T_Z s + 1} \\ E_Z(s) = K_{ZE} > 0 \text{ and } M_Z(s) = K_{ZM} > 0 \end{cases} \tag{7}$$

For $R(s)$ and $Z(s)$, we choose $K_R = K_Z = 1$ (lossless addition or removal of energy to and from storage), $T_R = T_Z = 1/4$ [ticks] to model that energy is added to the base system in one tick and does not suffer delays [5]. The poles of $R(s)$ and $Z(s)$ are $p_R = p_Z = -4 \in \mathbb{C}^-$, which means that the base processes of acquiring and expending energy are stable. Of note here is that we use the *tick* as the time unit of the ABM, but for a proper operational representation (so that $s = j\omega$, where ω is frequency in Hz), ticks must be transformed to seconds.

Replacing (7) into (5) and (6), we obtain:

$$R_o(s) = \frac{K_R K_B}{T_R s + 1 + K_R(K_{RM} - K_{RE})}, \tag{8}$$

$$Z_o(s) = \frac{K_Z}{T_Z s + 1 + K_Z(K_{ZM} - K_{ZE})}, \tag{9}$$

with the poles:

$$p_R = -\frac{1 + K_R(K_{RM} - K_{RE})}{T_R} = -4(1 + K_{RM} - K_{RE}), \tag{10}$$

$$p_Z = -\frac{1 + K_Z(K_{ZM} - K_{ZE})}{T_Z} = -4(1 + K_{ZM} - K_{ZE}), \tag{11}$$

where K_{RE} = rabbit-gain-feed [enp], K_{ZE} = zombie-gain-feed $\cdot$ $Z_{win}/100$ [enp], for $Z_{win} \in [0, 100]$ the probability that a *zombie* wins in an encounter with a *rabbit*; K_{RM} = rabbit-loss-move [enp], K_{ZM} = zombie-loss-move [enp]. For numerical compatibility, all gains should be defined or mapped over the same interval, e.g., $\in [0, 100]$, and as such scaling gains might be added. Here, the measuring unit *enp* represents energy points, an abstract unit for quantifying energy in the ABM.

3.3   Sensitivity to Initial Conditions

For the ABM, the scalar gains K_{RE}, K_{RM}, K_{ZE}, and K_{ZM} represent *initial conditions*. Their respective combinations determine if the behavior type of the agent is positive or negative feedback: as we can see from (10) and (11), the signs of the poles depend on the balance between energy gain and loss. For instance, a *zombie* agent that gains more energy from feeding than loses from movement will be able to continue existing in the ABM, spreading the infected genes throughout the *rabbit* population. For a *rabbit* with greater energy gain than loss, the species will breed uncontrollably until the ecosystem is overwhelmed and, ultimately, food scarcity will determine the collapse of the species. Individual agent behaviors determine ABM-level changes.

What happens during the interaction between the *rabbit* and *zombie* agents? As previously described, the meeting between a *rabbit* and a *zombie* results in a probabilistic decision for the *rabbit* agent to change species. Let Z_{win} be the probability that a *zombie* wins.

The ABM steady states we look at in this paper are:

- *rabbit* **survival**, in which the final population is formed of *rabbits* in equilibrium with their food source (grass). In this case, the *rabbit* agents are stable (negative feedback), i.e., gain less energy than they lose. Initial *rabbit* energy conditions and K_B matter, as the agents must survive long enough to start gaining energy: $e_{init}^R > move_1^R - breed_1^R$ for at least the first tick.
- *rabbit* **or** *zombie* **collapse**, in which only one of either species survives, overpopulates the ecosystem, and then becomes extinct without their food sources (grass or *rabbits*). In the former case, the *rabbits* have positive feedback or K_B too large, while the *zombies* have negative feedback or Z_{win} is too low. Vice-versa for the latter case, with Z_{win} too large. Interestingly, the time to

Fig. 4. Zombie infection as systems interaction

collapse is influenced by how large the difference between energy gain and loss is, i.e., by the parameters of (10) and (11), and thus by the poles of the closed loops $R_o(s)$ and $Z_o(s)$, and the gain of $R_o(s)$.

- **species dominant equilibrium**, in which the two species coexist, but one is more numerous than the other. In this case, the *rabbits* have negative feedback, the *zombies* have positive feedback, but the choice of Z_{win} allows for survival of *zombies* without overfeeding on *rabbits*.
- **species perfect equilibrium** (co-evolving), in which the two species maintain a balanced presence in the ABM. The number of agents in either species is approximately equal, with small variations around the same mean. This case is similar to the dominant equilibrium, for specific values of Z_{win}, dependant on the other initial conditions.

In this ABM, small changes in the *initial conditions* parameters (K_{RE}, K_{RM}, K_B, K_{ZE}, K_{ZM}, and Z_{win}) can drive the ABM to different steady states. For instance, in the case of *rabbit* win, either *zombies* do not survive long enough to propagate the infection or the chances of turning a *rabbit* are too low.

The infection mechanism replaces a *rabbit* with a *zombie*, which in systemic interpretation is a conditional switch. However, let us see how infection might look if modeled through feedback. Let the *rabbit* R_o be a process and let the *zombie* Z_o be the governor system, as in Fig. 4. We close this loop with either positive or negative feedback, which is given by:

$$F = \frac{Z_o R_o}{1 \mp Z_o R_o}. \tag{12}$$

Let $K_{RO} = 1/(1 + K_R(K_{RM} - K_{RE}))$, $T_{RO} = T_R/(1 + K_R(K_{RM} - K_{RE}))$, $K_{ZO} = 1/(1 + K_Z(K_{ZM} - K_{ZE}))$, and $T_{ZO} = T_Z/(1 + K_Z(K_{ZM} - K_{ZE}))$. From (8) and (9), we obtain:

$$F(s) = \frac{K_{RO} K_{ZO} K_B}{T_{RO} T_{ZO} s^2 + (T_{RO} + T_{ZO})s + (1 \mp K_{RO} K_{ZO} K_B)}. \tag{13}$$

According to the Hurwitz criterion [27], the coefficients of the denominator in (13) must have the same sign for stability and different signs for instability. Since $T_{RO}, T_{ZO} > 0$, F is stable for $\alpha = 1 \mp K_{RO} K_{ZO} K_B > 0$ and unstable for $\alpha < 0$. This comes back to the balance between energy loss and gain. When a *zombie* wins, i.e., feeds, its behavior has positive feedback, which leads to

$\alpha < 0$ for negative feedback *rabbits*. This suggests that the infection mechanism F might have negative feedback at *zombie* win (resulting in an unstable system, like the unstable positive feedback *zombie*), and positive feedback for *rabbit* win (resulting in a stable system, like a stable negative feedback *rabbit*). Vice-versa for positive feedback *rabbits* (when $\alpha > 0$). At limit, when $\alpha = 0$, the infection mechanism has integrator behavior (one origin pole), shooting off to infinity; however, this could only happen if $K_B = 1$, i.e. *rabbits* do not reproduce, in which case the ABM registers a collapse steady state.

Fortunately, the ABM NetLogo environment allows us to replace a *rabbit* with a *zombie* without jumping through systemic hoops; however, this analysis can provide hints on requirements in initial conditions (and thus process parameters) for a *rabbit* system to transform into a *zombie* system. This suggests that further analysis with complete agent dynamics could be worth pursuing.

4   Results

First, we illustrate the steady states described in Subsect. 3.3. Figure 5 shows examples of each ABM steady state categories, with the numbers of *rabbits* and *zombies* over time. The settings for each instance are in Tables 2 and 3, except for the rabbit collapse state, which is obtained with grass-regrowth-prob = 0 (always leads to collapse). Video demonstration: youtu.be/ihHBMwd496c.

In what follows, we map K_{RM} and K_{ZM} over $[0, 100]$ for numerical compatibility, i.e. K_{RM} = rabbit-loss-move $\cdot$ 10 and K_{ZM} = zombie-loss-move $\cdot$ 10, for rabbit-loss-move and zombie-loss-move $\in [0, 10]$.

Table 2 shows the ABM steady states and settling times for negative feedback *rabbits* and *zombies* as systems with either positive or negative feedback. For this, we ran simulations of 1000 ticks in duration, with 100 repetitions for each parameter configuration. Initial number of *rabbits* is 100 with a starting energy of 50. The grass regrowth probability is 50%, with one infected grass patch in the upper left quadrant. The fixed initial conditions parameters associated with the feedback models are: zombie-gain-feed = 85, K_{RE} = 15 *rabbit* feeding energy gain, K_{RM} = 50 *rabbit* movement energy loss, K_{ZM} = 50 *zombie* movement energy loss. The variable parameter is $Z_{win} \in [0, 100]$ probability for *zombie* win, which affects the value of K_{ZE} *zombie* feeding energy gain.

For $Z_{win} = 65$, we arrived close to a perfect equilibrium, so this steady state might be found for a $Z_{win} \in [61, 69]$. In Table 3, we take a closer look at this interval. In the state of perfect equilibrium, the numbers of *rabbits* and *zombies* are balanced. For this experiment, this state is found for values of Z_{win} between 63 and 64. Figure 6 shows the numbers of *rabbits* vs. *zombies* in two instances for $Z_{win} = 63.4$ and $Z_{win} = 63.5$. Figure 7 shows a simulation with *zombies* at limit. The ratio of food vs. total patches is on average between 50 and 60%.

We now take a closer look at the limit behavior. Table 4 shows the ABM steady states and settling times for simulations of 1000 ticks, over 100 repetitions for each parameter configuration. We keep most of the settings from the previous experiments, with the following changes: fixed $Z_{win} = 60$ (with $K_{ZE} = 51$), while

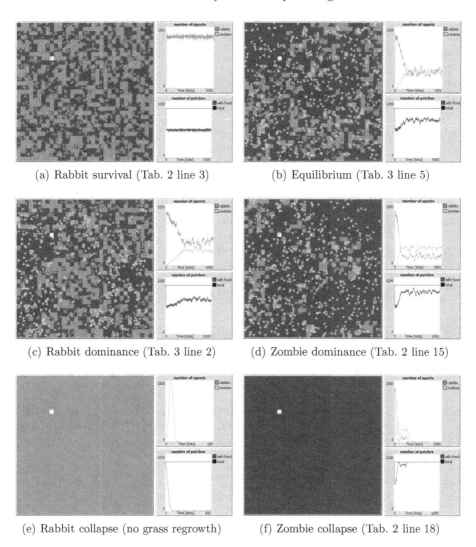

(a) Rabbit survival (Tab. 2 line 3)   (b) Equilibrium (Tab. 3 line 5)

(c) Rabbit dominance (Tab. 3 line 2)   (d) Zombie dominance (Tab. 2 line 15)

(e) Rabbit collapse (no grass regrowth)   (f) Zombie collapse (Tab. 2 line 18)

Fig. 5. ABM steady states examples

the *rabbit* feeding energy gain is variable $K_{RE} \in [45, 55]$. In this configuration, the *zombies* have limit behavior (neither stable nor unstable, Fig. 8). For $K_{RE} = 51$ we see what happens when the *rabbits* have limit behavior as well.

5   Discussion

In this paper we provide a proof-of-concept for the hypothesis that initial conditions effects can be analyzed through positive and negative feedback. The results show that the ABM is driven toward different steady states based on which behavior dominates the complex system: stable, unstable, or at limit.

72 C. Berceanu and M. Patrascu

Table 2. ABM steady states and settling times, averaged over 100 runs, for $K_{RE} = 15$ [enp], $K_{RM} = 50$ [enp], $K_{ZM} = 50$ [enp], and variable $Z_{win} \in [0, 100]$; settling time notation: R *rabbits*, Z *zombies*

K_{ZE} [enp]	Z_{win}	p_R	p_Z	Rabbit feedback	Zombie feedback	Mean rabbits	Mean zombies	ABM steady state	Settling time [ticks]
0	0	−144	−204	Negative	Negative	1846.62	0.97	Rabbit survival	19
4.25	5		−187			1847.18	0.99		18
8.5	10		−170			1847.50	1.02		18
12.75	15		−153			1844.05	1.16		17
17	20		−136			1844.20	1.44		17
21.25	25		−119			1846.30	1.53		18
25.5	30		−102			1850.27	1.82		19
29.75	35		−85			1847.48	2.13		19
34	40		−68			1845.19	2.61		15
38.25	45		−51			1844.21	3.66		16
42.5	50		−34			1841.66	4.18		19
46.75	55		−17			1718.42	9.45		17
51	60	−144	0	Negative	At limit	1718.42	72.08	Rabbit dominant equilibrium	Both oscillating
55.25	65	−144	17	Negative	Positive	530.06	613.54	Close to perfect equilibrium	140 R, 128 Z both oscillating
59.5	70	−144	34	Negative	Positive	414.70	563.41	Zombie dominant equilibrium	160 R, 115 Z
63.75	75		51			304.06	522.82		104 R, 98 Z
68	80		68			232.38	476.44		83 R, 56 Z
72.5	85	−144	85	Negative	Positive	75.24	48.33	Zombie collapse	85 R, 310 Z
76.5	90		102			82	46.57		82 R, 298 Z
80.75	95		119			84.87	46.31		86 R, 294 Z
85	100		136			71.74	45.78		84 R, 300 Z

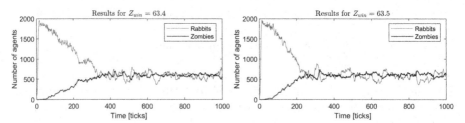

Fig. 6. ABM behavior close to equilibrium.

When both agents behave like negative feedback systems, the results are consistent (Table 2). For high zombie win probability and positive feedback *zombies*, the results are less consistent (not in table): some runs show zombie dominant

Table 3. ABM steady states, averaged over 100 runs, for $K_{RE} = 15$ [enp], $K_{RM} = 50$ [enp], $K_{ZM} = 50$ [enp], and variable $Z_{win} \in [61, 69]$

K_{ZE} [enp]	Z_{win}	p_R	p_Z	Rabbit feedback	Zombie feedback	Mean rabbits	Mean zombies	ABM steady state
51.85	61	-144	3.4	Negative	Positive	1130.78	388.24	Rabbit dominant equilibrium
52.7	62		6.8			816.52	525.48	
53.55	63		10.2			670.58	575.08	
53.89	63.4	-144	11.56	Negative	Positive	580.86	594.58	(Almost) perfect equilibrium
53.975	63.5		11.9			574.64	598.84	
54.4	64	-144	13.6	Negative	Positive	571.20	604.74	Zombie dominant equilibrium
55.25	65		17			530.06	613.54	
56.1	66		20.4			432.06	622.92	
56.95	67		23.8			380.54	619.62	
57.8	68		27.2			358.52	617.22	
58.65	69		30.6			319.88	620.98	

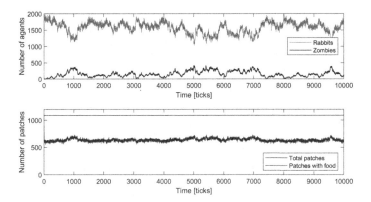

Fig. 7. ABM behavior with *zombies* at limit.

equilibrium instead of zombie collapse, with mean of *zombies* larger than mean of *rabbits*. We can see how the ratio of negative vs. positive feedback agents affects the outcome of the ABM.

The infection spread mechanism is driven by an initial condition parameter (win condition) that is not connected with either agent dynamic. Even small variations in this *interaction parameter* can cause the ABM to switch to a species dominant equilibrium state. In nonlinear systems terms, this behavior is one of metastable equilibrium [19], in which small disturbances can cause significant

Table 4. ABM behavior in number of agents, averaged over 100 runs, for $Z_{win} = 60$ [enp], $K_{RM} = 50$ [enp], $K_{ZM} = 50$ [enp], and variable $K_{RE} \in [45, 55]$

K_{RE} [enp]	p_R	p_Z	Rabbit feedback	Zombie feedback	Mean rabbits	Mean zombies	ABM steady state
45	−24	0	Negative	At limit	758.73	844.36	Oscillatory (around the same means) larger amplitudes for rabbits sometimes followed by collapse
46	−20				712.24	830.06	
47	−16				858.99	795.34	
48	−12				833.86	871.83	
49	−8				818.19	801.64	
50	−4				670.17	732.54	
51	0	0	At limit	At limit	735.75	738.32	Oscillatory (same mean)
52	4	0	Positive	At limit	808.25	757.94	Oscillatory (less consistent)
53	8				680.97	631.77	
54	12				731.05	661.73	Some oscillations often collapse
55	16				846.53	677.94	

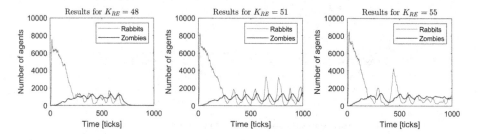

Fig. 8. ABM behavior around agent limits.

changes in behavior. It raises the question whether the ABM sensitivity to initial conditions could be measured with nonlinear systems tools, such as state-space trajectories and limit cycle analysis [25,26] or Lyapunov stability in the vicinity of equilibrium points [17].

When analyzing the small variations of two values for the interaction parameter (win condition), the differences between steady states are visually difficult to ascertain: both have an oscillatory behavior as the two species co-evolve. Only when looking at means over many runs can we draw a conclusion. Of course, we did not remove the probabilistic operators of this model, which naturally will produce variance in outcomes. However, this only shows the need for alternative and/or complementary measures of analysing complex system behaviors and states. There are still tools from systems theory and information theory that have yet to be exhausted in the context of complex systems and agent-based simulation models.

At limit, the numbers of both *rabbits* and *zombies* are oscillating with different amplitudes and periods, suggesting the existence of at least one limit cycle [29] in the ABM. This is a particularly interesting find, because although the behavior of the ABM is not coded into any one *zombie* agent, this behavior propagates to influence both species and the *rabbit* food source.

More interesting, however, is what we see when both *rabbits* and *zombies* are at limit. In dynamic systems, the response (to impulse or step, which for the ABM as a whole would be the equivalent of running the simulation) of an origin-pole system K/s is increasing steadily to infinity. Two of these integrator systems interacting in open loop continue to generate similar responses. However, when we close two integrators in a negative feedback loop, we obtain oscillations with consistent amplitudes. We get a hint of this in the ABM behavior for both species at limit (Fig. 8 center), which suggests that our hypothesis on modeling the *rabbit-zombie* encounter as a loop is worth further analysis.

With this case study we illustrated that the ABM steady states are dependent on the number of positive and negative feedback agents in the model, behaviors which are in turn determined by the initial conditions. We saw that some value intervals increase the ABM sensitivity to initial conditions, while for others the models displays consistent outcomes. This suggests that the sensitivity analysis of agent-based models might benefit from nonlinear systems tools, such as limit cycle methods.

An interesting question that arises is how resilient is an ABM, as a network of agents, to "bad" (i.e. positive feedback) nodes? If, for instance, we aim at modeling the spread of misinformation throughout a population, can we determine the limit condition for generating a butterfly effect in the network? In the ABM we used here, this limit condition was the switch from negative feedback *zombies* (or infected, or misinformed nodes) to positive feedback.

For this type of analysis, our feedback-based approach is able to integrate different agent dynamics, such as variable infection degrees, or spread mechanics, such as mitigation of infection over time. Moreover, the effect of probabilistic operators can be managed, via the systemic interpretation of their role in the ABM, either as part of the local agent dynamics or as part of agent interactions.

The generalization of our hypothesis resides in the very nature of systems: the steady states of a complex system are dependent on the ratio between stable, unstable, and at limit behaviors. The advantage is that this type of system stability can be derived even when there is no mathematical dynamic representations of behavior available, but merely a timewise measurement of the agent states that serve as outputs, which ABMs provide.

6   Conclusions

In this paper we propose a system representation based on feedback for agents in a two-species agent-based model. Results show that there is a dependency between ABM steady states on the type of agent feedback behavior. This is the first step for an alternate way to interpret initial conditions sensitivity in ABMs. A more extensive analysis without probabilistic operators has merit, to more accurately ascertain the ABM state trajectories and their dependence on the numbers of positive or negative feedback agents in the system.

For the particular two-species model we described in this paper, our future work will explore adding mechanisms such as *rabbit* agents being able to run from *zombie* agents, *rabbit-zombie* fight winner determined by the agents' energy levels or another variable (e.g., health status), probabilistic grass regrowth based on neighboring patches and times consumed, and infected grass spreading throughout the world.

In long-term, we plan on generalizing our approach to other types of complex systems and networks, and ultimately produce a methodology for initial-conditions sensitivity analysis in agent-based models.

Acknowledgements. The authors would like to thank our colleague Ioan Marica for his contribution to the implementation of the agent-based model.

References

1. NetLogo Community Models. http://ccl.northwestern.edu/netlogo/models/community/. Accessed 09 Aug 2022
2. NetLogo Patches. http://ccl.northwestern.edu/netlogo/bind/primitive/patches.html. Accessed 09 Aug 2022
3. Abreu, C.G., Ralha, C.G.: An empirical workflow to integrate uncertainty and sensitivity analysis to evaluate agent-based simulation outputs. Environ. Model. Softw. **107**, 281–297 (2018)
4. An, L., et al.: Challenges, tasks, and opportunities in modeling agent-based complex systems. Ecol. Model. **457**, 1–15 (2021)
5. Åström, K.J., Murray, R.M.: Feedback Systems: An Introduction for Scientists and Engineers. Princeton University Press, Princeton (2021)
6. Berceanu, C., Pătraşcu, M.: Engineering emergence: a survey on control in the world of complex networks. Automation **3**(1), 176–196 (2022)
7. Bertolotti, F., Locoro, A., Mari, L.: Sensitivity to initial conditions in agent-based models. In: Bassiliades, N., Chalkiadakis, G., de Jonge, D. (eds.) EUMAS/AT - 2020. LNCS (LNAI), vol. 12520, pp. 501–508. Springer, Cham (2020). https://doi.org/10.1007/978-3-030-66412-1_32
8. Bertolotti, T.: Generative and demonstrative experiments. In: Magnani, L. (ed.) Model-Based Reasoning in Science and Technology, pp. 479–498. Springer, Heidelberg (2014). https://doi.org/10.1007/978-3-642-37428-9_27
9. Birkin, M.: Microsimulation. In: Shi, W., Goodchild, M.F., Batty, M., Kwan, M.-P., Zhang, A. (eds.) Urban Informatics. TUBS, pp. 845–864. Springer, Singapore (2021). https://doi.org/10.1007/978-981-15-8983-6_44
10. Boccaletti, S., Grebogi, C., Lai, Y.C., Mancini, H., Maza, D.: The control of chaos: theory and applications. Phys. Rep. **329**(3), 103–197 (2000)
11. Bodine, E.N., Panoff, R.M., Voit, E.O., Weisstein, A.E.: Agent-based modeling and simulation in mathematics and biology education. Bull. Math. Biol. **82**(8), 1–19 (2020)

12. Crooks, A.T., Heppenstall, A.J.: Introduction to agent-based modelling. In: Heppenstall, A., Crooks, A., See, L., Batty, M. (eds.) Agent-based models of geographical systems, pp. 85–105. Springer, Dordrecht (2012). https://doi.org/10.1007/978-90-481-8927-4_5

13. Dreżewski, R.: A model of co-evolution in multi-agent system. In: Mařík, V., Pěchouček, M., Müller, J. (eds.) CEEMAS 2003. LNCS (LNAI), vol. 2691, pp. 314–323. Springer, Heidelberg (2003). https://doi.org/10.1007/3-540-45023-8_30

14. Dreżewski, R., Siwik, L.: Co-evolutionary multi-agent system with predator-prey mechanism for multi-objective optimization. In: Beliczynski, B., Dzielinski, A., Iwanowski, M., Ribeiro, B. (eds.) ICANNGA 2007. LNCS, vol. 4431, pp. 67–76. Springer, Heidelberg (2007). https://doi.org/10.1007/978-3-540-71618-1_8

15. Ghys, E.: The lorenz attractor, a paradigm for chaos. Chaos 1–54 (2013)

16. Ghys, É.: The butterfly effect. In: Cho, S.J. (ed.) The Proceedings of the 12th International Congress on Mathematical Education, pp. 19–39. Springer, Cham (2015). https://doi.org/10.1007/978-3-319-12688-3_6

17. Huang, R., Harinath, E., Biegler, L.T.: Lyapunov stability of economically oriented NMPC for cyclic processes. J. Process Control **21**(4), 501–509 (2011)

18. Janssen, S., Sharpanskykh, A., Curran, R., Langendoen, K.: Using causal discovery to analyze emergence in agent-based models. Simul. Model. Pract. Theory **96**, 1–21 (2019)

19. Kibele, A., Granacher, U., Muehlbauer, T., Behm, D.G.: Stable, unstable and metastable states of equilibrium: definitions and applications to human movement. J. Sports Sci. Med. **14**(4), 885 (2015)

20. Klasen, J.M., Lingard, L.A.: The butterfly effect in clinical supervision. Perspect. Med. Educ. **10**(3), 145–147 (2021)

21. Lenzitti, B., Tegolo, D., Valenti, C.: Prey-predator strategies in a multiagent system. In: Seventh International Workshop on Computer Architecture for Machine Perception (CAMP 2005), pp. 184–189. IEEE (2005)

22. Meluso, J., Austin-Breneman, J., Shaw, L.: An agent-based model of miscommunication in complex system engineering organizations. IEEE Syst. J. **14**(3), 3463–3474 (2019)

23. Miksch, F., Jahn, B., Espinosa, K.J., Chhatwal, J., Siebert, U., Popper, N.: Why should we apply ABM for decision analysis for infectious diseases?-an example for dengue interventions. PLoS ONE **14**(8), 1–19 (2019)

24. Miranville, A., Zelik, S.: Attractors for dissipative partial differential equations in bounded and unbounded domains. In: Handbook of Differential Equations: Evolutionary Equations, vol. 4, pp. 103–200 (2008)

25. Nagarajan, S.G., Mohamed, S., Piliouras, G.: Three body problems in evolutionary game dynamics: convergence, periodicity and limit cycles. In: 17th International Conference on Autonomous Agents and MultiAgent Systems, pp. 685–693 (2018)

26. Pasillas-Lépine, W.: Hybrid modeling and limit cycle analysis for a class of five-phase anti-lock brake algorithms. Veh. Syst. Dyn. **44**(2), 173–188 (2006)

27. Patil, A.: Routh-Hurwitz criterion for stability: an overview and its implementation on characteristic equation vectors using MATLAB. In: Hassanien, A.E., Bhattacharyya, S., Chakrabati, S., Bhattacharya, A., Dutta, S. (eds.) Emerging Technologies in Data Mining and Information Security. AISC, vol. 1286, pp. 319–329. Springer, Singapore (2021). https://doi.org/10.1007/978-981-15-9927-9_32

28. Polhill, J.G., et al.: Using agent-based models for prediction in complex and wicked systems. J. Artif. Soc. Soc. Simul. **24**(3) (2021)

29. Roenneberg, T., Chua, E.J., Bernardo, R., Mendoza, E.: Modelling biological rhythms. Curr. Biol. **18**(17), R826–R835 (2008)

30. Rzevski, G.: Modelling large complex systems using multi-agent technology. In: 2012 13th ACIS International Conference on Software Engineering, Artificial Intelligence, Networking and Parallel/Distributed Computing, pp. 434–437. IEEE (2012)
31. Seitbekova, Y., Bakibayev, T.: Predator-prey interaction multi-agent modelling. In: 2018 IEEE 12th International Conference on Application of Information and Communication Technologies (AICT), pp. 1–5. IEEE (2018)
32. Tang, M., Mao, X., Zhou, H.: Zombie-city: a new artificial society model. J. Comput. Inf. Syst. 9(12), 4989–4996 (2013)
33. Tian, Y., Sannomiya, N., Inoue, H., Shimohara, K.: Cooperation of multi-agent system and its composition. IFAC Proc. Vol. 38(1), 88–93 (2005)
34. Twu, P., Mostofi, Y., Egerstedt, M.: A measure of heterogeneity in multi-agent systems. In: 2014 American Control Conference, pp. 3972–3977. IEEE (2014)
35. Vyklyuk, Y., Manylich, M., Škoda, M., Radovanović, M.M., Petrović, M.D.: Modeling and analysis of different scenarios for the spread of COVID-19 by using the modified multi-agent systems-evidence from the selected countries. Results Phys. 20, 103662 (2021)
36. Wang, J., Xiong, J., Yang, K., Peng, S., Xu, Q.: Use of GIS and agent-based modeling to simulate the spread of influenza. In: 2010 18th International Conference on Geoinformatics, pp. 1–6. IEEE (2010)
37. Wilensky, U.: Netlogo. Center for Connected Learning and Computer-Based Modeling, Northwestern University, Evanston, IL (1999)
38. Williams, R.A.: Lessons learned on development and application of agent-based models of complex dynamical systems. Simul. Model. Pract. Theory 83, 201–212 (2018)
39. Yamada, J., Shawe-Taylor, J., Fountas, Z.: Evolution of a complex predator-prey ecosystem on large-scale multi-agent deep reinforcement learning. In: 2020 International Joint Conference on Neural Networks (IJCNN), pp. 1–8. IEEE (2020)

Proxy Manipulation for Better Outcomes

Gili Bielous[(✉)] and Reshef Meir

Technion-Israel Institute of Technology, Haifa, Israel
gili.bielous@campus.technion.ac.il, reshefm@ie.technion.ac.il

Abstract. This paper offers a framework for the study of strategic behavior in proxy voting, where non-active voters delegate their votes to active voters. It further studies how proxy voting affects the strategic behavior of non-active voters and proxies (active voters) under complete and partial information. We focus on the median voting rule for single-peaked preferences. Our results show strategyproofness with respect to non-active voters. Furthermore, while strategyproofness does not extend to proxies, we show that under mild restrictions strategic behavior can lead to socially optimal outcomes. For partial information settings, our results show that while convergence is guaranteed, it may be sub-optimal.

Keywords: Computational social choice · Proxy voting · Strategic voting · Strategyproofness

1 Introduction

In the age of internet, we see an increase of platforms and mechanisms for collective decision-making. However, many of these platforms suffer from low participation rates [13,22]. Thus, while there is an increase in the ability of individuals to influence collective decision-making in many areas, most decisions are made by a small, non-elected and non-representative groups of active voters. Partial participation may increase vote distortion [9] (the worst-case ratio between the social cost of the candidate elected and the optimal candidate, first defined in [17]); lead to counter-intuitive equilibria [5]; and significantly decrease the likelihood of selecting the Condorcet winner (when it exists) [8]. Above all, when the outcome of an election only considers a fraction of all opinions, it is unreasonable to assume that they accurately reflect the aggregated opinions of the collective.

Proxy voting, a long standing practice in politics and corporates [19], and an up-and-coming practice in e-voting and participatory democracies [16], aims at mitigating the adverse effects of partial participation. Non-active voters (followers) delegate their vote to another active voter (proxy), thereby at least having some influence on the outcome. In some cases, the outcome of proxy elections provide a better estimate of the aggregated social preference of all voters [3].

However, such delegation changes the power dynamic of voters by shifting some of the voting power to proxies. While much consideration is granted in

D. Baumeister and J. Rothe (Eds.): EUMAS 2022, LNAI 13442, pp. 79–95, 2022.
https://doi.org/10.1007/978-3-031-20614-6_5

the literature of social choice for the strategic behavior of voters [10,21] and candidates [7,20], there is little consideration of the *strategic behavior of proxies or followers* in proxy-mediated settings. Cohensius et al. [2017] consider strategic participation (i.e. selecting to participate or abstain) with mostly positive results; yet they pose the question of strategic behavior of proxies and followers as an open question, which was part of the inspiration to the current study.

Moreover, it is common to study strategic behavior in adversarial settings assuming complete information. However, this assumption may be unreasonable in the context of proxy voting. By delegating their vote, followers may wish to avoid the cognitive strain, time loss and other costs associated with determining and communicating their position. Thus, a setting that require followers to explicitly define their positions negates these benefits of proxy voting for followers. Reijngoud and Endriss [18] propose a framework for the study of strategic behavior in partial information settings. We apply it to study strategic behavior of proxies.

Our model considers a political spectrum over the real line [6,12], using the median voting rule for single-peaked preferences that was shown to be strategyproof [15]. Our initial study considers strategyproofness and manipulability with respect to both followers and proxies positions. Then, we consider sequences where proxies react to other proxies' actions. Finally, we turn to study strategic behavior in partial information settings. Our contribution is as follows:

- Strategyproofness of the median voting rule for single-peaked preferences extends to followers in proxy voting.
- Proxy voting with the median voting rule is manipulable with respect to proxy positions.
- Under mild restrictions, sequences of manipulations converge to an optimal equilibrium.
- Manipulations under partial information may converge to a worse equilibrium than without delegation.

2   Model and Preliminaries

We define the model of *Strategic Proxy Games (SPG)* as follows. There is a set of voters $N = \{1, ..., n\}$, and a set of proxies (active agents) $\Phi = \{\varphi_1, ..., \varphi_m\} \subseteq N$. Non-active voters, i.e. the set $N \setminus \Phi$ are called followers. Each voter $1 \leq i \leq n$ has a position $p_i \in \mathbb{R}$ along the political spectrum. Voters are assumed to have single-peaked preferences with peak at p_i. That is, for every $x, y \in \mathbb{R}$, if $x < y \leq p_i$, then Voter i prefers y to x, and if $p_i \leq x < y$, then Voter i prefers x to y. A *profile* is a vector $s \in \mathbb{R}^n$, such that s_i is the position Voter i declares. We denote by (s_{-i}, s_i') the profile that is equal to s except for the strategy of Voter i, that is s_i'. We adopt the model of [3], where followers each delegate their vote to the nearest proxy (as in [23]). That is, given a profile s, each Follower $i \in N \setminus \Phi$ delegates their vote to Proxy $\varphi_j \in \Phi$, where $\varphi_j = \text{argmin}_{\varphi_j \in \Phi} |s_j - s_i|$. All proxies delegate their vote to themselves. Voters' preferences are symmetric single-peaked for followers, that is, for every $x, y \in \mathbb{R}$, if $|x - p_i| < |y - p_i|$, then Follower i prefers x to y. Thus, voters' preferences are consistent with the delegation model. We assume that some tie-breaking scheme exists that only depends on positions of proxies.

Example 1. Consider the SPG appearing in Fig. 1.

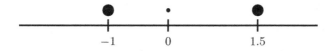

Fig. 1. An example SPG. Large dots indicate the positions of proxies, small dots indicate the positions of followers.

There are three voters $N = \{1, 2, 3\}$ with positions $p_1 = -1$, $p_2 = 0$, and $p_3 = 1.5$, where $\varphi_1 = 1, \varphi_2 = 3$ are proxies. In the truthful profile $s = (-1, 0, 1.5)$, the follower (voter 2) delegates their vote to the closer proxy φ_1. Thus, there are two votes to -1 and a single vote to 1.5.

Given a finite set $S \subseteq \mathbb{R}$ such that each element $s_i \in S$ has weight $w_{s_i} \in \mathbb{R}^+$, let $W = \sum_{s_i \in S} w_{s_i}$. The weighted median of S is an element $s_i \in S$ such that $\sum_{\{s_j \in S \setminus \{s_i\} : s_j \leq s_i\}} w_{s_j} \leq \frac{W}{2}$ and $\sum_{\{s_j \in S \setminus \{s_i\} : s_j \geq s_i\}} w_{s_j} \leq \frac{W}{2}$. That is, the sum of weights of elements that are smaller than s_i is at most half the total sum of weights, and the same holds for the sum of weights of elements that are larger than s_i.

Next, we define the Weighted Median voting rule. The weight if each proxy is defined as the number of delegations to them. Then, the *weighted median voting rule* (WM) selects the position that is the weighted median of proxy positions. Note that in this case, $W = n$. For example, the WM in Example 1 is the position -1, as there are 2 votes for -1 (the proxy at -1 and the single follower who delegates to them), and 1 vote for 1.5 (the proxy at 1.5 with no followers).

For a profile s, we denote the unweighted median of s by med_s, or med when clear from context. For a truthful profile p the *median voter* is a voter i such that $p_i = med_p$.

We say that a voter is *truthful* if they declare their true location, i.e. $p_i = s_i$. Voters may lie about their positions, i.e. $p_i \neq s_i$. We assume that voters are rational, that is, voters lie only if the outcome changes in their favor. We say that Voter i *has a manipulation* in p if there is $s_i \neq p_i$ such that Voter i strictly prefers the outcome by reporting s_i to the outcome by reporting p_i. A voting rule is *strategyproof* if for every p, no voter has a manipulation, otherwise, it is *manipulable*. The Median voting rule is known to be (group) strategyproof for single-peaked preferences [2,15].

3   Strategyproofness for Median Proxy Voting

We begin our analysis by showing that strategyproofness extends to Median Proxy Voting with respect to followers' positions. In [3] the authors show that for an infinite population of non-atomic voters given by some distribution where proxies are randomly selected, the winner of median proxy voting is the proxy nearest to the true median. The following Lemma shows that this result extends to our setting. A similar variant appears in [20].

Lemma 1. *Let s be a profile, and let med_s be the median of s. Then the reported position s_j of $\varphi_j = \arg\min_{\varphi_i \in \Phi} |s_i - med|$ is the winner by WM.*

Proof. W.l.o.g, assume $s_j \leq med$. As there are at most $\frac{n}{2}$ voters with positions smaller than med_s, the sum of votes to proxies left of s_j is at most $\frac{n}{2}$. As all median followers (followers that report position s_j) delegate their vote to φ_j, and there are at most $\frac{n}{2}$ voters with positions greater than med_s, the sum of votes to proxies with positions greater than s_j is at most $\frac{n}{2}$. Thus, s_j is the weighted median of s. $\square$

Next, we prove that for WM, followers do not have manipulations. Note that for followers manipulation implies delegation to another proxy.

Theorem 1. *WM is strategyproof w.r.t followers' positions.*

Proof. Assume towards contradiction that for some truthful profile s, there is a follower $i \in N \setminus \Phi$ that has a manipulation. W.l.o.g, assume $p_i \geq med_s$. Let φ be the proxy that is the winner for s, and let s_i' be the manipulation for Follower i. As s_i' is a manipulation, it must be that the winner for $s' = (s_{-i}, s_i')$ changed. Let $\varphi' \neq \varphi$ be the winner for s'. By Lemma 1, $med_s \neq med_{s'}$. Therefore, it must be that $s_i' < med_s$, and therefore $med_{s'} < med_s$, hence $s_{\varphi'} < s_\varphi$. One of the following must hold:

- $p_i < s_{\varphi'} < s_\varphi$: Since $med_s \leq p_i$, it follows that $s_{\varphi'}$ is closer to med_s than s_φ, in contradiction to Lemma 1.
- $s_{\varphi'} < s_\varphi < p_i$ by single-peakedness, Follower i prefers s_φ to $s_{\varphi'}$, in contradiction to s_i' being a manipulation.
- $s_{\varphi'} < p_i < s_\varphi$: as $p_i \geq med_s$, and since by Lemma 1 $|med_s - s_\varphi| < |med_s - s_{\varphi'}|$, we get $|p_i - s_\varphi| < |p_i - s_{\varphi'}|$. Thus by symmetric single-peakedness Follower i prefers s_φ to $s_{\varphi'}$, in contradiction to s_i' being a manipulation. $\square$

As Theorem 1 shows that WM is strategyproof with respect to followers' positions, we can henceforth consider them as non-strategic agents. In what follows, followers are considered to always be truthful, and we abuse the notation of a profile restricted to the strategic agents, i.e., the proxies.

We continue to analyze the strategic behavior of proxies. While we obtain a positive result of strategyproofness when only followers are considered strategic, the same does not hold for proxies, as demonstrated by the following example.

Example 2. Recall the SPG appearing in Example 1. When proxies are truthful, $s_1 = -1$ is the winner by the Weighted Median voting rule.

Next, consider the profile $s' = (-1, 1 - \varepsilon)$ for some $0 < \varepsilon < 2$ (Fig. 2).

Follower 2 delegates their vote to φ_3. There are two votes to $s_2 = 1 - \varepsilon$ and a single vote to $s_1 = -1$, thus, $1 - \varepsilon$ is the winner by WM.

Fig. 2. The SPG with φ_3 manipulation. Large empty dot is φ_3's true position, the manipulation is re-positioning strategically at $1 - \varepsilon$. Follower 2 delegates their vote to Proxy 3.

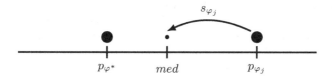

Fig. 3. A proxy with a manipulation.

As preferences are single-peaked and φ_3's peak is at $p_3 = 1.5$, we get that φ_3 prefer $1 - \varepsilon$ to -1. Hence, s' is a manipulation for φ_3.

The counter-example of Theorem 2 can be easily expanded to any number of followers and proxies. However, rather than formally constructing such example, The following theorem provides a complete characterization of manipulable scenarios. As a consequence, it shows that manipulations exist under very simple and reasonable conditions.

Theorem 2. *There is a proxy that has a manipulation in the profile s iff it holds that $s_{\varphi_i} \neq med$ for all $1 \leq i \leq m$, and there are proxies $\varphi_i, \varphi_j \in \Phi$ such that $p_{\varphi_i} < med < p_{\varphi_j}$.*

Proof. First, assume the winner is φ^* with position p_{φ^*}, and assume $p_{\varphi^*} < med$. For proxy φ_j we have that $p_{\varphi^*} < med < p_{\varphi_j}$. As preferences are single-peaked, φ_j prefers med to p_{φ^*}. We proceed by showing that $s_{\varphi_j} = med$ is a manipulation for Proxy φ_j, as in Fig. 3.

The median of (p_{-j}, s_{φ_j}) remains med, as there are at most $\frac{n}{2}$ voters with position that are smaller than med, hence the sum of votes to all proxies with positions smaller than med is at most $\frac{n}{2}$; and the same holds for the sum of votes to proxies with position larger than med. Since φ_j reports position $s_{\varphi_j} = med$, by Lemma 1 their position med is the winner by WM. Since φ_j prefer med to p^*, that is a manipulation for φ_j. When $p^*_\varphi > med$, by the same reasoning $s_{\varphi_i} = med$ is a manipulation for φ_i. Hence, no proxy has position at med, and there are φ_i, φ_j such that $p_{\varphi_i} < med < p_{\varphi_j}$, then there is a proxy that has a manipulation.

Next, if there is some proxy φ_k such that $s_{\varphi_k} = med$, then by Lemma 1 med is the winner and no proxy with position that is not med can change the outcome by reporting a position that is closer to med. Furthermore, every proxy with position at med have their peak outcome, so they cannot improve the outcome for them. Therefore, the only possible manipulations are by proxies with positions other

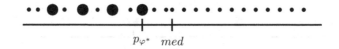

Fig. 4. If all proxies have positions on the same side of *med*, then non of them have a manipulation.

than *med*, and they can only manipulate by reporting a position that changes the location of the median. Assume towards contradiction that there is such a proxy φ, and w.l.o.g assume that $p_\varphi > med$. Then, to change the location of the median φ must report a position $s_\varphi < med$. Denote the median of $(p-\varphi, s_\varphi)$ by med'. We get that $med' < med$. Since s_φ is a manipulation, the outcome is at position $p' \leq med' < med < p_\varphi$. By single-peakedness φ prefers *med* to p', in contradiction to s_φ being a manipulation.

Finally, assume that for all proxies $p_{\varphi_i} \leq p_{\varphi^*} < med$ (Fig. 4).

By the same reasoning as for the case where there is a proxy with position at *med*, no proxy can change the outcome in their favor by reporting a position larger than *med*. Then, by Lemma 1 the only way to change the outcome is to get closer to the true median, i.e. set a strategy s_φ such that $p_{\varphi^*} < s_\varphi \leq med$. As proxy preferences are single-peaked, every proxy prefer p_{φ^*} to any position $p_{\varphi^*} < s_\varphi$, thus, they do not have a manipulation.   □

4   Manipulations for Better Outcomes

So far, we showed not only that proxy voting using WM is manipulable, but also that manipulations exist in common voting scenarios. Though strategyproofness is usually considered as a desirable property for voting rules, in what follows we argue that in the case of proxy voting, manipulations can actually be proven useful.

Recall that one of the motivations for proxy voting is to mitigate the caveats of partial participation. In [3], the authors show that proxy voting can better aggregate voter preferences as it can only reduce the distance from the true median over partial participation. The true median is the outcome of the median voting rule. It is both Condorcet consistent and the minimal sum of distances from voters' true preferences. It is common in Hotelling-Downs-like settings [6, 12] to measure the social cost of outcomes using the sum of distances of all agents positions to the outcome. Thus, the median of all voters reflects the social optimum. Moreover, reducing the distance of the outcome from the median may improve the social welfare, and generally can better reflect the collective preference.

4.1   Dynamics and Convergence

While manipulations are actions that agents may take from their truthful profile to get a better outcome, proxies may continue to take actions and reposition themselves to get better outcomes. In this section, we discuss on-going dynamics for proxies.

Our model offers an infinite action set. Therefore, the terminology of Iterative Voting [14], the standard setting for the study of on-going dynamics in voting, cannot be applied straightforward. We address it when relevant.

In what follows, we assume scenarios where manipulations exist, i.e., that meet the conditions of Theorem 2.

For every $\varphi_i \in \Phi$ and every profile $s_{-\varphi_i}$, we say that the position s'_{φ_i} is a *better-response* to s if φ_i prefers the outcome of $\left(s_{-\varphi_i}, s'_{\varphi_i}\right)$ to the outcome of s. We denote the set of better-responses for a profile s and proxy φ_i by $\mathcal{B}_s^{\varphi_i}$. We abuse the terminology of manipulations, such that a better-response from any profile s is a manipulation. A profile s is a *pure Nash equilibrium* (PNE) if for every $\varphi_i \in \Phi$ it holds that $\mathcal{B}_s^{\varphi_i} = \varnothing$, that is, no proxy have a manipulation for s.

A *policy* for proxy $\varphi_i \in \Phi$ is a function that maps a profile to a manipulation in the better-response set. Formally, let $\mathcal{S}$ be the set of all possible profiles for the proxies, and let $\mathcal{S}^* = \bigcup_{k=1}^{\infty} \mathcal{S}^k$. Then, a policy for φ_i is a function $\pi_{\varphi_i} : \mathcal{S} \to \mathbb{R}$ such that $\pi_{\varphi_i}(s) \in \mathcal{B}_s^{\varphi_i}$. One particular policy is the *best-response policy*, which selects a position with an outcome that the proxy prefers to all other positions in the better-response set, when one exists.

A *better-response dynamics* is a series of profiles, such that for every two consecutive profiles s^i, s^{i+1} in the series s^*, there is a proxy φ_j such that $s^{i+1} = \left(s^i_{-\varphi_j}, \pi_{\varphi_j}\left(s^i\right)\right)$. That is, every profile in the series is created by a single manipulation made by some proxy, according to that proxy's policy. We say that a dynamics s^* *converges* if the series s^* has a limit.

4.2 Monotone Policies

For proxies that are on the other side of the median than the outcome, it is reasonable to assume that their policies select a position that is on the side of the median as their position. This is due to the fact that every position on the side of the median is a better-response to every position on the opposite side of the median. Therefore, in the following discussion, we restrict policies to ones that preserves the integrity of proxies positions with respect to the median.

Formally, we say that a better-response dynamics s^* is *monotone* if for every $\varphi_i \in \Phi$, we have that $p_\varphi \leq med$ iff for every s^t it holds that $\pi_{\varphi_i}(s^t) \leq med$. Note that for every monotone better-response s^* starting from the truthful profile, for every s^t of s^* it holds that the median of s^t is med. We discuss non-monotone dynamics in Subsect. 4.4.

For a better-response dynamics s^*, and for a profile s^t of s^*, we say that $\varphi(t)$ is the *moving* proxy at t if $s^{t+1} = \left(s^t_{-\varphi(t)}, \pi_{\varphi(t)}\left(s^t\right)\right)$. We denote the manipulation of $\varphi(t)$ at s^t by $s'(t) = \pi_{\varphi(t)}\left(s^t\right)$. We say that $\varphi^*(t)$ is a *winning* proxy at s^t if the outcome of s^t is $s_{\varphi^*(t)}$, and denote $s^*(t) = s^t_{\varphi^*(t)}$. Finally, denote $\Delta_t = |med - s^*(t)|$, i.e. the distance between the median and the outcome of s^t.

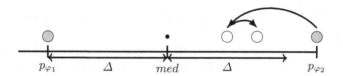

Fig. 5. Consecutive steps that increase the distance to the median. Gray dots indicate truthful positions of proxies, empty dots indicate positions of manipulation. Arrows indicate repositions. A small full dot is the position of a (single) follower.

The following Lemma shows that any manipulation in a monotone better-response dynamics where the winning proxy is not the moving proxy decreases the distance to the median.

Lemma 2. *For every monotone better-response dynamics s^* starting from the truthful profile $s^1 = p$, for every $t \geq 1$ if $\varphi(t) \neq \varphi^*(t)$, then $\Delta_{t+1} < \Delta_t$.*

Proof. By Lemma 1, we have that for s^{t+1} it holds that $\varphi^*(t+1) = \arg\min_{\varphi_k \in \Phi} |s^{t+1}_{\varphi_k} - med|$, therefore, for every $\varphi_k \in \Phi$ it holds that $|s^*(t+1) - med| \leq |s^{t+1}_{\varphi_k} - med|$. In particular, this holds for $\varphi^*(t)$. We get:

$$|s^*(t+1) - med| \leq |s^{t+1}_{\varphi^*(t)} - med|$$

Since $\varphi(t) \neq \varphi^*(t)$, it holds that $s'(t)$ is a manipulation for $\varphi(t)$, so $|s^{t+1}_{\varphi^*(t+1)} - med| \neq |s^{t+1}_{\varphi^*(t)} - med|$. Hence:

$$\Delta_{t+1} = |s^*(t+1) - med| < |s^*(t) - med| = \Delta_t.$$

$\square$

Lemma 2 suggests that manipulations made by proxies that do not have strategic positions at the current outcome reduce the distance to the true median. However, it is possible for winning proxies to manipulate in a way that increase the distance to the median. Figure 5 describe a proxy with 2 consecutive steps. The first makes them the winning proxy, the next is a better-response as they remain the winning proxy with a position that is closer to their true position.

We call sequences of consecutive manipulations by the same winning proxy *meta-move*. The following shows that while local manipulations within a meta-move can increase the current distance to the true median (as Fig. 5 demonstrates), meta-moves globally decrease the distance to the true median.

Lemma 3. *Let s^* be a monotone better-response dynamics starting from the truthful profile $s^1 = p$. Then, every meta-move strictly decreases the distance between the winning position and med.*

Proof. We start by giving a formal description of meta-moves. Let s^k such that $\varphi(k) \neq \varphi^*(k)$ and $\varphi^*(k+1) = \varphi(k)$. That is, in profile s^k, a proxy $\varphi(k)$ manipulates such that the manipulation makes them the winner. Next, let $t \geq 1$ such that for every $1 \leq i \leq t$ it holds that $\varphi(k+i) = \varphi(k) = \varphi^*(k+1)$.

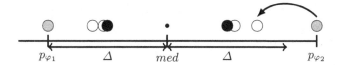

Fig. 6. A dynamics that diverges. The two large black dots indicate oscillation positions. The arrow indicates the first manipulation.

That is, once $\varphi(k)$ becomes the winning proxy, they keep making consecutive manipulations for t steps. We show that $\Delta_{k+t} < \Delta_k$.

By Lemma 1, monotonicity and since for every $1 \le i \le t$ it holds that $\varphi(k+i) = \varphi^*(k+1) \ne \varphi^*(k)$, we get that $\Delta_{k+i} \le \Delta_k$. Furthermore, since $s'(k)$ is a manipulation for $\varphi(k)$, it must be that the outcome of s^{k+1} is not equal to the outcome of s^k. We get that for every i, s^{k+i} is a manipulation and therefore $s^{k+i} \ne s^k$. Thus $\Delta_{k+i} \ne \Delta_k$. □

Lemma 2 and Lemma 3 together provide a complete analysis of the better-response sets for proxies, and show that the better-response set strictly decreases after each (meta) move. However, this alone is not sufficient for convergence.

Example 3. Recall the setting appearing in Example 1. Define $\alpha_1 = \frac{1}{4}$, and for every $t \in \mathbb{N}$, define $\alpha_{t+1} = \frac{1}{2}\alpha_t$. We define the following policy for $\varphi_i \in \Phi$:

$$\pi_{\varphi_i}(s^t) = med - sign(med - p_{\varphi_i})(\Delta_t - \alpha_t)$$

For every $t \in \mathbb{N}$ we get that

$$\begin{aligned}
\Delta_{t+1} &= |s_{\varphi_{t+1}}^{t+1} - med| \\
&= |med - sign(med - p_{\varphi_{t+1}})(\Delta_t - \alpha_t) - med| \\
&= |-sign(med - p_{\varphi_{t+1}})(\Delta_t - \alpha_t)| = \Delta_t - \alpha_t
\end{aligned}$$

As $\alpha_t = \frac{1}{2}\alpha_{t-1}$, we get $\Delta_{t+1} = \Delta_1 - \sum_{i=0}^{t-2}\frac{1}{2^i}\alpha_1 = \Delta_1 - \alpha_1\sum_{i=0}^{t-2}\frac{1}{2^i}$. As $t \to \infty$, we get that the distance to the median converges to $\Delta_1 - 2\alpha_1 = \Delta_1 - 2\frac{1}{4}\Delta_1 = \frac{1}{2}\Delta_1$, and the outcome oscillates between $-\frac{1}{2}$ and $\frac{1}{2}$, thus the best-response dynamics diverges. Figure 6 shows a schematic of this dynamic.

Note that Example 3 not only shows that monotone better-response dynamics need not converge, it also shows a key difference between our setting and Iterative Voting. We say that a dynamic is *acyclic* if there are no recurring states. For finite action sets, i.e., when the space of available manipulations for each agent is finite, acyclicity implies convergence. Example 3 shows that for infinite action spaces this does not hold.

In effect, α_t is the amount by which the outcome gets closer to the true median between steps. As Δ_t decreases, so does the leeway that proxies have to improve the outcome for themselves. While it is reasonable that α_t decreases as Δ_t decreases, Example 3 captures the behavior in which α_t decreases at a higher rate than Δ_t.

By restricting policies such that α_t and Δ_t decrease at the same rate, we can obtain convergence. Moreover, this guarantees that Δ_t itself converges to 0, meaning that the outcome converges to the true median.

Theorem 3. *Under some restrictions, every monotone better-response dynamics starting from the truthful profile converges, and the limit is a PNE where the outcome is the true median.*

Proof. We first define the necessary restriction on policies to achieve convergence. Let s^* be a monotone better-response dynamics that starts from the truthful profile $s^1 = p$ with policies π_{φ_i}, and let $0 \leq \alpha < 1$. We restrict policies such that manipulations must create a noticeable difference in the outcome. In particular, as Δ_t defines the interval in which manipulations are possible, such a restriction bounds the outcome away from Δ_t. Formally, for every $t \geq 1$, if $\varphi^*(t) \neq \varphi(t)$ then we require $|med - \pi_{\varphi_i}(s^t)| \leq \alpha \cdot \Delta_t$. For every t, l such that for every $0 \leq i \leq l$ it holds that $\varphi(t + i) = \varphi(t) = \varphi^*(t + 1) \neq \varphi^*(t)$, we require $|med - \pi_{\varphi_i}(s^{t+i})| \leq \alpha \cdot \Delta_t$.

First, if the series $\{\Delta_t\}_{t=1}^{\infty}$ converges to 0, then by definition of Δ_t, the distance between the outcome and the true median in s^* converges to 0. By Lemma 1, this implies that no proxy can change the outcome, thus, the better response set of every proxy is empty, and this is a PNE. Moreover, the outcome is the true median *med*.

Next, we argue that under the policy restrictions, $\Delta_t \to 0$ as $t \to \infty$. We construct a series $\{\Gamma_t\}_{t=1}^{\infty}$ as follows. $\Gamma_1 = \Delta_1$. If $\varphi^*(t) \neq \varphi(t)$, then set $\Gamma_{t+1} = \alpha \cdot \Gamma_t$. Otherwise, set $\Gamma_{t+1} = \Gamma_t$. We get that for every $t \geq 1$, it holds that $\Delta_t \leq \Gamma_t$. For the case where $\Gamma_{t+1} = \alpha \cdot \Gamma_t$ due to assumption and Lemma 2, and for the case where $\Gamma_{t+1} = \Gamma_t$ by Lemma 3.

Note that as long as $\Delta_t > 0$, there is a proxy with position not in $s^*(t)$, therefore, every manipulation for them strictly reduces the distance to the median. We therefore get that the amount of cases where $\Gamma_{t+1} = \Gamma_t$ is finite, and therefore for convergence it is sufficient to consider only the case where $\Gamma_{t+1} = \alpha \cdot \Gamma_t$. We get that $\Gamma_{t+1} = \alpha^t \cdot \Gamma_1 = \alpha^t \Delta_1$. As $\alpha < 1$, we get that $t \to \infty$ implies $\Gamma_t \to 0$.

Finally, since $\{\Gamma_t\}_{t=1}^{\infty}$ bounds $\{\Delta_t\}_{t=1}^{\infty}$ from above, and $\{\Gamma_t\}_{t=1}^{\infty}$ converges to 0, then $\{\Delta_t\}_{t=1}^{\infty}$ also converges to 0. □

As the true median of voters is the socially optimal outcome, Theorem 3 implies that the strategic behavior of proxies can in fact produce a socially optimal outcome.

4.3 Discretization

In many real-world applications, the assumption that voters can express any position on the political spectrum $\mathbb{R}$ is unreasonable. Voters are unlikely to distinguish between positions that are too similar, and this is the case both for selecting their truthful position, and distinguishing between different proxy positions for delegation. In computerized settings, there is some limited resolution to the expression of preferences (e.g. a temperature or a monetary amount). As it turns out, any such limit eliminates the possibility of oscillation we encountered in the previous section.

In this section, we assume w.l.o.g that the political spectrum is restricted to the set of all integers $\mathbb{Z}$.

For discrete spaces, every policy meets the conditions of Theorem 3. This is due to the fact that every manipulation made by a proxy with position that is not the current weighted median must decrease the distance to the true median by at least 1 (as the minimal distance between every distinct possible positions). Thus, the conditions are met for $\alpha = 1 - \frac{1}{\Delta_1}$. Therefore, for discrete spaces, every better-response dynamics converges, and the outcome is the true median, which is the socially optimal outcome.

Furthermore, for discrete spaces (in contrast to continuous) there is a well-defined best-response, that is to reposition at a distance that is one step closer to the true median than the current winner on their opposite side of the median. In particular, the best-response is monotone. Following the terminology of [14], a game has the *Finite Best Response Property (FBRP) from truth* if from any truthful profile, when restricted to best-responses, the dynamics converges. Thus, SPGs with WM are FBRP from truth.

4.4 Non-monotone Policies

In the previous sections we restricted the set of policies to those that maintain the integrity of proxies. That is, proxies always position themselves in the same side of the median as their truthful positions. However, there may be cases where it might be beneficial for a proxy to deviate to a position that is on the other side of the median. Proxies might attempt this in an intention to divert the positions of proxies on the opposite side of the median, or they might be willing to shift the median a little in an attempt to cause convergence to this new position. The following example demonstrate such a scenario.

Example 4. Consider the SPG appearing in Fig. 7

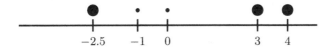

$$-2.5 \quad\quad -1 \quad 0 \quad\quad\quad\quad 3 \quad 4$$

Fig. 7. The SPG, large dots indicate proxies, small dots are followers.

The positions are $p = (-2.5, -1, 0, 3, 4)$. There are 3 proxies $\Phi = \{\varphi_1, \varphi_2, \varphi_3\}$ with positions $p_{\varphi_1} = -2.5, p_{\varphi_2} = 3, p_{\varphi_3} = 4$. There are 2 followers with positions $p_2 = -1, p_3 = 0$. The median is 0, and the outcome by the Weighted Median voting rule is the position $p_{\varphi_1} = -2.5$.

Assume that φ_2 manipulates to $s^1_{\varphi_2} = -2$. Now, the median is $p_2 = -1$, and the weighted median is $s^1_{\varphi_2}$. Note that φ_2 prefers this outcome to -2.5 by single-peakedness. Therefore, this is a manipulation for φ_2

Next, assume that φ_3 manipulates to $s_{\varphi_3}^2 = -1.5$. Now, the median in $s_{\varphi_3}^2 = -1.5$, and it is also the position of the closest proxy, thus, this is the weighted median. This outcome is preferable to φ_3 than -2.

Finally, φ_2 manipulates to $s_{\varphi_2}^3 = -1$. Now both the median and the weighted median is -1. Furthermore, both φ_1 and φ_3 can change the outcome in their favor.

Note that this does not imply convergence, as φ_2 still has a manipulation.

This example shows that a similar potential argument as used in the proof of Theorem 3, even with the added assumption that proxies make substantial enough steps to decrease the distance to the median, is unlikely to work. Our conjecture is that convergence holds for the unrestricted case as well, and that ultimately proxies would have an incentive to deviate back to their original side of the median, yet this is a matter of future research.

5   Partial Information

In previous sections we assumed that the proxies have complete information about the positions of proxies and followers alike. This assumption is common when analyzing adversarial behavior. However, is it reasonable in a proxy voting setting?

Recall that one of the applications of proxy voting is to mitigate the adverse effects of partial participation, where voters choose not to report their positions, rather only delegate their vote. Moreover, followers may not even know their exact position, rather they only know how to rank proxies by proximity. Thus, followers can still delegate their vote without the added cognitive strain of figuring what is their exact position.

When proxies have no information about positions of followers, then proxy voting is strategyproof. To see this, consider the profiles appearing in Fig. 8

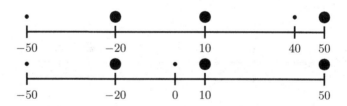

Fig. 8. An example of two profiles that are indistinguishable if followers positions are not public.

For the bottom profile, the proxy at -20 has a manipulation by deviating to -5. However, for the top profile, the proxy has no manipulation. When proxies have no information except proxies positions, the proxies cannot distinguish between the two profiles. Thus, proxies do not even know if the have a valid manipulation, let alone their better-responses.

This example shows that restricting the information available to proxies to reported proxy positions is too severe of an assumption.

In this section we relax the assumption of complete information. We first describe formally a less restrictive setting for the study of partial information. Next, we show that when only partial information is made available to voters, the strategic behavior of proxies may converge to a worse position than without delegation.

We employ the framework described in [18]. In this setting, a *poll information function (PIF)* σ maps each profile s to an information set $\sigma(s)$. For example, σ returns the outcome by WM, the number of delegations for each proxy, and even s itself. The set $\sigma(s)$ is then communicated to all voters.

In this setting, proxies cannot distinguish between profiles that yield the same information by σ. Recall the two profiles from Fig. 8. When only proxy positions are communicated by σ, the profiles are indistinguishable by the proxies. Therefore, they must assume the profiles are equally likely. However, proxies can deduce an equivalent set of profiles that are consistent with the information they have. In particular, both profiles in Fig. 8 would be in the same set.

Formally, Each proxy φ_i, based on their knowledge of their own preferences and the additional information $\sigma(s)$, deduce a set $W_{\varphi_i}^{\sigma(s)}$ of the possible positions of other followers (and proxies) that are compatible with the information set. That is, each profile s_{-i}' in $W_i^{\sigma(s)}$ is a profile of all voters except i such that (s_{-i}', s_i) is mapped by σ to the same information set they received $\sigma(s)$, i.e. $\sigma(s_{-i}', s_i) = \sigma(s)$.

Following the terminology of [4], we say that a position $s_{\varphi_i}^*$ is a *dominating manipulation* for Proxy φ_i if by reporting $s_{\varphi_i}^*$, there is some profile in $W_i^{\sigma(s)}$ that will produce a preferable outcome, and for all other profiles in $W_i^{\sigma(s)}$, it holds that φ_i weakly prefers them over the current outcome. More formally, let F be a resolute voting rule, and let $\succ_{\varphi_i}$ be a full order over all possible outcomes that define φ_i's true preferences. Then, $s_{\varphi_i}^*$ is a dominating strategy if there is a profile $s_{-i}' \in W_i^{\sigma(s)}$ such that $F(s_{-i}', s_{\varphi_i}^*) \succ_i F(s_{-i}', s_i)$ and for all profiles $s_{-i}' \in W_i^{\sigma(s)}$ it holds that $F(s_{-i}', s_{\varphi_i}^*) \succcurlyeq_i F(s_{-i}', s_i)$. Note that if σ returns the profile s, then the set of dominating strategies coincides with the set of better-responses. Moreover, dominating manipulations are the only rational actions that a risk-averse agent may take.

For the rest of this discussion, We also assume that the positions of the proxies are known as a choice of modeling, as followers need to know their positions to delegate their vote.

In this section, we assume that followers keep their positions as private information, and only delegate their vote to the proxy that is nearest to them. Therefore, for feasibility of delegation, we assume that proxies reveal their reported positions to all voters. Finally, we use σ_{winner}, the PIF that maps a profile s to the outcome of s by WM.

Next, we derive a similar positive result of convergence as in the complete information setting. First, as the PNE is defined with respect to better-responses, we consider convergence to a stable state (equilibrium) where none of the proxies have a dominating manipulation. However, as the position of the median is unknown to proxies, there is no straighforward interpretation of monotonicity. Instead, we consider a setting where proxies do not have a vote themselves. That is, votes are only delegated to them by followers. In this case, the position of the median is not affected by manipulations as is the case for monotone dynamics. This setting is closely related to the models of [3,20].

We begin our analysis by characterizing the set of dominating manipulations for proxies.

Theorem 4. *For any profile s and proxy $\varphi \in \Phi$, the set of dominating manipulations of φ is the interval between the position of the current winner and the closest proxy to the winner on the same side as p_φ (including their truthful position).*

Proof. First, every position s'_φ in the set is a dominating manipulation. Consider the profile $(s_{-\varphi}, s'_\varphi)$. There are only two possible winners, either $s_{\varphi^*(s)}$ (the position of the current winner) or s'_φ. W.l.o.g assume $p_\varphi < s_{\varphi^*(s)}$. By single-peakedness we get $p_\varphi \leq s'_\varphi < s_{\varphi^*(s)}$, thus φ weakly prefers the outcome. Next, there is a profile where φ wins, thus it is a dominating manipulation.

Next, for every position that is farther than the closest proxy on the same side as φ's truthful position, the outcome of $(s_{-\varphi}, s'_\varphi)$ is $\varphi^*(s)$ no matter the positions of followers. Thus, it is not a dominating manipulation. For positions that are on the other side of the current winner than φ's truthful position, consider the profile where $s_{\varphi^*(s)}$ is the median, and there are no followers between $s_{\varphi^*(s)}$ and the position of the closest proxy on the other side of $s_{\varphi^*(s)}$ than φ. The outcome must be a position that is further from the truthful position of φ than $s_{\varphi^*(s)}$, thus it is not a dominating manipulation.   □

Next, we show that the distance to the true median decreases by dominating manipulations.

Theorem 5. *Let s^* be a dynamics, then for every $t \geq 1$ it holds that $\Delta_{t+1} \leq \Delta_t$.*

Proof. Following Theorem 4, by repositioning to a dominating manipulations, the outcome either does not change, in which case $\Delta_{t+1} = \Delta_t$, or the moving proxy becomes the winner, in which case by Lemma 1 we get $\Delta_{t+1} < \Delta_t$.   □

We get that the distances between the winner and the true median is a decreasing monotone sequence that is bounded from below, thus, it converges. Therefore, under weak additional assumptions similarly to those made in the previous section (e.g. discretization) the step size is lower bounded so the dynamics converges. However, it is not guaranteed to converge to the true median, and in fact, may converge to a worse position than without delegation.

Consider the SPG appearing in Fig. 9.

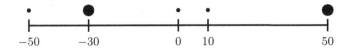

Fig. 9. The SPG, large dots are proxies, small dots are followers.

The true positions are $p = (-50, -30, 0, 10, 50)$. There are two proxies $\Phi = \{\varphi_1, \varphi_2\}$ with positions $p_{\varphi_1} = -30$ and $p_{\varphi_2} = 50$, and 3 followers. Note that proxies and followers are unaware to the positions of other followers. The median is 0, and the weighted median is -30. The social cost, or sum of distances from the weighted median to each position is

$$
\begin{aligned}
SC = & \ |-50 - (-30)| + |-30 - (-30)| \\
& + |-30 - 0| + |-30 - 10| + |-30 - 50| \\
& = 20 + 0 + 30 + 40 + 80 = 170
\end{aligned}
$$

Next, for φ_2, consider the position $s_{\varphi_2}^1{}' = 25$. From Theorem 4, it is a dominating manipulation.

Next, for φ_1 in $s^2 = \left(s_{-\varphi_2}^1, s_{\varphi_2}^1{}'\right)$, the only information that φ_1 has is that their position is -30, and that the position of φ_2 in s^2 is 25, and it is the outcome of s^2. Consider the position $s_{\varphi_1}^2{}' = 20$. Again, by Theorem 4 this is a dominating manipulation for φ_1.

Moreover, φ_1 has no dominating manipulation in $s^3 = \left(s_{-\varphi_1}^2, s_{\varphi_1}^2{}'\right)$. Additionally, this holds for every $s^t = \left(s_{-\varphi_2}^2, s_{\varphi_2}^t{}'\right)$ where $s_{\varphi_2}^t{}' \in \left(s_{\varphi_1}^2, s_{\varphi_2}^1\right] = (20, 25]$.

Finally, for every $s^t = \left(s_{-\varphi_2}^2, s_{\varphi_2}^t{}'\right)$ where $s_{\varphi_2}^t{}' \in \left(s_{\varphi_1}^2, s_{\varphi_2}^1\right] = (20, 25]$, the set of dominating strategies for φ_2 is $\left(20, s_{\varphi_2}^t{}'\right]$. Figure 10 demonstrates the dynamics.

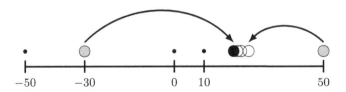

Fig. 10. An example that converges to a worse position than without delegation. Gray dots indicate truthful positions of proxies, empty dots indicate positions of dominating manipulations, full dot indicate convergence positions. Small full dots are followers.

We get that the distance between the position of φ_1 and φ_2 converges to 0, and therefore the dynamics ultimately converges to a PNE where the positions of both proxies is $s_{\varphi_1}^2 = 20$. The social cost of this outcome is $sum_{i=1}^5 |20-p_i| = 180$, that is greater than the social cost of the outcome of p.

Note that in the case of complete information, this counter-example would not converge in the same way. This is due to the fact that once φ_1 repositions and becomes the winner again, as they know the position of the median, their better-response set is not empty.

6   Conclusions and Future Work

We introduced *Strategic Proxy Games*, a framework to study strategic behavior of proxies in voting mechanisms.

First, we demonstrated that in this model, the extension of the median voting rule to the weighted median voting rule via proxy voting maintains strategyproofness with respect to followers' positions. In particular, this suggests that with respect to follower positions, the delegation scheme is optimal for followers preferences. Our study uses the Tullock delegation scheme, however other delegation models have been studied in the literature. In the one-step delegation domain, [11] consider delegation that accounts for small errors in assessment of positions, and [1] consider social connections that influence the weight of proxies. It would be interesting to see how the delegation model affects the outcome of proxy voting and the strategic behavior of followers and proxies.

We continued to study the strategic behavior of proxies, and showed that while strategyproofness does not extend to proxy voting, when proxies maintain the integrity of their positions with respect to the median, the outcome converges to the true median of all voters. This result implies that by relaxing truthfulness to integrity, strategic behavior can improve the outcome with respect to the truthful profile. In future work we would like to study the outcome without this restriction, and it is our conjecture that the outcome converges to the true median as well.

Finally, we study the implications of partial information to the strategic behavior of proxies. While we get a positive result of convergence, our results also show that in this case the outcome may increase the social cost.

In this research we focused on the median voting rule. We plan to study the implication of strategic proxy behavior in higher dimensions, as well as with other voting rules.

Acknowledgement. This research was supported by the Israel Science Foundation (ISF; Grant No. 2539/20).

References

1. Alon, N., Feldman, M., Lev, O., Tennenholtz, M.: How robust is the wisdom of the crowds? In: Twenty-Fourth International Joint Conference on Artificial Intelligence. Citeseer (2015)
2. Black, D.: On the rationale of group decision-making. J. Polit. Econ. **56**(1), 23–34 (1948)

3. Cohensius, G., Manor, S., Meir, R., Meirom, E., Orda, A.: Proxy voting for better outcomes. In: AAMAS 2017 (2017)
4. Conitzer, V., Walsh, T., Xia, L.: Dominating manipulations in voting with partial information. In: Twenty-Fifth AAAI Conference on Artificial Intelligence (2011)
5. Desmedt, Y., Elkind, E.: Equilibria of plurality voting with abstentions. In: Proceedings of the 11th ACM Conference on Electronic Commerce, pp. 347–356 (2010)
6. Downs, A.: An Economic Theory of Democracy. Harper & Row, New York (1957)
7. Dutta, B., Jackson, M.O., Le Breton, M.: Strategic candidacy and voting procedures. Econometrica **69**(4), 1013–1037 (2001)
8. Gehrlein, W.V., Lepelley, D.: Voting Paradoxes and Group Coherence: The Condorcet Efficiency of Voting Rules. Springer, Heidelberg (2010). https://doi.org/10.1007/978-3-642-03107-6
9. Ghodsi, M., Latifian, M., Seddighin, M.: On the distortion value of the elections with abstention. In: Proceedings of the AAAI Conference on Artificial Intelligence, vol. 33, pp. 1981–1988 (2019)
10. Gibbard, A.: Manipulation of voting schemes: a general result. Econom.: J. Econom. Soc. **41**, 587–601 (1973)
11. Green-Armytage, J.: Direct voting and proxy voting. Const. Polit. Econ. **26**(2), 190–220 (2015)
12. Hotelling, H.: Stability in competition. Econ. J. **39**(153), 41–57 (1929)
13. Jönsson, A.M., Örnebring, H.: User-generated content and the news: empowerment of citizens or interactive illusion? Journal. Pract. **5**(2), 127–144 (2011)
14. Meir, R.: Iterative voting. In: Trends in Computational Social Choice, pp. 69–86 (2017)
15. Moulin, H.: On strategy-proofness and single peakedness. Public Choice **35**(4), 437–455 (1980). https://doi.org/10.1007/BF00128122
16. Petrik, K.: Participation and e-democracy how to utilize web 2.0 for policy decision-making. In: 10th Annual International Conference on Digital Government Research: Social Networks: Making Connections between Citizens, Data and Government, pp. 254–263 (2009)
17. Procaccia, A.D., Rosenschein, J.S.: The distortion of cardinal preferences in voting. In: Klusch, M., Rovatsos, M., Payne, T.R. (eds.) CIA 2006. LNCS (LNAI), vol. 4149, pp. 317–331. Springer, Heidelberg (2006). https://doi.org/10.1007/11839354_23
18. Reijngoud, A., Endriss, U.: Voter response to iterated poll information. In: Proceedings of the 11th International Conference on Autonomous Agents and Multiagent Systems, vol. 2, pp. 635–644 (2012)
19. Riddick, F.M., Butcher, M.H.: Riddick's Rules of Procedure: A Modern Guide to Faster and More Efficient Meetings. Madison Books, Seattle (1991)
20. Sabato, I., Obraztsova, S., Rabinovich, Z., Rosenschein, J.S.: Real candidacy games: a new model for strategic candidacy. In: Proceedings of the 16th Conference on Autonomous Agents and MultiAgent Systems, pp. 867–875 (2017)
21. Satterthwaite, M.A.: Strategy-proofness and arrow's conditions: existence and correspondence theorems for voting procedures and social welfare functions. J. Econ. Theor. **10**(2), 187–217 (1975)
22. Schaupp, L.C., Carter, L.: E-voting: from apathy to adoption. J. Enterp. Inf. Manag. (2005)
23. Tullock, G.: Proportional representation. In: Toward a Mathematics of Politics, pp. 44–157 (1967)

The Spread of Opinions via Boolean Networks

Rachael Colley$^{(\boxtimes)}$ and Umberto Grandi

IRIT, University of Toulouse, Toulouse, France
{rachael.colley,umberto.grandi}@irit.fr

Abstract. Opinion diffusion models the spread of information among agents whose connections are given by a social network. We study opinion diffusion via Boolean networks, in which agents update their (binary) opinion according to a Boolean function that we assume is compactly represented as a propositional formula. The classical threshold models, where opinion updates depend on the proportion of an agent's influencers having a differing opinion, are a special case of our model. Boolean networks are a well-studied mathematical model for biology, and in this paper we analyse it through the lens of opinion diffusion. Most notably, we analyse the computational complexity of deciding if opinions converge from a given initial point, the existence of an asynchronous update that maximises the global agreement among the agents, and we explore connections with delegative voting.

Keywords: Multiagent systems · Social networks · Influence maximisation

1 Introduction

Opinion diffusion models how an opinion on an issue can spread throughout a social network. In the network, every node represents an agent who has an opinion on a given issue, which we will assume to be binary. The network's edges determine who influences each agent. A classical assumption is to use threshold functions to update an agent's opinion, changing it when a given proportion of their influencers have a different opinion (see, e.g., the seminal work of Granovetter [25]). Some typical problems studied in the literature on opinion diffusion are stable diffusion and opinion control. In the former, we recognise whether the diffusion process will stabilise such that no agent wants to update their opinion. In the latter, how to control certain opinion characteristics, such as there being a consensus on the issue, by changing some initial opinions or the structure of the network (see Sect. 1.2 for an overview).

In this paper we show that Boolean networks, a well-studied mathematical model from biology, generalise classical models of opinion diffusion and can be used to model fine-grained influence updates among the agents. Boolean networks are graphs where each node has a state, typically on or off, 1 or 0, yes or no. A discrete-time dynamical process starts from an initial state, and the state in following iterations of the network is determined by a set of Boolean update functions, one per node, that input the states of the node's neighbours. Akutsu et al. [3], Cheng et al. [11], Kauffman [28] provide good introductions to this model. There have been many mathematical advancements in the study of Boolean networks due to their ability to model gene regulatory networks in biology (see, e.g., Kauffman et al. [29] and Shmulevich and Zhang [39]).

Boolean networks can model opinion diffusion on binary issues where update functions are arbitrary Boolean functions. We assume that such functions are represented as logical formulas built from the standard connectives, $\wedge, \vee, \neg, \cdots$, where the atomic propositions are the influencers of the agent. These functions allow us to study fine-grained relationships between the agents, as showcased in the following example:

Example 1. A group is deciding whether they should go on holiday together. Alex organises a holiday to suit themself and their friends Bernie, Charlie and Dom. Alex believes it is the perfect holiday for the group and wants to go. However, the opinions of the rest of the group on the holiday may correspond to the following formulas:

- Bernie's closest friend is Dom, and Bernie will go if Dom decides to go as well. However, Bernie would also go on the holiday if both Alex and Charlie decided to go as well. Therefore, Bernie's opinion would be updated with respect to the following propositional formula: $(Alex \wedge Charlie) \vee Dom$.
- Charlie has currently fallen out with Alex. Therefore, Charlie will only go on the holiday if Bernie and Dom are both going and Alex is not. This could be expressed as $Bernie \wedge Dom \wedge \neg Alex$.
- Dom is reluctant to go on the holiday, and thus, will only go on the holiday if all of their friends go as well: $Alex \wedge Bernie \wedge Charlie$.

Consequently, as Alex will attend, this means that Charlie will not, given that they will only go if Alex does not. As Alex will attend and Charlie will not, Bernie will only go if Dom does. However, as Charlie will not go, neither will Dom. In turn, nor will Bernie.

1.1 Our Contribution

This paper studies Boolean networks as opinion diffusion models. As such, we focus on classical studies in opinion diffusion and show that:

- The computational complexity of determining if a given boolean network and set of initial opinions lead to a stable state under synchronous updates is PSPACE-complete, building on the result of Chistikov et al. [13] from majoritarian to arbitrary update functions via a non-trivial lemma (Sect. 3).
- There does not necessarily exist a sequence of asynchronous updates that leads to a stable profile (and maximises agreement), as shown by Bredereck and Elkind [8] for majority update functions. However, when update functions are restricted to contain only positive (or only negated) literals, we give a procedure that finds a stable state of opinions with a maximal number of agreements (Sect. 4).

- Synchronous opinion diffusion always terminates if the Boolean network models a multi-agent delegative voting problem (*aka* liquid democracy). Moreover, it does so in polynomial time and gives the same outcomes as the polynomial unravelling procedures defined by Colley et al. [16]. We also show that manipulating collective opinions in this setting is a NP-complete problem (Sect. 5).
- Known results from the vast literature on Boolean networks can be applied to classical problems of opinion diffusion (Sect. 6).

1.2   Related Work

In this section we overview existing work on Boolean networks and opinion diffusion, notably threshold models, multi-issue opinion diffusion, and delegative voting.

Algorithmic Approaches to Boolean Networks. A recent stream of papers provided algorithmic results that are closer to our purposes. Most notably, Akutsu et al. [1] study the complexity of choosing which nodes to control to gain a specific outcome, showing that the problem is NP-hard. Inoue [26] gives a logical language by which Boolean networks can be expressed. Kosub [33] studies fixed points in social networks, relating to our notion of stability. In Sect. 6 we expand on this related work by importing and rephrasing some of their results in the opinion diffusion terminology.

Threshold Models. Much opinion diffusion research has focused on threshold models, where agents update their opinion when a certain proportion of their influencers have differing opinions. The problem of convergence for binary opinions has been studied, e.g., by Goles and Olivos [22] who showed that threshold models either terminate or cycle between two different collections of opinions, and by Christoff and Grossi [15], who give the conditions by which a social network stabilises on majority updates. Another popular problem is maximising influence in the network (see, e.g., [19,37]). In particular, Zhuang et al. [41] define graph-theoretic notions when using a threshold model which determines how to reach a consensus among the opinions. Auletta et al. [6] identifies conditions on the graph structure that allows a minority to influence the majority. Furthermore, they also show that deciding whether the two opinions can coexist in some stable configuration is an NP-hard problem. Bredereck and Elkind [8] study an asynchronous model with majority updates to maximise the number of agreements in the model with polynomial algorithms.

Multi-issue Opinion Diffusion. General models of opinion diffusion have been proposed assuming that agents have opinions on multiple interconnected issues. Here the problem is how to ensure that influence results in consistent opinions for each of the agents: Brill et al. [9] need to ensure that individual preference orders remain transitive and acyclic, Botan et al. [7] use arbitrary integrity constraints. Both focus on majoritarian update functions. The closest work to ours in this context is that of Grandi et al. [24], which considers opinion diffusion with arbitrary update functions on multiple interconnected issues. When considering a single binary issue, this model corresponds to Boolean networks, with the only difference that Grandi et al. [24] give an explicit representation of the update formulas, while we assume they are compactly represented as propositional formulas.

Opinion Diffusion with Complex Opinion Updates. Rosenkrantz et al. [38] focuses on opinion diffusion where the updates are also determined by Boolean functions. This work, however, only considers social networks that are directed acyclic graphs. Another model of opinion diffusion extending the update functions is that of Morrison and Naumov [35], where agents can have many thresholds depending on the labels of the other nodes. For example, allowing different thresholds for different groups, updating their opinion if 80% of their work colleagues have a different opinion or if 30% of their close friends do.

Multiagent Delegations. The connection between models of delegative democracy, such as liquid democracy, and opinion diffusion was first observed by Christoff and Grossi [14]. The authors express liquid democracy as a model of opinion diffusion where every agent is influenced by at most one agent. Models of delegative democracy have recently been improved to account for multi-agent delegations: Degrave [18] allowed delegations to be fractionally spread among their delegates, and Colley et al. [16] let voters express a ranking of Boolean functions to model delegations. In Sect. 5 we expand the work of Christoff and Grossi [14] to the more general latter model.

2 The Model

A set of agents $\mathcal{N} = \{1, \cdots, n\}$ can influence each other's opinion via a social network $G = (V, E)$, where the agents are the nodes $V = \mathcal{N}$ and the directed edges represent influence, $(i, j) \in E$ if agent i can influence j's opinion. Furthermore, we let the *influence neighbourhood* of agent $i \in \mathcal{N}$ be $N_i = \{j \mid (j, i)\}$, therefore $j \in N_i$ means that j can influence i's opinion on the issue (sometimes this is referred to as i's in-neighbours). An agent i can influence themselves, thus allowing $(i, i) \in E$, as an agent's current opinion can affect their future opinions. We study a setting with a single binary issue; therefore, we denote agent i's opinion as $o_i \in \{0, 1\}$. As the agents' opinions are not static, we let o_i^t be i's opinion at time $t \in \mathbb{N}$, and thus o_i^0 is agent i's *initial opinion*. The collection of the agents' opinions, which we refer to as a *profile of opinions* at time t is denoted by $O^t = (o_1^t, \cdots, o_n^t)$.

In this model, each agent has a Boolean function γ_i that represents when agent i's opinion changes, known as their *update function*. The update function γ_i for agent i is represented as a compact propositional formula in DNF built from the connectives $\neg, \wedge, \vee$ where the atomic variables are given by N_i, assuming that $\text{Var}(\gamma_i) = N_i$. If for some $i \in \mathcal{N}$, $N_i = \emptyset$, then their update function is either $\gamma_i = \top$ or $\bot$, i.e., a constant function. The collection of the agents' update functions is denoted by $\overline{\gamma} = (\gamma_1, \cdots, \gamma_n)$.

Most of this paper is concerned with a synchronous update $\circ$ on the agents' opinions. For all agents, $\circ$ at time $t+1$ checks if each agent's neighbours' opinions at t induce that agent's opinion to change. Thus, $\circ$ iteratively lets $o_i^{t+1} = 1$ at time $t + 1$ if and only if $\bigwedge_{j \in N_i} o_j^t \models \gamma_i$ and lets $o_i^{t+1} = 0$, otherwise. We denote an instance of opinion diffusion with $\langle G, \overline{\gamma}, O^0 \rangle$. We denote t iterations of the diffusion process as $\circ(G, \overline{\gamma}, O^0, t) = O^t$. We say that the synchronous update is *stable* if there is some $t \in \mathbb{N}$ such that for all $t' > t$ we have that $\circ(G, \overline{\gamma}, O^0, t) = \circ(G, \overline{\gamma}, O^0, t')$, i.e., no more changes to the opinion profile can happen. At times we refer to the stable profile of opinions as O^T. In the literature, the notion of the diffusion process stabilizing is also referred to as the process converging [13]. As there are a finite number of opinion profiles of the agents, namely 2^n, this means that if the synchronous update does not lead to a stable opinion profile, the process is cyclic.

Example 2. Let the set of agents be $\mathcal{N} = \{a, b, c, d, e, f, g\}$ who have the following initial opinions $O^0 = (0, 1, 0, 0, 1, 1, 1)$. On the right-hand side of Fig. 1 we see the social network G, where $V = \mathcal{N}$ are the nodes and E represents by the directed edges. The neighborhoods of influence for each agent can be seen from G, for example, a has two incoming edge from d and g, thus $N_a = \{d, g\}$. On the left-hand side of Fig. 1, Table (a) lists each agent's neighbourhood of influence, update function and initial opinion. Consider the update function $\gamma_b = a \wedge \neg d$, the intuition behind this function is that b will only update their opinion at time $t + 1$ to be $o_b^{t+1} = 1$ if and only if at time t, a is for the issue $o_a^t = 1$ and d is against the issue $o_d^t = 0$. Note that in all other scenarios for b (dictated by the different combinations of opinions of a and d, excluding b's initial opinion) that b's opinion is against the issue.

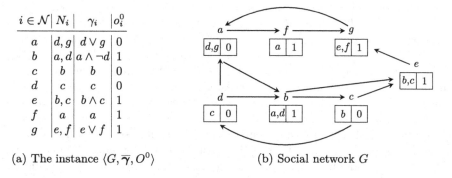

$i \in \mathcal{N}$	N_i	γ_i	o_i^0
a	d, g	$d \vee g$	0
b	a, d	$a \wedge \neg d$	1
c	b	b	0
d	c	c	0
e	b, c	$b \wedge c$	1
f	a	a	1
g	e, f	$e \vee f$	1

(a) The instance $\langle G, \overline{\gamma}, O^0 \rangle$ (b) Social network G

Fig. 1. This figure describes the social network and initial opinions of the agents in Example 2. Table (a) on the left-hand side gives every agent: their neighbourhood, update function, and initial opinion. On the right-hand side, Figure (b) depicts the social network G where the box under the agent's name gives their neighbourhood of influencers and their initial opinion.

We now follow the synchronous diffusion $\circ$ on $\langle G, \overline{\gamma}, O^0 \rangle$. Agent a updates their opinion from 0 to 1 when either d or g are for the issue in the previous iteration, as $o_g^0 = 1$, we see that $o_a^1 = 1$. Next we address the opinion update of

b at time $t = 1$, as at $t = 0$, $o_a^0 = 0$, we see that b's update function evaluates to false, therefore, $o_b^1 = 0$. Following this we arrive at $\circ(G, \overline{\gamma}, O^0, 1) = O^1 = (1, 0, 1, 0, 0, 0, 1)$. The opinions at $t = 1$ are used at time $t = 2$, giving $O^2 = (1, 1, 0, 1, 0, 1, 0)$. Following this, we have:

$$O^3 = (1, 0, 1, 0, 0, 1, 1); \quad O^4 = (1, 1, 0, 1, 0, 1, 1); \quad O^5 = (1, 0, 1, 0, 0, 1, 1).$$

The instance is not stable using $\circ$, as $O^3 = O^5 \neq O^4$. Thus, the process would alternate between O^3 and O^4. Note that the opinions of a, e, f and g are stable.

2.1 Restricted Languages for Update Functions

We let $\mathcal{L}$ denote a language for update functions, such that $\gamma \in \mathcal{L}$ if and only if γ abides by the criteria of $\mathcal{L}$. Generally, we assume that all Boolean formulas are in DNF. In threshold models, update functions are compactly represented as quota, i.e., $i \in \mathcal{N}$ has opinion $o_i^{t+1} = 1$ if and only if $\sum_{j \in N_i} o_j^t \geq q$, for some quota $q \in \mathbb{N}$. Expressing such a quota as a propositional formula leads to an exponential blow-up in constraint size. We denote the set of formulas corresponding to quota rules with $\mathcal{L}^{\text{quota}}$. Another restriction on the update functions that we study is that of $\mathcal{L}^+$, where update functions are Boolean functions that do not contain negated literals.

3 The Complexity of Convergence

In this section we examine the computational complexity of stability, i.e., the problem of detecting if a given initial configuration leads to a stable state. To follow the literature, we refer to the problem as *convergence*.

Convergence-$\mathcal{L}$	
Given:	An instance of Boolean opinion diffusion $\langle G, \overline{\gamma}, O^0 \rangle$ with every $\gamma \in \overline{\gamma}$ such that $\gamma \in \mathcal{L}$
Question:	Does the diffusion process stabilise on $\langle G, \overline{\gamma}, O^0 \rangle$?

To prove PSPACE-completeness for CONVERGENCE-$\mathcal{L}$, we use the reduction given by Chistikov et al. [13] for CONVERGENCE-**Maj**, where **Maj** is the majority update. In their proof, however, **Maj** is represented compactly as a quota rule for each agent. In contrast, it can only be represented as an exponential Boolean formula (for example, listing all the possible majorities). We refer to an instance of their model as $\langle G, \textbf{Maj}, O^0 \rangle$. We first prove a lemma that allows us to translate an instance $\langle G, \textbf{Maj}, O^0 \rangle$ into our model using Boolean formulas in polynomial time, with the addition of some dummy agents.

Lemma 1. *For every majoritarian opinion diffusion instance $\langle G, \textbf{Maj}, O^0 \rangle$ we can create a Boolean opinion diffusion instance $\langle G', \overline{\gamma}, O'^0 \rangle$ in $\mathcal{O}(n^3)$ time that converges exactly when $\langle G, \textbf{Maj}, O^0 \rangle$ does.*

Proof. Our proof relies on the fact that every budget constraint can be translated into Boolean circuits in decomposable negation normal form (DNNF) in polynomial time [17]. A circuit has leaf nodes which are labelled with either $\top, \bot, x, \neg x$ for any variable x. Furthermore, each internal node is labelled with $\wedge$ or $\vee$ dictating the operation performed on its children's nodes to determine its value. A DNNF circuit must be directed, acyclic, and have a single root. Moreover for every conjunction in the circuit, each of its conjuncts cannot share variables. Finally, note that any budget constraint over a set of costed issues $\mathcal{I}$ and budget limit B can be represented by a DNNF circuit that can be found in polynomial-time, in particular, $B + |\mathcal{I}|$-time [17, Theorem 16]. We will not describe how to build the circuits in detail; however, a clear connection to Boolean opinion diffusion can be made where parent nodes are influenced with respect to their label by their children. Furthermore, the circuit's leaf nodes either represent an issue being accepted or rejected (negation). Thus the input of a circuit is the opinions of an agent's influencers.

We use these DNNF circuits to encode the majoritarian opinion diffusion in our Boolean setting (moving from $\langle G, \mathbf{Maj}, O^0 \rangle$ to $\langle G', \overline{\gamma}, O'^0 \rangle$). We create dummy agents between each agent $i \in \mathcal{N}$ from G and their in-neighbours $N_i \neq \emptyset$ (recall that if $N_i = \emptyset$ then their opinions never update). These dummy agents are either part a DNNF circuit C_i or are *regulatory* agents in R_i. The dummy agents in C_i allow the final agent in the circuit's opinion to reflect the majority opinion of i's in-neighbours. The dummy agents in R_i ensure that every path from agents in N_i to i are of length k (the maximum path length of any required circuit). This ensures that the opinions of the original agents will update at the same time.

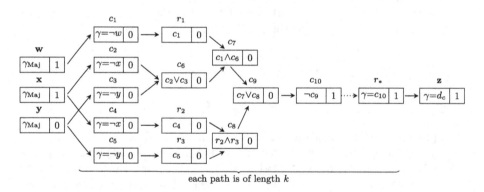

each path is of length k

Fig. 2. This diagram shows how to create a DNNF circuit to mimic the majority update function of agent $\mathbf{z}$ who is influenced by $\mathbf{w}, \mathbf{x}$ and $\mathbf{y}$. The circuit nodes, $C_\mathbf{z}$ represent a circuit reflecting if *at most one* of their influencers are for the issue with c_9 giving this outcome. Thus, c_{10}'s opinion reflects the majority opinion of $\mathbf{z}$'s influencers. The regulatory nodes ensure that each path from the influencers to $\mathbf{z}$ is of length k, either within the circuit (as seen by r_1, r_2 or r_3) or the nodes which can appear between c_{10} and r_* (represented by the dotted line).

We give an example of this translation in Fig. 2. It translates the majority update function of $\mathbf{z}$ who is influenced by $\mathbf{w}$, $\mathbf{x}$ and $\mathbf{y}$ via a DNNF circuit. The dummy agents who are part of the budget limit circuit $C_{\mathbf{z}}$ ensure that the opinion of c_9 is 1 if at most one of the agents $\mathbf{w}$, $\mathbf{x}$ or $\mathbf{y}$ has the opinion 1. Thus, the opinion of c_{10}, being the negation of c_9, reflects the majority opinion of $\mathbf{w}$, $\mathbf{x}$ and $\mathbf{y}$. The regulatory nodes $R_{\mathbf{z}}$ before c_{10} ensure that the opinions of $\mathbf{w}$, $\mathbf{x}$ and $\mathbf{y}$ reach c_{10} after the same number of steps. The regulatory nodes from c_{10} to r_* ensure that this majority opinion reaches the original agents of $\mathcal{N}$ at the same step. Observe that when an agent has an even number of influencers ($|N_i|$ is even), the strict majority rule on N_i requires a different budget limit depending on the agent's current opinion. Thus we would require two circuits for the two different budget limits.

The translation requires at most $2n$ circuits, with each circuit being found in $B + |\mathcal{I}| = \lfloor \frac{|N_i|}{2} \rfloor \pm 1 + |N_i|$ time. Hence, in total, at most $\mathcal{O}(2n^2)$ time is required to build every circuit, including adding the regulatory nodes. The initial opinions of these agents are the final information needed to create $\langle G', \overline{\gamma}, O'^0 \rangle$. All original agent retain their initial opinion. If the dummy agents of agent i appear before the final circuit agent (c_{10} in Fig. 2), then they have the opposite initial opinion to agent i, $1 - o_i^0$. All subsequent dummy agents (in Fig. 2 being c_{10} or after) have the same initial opinion o_i^0. This translation can be found in polynomial time.

Claim: For any step t and any $\ell \in [1, k]$ (where k is the largest depth of any C_i), it is the case that $O_i^t = O_i'^{((t-1)k+\ell) \mod k}$ always holds any non-dummy agent $i \in \mathcal{N}$.

We prove this claim by induction. Starting when $t = 0$, $\langle G, \mathbf{Maj}, O^0 \rangle$ has the initial opinions O^0, we need to check that in the first k steps ($\ell \in [1, k]$) of $\langle G', \overline{\gamma}, O'^0 \rangle$ that for all $i \in \mathcal{N}$ that $o_i'^\ell = o_i^0$. In the first k steps of $\langle G', \overline{\gamma}, O'^0 \rangle$, an agent's influencers' initial opinions have not reached them yet. This is due to their being k agents between i and the agents in N_i, namely the agents in C_i and R_i. Secondly, the opinion of i will not change before then due to the initial opinions of the dummy agents being chosen so that they will not change i's opinion. The inductive hypothesis assumes that for all previous steps t and for any $\ell \in [1, k]$ that $o_i^t = o_i'^{((t-1)k+\ell) \mod k}$. We now show this for $t + 1$. At the step kt of $\langle G', \overline{\gamma}, O'^0 \rangle$, we see that for an arbitrary agent $i \in \mathcal{N}$ that their influencers in N_i will influence the leaf nodes of C_i. By the inductive hypothesis, we know that the opinions of these agents from N_i have been static for the last k iterations. Thus, the opinions of the agents in N_i update at time kt and these will affect the opinion of i only after k steps, as this is the number of agents between i and N_i. Thus, $o_i'^{kt}$ is static for the next k steps.

By the previous claim, when $\langle G', \overline{\gamma}, O'^0 \rangle$ is built from $\langle G, \mathbf{Maj}, O^0 \rangle$, then either both or neither will converge. The isolated nature of the dummy agents (as $(C_i \cup R_i) \cap (C_j \cup R_j) = \emptyset$ for any $i \neq j \in \mathcal{N}$) means that their opinions only update to update the non-dummy agents. Due to the periodic nature of opinion updates in $\langle G', \overline{\gamma}, O'^0 \rangle$, when there is no new input to the circuit, the opinions of the dummy agents $C_i \cup R_i$ also do not change and thus, neither does the opinion of i.

Finally, this process can be completed in $\mathcal{O}(n^3)$ time: $\mathcal{O}(2n^2)$ needed to build the circuits; $\mathcal{O}(n^3)$ time is needed to alter all of the circuits to be of the same length; then at most $\mathcal{O}(nk)$ time is needed to add the remaining agents in R_i.

Proposition 1. CONVERGENCE-$\mathcal{L}$ *is* PSPACE-*complete.*

Proof. To show membership of CONVERGENCE-$\mathcal{L}$ in PSPACE, we need to ensure that it requires no more than polynomial space. We require two vectors with n entries, the first storing the current opinions and another for the updated opinions which use the current opinions. Furthermore, we have a counter that counts the number of iterations completed in the diffusion process (this counts maximally to $2^n + 1$, which can be represented with a polynomial amount of space, namely $n + 1$ bits when writing the number in binary). In addition, we need a polynomial amount of space to compute each agent's update function. Since model checking of Boolean functions can be done in polynomial time, it can be done in polynomial space as well. When the two vectors are equal, the answer is a "yes" answer. However, the answer is "no" when the counter has reached $2^n + 1$, as at this point, we are sure there is a cycle among the opinions. Thus, CONVERGENCE-$\mathcal{L}$ is in PSPACE.

To prove PSPACE-hardness for CONVERGENCE-$\mathcal{L}$, we reduce from the problem CONVERGENCE-**Maj**, which was shown to be PSPACE-complete by Chistikov et al. [13, Theorem 1]. The reduction is provided by Lemma 1, which shows that we can translate every instance of majoritarian opinion diffusion to Boolean opinion diffusion in polynomial time.

As CONVERGENCE-$\mathcal{L}$ is in PSPACEand PSPACE-hard, we can conclude that CONVERGENCE-$\mathcal{L}$ is PSPACE-complete.

Remark 1. A consequence of Proposition 1 is that checking the necessary and sufficient stability conditions given by Christoff and Grossi [15, Lemma 3] is a PSPACE-complete problem.

We study another decision problem from Chistikov et al. [13], asking if there is an initial set of opinions for a social network such that the process does not stabilise.

Guarantee-Convergence-$\mathcal{L}$
Given: A network G and $\overline{\gamma}$ such that for all $\gamma \in \overline{\gamma}$, $\gamma \in \mathcal{L}$
Question: Is there an O^0 such that $\langle G, \overline{\gamma}, O^0 \rangle$ does not stabilise?

Proposition 2. GUARANTEE-CONVERGENCE-$\mathcal{L}$ *is* PSPACE-*complete.*

Proof (Sketch). Membership of GUARANTEE-CONVERGENCE-$\mathcal{L}$ in PSPACEuses the basic idea used for proving membership in Proposition 1. The only difference is that we need to repeat the process for all initial opinions until one stabilises. Hence we store an extra vector with the current initial set of opinions in a vector with n entries. A "yes" answer is found when a diffusion process stabilises, whereas a "no" answer is found when all possible initial opinions have been shown not to stabilise. Note that both can be done with polynomial space. Thus, GUARANTEE-CONVERGENCE-$\mathcal{L}$ in PSPACE.

A similar reduction can obtain hardness to the one in Proposition 1, this time using Theorem 2 from Chistikov et al. [13]. Hence, GUARANTEE-CONVERGENCE-$\mathcal{L}$ is PSPACE-complete.

Remark 2. When restricting the network to be such that for every $i \in \mathcal{N}$, $|N_i| \leq 1$, then CONVERGENCE-$\mathcal{L}$ and GUARANTEE-CONVERGENCE-$\mathcal{L}$ are in P. This relates to the correspondence between opinion diffusion and liquid democracy observed by Christoff and Grossi [14].

Remark 3. To the best of our knowledge, this result is not present in the literature on Boolean networks. The closest being that checking if an agent's opinion is stable when updates happen block-sequentially is a PSPACE-complete problem [21]. Hence, our results are potentially useful for applications of BN, such as checking if there is a fixed point in a gene regulatory network from a given initial state.

4 Asynchronous Updates

In this section we extend the results from the asynchronous majoritarian opinion diffusion model from Bredereck and Elkind [8] to see if they still hold in our model. In particular, they give an asynchronous procedure to find a sequence of agents such that the diffusion process stabilises on a profile of opinions which maximises agreement on the issue. We now extend our model to be able to account for asynchronous updates.

Following the notation of Bredereck and Elkind [8], we let $\sigma \in 2^{\mathcal{N}} \times \cdots \times 2^{\mathcal{N}}$ be the sequence in which the updates happen. Note that when $\sigma = (\mathcal{N}, \cdots, \mathcal{N})$, we regain the synchronous model (all agents updating at the same time). Generally, asynchronous updates ensure that every entry in σ is a singleton (one agent updating at a time). Most cases between these two extremes relate to the notion of *block sequencing* when subsets of agents can update their opinions synchronously [21]. We slightly abuse notation by letting $\circ$ denote the asynchronous update function, which takes an instance $\langle G, \overline{\gamma}, O^0 \rangle$ and a sequence σ, then it returns a profile of opinions $O^{|\sigma|}$ found by following σ, thus $\circ[\langle G, \overline{\gamma}, O^0 \rangle, \sigma] = O^{|\sigma|}$. If we want to look at a certain step t of this sequence, we let $\circ[\langle G, \overline{\gamma}, O^0 \rangle, \sigma, t] = O^t$. One can distinguish an asynchronous update from a synchronous update by the presence of σ in the input.

Bredereck and Elkind [8] show that when all agents use the majority update function, there always exists an asynchronous update sequence such that the process stabilises. However, this is not the case in our general model due to the possibility of negations in the update functions.

Proposition 3. *For some* $\langle G, \overline{\gamma}, O^0 \rangle$, *there may exist no* σ *such that* $\circ[\langle G, \overline{\gamma}, O^0 \rangle, \sigma] = O^{|\sigma|}$ *where* $O^{|\sigma|}$ *is stable.*

Proof. Consider the following counter-example where there are no stable profiles. Let $\mathcal{N} = \{a, b\}$ with update functions $\gamma_a = b$ and $\gamma_b = \neg a$, and say $O_a^0 = 1$ and $O_b^0 = 0$. Consider the following profiles of opinions for $x \in \{0, 1\}$:

(x, x): this is not stable as b wants to update their opinion to $1 - x$;

$(x, 1 - x)$: this is not stable as a wants to update their opinion to $1 - x$.

As there is no stable profile of opinions for this social network, this entails that there is no sequence that leads to a stable profile of opinions.

Proposition 3 is a negative result showing that when the update functions use negated literals there is no longer a guarantee of a stable outcome. However, we show this is no longer true when restricting update functions to be in $\mathcal{L}^+$. Although we focus on $\mathcal{L}^+$, an analogous result can be shown when update functions only contain negated literals.

Bredereck and Elkind [8] look at sequences that not only stabilise the diffusion process but also maximise or minimise the number of 1s in the stable profile, namely, the *optimistic* or *pessimistic* updates. An update sequence is optimistic (respectively, pessimistic) if the sequence leads to a stable profile of opinions and it maximises (respectively, minimises) the number of 1s in the final state. We now show that Proposition 1 from Bredereck and Elkind [8] carries over to positive Boolean functions.

Proposition 4. *For every instance of Boolean opinion diffusion* $\langle G, \overline{\gamma}, O^0 \rangle$ *with every* $\gamma \in \overline{\gamma}$ *such that* $\gamma \in \mathcal{L}^+$, *there exists an optimist (resp. pessimistic) update sequence* σ *such that (i)* σ *is asynchronous, (ii)* $|\sigma| \leq 2n$, *(iii) every agent* $i \in \mathcal{N}$ *changes its opinion at most twice, (iv)* σ *can be computed in* $\mathcal{O}(\ell n^2)$ *time (where* ℓ *is the maximum time for model checking for any* $\gamma_i \in \overline{\gamma}$), *(v) if* σ *leads to the stable collective opinion* $O^{|\sigma|}$, *then every other optimistic (resp. pessimistic) update sequence* σ^* *also gives* $O^{|\sigma^*|}$.

Proof. We emphasise that the following proof follows the same steps and is very similar to the proof of Proposition 1 from Bredereck and Elkind [8]. We first give the procedure for the optimistic update, which has two phases, noting that the pessimistic update takes the two steps in the opposite order. Without loss of generality, we only give the proof sketch for the optimistic update, as the proof for the pessimistic update is very similar.

We initial start with an empty sequence σ and proceed with the following two phases, moving to phase two when there are no more changes available in phase one:

1. If $o_i^t = 0$ and $O_{\upharpoonright N_i}^t \vDash \gamma_i$ then append σ with $\{i\}$ and let $o_i^{t+1} = 1$;
2. If $o_i^t = 1$ and $O_{\upharpoonright N_i}^t \vDash \neg\gamma_i$ then append σ with $\{i\}$ and let $o_i^{t+1} = 0$.

This procedure is *(i)* asynchronous, as only a single agent's opinion is changed at any time. *(ii)* and *(iii)* are also true, as each agent can only have their opinion changed once in each phase. Thus each agent can maximally have their opinion changed twice in the sequence; moreover, the sequence's length is such that $|\sigma| \leq 2n$.

We now show *(iv)*: that the procedure terminates in $\mathcal{O}(\ell n^2)$ time. We let ℓ be the maximum time required to check if an opinion should be updated or not. This is model-checking and can be done in a polynomial time. In each phase, there are at most n iterations, where at each step t we have to check all agents who have the opposite opinion, which is at most $n - t$ checks, each taking ℓ steps. Thus, one phase can take at most $\mathcal{O}(\ell \frac{n(n+1)}{2})$ time. Thus, both phases can be computed in $\mathcal{O}(\ell n^2)$ time.

For *(v)* we first show that the procedure leads to a stable profile of opinions. We assume that there is an agent $i \in \mathcal{N}$ who wants to update their vote after the sequence given by the procedure to gain a contradiction. We now study two cases, the first case is if $O_i^{|\sigma|} = 1$ and the second if $O_i^{|\sigma|} = 0$. If $O_i^{|\sigma|} = 1$ yet $O_{\uparrow N_i}^t \vDash \neg \gamma_i$, then the procedure is not over as i's opinion would need to be updated at this point in phase 2. If $O_i^{|\sigma|} = 0$, yet $O_{\uparrow N_i}^t \vDash \gamma_i$, then it would have also been the case at the end of phase 1 (as $\gamma_i \in \mathcal{L}^+$, there is some cube of γ_i such that all of these neighbours have the opinion 1, which would have also been the case at the end of phase 1). Thus, at the end of phase 1, i's opinion should have been updated 1. In both cases, we have reached a contradiction and the procedure always leads to a stable profile of opinions.

Finally, we need to show that any other optimistic sequence σ^* gives the same profile of opinions, $\circ[\langle G, \overline{\gamma}, O^0 \rangle, \sigma] = \circ[\langle G, \overline{\gamma}, O^0 \rangle, \sigma^*]$. We show this via the following two cases: first, that every opinion changed from 0 to 1 in the sequence σ^* was also flipped under σ; second, that every vertex flipped from 1 to 0 under σ is also flipped under σ^*. As the two cases are similar, we only give the proof of the first case. We prove the first case via a contradiction, assuming that σ and σ^* do not give the same profile of opinions. Let $i^* \in \mathcal{N}$ be the first agent such that their opinion was changed from 0 to 1 under σ^* (at step k) yet not under σ. By assumption, for all steps $k' < k$, the agents' opinions that were changed from 0 to 1 under σ^* were also changed in σ as i^* was the first agent with a differing opinion. Thus, $\circ[\langle G, \overline{\gamma}, O^0 \rangle, \sigma*, k - 1]$ is such that $O_{\uparrow N_{i^*}}^{k-1} \vDash \gamma_{i^*}$. Therefore, if enough neighbours of i^* have the opinion 1 such that i^* can change their opinion to 1, then in phase 1 of σ, i^*'s opinion would be flipped from 0 to 1. Therefore, we have reached a contradiction, concluding that *(v)* is true.

5   Multi-agent Delegations as Boolean Opinion Diffusion

Following the work of Christoff and Grossi [14], we study the connection between opinion diffusion and delegative democracy. In liquid democracy an agent can either vote directly or delegate their vote to another agent, which can, in turn, be transitively delegated to another agent. Thus, a delegation can be seen as an agent being influenced by their delegate. There are, however, some differences between the two models. For instance, delegating agents in liquid democracy typically have no initial opinion and agents who have an initial opinion (a direct voter) are not influenced by other agents.

Table 1. For $i \in \mathcal{N}$, the left-hand-side table gives i's initial opinion and update function from their ballot; on the right-hand-side, it shows how to compute a delegating agent's opinion update.

if $B_i = 1$	$O_i^0 = 1;$	$\gamma_i = \top$
if $B_i = 0$	$O_i^0 = 0;$	$\gamma_i = \bot$
if $B_i = (S_i, F_i)$	$O_i^0 = *;$	$\gamma_i = F_i$

$$O_i^{t+1} = \begin{cases} 1 & \text{if } O_{\upharpoonright N_i}^t \vDash \gamma_i; \\ 0 & \text{if } O_{\upharpoonright N_i}^t \vDash \neg\gamma_i; \\ * & \text{, otherwise.} \end{cases}$$

Christoff and Grossi [14] were the first to make the connection explicit between liquid democracy and opinion diffusion for the case of delegations to a single agent. Given our interest in Boolean networks, we need to consider multi-agent delegations. Colley et al. [16] propose a model where ballots allow for multi-agent ranked delegations. This model extends liquid democracy in two regards: first, an agent's delegation can use the votes of many other agents; second, ballots can contain ranked delegations to avoid delegation cycles.

We now introduce a restricted version of the model from Colley et al. [16] which does not include ranked delegations. The model of multi-agent delegative voting has a set of $\mathcal{N} = \{1, \cdots, n\}$ agents (or voters) who vote on a single binary issue. Each agent $i \in \mathcal{N}$ gives a ballot $B_i \in \{(S_i, F_i) \mid S_i \subseteq \mathcal{N} \setminus \{i\}, F_i : S_i \rightarrow \{0,1\}\} \cup \{0,1\}$, thus, every agent either delegates or votes directly. Note that S_i is a subset of agents acting as i's delegates whose votes determine i's according to the Boolean function F_i. Colley et al. [16] define six *unravelling procedures* that take the ballots and return a profile of votes by resolving delegations. When considering ballots without ranked delegation, all of these procedures are equivalent; thus, we refer to them as UNRAVEL. UNRAVEL iteratively adds votes from delegations synchronously, stopping when no more votes can be added from one iteration to the next.

We now translate multi-agent delegative democracy into our synchronous Boolean opinion diffusion model as described in Sect. 2. The set of agents remains the same $\mathcal{N}$ and the edges of G are determined by the agent's delegates, thus $E = \{(j,i) \mid j \in S_i\}$. To allow the models to align, we introduce a third opinion, namely $*$, representing abstention. We now introduce a language for the update functions in this setting to account for the new ternary domain of opinions. This language, $\mathcal{L}_*$ follows from the language of ballots allowed by Colley et al. [16]. We say $\gamma \in \mathcal{L}_*$ if $\gamma : \{0, 1, *\} \rightarrow \{0, 1, *\}$ and for $O \in \{0, 1, *\}^{|\text{Var}(\gamma)|}$ computing $\gamma(O)$ can be done in polynomial time. This is equivalent to finding a necessary winner of a Boolean function on a partial assignment [32] for example, complete DNFs[1]

---

[1] The necessary winner of an update function γ in complete-DNF is 1 if and only if there exists at least one cube of the formula where every literal is true, and the necessary winner is 0 if and only if every cube of the formula is made false by at least one literal.

would fall into this category [16, Proposition 2]. On the left-hand side of Table 1, we see how we translate an agent's multi-agent delegative democracy ballot into an initial opinion and update function. Recall that if an agent's update function is $\top$ or $\bot$ then they do not have any influencers.

For a delegating agent $i \in \mathcal{N}$, their update function $\gamma_i = F_i$ can take as input $\{0, 1, *\}$ even though γ_i is represented as a propositional formula. The right-hand-side of Table 1 shows how to compute their opinion when the input of γ_i is can contain $*$s, $O^t_{\upharpoonright N_i} \in \{0, 1, *\}^{|N_i|}$.

Following the diffusion process described in Sect. 2, we prove a lemma that shows that the diffusion process always terminates to a stable state.

Lemma 2. Let $\langle G, \overline{\gamma}, O^0 \rangle$ be such that $\overline{\gamma} \in \mathcal{L}_*$, if at some time t $O^t_i = v \in \{0, 1\}$, then $O^{t'}_i = v$ for all steps $t' > t$.

Proof. We prove this lemma by induction on the step t, showing that if $O^t_i \in \{0, 1\}$ then for no $t' > t$ does it change.

Base Case: As $O^0_i \in \{0, 1\}$, this means that $\gamma_i = \bot$ or $\top$, respectively. As their update functions are constant, their opinion remains static at all steps $t \geq 1$, $O^t_i = O^0_i$.

Inductive Hypothesis: For some step t, every $i \in \mathcal{N}$ such that $O^t_i \in \{0, 1\}$, their opinion does not change in any subsequent step, $O^{t'}_i = O^t_i$ for all $t' > t$.

Inductive Step: We want to show that given the inductive hypothesis is true at t, it remains true at step $t + 1$. By assumption, we know that all agents with an opinion of 0 or 1 in O^t are such that their opinion will not change in future steps. For the agents in $S \subseteq \mathcal{N}$ such that $S = \{i \mid O^t_i = * \text{ and } O^{t+1}_i \in \{0, 1\}\}$, we want to show that for each $i \in S$ that their opinion will not change after $t + 1$. Taking an arbitrary $j \in S$ without loss of generality, we assume that $O^{t+1}_j = 1$. Therefore, $O^t_{\upharpoonright N_j} \vDash \gamma_j$. We let $V_j \subseteq N_j$ be the agents of N_j such that they have a vote in O^t, note that $O^t_{\upharpoonright V_j} \vDash \gamma_j$. By our inductive hypothesis, the votes of the agents in V_j will not change after time t. As j's vote changes at this step, a necessary winner of γ_j was found from the votes in V_j. As no vote from the agents in V_j will change, neither will the necessary winner of γ_j, no matter the votes of the agents in $N_j \backslash V_j$. As j was chosen arbitrarily, the votes of all agents in S do not change after $t + 1$. Our inductive hypothesis has been shown.

From Lemma 2 we see that the process terminates as only a finite number of opinion updates can be made.

Corollary 1. *The diffusion processes terminate on $\langle G, \overline{\gamma}, O^0 \rangle$ when $\overline{\gamma} \in \mathcal{L}_*$.*

We remark that although the process terminates, this does not necessarily mean that all agents have an opinion in $\{0, 1\}$. Furthermore, the outcome found by the diffusion process is the same as UNRAVEL. As UNRAVEL terminates in polynomial time [16, Proposition 4], we now show that the diffusion process also does. We let TERMINATE-$\mathcal{L}_*$ be the functional problem that given an instance $\langle G, \overline{\gamma}, O^0 \rangle$ with $\overline{\gamma} \in \mathcal{L}_*$, the problem finds the stable profile of opinions found by the diffusion process.

Proposition 5. TERMINATE-$\mathcal{L}_*$ *is in* P.

Proof. First recall that finding a necessary winner of a $\gamma \in \mathcal{L}_*$ can be done in polynomial time; let ℓ be the maximum amount of time required for any $\gamma \in \overline{\gamma}$. Lemma 2 tell us that when an opinion is in $\{0, 1\}$, it does not change. Thus, we have at most n diffusion iterations, in which all agents will have their update function checked for a necessary winner. Therefore, the process terminates in $\mathcal{O}(n^2 \ell)$ time.

Proposition 5 shows that our diffusion process can unravel a multi-agent delegation profile in polynomial time, giving the same computation complexity bound as UNRAVEL from Colley et al. [16].

5.1 Control in Multi-agent Delegation

One common area of research in opinion diffusion is opinion control, and we extend this to our model of opinion diffusion when focusing on multi-agent delegative democracy [1,34]. Thus, in this section we focus on the computational complexity of being able to change the outcome of the collective decision by bribing a given number of agents to change their vote. Here we look at ensuring that the collective outcome is for the issue, yet the problem of the collective decision being against the issue is equivalent. Here we focus on the collective outcome being determined by a quota rule while the update function remains expressed as propositional formulas in $\mathcal{L}_*$.

QUOTA-CONTROL	
Given:	An instance $\langle G, \overline{\gamma}, O^0 \rangle$ reflecting multi-agent delegative democracy such that for all $\gamma \in \overline{\gamma}$ we have that $\gamma \in \mathcal{L}_*$ and constants $k \in \mathbb{N}$ and $q \in [0, n]$
Question:	Is there a $D \subseteq \mathcal{N}$ such that $|D| \leq k$ and for all $i \in D$ changing $\gamma_i = \top$ and $O_i^0 = 1$ gives a stable profile of opinions O^T such that $\sum_{o_i \in O^T} o_i \geq q$?

Informally, QUOTA-CONTROL asks if there is a subset of agents D, who by bribing them to change their ballot to be for the issue will mean that there are at least q agents in the stable profile of opinions in favour of the issue.

Proposition 6. QUOTA-CONTROL *is an* NP-*complete problem.*

Proof. QUOTA-CONTROL can be shown to be in NP by checking a certificate in polynomial time. The certificate lists the agents in D whose update function and initial opinion will be changed to represent a direct vote for the issue. We make these changes to the instance, giving $\langle G', \overline{\gamma}', O'^0 \rangle$. As shown in Proposition 5, the diffusion process on such an instance terminates in polynomial time. Then it is required to check if the stable profile of opinions on termination exceeds the quota. Therefore, a certificate can be checked in polynomial time; thus, QUOTA-CONTROL is in NP.

We show NP-hardness of QUOTA-CONTROL by giving a reduction from the NP-complete problem *Feedback Vertex Set*, FVS [27]. FVS takes as input a directed graph $G = (V, E)$ and $k \in \mathbb{N}$ and then asks if there is a subset $X \subseteq V$ such that $|X| \leq k$ and the remaining graph, when only considering the vertices $V \backslash X$, is cycle free.

The translation of FVS is as such: the nodes remain the same $\mathcal{N} = V$ and for each $i \in \mathcal{N}$, N_i is determined by E. Each agent's update function depends on their neighbourhood as such: for each $i \in \mathcal{N}$ if $N_i = \emptyset$ then $O_i^0 = 1$ and $\gamma_i = \top$; else $O_i^0 = *$ and $\gamma_i = \bigwedge_{j \in N_i} j$. Note that the update functions of each delegating agent will update to 1 only when every one of their neighbours has the opinion 1, and against if one neighbour has the opinion 0, and $*$, otherwise. The quota represents unanimity $q = n$, i.e., the collective decision is 1 only when there is a consensus for the issue.

First, assume that we have a solution to FVS, and we want to show that there is also a solution to QUOTA-CONTROL. Given X, we change the update functions and the initial opinions of the agents in X. As X is a solution to FVS, we see that the remaining network is cycle free, and therefore, all votes can be assigned. As all direct voters vote for the issue, every opinion on termination will be 1, and our quota $q = n$ has been met. Next, we assume that there is no solution to FVS. Therefore, more than k nodes need to be removed to make the network cycle-free. Thus no matter which agents' initial opinions and update functions are changed, there will still be at least one cycle. For each i in this cycle, there will be no necessary winner found for $\gamma_i = \bigwedge_{j \in N_i} j$. Their opinion remains as $*$ (recall that there are no opinions of 0 at any stage of the diffusion, this means a necessary winner can only be found when all of i's neighbourhood is for the issue). Therefore, for every agent still in a cycle, their opinion at termination is $*$. Thus, the quota cannot be met and the final collective opinion is not 1. Therefore, there is no solution either for QUOTA-CONTROL. We have shown NP-hardness and membership for QUOTA-CONTROL, and thus, it is NP-complete.

This result is unsurprising given that an equivalent in majoritarian opinion diffusion is known to be an NP-hard problem [30] and manipulation via bribery remains an intractable problem in this voting scenario.

6   Results from the Boolean Network Literature

In this work we aim to make the connection between the well-established research area of Boolean networks (BN) and opinion diffusion. BN have impacted many different disciplines, most notably regulatory gene networks. The model used in this paper aligns with standard BN; thus many results can be translated into our model with only a few details to be checked. The following remarks give an idea of some results from the BN literature, rephrased in terms of Boolean opinion diffusion.

Remark 4. Akutsu et al. [5] showed that a unique Boolean network can be found in polynomial time from a sequence of profiles of opinions when the number of agents in any in-neighbourhood is bounded by some constant, $|N_i| \leq k$ for all $i \in \mathcal{N}$ and $k \in \mathbb{N}$.

Remark 5. Farrow et al. [20] showed that finding a stable profile of opinions for a Boolean opinion diffusion instance where the network is monotonic[2] is NP-complete. Furthermore, Zhao [40] showed it to be strongly NP-complete.

One BN topic that is not widely studied in opinion diffusion is negative influence. However, negative influence can be a key reason why a network does not stabilise (see Richard [36] for an overview of positive and negative cycles).

Remark 6. Goles and Salinas [23] showed that finding a stable profile of opinions can be done in polynomial time when every cycle in the network G has an even number of decreasingly monotonic arcs with respect to the update functions.

It may be sufficient for the opinion diffusion process not to stabilise in some cases if it only cycles through a small number of profiles.

Remark 7. Akutsu et al. [4] showed that in polynomial time a profile of opinions can be found that leads to a cycle among two profiles of opinions when all $\gamma \in \overline{\gamma}$ are such that $\gamma \in \mathcal{L}^{\vee} \cap \mathcal{L}^{+}$, thus, only contain positive literals and disjunction.

Fixed points are well studied in the BN literature; in our terminology, this equates to if there exists a stable collection of opinions for a network.

Remark 8. Kobayashi [31] showed that it is an NP-complete problem to check if a stable collection of opinions exists for a Boolean opinion diffusion instance.

This remark follows from the fact that this problem is equivalent to checking if there is a solution to an ILP where the set of constraints is for all $i \in \mathcal{N}$, $\gamma_i(O_{\restriction N_i}) = o_i$. In Sect. 3 we studied a similar problem, the difference being that in Proposition 1 we ask if there is a stable state coming from an initial profile of opinions. The increase in complexity from NP to PSPACE comes from the fact that it is hard to verify if a stable profile of opinions can come from a particular initial profile of opinions.

Boolean network control, as defined by Akutsu et al. [1], asks, from a given set of agents whose opinions can be controlled, if it is possible to gain a particular profile of opinions O^M in M steps by controlling only the given subset of agents.

Remark 9. Akutsu et al. [1] showed that Boolean network control is an NP-complete problem, yet is polynomial when the underlying graph is a tree.

---

[2] Take any Boolean function F and any $X \in \{0,1\}^{|F|}$ such that $F(X) = 1$, F is monotonic if and only if $F(X') = 1$ still holds for any X' found by changing a single 0 entry in X to a 1. A BN is monotonic if every Boolean function within it is also monotonic.

7   Conclusion

In this paper we have studied algorithmic problems from opinion diffusion on the model given by Boolean networks. We have shown that it is PSPACE-complete to recognise whether a given initial state leads to stability in synchronous diffusion, generalising a known result on majoritarian opinion diffusion. When moving to asynchronous diffusion, in contrast, we showed that the existence of a diffusion sequence leading to stability and maximising consensus cannot be guaranteed for arbitrary Boolean networks. However, we showed its existence when negative influence is not allowed. Finally, we showed that when a delegative voting problem induces the influence structure, stability is guaranteed, and influence maximisation is, perhaps unsurprisingly, NP-hard. We also rephrased known results from the Boolean network literature in terms of diffusion to showcase the synergy of the two research subjects.

This paper opens several directions for future work. Perhaps the most interesting is to explore the use of semi-tensor products in opinion diffusion, as they constitute the main technique used by recent research on Boolean networks (see, e.g., Cheng et al. [12] and Cheng [10]). We conjecture that this will draw a parallel between the use of DeGroot processes by Christoff and Grossi [14] to model delegative voting. Another area for future work is looking at probabilistic BNs for opinion diffusion, in particular, with respect to existing work on control [2].

Acknowledgements. The authors acknowledge the support of the ANR JCJC project SCONE (ANR 18-CE23-0009-01).

References

1. Akutsu, T., Hayashida, M., Ching, W.K., Ng, M.K.: On the complexity of finding control strategies for Boolean networks. In: Proceedings of the Fourth Asia-Pacific Bioinformatics Conference (2006)
2. Akutsu, T., Hayashida, M., Ching, W.K., Ng, M.K.: Control of Boolean networks: hardness results and algorithms for tree structured networks. J. Theor. Biol. **244**(4), 670–679 (2007)
3. Akutsu, T., Hayashida, M., Tamura, T.: Algorithms for inference, analysis and control of Boolean networks. In: International Conference on Algebraic Biology (2008)
4. Akutsu, T., Kosub, S., Melkman, A.A., Tamura, T.: Finding a periodic attractor of a Boolean network. IEEE/ACM Trans. Comput. Biol. Bioinf. **9**(5), 1410–1421 (2012)
5. Akutsu, T., Miyano, S., Kuhara, S.: Identification of genetic networks from a small number of gene expression patterns under the Boolean network model. In: Biocomputing 1999, pp. 17–28. World Scientific (1999)
6. Auletta, V., Ferraioli, D., Greco, G.: Reasoning about consensus when opinions diffuse through majority dynamics. In: Proceedings of the Twenty-Seventh International Joint Conference on Artificial Intelligence (IJCAI) (2018)
7. Botan, S., Grandi, U., Perrussel, L.: Multi-issue opinion diffusion under constraints. In: Eighteenth International Joint Conference on Autonomous Agents and Multiagent Systems (AAMAS) (2019)

8. Bredereck, R., Elkind, E.: Manipulating opinion diffusion in social networks. In: Proceedings of the Twenty-Sixth International Joint Conference on Artificial Intelligence (IJCAI) (2017)

9. Brill, M., Elkind, E., Endriss, U., Grandi, U.: Pairwise diffusion of preference rankings in social networks. In: Proceedings of the Twenty-Fifth International Joint Conference on Artificial Intelligence (IJCAI) (2016)

10. Cheng, D.: Semi-tensor product of matrices and its applications-a survey. In: Proceedings of the Fourth International Congress of Chinese Mathematicians (ICCM) (2007)

11. Cheng, D., Li, Z., Qi, H.: A survey on Boolean control networks: a state space approach. In: Hu, X., Jonsson, U., Wahlberg, B., Ghosh, B. (eds.) Three Decades of Progress in Control Sciences, pp. 121–139. Springer, Heidelberg (2010). https://doi.org/10.1007/978-3-642-11278-2_9

12. Cheng, D., Qi, H., Li, Z.: Analysis and Control of Boolean Networks: A Semi-tensor Product Approach. Springer, London (2010). https://doi.org/10.1007/978-0-85729-097-7

13. Chistikov, D., Lisowski, G., Paterson, M., Turrini, P.: Convergence of opinion diffusion is PSPACE-complete. In: Proceedings of the Association for the Advancement of Artificial Intelligence Conference on Artificial Intelligence (AAAI) (2020)

14. Christoff, Z., Grossi, D.: Binary voting with delegable proxy: an analysis of liquid democracy. In: Proceedings Sixteenth Conference on Theoretical Aspects of Rationality and Knowledge (TARK) (2017)

15. Christoff, Z., Grossi, D.: Stability in binary opinion diffusion. In: International Workshop on Logic, Rationality and Interaction (2017)

16. Colley, R., Grandi, U., Novaro, A.: Unravelling multi-agent ranked delegations. Auton. Agent. Multi Agent Syst. **36**(1), 1–35 (2022)

17. De Haan, R.: Hunting for tractable languages for judgment aggregation. In: Sixteenth International Conference on Principles of Knowledge Representation and Reasoning (2018)

18. Degrave, J.: Resolving multi-proxy transitive vote delegation. arXiv preprint arXiv:1412.4039 (2014)

19. Domingos, P., Richardson, M.: Mining the network value of customers. In: Proceedings of the Seventh ACM SIGKDD International Conference on Knowledge Discovery and Data Mining (2001)

20. Farrow, C., Heidel, J., Maloney, J., Rogers, J.: Scalar equations for synchronous Boolean networks with biological applications. IEEE Trans. Neural Netw. **15**(2), 348–354 (2004)

21. Goles, E., Montealegre, P., Salo, V., Törmä, I.: PSPACE-completeness of majority automata networks. Theoret. Comput. Sci. **609**, 118–128 (2016)

22. Goles, E., Olivos, J.: Periodic behaviour of generalized threshold functions. Discrete Math. **30**(2), 187–189 (1980). ISSN 0012-365X

23. Goles, E., Salinas, L.: Sequential operator for filtering cycles in Boolean networks. Adv. Appl. Math. **45**(3), 346–358 (2010)

24. Grandi, U., Lorini, E., Perrussel, L.: Propositional opinion diffusion. In: Fourteenth International Joint Conference on Autonomous Agents and Multiagent Systems (AAMAS) (2015)

25. Granovetter, M.: Threshold models of collective behavior. Am. J. Sociol. **83**(6), 1420–1443 (1978)

26. Inoue, K.: Logic programming for Boolean networks. In: Twenty-Second International Joint Conference on Artificial Intelligence (IJCAI) (2011)

27. Karp, R.M.: Reducibility among combinatorial problems. In: Miller, R.E., Thatcher, J.W., Bohlinger, J.D. (eds.) Complexity of Computer Computations. The IBM Research Symposia Series, pp. 85–103. Springer, Boston (1972). https:// doi.org/10.1007/978-1-4684-2001-2_9

28. Kauffman, S.: Homeostasis and differentiation in random genetic control networks. Nature **224**(5215), 177–178 (1969)

29. Kauffman, S.A., et al.: The Origins of Order: Self-organization and Selection in Evolution. Oxford University Press, New York (1993)

30. Kempe, D., Kleinberg, J., Tardos, É.: Maximizing the spread of influence through a social network. In: Proceedings of the Ninth ACM SIGKDD International Conference on Knowledge Discovery and Data Mining (2003)

31. Kobayashi, K.: Design of fixed points in Boolean networks using feedback vertex sets and model reduction. Complexity **5**, 1–9 (2019)

32. Konczak, K., Lang, J.: Voting procedures with incomplete preferences. In: Proceedings of IJCAI-2005 Multidisciplinary Workshop on Advances in Preference Handling, vol. 20 (2005)

33. Kosub, S.: Dichotomy results for fixed-point existence problems for Boolean dynamical systems. Math. Comput. Sci. **1**(3), 487–505 (2008)

34. Langmead, C.J., Jha, S.K.: Symbolic approaches for finding control strategies in Boolean networks. J. Bioinform. Comput. Biol. **7**(02), 323–338 (2009)

35. Morrison, C., Naumov, P.: Group conformity in social networks. J. Log. Lang. Inform. **29**(1), 3–19 (2020)

36. Richard, A.: Positive and negative cycles in Boolean networks. J. Theor. Biol. **463**, 67–76 (2019)

37. Richardson, M., Domingos, P.: Mining knowledge-sharing sites for viral marketing. In: Proceedings of the Eighth ACM SIGKDD International Conference on Knowledge Discovery and Data Mining (2002)

38. Rosenkrantz, D.J., Marathe, M.V., Ravi, S., Stearns, R.E.: Synchronous dynamical systems on directed acyclic graphs (DAGs): complexity and algorithms, Technical report 20-155. Biocomplexity Institute and Initiative, University of Virginia, Charlottesville, VA, USA (2020)

39. Shmulevich, I., Zhang, W.: Binary analysis and optimization-based normalization of gene expression data. Bioinformatics **18**(4), 555–565 (2002)

40. Zhao, Q.: A remark on "scalar equations for synchronous Boolean networks with biological applications" by C. Farrow, J. Heidel, J. Maloney, and J. Rogers. IEEE Trans. Neural Netw. **16**(6), 1715–1716 (2005)

41. Zhuang, Z., Wang, K., Wang, J., Zhang, H., Wang, Z., Gong, Z.: Lifting majority to unanimity in opinion diffusion. In: Twenty-Forth European Conference on Artificial Intelligence (ECAI) (2020)

Robustness of Greedy Approval Rules

Piotr Faliszewski[1]([✉]), Grzegorz Gawron[1,2], and Bartosz Kusek[1]

[1] AGH University, Krakow, Poland
faliszew@agh.edu.pl
[2] VirtusLab, Krakow, Poland

Abstract. We study the robustness of GreedyCC, GreedyPAV, and Phragmén's sequential rule, using the framework introduced by Bredereck et al. [6] for the case of (multiwinner) ordinal elections and adopted to the approval setting by Gawron and Faliszewski [15]. First, we show that for each of our rules and every committee size k, there are elections in which adding or removing a certain approval causes the winning committee to completely change (i.e., the winning committee after the operation is disjoint from the one before the operation). Second, we show that the problem of deciding how many approvals need to be added (or removed) from an election to change its outcome is NP-complete for each of our rules. Finally, we experimentally evaluate the robustness of our rules in the presence of random noise.

1 Introduction

We study the extent to which perturbing the input of several approval-based multiwinnner voting rules affects their outcome. We focus on GreedyCC, Greedy-PAV, and Phragmén rules, whose common feature is that they choose members of the winning committee in a sequential, greedy way.

In a multiwinner approval election, each voter indicates which candidates he or she finds appealing—i.e., which ones he or she approves—and a voting rule provides the winning committee (i.e., a fixed-size group of candidates). For example, the approval voting rule (AV) chooses committees of individually excellent candidates (i.e., the most approved ones), the proportional approval voting rule (PAV) ensures proportional representation of the voters, and the Chamberlin-Courant rule (CC) seeks a diverse committee. Unfortunately, while AV can be computed in polynomial time, finding the winning committees under the other two rules is intractable. Luckily, there are many workarounds for this issue. For example, instead of CC we can use its approximate variant GreedyCC, and instead of PAV we can either use GreedyPAV or the Phragmén rule (see the overview of Lackner and Skowron [17] for a discussion of these rules and their properties). While there is robustness analysis of AV, CC, and PAV [15], analogous results are missing for these greedy rules and our goal is to fill this hole.

---

*See `https://github.com/Project-PRAGMA/Greedy-Robust-EUMAS-2022` for the source code of the experiments performed in this paper.

D. Baumeister and J. Rothe (Eds.): EUMAS 2022, LNAI 13442, pp. 116–133, 2022.
https://doi.org/10.1007/978-3-031-20614-6_7

We use the robustness framework of Bredereck et al. [6], as adopted to the case of approval elections by Gawron and Faliszewski [15]. This framework consists of the following elements:

1. Evaluating the extent to which introducing a single small change may affect the outcome of a rule. For example, we say that a rule has ADD-robustness level equal to ℓ if adding a single approval results in, at most, replacing ℓ committee members. REMOVE-robustness level is defined analogously, but for the case of removing a single approval. Robustness levels of a rule describe its worst-case behavior under minimal perturbations of the input.[1]
2. Establishing the complexity of the ROBUSTNESS-RADIUS problem, which asks if a given number of basic operations (such as adding or removing approvals) suffices to change the election outcome. Solving this problem for various elections would measure a rule's robustness to targeted attacks on a per-instance basis. However, since ROBUSTNESS-RADIUS is NP-complete for many rules, neither Bredereck et al. [6] nor Gawron and Faliszewski [15] carried out such experiments and we follow them in this respect.
3. Computing for various elections how many randomly selected basic operations are needed, on average, to change their outcomes. This measures the rules' robustness to random noise.

Gawron and Faliszewski [15] considered AV, SAV (a rule similar in spirit to AV), CC, and PAV. They have shown that AV has {ADD, REMOVE}-robustness levels equal to 1, while the other rules have them equal to the committee size (although there are some intricacies for the case of SAV). Further, they have shown that ROBUSTNESS-RADIUS is in P for AV and SAV, but is NP-hard for CC and PAV. Given hardness of computing CC and PAV, this last result is not very surprising, but Gawron and Faliszewski have also shown fixed-parameter tractable algorithms for the respective problems. Unfortunately, Gawron and Faliszewski [15] did not pursue experimental studies (as some of their rules are NP-hard, even computing robustness to random noise would require nontrivial computing resources).

Our Contribution. We complement the work of Gawron and Faliszewski [15] by considering GreedyCC, GreedyPAV, and Phragmén. We show that their {ADD, REMOVE}-robustness levels are equal to the committee size and we show that the ROBUSTNESS-RADIUS problem is NP-complete for each of them. Since our rules are polynomial-time to compute, this result is not as immediate as in the case of CC or PAV. Finally, we experimentally evaluate the robustness of our rules, and of AV, to random noise.

Related Work. In addition to the works of Bredereck et al. [6] and Gawron and Faliszewski [15], our results are closely related to the line of work on the complexity of bribery in elections. In a bribery problem, we are given an election

---

[1] Whenever we speak of "robustness levels" without indicating whether we mean the ADD or REMOVE variant, we collectively refer to both.

and we ask if a certain outcome—such as including a certain candidate among the winners (in the constructive setting) or precluding a certain candidate from winning (in the destructive setting)—can be achieved by modifying the preferences of the voters with operations of a certain cost. The study of bribery was initiated by Faliszewski, Hemaspaandra, and Hemaspaandra [11] and was continued by many others (see the overview of Faliszewski and Rothe [12]). The ROBUSTNESS-RADIUS problem can be seen as a variant of destructive bribery. SWAP-BRIBERY, introduced by Elkind, Faliszewski, and Slinko [10], was used to study the robustness of single-winner voting rules by Shiryaev et al. [21], Baumeister and Hogrebe [3], and Boehmer et al. [5]. Magrino et al. [18], Cary [8], and Xia [25] used variants of destructive bribery to study margin of victory under various single-winner voting rules. The main difference between the studies of robustness and margin of victory is that in the former, the authors typically use fine-grained bribery variants that allow for making small modifications in the votes (in our case, these mean adding or removing single approvals), whereas in the latter the authors typically use coarse-grained bribery variants that allow operations that change the whole votes arbitrarily.

Our work is closely related to that of Faliszewski et al. [14], who study bribery of approval-based multiwinner rules under adding, removing, and swapping approvals. The main difference between our work and theirs is that they focus on the constructive setting and we study the destructive one.

2 Preliminaries

We write $\mathbb{N}_+$ to denote the set $\{1, 2, \ldots\}$ and for each integer t, by $[t]$ we mean the set $\{1, \ldots, t\}$. We use the Iverson bracket notation, i.e., given a logical expression P, we write $[P]$ to mean 1 if P is true and to mean 0 otherwise.

2.1 Approval Elections and Multiwinner Rules

An election is a pair $E = (C, V)$, where $C = \{c_1, \ldots, c_m\}$ is a set of candidates and $V = (v_1, \ldots, v_n)$ is a collection of voters. Each voter v_i has a set $A(v_i) \subseteq C$ of candidates that he or she approves. The approval score of a candidate is the number of voters that approve him or her.

A multiwinner voting rule $\mathcal{R}$ is a function that given an election E and committee size k outputs a family of size-k winning committees (i.e., a family of size-k subsets of C). If a rule always outputs a unique committee, then we say that it is resolute (in practice, non-resolute rules require tie-breaking rules, but we disregard this issue). For example, the approval voting rule (the AV rule) selects committees of k candidates with the highest approval scores. AV belongs to the class of Thiele rules, which are defined as follows: Consider an election $E = (C, V)$ and a nonincreasing function $\lambda \colon \mathbb{N}_+ \to [0, 1]$, such that $\lambda(1) = 1$ (we will refer to functions satisfying these conditions as OWA functions[2]). We define

---

[2] The name refers to the class of order-weighted operators (OWA operators), introduced by Yager [26] and used by Skowron et al. [22] to define a class of rules closely related to the Thiele ones.

the λ-score of a set $S \subseteq C$ of candidates as:

$$\lambda\text{-score}_E(S) = \sum_{v \in V} \left(\sum_{t=1}^{|S \cap A(v)|} \lambda(t) \right).$$

Given an election E and committee size k, the λ-Thiele rule outputs those size-k committees W that have the highest λ-score. For example, the AV rule uses the constant function $\lambda_{AV}(i) = 1$. This rule is meant to choose committees of individually excellent candidates, hence it considers the candidates with the highest individual approval scores. We are also interested in the Chamberlin–Courant rule (the CC rule) and the proportional approval voting rule (the PAV rule), which use functions $\lambda_{\text{CC}}(i) = [i = 1]$ and $\lambda_{\text{PAV}}(i) = 1/i$, respectively. Under CC, a voter assigns score 1 to a committee exactly if he or she approves at least one of its members, and assigns score 0 otherwise. This rule was introduced by Chamberlin and Courant [9] in the context of ordinal elections and was adapted to the approval setting by Procaccia et al. [19] and Betzler et al. [4]. Its purpose is to find diverse committees, so that as many voters as possible feel represented by at least one of the committee members. The PAV rule was introduced by Thiele [24] and its more elaborate scoring system is designed to ensure proportional representation of the voters [1,7].

Both CC and PAV are NP-hard to compute [2,19,22] and we are mostly interested in the rules defined by their greedy approximation algorithms. These algorithms run as follows (let $E = (C, V)$ be the input election, k be the committee size, and λ be the OWA function used):

We start with an empty committee $W = \emptyset$ and perform k iterations, where in each iteration we extend W with a single candidate c that maximizes the value $\lambda\text{-score}_E(W \cup \{c\}) - \lambda\text{-score}_E(W)$. If several candidates satisfy this condition then we break the tie according to a given tie-breaking order. We output W as the unique winning committee.

We refer to the incarnations of this algorithm for λ_{CC} and λ_{PAV} as GreedyCC and GreedyPAV, respectively. When analyzing an i-th iteration of these algorithms, for each candidate c we refer to the value $\lambda\text{-score}_E(W \cup \{c\}) - \lambda\text{-score}_E(W)$ as the score of c. For GreedyCC, we imagine that as soon as a candidate is included in the committee, all the voters that approve him or her are removed (indeed, these voters would not contribute positive score to any further candidates).

We are also interested in the Phragmén rule (or, more specifically, in the Phragmén's sequential rule, but we use the shorter name in this paper). The Phragmén rule proceeds according to the following scheme ($E = (C, V)$ is the input election and k is the committee size):

Initially, we have committee $W = \emptyset$. The voters start with no money, but they receive it at a constant rate (so, at each time point $t \in \mathbb{R}$, $t \geq 0$, each voter has in total received money of value t). At every time point for which there is a candidate c not included in W who is approved by voters that jointly have one unit of money, this candidate is "purchased." That is, candidate c is added to W and the voters that approve him or her have all their money reset to 0 (i.e., they pay for c). If several candidates can be purchased at the same time, we consider them in a given tie-breaking order. The process continues until W reaches size k or all the remaining candidates have approval score zero (in which case we extend W according to the tie-breaking order). We output W as the unique winning committee.

Similarly to PAV, Phragmén provides committees that ensure proportional representation of the voters [20]. For a detailed discussion of these rules we point the reader to the survey of Lackner and Skowron [17]. Faliszewski et al. [13] offer a general overview of multiwinner voting. Note that GreedyCC, GreedyPAV, and Phragmén are resolute.

2.2   Robustness of Multiwinner Voting Rules

We use the robustness framework introduced by Bredereck et al. [6] for the ordinal setting and adapted to the approval one by Gawron and Faliszewski [15]. In particular, we consider the ADD and REMOVE operations, where the former means adding a single approval to some vote and the latter means removing a single approval from a vote. Let us fix committee size k. For an operation OP $\in \{\text{ADD}, \text{REMOVE}\}$, we say that a multiwinner voting rule $\mathcal{R}$ is ℓ-OP-robust (or, that its OP-robustness level is ℓ) if ℓ is the smallest integer such that for every election $E = (C, V)$, where $|C| \geq 2k$,[3] and every election E' obtained from E with a single operation of type OP, the following holds:

> For each committee $W \in \mathcal{R}(E, k)$ there is a committee $W' \in \mathcal{R}(E', k)$ such that $|W \cap W'| \geq k - \ell$ (i.e., for every winning committee of E there is a winning committee of E' that differs in at most ℓ candidates).

Intuitively, if a rule is 1-ADD-robust then adding a single approval in an election held according to this rule may, at most, lead to replacing a single member of the winning committee. On the other hand, if a rule is k-ADD-robust, then adding a single approval sometimes leads to replacing the whole committee. Gawron and Faliszewski [15] have shown that AV is 1-{ADD,REMOVE}-robust, whereas both CC and PAV are k-{ADD,REMOVE}-robust (they also considered the SWAP operation, which means moving an approval from one candidate to another within a vote, and obtained analogous results for it).

Following Bredereck et al. [6] and Gawron and Faliszewski [15], we also study the ROBUSTNESS-RADIUS problem. Intuitively, in this problem we are interested in the smallest number of operations required to change the election result. The more are necessary, the more robust is the result on the given election.

Definition 1. *Let $\mathcal{R}$ be a multiwinner voting rule and let* OP *be either* ADD *or* REMOVE. *In the* $\mathcal{R}$-OP-ROBUSTNESS-RADIUS *problem we are given an election* E, *a committee size* k, *and a nonnegative integer* B *(referred to as the budget). We ask if it is possible to perform up to* B *operations of type* OP *so that for the resulting election* E' *it holds that* $\mathcal{R}(E, k) \neq \mathcal{R}(E', k)$.

---

[3] This is mostly a technical assumption, to ensure that there are enough candidates so that all members of a committee can be replaced with non-members.

3   Robustness Level

The results of Bredereck et al. [6] and Gawron and Faliszewski [15] give some intuitions regarding robustness levels that we may expect from multiwinner rules. On the one hand, simple, polynomial-time computable rules that focus on individual excellence tend to have robustness levels equal to 1 (this includes, e.g., AV in the approval setting, and a number of rules in the ordinal one). Indeed, Bredereck et al. [6, Theorem 6] have shown that if a rule selects a committee with the highest score, this score is easily computable, and the rule's robustness level is bounded by a constant, then some winning committee can be computed in polynomial time. On the other hand, more involved rules that focus on proportionality or diversity—in particular those NP-hard to compute—tend to have robustness levels equal to the committee size. However, regarding rules that form the committee sequentially, so far there was only one data point: Bredereck et al. [6] have shown that single transferable vote (STV; a well-known rule for the ordinal setting) has robustness levels equal to the committee size. We provide three more such examples by showing that GreedyCC, GreedyPAV, and Phragmén also have robustness levels equal to the committee size.

First, we consider the relationship between ADD-ROBUSTNESS and REMOVE-ROBUSTNESS for resolute rules and then we show that GreedyCC, GreedyPAV, and Phragmén are k-{ADD, REMOVE}-robust.

Proposition 1. *Let $\mathcal{R}$ be a resolute multiwinner voting rule, and let ℓ be a positive integer. $\mathcal{R}$ is ℓ-ADD-robust if and only if it is ℓ-REMOVE-robust.*

Theorem 1. *Let k be the committee size. For each multiwinner rule $\mathcal{R}$ in $\{GreedyCC, GreedyPAV, Phragmén\}$, $\mathcal{R}$ is both k-ADD-robust and k-REMOVE-robust.*

Proof. Let us fix committee size k. Since our rules are resolute, by Proposition 1 it suffices to show their k-ADD-robustness. To this end, we will form two elections, $E = (C, V)$ and $E' = (C, V')$, where E' can be obtained from E by adding a single approval, such that for each of our rules the unique winning committee for E is disjoint from the one for E'.

We let the candidate set be $C = A \cup B$, where $A = \{a_1, \ldots, a_k\}$ and $B = \{b_1, \ldots, b_k\}$, and we set the tie-breaking order to be:

$$a_1 \succ \cdots \succ a_k \succ b_1 \succ \cdots \succ b_k.$$

The voter collection of election E is as follows:

1. We have $k - 1$ voters approving $\{a_1, b_1\}$.
2. For each $i \in \{2, \ldots, k\}$ we have a single voter approving $\{a_1, b_i\}$.
3. For each $i \in \{2, \ldots, k\}$ we have a single voter approving $\{a_i, b_1\}$.
4. For each $i \in \{2, \ldots, k\}$ we have $2k - 3$ voters approving $\{a_i, b_i\}$.
5. We have voter v_0 with empty approval set.

As the reader can verify, every candidate from C is approved by exactly $2(k-1)$ voters. Election E' is defined in the same way, except that voter v_0 approves b_1. For each of our rules we will show that committee A wins in election E and committee B wins in election E'.

We first consider GreedyCC and election E. At the beginning of the first iteration, each candidate has score $2(k-1)$ and, due to the tie-breaking order, GreedyCC chooses a_1. As a consequence, in the second iteration the score of b_1 decreases by $k-1$ points and the scores of candidates $b_2, \ldots, b_k$ decrease by 1 point each. As there is no voter who approves two different candidates from A, each of the candidates in $\{a_2, \ldots, a_k\}$ still has $2(k-1)$ points. Hence a_2 is selected. The same reasoning applies to the following $k-2$ iterations, during which the remaining members of A are chosen.

On the other hand, for election E' GreedyCC outputs committee B. To see this, note that in the first iteration b_1 has score higher by one point than every other candidate and, so, is selected irrespective of the tie-breaking order. Then the scores of candidates in A decrease below $2(k-1)$, but the scores of candidates in $\{b_2, \ldots, b_k\}$ remain equal to $2(k-1)$. Hence these candidates are selected in the following iterations. Since GreedyCC outputs committee A for election E and committee B for election E', we see that GreedyCC is k-ADD-robust.

The case of GreedyPAV is analogous to that of GreedyCC. Indeed, the only difference between the operation of GreedyPAV and GreedyCC on elections E and E' is that when under GreedyCC the score of some candidate drops by x, the score of the same candidate drops by $x/2$ under GreedyPAV (naturally, this is not a general feature of these rules, but one that is specific to our two elections). As a consequence, both rules choose the same committees for E and E' and, so, GreedyPAV is k-ADD-robust.

Finally, we consider the Phragmén rule. Since in election E each candidate is approved by $2(k-1)$ voters, the first moment when a group of voters can purchase a candidate is $1/2(k-1)$. Due to the tie-breaking order, they first buy a_1, followed by a_2 and all the other members of A (as no two members of A are approved by the same voter, for each member of A there is a group of voters with sufficient funding). Thus the rule outputs committee A. In election E', candidate b_1 has $2k-1$ approvals and is purchased at time $1/2k-1$. As a consequence, all voters who approve b_1 have their budgets reset to 0. The next time when there is a group of voters that can purchase a candidate is $1/2(k-1)$. One can verify that at this point for each candidate in $\{b_2, \ldots, b_k\}$ there is a disjoint group of voters that has a unit of money, whereas there is no such group for any member of A. Hence, Phragmén outputs committee B. As in the previous two cases, this means that Phragmén is k-ADD-robust. □

The reader may worry that the above results hold due to the fact that our rules are resolute, but this is not the case. For example, if one used parallel-universes tie-breaking (where a rule outputs all the committees that could win for some way of resolving the internal ties) then the result would still hold. For example, for GreedyCC it would suffice to add one more voter approving both a_1 and b_1 to elections E and E'. Then, GreedyCC with parallel-universes tie-breaking would output both A and B as the winning committees for E, but for E' it would output only B. This would show its k-ADD-robustness (from the point of view of committee A).

4 Robustness Radius: Complexity Results

In this section we show that the ROBUSTNESS-RADIUS problem is NP-complete for each of our rules, for both adding and removing approvals. We observe that for each of our rules and operation type, the respective ROBUSTNESS-RADIUS problem is clearly in NP. Indeed, it suffices to nondeterministically guess which approvals to add/remove, compute the winning committees before and after the change (since our rules are resolute, in each case there is exactly one), and verify that they are different. Hence, in our proofs we will focus on showing NP-hardness. To this end, we give reductions from the following variant of the X3C problem (it is well known that this variant of the problem remains NP-complete [16]; note that in the standard variant of X3C one does not assume that each member of U belongs to exactly three sets).

Definition 2. *An instance of* RX3C *consists of a universe set* $U = \{u_1, \ldots, u_{3n}\}$ *and a family* $\mathcal{S} = \{S_1, \ldots, S_{3n}\}$ *of three-element subsets of* U, *such that each member of* U *belongs to exactly three sets from* $\mathcal{S}$. *We ask if there is a collection of* n *sets from* $\mathcal{S}$ *whose union is* U *(i.e., we ask if there is an exact cover of* U *).*

All our reductions follow the same general scheme: Given an instance of RX3C we form an election where the sets are the candidates and the voters encode their content. Additionally, we also have candidates p and d. Irrespective which operations we perform (within a given budget), all the set candidates are always selected, but by performing appropriate actions we control the order in which this happens. If the order corresponds to finding an exact cover, then additionally candidate p is selected. Otherwise, our rules select d.

We first focus on adding approvals and then argue why our proofs adapt to the case of removing approvals.

Theorem 2. *GreedyCC-*ADD-ROBUSTNESS-RADIUS *is* NP*-complete.*

Proof. We give a reduction form the RX3C problem. Our input consists of the universe set $U = \{u_1, \ldots, u_{3n}\}$ and family $\mathcal{S} = \{S_1, \ldots, S_{3n}\}$ of three-element subsets of U. We know that each member of U belongs to three sets from $\mathcal{S}$. We introduce two integers, $T = 10n^5$ and $t = 10n^3$ and we interpret both as large numbers, with T being significantly larger than t. We form an election $E = (C, V)$ with candidate set $C = \{S_1, \ldots, S_{3n}\} \cup \{p, d\}$, and with the following voters:

1. For each $S_i \in \mathcal{S}$, there are T voters that approve candidate S_i.
2. For each two sets S_i and S_j, there are T voters that approve candidates S_i and S_j.

3. There are $2nT + 4nt$ voters that approve p and d.
4. For each $u_\ell \in U$, there are t voters that approve d and those candidates S_i that correspond to the sets containing u_ℓ.
5. There are n voters who do not approve any candidates.

The committee size is $k = 3n + 1$ and the budget is $B = n$. We assume that the tie-breaking order among the candidates is:

$$S_1 \succ S_2 \succ \cdots \succ S_{3n} \succ p \succ d.$$

Prior to any bribery, each candidate S_i is approved by $3nT + 3t$ voters, p is approved by $2nT + 4nt$ voters, and d is approved by $2nT + 7nt$ voters.

Let us now consider how GreedyCC operates on this election. Prior to the first iteration, all the set candidates have the same score, much higher than that of p and d. Due to the tie-breaking order, GreedyCC chooses S_1. As a consequence, all the voters that approve S_1 are removed from consideration and the scores of all other set candidates decrease by T (or by $T + t$ or $T + 2t$, for the sets that included the same one or two elements of U as S_1). GreedyCC acts analogously for the first n iterations, during which it chooses a family $\mathcal{T}$ of n set elements (we will occasionally refer to $\mathcal{T}$ as if it really contained the sets from $\mathcal{S}$, and not the corresponding candidates).

After the first n iterations, each of the remaining $2n$ set candidates either has $2nT$, $2nT + t$, $2nT + 2t$, or $2nT + 3t$ approvals (depending how many sets in $\mathcal{T}$ have nonempty intersection with them). Let x be the number of elements from U that do not belong to any set in $\mathcal{T}$. Candidate p is still approved by $2nT + 4nt$ voters, whereas d is approved by $2nT + 4nt + xt$ voters. Thus at this point there are two possibilities. Either $x = 0$ and, due to the priority order, GreedyCC selects p, or $x > 0$ and GreedyCC selects d. In either case, in the following $2n$ iterations it chooses the remaining $2n$ set candidates (because after the $n + 1$-st iteration the score of that among p and d who remains drops to zero or nearly zero). If candidate p is selected without any bribery, then it means that we can find a solution for the RX3C instance using a simple greedy algorithm. In this case, instead of outputting the just-described instance of GreedyCC-ADD-ROBUSTNESS-RADIUS, we output a fixed one, for which the answer is *yes*. Otherwise, we know that without any bribery the winning committee is $\{S_1, \ldots, S_{3n}, d\}$. We focus on this latter case.

We claim that it is possible to ensure that the winning committee changes by adding at most n approvals if and only if there is an exact cover of U with n sets from $\mathcal{S}$. Indeed, if such a cover exists, then it suffices to add a single approval for each of the corresponding sets in the last group of voters (those that originally do not approve anyone). Then, by the same analysis as in the preceding paragraph, we can verify that the sets forming the cover are selected in the first n iterations, followed by p, followed by all the other set candidates.

For the other direction, let us assume that after adding some t approvals the winning committee has changed. One can verify that irrespective of which (up-to) n approvals we add, in the first n iterations GreedyCC still chooses n set candidates. Thus, at this point, the score of p is at most $2nT + 4nt + n$ and the score of d is at least $2nT + 4nt + xt - n$ (where x is the number of elements from U not covered by the chosen sets; we subtract n to account for the fact that n voters that originally approved d got approvals for the candidates selected in the first n iterations). If at this point d is selected, then in the following $2n$ iterations the remaining set candidates are chosen and the winning committee does not change. This means that p is selected. However, this is only possible if $x = 0$, i.e., if the set candidates chosen in the first n iterations correspond to an exact cover of U. □

A very similar proof also works for the case of GreedyPAV. The main difference is that now including a candidate in a committee does not allow us to forget about all the voters that approve him or her (the proof is in the appendix).

Theorem 3. *GreedyPAV*-ADD-ROBUSTNESS-RADIUS *is* NP-*complete.*

The proof for the case of Phragmén-ADD-ROBUSTNESS-RADIUS is similar in spirit to the preceding two, but requires careful calculation of the times when particular groups of voters can purchase respective candidates.

Theorem 4. *Phragmén*-ADD-ROBUSTNESS-RADIUS *is* NP-*complete.*

Proof. We give a reduction from RX3C. As input, we get a universe set $U = \{u_1, \ldots, u_{3n}\}$ and a family $\mathcal{S} = \{S_1, \ldots, S_{3n}\}$ of size-3 subsets of U. Each element of U appears in exactly three sets from $\mathcal{S}$. We ask if there is a collection of n sets that form an exact cover of U.

Our reduction proceeds as follows. First, we define two numbers, $T = 900n^{12}$ and $t = 30n^5$. The intuition is that both numbers are very large, T is significantly larger than t^2, and t is divisible by $6n$ (the exact values of T and t are not crucial; we did not minimize them but, rather, used values that clearly work and simplify the reduction). We form an election $E = (C, V)$ with candidate set $C = \{S_1, \ldots, S_{3n}\} \cup \{p, d\}$ and the following voters:

1. For each $S_i \in \mathcal{S}$, there are T voters that approve candidate S_i. We refer to them as the $\mathcal{S}$-voters.
2. For each $u_\ell \in U$, there are t^2 voters that approve those candidates S_i that correspond to the sets containing u_ℓ. We refer to them as the universe voters. For each $u_\ell \in U$, $\frac{t}{3n}$ of u_ℓ's universe voters additionally approve candidate d. We refer to them as the d-universe voters.
3. There are $T + 3t^2 - 2t$ voters that approve both p and d. We refer to them as the p/d-voters.
4. There are $\frac{t}{6n}$ voters that approve p. We refer to them as the p voters.
5. There are n voters who do not approve any candidate, and to whom we refer as the empty voters.

The committee size is $k = 3n + 1$ and the budget is $B = n$. The tie-breaking order is:
$$S_1 \succ S_2 \succ \cdots \succ S_{3n} \succ d \succ p.$$

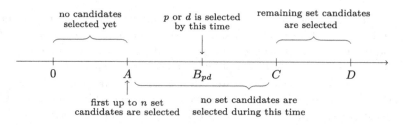

no candidates selected yet

p or d is selected by this time

remaining set candidates are selected

0   A B_{pd} C D

first up to n set candidates are selected

no set candidates are selected during this time

Fig. 1. Timeline for the Phragmén rule acting on the election from Theorem 4.

In this election, each candidate S_i is approved by exactly $T + 3t^2$ voters, d is approved by $(T + 3t^2 - 2t) + t$ voters, and p is approved by $(T + 3t^2 - 2t) + \frac{t}{6n}$ voters.

Let us consider how Phragmén operates on this election (we encourage the reader to consult Fig. 1 while reading the following text). First, we observe that when we reach time point $D = \frac{1}{T}$ then all the not-yet-selected set candidates (for whom there still is room in the committee) are selected. Indeed, at time D the $\mathcal{S}$-voters collect enough funds to buy them. On the other hand, the earliest point of time when some voters can afford to buy a candidate is $A = \frac{1}{T+3t^2}$. Specifically, at time A set voters and universe voters jointly purchase up to n set candidates (selected sequentially, using the tie-breaking order and taking into account that when some candidate is purchased then all his or her voters spend all their so-far collected money). Let us consider some candidate S_i that was not selected at time point A. Since S_i was not chosen at A, at least t^2 of the $3t^2$ universe voters that approve S_i paid for another candidate at time A. Thus the earliest time when voters approving S_i might have enough money to purchase him or her is C, such that:

$$\underbrace{C(T + 2t^2)}_{\substack{\text{money earned by those voters} \\ \text{who did not spend it at time } A}} + \underbrace{(C - A)t^2}_{\substack{\text{money earned between times } C \text{ and } A \text{ by uni-} \\ \text{verse voters who paid for candidates at time } A}} = 1.$$

Simple calculations show that $C = \frac{1+At^2}{T+3t^2}$. Noting that $A = \frac{1}{T+3t^2}$, we have that $C = A + A^2t^2$. However, prior to reaching time point C, either candidate p or candidate d is selected. Indeed, at time point $B_{pd} = \frac{1}{T+3t^2-2t}$ the p/d voters alone would have enough money to buy one of their candidates: We show that $B_{pd} < C$, or, equivalently, that $\frac{1}{B_{pd}} > \frac{1}{C}$. It holds that $\frac{1}{B_{pd}} = T + 3t^2 - 2t$ and:

$$\frac{1}{C} = \frac{1}{A + A^2t^2} = \frac{1}{A} \cdot \frac{1}{1 + At^2} = \frac{T + 3t^2}{1 + \frac{t^2}{T+3t^2}} = \frac{(T + 3t^2)^2}{T + 4t^2}.$$

By simple transformations, $\frac{1}{B_{pd}} > \frac{1}{C}$ is equivalent to:

$$(T + 3t^2 - 2t)(T + 4t^2) > (T + 3t^2)^2.$$

The left-hand side of this inequality can be expressed as:

$$((T + 3t^2) - 2t)((T + 3t^2) + t^2) = (T + 3t^2)^2 + \underbrace{(t^2 - 2t)(T + 3t^2) - 2t^3}_{\substack{\text{positive because } t^2 - 2t > 2t \\ \text{due to our assumptions}}},$$

and, hence, our inequality holds. All in all, we have $A < B_{pd} < C < D$.

It remains to consider which among p and d is selected. If p were to be selected, then it would happen at time point $B_p = \frac{1}{T^2 + 3t^2 - 2t + \frac{t}{6n}}$. This is when the p/d- and p voters would collect enough money to purchase p (assuming the former would not spend it on d earlier). Now, if at time A fewer than n set candidates were selected, then at least $\frac{t}{3n}$ of the d-universe voters would retain their money and, hence, d would be selected no later than at time point $B_d = \frac{1}{T^2 + 3t^2 - 2t + \frac{t}{3n}} < B_p$. On the other hand, if at time point A exactly n set candidates were selected (who, thus, would have to correspond to an exact cover of U) then all the d-universe voters would lose their money and voters who approve d would not have enough money to buy him or her before time B_p. Indeed, in this case the money accumulated by voters approving d would at time B_p be:

$$X = \underbrace{\frac{T + 3t^2 - 2t}{T + 3t^2 - 2t + \frac{t}{6n}}}_{\text{money of the } p/d \text{ voters}} + t \underbrace{\left(\frac{1}{T + 3t^2 - 2t + \frac{t}{6n}} - \frac{1}{T + 3t^2} \right)}_{\substack{\text{money collected by the } d-\text{universe} \\ \text{voters between time points } A \text{ and } B_p}}$$

We claim that $X < 1$, which is equivalent to the following inequality (where we replace $T + 3t^2$ with M; note that $M = \frac{1}{A}$):

$$\frac{M - t}{M - 2t + \frac{t}{6n}} < 1 + \frac{t}{M} = \frac{M + t}{M}$$

By simple transformations, this inequality is equivalent to $0 < \frac{Mt + t^2}{6n} - 2t^2$, which holds as $t > 6n$ and $M > 2t^2$. To conclude, if at time point A there are n set candidates selected for the committee, then p is selected for the committee as well.

Finally, we observe that irrespective of which among p and d is selected for the committee, the voters that approve the other one do not collect enough money to buy him or her until time D. Thus the winning committee either consists of all the set candidates and d, or of all the set candidates and p, where the latter happens exactly if at time A candidates corresponding to an exact cover of U are selected.

If at point A Phragmén would choose candidates corresponding to an exact cover of U then our reduction outputs a fixed yes-instance of Phragmén-ADD-ROBUSTNESS-RADIUS (as we have just found that an exact cover exists). Otherwise we output the formed election with committee size $k = 3n + 1$ and budget $B = n$. To see why this reduction is correct, we make the following three observations:

1. By adding n approvals, we cannot significantly modify any of the time points A, B_d, B_p, B_{pd}, C, and D from the preceding analysis, except that we can ensure which (up to) n sets are first considered for inclusion in the committee just before time point A.
2. If there is a collection of n sets in $\mathcal{S}$ that form an exact cover of U, then—by the above observation—we can ensure that these sets are selected just before time point A (by adding one approval for each of them among n distinct empty voters). Hence, if there is an exact cover then—by the preceding discussions—we can ensure that the winning committee changes (to consist of all the set candidates and p).
3. If there is no exact cover of U, then no matter where we add (up to) n approvals, candidate d gets selected and, so, the winning committee does not change (in particular, even if we add n approvals for p).

Since the reduction clearly runs in polynomial time, the proof is complete.   □

It remains to argue that REMOVE-ROBUSTNESS-RADIUS also is NP-complete for each of our rules. This, however, is easy to see. In each of the three proofs above, we had budget $B = n$ and n voters with empty approval sets. We were using these n voters to add a single approval for each of the n sets forming an exact cover, leading to the selection of p instead of d. For the case of removing approvals, it suffices to replace the n empty voters with $3n$ ones, such that each set candidate is approved by exactly one of them, and to set the budget to $B = 2n$. Now we can achieve the same result as before by deleting approvals for those set candidates that do not form an exact cover. Hence the following holds.

Corollary 1. *Let $\mathcal{R}$ be one of GreedyCC, GreedyPAV and Phragmén.* $\mathcal{R}$-REMOVE-ROBUSTNESS-RADIUS *is* NP-*complete.*

5   Robustness to Random Noise: Experimental Results

Let us now move on to an experimental analysis of our rules' robustness to random noise. The main idea of the experiment is as follows: First, we generate a number of elections from a given distribution and, for each of them, we compute its winning committee. Then, we perform a given number of random operations, such as adding or removing approvals (specified via a *perturbation level*, described below), and we compute the proportion of elections that change their outcome and the average number of committee members that get replaced. We do so for each of our rules (including AV), for several distributions, and for a range of perturbation levels. Our main observation is that the results for AV, PAV, and Phragmén are quite similar to each other, but those for CC stand out. Further, the results may quite strongly depend on the distribution of votes. Below we describe our setup and present the results in more detail.

Generating Elections. To generate synthetic elections, we use the *resampling* model recently introduced by Szufa et al. [23]. This model is parameterized by two numbers, $p, \phi \in [0, 1]$, and to generate an election with candidate set $C = \{c_1, \ldots, c_m\}$ and voter collection $V = (v_1, \ldots, v_n)$ it proceeds as follows: First, we choose a central approval set A of $\lfloor p \cdot m \rfloor$ candidates from C (uniformly at random from all subset of C of this cardinality). Then, for each voter v_i we set their initial approval set $A(v_i)$ to be equal to A. Finally, for each voter v_i and each candidate c_j, with probability ϕ, we perform resampling of v_i's approval for c_j, i.e. we make it approve the candidate with probability p. In other words, initially all voters have the central approval set, but for each candidate we resample its approval with probability ϕ. For example, for $\phi = 0$ each voter has identical approval set, which includes $\lfloor p \cdot m \rfloor$ candidates, whereas for $\phi = 1$ each voter approves each candidate independently, with probability p. The closer ϕ is to 0, the more similar are the votes, and the closer it is to 1, the more diverse they are.

Perturbation Levels. Given an election $E = (C, V)$, a perturbation level $\ell \in [0, 1]$ specifies how many operations of adding or removing approvals we are supposed to perform. For the ADD operation, perturbation level ℓ means that we add an ℓ fraction of all the approvals not appearing in the election, chosen uniformly at random. (In our election E, there are $X = \sum_{v \in V} |A(v)|$ approvals in total, but if each voter approved each candidate then there would be $|C| \cdot |V|$ approvals. Thus the number of not appearing approvals is $|C| \cdot |V| - X$.) For the REMOVE operation, perturbation level ℓ means removing an ℓ fraction of the approvals in the election, chosen uniformly at random.

Performing the Experiment. To perform our experiment for a given multiwinner rule $\mathcal{R}$, we consider values of $p \in \{0.1, 0.3\}$, values of $\phi \in \{0.25, 0.5, 0.75, 1\}$, perturbation levels ℓ between 0 and 0.95, with a step of 0.05 (but also including perturbation level 0.01), and operations OP $\in \{$ADD, REMOVE$\}$. For each combination of these parameters we generate 200 elections with 100 candidates and 100 voters from the resampling model with parameters p and ϕ. For each of these elections we compute its $\mathcal{R}$ winning committee of size $k = 10$, apply operations OP as specified by the perturbation level, and compute the winning committee of the resulting election (of the same size). We report the fraction of elections for which the two committees differ and the average number of candidates by which they differ. We show the results in Figs. 2 and 3.

Analysis. The results in Figs. 2 and 3 show several interesting patterns. Most strikingly, the results for AV, PAV, and Phragmén are very similar to each other (to the point that it is often quite difficult to distinguish respective plots), whereas those for CC stand out sharply. This suggests that the nature of choosing diverse committees, as done by CC, is quite different from that of choosing individually excellent ones (as done by AV) or proportional ones (as done by PAV and Phragmén).

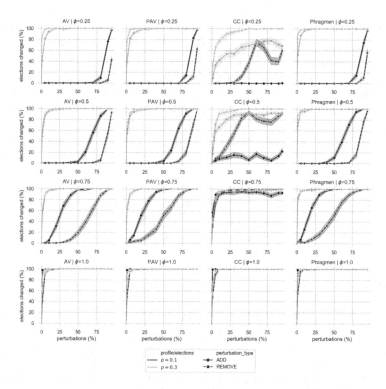

Fig. 2. Probabilities of changing elections results for the resampling model with $p = 0.1$ (blue lines) and $p = 0.3$ (orange lines) for different rules (columns of the plot) and different values of ϕ (rows of the plot) and different perturbation levels (x axis). Each data point corresponds to 200 elections with 100 candidates, 100 voters, and committee size 10. Wide light blue and light orange lines represent standard deviation. (Color figure online)

Second observation is that it is much easier to affect the results of elections where the votes approve, on average, $p = 0.3$ fraction of the candidates (orange lines in Figs. 2 and 3) than those where they approve, on average, $p = 0.1$ fraction of them (blue lines in Figs. 2 and 3). This is somewhat counterintuitive. For example, in AV one would expect that with fewer approvals in total it would be easier to push some non-winning candidate into the committee by, say, adding approvals, because the bar for entering the committee should be low. On the other hand, the added approvals come from a wider set of possibilities.

The next observation is that the higher the value of ϕ, the easier it is to affect the output committees. This is intuitive as for small values of ϕ the votes are highly correlated, whereas for larger ϕ the votes are more random and more fragile to adding noise.

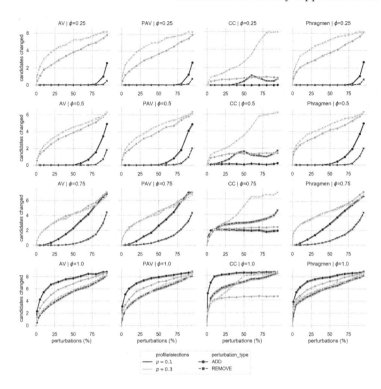

Fig. 3. Average number of replaced committee members (the setup of the plot is analogous to the one in Fig. 2. (Color figure online)

6 Summary

We have complemented the results of Brederek et al. [6] and Gawron and Faliszewski [15] by considering the robustness of GreedyCC, GreedyPAV, and Phragmén. We have found that their robustness levels are equal to the committee size (which means that even a minimal change to the votes can lead to completely replacing the winning committee), that the problems of deciding if modifying their input to a certain extent may change their outcomes are NP-complete, and we have observed how these rules react to random noise.

Acknowledgments. This project has received funding from the European Research Council (ERC) under the European Union's Horizon 2020 research and innovation programme (grant agreement No. 101002854). Grzegorz Gawron was supported in part by AGH University of Science and Technology and the "Doktorat Wdrozeniowy" program of the Polish Ministry of Science and Higher Education.

References

1. Aziz, H., Brill, M., Conitzer, V., Elkind, E., Freeman, R., Walsh, T.: Justified representation in approval-based committee voting. Soc. Choice Welfare **48**(2), 461–485 (2017)
2. Aziz, H., Gaspers, S., Gudmundsson, J., Mackenzie, S., Mattei, N., Walsh, T.: Computational aspects of multi-winner approval voting. In: Proceedings of AAMAS 201, pp. 107–115 (2015)
3. Baumeister, D., Hogrebe, T.: On the complexity of predicting election outcomes and estimating their robustness. In: Proceedings of EUMAS-2021, pp. 228–244 (2021)
4. Betzler, N., Slinko, A., Uhlmann, J.: On the computation of fully proportional representation. J. Artif. Intell. Res. **47**, 475–519 (2013)
5. Boehmer, N., Bredereck, R., Faliszewski, P., Niedermeier, R.: Winner robustness via swap- and shift-bribery: parameterized counting complexity and experiments. In: Proceedings of IJCAI-2021, pp. 52–58 (2021)
6. Bredereck, R., Faliszewski, P., Kaczmarczyk, A., Niedermeier, R., Skowron, P., Talmon, N.: Robustness among multiwinner voting rules. In: Bilò, V., Flammini, M. (eds.) SAGT 2017. LNCS, vol. 10504, pp. 80–92. Springer, Cham (2017). https://doi.org/10.1007/978-3-319-66700-3_7
7. Brill, M., Laslier, J., Skowron, P.: Multiwinner approval rules as apportionment methods. J. Theor. Polit. **30**(3), 358–382 (2018)
8. Cary, D.: Estimating the margin of victory for instant-runoff voting (August 2011), In: Presented at 2011 Electronic Voting Technology Workshop/Workshop on Trushworthy Elections (2011)
9. Chamberlin, B., Courant, P.: Representative deliberations and representative decisions: proportional representation and the Borda rule. Am. Pol. Sci. Rev. **77**(3), 718–733 (1983)
10. Elkind, E., Faliszewski, P., Slinko, A.: Swap bribery. In: Mavronicolas, M., Papadopoulou, V.G. (eds.) SAGT 2009. LNCS, vol. 5814, pp. 299–310. Springer, Heidelberg (2009). https://doi.org/10.1007/978-3-642-04645-2_27
11. Faliszewski, P., Hemaspaandra, E., Hemaspaandra, L.: How hard is bribery in elections? J. Artif. Intell. Res. **35**, 485–532 (2009)
12. Faliszewski, P., Rothe, J.: Control and bribery in voting. In: Brandt, F., Conitzer, V., Endriss, U., Lang, J., Procaccia, A.D. (eds.) Handbook of Computational Social Choice, chap. 7. Cambridge University Press, Cambridge (2015)
13. Faliszewski, P., Skowron, P., Slinko, A., Talmon, N.: Multiwinner voting: a new challenge for social choice theory. In: Endriss, U. (ed.) Trends in Computational Social Choice. AI Access Foundation. Springer, Cham (2017). https://doi.org/10.1007/978-3-031-09016-5_1
14. Faliszewski, P., Skowron, P., Talmon, N.: Bribery as a measure of candidate success: Complexity results for approval-based multiwinner rules. In: Proceedings of AAMAS-2017, pp. 6–14 (2017)
15. Gawron, G., Faliszewski, P.: Robustness of approval-based multiwinner voting rules. In: Proceedings of ADT-2019, pp. 17–31 (2019)
16. Gonzalez, T.: Clustering to minimize the maximum intercluster distance. Theoret. Comput. Sci. **38**, 293–306 (1985)
17. Lackner, M., Skowron, P.: Multi-winner voting with approval preferences. Tech. Rep. arxiv:2007.01795, arXiv.org (2022)

18. Magrino, T., Rivest, R., Shen, E., Wagner, D.: Computing the margin of victory in IRV elections In: Presented at 2011 Electronic Voting Technology Workshop/Workshop on Trushworthy Elections, August 2011
19. Procaccia, A., Rosenschein, J., Zohar, A.: On the complexity of achieving proportional representation. Soc. Choice Welf. **30**(3), 353–362 (2008)
20. Sánchez-Fernández, L., et al.: Proportional justified representation. In: Proceedings of AAAI-2017, pp. 670–676 (2017)
21. Shiryaev, D., Yu, L., Elkind, E.: On elections with robust winners. In: Proceedings of AAMAS-2013, pp. 415–422 (2013)
22. Skowron, P., Faliszewski, P., Lang, J.: Finding a collective set of items: From proportional multirepresentation to group recommendation. Artif. Intell. **241**, 191–216 (2016)
23. Szufa, S., et al.: How to sample approval elections? In: Proceedings of IJCAI-2022, pp. 496–502 (2022)
24. Thiele, T.: Om flerfoldsvalg. In: Oversigt over det Kongelige Danske Videnskabernes Selskabs Forhandlinger, pp. 415–441 (1895)
25. Xia, L.: Computing the margin of victory for various voting rules. In: Proceedings of EC-2012, pp. 982–999. ACM Press, June 2012
26. Yager, R.: On ordered weighted averaging aggregation operators in multicriteria decisionmaking. IEEE Trans. Syst. Man Cybern. **18**(1), 183–190 (1988)

Using Multiwinner Voting to Search for Movies

Grzegorz Gawron[1,2] and Piotr Faliszewski[1(✉)]

[1] AGH University, Krakow, Poland
faliszew@agh.edu.pl
[2] VirtusLab, Krakow, Poland

Abstract. We show a prototype of a system that uses multiwinner voting to suggest resources (e.g., movies) related to a given query. For example, a user provides a movie and the system answers with a list of movies that, depending on the voting rule used, are either very closely or more loosely related to the input one. This gives a way of controlling the diversity of the results (and an ability to escape one's filter bubble). We test our system both on synthetic data and on the MovieLens dataset.

1 Introduction

The idea of multiwinner voting is to provide a committee (i.e., a subset) of candidates based on the preferences of the voters. In principle, such mechanisms have many applications, ranging from choosing parliaments, through selecting finalists of competitions, to suggesting items in Internet stores or services. While the first two types of applications indeed are quite common in practice, the last one, so far, was viewed mostly as a theoretical possibility. Our goal is to change this view. To this end, we design a prototype of a voting-based search system that given a movie (or, a set of movies), finds related ones. The crucial element of our system—enabled by the use of multiwinner voting—is that one may specify to what extent he or she wants to focus on movies very tightly related to the input one(s), and to what extent he or she wants to explore a broader spectrum of movies that are related in some less obvious ways. If someone is looking for movies exactly like the specified one(s), then using focused search is natural, but if someone is not really sure what he or she really seeks, or wants to escape his or her filter bubble, then looking at a broader spectrum is more desirable.

Viewed more formally, our system belongs to the class of non-personalized recommendation systems based on collaborative filtering. That is, the users posing queries are anonymous and we do not target the results toward particular individuals, but we try to find movies related to the ones they ask about. In this sense, our system is more of a search tool than a recommendation one.

To find the relationships between the movies, we use a dataset of movie ratings (in our case, the MovieLens dataset of Harper and Konstan [18]), which

---

*See https://github.com/Project-PRAGMA/Movies-EUMAS-2022 for the code used in the experiments from this paper.

© The Author(s), under exclusive license to Springer Nature Switzerland AG 2022
D. Baumeister and J. Rothe (Eds.): EUMAS 2022, LNAI 13442, pp. 134–151, 2022.
https://doi.org/10.1007/978-3-031-20614-6_8

consists of a set of agents who each rated some movies. We represent this dataset as a *global election*, where the agents are the voters, the movies are the candidates, and each agent indicates which movies he or she likes. Then, given a query, i.e., either a single movie or a set of movies, we restrict the set of agents to those who liked the movies from the query and output a winning committee for the resulting *local election* (we also take special measures to avoid globally popular movies such as, e.g., *The Pirates of the Caribbean*, which are not necessarily relevant to the query). We use a family of voting rules parameterized by a value $p \geq 0$, such that for $p = 0$ we get the most focused results, and for larger p's the results become broader.

Our Contribution.   Our main contribution is designing a voting-based search system and testing it in the context of selecting movies. We evaluate its performance as follows: (1) Using both synthetic and MovieLens data, we show that the voting rules that are meant to pick either more closely or more loosely related movies indeed do so. (2) Using our system, we analyze and visualize similarities between movies. For example, the system can distinguish between the movies from the original *Star Trek* timeline and the reboot of the series. (3) We compare the performance of the two heuristics that we use to compute the winning committees (we resort to heuristic algorithms because our voting rules are NP-hard to compute).

Related Work.   Regarding multiwinner voting, we point the readers to the surveys of Faliszewski et al. [13] and Lackner and Skowron [22]; the former is more general and the latter focuses on approval voting. It is also interesting to consider the work of Elkind et al. [10], where the idea of using multiwinner voting for selecting movies was suggested (albeit, in a somewhat different setting). While multiwinner voting is not yet a mainstream tool in applications, some researchers have used it successfully. For example, Chakraborty et al. [6] have used it to select trending topics on Twitter or popular news on the Internet. For the latter task, Mondal et al. [25] also designed a voting-based solution. Pourghanbar et al. [29] and Faliszewski et al. [11] used diversity-oriented multiwinner voting rules to design genetic algorithms that would avoid getting stuck in a plateau regions of the search space.

For a broad discussion of modern recommendation systems, see the handbook edited by Ricci et al. [31], and, for an early account of collaborative filtering methods, see the work of Sarwar et al. [33]. As examples of works on movie recommendations, we mention the paper of Ghosh et al. [15], who describe a movie recommendation system using Black's voting rule with weighted user preferences, the paper of Azaria et al. [1], who focus on maximizing the revenue of the recommender, the paper of Choi et al. [8], who discuss recommendations based on movie genres, and the paper of Phonexay et al. [28], who adapt some techniques from social networks to recommendation systems. While most of this literature aims at finding the most tightly related movies—and as such is less relevant to our study. There are works on recommendation systems that focus on diversifying the results, such as, e.g., the work of Kim et al. [21], but in this paper the authors use neural networks and rely on a number of features, whereas we use multiwinner voting and simple collaborative filtering. Further, they do not focus on movies so it is difficult to compare the results.

2   Preliminaries

Let $\mathbb{R}_+$ denote the set of nonnegative real numbers, and for a positive integer i, let $[i]$ denote the set $\{1,\ldots,i\}$.

Utility and Approval Elections. Let $R = \{r_1,\ldots,r_m\}$ be a set of *resources* and let $N = \{1,\ldots,n\}$ be a set of *agents* (in voting literature these are *candidates* and *voters*, respectively). Each agent i has a utility function $u_i \colon R \to \mathbb{R}_+$, which specifies how much he or she appreciates each resource. The utilities are comparable among the agents, but not normalized (this means that some agents may feel more strongly about the resources than the others). Utility of zero means that an agent is completely uninterested in a given resource. Committees are sets of resources, typically of a given size k. For a committee $S = \{s_1,\ldots,s_k\}$ and an agent i, by $u_i(S)$ we mean the vector $(u_i(s_1),\ldots,u_i(s_k))$, where the utilities appear in some fixed order over the resources (this order will never be relevant). We write $U = (u_1,\ldots,u_n)$ to denote a collection of utility functions, referred to as a *utility profile*. A *utility election* $E = (R,U)$ consists of a set of resources and a utility profile over these resources. An *approval election* is a utility election where each utility is either 1, meaning that an agent approves a resource, or 0, meaning that he or she does not approve it. For approval elections we typically denote the utility profile as $A = (a_1,\ldots,a_n)$ and call it an *approval profile*. For a resource r_t, we write $A(r_t)$ to denote the set of agents that approve it.

OWA Operators. An *ordered weighted average* (OWA) operator is given by a vector of numbers $\lambda = (\lambda_1,\ldots,\lambda_k)$ and operates as follows. For vectors $x = (x_1,\ldots,x_k) \in \mathbb{R}^k$ and $x' = (x'_1,\ldots,x'_k)$, where x' is obtained by sorting x in nonincreasing order, we have $\lambda(x) = \lambda_1 x'_1 + \lambda_2 x'_2 + \cdots + \lambda_k x'_k$. E.g., operator $(1,\ldots,1)$ means summing the elements of the input vector, and $(1,0,\ldots,0)$ means taking the maximum. OWA operators are due to Yager [36].

(OWA-Based) Multiwinner Voting Rules. A *multiwinner voting rule* is a function f that given an election E and an integer k returns a family of size-k winning committees. Consider a utility election $E = (R,U)$, where $R = \{r_1,\ldots,r_m\}$ and $U = (u_1,\ldots,u_n)$, and an OWA operator $\lambda = (\lambda_1,\ldots,\lambda_k)$. Let S be a size-k committee. The λ-score of committee S in election E is $\lambda - score_E(S) = \sum_{i=1}^{n} \lambda(u_i(S))$. We say that a multiwinner rule f is OWA-based if there is a family $\Lambda = (\lambda^{(k)})_{k \geq 1}$ of OWA operators, one for each committee size k, such that for each election E and each committee size k, $f(E,k)$ consists exactly of those size-k committees S for which $\lambda^{(k)} - score_E(S)$ is highest.

HUV Rules. We use rules based on OWA operators of the form $\lambda^p = (1, 1/2^p, 1/3^p, \ldots)$, where $p \geq 0$, and we refer to them as *p-Harmonic Utility Voting* rules (*p*-HUV rules). The name stems from the fact that for $p = 1$ their OWA operators sum up to harmonic numbers:

1. For a committee size k, the 0-HUV rule chooses k resources whose sum of utilities over all the agents is highest; its OWA operator is $(1, \ldots, 1)$. Under approval elections, 0-HUV is the classic *Multiwinner Approval Voting* rule (AV).
2. The 1-HUV rule uses OWA operators $(1, 1/2, 1/3, \ldots)$; for approval elections this is the *Proportional Approval Voting* rule (PAV) of Thiele [35].
3. ∞-HUV uses OWA operators $(1, 0, \ldots, 0)$ and is known as the *Chamberlin–Courant* rule (CC). It was first introduced for the ordinal setting by Chamberlin and Courant [7] and then adapted to the approval one by Procaccia et al. [30] and Betzler et al. [4].

AV, PAV, and CC correspond to the three main principles of choosing committees: AV chooses *individually excellent* resources that are appreciated by the largest number of agents, PAV chooses committees that proportionally represent the preferences of the agents [2,5], and CC focuses on *diversity*, i.e., it seeks a committee so that as many agents as possible appreciate at least one resource in the committee. For more details, see the overviews of Faliszewski et al. [13] and Lackner and Skowron [22], and the work on the opposition between AV and CC [23]. For $p > 0$, *p*-HUV provides a compromise between individually excellent 0-HUV and diverse ∞-HUV (as shown by the results of Faliszewski et al. [12], as well as those of Elkind et al. [9] and Godziszewski et al. [16]).

Computing HUV Committees. For each $p > 0$, it is NP-hard to tell if there is a committee with at least a given score under the *p*-HUV rule ([3,34]). Thus, to compute a winning *p*-HUV committee of size-k (for some $p \geq 0$), we use the standard greedy heuristic, which starts with an empty committee and performs k iterations, where in each it extends the committee with a single resource whose inclusion maximizes the committee's *p*-HUV score. A classic result on submodular optimization shows that the committees computed this way achieve at least $1 - 1/e \approx 0.63$ fraction of the highest possible score ([24,26]) (for $p = 0$ this algorithm gives exact results). We also use the simulated annealing heuristic, as implemented in the *simanneal* library, version 0.5.0. We set the number of steps to 50 000 and the temperature to vary between 9900 and 0.6.

3   System Design

The main idea of our system is that for a *query set* of resources we form an election whose winning committee is our *result*. The system consists of three main components, the data model (responsible for representing the raw data as a global election), the search model (responsible for forming local elections based on queries), and winner determination (responsible for computing the results).

3.1   Data Model

The data model converts domain-specific data into a *global (approval) election*. The interpretation is that the agents in this election are users who interacted with some resources, and approve those that they enjoyed. Lack of an approval means that the interaction was negative or that there was no interaction.

Example 1. The MovieLens 25M dataset [18] contains 25'000'095 ratings of 62'423 movies, provided by 162'541 users (on average, each user rated almost 154 movies). Each rating is between one and five stars and was provided between 1995 and 2019 on the MovieLens website. We form a global election where each user is an agent, each movie is a resource, and a user approves a movie if he or she gave it at least four stars. We disregard those movies that were approved by fewer than 20 agents.

3.2   Search Model

The search model deals with forming a *local election*, specific to a particular query. The idea is that this election's winning committees would be our result sets. We first form a *local approval election* and then derive more fine-grained utilities for the agents, leading to a *local utility election*.

Let $E = (R, A)$ be the global approval election and let $Q \subseteq R$ be the query set (typically a singleton). Let $N = \{1, \ldots, n\}$ be the agents from E and let N_{loc} be the subset of N containing those agents who approve at least one member of Q. Then, let R_{loc} consist of those resources that are approved by at least one agent from N_{loc}, except for the resources from the query. Finally, let A_{loc} be the approval profile of the agents from N_{loc}, restricted to the resources from R_{loc}; $E_{loc} = (R_{loc}, A_{loc})$ is our local approval election. Intuitively, it contains the knowledge about Q. Unfortunately, as shown below, it may be insufficient to provide relevant search results.

Example 2. Consider the MovieLens global election from Example 1 and let the query set Q consist of a single movie, *Hot Shots!* (a quirky/absurd comedy). The three most-approved movies in the local approval election for Q are: (1) *The Matrix (1999)*, (2) *Back to the Future (1985)*, and (3) *Fight Club (1999)*. This is also the winning committee under the AV rule with $k = 3$. Neither of these movies has much to do with *Hot Shots!*, but they are popular both globally and among people who enjoyed *Hot Shots!*.

To address such issues, we derive a local utility election $E_{util} = (R_{util}, U_{util})$. We let the set of resources be the same, i.e., $R_{util} = R_{loc}$, but we modify the utilities to promote the relevant resources. We do so by employing the *term frequency-inverse document frequency* mechanism.

The goal of TF-IDF is to evaluate how specific a given term t is for a document d from a document corpus D (it was introduced by Jones [19,20]; see also the works of Robertson and Walker [32] and Ounis [27]). The main idea is that the specificity value of t in d is proportional to the frequency of t in d

Table 1. Results of our system for the movie *Hot Shots!* with the winning committee size set to 10 (see Examples 1, and 4).

#	Exact algorithm 0-HUV	Simulated annealing 1-HUV	2-HUV
1.	The Naked Gun 2 1/2 (1991)	Hot Shots! Part Deux (1993)	Hot Shots! Part Deux (1993)
2.	Hot Shots! Part Deux (1993)	The Loaded Weapon 1 (1993)	The Loaded Weapon 1 (1993)
3.	The Naked Gun (1988)	The Naked Gun (1988)	The Naked Gun 2 1/2 (1991)
4.	Top Secret! (1984)	The Naked Gun 2 1/2 (1991)	Men at Work (1990)
5.	The Loaded Weapon 1 (1993)	Blind Fury (1989)	Top Secret! (1984)
6.	Police Academy (1984)	Top Secret! (1984)	Hudson Hawk (1991)
7.	Spaceballs (1987)	Commando (1985)	Silent Movie (1976)
8.	Last Boy Scout, The (1991)	Hudson Hawk (1991)	Freaked (1993)
9.	Commando (1985)	Major League II (1994)	Major League II (1994)
10.	The Naked Gun 33 1/3 (1994)	Yamakasi (2001)	Yamakasi (2001)
#		Greedy algorithm 1-HUV	2-HUV
1.		The Naked Gun 2 1/2 (1991)	The Naked Gun 2 1/2 (1991)
2.		Hot Shots! Part Deux (1993)	Hot Shots! Part Deux (1993)
3.		Top Secret! (1984)	The Loaded Weapon 1 (1993)
4.		The Loaded Weapon 1 (1993)	Major League II (1994)
5.		Major League II (1994)	Top Secret! (1984)
6.		Last Boy Scout, The (1991)	Yamakasi (2001)
7.		Yamakasi (2001)	Hudson Hawk (1991)
8.		The Naked Gun (1988)	Silent Movie (1976)
9.		Hudson Hawk (1991)	Freaked (1993)
10.		Silent Movie (1976)	Last Boy Scout, The (1991)

(term frequency; *TF*) and is inversely proportional to the frequency of t in all the documents D (inverse document frequency; *IDF*). Given our global election $E = (R, A)$ and the local approval election $E_{loc} = (R_{loc}, A_{loc})$, we implement the TF-IDF idea as follows. We interpret the resources as the terms, and we take the document corpus to consist of two "documents," election E_{loc} and election $E' = (R_{loc}, A')$, where A' is the approval profile for those agents from the global election that do not appear in E_{loc}. Let n be the total number of agents. For a resource $r \in R_{loc}$, we let its *term frequency* be the number of agents that approve it in the local election, i.e., $\mathrm{tf}(r) = |A_{loc}(r)|$. We let r's inverse document frequency be $\mathrm{idf}(r) = \ln\left(n/|A(r)|\right)$. We also assume some constant γ to balance TF and IDF values, and we define $\text{tf-idf}_\gamma(r) = \mathrm{tf}(r)\gamma^{\mathrm{idf}(r)} = \frac{|A_{loc}(r)|}{|A(r)|^{\ln \gamma}} \cdot \left(n^{\ln \gamma}\right)$.

Example 3. Consider resources r_1, r_2, and r_3 where: $|A_{loc}(r_1)| = 1$, $|A(r_1)| = 2$, $|A_{loc}(r_2)| = 10$, $|A(r_2)| = 20$, and $|A_{loc}(r_3)| = 100$, $|A(r_3)| = 2000$. If we focused on the number of approvals in the local election (by taking $\ln \gamma = 0$), then we would view r_3 as the most relevant resource. This would be unintuitive as only a small fraction of r_3's approvals come from the agents who enjoy the items in the query set. For $\gamma \approx 2.71$ (i.e., $\ln \gamma = 1$), we would focus on the ratios $|A_{loc}(r_i)|/|A(r_i)|$, so r_1 and r_2 would be equally relevant, and r_3 would come third.

This is better, but still unsatisfying as r_2 is more popular than r_1. By taking, e.g., $\gamma = 2$ (i.e., $\ln \gamma \approx 0.69$) we would focus on ratios $|A_{loc}(r_i)|/|A(r_i)|^{0.69}$ and r_2 would come first.

We have found that $\gamma = 1.85$ works best for our scenario (see Sect. 4.1). Let i be some agent and let r be a resource from the local utility election. If agent i approves r in the local approval election, then in the local utility election we set $u_i(r) = \text{tf-idf}(r)/|A_{loc}(r)|$. Otherwise, we set $u_i(r) = 0$. The utilities of a given resource sum up to its TF-IDF value.

3.3 Winner Determination

If we are looking for resources that are closely connected to the query set, then we compute the results of the local utility election using 0-HUV. For a broader search, we use p-HUV rules with $p \in \{1, 2, 3, \ldots\}$. To compute a (close to) winning committee, we either use the greedy algorithm or simulated annealing. The former orders the committee by the iteration number in which a given resource was added, and the latter uses arbitrary ordering.

Example 4. Consider the local utility election for the *Hot Shots!* movie. In Table 1 we show the p-HUV committees for $p \in \{0, 1, 2\}$. Let us discuss the contents of these committees (for $p \in \{1, 2\}$, we focus on simulated annealing): The first seven movies selected by 0-HUV are quirky, absurd comedies, quite in spirit of *Hot Shots!*. Among the next three movies, two are comedies (one of which is very much in spirit to the first seven) and one is an action movie. Except for *Yamakasi*, all movies selected by 1-HUV are either comedies of different styles (7 movies) or action movies (2 movies). 2-HUV selects a somewhat more varied set of comedies than 1-HUV. *Yamakasi* is an outlier (it has very few approvals, only 53, of which 27 come from people who enjoyed *Hot Shots!*).

3.4 Final Search Process

To summarize, the search process is divided into the following steps: (1) convert the domain specific user preferences (e.g., movie rankings) into *global* approval election, (2) define a query (e.g., a movie or a set of movies), (3) generate a *local* approval election to contain only the voters approving of the movies from the query and the candidates (e.g., movies) approved by these voters, (4) transform the *local* approval election to utility election by evenly spreading the candidate's TF-IDF score among its approvals, (5) choose the search focus parameter p, (the lower, the more focused is the search) and finally (6) use a p-HUV multiwinner rule to find the required winning committee (e.g., a set of movies).

4 Experiments

In this section we present four experiments. All but the second one are conducted on the MovieLens dataset.

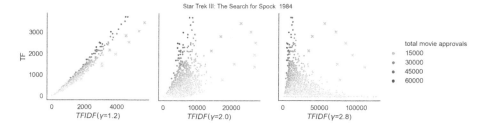

Fig. 1. Each dot (cross) represents a movie (a *Star Trek* movie) in the local election generated for *Star Trek III: The Search for Spock (1984)* and shows the relation between its popularity (its *TF* value) on the y axis and its final TF-IDF score on the x axis for various values of γ. The hue of the dot (cross) represents the number of its approvals in the global election.

4.1   Calibrating the TF-IDF Metric

Intuitively, γ is used to give more weight to the IDF component relative to the TF one. In other words, replacing γ with a larger value more strongly diminishes the TF-IDF values of the globally more popular movies than of the less popular ones. This balance is visualized in Fig. 1, where we consider the movie *Star Trek III: The Search for Spock (1984)* as a singleton query, and for each movie in the local approval election we draw a dot whose y coordinate is its number of approvals in the local election (i.e., its TF value) and whose x coordinate is its TF-IDF value, for several values of γ. The hue of the dot represents the number of approvals of the movie in the global election. The top movies according to TF-IDF (for a given γ) are the rightmost dots in the respective diagram. Note that the higher the γ is, the more dots with low TF value appear to the right. For $\gamma = 1.2$, quite a few generally popular items (with darker hue) make it to the top, simply because they are popular overall and not only in the context of the query. For $\gamma = 2.0$, there seems to be a good balance between the popular and not so popular movies, while for $\gamma = 2.8$ there are only unpopular movies in the top.

The above argument for using $\gamma = 2$ is based on intuition and, indeed, it turns out that a slightly different value gives somewhat better result. To find this value we have performed the following experiment. Our basic premise is that the γ value should be such that when searching for a singleton query, its most similar movies should appear among the top ten with respect to the TF-IDF metric. While deciding what is "the most similar movie" is subjective, we assumed that we can identify certain clusters of movies, which are similar to one another within the same cluster. Taking as an example the movies from the *Star Trek* series, other *Star Trek* movies are the most similar ones. The MovieLens dataset contains fourteen *Star Trek* movies (that are approved by at least 20 users). We used each *Star Trek* movie as a singleton query set, computed its local approval election, ranked the movies from this election with respect to their TF-IDF values for γ between 1.1 and 2.80 (with a step of 0.05) and for

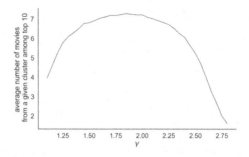

Fig. 2. A joint calibration graph, averaging the results from the clusters of *Star Trek*, *Indiana Jones*, *James Bond*, and *Marvel* movies. The x axis shows the γ value and the y axis shows how many movies from a given cluster appear, on average, among top 10 ones according to the 0-HUV rule when we search for a movie from that cluster.

each of these values calculated how many other *Star Trek* movies are among the top ten ones. Then, we averaged these values over all the fourteen movies for each γ. We found that for $\gamma \in \{1.9, 1.95, 2.0\}$ we get the highest value (7.21; see the appendix).

However, we found that for other such clusters we obtain different γ values. We checked four movies from the *Indiana Jones* series (and found $\gamma = 1.6$), 25 movies from the *James Bond* series (and found $\gamma = 1.85$) and 31 movies from the *Marvel* universe (and found $\gamma = 1.6$). Since there is not a single optimal γ value for all clusters, we decide to use the average of the top 10 movie counts across all the movies from the mentioned clusters. The results are presented in Fig. 2. We fix the $\gamma = 1.85$, for which we obtained the highest average.

4.2 Testing the Rules: Synthetic Data

In the second experiment we generate the global election synthetically. The point is to observe the differences between committees computed according to p-HUV rules for different values of p in a controlled environment.

Generating Global Elections. We assume that we have nine main categories of movies (such as, e.g., a comedy or a thriller) and each category has nine sub-categories (such as, e.g., a romantic comedy, or a psychological thriller). For each pair of a category $u \in \{1, \ldots, 9\}$ and its subcategory $v \in \{1, \ldots, 9\}$, we generate 25 movies, denoted $u.v(1), \ldots, u.v(25)$. Given a movie $u.v(i)$, we set its *quality factor* to be $q(i) = -\arctan \frac{i-13}{10} + 2$. That is, for each subcategory the first movie has the highest quality, about 2.87, and the qualities of the following movies decrease fairly linearly, down to about 1.12 (naturally, this choice is quite arbitrary). We have $n = 2000$ voters. Each voter i has a probability distribution P_i over the main categories and for each category u, he or she has probability distribution P_i^u over its subcategories. For each voter, we choose each of these distributions as permutations of $(0.5, 0.1, 0.1, 0.1, 0.1, 0.025, 0.025, 0.025, 0.025)$,

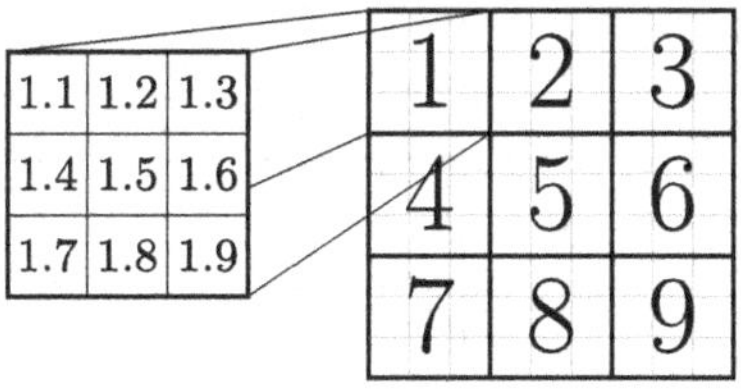

Fig. 3. Visual arrangement of the movie categories and subcategories for the synthetic experiment.

chosen uniformly at random: Each voter has the most preferred category, four categories that he or she also quite enjoys, and four categories that he or she rarely enjoys (the same applies to subcategories). To generate an approval of a voter i we do as follows: (1) We choose a category u according to distribution P_i and, then, a subcategory v according to distribution P_i^u. (2) We choose a movie among $u.v(1), \ldots, u.v(25)$ with probability proportional to its quality factor. The voter approves the selected movie. We repeat this process 162 times for each voter, leading to a bit fewer approvals due to repetitions in sampling (recall that in MovieLens the average number of approvals is 154). While this process is certainly quite ad-hoc, we believe that it captures the main features of preferences regarding movies. Further, in this model two movies are very similar if they come from the same subcategory, are somewhat similar if they come from the same category but different subcategories, and are very loosely related otherwise.

Running the Experiment. For each number $p \in \{0, 1, 2\}$ and both algorithms for computing approximate p-HUV committee we repeat the following experiment. We generate 100 global elections as described above and for each of them we compute a committee of size $k = 10$ for the query set consisting of movie 1.1(13), i.e., the middle-quality movie from subcategory 1.1 (since the (sub)categories are symmetric, their choice is irrelevant; results for other movies are similar). Considering all runs of the experiment, altogether 1000 movies are selected (some are selected more than once and we count each occurrence separately). Then, for each subcategory $u.v$, we sum up how many movies from this subcategory are among the 1000 selected movies, obtaining a histogram.

To present these histograms visually, we arrange the categories into a 3×3 square, where each category is further represented as a 3×3 subsquare of subcategories, as shown in Fig. 3. We show thus-arranged histograms for the greedy algorithm in Fig. 4 and for simulated annealing in Fig. 5. Each subcategory/square is labeled with the number of movies selected from this subcategory and its background reflects this number (darker backgrounds correspond to higher numbers). Further, next to the name of each p-HUV rule we report a vector (x, y, z), where x means the number of movies selected from subcategory 1.1, y means the number of movies selected from category 1 except for those in subcategory 1.1, and z refers to the number of all the other selected movies. Thus we always have that $x + y + z = 1000$.

0-HUV, $(985, 15, 0)$ 1-HUV, $(670, 222, 108)$ 2-HUV, $(437, 249, 314)$

Fig. 4. Histograms for the synthetic experiment and the greedy algorithm.

0-HUV, $(980, 20, 0)$ 1-HUV, $(646, 214, 140)$ 2-HUV, $(403, 265, 336)$

Fig. 5. Histograms for the synthetic experiment and simulated annealing.

Analysis. Our main conclusion is that, indeed, 0-HUV focuses on very similar movies (almost all the selected movies come from category 1.1) and as p increases, approximate p-HUV committees include more and more movies from other subcategories of category 1, and, eventually, even more movies outside of it. It would be desirable to have a value of p for which we would get a vector (x, y, z) close to, say, $(450, 450, 100)$, so that about half of the movies would be very related to the query, about half would be quite related, and few would be rather loosely related. Our algorithms do not seem to provide committees with such vectors and finding rules that would provide them would be interesting.

4.3 Testing the Rules: Movies Data

In this section we observe how varying the value of p affects the results of p-HUV rules on the MovieLens dataset, and how our system can find relations between movies. Our strategy is as follows: First, we derive a (dis)similarity measure between movies. We select some movies that we would like to compare, e.g. movies from the Star Trek series. Then, we gather a set of movies (including some that we want to focus on and some that appear as search results when we query for the former ones) and present them on a 2D plane, so that the more similar two movies are, the closer they are to each other. We annotate this visualization with the movies that we query for and the search results. This way we see how 0-HUV selects movies very similar to the query, while other rules choose more spread-around sets. Next, as a bit of an anecdotal example, we apply our dissimilarity measure to the *Star Trek* movies and find that it clusters them in a meaningful way. This reinforces our belief that the measure is truly useful. In this section we focus on the greedy algorithm.

Similarity Among Movies. Let us consider two movies, x and y. We take the following approach to obtain a number that, in some way, is related to their similarity. First, we form a local utility election using x as the singleton query set. If y does not appear in this election, then we consider it as completely dissimilar from x. Otherwise, we sort the movies from the local election in the ascending order of their TF-IDF values and we define the rank of y with respect to x, denoted $\mathrm{rank}_x(y)$, to be the position on which y appears. (So if y has the highest TF-IDF value then $\mathrm{rank}_x(y) = 1$, if it has the second highest TF-IDF then $\mathrm{rank}_y(x) = 2$, and so on; recall that the idea of TF-IDF is that the higher it is, the more relevant a movie is for the search query and, so, we equate relevance with similarity). We define the dissimilarity between x and y as $\mathrm{diss}(x, y) = \frac{1}{2}(\mathrm{rank}_x(y) + \mathrm{rank}_y(x))$. This ensures that $\mathrm{diss}(x, y) = \mathrm{diss}(y, x)$ and that the larger $\mathrm{diss}(x, y)$ is, the less related—and, hence, less similar—are the two movies.

Gathering Movies for Comparison. We would like to compare the outcomes of various p-HUV rules on each of the movies from some set A. To do so, we form an extension of A as follows (we consider p values in $\{0, 1, 2, 3\}$ and committee size $k = 10$, unless we say otherwise): (1) For each movie $x \in A$ and each $p \in \{0, 1, 2, 3\}$, we compute the p-HUV winning committee for the local utility election based on the singleton query x. We take the union of these committees and call it B. (2) For each movie $y \in B$, we compute 0-HUV winning committee of size two for the local utility election based on y. We refer to the union of these committees as C. (3) We let $\mathrm{ext}(A) = A \cup B \cup C$ be the extension of A. We use set B because we are interested in relations between the contents of the committees provided by all our rules for all the movies in A, and we add set C because we also want to ensure that each movie from $A \cup B$ has a similar one in the extension.

Visualizing Relations Between the Movies. Given a set A of movies and its extension $\mathrm{ext}(A)$, we first compute the value $\mathrm{diss}(x, y)$ for all distinct movies x and y in $\mathrm{ext}(A)$. Then, we form a complete graph where members of $\mathrm{ext}(A)$ are the nodes and for each two movies x and y, the edge connecting them has weight $\mathrm{diss}(x, y)$. Then we compute an embedding that maps each movie in $\mathrm{ext}(A)$ to a point on a two-dimensional plane, so that the Euclidean distances between these points correspond (approximately) to the weights of the edges. To this end, we use the force-directed algorithm of Fruchterman and Reingold [14]. We use the implementation provided in the *networkx* library (version 2.6.3), ran for 10'000 iterations. For a description of the library we refer the reader to [17].

The Fruchterman-Reingold algorithm does not take the weights of the edges in the graph whose embedding it is to compute as input, but the forces that act to bring the nodes of a given edge closer. Since this value should be inverse to

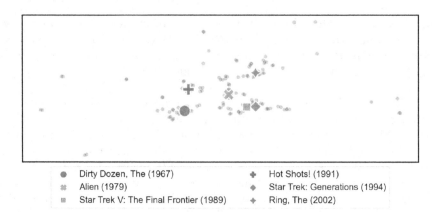

●	Dirty Dozen, The (1967)	✚	Hot Shots! (1991)
✻	Alien (1979)	◆	Star Trek: Generations (1994)
▪	Star Trek V: The Final Frontier (1989)	✦	Ring, The (2002)

Fig. 6. Embedding of the movies.

our dissimilarity, for each two movies x and y we use force $(\mathrm{diss}(x,y))^{-2}$ (by experimenting with different force functions we found this value to work well).

Comparing p-HUV Rules. Next we use the visualization methodology to analyze the outcomes of different p-HUV rules. Set A consists of movies *Hot Shots! (1991), Star Trek V: The Final Frontier (1989), Star Trek: Generations (1994), Alien (1979), Ring, The,* and *Dirty Dozen, The. Hot Shots!* is a quirky comedy, *Star Trek* movies are examples of science-fiction, and so is *Alien*, which also has strong elements of a horror movie. *Ring, The* is a horror movie and *Dirty Dozen, The* is a classic war movie. We show an embedding of these movies (and the movies from their extension) in Fig. 6. In particular, we see that the two *Star Trek* movies are correctly presented as very similar, whereas the other movies are farther away from each other.

In Fig. 7 we visualize the committees provided by p-HUV rules for $p \in \{0,1,2\}$ and singleton query sets from A. Specifically, each column corresponds to a value of p and each row to a different query. The query is marked with a black diamond and the members of selected committees have surrounding black circles (they are guaranteed to be present in the extension of A).

We see that the 0-HUV rule always chooses movies very close (very similar) to the one from the query. Indeed, we have defined our dissimilarity function to encode this effect. It is more interesting to consider p-HUV rules for $p \geq 1$. In this case, we see that the selected movies are always farther away from the query than for 0-HUV, but the extent to which this happens varies. For example, for *Hot Shots!* the committees get more and more spread as p increases, whereas for *Star Trek: Generations* the outcomes are very similar for all $p \geq 1$. Yet, altogether, our system achieves its main goals: The 0-HUV rule gives tightly focused results, closely connected to the query, and p-HUV rules for $p \geq 1$ give more diverse results.

Star Trek Movies. Our dissimilarity measure can identify interesting features of the movies. Let A consist of the fourteen *Star Trek* movies from MovieLens. We

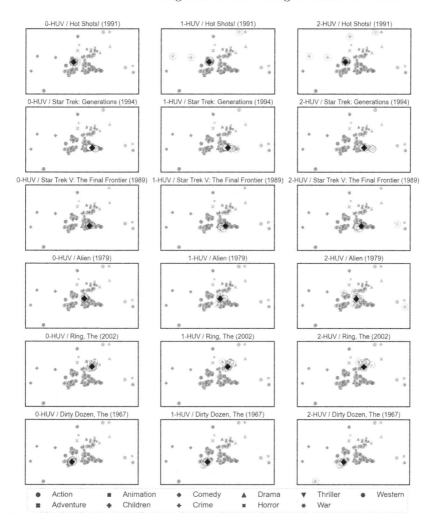

Fig. 7. Search results for different queries and different p-HUV rules. Each row corresponds to a movie used for the singleton query and each column corresponds to the voting rule used. The query movie is marked with a black diamond and the members of the winning committee are marked with black circles.

show the visualization of the extension of this set of movies in Fig. 8. The first ten movies, released between 1979 and 2002 and marked with blue symbols, are clustered closely together. These movies come from the original series and *The Next Generation* series (the transition between the two series was quite gentle, hence it is not surprising that the two groups are merged). The next cluster consists of the three movies from 2009, 2013, and 2016, and is marked in green. These movies form a new, reboot series (so-called *Kelvin Timeline*). Finally, the 2015 movie is a fan film and does not belong to the official set. Altogether, we

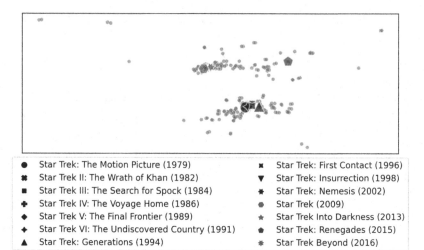

● Star Trek: The Motion Picture (1979)	✖ Star Trek: First Contact (1996)
✱ Star Trek II: The Wrath of Khan (1982)	▼ Star Trek: Insurrection (1998)
■ Star Trek III: The Search for Spock (1984)	✳ Star Trek: Nemesis (2002)
✚ Star Trek IV: The Voyage Home (1986)	⬢ Star Trek (2009)
◆ Star Trek V: The Final Frontier (1989)	★ Star Trek Into Darkness (2013)
✦ Star Trek VI: The Undiscovered Country (1991)	⬟ Star Trek: Renegades (2015)
▲ Star Trek: Generations (1994)	✻ Star Trek Beyond (2016)

Fig. 8. Star Trek movies.

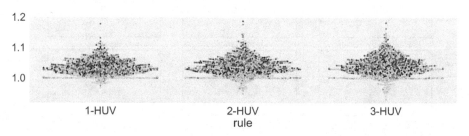

Fig. 9. Effectiveness of the greedy algorithm versus simulated annealing on the Movie-Lens 25M dataset. Each dot represents a single movie (from a set of 1000 randomly selected ones), and is used as a singleton query set. Its position on the y axis is the ratio of the scores of the committees computed for this movie using the greedy algorithm and simulated annealing. The position on the x-axis is perturbed to show all the dots. The shade of the dot represents the number of approvals of the movie in the global election (the darker it is, the more approvals).

see that similar movies are grouped together even if they were released over a long period of time, whereas significant changes, such as making a reboot or shooting a fan film, are clearly separated. In the appendix we show such figures for the *Indiana Jones*, *Star Wars*, *James Bond*, and *Marvel* movie series. The fact that our dissimilarity measure identifies such details as described above is an indication of its usefulness and quality.

4.4 Effectiveness of the Heuristics

In the final experiment we compare the quality of the committees computed by the greedy algorithm and by simulated annealing, for the MovieLens dataset.

Table 2. Average ratios of committee scores computed using the greedy algorithm and using the simulated annealing algorithm on the MovieLens 25M dataset. We provide both the mean values of the scores and their standard deviations.

Rule	Mean	Std. Dev.
1-HUV	1.033	0.026
2-HUV	1.036	0.029
3-HUV	1.040	0.034

We sampled 1000 movies and used them as singleton query sets. For each, we computed the local utility election and computed approximate winning committees for 1-HUV, 2-HUV, and 3-HUV, using both our algorithms. For each movie we calculated the ratio of the score obtained using the greedy algorithm and simulated annealing (if the ratio is above 1 then the greedy algorithm performs better, and if it is below 1 then simulated annealing is better). The results are in Fig. 9 and, in a more aggregate form, in Table 2. On average, the greedy algorithm finds committees with about 3% higher scores, which is not a substantial advantage.

5   Conclusions

Our system is a prototype and can be improved in many ways. For example, in addition to using the TF-IDF heuristic, we could use the features of the movies to identify which ones are the most relevant to a query. We could also allow the user to specify which features of the movies they would like to explore. Yet, it already shows that multiwinner voting can be useful for designing search systems, allowing the users to specify how strongly related items they are looking for.

Acknowledgments. This project has received funding from the European Research Council (ERC) under the European Union's Horizon 2020 research and innovation programme (grant agreement No. 101002854). Grzegorz Gawron was supported in part by AGH University of Science and Technology and the "Doktorat Wdrozeniowy" program of the Polish Ministry of Science and Higher Education.

References

1. Azaria, A., Hassidim, A., Kraus, S., Eshkol, A., Weintraub, O., Netanely, I.: Movie recommender system for profit maximization. In: Proceedings of RecSys-2013, pp. 121–128 (2013)

2. Aziz, H., Brill, M., Conitzer, V., Elkind, E., Freeman, R., Walsh, T.: Justified representation in approval-based committee voting. Soc. Choice Welfare **48**(2), 461–485 (2017)
3. Aziz, H., Gaspers, S., Gudmundsson, J., Mackenzie, S., Mattei, N., Walsh, T.: Computational aspects of multi-winner approval voting. In: Proceedings of AAMAS-2015, pp. 107–115 (2015)
4. Betzler, N., Slinko, A., Uhlmann, J.: On the computation of fully proportional representation. J. Artif. Intell. Res. **47**, 475–519 (2013)
5. Brill, M., Laslier, J.F., Skowron, P.: Multiwinner approval rules as apportionment methods. J. Theor. Polit. **30**(3), 358–382 (2018)
6. Chakraborty, A., Patro, G., Ganguly, N., Gummadi, K., Loiseau, P.: Equality of voice: Towards fair representation in crowdsourced top-k recommendations. In: Proceedings of FAT-2019, pp. 129–138 (2019)
7. Chamberlin, B., Courant, P.: Representative deliberations and representative decisions: proportional representation and the Borda rule. Am. Polit. Sci. Rev. **77**(3), 718–733 (1983)
8. Choi, S., Ko, S., Han, Y.: A movie recommendation algorithm based on genre correlations. Expert Syst. Appl. **39**(9), 8079–8085 (2012)
9. Elkind, E., Faliszewski, P., Laslier, J., Skowron, P., Slinko, A., Talmon, N.: What do multiwinner voting rules do? An experiment over the two-dimensional Euclidean domain. In: Proceedings of AAAI-2017, pp. 494–501 (2017)
10. Elkind, E., Faliszewski, P., Skowron, P., Slinko, A.: Properties of multiwinner voting rules. Soc. Choice Welfare **48**(3), 599–632 (2017)
11. Faliszewski, P., Sawicki, J., Schaefer, R., Smolka, M.: Multiwinner voting in genetic algorithms. IEEE Intell. Syst. **32**(1), 40–48 (2017)
12. Faliszewski, P., Skowron, P., Slinko, A., Talmon, N.: Multiwinner rules on paths from k-Borda to Chamberlin-Courant. In: Proceedings of IJCAI-2017, pp. 192–198 (2017)
13. Faliszewski, P., Skowron, P., Slinko, A., Talmon, N.: Multiwinner voting: a new challenge for social choice theory. In: Endriss, U. (ed.) Trends in Computational Social Choice. AI Access Foundation (2017)
14. Fruchterman, T., Reingold, E.: Graph drawing by force-directed placement. Software: Pract. Exp. **21**(11), 1129–1164 (1991)
15. Ghosh, S., Mundhe, M., Hernandez, K., Sen, S.: Voting for movies: the anatomy of recommender systems. In: Proceedings of the 3rd Annual Conference on Autonomous Agents, pp. 434–435 (1999)
16. Godziszewski, M., Batko, P., Skowron, P., Faliszewski, P.: An analysis of approval-based committee rules for 2d-Euclidean elections. In: Proceedings of AAAI-2021. pp. 5448–5455 (2021)
17. Hagberg, A., Swart, P., Chult, D.: Exploring network structure, dynamics, and function using NetworkX. Tech. rep., Los Alamos National Lab. (LANL), Los Alamos, NM (United States) (2008)
18. Harper, F.M., Konstan, J.: The movielens datasets: History and context. ACM Trans. Interact. Intell. Syst. **5**(4), 19:1–19:19 (2016)
19. Jones, K.S.: Index term weighting. Inf. Storage Retrieval **9**(11), 619–633 (1973)
20. Jones, K.S.: A statistical interpretation of term specificity and its application in retrieval. J. Docum. **60**(5), 493–502 (2004)
21. Kim, Y., Kim, K., Park, C., Yu, H.: Sequential and diverse recommendation with long tail. In: Proceedings of IJCAI-2019, pp. 2740–2746 (2019)
22. Lackner, M., Skowron, P.: Approval-based committee voting: Axioms, algorithms, and applications. Tech. Rep. arXiv:2007.01795 [cs.GT], arXiv.org (Jul 2020)

23. Lackner, M., Skowron, P.: Utilitarian welfare and representation guarantees of approval-based multiwinner rules. Artif. Intell. **288**, 103366 (2020)
24. Lu, T., Boutilier, C.: Budgeted social choice: from consensus to personalized decision making. In: Proceedings of IJCAI-2011, pp. 280–286 (2011)
25. Mondal, A., Bal, R., Sinha, S., Patro, G.: Two-sided fairness in non-personalised recommendations. Tech. Rep. arXiv:2011.05287 [cs.AI], arXiv.org (Nov 2020)
26. Nemhauser, G., Wolsey, L., Fisher, M.: An analysis of approximations for maximizing submodular set functions. Math. Program. **14**(1), 265–294 (1978)
27. Ounis, I.: Inverse document frequency. In: Liu, L., Ozsu, M.T. (eds.) Encyclopedia of Database Systems. Springer, Boston (2018). https://doi.org/10.1007/978-0-387-39940-9_933
28. Phonexay, V., Park, D., Xinchang, K., Hao, F.: An efficient movie recommendation algorithm based on improved k-clique. Hum. Cent. Comput. Inf. Sci. **8**, 38 (2018)
29. Pourghanbar, M., Kelarestaghi, M., Eshghi, F.: EVEBO: a new election inspired optimization algorithm. In: Proceedings of CEC-2015. pp. 916–924 (2015)
30. Procaccia, A., Rosenschein, J., Zohar, A.: On the complexity of achieving proportional representation. Soc. Choice Welfare **30**(3), 353–362 (2008)
31. Ricci, F., Rokach, L., Shapira, B. (eds.): Recommender Systems Handbook. Springer, New York (2015). https://doi.org/10.1007/978-0-387-85820-3
32. Robertson, S., Walker, S.: On relevance weights with little relevance information. In: Proceedings of SIGIR-1997, pp. 16–24 (1997)
33. Sarwar, B., Karypis, G., Konstan, J., Riedl, J.: Item-based collaborative filtering recommendation algorithms. In: Proceedings of WWW-2001, pp. 285–295 (2001)
34. Skowron, P., Faliszewski, P., Lang, J.: Finding a collective set of items: From proportional multirepresentation to group recommendation. Artif. Intell. **241**, 191–216 (2016)
35. Thiele, T.: Om flerfoldsvalg. In: Oversigt over det Kongelige Danske Videnskabernes Selskabs Forhandlinger, pp. 415–441 (1895)
36. Yager, R.: On ordered weighted averaging aggregation operators in multicriteria decisionmaking. IEEE Trans. Syst. Man Cybern. **18**(1), 183–190 (1988)

Allocating Teams to Tasks: An Anytime Heuristic Competence-Based Approach

Athina Georgara[1,2]($\boxtimes$), Juan A. Rodríguez-Aguilar[1], and Carles Sierra[1]

[1] Artificial Intelligence Research Institute, CSIC, Barcelona, Spain
`ageorg@iiia.csic.es`
[2] Enzyme Advising Group, Barcelona, Spain

Abstract. Many practical applications often need to form a team of agents to solve a task since no agent alone has the full set of required competencies to complete the task on time. Here we address the problem of distributing individuals in non-overlapping teams, each team in charge of a specific task. We provide the formalisation of the problem, we encode it as a linear program and show how hard it is to solve it. Given this, we propose an anytime heuristic algorithm that yields feasible team allocations that are good enough solutions. Finally, we report the results of an experimental evaluation over the concrete problem of matching teams of students to internship programs in companies.

Keywords: Team formation · Task allocation · Optimisation · Heuristics

1 Introduction

Many real-world problems require allocating teams of individuals to tasks. For instance, forming teams of robots for search and rescue missions [6], forming teams of Unmanned Aerial Vehicles (UAVs) for surveillance [28], building teams of people to perform projects in a company [31], or grouping students to undertake school projects [4]. In this paper, we study the allocation of many teams to many tasks with size constraints, permitting no overlaps. That is, each agent can be part of at most one team, each team can be allocated to at most one task, and each task must be solved by at most one team. We illustrate our results in the domain of education, where it is very common that students shall form teams and collaborate with their teammates towards some common goal. For example, in primary and secondary schools teachers usually need to divide their students into study groups (teams) to carry out some school projects. Similarly, in universities, students are usually requested to work in teams in order to carry out semester projects. Moreover, educational authorities often need to form student teams and match them with internship programs, as it is more and more

*Research supported by projects AI4EU (H2020-825619), TAILOR (H2020-952215), 2019DI17, Humane-AI-Net (H2020-952026), Crowd4SDG (H2020-872944), and grant PID2019-104156GB-I00 funded by MCIN/AEI/10.13039/501100011033.

D. Baumeister and J. Rothe (Eds.): EUMAS 2022, LNAI 13442, pp. 152–170, 2022.
https://doi.org/10.1007/978-3-031-20614-6_9

common that students spend time with companies to gain experience in the industry. Currently, teachers and education authorities obtain such allocations mainly by hand, but given the combinatorial nature of the problem, manual allocation requires a large amount of work. Beyond the activities within classrooms, the problem of allocating non-overlapping teams to tasks can also be found in events and competitions where participants need to work in teams and compete with each other, such as hackathons; or in situations where different teams need to work in parallel towards a common goal, and individuals cannot be in more than one team at a time, such as in search and rescue missions.

The multi-agent systems (MAS) literature has tackled the problem of allocating teams to tasks in several ways. The existing literature includes research on how to form a *single team* and allocate it to a *single* task [1,2,23]; how to form a *single team* and match it with *multiple tasks* [11]; and how to form *multiple teams* to solve the *very same* task [4]. Moreover, there is a handful of research works on forming *multiple teams* to match with *multiple tasks*, either by allowing *agent overlaps* (agents participate in multiple teams [6]), and/or *task overlaps* (different teams jointly solve a task [5]). However, the problem of distributing agents in non-overlapping teams, each to solve a different task, has deserved little attention, with the exception of [12,29,30]. This *non-overlapping many teams to many tasks* (NOMTMT) allocation problem is the one we address in this paper.

In most works, regardless of the type of team allocation problem, the allocation is decided based on due to agents' competences. As noted in [4], the literature on team composition and formation considers either a Boolean model of competences (an agent has or has not a competence) [1,2,12,23], or a graded model (an agent has a competence up to some degree) [3,4,7]. In many cases, competences are not explicitly considered, but they are 'concealed' behind some utility function [5,6,29]. Common to all these models is the assumption that a team assigned to a task must possess the competences *exactly* as required by the task. This is rather limiting to cope with real-world problems. For instance, even if a student does not posses a specific competence, they might still be qualified for a task if any of their already-acquired competences is similar enough. However, the semantic relationship between competences has been disregarded when matching teams to tasks. This prevents, for instance, that a team is allocated to a task requiring competences *similar* to those offered by the team. Against this background, here we make headway in the non-overlapping "many teams to many tasks" matching problem through the following novel contributions:[1]

1. A method for computing the semantic matching between a task and a team based on an ontology of competences.
2. A formalisation of the NOMTMT allocation problem as an optimisation problem together with a complexity analysis.
3. An integer linear programming (ILP) encoding for solving optimally the NOMTMT allocation problem.
4. An anytime heuristic algorithm to solve the NOMTMT allocation problem.
5. A threefold empirical evaluation: *(a)* we compare our heuristic algorithm against CPLEX [20] using synthetic data, and show that it outperforms CPLEX

---

[1] This work is an extended version of our earlier work presented in [16,17].

in terms of solving time; *(b)* we use real-world data from students that must be allocated to internships, and show that our heuristic algorithm solves large problem instances that CPLEX cannot handle; and *(c)* a group of experts in education confirm that the allocations produced by our heuristic algorithm are better than those manually produced by experienced teachers.

2   The NOMTMT Allocation Problem

This section formally casts our problem as an optimisation one. To do so, we first refer to the basic concepts of the problem, then we discuss the competence model to be used, and finally we define the problem as an optimisation problem.

2.1   Basic Concepts

A *competence* corresponds to a specified capability, skill, or knowledge. We assume there is a known, predefined and fixed set of competences, denoted by $\mathcal{C}$. A *task* is characterised by a set of requirements on agents' competences and team size constraints. For instance, an internship program in a computer tech company might require three competences (ML principles, coding in Python, and web development), and a team of size four. Thus, the company needs four employees that together possess the three required competences. In general, there might be further constraints, such as temporal or spatial constraints (i.e., when and where the task can be realised). However, within the scope of this paper, we only focus on team size constraints. The competences' relative importance is often part of the task description. Formally, a *task* τ is a tuple $\langle \text{t\_id}, C, w, s \rangle$, where t_id is a unique task identifier, $C \subseteq \mathcal{C}$ is the set of required competences, $w : C \rightarrow (0,1]$ is a function that weighs the importance of competences, and $s \in \mathbb{N}_+$ is the required team size. The set of all tasks to perform is denoted by T, with $|T| = m$. We describe each *agent* via its acquired competences. Thus, an agent a is given by a tuple $\langle \text{a\_id}, C' \rangle$, where a_id is a unique agent identifier, and $C' \subseteq \mathcal{C}$ is a set of acquired competences. The set of agents is denoted by A, with $|A| = n$. Given $\tau \in T$, we denote the set of all size-compliant teams for τ as $\mathcal{K}_\tau = \{K \subseteq A : |K| = s_\tau\}^2$, where s_τ is the team size required by task τ.

2.2   Competence Coverage and Affinity

To match a team with a task, it is essential that the team is capable of solving the task. That is, before allocating a team of agents K to some task τ, we need to verify whether the agents, as a team, are equipped with the necessary competences, as determined by C_τ. Given a task τ and a team of agents K, we say that K is suitable for τ if K can *cover the required competences* of τ. That is, for each required competence $c \in C_\tau$, there is at least one agent $a \in K$ with

---

[2] Note: we use subscript a to refer to the set of competences and the identifier of an agent $a \in A$, and subscript τ to refer to the elements of task $\tau \in T$.

competence c. As mentioned above, the existing literature considers competences as Boolean or graded features and determines the 'matching quality' of a team when assigned to a task through some function, usually expressed as a utility function. As already mentioned, the existing models are limiting. To overcome such limits we consider the matching quality in terms of the semantic similarity between competences required by tasks and offered by teams. Here we present an intuitive way of determining this 'matching quality' as *competence coverage*.

Given some domains, competences are usually structured by an ontology which determines similarities between different competences. For example, competences c_1 (coding in Python) and c_2 (coding in Java), are different, but share essential principles (e.g. both are object-oriented languages). We can therefore assume that an agent with competence c_1 can somewhat be adequate for a task requiring competence c_2.

We assume that there is a known competence ontology which structures the competences in $\mathcal{C}$ according to their semantics, and for every pair of competences c, c' provides a *similarity degree* $\text{sim}(c, c') \in [0, 1]$. Let assume that the ontology is structured as an acyclic directed graph, where each node is a specialised, refined version of its parent node. In Sect. 5, we exploit well-established ontologies with such properties. We compute the semantic similarity between two competences c, c' as: $\text{sim}(c, c') = e^{-\lambda l} \frac{e^{\kappa h} - e^{-\kappa h}}{e^{\kappa h} + e^{-\kappa h}}$ if $l \neq 0$ and 1 otherwise, where: l is the shortest path in the graph between c and c'; h is the depth of the deepest competence subsuming both c and c'; and $\kappa, \lambda \in [1, 2]$ are parameters regulating the influence of l and h on the similarity metric. Our semantic similarity function is a variation of the metric introduced in [24], which guarantees the reflexive property of similarity: a node is maximally similar to itself, independently of its depth. In other words, nodes at zero distance ($l = 0$) have maximum similarity. Similarly to [27], the values of semantic similarities lie in $[0, 1]$.

Given this, we assume that an agent a can cover competence c with degree $\text{cvg}(c, a) = \max_{c' \in C_a} \text{sim}(c, c')$. Then, given a task τ with required competences C_τ and an agent a with acquired competences C_a, the competence coverage of task τ by agent a is: $\text{cvg}(a, C_\tau) = \prod_{c \in C_\tau} \text{cvg}(c, a) = \prod_{c \in C_\tau} \max_{c' \in C_a} \{\text{sim}(c, c')\}$. The product captures a's competence coverage over *all* competences.

Moving now from a single agent to a team of agents, allocating a team to a task requires to solve a *competence assignment problem*.[3] That is, given a task τ, we need to assign to each agent a in a team K a subset of competences of C_τ for which it will be responsible. As such, for each pair $\langle \tau, K \rangle$ we need a *competence assignment function* $\eta_{\tau \to K} : K \to 2^C_\tau$ that maps each agent in K with a subset of the required competencies. According to [4], a competence assignment function (CAF) for a size-compliant team of agents $K \in \mathcal{K}_\tau$ and a task τ is such that $\bigcup_{a \in K} \eta_{\tau \to K}(a) = C_\tau$. Moreover, we consider the reverse competence assignment function (r-CAF), denoted by $\theta_{\tau \to K} : C_\tau \to 2^K$, where $\theta_{\tau \to K}(c)$ indicates the agents that are assigned to cover competence c. Note that $\Theta_{\tau \to K}$

---

[3] As noted by [22], recent definitions on the term team refer to the specific subtask/ competences that will be performed by each agent.

contains $|C_\tau| \cdot (2^{|K|-1})$ different CAFs. However, not all CAFs are equivalent or equally desired. Hence, here we adopt the concept of *fair competence assignment function (FCAF)* following the notion of *inclusive assignments* in [3] by adding an upper bound on the number of competences that can be assigned to an agent. An FCAF ensures that each competence required by the task τ is covered by at least one agent, and each agent covers at least one and at most $\left\lceil \frac{|C_\tau|}{|K|} \right\rceil$ competences. This bound avoids overloading a few very competent agents with excessive responsibilities.

Therefore, given an FCAF $\eta_{\tau \to K}$, we want to evaluate the suitability of a given team K for task τ. To do so, we first define a team's *competence affinity* with respect to a task taking into consideration the importance of each competence and the agents' assigned competences while satisfying the following requirements: *(i)* the higher the coverage of an assigned competence, the higher the competence affinity; *(ii)* the lower the importance of an assigned competence, the higher the competence affinity; and *(iii)* the competence affinity is at most equal to the coverage of any assigned competence with maximal importance. Formally, we define an agent's competence affinity as:

Definition 1 *(Agents' Competence Affinity).* Given an agent $a \in A$, a task $\tau \in T$, and a competence assignment function $\eta_{\tau \to K}$, the competence affinity of a to τ is:

$$\text{aff}(a, \tau, \eta_{\tau \to K}) = \prod_{c \in \eta_{\tau \to K}(a)} \max\left\{ (1 - w_\tau(c)), \text{cvg}(c, a) \right\}. \tag{1}$$

Since we are targeting FCAFs, i.e., we want balanced assignments of responsibilities, the competence affinity of a team of agents $K \subseteq A$ to task τ is defined a-la-Nash, as the product[4] of the competence affinity of the individuals in K to τ with respect to some fair competence assignment function $\eta_{\tau \to K}$ The product assigns a larger value to teams where all agents equally contribute to a task, rather than to teams with unbalanced contributions.

Definition 2 *(Team's Competence Affinity).* Given a team of agents $K \subseteq A$, a task $\tau \in T$, and a fair competence assignment $\eta_{\tau \to K}$, the competence affinity of K to τ is:

$$\text{aff}(K, \tau, \eta_{\tau \to K}) = \prod_{a \in K} \text{aff}(a, \tau, \eta_{\tau \to K}). \tag{2}$$

Observe that the competence affinity of a team to a task depends on the competence assignment function. In other words, for a given team K and a given task τ, different competence assignment functions result in different competence affinities. Finding the competence assignment function that yields the highest competence affinity is in fact an optimisation problem in itself:

$$\eta^*_{\tau \to K} = \underset{\eta \in \Theta_{\tau \to K}}{\text{argmax}} \ \text{aff}(K, \tau, \eta) \tag{3}$$

---

[4] As noted in [9], the product favours both increases in overall team utility and inequality-reducing distributions of individuals' contributing values.

where $\Theta_{\tau \to K}$ denotes the family of all CAFs for task τ and team K.

However, considering that, in practice, for a task τ both team size s_τ and the number of required competences $|C_\tau|$ are relatively small (2–5 members, and ≤ 10, respectively), solving this sub-problem optimally, e.g. by means of a linear program, is rather inexpensive. With this in mind, the optimum team for task τ is the one that: (i) maximises competence affinity; and (ii) satisfies the team size requirement. Note that the size of $\mathcal{K}_\tau$, which is the set of all size-compliant teams, is $\binom{n}{s_\tau}$. The optimum team K^* is the one that maximises competence affinity, under an optimal competence assignment function: $K^* = arg\,max_{K \in \mathcal{K}_\tau}\ \text{aff}(K, \tau, \eta^*_{\tau \to K})$.

2.3   The Optimisation Problem

Finding a good allocation of agents for a collection of tasks is yet another optimisation problem that tries to maximise the *overall* competence affinity of all teams for their assigned tasks. For a single task τ, the best candidate would be the team that maximises the competence affinity, that is, $K^* = arg\,max_{K \in \mathcal{K}_\tau}\ \text{aff}(K, \tau, \eta^*_{\tau \to K})$. For a collection of tasks T, with $|T| > 1$, we must maximise the competence affinity of all candidate teams with the tasks each one is matched to, given that each agent can participate in at most one team, each team can be allocated to at most one task, and each task can be assigned to at most one team. First we need to formally define what is a Feasible Team Allocation Function (FTAF), and then proceed on finding the optimum one, i.e., the one that maximises the competence affinity.

Definition 3 *(Feasible Team Allocation Function (FTAF))*. Given a set of tasks T, and a set of agents A, a feasible team allocation function g is a function $g : T \to 2^A$ such that: (1) every task $\tau \in T$ is allocated its requested number of agents, so that $|g(\tau)| = s_\tau$; and (2) an agent can only be assigned to one team: for every pair of tasks $\tau, \tau' \in T$, such that $\tau \neq \tau'$, it holds that $g(\tau) \cap g(\tau') = \emptyset$.

The family of all feasible team allocation functions is denoted by G. To achieve balanced allocations, the optimum team allocation function g^* maximises the product of competence affinities of the teams to their assigned tasks.

Definition 4 *(Non-Overlapping   Many   Teams   to   Many Tasks (NOMTMT) Allocation Problem)*. Given a set of tasks T, and a set of agents A, the *Non-Overlapping Many Teams to Many Tasks Allocation Problem* is to find a team allocation function $g^* \in G$ that maximises the overall team affinity:

$$g^* = \underset{g \in G}{\text{argmax}} \prod_{\tau \in T} \text{aff}(g(\tau), \tau, \eta^*_{\tau \to g(\tau)}) \tag{4}$$

Note that in a NOMTMT allocation problem, for each team allocation $g \in G$ and each task τ we need to find the competence assignment function with the highest competence affinity for team $g(\tau)$, namely $\eta^*_{\tau \to g(\tau)}$. Thus, for each team allocation we need to solve $|T|$ optimisation problems (one per task) in order to determine $\eta^*_{\tau \to g(\tau)}$.[5] Here we want to highlight that the problem we address here is a non-trivial generalisation of the problem tackled in [4], which unlike us only copes with forming teams for a single task. Next, we show that the NOMTMT allocation problem is $\mathcal{NP}$-complete by reduction to a well-known problem.

Theorem 1. *The NOMTMT allocation problem for more than one task is $\mathcal{NP}$-complete.*

Proof. Due to space limitations, the proof can be found in: https://bit.ly/3A2uoSK.

Notably, the problem we solve here can be cast as a cooperative game [8] where the agents and the tasks correspond to the players—with the constraint that exactly one task-player must exist in each coalition—and the competence affinity comprise the game's utility function. Therefore, we would seek for the a coalition structure that maximizes the *Nash Social Welfare* [26].

3 Solving the NOMTMT Allocation Problem Optimally

Here we encode the NOMTMT allocation problem (Definition 4) as a linear program. First, for each task $\tau \in T$ and each size-compliant team $K \in \mathcal{K}_\tau$, we use a binary decision variable x^τ_K to indicate whether team K is assigned to task τ in the solution. Then, solving a NOMTMT allocation problem amounts to solving the following non-linear program:

$$\max \prod_{\tau \in T} \prod_{K \in \mathcal{K}_\tau} \left(\text{aff}(K, \tau, \eta^*_{\tau \to K}) \right)^{x^\tau_K} \tag{5}$$

subject to:

$$\sum_{K \subseteq \mathcal{K}_\tau} x^\tau_K \leq 1 \qquad \forall \tau \in T \tag{5a}$$

$$\sum_{\substack{\tau \in T}} \sum_{\substack{K \subseteq \mathcal{K}_\tau \\ a \in A}} x^\tau_K \leq 1 \qquad \forall a \in A \tag{5b}$$

$$x^\tau_K \in \{0, 1\} \qquad \forall K \subseteq A, \tau \in T \tag{5c}$$

Constraints (5b) ensure that each agent will be assigned to at most one task; while constraints (5a) guarantee that each task is assigned to at most one team. Notice that the objective function (Eq. (5)) is non-linear. Nevertheless, we linearise it by maximising the logarithm of $\prod_{\tau \in T} \prod_{K \in \mathcal{K}_\tau} \left(\text{aff}(K, \tau, \eta^*_{\tau \to K}) \right)^{x^\tau_K}$. Thus, solving the non-linear program above is equivalent to solving the following binary linear program:

---

[5] Note that the NOMTMT allocation problem is interrelated with the $|T|$ optimisation problems. However, for a fixed team allocation, the inner optimisation problems are independent from one another.

$$\max \sum_{\tau \in T} \sum_{K \in \mathcal{K}_\tau} x_K^\tau \cdot \log \left(1 + \mathrm{aff}(K, \tau, \eta_{\tau \to K}^*) \right) \tag{6}$$

subject to: Eqs. (5a), (5b), and (5c). Note that the above is an equivalent optimisation problem: without affecting the monotonicity of the function *(i)* we use the $\log(\cdot)$ to convert the double product to double sum, and the powered factor into a product; and *(ii)* we change the function's domain to avoid $\log(0)$. We can solve this LP with the aid of an off-the-shelf solver (e.g. CPLEX [20], Gurobi [19]), GLPK [18], or SCIP [15]). Given sufficient time, an LP solver will return an optimal solution to the NOMTMT allocation problem.

Note that building such an LP requires to pre-compute the values of $\mathrm{aff}(K, \tau, \eta_{\tau \to K}^*)$, which amounts to solving an optimisation problem for each pair of team and task. This leads to large LPs as the number of agents and tasks grow.

4   An Algorithm for the NOMTMT Allocation Problem

Our proposed algorithm consists of two stages in a similar manner as in [4]—as we already said, our problem is a generalisation. The first stage finds an initial feasible allocation of teams to tasks. The second one iteratively improves the allocation by swapping agents between pairs of teams using different strategies.

4.1   Building an Initial Team Allocation

The algorithm finds an initial, feasible, and *promising* team allocation. It sequentially picks up a team for each task, starting from the 'hardest' task to the 'lightest' one. We consider that a task is 'hard' if there are just a few agents that can cover its competences. Picking teams for the harder tasks first is a heuristic to avoid that the few agents that can cover it are picked by other 'simpler' tasks.

Computing the Allocation Hardness of Tasks. We measure the *allocation hardness* of each task (referred as 'hardness' hereafter) by considering the competences required by the task with respect to the capabilities of *all* available agents. Intuitively, the more agents offering high coverage of competence c, the less hard a task requiring c is. Specifically, to characterise the hardness of competences, and therefore the hardness of tasks, we exploit the notion of *moment of inertia* based on [25]. We measure the hardness of a task as the hardness to cover its competences based on the agent's competences. That is, each agent can cover each competence with an affinity in range $[0, 1]$. Thus, we capture the effort to cover a competence as best as possible similar to the effort to rotate a rigid body around some axis. In other words, we see the distribution of all agents' coverage of a competence as the mass distribution of a rigid body. In our case, the chosen axis to rotate around represents the ideal competence coverage, i.e., where all agents cover the competence with utmost affinity. We compute the moment of inertia for c as: $I(c) = \sum_{J \in \mathcal{I}} n_J^c \cdot (1 - mid(J))^2$, where: (i) $\mathcal{I} = \{[0, 0.1),$ $[0.1, 0.2), [0.2, 0.3), [0.3, 0.4), [0.4, 0.5), [0.5, 0.6), [0.6, 0.7), [0.7, 0.8), [0.8, 0.9),$

$[0.9, 1]\}$ is an interval partition of the domain of competence coverage $[0, 1]$; (ii) $n_J^c = |\{a \in A|\text{cvg}(c, a) \in J\}|$ is the number of agents in A whose coverage of competence c lies within interval J, and hence represents the *mass* of c in the interval; and (iii) $mid(J)$ corresponds to the midpoint of interval J.

Now, we compute the hardness of each task from the hardness of each one of the competences that it requires (inversely proportional to the moment of inertia of its competences) as well as their relative importance weights. Thus, given task τ, we define its hardness as $h(\tau) = \omega \cdot \sum_{c \in C_\tau} w_\tau(c) \cdot I(c)$, where $\omega = \frac{1}{\sum_{c \in C_\tau} w_\tau(c)}$, is a normalising factor over the weights.

Building an Initial Team Allocation. Our algorithm sorts tasks according to their hardness and proceeds by sequentially allocating a team for each task starting from the hardest one. Let $A_\tau \subseteq A$ be the set of available agents to allocate to τ. First, the algorithm sorts the task's competences, C_τ, based on their relative importance, into a sequence $\bar{C}_\tau$. We note as $\bar{C}_\tau^i$ the i-th competence in $\bar{C}_\tau$. To allocate an agent to the top competence in the sequence, $\bar{C}_\tau^1$, we select the agent that best covers the competence. Formally, we compute the agent to allocate to $\bar{C}_\tau^1$ as $\sigma(\bar{C}_\tau^1) = arg\,max_{a \in A_\tau}\{\text{cvg}(\bar{C}_\tau^1, a)\}$. After allocating that agent to $\bar{C}_\tau^1$, the set of agents available to allocate to the rest of competences is $A_\tau - \{\sigma(\bar{C}_\tau^1)\}$. In general, given the i-th competence $\bar{C}_\tau^i$, we obtain the agent to allocate to the comptence as: $\sigma(\bar{C}_\tau^i) = arg\,max_{a \in A_\tau - \Sigma_{i-1}}\{\text{cvg}(\bar{C}_\tau^i, a)\}$, where $\Sigma_{i-1} = \bigcup_{k=1}^{i-1}\{\sigma(\bar{C}_\tau^k)\}$ stands for the agents allocated so far up to competence $\bar{C}_\tau^{i-1}$. The selected team for task τ is $K = \bigcup_{i=1}^{s_\tau}\sigma(\bar{C}_\tau^i)$. The agents in K are no longer available for being chosen to participate in another team.

4.2   Improving Team Allocation

The second stage of our algorithm applies several heuristics implemented as *agent swaps*. This stage is similar to the approach proposed in [4], with the addition of an exploring step. The heuristics are applied until either: (1) the global maximum competence affinity is reached; (2) no solution improvement occurs for a number of iterations; or (3) the algorithm is stopped by the user. In all cases, the most recently found solution is returned. This stage performs two types of iterations:

1. **Single pairing.** We randomly select two tasks, and we apply over them the following swaps:
   (a) **Exploiting swap.** Find the optimal team allocation just considering the agents in the teams currently allocated to both tasks.
   (b) **Exploring swap.** Try a maximum of k times the following: (i) randomly select one of the two tasks, one agent within that task and an unassigned agent (if any); (ii) swap them; (iii) if the competence affinity is improved, keep the change and stop the exploring swaps.
2. **Exhaustive pairing.** For *every* pair of tasks, swap every possible pair of agents within them. If the competence affinity is improved, keep the change and stop the exhaustive pairing.

5   Empirical Analysis

We evaluated our algorithm regarding: (1) the quality of solutions; (2) the time required to produce optimal solutions; (3) its performance when solving a real-world problem. Importantly, our algorithm was validated by experts on team formation by comparing the allocations computed by our algorithm with respect to the allocations provided by teachers with expertise in team formation.

Table 1. Time savings to reach optimality *wrt.* CPLEX.

Scenario	Time Savings *wrt.* CPLEX(%)
Small (10 Tasks)	60%
Medium (15 Tasks)	55%
Large (20 Tasks)	71%

We ran all the experiments on a PC with Intel Core i7 CPU, 8 cores, and 8GB RAM. The implementation of our algorithm, along with all the necessary supporting code, was made in Python3.7. In all experiments, we set our algorithm's parameters as follows: to compute similarities we used $\kappa = 0.35, \lambda = 0.75$; we performed one exhaustive-pairing every 50 single-pairings; we stopped the algorithm after completing two rounds of 50 single-pairings and after two rounds of exhaustive pairings elapsed with no improvements. In what follows, in Sect. 5.1, we pitch our algorithm against CPLEX to study its quality, as well as its runtime and anytime performance. In Sect. 5.2, we solve a real-world problem and study our algorithm's behaviour as the team-size parameter changes. Finally, in Sect. 5.3, we compare the quality of our algorithm's allocations with the ones obtained by experts in team formation.

5.1   Quality, Runtime and Anytime Analysis

Generating Problem Instances. In this analysis, we used as competence ontology the taxonomy developed by the Institute for the Development of Vocational Training for Workers (ISFOL) [21]. For comparison purposes, we built 3 families of problem instances of different sizes (small, medium, large) that could all be solved by CPLEX within acceptable time limits. We synthetically generated agents, competencies and tasks as follows. First, we generated the tasks to perform. We started by fixing a number of tasks from $\{10, 15, 20\}$. After that, for each task τ we sampled: its required team size $m_\tau \sim \mathcal{U}\{1, 3\}$; its number of required competencies $|C_\tau| \sim \mathcal{U}\{2, 5\}$; and its importance weights $c \in C_\tau$ is $w_\tau(c) \sim \mathcal{N}\big(\mu = \mathcal{U}(0, 1), \sigma \sim \mathcal{U}(0.01, 0.1)\big)$. Second, we generated agents to perform tasks. For each task τ, we generated m_τ agents such that the competencies of each agent contain competencies that are either identical or a child-node in the ISFOL taxonomy of some required competence in τ. Our experiments involve 60 problem instances distributed in three families: (1) 20 instances with 10 tasks and ~20.5 agents (average number of agents over 20 problem instances); (2) 20 instances with 15 tasks and ~30.6 agents (average over 20); and (3) 20 instances with 20 tasks and ~41.35 agents (average over 20).

Quality Analysis. Figure 1a shows the evolution of the *quality* of our heuristic algorithm calculated as the ratio between the competence affinity of the solutions computed by our algorithm and the optimal competence affinity computed by CPLEX. The figure plots the average of the quality ratio achieved by our algorithm along time over 20 problem instances per scenario: low-size (10 tasks), medium-size (15 tasks), large-size (20 tasks). Variances for all cases are insignificant, $\leq 5 \cdot 10^{-4}$, and hence we do not plot them. The timestamps are also averages over the 20 problem instances. Notice that our heuritic algorithm reaches optimality (quality 1), likewise CPLEX, in the three scenarios.

Runtime Analysis. The greatest advantage of our heuristic algorithm is that it is much faster than CPLEX. Table 1 shows the time we can save with respect to CPLEX to reach optimality. Overall, using our heuristic can save from ~55% to ~71% time with respect to CPLEX. Specifically, for problem instances with 10 tasks (small scenario), we save 60% time *wrt.* CPLEX; for problem instances with 15 tasks (medium scenario), we save 55% time; and, for problem instances with 20 tasks (large scenario) we save 71% time *wrt.* CPLEX. Note that the main time consuming task for CPLEX is building of the LP encoding the problem.

Anytime Analysis. Let t_{opt} be the seconds required by CPLEX to reach optimality. Our algorithm finds the first solution: (1) after $10^{-3} \cdot t_{opt} \, (= 0.06)$ seconds with a quality at 80% of the quality of the optimal in the small scenario, (2) after $25 \cdot 10^{-3} \cdot t_{opt} \, (= 0.12)$ seconds and 70% in the medium scenario, and (3) after $2 \cdot 10^{-4} \cdot t_{opt} \, (= 0.29)$ seconds and 65% in the large scenario (see Table 2).

5.2   Solving a Real-World Problem

As mentioned earlier, in the domain of education there is a need to allocate teams of students to internship programs. Each student is equipped with competencies, determined through the student's educational background (type of school, enrolment year, completed courses, past educational activities, etc.), while each internship specifies a set of required competencies for the team. In this part of the experimental analysis, we used *real-world data*. Specifically, we count on

Table 2. Quality of the initial solution, the time needed in seconds, and the proportion of time compared to the time required by CPLEX (t_{opt}).

Scenario	Quality	Time in sec	Proportion of t_{opt}
Small (10 Tasks)	80%	0.06 s	10^{-3}
Medium (15 Tasks)	70%	0.12 s	$25 \cdot 10^{-3}$
Large (20 Tasks)	65%	0.29 s	$2 \cdot 10^{-4}$

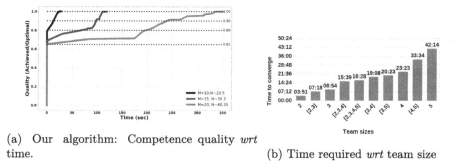

(a) Our algorithm: Competence quality *wrt* time.

(b) Time required *wrt* team size

Fig. 1. Quality analysis and scalability.

a collection of 100 students whose competencies are described in the European Skills/Competences qualifications and Occupations (ESCO) [13] ontology. ESCO consists of a dictionary that describes, identifies and classifies professional occupations, skills, and qualifications relevant for the EU labour market and education and training. The ESCO ontology is a directed acyclic graph structure of 6547 different competencies, with 7 levels, and an average branching factor of 1.26 (maximum branching factor 15). The collection of students in our dataset is equipped with 118 different competencies, on average with 11.98 each. We also used a collection of 50 real internship programs, whose competencies are also described in ESCO. All 50 internships required 34 different competencies, while each internship required on average 4 competencies.

Our following analysis shows the problem's scalability as required team sizes grow, and investigates the ability of our algorithm to handle the problem. Due to the fact that the actual data regarding tasks (internship programs) did not specify a required team size, we synthetically created problem instances of certain team sizes. Specifically, we used datasets where all tasks required the same team size, i.e., where all tasks required *equal* team sizes (either 2, 3, 4, or 5). These team sizes are based on the following observation in [3]: "teams that are formed within an educational environment shall not exceed 5 members." Moreover, we also created problem instances where tasks required *varying* team sizes (team sizes in $[2, 3]$, in $[2, 4]$, in $[2, 5]$, in $[3, 4]$, in $[3, 5]$, and in $[4, 5]$), where the team sizes are equally distributed across the tasks within each problem instance. Consider the scenario requiring teams of equal size 5 and 100 agents. The search space has $\sim 7.5 \cdot 10^7$ different teams of size 5. To solve such a hard scenario instance optimally (e.g., by using CPLEX), we would need to produce ~ 75 millions of decision variables just for a single internship with team size 5. Thus, generating the LP encodings for the problem instances considered here is totally infeasible.

Analysis. Figure 1b shows the time required to converge to a solution as the average over 20 different problem instances with 100 agents and 20 tasks. The bars illustrate the average time (in minutes:seconds) needed by our algorithm to output an allocation per team size. As expected, settings with smaller team sizes require much less time until they converge to a solution. In general, the time needed by a problem instance requiring team sizes in $[a, b]$ falls between the times needed *(a)* by the problems requiring team sizes a and b, and *(b)* by the problems requiring team sizes in $[a, b-1]$ and $[a+1, b]$. Notably, we need less than 50 minutes to yield a solution in settings where each task requires a team of size 5, which is the hardest scenario. We deem this is acceptable considering that this process is not required to run in real time with very demanding time constraints. Note that the current practice is to match students to internships by hand, which is much more time consuming, while LP solvers cannot even generate the program in time. Hence, our results show the feasibility of employing our algorithm to perform team allocation in the education scenario that we address.

5.3 Validation

Our last analysis focuses on having our algorithm validated by teachers experienced in team formation. For that, we pitched our algorithm against some experts (teachers) with experience in allocating students to internships. Specifically, we synthesised an instance of a task allocation problem involving 50 internships ($m = 50$) and 100 students ($n = 100$) with team sizes within $\{1, 2, 3\}$. Notice that such settings are similar to those employed in our actual-world evaluation in Sect. 5.2. The problem instance used here is the largest one regarding the number of tasks that we can generate with the 100 student profiles at hand. Notably, to solve this problem optimally (e.g. by using CPLEX) would require more than 1.8 million decision variables.

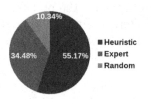

(a) **Single Winner**: Percentage out of 29 tournaments.

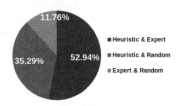

(b) **Tie with 2 Winners**: Percentage out of 17 tournaments.

Fig. 2. Heuristic vs expert vs random.

Thereafter, we proceed as follows. For the very same problem instance: (1) we task an expert with matching by hand teams of students with tasks; (2) we employ our algorithm to compute an allocation; and (3) we compute a random allocation of teams of students to tasks. Henceforth, we note those three allocation methods as g_{expert}, $g_{\text{heuristic}}$, and g_{random} respectively. Then, eight evaluators (teachers as well), who are regularly engaged with the process of allocating

student to internships, were tasked to compare the quality of the three allocations, without knowing the method that produced each allocation. Notably, our
algorithm yielded an allocation in less than 1 h and 45 min, while the experts
reported that they approximately needed a whole working week in order to study
and analyse the students and internship data, and manually build an allocation.

Evaluation Process. Each evaluator was asked to mark the internship assignments produced by each one of the three allocation methods. Thus, each evaluator marked each internship assignment with one of the following marks: 1 for
first option, 2 for second option, and 3 for third option. Notice that we allowed
the evaluators to mark two assignments produced by two different allocation
methods with the same value if they considered them to be equivalent.

Handling Missing Data. Here we want to point out that during this final
analysis, we faced the problem of missing data. That is, the expert did not manage to find a team for every internship. Specifically, the expert did not provide
a team assignment to 13 internships (out of 50), leaving 23 students (out of
100) without internship. This led the evaluators work with incomplete data (two
complete allocations, and a partial one), and, in their turn, provide incomplete
evaluations. In particular, since for some tasks g_{expert} was missing, the evaluators were unable to mark the three allocation methods (g_{expert}, $g_{heuristic}$, and
g_{random}). For this reason we used the auxiliary mark 4 indicating absence, which
is considered worse than third option (mark 3). Therefore, any missing allocation was marked with a 4 by all evaluators. Moreover, eventually the evaluators
missed marking some internships (different interships for each evaluator). In that
case, we generated a third-option mark (3) for missing evaluations.

Analysis. Our analysis is founded on finding the best allocation method for
each internship assignment based on the evaluators' assessments. We consider
the evaluation of each internship assignment as a *tournament* consisting of three
competing rounds between pairs of allocation methods: (1) Heuristic vs Expert;
(2) Heuristic vs Random; (3) Expert vs Random.

The marks set by evaluators allow to pick the winning allocation method
of each round and of the tournament as a whole.[6] The winning allocation
method of each round results from the aggregated marks of evaluators: the
internship assignment with greater aggregated mark wins one point for its allocation method. In case there is a tie between two internship assignments in a
round, their corresponding allocation methods earn half a point each. Using the
points accumulated from each round of a tournament, we apply a Copeland$_\alpha$
voting rule [10] (with $\alpha = 0.5$) to declare the winner of the tournament. As
shown in [14] this voting rule is "resistant to all the standard types of (constructive) electoral control". In short, the allocation method that accumulates more
points throughout the three rounds wins the tournament. Again, in case of a tie
between two allocation methods, each one earns half a point. As an illustratory
example, say that for a given tournament: the 8 evaluators considered that our

---

[6] Notably, the marks applied by the evaluators indicate rankings and therefore these
numbers are meaningless; thus we turn to tournaments.

heuristic algorithm provided the best assignment, 5 evaluators considered that the human expert provided a better assignment than random, and 2 evaluators equally preferred the assignments produced by the human expert and random. That would lead to the following scores: our heuristic algorithm would get $8 \cdot 1$ points, the expert's allocation would get $5 \cdot 1 + 2 \cdot 0.5 = 6$ points, and random would get $2 \cdot 0.5 + 1 \cdot 1 = 2$ points. Therefore, the winner of this tournament would be our algorithm.

Each tournament may have *a single winner*, *a tie with two winners*, or *no winner*. In our evaluation, we encounter 58% over 50 tournaments (i.e., internship assignments) that announced a single winner, and 34% that announced two winners in a tie. Considering only the tournaments that announce a **single winner**, in Fig. 2a we observe that 55.17% of these tournaments announced as winner the allocation yielded by our heuristic algorithm, while 34.48% of the tournaments announced as winner the allocation provided by the human expert. The random allocation method only won 10.34% of the tournaments. Therefore, the evaluators preferred the assignments produced by our algorithm to those produced by a human expert. Consider now the tournaments declaring **2 winners (tie)**. Figure 2b shows that, as expected, our heuristic algorithm and the human expert jointly won more than half of the tournaments (52.94%). Overall, regarding the tournaments declaring a tie with two winners, our heuristic algorithm was part of the winning tie 88.23% of the times. To summarise, our analysis indicates that expert evaluators deem our proposed heuristic algorithm as the method of choice to assign teams of students to internships.

6   Related Work

Team formation has received much attention by the AI and MAS community. Anagnostopoulos et al. in [1] thoroughly study the problem of forming a single team to resolve a single task, and show the employability of several algorithms in large scale communities. Lappas et al. in [23] tackle the problem of finding a single team of experts for a given task in an attempt to minimize the communication cost among the team. [2] study an online version of the team formation problem and propose algorithms in order to form teams as a stream of tasks sequentially arrives (one task at a time). Notably, [2] form a single team for a single task at a time; while agents can be 'reused' in teams of different tasks, permitting overlapping teams. Kurtan et al. [22] study the dependencies between subtasks of a given task, and propose algorithms for building a single team for a single task considering some desired qualities, such as preserving privacy.

Chad et al. [11] add a new dimension to the problem by considering robustness, and focus on finding a single robust team to perform several tasks. Andrejczuck et al. [4] tackle the many teams to single task problem and present algorithms for partitioning a set of agents into equal-size teams in order to perform resolve the very same task. Capezzuto et al. in [6] tackle the many teams to many tasks team formation problem considering temporal and spacial constraints, and propose an anytime, efficient algorithm. However, compared to the problem we tackle here, the proposed algorithm in [6] provides solutions with overlapping teams, and aims to maximise the number of tasks solved per team.

Regarding the many teams to many tasks team formation problem with no overlaps—i.e., problems for which different teams share no common agents, each team can be allocated to only one task, and each task can be assigned to only one team—we can find a handful of works in the literature. Specifically, we have singled out two works, namely [12,29], which can be considered as the most directly related to ours. Although these papers tackle the general *many teams to many tasks* problem, their version of the problem is essentially different to ours, hence preventing us from conducting meaningful comparisons. In more detail, [29] propose a branch-and-bound technique to determine the optimal team size structure and then they proceed with a brute-force search. Given that the problem we tackle in this work assumes that team sizes are known a priori (team size is part of each task's requirements), comparing against [29] would be equivalent to compare against brute-force search. Notably, brute-force search becomes prohibitive as the number of agents and tasks rise; and considering the problem instances in our analysis such a comparison would be infeasible.

On the other hand, Czatnecki and Dutta [12] propose an algorithm for matching non-overlapping teams of robots with tasks. Similarly to [29], [12] sets no constraints on the team sizes. However, even if we could 'bypass' the team size misalignment (by allowing [12] to yield a result, and use these team sizes in our version), there is yet another essential difference between [12] and our approach. Our algorithm pursues to *optimise* the competence affinity between all teams with their assigned tasks while targeting at balanced allocations (i.e., all teams are more or less equally competent for their task). Instead, [12] targets at finding *Nash stable* teams, i.e., teams whose agents have not incentive to unilaterally abandon their current team and task without harming the others. As such, [12] and our approach differ notably in their objectives.

Regardless of the type of team allocation problem, all the works above use a rather simplistic competence model. That is, following the observation in [3], all these works assume either that an agent may have or have not a competence (Boolean) [1,2,12,22,23]; or that an agent may have a competence up to a degree (Graded) [3,4,7]. Nonetheless, all works consider that a team must collectively possess all the required competences, *exactly as requested*. However, in this work we identify that an agent, and therefore a team, can perform a task when they count on competences that are *similar* to the ones required, even if they are not exactly the same. This is natural, especially when the agents correspond to humans. Given that ontologies such as ESCO [13] describe semantic relations among competences, not having a specific competence for a tasks is not an obstacle provided that agents have similar enough competences. For example, when students move from school to industry, they count on competences, acquired at the school, which are not exactly the same as those required by industry. And yet, these student can be considered adequate for jobs in industry. As such, in this work we put forward a methodology to resolve such issues.

7 Conclusions and Future Work

In this work, we studied a particular type of team formation problem, and hence we focused on the *Non-Overlapping Many Teams to Many Tasks* (NOMTMT) allocation problem. First, we provided the formulation of the problem. At this point, we identified and tackled an existing issue regarding the competence models that we find essential when solving real-world cases. As such, we introduced a new ontology-based competence model, and proposed a methodology to compute semantic similarities between the competencies required by a task and those offered by a team. Then, we cast the NOMTMT allocation problem as an optimisation one, and show how to solve optimally it by the means of LP. Thereafter, motivated by the practical limitations of solving the problem optimally, we introduced a novel anytime, heuristic algorithm. Finally, we conducted a three-fold evaluation of our proposed algorithm. Our results: *(i)* showed that our heuristic algorithm can reach optimality in notably less time than an LP solver, saving up to 71% of time; *(ii)* showed that our algorithm can handle large, real-world problems with 100 agents and 20 tasks in less than an hour, while solving the problem optimally is infeasible; and *(iii)* our algorithm outperformed experts while requiring much less time (one hour and half vs a whole working week). Notably, besides the problem's size, another time consuming factor for the human experts is the need of manually discerning the similarities between the competences required by a task and those offered by a team. As future work, we plan to relax our team size constraints, and use instead allowable intervals—e.g., at least 2 and at most 5 members—since, these assumptions are not fundamental to our model. Moreover, we will address the notion of "robustness", and work towards not only forming good allocations, but also forming robust allocations.

References

1. Anagnostopoulos, A., Becchetti, L., Castillo, C., Gionis, A., Leonardi, S.: Power in unity: forming teams in large-scale community systems. In: Proceedings of the 19th ACM Conference on Information and Knowledge Management, CIKM 2010, Toronto, Ontario, Canada, 26-30 October 2010, pp. 599–608, January 2010
2. Anagnostopoulos, A., Becchetti, L., Castillo, C., Gionis, A., Leonardi, S.: Online team formation in social networks. In: Proceedings of the 21st International Conference on World Wide Web. pp. 839–848. WWW 2012, Association for Computing Machinery, New York, NY, USA (2012)
3. Andrejczuk, E., Berger, R., Rodríguez-Aguilar, J.A., Sierra, C., Marín-Puchades, V.: The composition and formation of effective teams: computer science meets organizational psychology. Knowledge Eng. Rev. **33**, e17 (2018)
4. Andrejczuk, E., Bistaffa, F., Blum, C., Rodríguez-Aguilar, J.A., Sierra, C.: Synergistic team composition: a computational approach to foster diversity in teams. Knowl.-Based Syst. **182**, 104799 (2019)
5. Bachrach, Y., Meir, R., Jung, K., Kohli, P.: Coalitional structure generation in skill games. In: Proceedings of the Twenty-Fourth AAAI Conference on Artificial Intelligence, , vol. 2, AAAI 2010, AtlantaGeorgia, USA, July 11–15 (2010)

6. Capezzuto, L., Tarapore, D., Ramchurn, S.: Anytime and efficient coalition formation with spatial and temporal constraints. In: Bassiliades, N., Chalkiadakis, G., de Jonge, D. (eds.) EUMAS/AT -2020. LNCS (LNAI), vol. 12520, pp. 589–606. Springer, Cham (2020). https://doi.org/10.1007/978-3-030-66412-1_38

7. Chalkiadakis, G., Boutilier, C.: Sequentially optimal repeated coalition formation under uncertainty. Auton. Agent. Multi-agent Syst. **24**(3), 441–484 (2012)

8. Chalkiadakis, G., Elkind, E., Wooldridge, M.: Computational Aspects of Cooperative Game Theory (Synthesis Lectures on Artificial Inetlligence and Machine Learning), , 1st edn. Morgan & Claypool Publishers (2011)

9. Chevaleyre, Y., et al.: Issues in multiagent resource allocation. Informatica **30**, 3–31 (2006)

10. Conitzer, V., Sandholm, T.: Complexity of manipulating elections with few candidates. In: Eighteenth National Conference on Artificial Intelligence, pp. 314–319. American Association for Artificial Intelligence, USA (2002)

11. Crawford, C., Rahaman, Z., Sen, S.: Evaluating the efficiency of robust team formation algorithms. In: Osman, N., Sierra, C. (eds.) Autonomous Agents and Multiagent Systems, pp. 14–29. Springer, Cham (2016). https://doi.org/10.1007/978-3-319-46882-2_2

12. Czatnecki, E., Dutta, A.: Hedonic coalition formation for task allocation with heterogeneous robots. In: 2019 IEEE International Conference on Systems, Man and Cybernetics (SMC), pp. 1024–1029 (2019)

13. ESCO: European skills, competences, qualifications and occupations. https://ec.europa.eu/esco/portal (2010)

14. Faliszewski, P., Hemaspaandra, E., Hemaspaandra, L.A., Rothe, J.: Llull and copeland voting broadly resist bribery and control. In: Proceedings of the Twenty-Second AAAI Conference on Artificial Intelligence, AAAI 2007, pp. 724–730. AAAI Press (2007)

15. Gamrath, G., et al.: The SCIP Optimization Suite 7.0. Technical report, Optimization Online (March 2020). www.optimization-online.org/DB_HTML/2020/03/7705.html

16. Georgara, A., Rodríguez-Aguilar, J.A., Sierra, C.: Towards a Competence-Based Approach to Allocate Teams to Tasks, pp. 1504–1506. International Foundation for Autonomous Agents and Multiagent Systems, Richland, SC (2021)

17. Georgara, A., Rodríguez-Aguilar, J.A., et al.: An anytime heuristic algorithm for allocating many teams to many tasks. In: Proceedings of the 21st International Conference on Autonomous Agents and Multiagent Systems, pp. 1598–1600. AAMAS '22, International Foundation for Autonomous Agents and Multiagent Systems, Richland, SC (2022)

18. GLPK: Glpk: Gnu linear programming kit) (2018). www.gnu.org/software/glpk/

19. GUROBI: Gurobi optimizer 8.0 (2018). www.gurobi.com/

20. IBM: Ibm ilog cplex optimization studio 12.10 (2019). www.ibm.com/us-en/marketplace/ibm-ilog-cplex

21. ISFOL: Professioni, occupazione, fabbisogni (2017). https://fabbisogni.isfol.it

22. Kurtan, C., Yolum, P., Dastani, M.: An ideal team is more than a team of ideal agents. In: ECAI (2020)

23. Lappas, T., Liu, K., Terzi, E.: Finding a team of experts in social networks. In: Proceedings of the 15th ACM SIGKDD International Conference on Knowledge Discovery and Data Mining. KDD 2009, pp. 467–476. Association for Computing Machinery, New York, NY, USA (2009)

24. Li, Y., Bandar, Z.A., Mclean, D.: An approach for measuring semantic similarity between words using multiple information sources. IEEE Trans. Knowl. Data Eng. **15**(4), 871–882 (2003)

25. Morrison, R.W., De Jong, K.A.: Measurement of population diversity. In: Collet, P., Fonlupt, C., Hao, J.K., Lutton, E., Schoenauer, M. (eds.) Artificial Evolution, pp. 31–41. Springer, Berlin (2002). https://doi.org/10.1007/3-540-46033-0_3

26. Nguyen, T.T., Rothe, J.: Minimizing envy and maximizing average Nash social welfare in the allocation of indivisible goods. Discret. Appl. Math. **179**, 54–68 (2014)

27. Osman, N., Sierra, C., Mcneill, F., Pane, J., Debenham, J.: Trust and matching algorithms for selecting suitable agents. ACM Trans. Intell. Syst. Technol. **5**(1), 16:1–16:39 (2014)

28. Ponda, S.S., Johnson, L.B., Geramifard, A., How, J.P.: Cooperative mission planning for multi-UAV teams. In: Valavanis, K.P., Vachtsevanos, G.J. (eds.) Handbook of Unmanned Aerial Vehicles, pp. 1447–1490. Springer, Dordrecht (2015). https://doi.org/10.1007/978-90-481-9707-1_16

29. Präntare, F., Heintz, F.: An anytime algorithm for simultaneous coalition structure generation and assignment. In: Miller, T., Oren, N., Sakurai, Y., Noda, I., Savarimuthu, B.T.R., Cao Son, T. (eds.) PRIMA 2018. LNCS (LNAI), vol. 11224, pp. 158–174. Springer, Cham (2018). https://doi.org/10.1007/978-3-030-03098-8_10

30. Präntare, F., Heintz, F.: An anytime algorithm for optimal simultaneous coalition structure generation and assignment. Auton. Agent. Multi-Agent Syst. **34**(1), 1–31 (2020)

31. Sa Silva, I.E., Krohling, R.A.: A fuzzy sociometric approach to human resource allocation. In: 2018 IEEE International Conference on Fuzzy Systems (FUZZ-IEEE), pp. 1–8. IEEE (2018)

Collaborative Decision Making for Lane-Free Autonomous Driving in the Presence of Uncertainty

Pavlos Geronymakis$^{(\boxtimes)}$ (ID), Dimitrios Troullinos (ID), Georgios Chalkiadakis (ID),
and Markos Papageorgiou (ID)

Technical University of Crete, Chania 73100, Greece
`pgeronymakis@isc.tuc.gr`, {`dtroullinos,markos`}`@dssl.tuc.gr`,
`gehalk@intelligence.tuc.gr`

Abstract. The recently introduced *lane-free traffic* paradigm removes the restrictions of the traffic lanes, so that autonomous vehicles can move anywhere laterally across the road's width. Previous research in this domain has employed the celebrated max-plus message-passing algorithm in order to allow the coordination of all (connected and autonomous) vehicles in the environment. However, when allowing for the realistic perspective that there exist vehicles that are unable or unwilling to communicate with others, the uncertainty introduced renders the aforementioned coordination approach ineffective. To combat this, in this paper we adjust the Max-plus algorithm accordingly so that agents using max-plus for coordination can also observe and take into consideration independent agents via emulated messages. We put forward different methods to form these messages—namely the Maximax, Maximin, Hurwicz, Minimax Regret and Laplace decision-making criteria. Finally, we provide a thorough evaluation of our approach, including a detailed comparison of all criteria used for message-forming.

Keywords: Max-plus algorithm · Uncertainty · Lane-free traffic

1 Introduction

In recent years, there have been significant advancements in the field of automobiles and the automation of vehicular traffic. While research in this field mainly focuses on lane-based traffic, a recent development is the investigation of the novel lane-free traffic paradigm [10,11].

In our work, we also consider agents operating in a lane-free environment, specifically on a lane-free one-way highway. As such, vehicles are not restricted by the lanes as in traditional highways, but can instead move freely across the

The research leading to these results has received funding from the European Research Council under the European Union's Horizon 2020 Research and Innovation programme/ERC Grant Agreement n. [833915], project TrafficFluid.

entire highway width. Connected and Autonomous Vehicles (CAVs) enter the highway at random positions, with randomly assigned desired speeds. In their attempt to reach their desired speed and exit the highway with minimum delay, they may accelerate and move past other agents, and this kind of maneuvers may result into collisions among them.

Now, in existing work, the max-plus algorithm [7,14] is used to coordinate the movement of the CAV agents, and assist them in reaching their desired speeds while avoiding collisions. Note that this line of work has only focused on homogeneous environments, where every agent in the highway decides upon its actions using the max-plus algorithm. By contrast, we introduce additional agents whose movement is independent of the max-plus algorithm, and modify max-plus in order to incorporate them within the algorithm. However, due to the lack of communication, this imposes uncertainty for max-plus agents. To this end, we adopt a range of different decision-making criteria to be embedded in our adjusted version of max-plus, so as to incorporate uncertainty within the algorithm. The incorporated criteria include: *Maximax, Maximin, Hurwicz, Minimax Regret, Laplace*; and also a simple opponent modelling technique we devised for our domain. Our experimental evaluation shows that the embedding of decision-making criteria in the face of uncertainty within max-plus, does in fact reduce collision occurrences; and that the more elaborate criteria provide incremental improvements.

In what follows, in Sect. 2 we provide the relevant background work, that will be used as our foundation to address the issues of uncertainty in the lane-free environment, while in Sect. 3 we present our approach involving the adjustment of max-plus algorithm and the incorporation of multiple criteria that address the uncertainty imposed by individual agents. In Sect. 4 we present our experimental evaluation and discuss the effectiveness of our approach by comparing each criterion in terms of reducing collisions among max-plus-coordinated and independent agents. Finally, in Sect. 5 we conclude our work and address potential future endeavors.

2   Background and Related Work

In this section, we present the technical background of this work, namely the framework of Coordination Graphs and the max-plus Algorithm, along with related work, with more focus towards the existing work that we build upon.

2.1   Coordination Graphs

Coordination Graphs (CGs) [4] are used in multi-agent systems to model coordination among agents. In a multi-agent environment, there is not always a need for explicit coordination among all agents. Local coordination between agents that interact with each other is often enough to achieve the global coordination task. CGs take advantage of this, allowing for scalability in the number of participating agents, and making the joint action of a set of agents that maximizes the global utility more easily obtainable.

In CGs, the agents are represented by a node in the graph, and the cross-agent interactions take the form of edges denoting a need for coordination between the connected agents. Each agent $i \in N$, where N is the set of nodes (agents), performing an action $a_i \in A$, where A is the action domain of a_i, has a local utility $f_i(a_i)$, while $f_{ij}(a_i, a_j)$ corresponds to a shared utility related to the edge $i, j \in E$, where N is the set of edges. As such, the global utility $u(a)$ is defined as :

$$u(a) = \sum_{i \in N} f_i(a_i) + \sum_{(i,j) \in E} f_{ij}(a_i, a_j) \qquad (1)$$

2.2   The Max-Plus Algorithm

The Max-plus algorithm [7] is a message-passing algorithm that provides a solution to a CG representation of a coordination problem, i.e., provides an action for each participating agent i.

In every iteration, each agent i sends locally maximized messages $\mu_{ij}(a_j)$ according to their current maximizing action a_i, to each one of their neighboring agents j connected with an edge in the graph $i((i,j) \in E \forall j \in N_i$. Each message can be calculated by:

$$\mu_{ij}(a_j) = max_{a_i}\{f_i(a_i) + f_{ij}(a_i, a_j) + \sum_{k \in N_i \setminus \{j\}} \mu_{ki}(a_i)\} + c_{ij} \qquad (2)$$

Convergence is only guaranteed when the CG does not contain cycles. A normalizing value of $c_{ij} = -\frac{1}{|N_k|}\sum_k \mu_{ik}(a_k)$ can be added to normalize the values of messages, so that they do not constantly accumulate when cycles exist in the graph. Finally, each agent i selects the action a_i that maximizes the received local messages $\mu_{ji}(a_i)$ along with i's local payoff $f_i(a_i)$: $a_i = argmax_{a_i}\{f_i(a_i) + \sum_{j \in N_i} \mu_{ji}(a_i)\}$. Max-plus is an iterative algorithm, and is executed until convergence of the passing messages μ_{ij}, or until a stopping criterion is met.

2.3   Max-Plus in the Lane-Free Environment

The adoption of the max-plus algorithm in the lane-free environment involves the construction of a CG as defined by the local interaction among agents [13]. Each lane-free vehicle is an agent i depicted by a node $i \in N$ in the graph. Its interaction with nearby agents depends primarily on the distance between them. An agent i considers nearby vehicles on the front and back within a certain longitudinal distance dx, which is set at 50 m. Now, each agent does not form connections with all observed agents, but only with those that there is an actual need for coordination, so as to avoid a potential collision. As such, the authors in [13] adopt Artificial Potential Fields to quantify the danger of collision between two agents i and j, and incorporate this function into the local utilities. For that, the authors select the ellipsoid function to capture the potential collision in this domain. The form of the ellipsoid used is:

$$E(dx, dy) = \frac{m}{\left(\left(\frac{|dx|}{\alpha}\right)^{p_x} + \left(\frac{|dy|}{b}\right)^{p_y} + 1\right)^{p_t}} \tag{3}$$

where dx, dy are the longitudinal and lateral distance of the respective center points of the vehicles i, j. The parameters a, b are used to adjust the range of the field for the x, y axis, while the $p_x . p_y, pt$ affect the overall shape, and m defines the magnitude when the distances are close to 0.

The local utility function contains two components, namely the "critical region" and "broader regions", as:

$$U_{ij}(s_{ij}) = E_c(dx_{ij}, dy_{ij}) + E_b(dx_{ij}, dy_{ij}, dv_{x,ij}, dv_{y,ij}) \tag{4}$$

Authors use a tuple of information relevant to the local state among the two agents with s_{ij}. The critical region E_c is based solely on the distance of the agents, providing a positive value when agents are too close, while the broader region E_b also accounts for the relative speed of the vehicles in both axes, capturing a broader view of the vehicles, informing when a collision is about to happen when vehicles approach one another with high speed. For more information on the Artificial Potential Fields used for the local utilities, we refer the interested reader to [13]. The maximum number of edges for forwards and backwards agents is also restricted, in order to control the graph's density. This selection process is performed based on the euclidean distance between agent i and each neighbor agent j.

The agents' goal is to avoid collisions with their neighboring agents while trying to reach and/or maintain their assigned desired speed $v_{d,i}$. The local payoff $f_{ij}(a_i, a_j)$ incorporates that as a local edge utility function. The transition function is used for all combinations of joint action pairs, to provide the value of the potential field for the resulting state at the next time-step (depicted with s'_{ij}) to the local payoff $f_{ij}(a_i, a_j)$, that "informs" the agents on the outcome of their interaction.

Thus, the local payoff function $f_{ij}(a_i, a_j)$ shared by i, j at local state s_{ij} is:

$$f_{ij}(a_i, a_j) = \begin{cases} -U_{ij}(s'_{ij}), & U_{ij}(s'_{ij}) \neq 0 \\ c_s \cdot r_{v,ij}, & else \end{cases} \tag{5}$$

$$r_{v,ij} = r_{v,i} \cdot \frac{1}{|N_i|} + r_{v,j} \cdot \frac{1}{|N_j|} \tag{6}$$

where $|N_i|$ is the number of edges that contain agent i. The form of $r_{v,ij}$ is a linear function based on current speed $v_{x,i}$, normalized according to the desired speed $v_{d,i}$. This speed utility component is defined as: $r_{v,i} = (v_{d,i} - |v_{d,i} - v_{x,i}|)/v_{d,i}$. When the agents are close enough and in danger of a collision, the local payoff $f_{ij}(a_i, a_j)$ is negative. Otherwise, it is positive and reflects the goal of reaching the desired speed.

Finally, the action domain A is discretized in order to comply with the max-plus algorithm, and each agent considers a set of 5 possible actions:

- a0: zero acceleration in both axes.
- a1: longitudinal acceleration of $2\,\mathrm{m/s}^2$.

- a2: longitudinal deceleration of $2 \, \text{m/s}^2$.
- a3: lateral acceleration $1 \, \text{m/s}^2$ towards left.
- a4: lateral acceleration $1 \, \text{m/s}^2$ towards right.

2.4   Related Work

Regarding the lane-free traffic application domain, many works already exist that propose relevant vehicle movement strategies, which tackle the problem from different research fields. First, the authors in [11] propose a rule-based vehicle movement strategy by adopting the notion of forces being applied to nearby vehicles, and this strategy is employed by the independent vehicles we introduce in the lane-free environment. Moreover, the work of [16] introduces an optimal control approach for the problem of lane-free driving, with vehicles optimizing their behavior by considering a future horizon and updating their trajectories online based on model-predictive control. Finally, the authors in [6] design a two-dimensional lane-free cruise controller with more emphasis on control theory.

Within the framework of CGs, there are works that tackle uncertainty in the environment already, but to the best of our knowledge, there is no work that extends max-plus based on our formulation, addressing the uncertainty of independent agents with decision-making criteria. In more detail, authors in [1] tackle coordination problems under uncertainty by devising Fuzzy Coordination Graphs, as they view the problem from the perspective of fuzzy games [8] and propose a variant of the variable elimination algorithm [4] to obtain the joint action. Moreover, in [9], agents' interactions are depicted in a graph structure, as in CGs, and the authors address the uncertainty for decentralized planning under uncertainty regarding the agents' observations. To do so, they incorporate the notion of beliefs into the Monte Carlo Tree search algorithm used for planning and use heuristic-based policies to predict other agents' actions.

3   Max-Plus Under Uncertainty

The main goal of this work is to extend the use of the max-plus algorithm to non-homogeneous lane-free environments. A non-homogeneous lane-free environment consists of additional agents that do not operate following the max-plus algorithm. We introduce new independent agents, with different behavior, that have no form of communication with other agents. This restriction imposes the challenge of predicting and modeling these agents in a way that is compatible with the max-plus algorithm, i.e., the message-passing operation of locally maximized messages sent among communicating agents. As such, to incorporate this new type of agent into the max-plus algorithm we emulate the messages that would be sent from independent agents to max-plus agents.

3.1   Emulated Messages

To apply the max-plus algorithm in a non-homogeneous lane-free environment, we first incorporate the independent agents in the CG accordingly. We consider a CG modeled as in [13], where each agent is represented by a node in the graph. Now, as in [13], we assume that each agent possesses observational capabilities, therefore agents can observe their surrounding vehicles' current status (position, speed, dimensions). As such, max-plus agents also observe independent agents nearby. Therefore, the observed independent agents are again represented by nodes, and edges that indicate a need for coordination can be formed (only) from the perspective of max-plus agents. However, the coordination between max-plus and independent agents cannot be achieved since there is no actual communication with independent agents.

The inability of non-cooperative agents to receive and read messages sent from max-plus agents means that sending any messages to them is ineffective. Thus, we establish a one-way communication between non-cooperative and max-plus in the form of emulated messages sent only from (observed) independent to max-plus agents. These messages are only emulated when the respective max-plus agents do observe independent agents and an edge that connects them exists within the CG. As mentioned, max-plus agents' can detect their neighbors' position and speed. This means that during the calculation of these messages, the longitudinal and lateral position of non-cooperative agents can be considered known, as well as the speed of the vehicles in both axes.

In Fig. 1 we present an example of our non-homogeneous environment and visualize the messages exchanged or emulated. Agents 2 and 3 follow the max-plus algorithm, while the agents 1 and 4 are independent, and they receive no messages. Agents 2 and 3 exchange messages for their actions, and also emulate messages from the observed agents 1 and 4.

3.2 Prediction Under Uncertainty

We reformulate the max-plus algorithm in order to incorporate emulated messages from other agents and take them into account for the decision-making process regarding the actions of the max-plus agents. For each neighbor, the agent checks if it is a max-plus agent, a fact ascertained by the receipt of the corresponding μ_{ij} message from that agent. Otherwise, they emulate the message from that agent. The pseudocode of our max-plus extension is provided

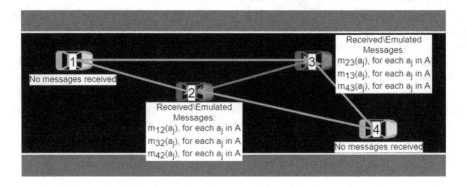

Fig. 1. The messages that each agent will receive.

Algorithm 1. Max-plus algorithm with independent agents

1: **procedure** MAX_PLUS($N, E, A, class$)
2:     **for** $i \in N$ **do**   ▷ N is the set of agents
3:         $neighbors \leftarrow \cup_{\forall(i,j) \in E}\{j\}$ ▷ $\forall(i,j) \in E$, only i may be independent
4:         **for** $j \in neighbors$ **do**
5:             **for** $a\_j \in A$ **do**
6:                 **if** $class(i) \in maxplus$ **then**
7:                     $\mu_{ij}(a_j) \leftarrow max_{a_i}[f_i(a_i) + f_{ij}(a_i, a_j) + \sum_{k \in neighbors\backslash i} \mu_{ki}(a_i)] + c_{ij}$
8:                     $action[i] \leftarrow max\_g\_action(A, i, \mu, neighbors)$
9:                 **else**
10:                    $\mu_{ij}(a_j) \leftarrow \mu\_toEmulate(a_j, i, j, A)$
11:                **end if**
12:            **end for**
13:        **end for**
14:    **end for**
15:    **return** $action$
16: **end procedure**

---

in Algorithm 1. Messages emulated from observed agents that are not operating according to max-plus, are calculated based on the "$\mu\_toEmulate$". Finally, the "max_g_action" simply returns the action for agent i that maximizes its received messages $\mu_{ji}(a_i)$ (see [7] for more details). We should note that we also employ the anytime implementation of max-plus [7], but do not include it in this pseudocode in order to maintain simplicity. In what follows, we provide multiple criteria for the calculation of emulated messages, i.e., the implementation of "$\mu\_toEmulate$".

We now must specify the content of those emulated messages. Max-plus agents shall choose the best action for them and their neighbors, while still abiding by the max-plus algorithm, by choosing the action that maximizes the summation of the received messages. Considering there is no way of knowing for certain the intentions of non-communicative agents, our best option is to make assumptions regarding their action and the emulated messages should reflect this. These conditions of uncertainty, render the use of *decision rules (or decision-making criteria) under uncertainty* necessary. The ones examined in this paper are: the *Maximax criterion*; the *Wald's Maximin criterion*; the *Hurwicz criterion*; the *Savage's Minimax Regret*; and the *Laplace's criterion*.

Maximax, Maximin and Hurwicz's Criterion. First, we examine three standard approaches for problems under uncertainty, the Maximax, Wald's Maximin [15] and Hurwicz [5] criteria. The Maximax criterion is an optimistic approach, since it makes the assumption that the best case scenario will always occur, and suggests an action that fits those conditions. On the contrary, Maximin considers the worst-case scenario due to the uncertainty that is associated with the complete lack of information about the possibilities, leading to a more pessimistic decision-making process. The Hurwicz criterion [5], introduced by

Leonid Hurwicz in 1951, offers a "middle ground" option between the Maximax and Maximin criteria. The Hurwicz criterion attempts to find a balance between the extremes of the pessimism of Maximin and the optimism of Maximax. Hurwicz makes use of a β temperature parameter, which acts as a measure of confidence in the decision maker regarding the probability of the best case scenario occurring, i.e., the β value reflects the decision maker's willingness to take risks. The variable β can take any value between 0 and 1.

When β is set to 1, the Hurwicz criterion is reduced to the Maximin criterion, while $\beta = 0$ reduces Hurwicz to the Maximax criterion.

When the Maximax criterion is adopted, for an independent agent i and a max-plus agent j, the message associated with an action a_j of agent j in accordance to the actions of agent i is calculated as:

$$\mu_{max,ij}(a_j) = max_{a_i}\{f_{ij}(a_i, a_j)\} \tag{7}$$

Likewise, for the Maximin criterion:

$$\mu_{min,ij}(a_j) = min_{a_i}\{f_{ij}(a_i, a_j)\} \tag{8}$$

For the Hurwicz criterion, the message associated with each a_j results from the weighted average of maximum payoff (multiplied by β) and minimum payoff (multiplied by $1 - \beta$). For any value assigned to β, the message value that will be sent is formed by:

$$\mu_{ji}(a_j) = \beta \cdot \mu_{max,ji}(a_i) + (1 - \beta) \cdot \mu_{min,ji}(a_i) \tag{9}$$

Dynamic Calculation of β in Hurwicz Criterion. Typical uses of the Hurwicz criterion make use of β as a constant, with a value between 0 and 1. However, our lane-free environment contains dynamic interactions among agents, and they encounter situations of interactions where a predetermined degree of optimism/pessimism may not be appropriate. As such, we consider that the distance between agents i and j can affect the optimism for the outcome of i's action. A simple way of modelling a dynamic β based on the distance between two agents is calculating the longitudinal distance between them and normalizing that value accordingly so that $\beta \in [0, 1]$. Therefore, β is calculated as:

$$\beta = \frac{|dx_{ij}|}{dx_{max}} \tag{10}$$

where $|dx_{ij}|$ is the longitudinal distance between i and j, and dx_{max} is the maximum distance that two vehicles can be apart in the x axis, and still be considered neighbors in the CG.

Savage's Minimax Regret. Savage's Minimax Regret criterion [12] is an extension of Wald's Maximin criterion. Minimax Regret provides an alternative approach that tackles the unpredictability of the environment, by incorporating the notion of regret. To handle the uncertainty of the choices of other agents, instead of just maximizing the minimum possible payoff, we calculate the regret of each action. An action's regret in a specific state refers to the difference between the best payoff in that state, and the actual payoff produced when a particular action is performed. The Minimax Regret criterion minimizes the maximum regret an action of agent j may have across all actions of agent i.

In systems with two agents i and j, the regret of an action of j is defined based on the possible outcomes when i performs any of its available actions (of the set of actions A). Consequently, there are $|A|$ possible states. In the lane-free environment, a max-plus agent may have multiple neighbors, whose combination of actions result into different states. If $|N_j|$ is the number of agents neighboring a max-plus agent j in the CG, the number of possible states occuring are $|A|^{|N_j|}$. First, considering only one independent agent i observed by a max-plus agent j, for any state that is generated by the selected action a_i, the maximum regret of an action a_j is defined as:

$$R(a_j) = max_{a_i \in A}\{max_{a_k \in A}\{f_{ij}(a_i, a_k)\} - f_{ij}(a_i, a_j)\} \tag{11}$$

where the calculation within the max operator for the actions of i depicts the element a_i, a_j of the regret table.

The criteria we examined so far only form messages based on the actions of individual neighbors. However, for Minimax Regret, viewing each neighbor individually is inappropriate, as the resulting messages, consisting of regret values are not properly combined through a simple summation process. As such, Minimax Regret takes into account all independent neighbors from the perspective of each max-plus agent. Consequently, we must calculate the payoffs for each state created by the combination of action of the neighbors. Thus, given a max-plus agent j, and a set of p independent agents $\{i_1, \cdots, i_p\}$ connected with j within the CG, the maximum regret of each action a_j is calculated as:

$$R(a_j) = max_{\{a_{i_1}, \cdots, a_{i_p}\} \in A^p}\left\{ max_{a_k \in A}\left\{ \sum_{i=i_1}^{i_p} f_{ij}(a_i, a_k)\right\} - \sum_{i=i_1}^{i_p} f_{ij}(a_i, a_j)\right\} \tag{12}$$

where we are interested in minimizing $R(a_j)$ instead of maximizing. As such, the associated message is: $\mu_{ij}(a_j) = -R(a_j)$, where the index i now reflects the whole set of independent agents that j observes and is connected to, meaning that in contrast to all other criteria, we emulate a single set of messages for all independent agents connected to j.

To calculate $R(a_j), \forall j \in A$, we use a tree to construct the joint action space, and obtain the sum of the local functions associated with each independent agent. Starting at the root, we create $|A|$ children and attach to them the associated local message payoff, resulting from the joint action of j with the neighbor i_1. We then iteratively expand each child node according to the actions of the i_k neighbor and attach to each node the associated local message payoff plus the value of parent node. This is repeated for all neighbors p. As such, each leaf node will contain the sum of local payoffs associated with the corresponding joint action of all neighbors.

Laplace's Equal Likelihood Criterion. The Laplace criterion [3] is based on the principle of insufficient reason. Essentially, it states that if there is no sufficient reason to assume the probabilities of any scenario occurring, we can only infer that all possible outcomes occur with the same probability. For each action agent i may take, we assign the same probability. Since we consider all agents in our environment have the same set of available actions as our agents, the probability assigned to each action is $\frac{1}{5} = 0.2$. The message attached to the action a_j of max-plus agent j from non-cooperative agent i, is formed by calculating the average payoff for all actions of i:

$$\mu_{ij}(a_j) = \sum_{a_i \in A} \frac{1}{|A|} \cdot (f_{ij}(a_i, a_j)) \tag{13}$$

Thus, the Laplacian criterion considers each action to be occurring with the same frequency. This of course cannot possibly hold true for autonomous agents in a lane-free environment, which are expected to be adopting different driving behaviours and strategies. As such, we expect that classifying independent agents into different behavioural types, and tracking their actions in an opponent modelling fashion, could be beneficial in terms of computing more accurate average payoff estimates and thus coordination messages.

As a first step towards that direction, we devise a simple opponent model by classifying each independent agent according to its surroundings. We detail that model immediately below.

Opponent Modelling. The behavior of drivers in real-life scenarios is heavily dependent on the vehicles in close proximity. For instance, a driver will not accelerate when another is directly in front of her and will be reluctant to slow down to avoid hitting cars that are in her rear.

We use a simple heuristic in order to classify each independent agent by the number of their respective neighbors. For an independent agent i, we distinguish each neighbor k (within distance of $d_o = 50m$ from the perspective of i) based on the relative position from i, i.e., we recognize that k is in front of i when its relative longitudinal position is greater than 0 $(dx = x_k - x_i)$. Similarly, k is considered to be on the left or right w.r.t. i based on their respective lateral placement. Based on these values we consider each neighbor of the independent agent to be either at its *front-left, front-right, rear-left* or *rear-right*.

An illustrative example is provided in Fig. 2, where vehicle 0 is an independent agent with five other agents 1, 2, 3, 4 and 5 in its surroundings. Each neighboring agent of 0 must be in one of the 4 regions to be characterised as a front-left, front-right, rear-left or rear-right neighbor. Based on these areas, we consider be 1 on the rear-left, 2 and 3 on the rear-right, 4 on the front-right, and 5 on the front-left of independent agent 0.

Then, for independent agent i we count the number of neighbors on each region and classify i by this information. To bound the number of classes, we consider at most five agents within each aforementioned region, prioritizing according to the agents' distance from i. That means each agent i belongs to a category

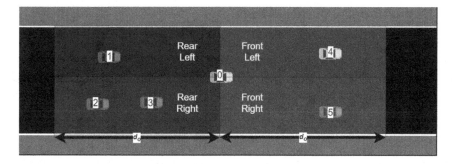

Fig. 2. Showcasing the assignment of an independent agent's neighbors to each region.

described by a tuple: $\langle n_0, n_1, n_2, n_3 \rangle$, where elements are the number of front-left, front-right, rear-left, and rear-right neighbors respectively. This results in $6^4 = 1296$ different classes of agents (each element has six possible states, from 0 to 5 agents). To determine the probability of an action that an independent agent may take, we first observe their actions and update the frequencies of their actions accordingly.

Notice that the acceleration of independent agents can be observed implicitly by the max-plus agents at each time-step, through the speed update. Thus, the acceleration of an independent vehicle is calculated by $a_c = \frac{v_t - v_{t-1}}{time\_step}$, where v_{t-1}, v_t is the longitudinal speed of an independent agent at two consecutive time-steps. Any independent agent may operate directly in the continuous domain, i.e., have continuous values for acceleration. We convert these to the available set of discrete actions in order to be compatible with max-plus. We remind the reader that we have a set of 5 discrete actions, with action a_0 being equivalent to zero acceleration across all axes. We set a threshold value of c_t. If the acceleration of an independent agent does not exceed these threshold in both axes, we assume they perform the action a_0. The actions a_1, a_2 that correspond to movement in the x axis (acceleration and deceleration respectively), are assumed when the agent's longitudinal acceleration exceeds c_t in the corresponding direction. Similarly for the lateral acceleration.

Finally, after collecting information from independent agents, the emulated message attached to the action a_j of a max-plus agent from an independent agent i, is formed by calculating the weighted average payoff for all actions of i, and Eq. 13 now becomes:

$$\mu_{ij}(a_j) = \sum_{a_i \in A} w_{class}(i, a_i) \cdot (f_{ij}(a_i, a_j)) \tag{14}$$

where $w_{class}(i, a_i)$ returns the measured weight (i.e., frequency of occurrence) of action a_i for the associated class of i, by accessing information regarding i's neighbors for the classification.

4   Experimental Evaluation

In this section we present our experimental evaluation where we first introduce independent lane-free agents. In order to investigate more "extreme" conditions, we also examine independent agents with added noise, which naturally adds to the uncertainty. Then, we provide our experimental results for 2 different distributions of lane-free agents and independent agents, and for all levels of noise considered.

4.1   Lane-Free Independent Agents (with Noise)

We introduce independent agents based on a rule-based approach in lane-free traffic environments [11]. These agents behave rationally, in the sense that they try to maximize speed while actively trying to avoid collisions with other agents by observing nearby vehicles. We refer the interested reader to [11] for more information on these agents' movement strategy. In order to properly evaluate our proposed approach, and increase the uncertainty induced, we add noise to the control of these independent agents. The two acceleration values a_x, a_y of each independent agent in a particular time step, resulting from its policy, is filtered with additional noise. The actions a'_x and a'_y that the agent will actually perform are: $a'_x = a_x + n_{px} \cdot a_x$ & $a'_y = a_y + n_{py} \cdot a_y$, where $n_p \sim \mathcal{U}(-c_p, c_p)$ and $\mathcal{U}$ is a uniform distribution. Note that for small values of a_x, a_y, i.e., when the agents maintain the same speed, the added noise will have a negligible effect since it depends on the values of the initially chosen accelerations a_x, a_y. As such, we also examine a second type of noise, n, which is independent of the accelerations of the new vehicles, $a'_x = a_x + n_x$ & $a'_y = a_y + n_y, n \sim \mathcal{U}(-c', c')$, and has an increased effect as we observe from the experimental evaluation.

Summarizing, the three types of independent agents we introduce to our environment are:

- Type A: Lane-free agents with no noise
- Type B: Lane-free agents with noise $n_p \sim \mathcal{U}(-0.5, 0.5)$
- Type C: Lane-free agents with noise $n \sim \mathcal{U}(-1.0, 1.0)$

As mentioned, the independent agents incorporate a different policy, that does not rely on communication/coordination among agents. Also, their acceleration values are continuous, while max-plus agents operate on a discretized action domain, thus making the prediction of what the next action for each agent will be even more difficult.

4.2   Simulation Environment

To examine the effectiveness of each criterion we use an extension of SUMO, designed for lane-free traffic [13]. We extend the SUMO environment setup in [7], to include both max-plus agents and agents based on [11], and can adjust the distribution of the different varieties of agents (e.g., max-plus and independent in

Table 1. Simulation parameters.

Parameter	Value
Highway length	$5\,km$
Highway width	$10.2\,m$
Vehicle length	$3.2\,m$
Vehicle width	$1.6\,m$
Simulation time	$1\,h$
Time-interval	$0.25\,s$
v_d (desired speed)	$[25, 35]\frac{m}{s}$
$v_{x,init}$ (initial speed)	$25\frac{m}{s}$
Inflow rate	$7200\frac{veh}{hr}$

our case) entering the simulation environment. This gives us the opportunity to control the penetration rate of max-plus and independent agents in the highway, and observe the interaction between them. In this environment, we examine and compare the number of collisions between max-plus agents and independent ones. In every time-step, we consider that a collision occurs when two vehicles' positions overlap.

4.3   Experiments and Results

For our evaluation, we introduce a baseline criterion with a simplistic assumption, to provide more incentives for the use of decision-making criteria. Specifically, as a baseline criterion, we assume that independent agents always perform action a_0, i.e., 0 acceleration in both axes, meaning that the emulated messages have the form: $\mu_{ij}(a_j) = f_{ij}(a_0, a_j)$.

The parameters relevant to the lane-free scenario we examined are shown in Table 1. We examined two different configurations regarding the distribution of vehicles. Specifically, in our first scenario, 40% of our CAVs population consists of independent agents; while in the second scenario, the independent agents are 60% of all CAVs. Both distributions contain results for the three types of independent agents (i.e., types A, B, and C), as discussed in Sect. 4.1.

Results. Experimental results are provided in Figs. 3 and 4, for our first and second scenario respectively. The results shown are averages across 10 runs with different seed values each (the seed value for each run are the same across all experimental configurations). Code was written in Python 3, and simulations were executed on a PC with an Intel i7-7700k CPU and 16 GB of RAM. Each run of 1 h of simulation required approximately 45 min, with the Minimax Regret criterion adding a small overhead of around 5 min. We report that we observed an average speed within the range $[28.6, 29.3]$ m/s for all different seed values.

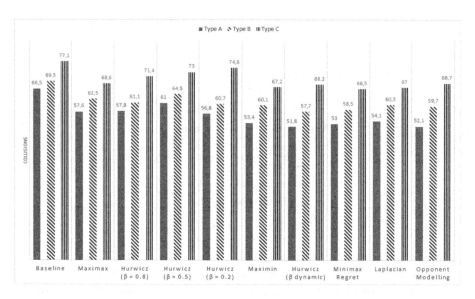

Fig. 3. Collisions per hour for experiments with a distribution of 60% max-plus agents and 40% non-max-plus agents.

The speed deviation between each criterion was not significant, and variations were observed due to the different seed values.

Regarding collisions, a first observation is that the baseline criterion exhibits more collisions than any of the criteria we used: as shown in both figures, for each independent agent type, the performance of the baseline approach is consistently worse than any decision-making criterion used. This motivates the use of more elaborate ways to address the uncertainty regarding other agents, as it clearly affects performance. It is important to note that while the baseline performs worse when compared to the agents following the more elaborate decision-making criteria, agents using the baseline criterion still use our extension of the max-plus algorithm and do observe the other vehicles in the highway.

Hurwicz allows us to balance both the best- and worst-case scenarios. However, standard uses of Hurwicz under-perform, resulting into more collisions when compared even to the more naive Maximax criterion. Only the use of a dynamic β provides a noticeable improvement, which allows us to adjust our optimism depending on how close the vehicles are. This leads to fewer collisions compared to the use of the Hurwicz criterion with fixed β. Intuitively, one could assume that the pessimism of Maximin may be excessive, especially when there is no noise added. This intuition proved false, as Maximin performs better than both Maximax and Hurwicz with constant β, presumably due to the fact that independent agents have a distinct methodology of choosing their actions that does not match with the local functions of max-plus agents. That means the conservative approach of Maximin fairs better with them than initially expected.

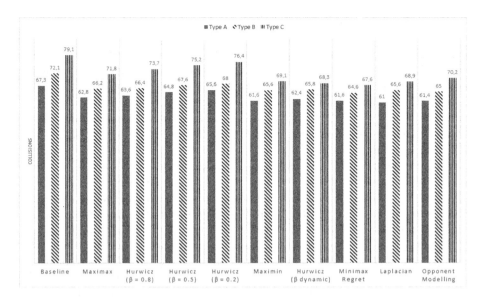

Fig. 4. Collisions per hour for experiments with a distribution of 40% max-plus agents and 60% non-max-plus agents.

The performance of the Minimax Regret approach lies between that of Maximin and Hurwicz with dynamic β, but Minimax Regret provides somewhat better results for the high noise levels (Type C agents), as can be observed in both figures. Apparently, the notion of regret along with the joint view of all independent agents, helps in environments with higher unpredictability (increased noise levels).

The Laplacian approach provides similar results with all aforementioned criteria, and has a slight advantage when the levels of noise are high.

However, for lower noise levels (i.e., for independent agents of Type A & B), the Hurwicz with dynamic β provides slightly better results, indicating that our heuristic function for β performs better in low noise environments.

For the opponent model, we set the associated threshold to $c_t = 0.5$, and collect data from 10 1-h simulations (with different seed values) using the Laplacian approach. Opponent modeling provides only a marginal improvement w.r.t. the Laplacian when the vehicles do not have noise for the first configuration (cf Fig. 3), since the observations used for estimating the frequencies of actions for each class do coincide with the policy of the independent agents (not filtered with noise). Of course, this is not the case when noise is added, due to the observed behavior being partially inconsistent. We believe that a more refined opponent model would enhance the results, and therefore it constitutes an imminent future research endeavor.

In general, replacing max-plus agents with more independent agents leads to more uncertainty in our decision making (cf Fig. 4), resulting in more collisions and smaller margins between both the different criteria, and the different types.

5   Conclusions and Future Work

In this paper we extended the application of the max-plus algorithm to the lane-free environment [13] in order to render it compatible with agents not obeying the same algorithm. We did so by estimating the actions of the other agents using different criteria that tackle uncertainty, and our experimental evaluation exhibited improvement when those criteria are in effect. Notably, max-plus agents now encounter vehicles whose available range of actions is significantly larger than their own set of actions.

In future work, we plan to expand our work and establish ways to incorporate continuous actions of observed agents on the emulated messages. Moreover, it would be interesting to combine the proposed approach with the work of [14] which introduces a dynamic discretization variant of the algorithm, that enables its use in continuous action domain by lifting the task of predetermining a constant number of appropriate discrete actions. Furthermore, as mentioned already, the opponent model is quite simplistic, and can be re-examined so as to incorporate more features that are important (such as the speed of the vehicles)—and to also address the quantification of uncertainty, potentially by using probabilistic opponent modelling techniques [2] along with incorporation of domain knowledge (i.e., the expected behavior of vehicles). Finally, we intend to investigate the application of the distributed max-plus variant [7], and compare with our work in this paper.

References

1. Ahmadzadeh, H., Masehian, E.: Fuzzy coordination graphs and their application in multi-robot coordination under uncertainty. In: 2014 Second RSI/ISM International Conference on Robotics and Mechatronics (ICRoM), pp. 345–350. IEEE (2014)
2. Albrecht, S.V., Stone, P.: Autonomous agents modelling other agents: a comprehensive survey and open problems. Artif. Intell. **258**, 66–95 (2018)
3. Aldea, C., Olariu, C.: Selecting the optimal software solution under conditions of uncertainty. Procedia Soc. Behav. Sci. **109**, 333–337 (2014)
4. Guestrin, C., Koller, D., Parr, R.: Multiagent planning with factored MDPS. In: Advances in Neural Information Processing Systems, vol. 14. MIT Press (2001)
5. Hurwicz, L.: Some specification problems and applications to econometric models. Econometrica **19**(3), 343–344 (1951)
6. Karafyllis, I., Theodosis, D., Papageorgiou, M.: Two-dimensional cruise control of autonomous vehicles on lane-free roads. In: 60th IEEE Conference on Decision and Control, pp. 2683–2689. CDC (2021)
7. Kok, J.R., Vlassis, N.: Collaborative multiagent reinforcement learning by payoff propagation. J. Mach. Learn. Res. **7**, 1789–1828 (2006)
8. Larbani, M.: Non cooperative fuzzy games in normal form: a survey. Fuzzy Sets Syst. **160**(22), 3184–3210 (2009)
9. Li, M., Yang, W., Cai, Z., Yang, S., Wang, J.: Integrating decision sharing with prediction in decentralized planning for multi-agent coordination under uncertainty. In: Proceedings of the 28th International Joint Conference on Artificial Intelligence, pp. 450–456. IJCAI (2019)

10. Mulla, A.K., Joshi, A., Chavan, R., Chakraborty, D., Manjunath, D.: A microscopic model for lane-less traffic. IEEE Trans. Control Netw. Syst. **6**(1), 415–428 (2019)
11. Papageorgiou, M., Mountakis, K.S., Karafyllis, I., Papamichail, I., Wang, Y.: Lane-free artificial-fluid concept for vehicular traffic. Proc. IEEE **109**(2), 114–121 (2021)
12. Pérez-Galarce, F., Álvarez Miranda, E., Candia-Vejar, A., Toth, P.: On exact solutions for the minmax regret spanning tree problem. Comput. Oper. Res. **47**, 114–122 (2014)
13. Troullinos, D., Chalkiadakis, G., Papamichail, I., Papageorgiou, M.: Collaborative multiagent decision making for lane-free autonomous driving. In: Proceedings of the 20th International Conference on Autonomous Agents and MultiAgent Systems, AAMAS, pp. 1335–1343 (2021)
14. Troullinos, D., Chalkiadakis, G., Samoladas, V., Papageorgiou, M.: Max-sum with quadtrees for decentralized coordination in continuous domains. In: Proceedings of the Thirty-First International Joint Conference on Artificial Intelligence, IJCAI-22, pp. 518–526. International Joint Conferences on Artificial Intelligence Organization (2022)
15. Wald, A.: Statistical decision functions which minimize the maximum risk. Ann. Math. **46**(2), 265–280 (1945)
16. Yanumula, V.K., Typaldos, P., Troullinos, D., Malekzadeh, M., Papamichail, I., Papageorgiou, M.: Optimal path planning for connected and automated vehicles in lane-free traffic. In: 2021 IEEE International Intelligent Transportation Systems Conference (ITSC), pp. 3545–3552 (2021)

Maximin Shares Under Cardinality Constraints

Halvard Hummel$^{(\boxtimes)}$ and Magnus Lie Hetland

Norwegian University of Science and Technology, Trondheim, Norway
{halvard.hummel,mlh}@ntnu.no

Abstract. We study the problem of fair allocation of a set of indivisible items among agents with additive valuations, under cardinality constraints. In this setting, the items are partitioned into categories, each with its own limit on the number of items it may contribute to any bundle. We consider the fairness measure known as the *maximin share* (MMS) *guarantee*, and propose a novel polynomial-time algorithm for finding 1/2-approximate MMS allocations for goods—an improvement from the previously best available guarantee of 11/30. For single-category instances, we show that a modified variant of our algorithm is guaranteed to produce 2/3-approximate MMS allocations. Among various other existence and non-existence results, we show that a $(\sqrt{n}/(2\sqrt{n}-1))$-approximate MMS allocation always exists for goods. For chores, we show similar results as for goods, with a 2-approximate algorithm in the general case and a 3/2-approximate algorithm for single-category instances. We extend the notions and algorithms related to *ordered* and *reduced instances* to work with cardinality constraints, and combine these with *bag filling* style procedures to construct our algorithms.

Keywords: Constrained fair allocation · Indivisible goods · Indivisible chores · Maximin share · Matroid constraints · Cardinality constraints

1 Introduction

The problem of fair allocation is one that naturally occurs in many real-world settings, for instance when an inheritance is to be divided or limited resources are to be distributed. For a long time, the research in this area primarily focused on the allocation of divisible items, but lately the interest in the more computationally challenging case of indivisible items has seen a surge. (Bouveret et al. provide a somewhat recent overview [8]). For this variant of the problem, many of the central fairness measures in the literature on divisible items, such as *envy-freeness* and *proportionality*, are less useful. Instead, relaxed fairness measures, such as the *maximin share* (MMS) *guarantee* [10], have been introduced, where all agents receive at least as much as if they partitioned the items but were

---

A preliminary version of this paper appeared at AAMAS 2022 as an extended abstract [21].

D. Baumeister and J. Rothe (Eds.): EUMAS 2022, LNAI 13442, pp. 188–206, 2022.
https://doi.org/10.1007/978-3-031-20614-6_11

the last to select a bundle. It is not always possible to find an MMS allocation [12,22,26], but good approximations exist [15,16].

Fairly allocating items in the real world often involves placing constraints on the bundles allowed in an allocation. For example, consider the problem where a popular physical conference or convention offers a variety of talks and panels organized across several synchronized parallel tracks. Due to space constraints, each talk is limited to some maximum number of participants, fewer than the total number of participants at the conference. Consequently, there may be more people interested in attending some talks than there are available seats. To mitigate this, the conference wants to fairly allocate the available seats, based on participants' preferences, so that no participant receives seats they cannot use, i.e., multiple seats at the same talk or seats at multiple talks in the same time slot. In order to solve this problem, we need to be able to express that some items belong to the same category (seats at talks in the same time slot) and that there is a limit on the number of items each category can contribute to any bundle (in this case 1). This kind of constraints is called *cardinality constraints* and was introduced by Biswas and Barman [6].

The conference example highlights a general type of problems for which cardinality constraints are useful, where each agent should not receive more items of a certain type than she could possibly have use for. Another such problem is the motivating example of Biswas and Barman [6]: A museum is to fairly allocate exhibits of different types to newly opened branches. To make sure that each branch can handle its allocated exhibits, so that no exhibits go to waste, an upper limit is placed on the number of exhibits each branch can be allocated of each exhibit type. The constraints may also provide each agent with some diversity in the type of items she receives. For example, with sufficiently small limits in the museum example, each branch must receive a somewhat diverse collection of exhibits.

Another application is making sure that items of certain types are guaranteed to be roughly evenly distributed among the agents. This can be achieved by setting the number of items each agent can receive from a given category close to the number of items in this category divided by the number of agents. For example, consider a situation where a set of donated items, including a limited number of internet-capable devices, are to be fairly allocated to low-income families. A single family can make use of many internet-capable devices. However, the organization behind the allocation process may want to make sure that as many families as possible have access to the internet. By placing all the internet-capable devices in the same category and giving each family at most one item from this category, the internet-capable devices will be distributed to as many families as possible.

Biswas and Barman [6] showed that under cardinality constraints, with additive valuations, it is always possible to find an allocation of goods where each agent gets at least $1/3$ of her MMS. This is achieved by a reduction to an unconstrained setting with submodular valuations, where the approximate allocation is found using an algorithm described by Ghodsi et al. [16]. More recently, Li and Vetta showed that $11/30$-approximate MMS allocations are guaranteed to exist under hereditary set system constraints [24]. This approximation guarantee is achievable in polynomial time for certain classes of set systems, including set systems representing cardinality constraints.

1.1 Contributions

We develop a polynomial-time algorithm for finding 1/2-approximate MMS allocations for goods under cardinality constraints, improving on the 1/3 and 11/30 guarantees of Biswas and Barman [6] and Li and Vetta [24], which are, to our knowledge, the best guarantees previously available. To construct the algorithm, we extend the notions and algorithms related to *ordered* and *reduced instances* to work with cardinality constraints, and combine these with a *bag-filling* style algorithm. Combining this algorithm with a lone-divider style [1] preprocessing step, we show that $(\sqrt{n}/(2\sqrt{n}-1))$-approximate MMS allocations always exist for goods—a large improvement for few agents. The preprocessing step unfortunately relies on finding MMS-partitions, an NP-hard problem [29]. However, the 1/2-approximate MMS algorithm is able to find both $(n/(2n-1))$-approximate MMS allocations and 1-out-of-$(2n-1)$ MMS allocations by changing a constant.

For chores, we show that a similar approach finds 2-approximate (or, more precisely, $((2n-1)/n)$-approximate) MMS allocations in polynomial time. This is, to our knowledge, the first MMS result for chore allocation under cardinality constraints.

We also examine a special case of cardinality constraints, in which all the items belong to the same category. This case is equivalent to placing a restriction on the number of items in each bundle, or equivalently restricting bundles to independent sets of a *uniform matroid*. This is a setting of interest in itself, especially for chores, where it can be useful to make sure that no agent is stuck with a much larger number of chores than anyone else. By modifying our general algorithms, we show that in this special case, (2/3)-approximate MMS allocations for goods and (3/2)-approximate MMS allocations for chores can be found in polynomial time.

1.2 Related Work

Several other constraint types have been examined in the recent literature. (See Suksompong's recent survey for a detailed overview [28].) One such constraint is that all agents must receive exactly the same number of items [13], a more restrictive version of our single-category instances. Another, studied by Bouveret et al., uses an underlying graph to represent connectivity between the items and requires each bundle to form a connected component [7]. Such connectivity constraints have since been explored in many papers [e.g., 5,19,25]. A variation is the allocation of *conflicting items*, where each bundle must be an independent set in the graph [11,20]. There is some overlap between this scenario and cardinality constraints with threshold 1 [cf. 20], but neither is a generalization of the other. Cardinality constraints have recently been studied by Shoshan et al., who considered the problem of finding allocations that are both Pareto optimal and EF1 for instances with two agents [27].

Matroids have been used to constrain allocations in several different ways [18]. The cardinality constraints placed on a single bundle may in fact be represented by a *partition matroid* or for single-category instances a *uniform matroid*. The 1/2-approximate MMS algorithm of [17] applies to the superficially similar problem where a single matroid constraint is placed on the union of *all* bundles. As pointed out by [6], this algorithm cannot be applied to the cardinality constraint scenario.

2 Preliminaries

For a given instance, $I = \langle N, M, V \rangle$, of the fair allocation problem, let $N = \{1, 2, \ldots, n\}$ denote a set of *agents*, $M = \{1, 2, \ldots, m\}$, a set of *items*, and $V = \langle v_1, v_2, \ldots, v_n \rangle$, the *valuation profile*, i.e., the collection of the agents' *valuation functions* $v_i : 2^m \to \mathbb{R}$ over the subsets $S \subseteq M$. For simplicity, the valuation of a single item $v_i(\{j\})$ will be denoted by both $v_i(j)$ and v_{ij}. We assume that the valuations are additive, i.e., $v_i(S) = \sum_{j \in S} v_{ij}$. We wish to find an allocation $A = \langle A_1, A_2, \ldots, A_n \rangle$ that forms a partition of M into n possibly empty subsets, or *bundles*, one for each agent. We say that an instance I consists of *goods* if $v_{ij} \geq 0$ for all $i \in N, j \in M$, and *chores* if $v_{ij} \leq 0$ for all $i \in N, j \in M$. We consider both instances consisting of goods and ones consisting of chores. However, we do not consider instances consisting of a mix of goods and chores. For simplicity, we will throughout the paper assume that all instances consist of goods, except for in Sect. 7, which covers our results on chores.

For the fair allocation problem *under cardinality constraints*, an instance is given by $I = \langle N, M, V, C \rangle$, where C is a set of ℓ pairs $\langle C_h, k_h \rangle$ of *categories* C_h and corresponding *thresholds* k_h. The categories constitute a partition of the items, M. An allocation A is *feasible* for the instance if no agent receives more than k_h items from any category C_h, i.e., if $|A_i \cap C_h| \leq k_h$ for all $i \in N, h \in \{1, \ldots, \ell\}$. We let $\mathcal{F}_I$ denote the set of all feasible allocations for I, with the subscript omitted if it is clear from context. To guarantee that there is at least one feasible allocation, i.e., $\mathcal{F} \neq \emptyset$, no category may contain more items than we can possibly distribute, i.e., we require that $|C_h| \leq nk_h$ for all $h \in \{1, \ldots, \ell\}$[1].

We are concerned with the fairness criterion known as the *maximin share guarantee* [10]. The *maximin share* (MMS) of an agent is the value of the most preferred bundle the agent can guarantee herself if she were to divide the items into feasible bundles and then choose her own bundle last. More formally:[2]

Definition 1. *Let* $I = \langle N, M, V, C \rangle$ *be an instance of the fair allocation problem under cardinality constraint. The* maximin share *of an agent* i *for the instance* I *is given by*

$$\mu_i^I = \max_{A \in \mathcal{F}_I} \min_{A_j \in A} v_i(A_j),$$

---

[1] Instances with more than nk_h items in category C_h can be handled by ordering the instance (see Sect. 3) and ignoring the worst items in the category.

[2] The definition is equivalent for chores.

where $\mathcal{F}_I$ is the set of feasible allocations for I. If I is obvious from context, we write simply μ_i.

An allocation is said to *satisfy the MMS guarantee*, or *to be an MMS allocation*, if each agent gets a bundle valued at least as much as the agent's MMS, i.e., $v_i(A_i) \geq \mu_i$ for all agents i. We concern ourselves with allocations that satisfy this guarantee *approximately*, where an allocation is said to be an α-*approximate MMS allocation* for some $\alpha > 0$ if $v_i(A_i) \geq \alpha\mu_i$ for all agents i. An allocation A is said to be an *MMS partition* of an agent i, if $v_i(A_j) \geq \mu_i$ for all $A_j \in A$. By definition, at least one MMS partition exists for any agent in any instance. As MMS allocations are not guaranteed to exist [12,22,26], there exists a generalized and relaxed version of MMS, called the *l-out-of-d MMS* [3].[3] This fairness criterion works like MMS, except that the agent is to partition the goods into d feasible bundles maximizing the combined value of the l least valuable bundles in the partition. Our algorithms require some knowledge about the value of μ_i in order to determine when a bundle is worth at least $\alpha\mu_i$ to an agent i. Finding the MMS of an agent is known to be NP-hard for the unconstrained fair allocation problem [29]. Since unconstrained fair allocation is simply the special case of $\ell = 1$ and $k_1 = m$, finding an agent's MMS is at least as hard under cardinality constraints.[4] In order to provide polynomial-time algorithms, we exploit the fact that μ_i cannot be larger than the average bundle value, i.e., $\mu_i \leq v_i(M)/n$, and we can scale all values so that $v_i(M) = n$, so that $\mu_i \leq 1$, as shown in the following theorems. Due to space constraints, their proofs have been omitted, but can be found in the extended version on arXiv, along with all other omitted proofs.[5] The proofs from ordinary fair for the two succeeding theorems do in fact extend to cardinality constraints without any modification [see, e.g., 2,14]. We assume, without loss of generality, that $v_i(M) > 0$ for each agent i.[6]

Theorem 1. (Scale invariance). *If A is an MMS allocation for the instance $I = \langle N, M, V, C \rangle$, then A is also an MMS allocation for $I' = \langle N, M, V', C \rangle$, where $v_i'(S) = a_i v_i(S), a_i > 0$, for some agent i.*

Theorem 2. (Normalization). *Let $I = \langle N, M, V, C \rangle$ be an instance of the fair allocation problem of under cardinality constraints and $v_i(M) = |N|$ for some agent i. Then $\mu_i \leq 1$.*

Once valuations have been normalized, constructing an α-approximate MMS allocation reduces to providing each agent with a bundle worth at least α.

---

[3] We use l instead of the usual ℓ to avoid conflicting use of symbols.

[4] In the unconstrained setting, a PTAS exists for finding the MMS of each individual agent [29], but this PTAS does not extend to fair allocation under cardinality constraints and there does not, to our knowledge, exist a PTAS for this problem.

[5] Available at https://arxiv.org/abs/2106.07300, together with an earlier preprint version (v1) containing some preliminary experiments and corresponding source code.

[6] If $v_i(M) = 0$, normalization does not work. However, since this implies $\mu_i = 0$, Corollary 1 can be used to eliminate agent i from the instance.

3   Ordered Instances

In the unconstrained setting, Bouveret and Lemaître showed that each instance can be reduced to an instance where all agents have the same preference order over all goods [9]. That is, in such an instance there exists an ordering of the goods such that when $j < k$, we have $v_{ij} \geq v_{ik}$ for all agents i. While Bouveret and Lemaître introduced these as instances that satisfy *same-order preferences*, we will refer to them as *ordered instances*, as is the norm for MMS-approximation algorithms [4, 14].

The reduction works as follows. For each agent, sort the good values and reassign these to the goods, which are listed in some predetermined order, common to all agents. Allocations for the reduced instance are converted into allocations for the original instance, without diminishing their value, by going through the goods in the predetermined order; the agent who originally received a given good instead chooses her highest-valued remaining good.

Since only the permutation of value assignments to goods changes, the reduction does not change the MMS of each agent. Thus, any α-approximate MMS allocation in the ordered instance will also be α-approximate in the original instance. Ordered instances are therefore at least as hard as any other instances, and it suffices to show that an algorithm produces an α-approximate MMS allocation for ordered instances.

The standard definition of an ordered instance does not work under cardinality constraints, due to an inherent loss of information about which goods belong to which category. Without this information, one is not guaranteed to be able to produce a feasible α-approximate MMS allocation when converting back to the original instance. We generalize the definition to fair allocation under cardinality constraints. In the special case where $\ell = 1$, this definition and the later conversion algorithms are equivalent to those of Bouveret and Lemaître.

Definition 2. *An instance $I = \langle N, M, V, C \rangle$ of the fair allocation problem under cardinality constraints is called an* ordered *instance if each category $C_h = \{c_1, c_2, \cdots, c_{|C_h|}\}$ is ordered such that for all agents i, $v_i(c_1) \geq v_i(c_2) \geq \cdots \geq v_i(c_{|C_h|})$.*

With the generalized definition, the reduction of MMS-approximation to ordered instances can be extended to cardinality constraints by applying the algorithms of Bouveret and Lemaître to each category C_h individually, as shown in algorithms 1 and 2.

Lemma 1. *Let $I = \langle N, M, V, C \rangle$ be an instance of the fair allocation problem under cardinality constraints, and A' a feasible α-approximate MMS allocation for the ordered instance I' produced by Algorithm 1. Then the allocation produced by conversion of A' with Algorithm 2 is a feasible α-approximate MMS allocation for I.*

Repeating the ordering and deordering procedure for each category does not affect the polynomial nature of the procedures. As a result, the reduction to ordered instances holds.

Algorithm 1 Order instance	**Algorithm 2** Recover solution
Input: Instance $I = \langle N, M, V, C \rangle$	**Input:** Instance $I = \langle N, M, V, C \rangle$ and al-
Output: Ordered $I' = \langle N, M, V', C \rangle$	location A' for corresponding I'
1 **for** $(C_h, k_h) \in C$	**Output:** Allocation A for I
2 **for** $j = 1$ **to** $|C_h|$	1 $A = \langle \emptyset, \ldots, \emptyset \rangle$
3 **for** $i \in N$	2 **for** $(C_h, k_h) \in C$
4 $v'_i(c_j) = i$'s jth highest	3 **for** $j = 1$ **to** $|C_h|$
5 value in C_h	4 $i = $ agent for which $c_j \in A'_i$
6 **return** $\langle N, M, V', C \rangle$	5 $j^* = i$'s preferred item in C_h
	6 $A_i = A_i \cup \{j^*\}$
	7 $C_h = C_h \setminus \{j^*\}$
	8 **return** A

Theorem 3. *For fair allocation under cardinality constraints, MMS-approximation reduces to MMS-approximation of ordered instances in polynomial time.*

Proof. By Lemma 1 it is sufficient to find an α-approximate MMS allocation for the reduced instance produced by Algorithm 1. Since both algorithms 1 and 2 are polynomial in the number of agents and goods for each category, the reduction is polynomial in the number of agents, goods and categories.

4   Reduced Instances

High-valued goods are generally harder to handle than low-valued goods in MMS-approximation. Low-valued goods can easily be distributed across bundles in an approximately even manner and to a certain extent in a way that makes up for an uneven value distribution due to the high-valued goods. High-valued goods, on the other hand, allow only for a rough and usually uneven distribution. In order to simplify the problem instances, we wish to minimize both the number of high-valued goods and the maximum value of a good.

If we remove an agent i and a bundle $B \subseteq M$ from an instance, the result is called a *reduced* instance. If the bundle's value is sufficiently high $(v_i(B) \geq \alpha\mu_i)$ and the MMS of the remaining agents are at least as high after the removal, this is called a *valid reduction* [15], a concept used in many MMS approximation algorithms for the unconstrained fair allocation problem [e.g., 14,16,23].[7] With a valid reduction we can both guarantee agent i a bundle with a value of at least $\alpha\mu_i$ and reduce the original instance to a smaller problem instance.

Given the above definition, a valid reduction could leave an instance without any feasible (complete) allocations, as there may be more goods left in a category than can be allocated to the remaining agents. We require that a valid reduction leaves the reduced instance with at least one feasible allocation.

---

[7] The term *reduction* here refers to data reduction, as the term is used in parameterized algorithm design, rather than to the problem transformations of complexity theory.

Definition 3. *Let $I = \langle N, M, V, C \rangle$ be an instance of the fair allocation problem under cardinality constraints, B a feasible bundle, i an agent, and $I' = \langle N \setminus \{i\}, M \setminus B, V', C' \rangle$, where V' and C' are equivalent to V and C, with agent i and the items in B removed. If $v_i(B) \geq \alpha \mu_i^I$, $\mathcal{F}_{I'} \neq \emptyset$ and $\mu_{i'}^{I'} \geq \mu_{i'}^I$ for all $i' \in N \setminus \{i\}$, then allocating B to i is called a valid reduction.*

Most of the valid reductions used in unconstrained fair allocation are based on the pigeonhole principle. If you can find a set of goods that are worth at least $\alpha \mu_i$ to some agent i and show that all agents must have an MMS partition with a bundle containing an equivalent number of equally or higher valued goods, then you have a valid reduction. The latter part is exactly what the pigeonhole principle promises if we, e.g., look at the bundle $\{n, n + 1\}$ in unconstrained fair allocation. Under cardinality constraints, we can also utilize the pigeonhole principle to find valid reductions. The usefulness is, somewhat reduced, due to both a lack of a common preference ordering across categories and the restrictiveness of the category thresholds. We can, however, show a general result for valid reductions based on the pigeonhole principle.

Theorem 4. *Let $I = \langle N, M, V, C \rangle$ be an ordered instance of the fair allocation problem under cardinality constraints, and let $B = \{j_1, \ldots, j_k\}$ be a feasible bundle of $k \geq 1$ goods such that $v_i(B) \geq \alpha \mu_i$ for an agent $i \in N$ and $\alpha > 0$. Let each agent $i' \in N \setminus \{i\}$ have a bundle $B_{i'}$ in one of her MMS partitions such that there is an injective map $f : B \to B_{i'}$ where, for each $j \in B$, j and $f(j)$ belong to the same category, and $v_{i'}(f(j)) \geq v_{i'}(j)$. Let B' be the bundle consisting of the goods in B and for each $C_h \in C$ the $\max(0, |C_h \setminus B| - (|N| - 1)k_h)$ lowest-valued goods in $C_h \setminus B$. Then, B' and i form a valid reduction for I and α.*

Proof sketch. (full proof in the extended version). For any agent $i' \neq i$, the injective map and the construction of B' guarantees that there is a way to modify the MMS partition of i' through trades and transfers of goods, such that one bundle is turned into B' and the value of any other bundle is at least as high as in the MMS partition originally. The construction of B' also guarantees a valid instance after the reduction. Since $v_i(B') \geq v_i(B) \geq \alpha \mu_i$, B' and i form a valid reduction for I and α.   □

We can easily use the general result of Theorem 4 to construct similar valid reductions to those in the unconstrained setting. Any good i valued at more than $\alpha \mu_i$ for some agent i can be used for a reduction, as the identity function $f : \{j\} \to \{j\}$ satisfies the criteria of Theorem 4. Similarly, by the pigeonhole principle, we can create valid reductions with the n-th and $(n + 1)$-th most valuable goods in a single category.

Corollary 1. *Let $I = \langle N, M, V, C \rangle$ be an ordered instance of the fair allocation problem under cardinality constraints, where there is an agent $i \in N$ and a good $j \in M$ such that $v_{ij} \geq \alpha \mu_i$ for $\alpha > 0$. Then, a valid reduction can be constructed from the bundle $B = \{j\}$.*

Corollary 2. *Let $I = \langle N, M, V, C \rangle$ be an ordered instance of the fair allocation problem under cardinality constraints, with a category $C_h = \langle c_1, c_2, \ldots, c_{|C_h|} \rangle$, $|C_h| \geq |N| + 1$, where $v_i(\{c_{|N|}, c_{|N|+1}\}) \geq \alpha \mu_i$ for some $i \in N$ and $\alpha > 0$. Then, a valid reduction can be constructed from the bundle $B = \{c_{|N|}, c_{|N|+1}\}$.*

It can be tempting to think that we can employ the same valid reductions within a single category as is possible in the unconstrained setting. This is not the case, even when the instance only has a single category and three agents with identical valuations. For example, in the unconstrained setting, any bundle B consisting of two goods, with $v_i(B) \geq \alpha \mu_i$ for an agent $i \in N$ and $v_{i'}(B) \leq \mu_{i'}$ for all other agents $i' \in N \setminus \{i\}$, can be used for a valid reduction. This, is not the case under cardinality constraints, even when removing B and i produces a feasible instance without removing any other goods.[8]

5   MMS Results Under Cardinality Constraints

The reductions of Theorems 2 and 3 and Corollary 1, which can be performed in polynomial-time, let us restrict finding α-approximate MMS allocations to normalized ordered instances where each good is worth less than α, without loss of generality. For such instances, Algorithm 3 can be used to find $(|N|/(2\,|N|-1))$-approximate MMS allocations, which for any number of agents is at least a $1/2$-approximate MMS allocation.

The algorithm works in a somewhat similar manner to bag filling algorithms for unconstrained fair allocation [see, e.g., 14,16], i.e., by incrementally adding goods to (and, in our case, removing goods from) a "bag," or partial bundle, B, until $v_i(B) \geq \alpha$ for some agent i. The major difference is the initial content of the bundle. To make sure that a complete feasible allocation is found, the bundle initially contains the $\lfloor |C_h|/n \rfloor$ least-valuable remaining goods in each category C_h (denoted by C_h^L). This guarantees that the required number of goods is given away from each category. The value of the bundle is then incrementally increased, so as to not increase the value by more than α in each step, by exchanging one of the goods in B from some C_h^L, for one of the $\lfloor |C_h|/n \rfloor$ most valuable remaining goods in the same category (denoted C_h^H). To mitigate possible effects of rounding $|C_h|/n$, one additional good may be added from any category where $|C_h|/n > \lfloor |C_h|/n \rfloor$.

Before proving that the algorithm does indeed find a $1/2$-approximate MMS allocation, we first need a lower bound on the value of the remaining goods at any point during the execution of the algorithm.

Lemma 2. *Let $I = \langle N, M, V, C \rangle$ be a normalized ordered instance of the fair allocation problem under cardinality constraints where all goods are worth less than α for some $\alpha \geq 1/2$. Let n denote the number of remaining agents at any given point during the execution of Algorithm 3. Then each remaining agent assigns a value of at least $|N| - 2(|N| - n)\alpha$ to the set of unallocated goods.*

---

[8] See Example 1 in the extended version for a simple instance where this fails.

Algorithm 3 Find a α-MMS solution to ordered instance

Input: A normalized ordered instance $I = \langle N, M, V, C \rangle$ with all $v_{ij} < \alpha$
Output: Allocation A consisting of each bundle B allocated
1 **while** there is more than one agent left
2    $B = \cup_{h=1}^{\ell} C_h^L$
3   **while** $v_i(B) < \alpha$ for all agents i
4   **if** $B \cap C_h^L \neq \emptyset$ for some C_h
5        $j = $ any element of $C_h^H \setminus B$
6        $j' = $ any element of $B \cap C_h^L$
7        $B = (B \setminus \{j'\}) \cup \{j\}$
8   **else** $j = $ any $c_{\lceil |C_h|/n \rceil}$ not in B
9        $B = B \cup \{j\}$
10   allocate B to some agent i with $v_i(B) \geq \alpha$
11   remove B and i from I and update n, and C_h^H and C_h^L for all h
12 allocate the remaining goods to the last agent

Proof. Because the instance is normalized, the lemma holds at the start of the algorithm. Assume that there are n remaining agents at the start of an iteration, and for each remaining agent i, $v_i(M) \geq |N| - 2(|N| - n)\alpha$. Let i' be the agent receiving B in the iteration. For any remaining agent $i \neq i'$, we wish to show that $v_i(M \setminus B) \geq |N| - 2(|N| - n + 1)\alpha$. Because the valuations are additive, the only way this cannot hold is if $v_i(B) > 2\alpha$. Since any change to B after the initial creation adds a good to B or exchanges a good in B for another, any individual change cannot increase the value of B by more than α. Thus, because the loop at line 3 terminates as soon as $v_i(B) \geq \alpha$, the only way we may have $v_i(B) > 2\alpha$ is if it holds initially, i.e., $B = \bigcup_{h=1}^{\ell} C_h^L$ and $v_i(\bigcup_{h=1}^{\ell} C_h^L) > 2\alpha$. However, by definition $v_i(C_h^L) \leq v_i(C_h)/n$ which implies $v_i(B) \leq v_i(M)/n$. Consequently, $v_i(M \setminus B) \geq (n-1)v_i(B) \geq (n-1)2\alpha \geq (n-1) \geq |N| - 2(|N| - n + 1)\alpha$. □

With Lemma 2 we have a sufficient lower guarantee for the remaining value. We are now ready to show the guarantees of the algorithm.

Lemma 3. *Given a normalized ordered instance $I = \langle N, M, V, C \rangle$ of the fair allocation problem under cardinality constraints where all goods are worth less than $\alpha = |N|/(2|N| - 1)$, Algorithm 3 finds a feasible $(|N|/(2|N| - 1))$-approximate MMS allocation in polynomial time in the number of agents and goods.*

Proof. When allocating the remaining goods to the last agent, Lemma 2 guarantees that the goods are worth at least α, if $|N| - 2(|N| - 1)\alpha \geq \alpha$, which holds for $\alpha \leq |N|/(2\,N| - 1)$. Additionally, as long as B reaches a value of α before running out of improvement operations, any other agent is also guaranteed to receive a bundle they value at no less than α. Since B contains the $\lceil C_h/n \rceil$ most valuable goods in each category C_h when the algorithm runs out of operations, B reaches a value of at least $1/n$ of the remaining value. We thus only need to show that the remaining value is always at least $n\alpha$ for any remaining agent. Lemma 2 guarantees that the remaining value is at least $|N| - 2(|N| - n)\alpha$. Since, this value is at least α for $n = |N| - 1$, the value is at least $2(n-1)\alpha + \alpha \geq n\alpha$ for any other n, and we are guaranteed that the value of B reaches at least α in any iteration. Since $\mu_i \leq 1$ for $i \in N$, each agent i receives at least $\alpha\mu_i$ value.

It remains to show that any bundle allocated is feasible. As long as $|C_h| \leq nk_h$, it holds that $\lceil |C_h|/n \rceil \leq k_h$ and any bundle allocated is feasible. Obviously, $|C_h| \leq nk_h$ holds when $n = |N|$, as all instances are assumed to have at least one feasible complete allocation. Assume that $|C_h| \leq nk_h$ holds at the start of an iteration. The bundle B starts with $\lfloor |C_h|/n \rfloor \geq |C_h| - (n-1)k_h$ of the goods in C_h and no good is removed without adding another from the same C_h. Thus, $|C_h \setminus B| \leq (n-1)k_h$ and the condition holds for $n-1$ after allocating B. Consequently, each allocated bundle, including the bundle allocated to the last agent, is feasible.

In each iteration of the algorithm, goods are added to and exchanged through a set of operations. As no good is added back into B after being removed, the number of operations in each iteration is polynomial in the number of agents and goods. Since there are $|N| - 1$ iterations, the running time of the algorithm is also polynomial in the number of agents and goods. □

We have now showed everything needed to show that 1/2-approximate MMS allocations exist and can be found in polynomial time.

Theorem 5. *For an instance $I = \langle N, M, V, C \rangle$ of the fair allocation problem under cardinality constraints, a $(|N|/(2|N| - 1))$-approximate MMS allocation always exists and can be found in polynomial time.*

Proof. By Theorems 2 and 3 and Corollary 1, any instance I can in polynomial time be converted to one, I', that Algorithm 3 accepts. Since I' has no more agents than I, Lemma 3 guarantees that for I' an at least $(|N|/(2|N| - 1))$-approximate MMS allocation is found in polynomial time by Algorithm 3. The allocation for I' can then be turned back to one for I in polynomial time. □

Algorithm 3 is guaranteed to find α-approximate MMS allocations for *all* possible problem instances when $\alpha \leq |N|/(2N| - 1)$. However, there exist many types of problem instances for which the algorithm will find a feasible α-approximate MMS allocation when a larger α is used. For example, for an instance where $v_{ij} \leq \mu_i/4$ for all $i \in N$, $j \in M$, the algorithm will always find a feasible α-approximate MMS allocation when $\alpha = 3/4$, because then each bundle allocated in the bag filling step is worth no more than 1, unless the bundle is the starting bag. Generally, increasing α might in the worst case result in the remaining value decreasing to the point where $v_i(B) < \alpha$ for any remaining agent i after all improvements have been performed on B. However, for many problem instances, the average value of each allocated bundle is quite a bit smaller than 2α for any remaining agent i. Thus, even for larger values of α, the algorithm can often find a α-approximate MMS allocation. While it is hard to determine the largest α that works for a certain problem instance through calculation, it is possible to simply check if the algorithm finishes for various values of α. Preliminary experiments suggest that trying the algorithm for a limited number of different values of α often provides much better approximations.

Since Theorem 5 in fact guarantees each agent a bundle of value at least $(|N|/(2|N| - 1))v_i(M)$, it directly allows us to show that a 1-out-of-$(2|N| - 1)$ MMS allocation always exists and can be found in polynomial time.

Corollary 3. *For an instance $I = \langle N, M, V, C \rangle$ of the fair allocation problem under cardinality constrains, a 1-out-of-$(2|N| - 1)$ MMS allocation always exists and can be found in polynomial time.*

Proof. In a similar fashion to Theorem 2, the 1-out-of-$(2|N| - 1)$ MMS of any agent can at most be $v_i(M)/(2|N| - 1)$. The proof of Lemma 3 shows that Algorithm 3 gives each agent a bundle valued at least $|N|/(2|N| - 1)$ when $v_i(M) = |N|$, which is at least the 1-out-of-$(2|N| - 1)$ MMS of any agent.   □

It is possible to improve the existence guarantee for MMS approximation by using bag filling in combination with the lone-divider technique of Aigner-Horev and Segal-Halevi [1]. In the lone-divider technique, agent i, one of the remaining agents, is chosen to partition the remaining goods into bundles that all have a value of at least $\alpha\mu_i$ to i. Then, a non-empty subset of the bundles is allocated to some subset of the remaining agents, through an *envy-free matching* which is guaranteed to exist. An envy-free matching is here a matching where each agent matched to a bundle values it at no less than $\alpha\mu_i$ and all non-matched remaining agents value the matched bundles at less than $\alpha\mu_i$. Aigner-Horev and Segal-Halevi showed that an envy-free matching always exists [1]. The process is then repeated until no agent remains. In order to improve the existence guarantee, we first use the lone-divider technique with a partition scheme that only works when a large number of agents remain. When the partition scheme no longer works, the ratio of remaining value to remaining agents has increased, since $\alpha < 1$ and any bundle already allocated is worth less than $\alpha\mu_i$ to any remaining agent. The increased ratio allows Algorithm 3 to be able to provide each remaining agent with a greater value than before the allocations. Unfortunately, the existence result is only of an existential nature, as the partition scheme depends on finding arbitrary MMS-partitions, which is known to be NP-hard [29].

Theorem 6. *For an instance $I = \langle N, M, V, C \rangle$ of the fair allocation problem under cardinality constraints, a $(\sqrt{|N|}/(2\sqrt{|N|} - 1))$-approximate MMS allocation always exists.*

Proof sketch. (full proof in the extended version). When only a few bundles have been given away, any MMS-partition of I for any remaining agent contains at least as many bundles with a remaining value of $\alpha\mu_i$ or higher, as there are remaining agents. The goods in the other bundles in the MMS-partition can then arbitrarily be moved to one of these bundles with remaining value $\alpha\mu_i$. On the other hand, since $\alpha < 1$, as the number of allocated bundles increases, each remaining agent's proportional share of the value of the remaining goods increases. Thus, Algorithm 3 will be able to guarantee a partition with higher and higher minimum bundle value. The value of α must then be set so that in any situation, one of the two methods works. It can be shown that $\sqrt{|N|}/(2\sqrt{|N|}-1)$ is the largest value of α that works.   □

6   Uniform Matroid Constraints

In this section we deal with the special case of cardinality constraints in which there is only a single category, i.e., $\ell = 1$. In this case, the cardinality constraints are equivalent to simply limiting the maximum number of goods in a bundle, or, equivalently, restricting bundles to be independent sets of a *uniform matroid*. Throughout the section we will assume that for any ordered instance, which provides a total ordering of goods, the goods are numbered in a way such that $v_i(j) \geq v_i(j')$ for all $i \in N$ and $j, j' \in M$ with $j < j'$. In other words, the goods are numbered from most preferred (1) to least preferred ($|M|$). Our main result (Theorem 7) for single-category instances is the existence of $(2/3)$-approximate MMS allocations and the ability to find these in polynomial time.

Theorem 7. *For an instance $I = \langle N, M, V, \langle (C_1, k_1) \rangle \rangle$ of the fair allocation problem under cardinality constraints, a $(2/3)$-approximate MMS allocation always exists and can be found in polynomial time.*

In order to prove Theorem 7 we need the following observation about the value of certain subsets of goods.

Lemma 4. *Let $I = \langle N, M, V, \langle (C_1, k_1) \rangle \rangle$ be an ordered instance of the fair allocation problem under cardinality constraints. For any $r \in \{1, 2, \ldots, |N|\}$, let $B_r = \{r, r+1, \ldots, \min(|M|, r + k_1(|N| - r + 1) - 1)\}$. Then, for any $i \in N$, $v_i(B_r) \geq (|N| - r + 1)\mu_i$.*

Lemma 4 provides two useful properties. Most importantly, it can be used to show that the bundles created during a bag-filling style algorithm (Algorithm 4) will be worth at least μ_i before running out of improvements. At the same time, it provides a direct, polynomial way to improve our estimate of μ_i (in addition to Theorem 2) to the required accuracy for the algorithm. Lemma 4 can be used to show that 2/3-MMS allocations can be found in polynomial time for a restricted class of instances using Algorithm 4.

Lemma 5. *For an instance I of the fair allocation problem under cardinality constraints satisfying the requirements of Algorithm 4, the algorithm finds a $2/3$-approximate MMS allocation in polynomial time.*

Algorithm 4 Find (2/3)-MMS solution for single-category instance

---

Input: An ordered instance $I = \langle N, M, V, \langle C_1, k_1 \rangle \rangle$ with $|M| > |N|$, $\mu_i \leq 1$, $v_i(B_r) \geq |N| - r + 1$ (from Lemma 4), $v_i(1) < 2/3$, and $v_i(|N| + 1) < 1/3$ for every $i \in N$, $r \in \{1, 2, \ldots, |N|\}$

Output: Allocation A consisting of each bundle B_j' allocated

1 let $B_1' = \{1\}, B_2' = \{2\}, \ldots, B_{|N|}' = \{|N|\}$
2 **for** $j = |N|$ down to 1
3   **if** $|M| > k_1(j - 1) + 1$
4   add the $|M| - k_1(j - 1) - 1$ least-valuable goods in
              $M \setminus (B_1' \cup B_2' \cup \cdots \cup B_j')$ to B_j'
5   **while** $v_i(B_j') \leq 2/3$ for all $i \in N$ and $|B_j'| < k_1$
6   add the least-valuable good in $M \setminus (B_1' \cup B_2' \cup \cdots \cup B_j')$ to B_j'
7   **while** $v_i(B_j') \leq 2/3$ for all $i \in N$
8   exchange the least valuable $g \in B_j'$ for the least valuable
              $g' \in M \setminus (B_1' \cup B_2' \cup \cdots \cup B_j')$ with $g' < g$
9   find $i \in N$ such that $v_i(B_j') \geq 2/3$
10   allocate B_j' to i and set $N = N \setminus \{i\}$, $M = M \setminus B_j'$.

Proof sketch. (full proof in the extended version). The correctness of Algorithm 4 follows from two observations about the construction of B_j'. First, the construction guarantees that B_j' is feasible and contains at least the required number of goods so that after allocating B_j', there are at most $k_1(j-1)$ goods left. Second, Lemma 4, the incremental improvements of B_j' and the distribution of the $|N|$ most valuable goods into distinct bundles, together guarantee that when $j = r$, the value of the $\min(k_1, |B_r \cap M|)$ most valuable remaining goods in B_r is at least 1 for each remaining agent. Thus, B_j' will always be able to reach a value of at least 2/3. □

Proof sketch. for Theorem 7 (full proof in the extended version). The proof boils down to showing that for any instance I, we can either trivially, if $|M| \leq |N|$, find a (2/3)-approximate MMS allocation through valid reduction, or we can turn I into an instance accepted by Algorithm 4. The latter is achieved through repeated rescaling based on Theorem 2 and Lemma 4, together with applying all possible valid reductions based on Corollaries 1 and 2. □

In addition to existence of (2/3)-approximate MMS allocations, certain restricted classes of single-category instances allow for better approximation or existence guarantees. Specifically, when the number of goods is not much larger than the category threshold, approximation results for unconstrained fair allocation apply under cardinality constraints.

Lemma 6. *For an instance $I = \langle N, M, V, \langle (C_1, k_1) \rangle \rangle$ of the fair allocation problem under cardinality constraints, with $|M| < |N| + k_1$, MMS-approximation reduces to MMS-approximation for unconstrained fair allocation.*

As a result of Lemma 6, the following follows directly from the results of Garg and Taki on MMS approximation in unconstrained fair allocation [15].

Corollary 4. *For an instance $I = \langle N, M, V, \langle (C_1, k_1) \rangle \rangle$ of the fair allocation problem under cardinality constraints, with $|M| < |N| + k_1$, a $(3/4 + 1/(12n))$-approximate MMS allocation always exists and a $(3/4)$-approximate MMS allocation can be found in polynomial time.*

When the threshold is small enough, it is possible to show that MMS allocations always exist. For larger thresholds, on the other hand, it is possible to create instances for which there is no MMS allocation.

Lemma 7. *Let $I = \langle N, M, V, \langle (C_1, k_1) \rangle \rangle$ be an instance of the fair allocation problem under cardinality constraints. If $k_1 \leq 2$, an MMS allocation always exists. If $k_1 \geq 4$, an MMS allocation is not guaranteed to exist.*

7 Fair Allocation of Chores

So far we have only considered instances where the items are goods. In this section we instead consider instances where the items are chores. As our results on chores are similar in scope and technique to our results on goods, the results will only be covered briefly with all proofs given in the extended version. We assume, without loss of generality, that $v_i(M) < 0$.[9] Then concepts of scale invariance and normalization transfer directly to chores.

Theorem 8. (Scale invariance) *If A is an MMS allocation for the instance $I = \langle N, M, V, C \rangle$ of the fair allocation of chores problem under cardinality constraints, then A is also an MMS allocation of $I' = \langle N, M, V', C \rangle$, where $v_i'(S) = a_i v_i(S)$, $a_i > 0$, for some agent i.*

Theorem 9. (Normalization) *Let $I = \langle N, M, V, C \rangle$ be an instance of the fair allocation of chores problem under cardinality constraints and $v_i(M) = -|N|$ for some agent i. Then $\mu_i \leq -1$.*

Further, the reduction to ordered instances works for chores as well. As with goods, reassigning the valuations of the chores does not change the MMS of any agent. The earlier conversion algorithm for an allocation of the ordered instance provides each agent with a bundle of equal or higher value (less disutility), which provides an equal or better approximation.

Theorem 10. *For fair allocation of chores under cardinality constraints, MMS-approximation reduces to MMS-approximation of ordered instances in polynomial time.*

---

[9] As with goods, normalization does not work if $v_i(M) = 0$. In this case, i can be removed from the (ordered) instance by allocating i the k_h worst chores in each C_h. This would constitute a valid reduction.

For chores, the use of valid reductions does not make sense in the same way as for goods. While valid reductions could still exist and be used, there is a lack of simple rules for finding useful valid reductions. However, we can still bound the number of chores that have a large disutility by exploiting the pigeonhole principle on MMS partitions. Note that Theorem 11 provides a stronger upper bound on the number of high-valued chores than the bounds for goods when $\ell \geq 2$.

Theorem 11. *Let* $I = \langle N, M, V, C \rangle$ *be an instance of the fair allocation of chores problem under cardinality constraints, with* $|M| \geq |N|r + 1$ *for an* $r \in \{0, 1, \dots\}$. *For agent* $i \in N$, *let* $g_{i_j} \in M$ *denote the* j-*th most valuable chore in* M *for* i. *Then,*

$$v_i(\{g_{i_{|N|r+1-r}}, g_{i_{|N|r+2-r}}, \dots, g_{i_{|N|r+1}}\}) \geq \mu_i$$

Theorems 8, 9 and 11 allow for an easy adjustment of the valuation functions such that for each agent $i \in N$, $\mu_i \leq -1$, $v_i(M) \geq -|N|$ and there are at most $r|N|$ chores that i values at less than $-1/(r+1)$. Crucially, this guarantees that no chore is valued at less than -1, allowing a variant of the bag-filling algorithm used for goods to find 2-approximate MMS allocations.

Theorem 12. *For an instance* $I = \langle N, M, V, C \rangle$ *of the fair allocation of chores problem under cardinality constraints, a* $((2|N|-1)/|N|)$-*approximate MMS allocation always exists and can be found in polynomial time.*

For single-category instances we can also for chores find much better MMS approximate allocations using an algorithm similar to Algorithm 4.

Theorem 13. *For an instance* $I = \langle N, M, V, \langle (C_1, k_1) \rangle \rangle$ *of the fair allocation of chores problem under cardinality constraints, a* $(3/2)$-*approximate MMS allocation always exists and can be found in polynomial time.*

8   Discussion

We improved the currently best known MMS approximation guarantees for cardinality constraints by extending the concepts of ordered instances and valid reductions to this setting. Cardinality constraints do, however, impose additional challenges that do not exist in the unconstrained setting, limiting the achievable approximation guarantees. The apparent lack of a common preference ordering between distinct categories limits the degree to which the number of and maximum value of high-valued goods can be restricted—an important factor in improving the approximation guarantee of bag-filling style algorithms. Cardinality constraints also restrict the usability of other types of MMS-approximation algorithms. For example, the lone-divider method may easily allocate bundles that contain many items from a single category and few from others, which in turn can make all further feasible divisions very unbalanced.

Acknowledgment. The authors wish to acknowledge valuable input from anonymous reviewers.

References

1. Aigner-Horev, E., Segal-Halevi, E.: Envy-free matchings in bipartite graphs and their applications to fair division. Information Sci. **587**, 164–187 (2022). https://doi.org/10.1016/j.ins.2021.11.059. https://www.sciencedirect.com/science/article/pii/S0020025521011816
2. Amanatidis, G., Markakis, E., Nikzad, A., Saberi, A.: Approximation algorithms for computing maximin share allocations. ACM Trans. Algor. **13**(4), 1–28 (2017). https://doi.org/10.1145/3147173. https://doi.org/10.1145/3147173
3. Babaioff, M., Nisan, N., Talgam-Cohen, I.: Competitive equilibrium with indivisible goods and generic budgets. Math. Oper. Res. **46**(1), 382–403 (2021). https://doi.org/10.1287/moor.2020.1062. https://pubsonline.informs.org/doi/abs/10.1287/moor.2020.1062. publisher: INFORMS
4. Barman, S., Krishna Murthy, S.K.: Approximation algorithms for maximin fair division. In: Proceedings of the 2017 ACM Conference on Economics and Computation, pp. 647–664. EC 2017, Association for Computing Machinery, Cambridge, Massachusetts, USA (2017). https://doi.org/10.1145/3033274.3085136. https://doi.org/10.1145/3033274.3085136
5. Bilò, V., et al.: Almost envy-free allocations with connected bundles. In: Blum, A. (ed.) 10th Innovations in Theoretical Computer Science Conference (ITCS 2019). Leibniz International Proceedings in Informatics (LIPIcs), vol. 124, pp. 1–21. Schloss Dagstuhl-Leibniz-Zentrum fuer Informatik, Dagstuhl, Germany (2018). https://doi.org/10.4230/LIPIcs.ITCS.2019.14. https://drops.dagstuhl.de/opus/volltexte/2018/10107. iSSN: 1868-8969
6. Biswas, A., Barman, S.: Fair division under cardinality constraints. In: Proceedings of the Twenty-Seventh International Joint Conference on Artificial Intelligence, pp. 91–97. International Joint Conferences on Artificial Intelligence Organization, Stockholm, Sweden (2018). https://doi.org/10.24963/ijcai.2018/13. https://www.ijcai.org/proceedings/2018/13
7. Bouveret, S., Cechlárová, K., Elkind, E., Igarashi, A., Peters, D.: Fair division of a graph. In: Proceedings of the Twenty-Sixth International Joint Conference on Artificial Intelligence, pp. 135–141. International Joint Conferences on Artificial Intelligence Organization, Melbourne, Australia (2017). https://doi.org/10.24963/ijcai.2017/20. https://www.ijcai.org/proceedings/2017/20
8. Bouveret, S., Chevaleyre, Y., Maudet, N.: Fair Allocation of Indivisible Goods. In: Handbook of Computational Social Choice, pp. 285–310. Cambridge University Press, 32 Avenue of the Americas, New York, NY 10013–2473, USA, 1 edn. (2016). https://www.cambridge.org/no/academic/subjects/computer-science/artificial-intelligence-and-natural-language-processing/handbook-computational-social-choice?format=HB&isbn=9781107060432
9. Bouveret, S., Lemaître, M.c.: Characterizing conflicts in fair division of indivisible goods using a scale of criteria. Auton. Agents Multi-Agent Syst. **30**(2), 259–290 (2016). https://doi.org/10.1007/s10458-015-9287-3. https://link.springer.com/10.1007/s10458-015-9287-3
10. Budish, E.: The combinatorial assignment problem: approximate competitive equilibrium from equal incomes. J. Polit. Econ. **119**(6), 1061–1103 (2011). https://doi.org/10.1086/664613. https://www.journals
11. Chiarelli, N., Krnc, M., Milanič, M., Pferschy, U., Pivač, N., Schauer, J.: Fair packing of independent sets. In: Klasing, R., Radzik, T. (eds.) IWOCA 2020. LNCS, vol. 12126, pp. 154–165. Springer, Cham (2020). https://doi.org/10.1007/978-3-030-48966-3_12

12. Feige, U., Sapir, A., Tauber, L.: A tight negative example for MMS fair allocations. arXiv:2104.04977 (2021)
13. Ferraioli, D., Gourvès, L., Monnot, J.: On regular and approximately fair allocations of indivisible goods. In: Proceedings of the 2014 International Conference on Autonomous Agents and Multi-Agent Systems. pp. 997–1004. AAMAS 2014, International Foundation for Autonomous Agents and Multiagent Systems, Paris, France (2014). https://doi.org/10.5555/2615731.2617405
14. Garg, J., McGlaughlin, P., Taki, S.: Approximating maximin share allocations. In: Fineman, J.T., Mitzenmacher, M. (eds.) 2nd Symposium on Simplicity in Algorithms (SOSA 2019). OpenAccess Series in Informatics (OASIcs), vol. 69, pp. 1–11. Schloss Dagstuhl-Leibniz-Zentrum fuer Informatik, Dagstuhl, Germany (2019). https://doi.org/10.4230/OASIcs.SOSA.2019.20. https://drops.dagstuhl.de/opus/volltexte/2018/10046
15. Garg, J., Taki, S.: An improved approximation algorithm for maximin shares. In: Proceedings of the 21st ACM Conference on Economics and Computation. pp. 379–380. EC 2020, Association for Computing Machinery, New York, NY, USA (2020). https://doi.org/10.1145/3391403.3399526. https://doi.org/10.1145/3391403.3399526. arXiv: 1903.00029
16. Ghodsi, M., Hajiaghayi, M., Seddighin, M., Seddighin, S., Yami, H.: Fair allocation of indivisible goods: improvements and generalizations. In: Proceedings of the 2018 ACM Conference on Economics and Computation. pp. 539–556. EC 2018, Association for Computing Machinery, Ithaca, NY, USA (2018). https://doi.org/10.1145/3219166.3219238. https://doi.org/10.1145/3219166.3219238
17. Gourvès, L., Monnot, J.: On maximin share allocations in matroids. Theor. Comput. Sci. **754**, 50–64 (2019). https://doi.org/10.1016/j.tcs.2018.05.018. http://www.sciencedirect.com/science/article/pii/S0304397518303384
18. Gourvès, L., Monnot, J., Tlilane, L.: Near fairness in matroids. In: Proceedings of the Twenty-first European Conference on Artificial Intelligence. pp. 393–398. ECAI2014, IOS Press, Prague, Czech Republic (2014)
19. Greco, G., Scarcello, F.: The complexity of computing maximin share allocations on graphs. Proceed. AAAI Conf. Artif. Intell. **34**(02), 2006–2013 (2020). https://doi.org/10.1609/aaai.v34i02.5572,.https://ojs.aaai.org/index.php/AAAI/article/view/5572
20. Hummel, H., Hetland, M.L.: Fair allocation of conflicting items. Auton. Agents Multi-Agent Syst. **36**(1), 8 (2021). https://doi.org/10.1007/s10458-021-09537-3. https://doi.org/10.1007/s10458-021-09537-3
21. Hummel, H., Hetland, M.L.: Guaranteeing half-maximin shares under cardinality constraints. In: Proceedings of the 21st International Conference on Autonomous Agents and Multiagent Systems, pp. 1633–1635. AAMAS 2022, International Foundation for Autonomous Agents and Multiagent Systems (2022)
22. Kurokawa, D., Procaccia, A.D., Wang, J.: When can the maximin share guarantee be guaranteed? In: Proceedings of the Thirtieth AAAI Conference on Artificial Intelligence, pp. 523–529. AAAI2016, AAAI Press, Phoenix, Arizona (2016)
23. Kurokawa, D., Procaccia, A.D., Wang, J.: Fair enough: guaranteeing approximate maximin shares. J. ACM **65**(2), 1–27 (2018). https://doi.org/10.1145/3140756. https://doi.org/10.1145/3140756
24. Li, Z., Vetta, A.: The fair division of hereditary set systems. ACM Trans. Econ. Comput. **9**(2), 1–19 (2021). https://doi.org/10.1145/3434410. https://dl.acm.org/doi/10.1145/3434410

25. Lonc, Z., Truszczynski, M.: Maximin share allocations on cycles. In: Proceedings of the Twenty-Seventh International Joint Conference on Artificial Intelligence, IJCAI-18, pp. 410–416. International Joint Conferences on Artificial Intelligence Organization (2018). https://doi.org/10.24963/ijcai.2018/57. https://doi.org/10.24963/ijcai.2018/57

26. Procaccia, A.D., Wang, J.: Fair enough: guaranteeing approximate maximin shares. In: Proceedings of the fifteenth ACM conference on Economics and computation, pp. 675–692. EC 2014, Association for Computing Machinery, Palo Alto, California, USA (2014). https://doi.org/10.1145/2600057.2602835. https://doi.org/10.1145/2600057.2602835

27. Shoshan, H., Segal-Halevi, E., Hazon, N.: Efficient nearly-fair division with capacity constraints. arXiv:2205.07779 (2022). https://arxiv.org/abs/2205.07779. arXiv: 2205.07779

28. Suksompong, W.: Constraints in fair division. ACM SIGecom Exchanges 19(2), 46–61 (2021). https://doi.org/10.1145/3505156.3505162

29. Woeginger, G.J.: A polynomial-time approximation scheme for maximizing the minimum machine completion time. Operat. Res. Lett. 20(4), 149–154 (1997). https://doi.org/10.1016/S0167-6377(96)00055-7. http://www.sciencedirect.com/science/article/pii/S0167637796000557

Welfare Effects of Strategic Voting Under Scoring Rules

Egor Ianovski[1]([✉])[iD], Daria Teplova[2][iD], and Valeriia Kuka[3]

[1] HSE University, St. Petersburg, Russia
`george.ianovski@gmail.com`
[2] ITMO University, St. Petersburg, Russia
[3] Saint Petersburg State University, St. Petersburg, Russia

Abstract. Strategic voting, or manipulation, is the process by which a voter misrepresents his preferences in an attempt to elect an outcome that he considers preferable to the outcome under sincere voting. It is generally agreed that manipulation is a negative feature of elections, and much effort has been spent on gauging the vulnerability of voting rules to manipulation. However, the question of why manipulation is actually bad is less commonly asked. One way to measure the effect of manipulation on an outcome is by comparing a numeric measure of social welfare under sincere behaviour to that in the presence of a manipulator. In this paper we conduct numeric experiments to assess the effects of manipulation on social welfare under scoring rules. We find that manipulation is usually negative, and in most cases the optimum rule with a manipulator is different to the one with sincere voters.

Keywords: Strategic voting · Scoring rules · Social choice · Social welfare

1 Introduction

In the parlance of social choice, voting is the mechanism by which a group of agents aggregate their preferences over a set of outcomes to select a single outcome for the whole of society. The language naturally brings to mind a political election – and indeed, modern voting theory traces back to the proposals of electoral reform by Borda and Condorcet in 18th century France – but the model can equally well describe the process by which a panel of judges determines the winner of a contest, a firm makes its hiring decisions, or an ensemble of algorithms comes to a joint decision.

Strategic voting is the process by which an agent casts a vote not in agreement with his true preferences, but in an attempt to attain the most preferable outcome – the standard example is a supporter of a minor third party voting for

---

Support from the Basic Research Program of the HSE University is gratefully acknowledged.

D. Baumeister and J. Rothe (Eds.): EUMAS 2022, LNAI 13442, pp. 207–220, 2022.
https://doi.org/10.1007/978-3-031-20614-6_12

a major party closest to his ideological position. Strategic voting is also known as manipulation, a much more coloured term that is more readily associated with fraud, bribery, and other malfeasance, rather than the innocent act of not wasting one's vote. In a political context, one could even go so far as to claim it is the democratic duty of every citizen to "manipulate" in this fashion to make his voice heard. To understand why manipulation is perceived negatively, one needs to consider the other applications of voting, those involving a small panel of experts choosing among outcomes, particularly when some outcomes are objectively "better" or "more correct" than others. In the case of a sporting event, we would certainly hope the judges rank the athletes based on their objective performance rather than personal preference (though we understand well enough that this is not always the case [28]).

The Gibbard-Satterthwaite theorem [10,23] established that all non-trivial voting rules are vulnerable to manipulation, but that does not mean that all rules are equally vulnerable, and much attention has been focused determining that degree of vulnerability by measuring the likelihood of manipulation taking place [3,7,25], the complexity of finding such a manipulation [1,11,22], or the amount of information necessary to manipulate [6,8,26].

While these approaches greatly improved out understanding of how hard or how likely it is to affect the outcome of a voting rule, they said nothing about whether or not this manipulation is actually bad. In a sense, they did not have the vocabulary to do so – the twentieth century was dominated by the axiomatic approach to voting, studying which properties a voting rule does or does not satisfy, and the question of why we vote (presumably, to elect good outcomes) was rarely asked.

This was not always the case. Condorcet motivated his method as electing the objectively "correct" candidate [27], while Borda's contemporaries observed that his method can be seen to maximise voter satisfaction [13]. This welfare approach to voting has resurfaced in recent years, and suggests a clear means to measure the effect of manipulation on voting rules – the degree to which the final social welfare of society is affected.

In this paper we numerically explore the welfare effects of strategic voting under scoring rules, focusing on the case of a small number of voters making a choice between candidates, and the final outcome being evaluated in terms of Borda, Rawls, or Nash welfare.

1.1 Related Work

To our knowledge, the first authors to study the welfare effects of strategic voting were Chen and Yang [5]. In their work they consider voting in open primaries, where members of party B are allowed to vote for the candidate party A will nominate for the general election. Such primaries invite strategic behaviour in the form of "mischief voting" – voters of party B will strive to nominate the most extreme candidate of party A, to guarantee that party B's candidate will win the final election.[1] The authors model the situation in a one-dimensional Hotelling framework, and consider three scenarios: all voters are sincere, only voters of party B are strategic, or all voters are strategic. They find that the worst outcome in terms of social welfare is when only voters of party B are strategic, but the best outcome is when all voters strategise – the effect is explained by the fact that the voters of party A are motivated to vote for a more moderate candidate to counter the behaviour of the voters of party B.

In a series of papers, Lehtinen uses numeric experiments to assess the welfare effects of strategic voting under sequential majority [15], Borda [14], approval voting, and plurality [16]. In his framework voters have cardinal utility over three candidates, and receive a noisy signal about the support the other candidates have. Each voter assumes the other voters are acting sincerely, and then votes in accordance with expected utility maximisation. The result is that strategic voting allows voters to express intensity of preference – a voter for whom candidate a is only slightly better than b is less likely to manipulate in favour of a than a voter for whom a is much better. He finds that under sequential majority, Borda, and plurality utilitarian efficiency (the probability of electing the candidate maximising social welfare) increases under strategic behaviour, particularly if the correlation between the utilities of the different candidates is high. Under plurality the effect is particularly marked, the utilitarian efficiency increasing from $\approx 35\%$ to as much as 95%. The lower the correlation, the less pronounced the effect, and under approval voting there is very little difference between the sincere and strategic scenarios. In a second series of experiments the Condorcet efficiency of the rules is compared; here strategic behaviour is harmful.

Lu et al. [18] consider a setting where a group of manipulators want to elect a target candidate, but possess only partial, probabilistic knowledge of the preferences of the sincere voters. The main focus of their work is on how to compute the optimum strategy of the manipulators, but they also assess the damage the manipulators can do to social welfare, i.e. the difference in the utility derived by the sincere voters before and after manipulation. The authors train a Mallows model on Dublin West electoral data and simulate voter behaviour under the Borda rule. They find that while the probability of the manipulators being able to influence the election can be very high, the damage to social welfare is low – never more than 5%. This is explained by the fact that a manipulation is more likely to be successful in favour of a candidate that already enjoys broad support among the sincere voters, rather than a candidate who is reviled by everyone.

Bassi [4] studied the strategic behaviour of human voters in laboratory experiments. Every game in the experiment consisted of five voters and four candidates, using one of plurality, Borda, or approval voting. The main focus of the paper was on whether humans vote as predicted by the iterated elimination of dominated strategies, thus every profile used had a dominance solution. The welfare

---

[1] "Do it. I will personally write you a campaign cheque now, on behalf of this country, which does not want you to be president, but which badly wants you to run."
–John Oliver, on the prospect of Trump running in 2016.

of the outcomes was measured in terms of Condorcet efficiency and social welfare (the sum of the participants' monetary payoffs), and compared to the theoretical prediction for sincere agents and for strategic agents playing the equilibrium solution. Plurality voting was found to outperform Borda and approval voting in terms of social welfare, but lost in terms of Condorcet efficiency.

1.2 Our Contribution

We perform numeric experiments to evaluate the welfare effects of strategic voting by a small panel of voters. Our experiments cover 15 scoring rules, 3 measures of welfare, and 9 statistical cultures. Among our findings, we find that concave rules suffer the most welfare loss under manipulation, to the point that if our goal is to maximise Rawls or Nash welfare, it is rarely a good idea to use a rule that naïvely maximises said Rawls or Nash welfare; that convex rules are resistant to manipulation, which makes them more likely to elect the best outcome under a Mallows model; and that $(m/2)$-approval performs exceedingly well under Euclidean preferences, for all the welfare measures studied.

2   Preliminaries

2.1 Voting Concepts

Let $\mathcal{V}$, $|\mathcal{V}| = n$, be a set of voters, $\mathcal{C}$, $|\mathcal{C}| = m$, a set of candidates, and $\mathcal{L}(\mathcal{C})$ the set of linear orders over $\mathcal{C}$. Every voter is associated with some $\succeq_i \in \mathcal{L}(\mathcal{C})$, which denotes the voter's preferences. A profile $P \in \mathcal{L}(\mathcal{C})^n$ is an n-tuple of preferences, P_i is the ith component of P (the preferences of voter i), and P_{-i} the preferences of all the other voters.

A voting rule is a mapping:

$$f : \mathcal{L}(\mathcal{C})^n \to \mathcal{C},$$

I.e., it is a rule which associates each profile with a candidate, who is the *election outcome*.

We are interested in a class of voting rules known as scoring rules.

Definition 1. *A scoring rule is a voting rule defined by a sequence of scores, $s_1, \ldots, s_m$ satisfying $s_i \geq s_{i+1}$ and $s_1 > s_m$. Using $pos(i, c)$ to denote the position of candidate c in voter i's ballot, the score of c is:*

$$score(c) = \sum_{i \leq n} s_{pos(i,c)}.$$

The candidate with the highest score is the election outcome, ties are broken lexicographically.

In this paper we are interested in the following scoring rules:

- k-approval *is the scoring rule with* $s_i = 1$ *for* $i \leq k$, *and* $s_j = 0$ *for* $j > k$. *I.e., the best* k *candidates get one point, the rest* 0. *1-approval is also known as* plurality.
- k-Borda *is the scoring rule with* $s_i = \max(k - i + 1, 0)$. *I.e., the top candidate gets* k *points, then* $k - 1$, $k - 2$, *and so on.* $(m - 1)$-*Borda is also known as* Borda.
- *A* geometric scoring rule with parameter p *[12], or* geometric p *for short, is the scoring rule with* $s_i = p^{m-i}$ *if* $p > 1$ *(the* convex *rules) and* $s_i = 1 - p^{m-i}$ *if* $p < 0$ *(the* concave *rules). For example, with 5 candidates and* $p = 2$ *the scoring vector is* $16, 8, 4, 2, 1$.
- *The* Nash rule *is the scoring rule with* $s_i = \log(m - i)$ *for* $i < m$, *and* $s_m = -n \log(m - 1)$.

We will evaluate the election outcomes with three ordinal welfare functions, normalised to give an outcome between 0 and 100.

Definition 2. *Suppose c is the election outcome. The* Borda welfare *of the outcome is the sum of the Borda scores of c, normalised by the hypothetical Borda score of a candidate ranked first by all:*

$$Borda(c) = 100 \frac{\sum_{i \leq n}(m - pos(i, c))}{(m - 1)n}.$$

The Rawls welfare *of the outcome is the Borda score given to c by the voter that ranks c the lowest, normalised by* $(m - 1)$:

$$Rawls(c) = 100 \frac{\min_{i \leq n}(m - pos(i, c))}{(m - 1)}.$$

The Nash welfare *of the outcome is the product of the Borda scores of c, normalised by taking the nth root:*

$$Nash(c) = 100 \frac{\sqrt[n]{\prod_{i \leq n}(m - pos(i, c))}}{(m - 1)}.$$

Borda welfare is based on the utilitarian principle of choosing a candidate with the best average rank. Rawls welfare is based on the egalitarian notion of choosing a candidate that will minimise the misery of the unhappiest voter. Nash welfare, while originally proposed as a solution to a bargaining problem, is often proposed as a means to achieve a balance of the utilitarian and egalitarian principles [19,21]. It should be noted that, unlike Borda and Rawls welfare, the Nash-maximising outcome depends on the choice of the zero point. In this paper, we value the last position at 0, but the performance of the voting rules with respect to Nash welfare would have differed somewhat with a different choice.

Under sincere behaviour, the Borda rule, by definition, maximises Borda welfare.

Rawls welfare is maximised by generalised antiplurality, which is not a scoring rule per se, but a *generalised scoring rule* [24] – candidates are first ranked by their $(m-1)$-approval score, first-order ties are broken by the $(m-2)$-approval score, second-order ties by the $(m-3)$-approval score, and so on. We do not investigate generalised antiplurality directly, but the rule is equivalent to a geometric scoring rule with a sufficiently small p [12]; thus the geometric rule with $p = 0.5$ is a close proxy to the Rawlsian optimum.

Given that $\log(xy) = \log(x) + \log(y)$, a candidate maximises Nash welfare if and only if it maximises the sum of the logarithms of its Borda points; this is the motivation behind the Nash rule. Unfortunately this does not give us a scoring rule because $\log(0)$ is undefined, which is why we set $s_m = -n\log(m-1)$; thus, no amount of first places will compensate for a single last place.

The main interest of this paper is measuring the effect of strategic voting on these measures of welfare.

Definition 3. *Consider a voting rule f and a profile P. A strategic vote for voter i is a P_i' such that:*

$$f(P_i', P_{-i}) \succ_i f(P_i, P_{-i}).$$

In other words, if voter i casts P_i' instead of P_i, then the election outcome is preferable for voter i.

A voter may have many strategic votes available to him. We thus define his optimal strategy to be a P_i^* such that:

$$P_i^* \in \arg\max_{P_i'} f(P_i', P_{-i}),$$

the $\arg\max$ operator is understood with respect to voter i's preferences over the election outcomes.

Against this standard definition of manipulation two criticisms are often levied: 1) the probability of a single voter affecting the outcome of an election is negligibly small, and 2) it is unreasonable to suppose this voter has access to information about the other voters' preferences, which he needs to compute his strategic vote. In the political interpretation of voting, both arguments are undoubtedly valid, and a reasonable model should account for strategic voting by groups and incomplete information, such as the model of [18] or [14]. However, if we consider the interpretation of a small group of experts making a choice between candidates with the aim of identifying the one which is "best", then the standard definition is reasonable enough – it would not take a great deal of social engineering to find out how one's colleagues plan to rank interview candidates (say, ask them during a coffee break), and a single unethical judge can be enough to skew the outcome of a sporting context. Since our simulations will focus on the case where the number of voters is small and we are measuring the outcome in terms of numerical measures of welfare, we believe the standard definition of manipulation is sufficient.

2.2   Statistical Cultures

We will generate voter profiles from four theoretical families. In each case, the voters are sampled i.i.d.

- Impartial culture: given n voters and m candidates, each voter's preferences are drawn uniformly at random from all $m!$ possible preference orders.
- k-Euclidean: every voter and candidate is generated, uniformly at random, in $[0,1]^k$, the k-dimensional unit cube. A voter's preferences are determined by Euclidean distance to the candidates – the closer the candidate, the more preferred.
- Mallows model: given a dispersion parameter ϕ, $0 < \phi < 1$, and a reference order σ, a voter is assigned a preference order r with probably $\frac{1}{Z}\phi^{d(\sigma,r)}$. $d(\sigma,r)$ is the Kendall-tau distance between σ and r, and Z is a normalisation constant to make sure the probabilities add to one.
- Mixed Mallows model: given dispersion parameters $\phi_1,\ldots,\phi_k$, reference orders $\sigma_1,\ldots,\sigma_k$, and probabilities $p_1,\ldots,p_k$, a voter is assigned a preference order r with probably $\sum_{i\leq k} p_i \frac{1}{Z_i}\phi_i^{d(\sigma_i,r)}$. That is, each (ϕ_i,σ_i) defines a Mallows model, and we choose which Mallows model to sample from with the probabilities $p_1,\ldots,p_k$.

It should be noted that a mixed Mallows model will behave very differently depending on what reference orders are used, e.g. drawing profiles from a mixture of $a \succ b \succ c \succ d$ and $b \succ a \succ c \succ d$ will result in much more correlated preferences than a mixture of $a \succ b \succ c \succ d$ and $d \succ c \succ b \succ a$. In this paper, when we sample from the mixed Mallows model, it is understood that the reference orders are chosen randomly for each profile sampled.

In addition to these theoretical cultures we use two cultures based on empirical data from Preflib [20]. The first, Mallows sushi, is a mixed Mallows model trained by Lu and Boutilier [17] on a dataset of 5,000 preferences over 10 sushi types (https://www.preflib.org/data/ED/00014).

The second is based on skating data, consisting of judges' rankings of athletes in various events. The preferences in this data are highly correlated, and in most events the winner is unanimous. To deal with this we hand-picked an event with the most disagreement among the judges (https://www.preflib.org/data/ED/00006/00000046), and used a simple bag-of-preferences model (sampling the judges' rankings with replacement).

2.3   Experimental Setup

The simulations are based on varying the following parameters.
    Voting rules:

- Borda family ($m - 1$, $m/2$, $m/4$, 5).
- Approval family ($m/2$, $m/4$, 5, 1).
- Geometric family (2, 1.5, 1.2, 0.8, 0.65, 0.5).
- Nash rule.

    Theoretical cultures:

- Impartial culture.
- Euclidean family (1, 2, 5 dimensions).

- Mallows family (dispersion parameters 0.8, 0.5).
- Mixed Mallows (two equiprobable components, dispersion parameter 0.5).

Welfare measure:

- Borda welfare.
- Rawls welfare.
- Nash welfare.

Voter behaviour:

- All voters sincere.
- Voter 1 acts optimally.

The procedure for generating welfare results is as follows:

1. Fix $n = 10$. For each choice of $m \in \{3, \dots, 100\}$, voting rule, theoretical culture, behaviour, and welfare measure generate 10,000 profiles, measure the welfare of the election outcome, and return the average.
2. Fix $m = 10$. For each choice of $n \in \{3, \dots, 100\}$, voting rule, behaviour, and welfare measure generate 10,000 profiles from the Mallows sushi culture, measure the welfare of the election outcome, and return the average.
3. Fix $m = 30$. For each choice of $n \in \{3, \dots, 100\}$, voting rule, behaviour, and welfare measure generate 10,000 profiles from the skating bag culture, measure the welfare of the election outcome, and return the average.

3   Results

In this section we discuss the most interesting or representative results. The results for all the studied scenarios, along with the data, code, and instructions for replication, can be found on the Github.[2]

3.1   Impartial Culture

Impartial culture is often seen as a worst-case for manipulation, since it increases the odds of a close election where strategic voting can make a difference. In terms of consequences on welfare, however, this turns out to be rather benign; though most scoring rules lose welfare after manipulation, Borda (and its truncated version) remains the best choice for maximising Borda welfare (Fig. 1a), Geometric 0.5 for Rawls welfare, and Nash for Nash (at least for $m < 40$, after which it is overtaken by Borda. See Fig. 1b).

Nevertheless, the results with impartial culture allow us to make some general observations about the behaviour of scoring rules, which remain true in subsequent experiments.

Under sincere behaviour, concave rules expectedly do well in terms of Rawls and Nash welfare, while the Nash rule performs well in all three. However, these

---

[2] https://github.com/EIanovski/WelfareManipulation.

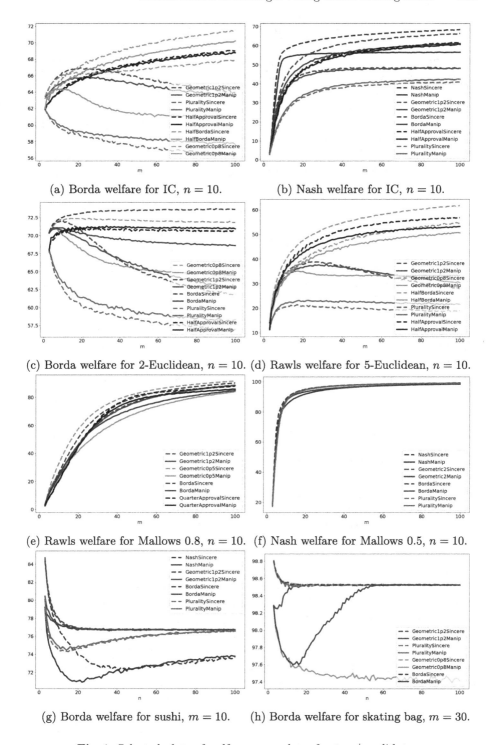

(a) Borda welfare for IC, $n = 10$.

(b) Nash welfare for IC, $n = 10$.

(c) Borda welfare for 2-Euclidean, $n = 10$. (d) Rawls welfare for 5-Euclidean, $n = 10$.

(e) Rawls welfare for Mallows 0.8, $n = 10$. (f) Nash welfare for Mallows 0.5, $n = 10$.

(g) Borda welfare for sushi, $m = 10$.   (h) Borda welfare for skating bag, $m = 30$.

Fig. 1. Selected plots of welfare vs number of voters/candidates.

rules are very susceptible to manipulation, and experience the largest welfare drops. In the case of impartial culture, these drops are insufficient to dethrone the geometric rule with $p = 0.5$ as the best choice for maximising Rawls welfare, but when we move on to other cultures we shall see the concave rules perform very poorly.

Convex geometric rules prove to be resistant to manipulation, and experience very minor welfare drops under strategic behaviour. However, their overall welfare properties are poor, so their stability does little to recommend them. Plurality is the most convex rule imaginable, and it is one of the few rules to consistently yield *higher* welfare in the presence of manipulation. However, even with the gain from manipulation, it consistently ranks as the worst rule in terms of welfare.

Borda lies on the border of convex and concave rules [12], and its properties lie between the two: loss of welfare after manipulation is tangible, but nowhere near the extent of concave rules. Though rarely the best rule in terms of welfare under manipulation, it routinely does pretty well.

5-approval and 5-Borda fare poorly, tending towards the plurality outcome as the number of candidates grows. This is unfortunate since the appeal of these rules is in their low cognitive burden on the voter, requiring the voter to rank 5 candidates rather than m; but it seems that if we value welfare, we rarely can get by without asking the voters for their full rankings. $(m/2)$-approval and $(m/2)$-Borda fare much better; $(m/2)$-Borda often outperforms full Borda, while $(m/2)$-approval is the clear winner under Euclidean preferences, to which we turn next.

3.2   Euclidean Cultures

The key feature of the Euclidean cultures is the existence of a centre – candidates close to the centre of the unit cube are reasonably close to all voters, and thus tend to have high Borda, Rawls, and Nash welfare. This goes a long way to explain the outstanding performance of $(m/2)$-approval in this setting (Fig. 1c, Fig. 1d) – the centre candidates are likely to be in the top half of most voters' ballots, and thus accumulate too many points for the manipulator to do much beyond choosing which centre candidate in particular should win.

As with impartial culture, the welfare of concave rules drops sharply under manipulation, but this time the effect is that these rules never maximise their respective welfare. Under 2- and 5-Euclidean, indeed, the Borda rule is the best choice for Rawls and Nash welfare after $(m/2)$-approval.

The dimension of the space seems to make a difference. Under 5-Euclidean the Borda rule performs a lot better, with $(m/2)$-Borda yielding the highest Borda welfare and Nash welfare for $m > 40$ (Table 1). Interestingly, $(m/4)$-approval also outperforms $(m/2)$-approval in terms of Borda welfare.

3.3   Mallows Models

The Mallows model models the situation where there is an underlying objective truth, and voter preferences are noisy signals of this true order. This noise is modelled as swaps of neighbouring candidates in the order (Kendall-tau distance), so the less swaps separate an order from the objective truth, the more likely it is to be generated. The result of this is that voter preferences are highly correlated, and as the number of candidates increases, so does the probability of the outcome being unanimous – with 100 candidates, the probability of a swap occurring at the very top of a voter's preferences is very low. The dispersion parameter affects how soon we reach the point where all voters are likely to agree on the top candidates (Fig. 1e vs Fig. 1f).

This is where convex rules come to the fore. The extra weight they give to the top candidates allows the candidates ranked high in the objective order to accumulate an overwhelming lead, reducing the manipulator's ability to harm social welfare. The result is that these rules are optimal at once with respect to Borda, Rawls, and Nash welfare. Concave rules, including Nash and Borda, give the manipulator enough power to bury a candidate ranked highly by the others, which harms their welfare for small values of m. However as we have observed, as m increases we head towards consensus, where the manipulator will have no incentive to manipulate.

The situation is different in our mixed Mallows model, which we remind the reader consists of two equiprobable components with dispersion parameters 0.5; the reference orders are sampled randomly for each profile. Convex rules again display poor welfare properties overall, while Nash and the concave geometric rules lose a lot from manipulation. The winners are members of the Borda and approval families, with $(m/2)$-Borda and $(m/4)$-approval performing well in terms of all welfare measures.

3.4   Mallows Sushi

As another Mallows mixture, one might expect the Mallows sushi model to perform similar to our mixed Mallows model, but this is not the case. It appears that there is such a thing as the objectively best sushi (fatty tuna, for the curious), and as the number of voters increases, all voting rules converge to this result (Fig. 1g). Borda, the convex rules, and the truncated rules converge rapidly; plurality and the highly concave rules slowly; Nash the slowest of all. Manipulation is only really tangible for the highly concave rules and Nash, as it gives voters the ability to effectively veto a choice of sushi.

3.5   Skating Bag

The skating bag culture is an example of a situation where there is a clear "best" candidate, who maximises at once Borda, Rawls, and Nash welfare, and all reasonable voting rules, plurality included, elect this best candidate. The damage of manipulation, therefore, measures the ability of a single voter to force through his preferred outcome in spite of overwhelming social consensus. A scoring rule needs to be top-heavy to resist this behaviour, so the high positions of the best candidate in the sincere voters' ballots will outweigh any shenanigans by the manipulator. As plurality is the top-heavy rule par excellence, this is one of the rare situations where this rule shines (Fig. 1h). Convex geometric rules are vulnerable when the number of voters is small, but from about 10 voters onwards the sincere votes begin to outweigh the manipulator's endeavours. The Borda rule is well-known for the scope it gives a manipulator to cause mischief, and it is only after we have 50 voters that the threat under Borda is liquidated.

As for concave rules, the threat never goes away. Even in an electorate of 100 voters, a single manipulator can force through a socially suboptimal outcome. A single last position does too much damage to the best candidate, giving the manipulator effective veto power over the outcome.

Table 1. Best scoring rules post manipulation with $n = 10$, $m > 10$. Boldface denotes rules that maximise welfare under sincere behaviour. Italics denote rules that are almost as good as the best, but much simpler.

Culture	Borda welfare	Rawls welfare	Nash welfare
Impartial culture	**Borda** $(m < 25)$, $(m/2)$-Borda $(m > 25)$	**Geometric 0.5**, $(m/2)$-approval $(m = 100)$	Borda $(m > 40)$, **Nash** $(m < 40)$, $(m/2)$-approval $(m > 40)$
1-Euclidean	**Borda** $(m < 12)$, $(m/2)$-approval $(m > 12)$	$(m/2)$-approval	$(m/2)$-approval
2-Euclidean	**Borda** $(m < 12)$, $(m/2)$-approval $(m > 12)$	$(m/2)$-approval	$(m/2)$-approval
5-Euclidean	$(m/2)$-Borda, $(m/4)$-approval $(m > 95)$	$(m/2)$-approval	$(m/2)$-approval $(m < 40)$, $(m/2)$-Borda $(m > 40)$
Mallows 0.8	Geometric 1.2	Geometric 1.2 $(m > 65)$, $(m/4)$-approval $(25 < m < 65)$, Borda $(m < 25)$	Geometric 1.2 $(m > 15)$, **Nash** $(m < 15)$
Mallows 0.5	Geometric $p > 1$, Plurality	5-approval	Geometric 2, *Plurality*
Mixed Mallows	$(m/2)$-Borda, $(m/4)$-approval $(m > 30)$	$(m/4)$-approval	$(m/4)$-approval $(m > 20)$, $(m/2)$-Borda $(m > 80)$, 5-approval $(m < 20)$

4   Conclusions

We summarise the three main takeaways of this study:

- Manipulation makes a difference. With the exception of impartial culture, or profiles with a small number of candidates, the welfare-maximising rule with a manipulator is never the same as under sincere behaviour (Table 1). The effect of manipulation in our framework is almost always negative.
- Top-heavy rules such as convex geometric rules and plurality are resistant to manipulation, losing little, or even gaining welfare in the presence of a manipulator. However, their welfare properties are so poor that this property does little to recommend them. The exception is in the case of highly correlated cultures such as Mallows models, where the additional weight these rules gives to the top candidate stymies attempts at manipulation.
- Concave geometric rules and the Nash rule are very susceptible to manipulation, to the point that Borda or even a convex rule is often better at maximising Rawls/Nash welfare than the rules designed for that purpose. This is an issue because empirical evidence suggests that humans value a mixture of the egalitarian and utilitarian principles, and given a choice will choose a voting rule that strikes a balance between the two [2,9,19]. If these rules fail to deliver in the face of strategic behaviour, the question must be posed: what voting rule should a society choose, if it seeks to strike a balance between utilitarian and egalitarian principles?

References

1. Aleskerov, F., Ivanov, A., Karabekyan, D., Yakuba, V.: Manipulability of aggregation procedures in impartial anonymous culture. Proc. Comput. Sci. **55**, 1250–1257 (2015)
2. Ambuehl, S., Bernheim, B.D.: Interpreting the will of the people: a positive analysis of ordinal preference aggregation. Working Paper 29389, National Bureau of Economic Research (2021). https://www.nber.org/papers/w29389
3. Bartholdi, J.J., Tovey, C.A., Trick, M.A.: The computational difficulty of manipulating an election. Soc. Choice Welf. **6**(3), 227–241 (1989)
4. Bassi, A.: Voting systems and strategic manipulation: an experimental study. J. Theoret. Polit. **27**(1), 58–85 (2015)
5. Chen, K.P., Yang, S.Z.: Strategic voting in open primaries. Public Choice **112**(1/2), 1–30 (2002)
6. Chopra, S., Pacuit, E., Parikh, R.: Knowledge-theoretic properties of strategic voting. In: Alferes, J.J., Leite, J. (eds.) JELIA 2004. LNCS (LNAI), vol. 3229, pp. 18–30. Springer, Heidelberg (2004). https://doi.org/10.1007/978-3-540-30227-8_5
7. Conitzer, V., Sandholm, T., Lang, J.: When are elections with few candidates hard to manipulate? J. ACM **54**(3), 14-es (2007)
8. Conitzer, V., Walsh, T., Xia, L.: Dominating manipulations in voting with partial information. In: Twenty-Fifth AAAI Conference on Artificial Intelligence (2011)
9. Frohlich, N., Oppenheimer, J.A., Eavey, C.L.: Laboratory results on Rawls's distributive justice. Br. J. Polit. Sci. **17**(1), 1–21 (1987)

10. Gibbard, A.: Manipulation of voting schemes: a general result. Econometrica **41**(4), 587–601 (1973)
11. Kelly, J.S.: Almost all social choice rules are highly manipulable, but a few aren't. Soc. Choice Welf. **10**(2), 161–175 (1993)
12. Kondratev, A.Y., Ianovski, E., Nesterov, A.S.: How should we score athletes and candidates: geometric scoring rules. arXiv preprint arXiv:1907.05082 (2019)
13. Laplace, P.S.: Œuvres complètes, vol. 7, chap. Théorie analytique des probabilités, pp. 277–279 (1886). https://gallica.bnf.fr/ark:/12148/bpt6k775950/f4
14. Lehtinen, A.: The Borda rule is also intended for dishonest men. Public Choice **133**(1–2), 73–90 (2007)
15. Lehtinen, A.: The welfare consequences of strategic voting in two commonly used parliamentary agendas. Theory Decis. **63**, 1–40 (2007)
16. Lehtinen, A.: The welfare consequences of strategic behaviour under approval and plurality voting. Eur. J. Polit. Econ. **24**, 688–704 (2008)
17. Lu, T., Boutilier, C.: Effective sampling and learning for Mallows models with pairwise-preference data. J. Mach. Learn. Res. **15**(117), 3963–4009 (2014)
18. Lu, T., Tang, P., Procaccia, A., Boutilier, C.: Bayesian vote manipulation: optimal strategies and impact on welfare. In: Uncertainty in Artificial Intelligence - Proceedings of the 28th Conference, UAI 2012 (2012)
19. Masthoff, J.: Group recommender systems: combining individual models. In: Ricci, F., Rokach, L., Shapira, B., Kantor, P.B. (eds.) Recommender Systems Handbook, pp. 677–702. Springer, Boston (2011). https://doi.org/10.1007/978-0-387-85820-3_21
20. Mattei, N., Walsh, T.: PrefLib: a library for preferences. In: ADT (2013). https://www.preflib.org
21. Moulin, H.: Fair Division and Collective Welfare. MIT Press, Cambridge (2004). chap. 3
22. Nitzan, S.: The vulnerability of point-voting schemes to preference variation and strategic manipulation. Public Choice **47**(2), 349–370 (1985)
23. Satterthwaite, M.A.: Strategy-proofness and Arrow's conditions: existence and correspondence theorems for voting procedures and social welfare functions. J. Econ. Theory **10**(2), 187–217 (1975)
24. Smith, J.H.: Aggregation of preferences with variable electorate. Econometrica **41**(6), 1027–1041 (1973)
25. Walsh, T.: Where are the hard manipulation problems? J. Artif. Int. Res. **42**(1), 1–29 (2011)
26. Xia, L., Conitzer, V.: Determining possible and necessary winners given partial orders. J. Artif. Intell. Res. **41**, 25–67 (2011)
27. Young, H.P.: Optimal voting rules. J. Econ. Perspect. **9**(1), 51–64 (1995)
28. Zitzewitz, E.: Nationalism in winter sports judging and its lessons for organizational decision making. J. Econ. Manag. Strat. **15**, 67–99 (2006)

Preserving Consistency for Liquid Knapsack Voting

Pallavi Jain[1], Krzysztof Sornat[2]([⊠])[iD], and Nimrod Talmon[3][iD]

[1] Indian Institute of Technology Jodhpur, Jodhpur, India
`pallavi@iitj.ac.in`
[2] IDSIA USI-SUPSI, Lugano, Switzerland
`krzysztof.sornat@idsia.ch`
[3] Ben-Gurion University of the Negev, Beer Sheva, Israel
`talmonn@bgu.ac.il`

Abstract. Liquid Democracy (LD) uses transitive delegations to facilitate joint decision making. In its simplest form, it is used for binary decisions, however its promise holds also for more advanced voting settings. Here we consider LD in the context of Participatory Budgeting (PB), which is a direct democracy approach to budgeting, most usually done in municipal budgeting processes. In particular, we study Knapsack Voting, in which PB voters can approve projects, however the sum of costs of voter-approved projects must respect the global budget limit. We observe inconsistency issues when allowing delegations, as the cost of voter-approved projects may go over the budget limit; we offer ways to overcome such inconsistencies by studying the computational complexity of a related combinatorial problem in which the task is to update as few delegations as possible to arrive—after following all project delegations—to a consistent profile.

Keywords: Participatory budgeting · Liquid democracy · Knapsack voting · Computational complexity · Parameterized complexity · Approximation algorithms

1 Introduction

Liquid Democracy (LD) provides voters with greater flexibility as each voter is free to decide whether to vote on her own or delegate her vote to another voter of her choice [6]. Importantly, these delegations are transitive, so, e.g., if voter u delegates her vote to voter v who in turn delegates her vote to voter w, then effectively the vote of u is delegated to w. As such, LD is usually framed as solving the scalability issue of direct democracy while avoiding the pitfalls of representative democracy [3,19]. Practically, however, LD is usually used only when voting on two proposals (i.e., a yes/no vote; we do mention, in Subsect. 1.1, some works considering other settings). Our motivation for this work is to investigate the possibility of using LD for the more involved setting of Participatory Budgeting (PB) [9].

In PB (specifically in *Combinatorial PB* [2]), voters express their preferences over a set of projects, where each project has its own cost. Then, the aggregation task is to choose a subset of these projects whose total cost does not exceed some given budget

---

An extended abstract of this work appeared in AAMAS 2021 [21].

© The Author(s), under exclusive license to Springer Nature Switzerland AG 2022
D. Baumeister and J. Rothe (Eds.): EUMAS 2022, LNAI 13442, pp. 221–238, 2022.
https://doi.org/10.1007/978-3-031-20614-6_13

limit. While there are many ballot types that can be used by voters in PB, usually voters express their preferences by providing approval ballots. In this paper we concentrate on one variant of approval ballots, referred to as *Knapsack Voting* [17]: in it, each voter can approve as many projects as she wishes, however the total cost of the projects approved by a voter must not exceed the given budget limit.

Note that, effectively, this means that each voter shall solve an instance of the Knapsack problem herself; this indeed makes the task of each voter much more involved than when voters are simply required to submit an arbitrary approval ballot (without solving a Knapsack instance). We argue that the main reason of requiring voters to satisfy such Knapsack constraints is that, by solving Knapsack constraints, voters appreciate that the global aggregation task of PB (which is, in essence, solving a Knapsack constraint while taking into consideration the preferences of the voters) is not trivial; as such, voters may be more accepting to the output bundle selected by the aggregation method in use. Goel et al. [17] discuss further advantages of this ballot type.

So, how can LD be used for elections in which voters are using Knapsack Voting? A simple way would be to allow each voter to choose between the following two options: (1) vote directly, by submitting a subset of projects she approves, while making sure that their total cost respects the budget limit; or (2) delegate her vote completely to another voter of her choice. While this way might be plausible, here we wish to explore the possibility of granting voters even greater flexibility, thus we propose "project-wise delegations": each voter v, for each project p, can choose between the following two options: (1) vote directly, deciding whether to approve p or disapprove p (i.e., whether to select p or not); or (2) delegate the decision on whether to approve p or disapprove p to another voter of her choice.

In other words, we wish to apply *fine-grained* Liquid Democracy (in contrast to standard *coarse-grained* Liquid Democracy) to Knapsack ballots for PB. That is, while coarse-grained Liquid Democracy in our context would mean that a voter can either vote directly or delegate her complete ballot to a voter of her choice, fine-grained Liquid Democracy in our context means that a voter can delegate parts of her ballot (i.e., subsets of projects) to voters of her choice. Our point of view is that the basic merit of Liquid Democracy is the greater flexibility it gives to voters participating in it. Thus, we strive to push this flexibility even further. Concretely, a voter that does not feel competent to decide (e.g. between several environmental projects) may delegate these projects to a voter of her choice, while directly deciding on other project that she feels more competent about. Thus, our results can be seen as showing that, at least in some cases, it is indeed possible to allow for more expressive power to the voters; generally speaking, this is useful as, in principle, greater voter flexibility has the potential of allowing to reach better joint decisions. Consider the following example.

Example 1. Consider 3 voters u, v, w, and 4 projects a, b, c, d, where voter u is positive towards approving project a but does not like project b. Then, u approves project a and disapproves project b. It is possible, that voter u is not sure about the project c due to the lack of information, knowledge, or some other reason. But, she trusts voter v on the decision for project c. So, she delegates her vote for c to v; and will take the same decision as of v. It is possible that u does not find v competent enough to take a decision for project d and trusts w more than v. So, she delegates her vote for d to w.

Indeed, our motivation for investigating LD for PB is to grant voters greater flexibility and expressive power. There are not, however, such thing as a free lunch—the price of this greater flexibility is the possibility, due to delegations, of ballot inconsistency: consider the example above and say that each project costs 1 and the budget limit is 2. If v decides to approve project c and also w decides to approve project d then effectively voter u would approve projects a, c, and d, thus in total she approves projects of cost 3, which is strictly above the budget limit. Thus, due to following the direct decisions and the delegations as expressed by voter u, we have that the vote of u violates the constraints of Knapsack Voting.

Our main aim, thus, in this paper is to explore possibilities of mitigating such possible inconsistencies. To this end, our approach is to look for the most delicate changes we can apply to the given votes to arrive to an instance in which such inconsistencies are avoided. We formulate our approach as the combinatorial problem of updating as few delegations as possible so that, after following all delegations, all votes satisfy the Knapsack constraint of Knapsack Voting.

Indeed, the reader may wonder why we take for us the freedom of changing the ballots submitted by the voters. Our point of view is that preserving consistency of the profiles after delegations (i.e., respecting the Knapsack constraints after following all the delegations) is crucial, as voters in a Liquid Democracy context expect to be able to see the ballots that were submitted on their behalf after taking into account their delegations. Thus, the system shall be able to provide such ballots; however, this conflicts with the desire to respect the Knapsack constraints. In particular, voters may feel that the system is unfair if some voters would effectively not respect the Knapsack constraint after following delegations. Thus, we take the natural approach of modifying the input we get as minimally as possible.

1.1 Related Work

Perhaps the closest work to ours is the work of Brill and Talmon on Pairwise Liquid Democracy [8] that deals with introducing LD to single winner ordinal elections in which each voter can delegate the decision on whether she prefers one alternative over the other, for each pair of alternatives, to another voter of her choice. Brill and Talmon show that, allowing this "pairwise" delegation might result in inconsistent ballots (e.g., voter u prefers a to b, delegates the decision on the pair $\{b, c\}$ to voter v who ends up preferring b to c, and delegates the decision on the pair $\{c, a\}$ to voter w who ends up preferring c to a, resulting in intransitive preference for voter u). Another closely related work is that of Christoff et al. [10], dealing with introducing LD to a more general, logic-based social choice setting, while dealing with logical inconsistencies resulting from per-formula delegations.

Some works on LD from a computational social choice perspective consider allowing a voter to delegate a single decision to several voters [11,18]; we, similar to Brill and Talmon [8] and Bloembergen et al. [5], consider delegating each decision to only one other voter, however voters can use delegations for several decisions at once (note that in our setting voters can delegate different decisions to different voters). Other papers propose different aggregation methods for PB [1,4,14,26] (see also the survey of Aziz and Shah [2]). For the most part of our paper, however, the specific aggregation method to be used is not relevant, as our aim is to arrive at a consistent profile of votes while allowing per-project delegations.

1.2   Our Contribution

We consider using fine-grained LD for PB by allowing per-project delegations for Knapsack Voting and consider a specific way of mitigating the possible inconsistencies resulting from following these delegations. In particular, from a computational complexity point of view, we show that the problem of finding the smallest set of delegations to update to arrive at a consistent profile, after following all remaining delegations, is computationally intractable (Subsect. 3.2), also for various special cases and for a number of natural parameters, except for the number of voters, for which it is fixed-parameter tractable (Theorem 11). We do, however, identify some special cases that allow for efficient algorithms (Proposition 8 and Observation 13), devise approximation algorithms for the problem (Sect. 5), and report on related computer-based simulations based on an Integer Linear Programming (ILP) formulation (Sect. 4).

2   Preliminaries

In this section we describe Knapsack Voting (Subsect. 2.1), our generalized model of per-project delegations (Subsect. 2.2), and formally define the combinatorial problem of updating as few delegations to arrive to a consistent profile (Subsect. 2.3).

For $n \in \mathbb{N}$, we define $[n] = \{1, \ldots, n\}$. By $\mathcal{O}^*(\cdot)$ we denote $\mathcal{O}(\cdot)$ notation when suppressing polynomial factors. By $o(\cdot)$ we denote little-o notation. By ETH we mean the Exponential Time Hypothesis [20].

2.1   Knapsack Voting

In Knapsack Voting [17] we are given a set of projects, $P = \{p_1, \ldots, p_m\}$, together with their cost function $c : P \rightarrow \mathbb{N}$ of projects, a budget limit B, and a set of voters, $V = \{v_1, \ldots, v_n\}$ such that each $v \in V$ is represented by its approval ballot respecting the budget limit, i.e., it holds that $v \subseteq P$ and $\sum_{p \in v} c(p) \leq B$. E.g., consider a simple instance of Knapsack Voting with a set of projects $P = \{p_1, p_2, p_3\}$ with $c(p_1) = c(p_2) = 3$, $c(p_3) = 5$, a budget limit $B = 6$, and a set of voters $V = \{v_1, v_2\}$ with $v_1 = \{p_1, p_2\}$ and $v_2 = \{p_3\}$. Indeed, the total cost of projects approved by v_1 and v_2, are 6 and 5 respectively, thus both voters respect the budget limit. Clearly, v_2 cannot approve p_2 as well without violating the Knapsack constraint. (Note that we use the terms "approve" and "disapprove" as they are the standard jargon for approval elections; in a way, a voter does not really "disapprove" of projects she did not select, but merely not support them.)

It is useful to view a vote in Knapsack Voting as a binary vector of length m, where the ith entry is 1 if the voter approves the ith project and 0 if the voter disapproves the ith project. Indeed, in Knapsack Voting a voter decides for each project, whether to approve it or not.

2.2   Liquid Knapsack Voting

In our per-project delegation model we allow voters to decide, for each project, whether to delegate the decision on whether to approve the project or disapprove it, to a voter of their choice. I.e., a voter can, for each project, either (1) approve the project; (2) disapprove the project; or (3) delegate the decision of whether to approve or disapprove the project to some other voter—her delegation for this project. Note that a voter can choose several delegates, assigning a different set of projects to each delegate, but cannot assign more than one delegate for a single project. Formally, in *Liquid Knapsack Voting* we are given a set of projects, $P = \{p_1, \ldots, p_m\}$, together with their cost function $c : P \to \mathbb{N}$ of projects, a budget limit B, and a set of voters, $V = \{v_1, \ldots, v_n\}$. Here, voter v is represented by an m-length vector L_v such that each element in L_v is either 1—denoting that the corresponding project is approved by voter v; 0—denoting that the corresponding project is disapproved by voter v; or the name of some other voter—denoting that v delegates her vote for the corresponding project to that voter. (Note that Liquid Knapsack Voting indeed generalizes Knapsack Voting: in Knapsack Voting L_v would simply be a binary vector.)

Example 2. Consider a simple instance of Liquid Knapsack Voting with a set of projects $P = \{p_1, p_2, p_3\}$ with $c(p_1) = c(p_2) = 3$, $c(p_3) = 5$, a budget limit $B = 6$, and a set of voters $V = \{v_1, v_2\}$. Say that v_1 decides to approve p_1, disapprove p_3, but is unsure regarding p_2; say also that v_1 decides to delegate the decision on p_2 to voter v_2. Say further that voter v_2 decides to approve p_3 but disapprove both p_1 and p_2. Then, effectively, following v_1's delegation of the decision regarding p_2 to v_2, we have that v_1 should be considered as disapproving p_2 as well. Viewed as vectors, $L_{v_1} = [1, v_2, 0]$ while $L_{v_2} = [0, 0, 1]$.

It will be useful also to consider the *delegation graph* implied by an instance of Liquid Knapsack Voting, with a vertex for each voter and an arc from vertex u to vertex v if u delegates some decisions (on at least one project) to v. Furthermore, we can also construct a delegation graph for each project—we call them *per-project delegation graphs*. Put differently, the arcs of the *delegation graph* are the union of the arcs of each of these *per-project delegation graphs*.

As every voter may delegate a decision on a specific project only to a single other voter, all vertices in a per-project delegation graph have an out-degree of at most 1. Thus, for every voter and every project we can follow its (unique) delegation chain in the corresponding per-project delegation graph.

Delegation Chains. A *delegation chain* for some project p is a sequence of voters, each delegates the decision on p to the next voter in the chain, where the last voter in the chain delegates the decision on p to some voter that (dis)approves p. (The voter that (dis)approves p is not contained in this delegation chain.) The *root* of a delegation chain for some project p is the last voter in the chain (in particular, the root is not a voter that (dis)approves p). A *delegation component* for some project p is a set of voters, each of which is part of some delegation chain for p that has the same root.

Remark 3. Two voters might be in different delegation chains but in the same delegation component. Moreover, a voter which (dis)approves a project p can receive a delegation on p from a few voters (which are the roots of disjoint delegation components for p).

TANSTAAFL.[1] The main merit of using Liquid Knapsack Voting is the additional expressiveness it offers to the voters. This additional expressiveness, however, comes with a price; in particular: (1) There could be **cycles**—e.g., say that u delegates the decision on p to v and then also v delegates the decision on p to u; then, it is not clear how to decide whether it should be taken that these voters approve or disapprove p. (2) Ballots may be **inconsistent**—say that u delegates the decision on several projects to some other voters. Then, it could be that, following the delegations, the resulting ballot of u exceeds the budget limit, thus not satisfying the Knapsack constraint.

Our main approach of dealing with the possibility of inconsistent ballots results from our per-project delegations is to look for the minimal set of delegations that, if updated (to approvals or disapprovals) would result in a *consistent profile* (i.e., a profile in which all votes, after following all delegations, satisfy the Knapsack constraint).

2.3   Consistent Knapsack Voting

Following the informal discussion above, next is the formal definition of the combinatorial problem we aim at solving here. By a *consistent* Knapsack Voting instance we mean that all voters satisfy the Knapsack constraint, after we follow all delegations. The CONSISTENT KNAPSACK VOTING (CKV) problem is formally defined as follows (Fig. 1 shows an example of solving an instance of CKV).

CONSISTENT KNAPSACK VOTING (CKV)
Input: A set of projects P, cost function $c\colon P \to \mathbb{N}$, a set of voters V, a set of votes $\{L_v : v \in V\}$, where $L_v \in \{0, 1, V \setminus \{v\}\}^{|P|}$, a budget limit B and an integer k.
Question: Can we update at most k delegations to 0 or 1 so that the resulting instance is a consistent Knapsack Voting instance?

Two remarks are in place:

1. We only allow to update delegations to an approval or a disapproval; in particular, we do not allow to change an approval to a disapproval. Our modeling is such as it seems too invasive to change a direct decision of voter.
2. Technically, the definition of CKV allows to change a delegation to an approval; however, as the task is to avoid violating Knapsack constraints, we assume w.l.o.g. that we use the available k delegations updates only to change delegations to disapprovals.

W.l.o.g. we assume that an instance of CKV can be made consistent by updating *all* delegations to disapprovals. Otherwise, it would be a NO instance trivially.

We wish to offer a different angle on the combinatorial problem we set to study here: the approach we take in the paper is to develop algorithms that take the whole input—with the delegations, and thus with the possibility of budget-infeasible votes—and find a minimum set of delegation-modifications so that we would arrive to a voting profile that respects the Knapsack constraints. In this context, our approach can be viewed as a preprocessing phase for any aggregation method defined on Knapsack ballots, and, indeed, our approach is agnostic to the aggregation method used.

---
[1] There ain't no such thing as a free lunch.

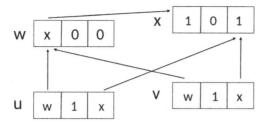

Fig. 1. An instance of CKV. There is a set of projects $P = \{p_1, p_2, p_3\}$, each of unit cost, and the budget limit is $B = 2$. There are voters $V = \{u, v, w, x\}$, whose votes are represented as vectors where the left entry corresponds to p_1, the middle entry to p_2, and the right entry to p_3; e.g., voter u delegates the decision on p_1 to w, approves p_2, and delegates the decision on p_3 to x. (u, w) is an example of delegation chain for project p_1. There is one delegation component for project p_1—it is $\{u, v, w\}$ with the root w. Regarding Remark 3, note that u and v are not in the same delegation chain but they are in the same delegation component. Furthermore, there are two delegation components for project p_3, mainly: $\{u\}$ and $\{v\}$ with roots u and v respectively. Note that if we follow the delegations then both u and v would violate the Knapsack constraints. If we update the delegation of voter w wrt. p_1 (i.e., change it so that w would disapprove p_1), however, then we will have a consistent instance, thus with $k = 1$, this is a yes-instance.

Parameters. We are interested in the parameterized complexity of CKV, wishing to identify certain instance parameters that allow for efficient algorithms for CKV. Next we discuss our choice of parameters: (1) **general parameters**: We consider several parameters visible in the definition of CKV: the number $|V|$ of voters, the number $|P|$ of projects, the budget limit B, and the number of updates k (we refer to k also as the *solution size*). (2) **delegation-specific parameters**: We consider further parameters that relate explicitly to the delegations; informally speaking, these parameters measure how complicated is the delegation structure of an instance: the number of delegations, the maximum number of delegations a single voter can use, the maximum length of a delegation chain. Note that, if any of these parameters is 0, then the problem reduces to the standard Knapsack Voting problem, in which validating consistency can be done in polynomial-time (by checking each voter individually).

3 Theoretical Results

In Subsect. 3.1, we describe preprocessing steps that allow us to assume, throughout the paper, that CKV instances have a certain, simplified structure. Then we discuss parameterized algorithms (Subsect. 3.2). (Note that, in Sect. 5, we discuss approximation algorithms.) Due to space limitation, we will defer some proofs to the full version of the paper.

3.1 Preprocessing Steps and Observations

Given an instance of CKV, throughout the paper we assume that we first apply the following two preprocessing steps.

Removing Cycles. Indeed, cycles are possible (e.g., voter u delegates the decision on p to voter v, which, in turn, delegates the decision on p "back" to voter u; longer cycles are also possible). Each cycle can be resolved only by changing at least one delegation from the cycle. For CKV, we can, however, simply change exactly one (arbitrary) delegation to disapproval (at cost 1, so optimally). Then all delegations in the cycle can be immediately resolved to be disapprovals. Such operation is proper because we are interested in minimizing the number of changes of delegations to have Knapsack-consistent ballots, so having only disapprovals on a cycle is always better (precisely, not worse) than having some approvals. Such operation of removing a cycle also decreases k by 1. Put differently, throughout the paper we assume w.l.o.g. that there are simply no delegation cycles in our CKV instances.

Removing Disapproval Chains. A *disapproval chain* is a delegation chain ending in a disapproval; e.g., voter u delegates the decision on p to v, v delegates the decision on p to w, and w disapproves p. Simply following the delegations, we will have disapprovals for all voters in a disapproval chain, for the corresponding project at hand. So, as having disapprovals is always better in the context of CKV, we can simply change all delegations in a disapproval chain to be disapprovals (at cost 0, so optimally). Put differently, throughout the paper we assume w.l.o.g. that there are simply no disapproval chains in our CKV instances. In particular, we can use this rule also when modifying an instance by changing a delegation to disapproval (which may create a disapproval chain; then we resolve it immediately at cost 0).

Remark 4. Assuming an exhaustive application of the above preprocessing steps, we assume w.l.o.g. throughout the paper that we only have *approval chains*; i.e., if we follow each delegation in an instance we end up in an approval (but never a disapproval and we never get stuck in a cycle). Therefore, we use names *delegation chains* and *approval chains* interchangeably.

3.2   Parameterized Complexity

We study the parameterized complexity of CONSISTENT KNAPSACK VOTING. While the problem is hard with respect to many parameters, we do identify some parameterized algorithms. In particular, the algorithm from Theorem 11 is efficient for instances with few voters. Indeed, while participatory budgeting is usually done with many voters (e.g., residents of a municipality) it can be performed with few voters (e.g., a city planning committee).

The next hardness result follows by a reduction from the VERTEX COVER problem (VC) in which, for a given graph G and integer k', we have to decide if there exists a subset $S, |S| \leq k'$ of vertices of graph G such that each edge of G has at least one endpoint in S.

Theorem 5. CKV *is* NP-*hard even when* $|P| = 4$ *and each voter can delegate to only one other voter.*

Proof. We give a polynomial-time reduction from VC on cubic graphs (i.e. 3-regular), which is known to be NP-hard [16]. Let (G, k') be an instance of VC, where G is a cubic graph. G is 4-colorable (that is, we can color the vertices of the graph using at most four colors such that for any edge in G, colors of its endpoints are not the same) and we can find such coloring in polynomial time through a greedy algorithm. We color the vertices using colors $1, 2, 3, 4$. We construct an instance of CKV as follows. We create four projects p_1, p_2, p_3, p_4 corresponding to vertex colors. The cost of every project is 1. Corresponding to every vertex $x \in V(G)$, we add two voters v_x and $\hat{v}_x$, which we call as VertexVoter and dummyVertexVoter, respectively. The dummyVertexVoter $\hat{v}_x$ approves the project corresponding to the color of the vertex x, and disapprove remaining 3 projects. The VertexVoter v_x delegates the project corresponding to the color of the vertex x to the dummyVertexVoter $\hat{v}_x$, and disapprove remaining 3 projects. Further, corresponding to every edge $e \in E(G)$ of G, we add a voter v_e, which we call as EdgeVoter. Let $e = xy$ be an edge and let i and j be the colors of x and y respectively (we have $i, j \in [4], i \neq j$). Then, the voter v_e delegates: 1) project p_i to the VertexVoter v_x; 2) project p_j to the VertexVoter v_y; and disapprove the remaining two projects. Finally, in the created instance of CKV we set $B = 1$ and $k = k'$. Next, we prove the correctness of the reduction.

In the forward direction, let S be a solution to (G, k'). For every vertex $x \in S$, we update the delegation of voter v_x to 0. Since S is a vertex cover, for every EdgeVoter v_e, where $e = xy$ in an edge in G, either we update delegation for the voter v_x or v_y. Thus, every EdgeVoter approves only one project, which is within the budget. Since $|S| \leq k' = k$, we only update at most k delegations. This completes the proof in the forward direction.

In the backward direction, we first note that for a yes-instance of the problem, there exists a solution in which we only update the delegations for VertexVoters as they are the only roots of delegation components. Indeed, suppose a delegation of the EdgeVoter voter v_e to the VertexVoter v_x is updated, then instead of it, we can update the delegation of the voter v_x to 0, and clearly it is still a solution. So, we consider a solution of size at most k in which we only update the delegations for VertexVoters. We create a subset $S \subseteq V(G)$ as follows: if we update the delegation of voter v_x, then add the vertex x to S. Clearly, $|S| \leq k'$ as $k' = k$. We claim that S is a vertex cover of G. Suppose it is not the case, then there exists an edge $e = xy$ such that neither x nor y is in S. This implies that we neither update delegation of v_x nor delegation of v_y. Thus, the voter v_e approves 2 projects. This results in a contradiction with the Knapsack constraint with $B = 1$ and completes the proof.   □

In fact, the reduction used in Theorem 5 shows NP-hardness even when some parameters are constant.

Corollary 6. CKV *is NP-hard even if all of the following hold:* $|P| = 4$, $B = 1$, *the maximum number of delegations in a vote is at most* 3*, the maximum number of approvals in a vote is at most* 1*; the maximum cost of a project is* 1*, the maximum length of a delegation chain is* 2*, the maximum in-degree in the delegation graph is at most* 3*.*

The next result follows by a reduction from the SET COVER problem, known to be W[2]-hard wrt. k [12, 13].

Theorem 7. CKV *is* W[2]-*hard wrt.* k *even if each voter can delegate to only one other voter.*

Next we describe some tractable cases. First, if we restrict each voter to be able to delegate only one of the projects, we have tractability (as we can check each voter individually).

Proposition 8. CKV *can be solved in polynomial-time when every voter delegates at most one project.*

Proof. A voter that does not delegate is consistent (due to our assumption). For a voter that delegates one project we check if she is consistent with replacing the delegation with 1 (recall, we assumed we do not have either cycles or disapproval chains). If so, we can skip this voter and resolve her delegation in the last phase (by just following its delegation chain). If not, then we know this delegation has to be resolved to 0 hence we can update the last delegation in the corresponding delegation component (i.e., in its root) at cost 1. Such operation resolves the delegation to 0 but also it affects in the same way the largest set under inclusion of other voters (still at cost 1). In particular, after update of the delegation of the root to 0 (at cost 1) we propagate this decision to all delegations in this delegation component (without paying extra cost). Note that such operation does not create any disapproval chain or delegation cycle. ☐

Deciding separately on each delegation component, we have the following.

Observation 9. *We can solve* CKV *in time* $\mathcal{O}^*(\binom{|C|}{k})) \le \mathcal{O}^*(2^{|C|})$, *where C is the set of delegation components.*

Proof. A solution to a yes-instance of CKV can be characterized by updating at most k delegations to disapprovals. W.l.o.g. the updates are made in the roots of delegation components. The result comes from a brute-force enumeration of all possible choices of updating some k delegations (delegation components) to disapprovals. Overall, we consider at most $2^{|C|}$ cases, each in polynomial-time, hence the total running time is $\mathcal{O}^*(2^{|C|})$. ☐

The number of delegation components $|C|$ is upper-bounded by the number of delegations D. Furthermore, $D \le |V| \cdot |P|$, hence CKV is FPT wrt. $|C|$, D, or $|V|+|P|$. We have the following corollary that gives us an algorithm that is almost tight, following the ETH-based lowerbound of Theorem 12.

Corollary 10. *We can solve* CKV *in time* $\mathcal{O}^*(2^{|V| \cdot |P|})$.

We can remove $|P|$ from the exponent in the result above, but then the dependence on $|V|$ is double-exponential.

Theorem 11. CKV *can be solved in* $\mathcal{O}^*(2^{\mathcal{O}(2^{|V|+\log|V|})})$ *time, hence the problem is* FPT *wrt.* $|V|$.

Proof. We solve the problem by outputting a subset S of delegation components, whose update to disapproval makes an instance consistent. For every subset of voters $V' \subseteq V$ we define a type $t_{V'}$ of a delegation component. So, we have $2^{|V|}$ types of delegation components. A delegation component dc, which is defined by a subset of voters V' and a project p, is of type $t_{V'}$ which we denote by $\mathrm{dc} \in t_{V'}$. We overload the notation by writing $c(\mathrm{dc}) = c(p)$. By $|t_{V'}|$ we denote the number of delegation components of type $t_{V'}$. Note that each type $t_{V'}$ consists of at most $|P|$ delegation components (at most one for each project); hence, we have at most $|P| \cdot 2^{|V|}$ delegation components.

We define a Mixed Integer Linear Program (MILP) with $2^{|V|}$ many integer variables (one for each delegation component type). The main idea is that if $\mathrm{dc}_1, \mathrm{dc}_2 \in t_{V'}$ and $c(\mathrm{dc}_1) > c(\mathrm{dc}_2)$ then it is better to update a component of the more expensive project dc_1 than that of the less expensive project dc_2. (Observe that the topological structure of delegations in dc_1 and dc_2 does not matter, only the subset of voters who will be affected if we change the root of the delegation component to disapproval.) Using this fact, we will split an integer variable into a sum of real variables—where the i-th variable represents updating the i-th most expensive project from a delegation component type.

Formally, for each $V' \subseteq V$ we define an integer variable $x_{V'} \in \{0, 1, \ldots, |t_{V'}|\}$ and $|t_{V'}|$-many real variables $y_{V',i} \in [0, 1]$, where $i \in \{1, 2, \ldots, |t_{V'}|\}$. We write the following constraint to connect the integer variable with its corresponding real-valued variables:

$$x_{V'} = \sum_{i=1}^{|t_{V'}|} y_{V',i} \, . \tag{1}$$

We need to add the knapsack constraint for every voter. To this end, we define $p(V', i) \in P$ to be the i-th most expensive project in a delegation component type $t_{V'}$ (by definition, there is at most one delegation component of that type that concerns a particular project). Then, for every $v \in V$ we define the knapsack constraint:

$$\sum_{p \in P: L_v(p)=1} c(p) + \sum_{V' \subseteq V: v \in V'} \sum_{i=1}^{|t_{V'}|} (1 - y_{V',i}) \cdot c(p(V', i)) \leq B \, .$$

The objective function is $\min \sum_{V' \subseteq V} x_{V'}$.

We can transform any optimal solution (x^*, y^*) of the MILP into an optimal solution (x^*, y^{int}) consisting of integer variables only: in particular, we define $y_{V',i}^{\mathrm{int}} = 1$ for $i \in \{1, \ldots, x_{V'}^*\}$ and $y_{V',i}^{\mathrm{int}} = 0$ for $i \in \{x_{V'}^* + 1, \ldots, |t_{V'}|\}$.

Optimality. The objective value of such a solution (x^*, y^{int}) is the same as for (x^*, y^*) (hence optimal), as the objective function depends only on $x_{V'}$ and both solutions have the same value for variables $x_{V'}$.

Feasibility. We can proceed as described above since the monotonicity of $c(p(V', i))$ wrt. i allows to move the value from $y_{V',i}$ to $y_{V',i-1}$, keeping consistency with the knapsack constraint.

Running Time. The MILP has at most $2^{|V|}$ integer variables, $|P| \cdot 2^{|V|}$ real variables, and $|V| + 2^{|V|}$ many constraints. We can solve an MILP using $\mathcal{O}(p^{2.5p+o(p)} \cdot |I|)$ arithmetic operations, where $|I|$ is the input size and p is the number of integer variables [7,22]. In particular, our MILP can be solved in $\mathcal{O}^*(2^{\mathcal{O}(2^{|V|+\log|V|})})$-time. $\qquad\square$

Note that $2^{|V|}$ in the proof above is only an upper-bound for the number of integer variables in the MILP. Indeed, we can write a more strict upper-bound. Let t be the number of non-empty types $t_{V'}$, i.e., $t = |\{t_{V'} : V' \subseteq V, |t_{V'}| > 0\}|$. Constraint (1) sets $x_{V'}$ to be 0 for empty types $t_{V'}$. It means that we have at most t free integer variables, hence CKV is FPT wrt. t.

The next result gives a lower bound on the running time of the algorithm assuming ETH. The reduction follows from $(3,4)$-CNF-SAT [27] and the ETH-based lower-bound for it [24, Corollary 17].

Theorem 12. *Unless ETH fails, there is no algorithm for* CKV *that runs in time* $2^{o(|P|+|V|+k+B)}$.

Consider an additional very restricted case in which the length of a delegation chain is at most one, i.e., the non-transitive proxy voting setting. For instance, say that there are several types of projects and there are several voters, each of which is an expert on some type of projects (e.g., a medical doctor is an example on health-related projects). Then, perhaps each voter either decides on each project on her own, or delegate projects of a certain type to an expert. This would result in delegation chains of length at most one. Such cases can be solved in polynomial-time, by greedily changing delegations on the most expensive projects each voter delegates until they satisfy the Knapsack constraint.

Observation 13. CKV *can be solved in polynomial-time if all delegation chains are of length at most one.*

4   ILP and Simulation Results

Optimization version of the CKV problem can be formulated as an ILP, thus one can use existing ILP solvers for it. (Note that this ILP is essentially different than MILP defined in Theorem 11.)

Theorem 14. *We can formulate* CKV *as an integer program with* $|C|$ *binary variables, where* C *is the set of delegation components.*

Proof. For each delegation component we have to decide if we update it to disapproval. Hence we make an arbitrary order on delegation components and define $|C|$ binary variables $x_1, x_2, \ldots, x_{|C|}$, where $x_i = 1$ means we update the i-th delegation component and we keep it otherwise. For each $v \in V$ and $p \in P$ such that $L_v(p) \notin \{0,1\}$ we define $l(v,p) \in [|C|]$ as the index of the delegation component to which the delegation by v on p belongs. Hence, for every $v \in V$ we define the following constraint that decodes the budget limit consistency of v:

$$\sum_{p:L_v(p)=1} c(p) + \sum_{p:L_v(p) \notin \{0,1\}} c(p) \cdot (1 - x_{l(v,p)}) \leq B.$$

The objective function of CKV is minimizing the number of delegation updates, hence it is decoded by $\min \sum_{i \in [|C|]} x_i$. This finishes the description of the ILP. $\square$

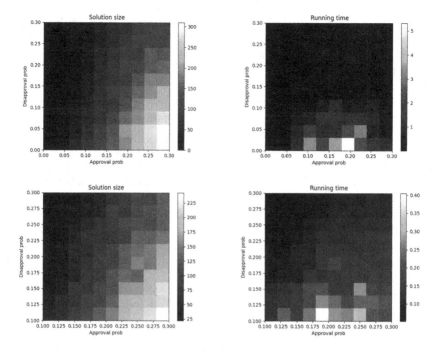

Fig. 2. Solution size and ILP running time (in seconds) for instances of CKV. The results for the artificial instances are on top while the results for the Bitcoin instances are on the bottom. Each square in each heatmap corresponds to different values of r_0 and r_1 and is averaged over 25 repetitions. Each instance consists of 200 voters, 20 projects with costs sampled from exponential distribution with mean 400, and budget limit 3000. See description in Subsect. 4.1.

We performed computer-based simulations to get a better feeling of the hardness of solving CKV. To this end, we implemented the above ILP and used it to solve different instances, recording the solution size and the running time of the ILP. In the next subsections we describe the experimental setup, provide the results, and discuss them.

4.1 Experimental Setup

We have two sets of instances: instances originating from real-world data and instances that are completely artificially-generated. The "real-world based data" only allows us to generate delegation graphs that resemble the real world, but the ballots are generated randomly as well. Below we describe how we generate our instances.

Artificial Instances. These are generated as follows: we fix a number n of voters, a number m of projects, a budget limit B, and probability values r_0, r_1 such that $r_0 + r_1 \in [0, 1]$. We set the cost of each project to be a value sampled form an exponential distribution with mean 400. For each voter we draw at random a set $S_v \subseteq V$ containing the voters that v is "allowed" to delegate to. S_v is constructed by adding to it each other voter $v' \neq v$ with probability 0.5, independently and uniformly at random. For each voter, we create a ballot as follows: for each project p, with probability r_0 the voter approves p; with probability r_1 the voter disapproves p; and with the remaining $1 - r_0 - r_1$, the voter delegates the decision on p to some other voter, chosen uniformly at random from S_v.

Real-World Based Instances. The instances originating from real-world instances are similar to the artificial instances, except for the definition of S_v. In particular, instead of having for each voter v, the set S_v of voters she might delegate to being a randomly-generated set, we proceeded as follows. We took the "Bitcoin Alpha trust weighted signed network" of Stanford Network Analysis Project (SNAP) [23]. This is a weighted directed graph in which each vertex corresponds to a user of Bitcoin, and the weight on a directed arc from some vertex u to some vertex v means the "level of trust" u have on v. After cleaning the data, we used each vertex of this Bitcoin graph as a voter v, and set its S_v to be all other voters that v trusts with a positive weight (the weights in the data might be negative, corresponding to a Bitcoin user that does not trust some other user). The ways in which the ballots are generated for these instances is similar to what explained above for the artificial instances.

4.2   Results and Discussion

Our results are given in Fig. 2 and in Fig. 3. In Fig. 2, both for the artificial instances and for the instances whose delegation graphs are derived from real-world data, we varied the values of r_0 (the probability of a voter approving a project) and r_1 (the probability of a voter disapproving a project) and recorded the average running time and the average solution size, when performing 25 repetitions for each choice of parameters. In Fig. 3, both for the artificial instances and for the instances whose delegation graphs are derived from real-world data, we varied the values of n (number of voters) and m (number of projects), and recorded again the average running time and the average solution size, when performing 25 repetitions for each choice of parameters.

Regarding Fig. 2, one can see that, as we increase the probability of approving and as we decrease the probability of disapproving, the instances become harder, as there are simply more delegations, thus more delegation components in particular. Regarding Fig. 3, one can see that even for quite large instances the ILP formulation performs well, with its running time increasing naturally as the number n of voters or the number m of projects increases.

5   Approximation Algorithms

There are two natural objectives we can violate, hence we can consider approximations for them: (1) the number of updates k and (2) the knapsack constraint B. We consider two separate problems: one, in which we fix the number of updates k and aim at violating the knapsack constraint B as little as possible; and another, in which we fix the knapsack constraint B (and do not allow to violate it) and aim at minimizing the number of updates k. To address these problems, it will be convenient to use the following notation: we call a solution for CKV an (α, β)-approximate solution, for some $\alpha, \beta \geq 1$,

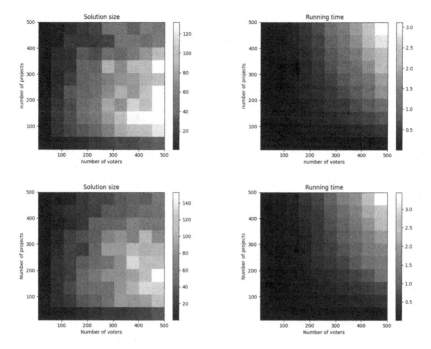

Fig. 3. Solution size and ILP running time (in seconds) for instances of CKV. The results for the artificial instances are on top while the results for the Bitcoin instances are on the bottom. Each square in each heatmap corresponds to different values of n and m and is averaged over 25 repetitions. For each instance, the probability of approving a project is 0.2, of disapproving a project is 0.6, and thus of delegating the decision on a project is 0.2. The budget limit B equals $0.3 \cdot 400 \cdot m$, where the project costs are sampled exponentially with mean 400. See description in Subsect. 4.1.

if it is: 1) at most α times larger than an optimal one and 2) the maximal violation of the knapsack constraint is by at most β factor. Let C be a set of delegation components. We solve a problem by outputting a subset $S \subseteq C$ of delegation components, whose update to disapproval makes an instance consistent. Updating all delegation components from C we achieve a trivial $(|C|, 1)$-approximation. Considering the whole C and all $1/\epsilon$-sized subsets of C as a solution ($\epsilon > 0$) we achieve $(\epsilon \cdot |C|, 1)$-approximation in $\mathcal{O}^*(|C|^{1/\epsilon})$ time, i.e., polynomial-time. On the other hand, we can consider achieving the minimum number of updates and violate the knapsack constraint only.

Theorem 15. *Let $\mathcal{I}$ be an instance of* CKV *and let $r \in [0, 1)$ be a fixed constant. There exists a polynomial-time algorithm that returns $(1, 1 + \max\{\frac{3\ln(2|V|)}{B}, \sqrt{\frac{3\ln(2|V|)}{B}}\})$-approximate solution for $\mathcal{I}$ with probability at least r.*

236 P. Jain et al.

Proof (sketch). The idea of the proof is as follows. We define an ILP to CKV (with reversed meaning of variables comparing to the ILP from Theorem 14). Then, we define its natural linear relaxation (LP) by replacing each binary variable with a variable in an interval $[0, 1]$. Then, we solve the LP in polynomial-time and scale the solution up to achieve sum of the variables being an integer (but still at most the value of the optimal integral solution). We can treat the values of variables in the obtained solution as probabilities and round the solution to an integral one using the DEPENDENTROUNDING procedure [15,25]. DEPENDENTROUNDING is a random process but with probability 1 it keeps the sum of all our variables, hence we get a solution with the number of delegations updates being at most the value of the optimal integral solution. What is more DEPENDENTROUNDING has the *Negative Correlation* property that makes the sum of any subset of variables being more concentrated around its expected value hence we can apply Chernoff-Hoeffding concentration bounds and argue that, with a constant probability, the solution does not exceed the knapsack constraint too much. Full formal proof can be found in the full version of the paper. □

Note that, in the case where $3\ln(2|V|) \leq B$ the ratio achieved by Theorem 15 is at most $(1, 2)$. In Theorem 15 we can replace $|V|$ by the number of voters that delegate at least 2 projects (which is potentially a smaller number). Indeed, we cannot exceed the budget limit for the voters that do not have delegations. Also, if a voter has one delegation we can resolve it in preprocessing. Then we do not need to count such voters in the union-bound used in the proof.

Further Work. It would be interesting to improve the approximation ratios. It is an open question whether we can achieve an (α, β)-approximation with constant α and β. On the other hand, one could provide inapproximability results to understand the limitations of this approach.

6 Discussion and Outlook

Motivated by the desire to get the benefits of LD for PB, we considered the option of allowing per-project delegations for Knapsack Voting. Observing that with the additional flexibility given to voters, there could be inconsistencies by naively following delegation chains, we considered altering as few delegations as possible to solve such inconsistencies. We have shown that this is computationally very hard; but it can be done efficiently (1) if $|V|$ is small and for other restricted cases; (2) if we settle for approximation algorithms; and (3) if we are using ILP solvers. This opens the way to solve many instances efficiently. We believe that it is worth-while to allow fine-grained transitive delegations to PB as we view our results as showing that it is possible to enable it, at least in certain cases.

The most pressing future research direction would be to develop and analyze other ways of solving such inconsistencies, such as: (1) having voters rank the projects she delegates so that we could go greedily over such rankings; (2) updating a set of delegations whose total cost is the minimum (and not its size, as we study here); (3) updating a set of delegations while not tackling only the roots of delegation chains, e.g., by minimizing the number of voters affected.

Acknowledgements. We would like to thank the anonymous reviewers for their helpful comments.

Krzysztof Sornat was partially supported by the SNSF Grant 200021_200731/1 and the European Research Council (ERC) under the European Union's Horizon 2020 research and innovation programme (grant agreement No 101002854). Nimrod Talmon was supported by the Israel Science Foundation (ISF; Grant No. 630/19).

References

1. Aziz, H., Lee, B.E., Talmon, N.: Proportionally representative participatory budgeting: axioms and algorithms. In: Proceedings of AAMAS 2018, pp. 23–31 (2018)
2. Aziz, H., Shah, N.: Participatory budgeting: models and approaches. In: Rudas, T., Péli, G. (eds.) Pathways Between Social Science and Computational Social Science. CSS, pp. 215–236. Springer, Cham (2021). https://doi.org/10.1007/978-3-030-54936-7_10
3. Behrens, J.: The origins of liquid democracy. Liquid Democracy J. **5**(2), 7–17 (2017)
4. Benadè, G., Nath, S., Procaccia, A.D., Shah, N.: Preference elicitation for participatory budgeting. Manag. Sci. **67**(5), 2813–2827 (2021)
5. Bloembergen, D., Grossi, D., Lackner, M.: On rational delegations in liquid democracy. In: Proceedings of AAAI 2019, pp. 1796–1803 (2019)
6. Blum, C., Zuber, C.I.: Liquid democracy: potentials, problems, and perspectives. J. Polit. Philos. **24**(2), 162–182 (2016)
7. Bredereck, R., Faliszewski, P., Niedermeier, R., Skowron, P., Talmon, N.: Mixed integer programming with convex/concave constraints: fixed-parameter tractability and applications to multicovering and voting. Theor. Comput. Sci. **814**, 86–105 (2020)
8. Brill, M., Talmon, N.: Pairwise liquid democracy. In: Proceedings of IJCAI 2018, pp. 137–143 (2018)
9. Cabannes, Y.: Participatory budgeting: a significant contribution to participatory democracy. Environ. Urban. **16**(1), 27–46 (2004)
10. Christoff, Z., Grossi, D.: Binary voting with delegable proxy: an analysis of liquid democracy. In: Proceedings of TARK 2017. EPTCS, vol. 251, pp. 134–150 (2017)
11. Colley, R., Grandi, U., Novaro, A.: Smart voting. In: Proceedings of IJCAI 2020, pp. 1734–1740 (2020)
12. Cygan, M., et al.: Parameterized Algorithms. Springer, Cham (2015). https://doi.org/10.1007/978-3-319-21275-3
13. Downey, R.G., Fellows, M.R.: Fixed-parameter tractability and completeness I: basic results. SIAM J. Comput. **24**(4), 873–921 (1995)
14. Freeman, R., Pennock, D.M., Peters, D., Vaughan, J.W.: Truthful aggregation of budget proposals. J. Econ. Theory **193**, 105234 (2021)
15. Gandhi, R., Khuller, S., Parthasarathy, S., Srinivasan, A.: Dependent rounding and its applications to approximation algorithms. J. ACM **53**(3), 324–360 (2006)
16. Garey, M.R., Johnson, D.S.: Computers and Intractability: A Guide to the Theory of NP-Completeness. W. H. Freeman, New York (1979)
17. Goel, A., Krishnaswamy, A.K., Sakshuwong, S., Aitamurto, T.: Knapsack voting for participatory budgeting. ACM Trans. Econ. Comput. **7**(2), 8:1–8:27 (2019)
18. Gölz, P., Kahng, A., Mackenzie, S., Procaccia, A.D.: The fluid mechanics of liquid democracy. ACM Trans. Econ. Comput. **9**(4), 23:1–23:39 (2021)
19. Green-Armytage, J.: Direct voting and proxy voting. Const. Polit. Econ. **26**(2), 190–220 (2015)
20. Impagliazzo, R., Paturi, R.: On the complexity of k-SAT. J. Comput. Syst. Sci. **62**(2), 367–375 (2001)

21. Jain, P., Sornat, K., Talmon, N.: Preserving consistency for liquid knapsack voting: extended abstract. In: Proceedings of AAMAS 2021, pp. 1542–1544 (2021)
22. Lenstra, H.W.: Integer programming with a fixed number of variables. Math. Oper. Res. **8**(4), 538–548 (1983)
23. Leskovec, J., Krevl, A.: SNAP Datasets: Stanford Large Network Dataset Collection (2014). http://snap.stanford.edu/data
24. Socała, A.: Lower bounds under strong complexity assumptions. Ph.D. thesis, University of Warsaw (2017)
25. Srinivasan, A.: Distributions on level-sets with applications to approximation algorithms. In: Proceedings of FOCS 2001, pp. 588–597 (2001)
26. Talmon, N., Faliszewski, P.: A framework for approval-based budgeting methods. In: Proceedings of AAAI 2019, pp. 2181–2188 (2019)
27. Tovey, C.A.: A simplified NP-complete satisfiability problem. Discret. Appl. Math. **8**(1), 85–89 (1984)

Strategic Nominee Selection
in Tournament Solutions

Grzegorz Lisowski[(✉)]

University of Warwick, Coventry, UK
Grzegorz.Lisowski@warwick.ac.uk

Abstract. Tournament solutions provide methods of selecting winners of a competition based on the results of pairwise comparisons. These methods have been studied in-depth from the perspective of social choice theory, where a comparison between two candidates indicates which of them is preferred to another by the majority of voters. In this paper we study the party setting, in which groups of candidates select their representatives. We consider the Uncovered Set tournament solution, in which a candidate i is selected if no other candidate beats all the options defeated by i, and contrast it with the Condorcet Winner rule, in which either Condorcet winner is chosen or no selection is made. We show that checking if a Nash equilibrium exists is NP-complete for both of these rules. Moreover, from the perspective of Uncovered Set, it is also NP-complete to check if a party has a potential winner.

Keywords: Tournaments solutions · Nash equilibria · Coalitional tournaments

1 Introduction

One of the key problems in representative democracy is how candidates participating in the elections are selected from a larger number of potential competitors. In fact, in most of political systems parties are only allowed to nominate a certain number of their members to run for a given position. Notably, in the US presidential elections parties nominate only one candidate, which is a strategic decision of great importance. As such, *primaries*, i.e., the process of selecting party candidates, gained substantial attention not only in political science literature (see, e.g., [8,9,28]), but also in multi-agent systems community ([4,15,16]).

Voting theory provides a vast amount of ways to reason about selection of candidates based on diverse preferences of individuals. In particular, *tournament solutions* are well-established methods of representing voters' preferences and of subsequent selection of a set of winners based on them (see, e.g., [14,20,21,25]). There, candidates are represented as vertices in a directed graph in which an edge between a pair of them determines the winner in a pairwise contest. This information can subsequently be used to select the best options among the entire set of candidates. As such, tournaments have been extensively researched in the context of social choice (see, e.g., [5] for an overview).

© The Author(s), under exclusive license to Springer Nature Switzerland AG 2022
D. Baumeister and J. Rothe (Eds.): EUMAS 2022, LNAI 13442, pp. 239–256, 2022.
https://doi.org/10.1007/978-3-031-20614-6_14

The choice of a winner of a tournament is clear when there is an option which beats all other contestants, which is called a *Condorcet winner*. However, it is possible for voters to submit preferences over candidates which result in a cyclic tournament, which implies that such an option might not exist. Hence, a number of methods of selecting sets of winners even in such a situation have been proposed. Among others, the well-studied *Uncovered Set* has been proposed independently by [13] and [24]. There, a candidate i is said to be a winner if there is no other candidate which beats all of the opponents that i does. This method has been shown to display important properties with respect to fairness. If the tournament relation is interpreted as which of the candidates is preferred by the majority of voters, a candidate i is said to be Pareto dominated if all voters prefer some candidate j over i. Importantly, Uncovered Set has been shown to select the largest set of winners which does not contain a Pareto dominated option [6].

It is natural from the perspective of the problem of primaries to consider the question of how parties striving to win the elections select their nominee in a system based on a tournament, assuming that pairwise comparisons between all potential candidates are known.

Example 1. The left subfigure of Fig. 1 depicts a tournament between six candidates, divided into three parties. Based on the information on which option is preferred between each pair of candidates, parties need to select exactly one representative. The right subfigure shows the tournament in which every group chooses the upper candidate. Observe that as the representative of the leftmost party dominates all other participants, they clearly win the tournament.

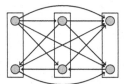 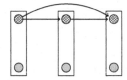

Fig. 1. The left figure depicts a tournament relation defined over all potential candidates, while the right figure presents a tournament including only those nominated to participate in the elections. For clarity, we omit edges between candidates belonging to the same parties in all figures.

In this paper we propose to study the described problem from the algorithmic game theory perspective. We define classical solution concepts in the proposed framework, focusing on *pure Nash equilibrium* (NE). The main focus of the paper is the study of computational complexity if a NE exists given a set of parties and relations between individual contestants.

It is worth noting that recently Lisowski, Ramanujan and Turrini [22] studied the coalitional tournaments setting from the perspective of *knockout tournaments*. In this setting, players are competing in rounds. So, at the start they are seeded at the leaves of a binary tree. Subsequently, the winner in each pairwise contests advances to a next round, until the winner is selected. It has been shown that checking if a NE exists in this setting is solvable in quasi-polynomial time.

However, the methods used to demonstrate the tractability of this problem in knockout tournaments strongly rely on the tree structure of the competition. It is therefore natural to investigate whether this result holds when other tournament solutions are considered. In this paper we address this problem.

Our Contribution. In this paper we establish algorithmic properties of the Uncovered Set rule. We contrast them with the Condorcet Winner rule, in which only the Condorcet winner is selected, if it exists. We consider three main computational questions. First, for a given method of selecting the winners from a tournament, we address the problem of checking whether a party can win in some strategy profile. We show that this problem is tractable for the Condorcet Winner rule, but NP-complete for Uncovered Set. Further, we analyse the problem of whether there exists a pure Nash equilibrium in the competition, for a given rule, and finally, we are interested in checking if a given party has a candidate which can win in some Nash equilibrium. We show that these two problems are NP-complete for both of the rules we consider.

Related Literature. Recently, Kondratev and Mazalov [19] studied coalitional tournaments from the perspective of cooperative game theory. As such, they analysed the behaviour of players who can form coalitions in order to get the best outcome for themselves. In our proposed approach instead, parties are already fixed. This approach is similar to the one proposed by Faliszewski, Gourvès, Lang, Lesca and Monnot [12] in which political parties select their representatives to compete in the elections which are based on the plurality rule. In their study, the investigation was limited to checking if a party has a necessary, or a possible winner. The problem of checking if a party has a possible winner from the perspective of the plurality rule has been shown to be NP-complete, which is analogous to our corresponding result in the context of the Uncovered Set rule. However, they leave the study of game theoretic solution concepts open in this scenario.

Our work is closely connected to *strategic voting*. In this key areas of computational social choice theory it is studied how agents striving to ensure that the best possible outcome of the elections from their perspective is obtained behave (see, e.g., [23]). Another research area related to primaries is *strategic candidacy*. There, it is studied how participants of the elections might want to drop out from the competition to prevent some opponents from winning (see, e.g., [7,10,11,26]).

Furthermore, our study is related to the analysis of possible and necessary winner problems in the context of partial tournaments [2]. There, the problem we consider involves tournaments with partial information about the results of pairwise contests, and whether an option is a winner in some, or in all completions of the partial tournament.

Finally, a related line of research involves manipulation in tournaments. One of the studied types of manipulation is the possibility of a pair of players to change the result the match between them in order to get a beneficial result (see, e.g., [1]). Another method of manipulation is situated in well-studied *knockout tournaments*. A natural way of manipulation in this setting is fixing a seeding ensuring that a given player is the winner (see, e.g., [3,17,18,27]).

Paper Structure. In Sect. 2 we define the key notions used later in the paper. Then, in Sect. 3 we present initial facts about all rules we consider. In Sect. 4 we investigate the properties of the Condorcet Winner rule, and in Sect. 5 we analyse the Uncovered Set rule. Finally, Sect. 6 concludes and provides directions for further research.

2   Preliminaries

Let us provide the definitions of needed concepts and of computational problems which we study in this paper.

Tournaments. Let N be the set of *candidates*. Then, a *tournament* is a directed graph (N, E), where E is an irreflexive, binary relation over N, in which, for every pair of candidates $i \neq j$ in N, exactly one of (i, j) and (j, i) belongs to E. If $(i, j) \in E$, we say that i *beats* j in E. We will say that i beats j when E is clear from the context. Given a tournament (N, E) and $i \in N$, we denote as $D(i)$ the set of candidates beaten by i. Formally, $D(i) = \{j \in N : i \text{ beats } j\}$.

Parties. We study the case in which candidates are partitioned into *parties*. For a given tournament (N, E), a party is a member of a partition $P = \{P_1, \ldots, P_m\}$ of N. We call such a partition a *set of parties* and denote a tuple (N, E, P) as a *party structure*. Further, we require each party to select exactly one candidate. So, a *strategy profile* is a tuple $(c_1, \ldots, c_m)$ such that for every c_i, we have that $c_i \in P_i$. For convenience, for a party structure (N, E, P) and $i \in N$, we denote as $\mathcal{P}(i)$ the party $P_j \in P$ such that $i \in P_j$.

To account for the competition between the selected candidates, given a party structure $T = (N, E, P)$ and a strategy profile $\mathbf{c} = (c_1, \ldots, c_m)$, a subtournament induced by $\mathbf{c}$, which we denote as $T_\mathbf{c}$, is a tournament $(\mathbf{c}, E')$ such that for every pair of candidates $c_i, c_j \in \mathbf{c}$, c_i beats c_j in E' if and only if c_i beats c_j in E. For simplicity, we will refer to such a subtournament as a *filtration of T*.

Tournament Rules. In the scenario we consider parties are interested in winning the competition. To determine the set of winners we consider *tournament solutions*. Let $\mathbf{T}_N$ be the set of all tournaments with the set of candidates N. Then, a tournament solution is a function $F : \mathbf{T}_N \to 2^N$. Further, given a party structure $T = (N, E, P)$, a strategy profile $\mathbf{c}$ and a tournament solution F, we say that a party P_i is a *winner* under F at $T_\mathbf{c}$, if $c_i \in F(T_\mathbf{c})$. When clear from the context, we just say that P_i is a winner of $T_\mathbf{c}$, or that P_i is a winner under $\mathbf{c}$ (when the party structure is not ambiguous). We also say that $c_i \in P_i$ is a winner in the initial tournament, if $c_i \in F((N, E))$.

In this paper we will consider two tournament solutions, namely the *Condorcet Winner* rule and the *Uncovered Set* rule. Given a tournament (N, E), a candidate $i \in N$ is a Condorcet winner if i beats any other candidate $j \in N$. Notice that the set of all Condorcet winners in a tournament is either a singleton or is empty. Then, the Condorcet Winner rule selects the set of all Condorcet winners. Observe that this rule might not select any candidate.

Definition 1 (Condorcet Winner Rule). *The Condorcet Winner rule (CW) is the tournament solution such that for every tournament (N, E), $CW(N, E)$ is the Condorcet winner if it exits, and the empty set otherwise.*

Furthermore, we are interested in one of the rules extending the Condorcet Winner rule, which guarantees that the set of winners is not empty. Given a tournament (N, E) and a pair $i, j \in N$ we say that i *covers* j ($i \succeq j$) if $D(j) \subseteq D(i)$. So, i covers j if i beats all of the candidates that j beats. Observe how the fact that $i \succeq j$ implies that i beats j. Then, the Uncovered Set rule selects all candidates which are not covered by any other candidate.

Definition 2 (Uncovered Set Rule). *The Uncovered Set rule (US) is the tournament solution such that for every tournament (N, E)*

$$US((N, E)) = \{i \in N : \text{ for every } j \in N, \ j \not\succeq i\}$$

Nash Equilibrium. We are interested in the game-theoretic study of the scenario we consider. We will study the properties of the well-studied solution concept of a *pure Nash equilibrium* (NE). Given a strategy profile $\mathbf{c}$, a party P_i and a candidate $c'_i \in P_i$, $(c'_i, \mathbf{c}_{-i})$ denotes the strategy set in which the candidate selected by P_i is c'_i and all other parties select the same candidate as in $\mathbf{c}$. Then, for a party structure $T = (N, E, P)$ and a tournament solution F, we say that $\mathbf{c}$ is a NE under F, if for every party P_i such that P_i is not a winner of $T_{\mathbf{c}}$ and $c'_i \in P_i$, it holds that P_i is not a winner of $T_{(c'_i, \mathbf{c}_{-i})}$.

Observe how the strategy profile which we consider in Fig. 1 is a NE both under CW and under US. Indeed the candidate selected by the leftmost party is a Condorcet winner in (N, E). Therefore, in every strategy profile in which it is selected, it beats and cover all other options, implying that it is the only winner in all such profiles from the perspective of both rules we consider.

Computational Problems. Let us define the computational problems studied in the setting we consider.

F-Possible Winner is the problem of checking whether a given party has a candidate who is a winner from the perspective of F under some strategy profile. Given a party structure $T = (N, E, P)$, we say that a candidate c is a *possible winner* of T from the perspective of F if there is a strategy profile $\mathbf{c}$ such that $\mathcal{P}(c)$ is a winner of $T_{\mathbf{c}}$ from the perspective of F under $\mathbf{c}$.

F-Possible Winner:
Input: Party structure $T = (N, E, P)$, party $P_i \in P$.
Question: Is there a candidate $c_i \in P_i$ such that P_i is a possible winner of T under F?

Further, F-Winner in NE is the problem of checking if a party is winner from the perspective of F in some NE.

F-Winner in NE:
Input: Party structure $T = (N, E, P)$, party $P_i \in P$.
Question: Is there a candidate $c_i \in C_i$ such that c_i is a winner of $T_{\mathbf{c}}$ under F for some strategy profile $\mathbf{c}$ which is a NE under F?

Finally, F-NE EXISTENCE is the problem of checking if there exists a strategy profile which is a NE from the perspective of F.

F-NE EXISTENCE:
Input: Party structure (N, E, P).
Question: Is there a strategy profile **c** which is a NE under F?

3   Initial Remarks

Even though we restrict ourselves to two specific tournament solutions, some properties are shared by larger classes of rules, such as *Condorcet consistent* rules. We say that a rule F is Condorcet consistent if for every tournament (N, E) in which $i \in N$ is the Condorcet winner, $F((N, E)) = \{i\}$. Observe that both CW and US are Condorcet consistent. We first observe that the existence of a NE is not guaranteed for any Condorcet consistent rule.

Proposition 1. *For every Condorcet consistent rule F there is a party structure (N, E, P) without a NE from the perspective of F.*

Proof. Consider a Condorcet consistent rule F and the party structure with parties $A = \{a_1, a_2\}$ and $B = \{b_1, b_2\}$ depicted in Fig. 2.

Let us show that there are no NE in this party structure from the perspective of F. Consider an arbitrary strategy profile (a_i, b_j) in this structure and let w.l.o.g a_i beat b_j. Note that then A is the unique winner from the perspective of F since F is Condorcet consistent. But then, by construction of the party structure, there is a $b_{3-j} \in B$ such that b_{3-j} beats a_i. Observe that B is the unique winner of (a_i, b_{3-j}) So, (a_i, b_j) is not a NE.

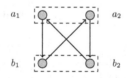

Fig. 2. Example of a party structure with no NE under any Condorcet consistent rule.

Further, given a party structure (N, E, P), parties $P_i, P_j \in P$ and a candidate $c_i \in P_i$, we say that c_i *dominates* P_j if for every $c_j \in P_j$, c_i beats c_j. Then, a NE from the perspective of any Condorcet consistent rule exists in a party structures with two parties exactly when there is a candidate which dominates the opposing party.

Proposition 2. *For every Condorcet consistent rule F and every party structure (N, E, P) such that $|P| = 2$ there exists a NE under F in (N, E, P) if and only if there is a candidate c which dominates the party $P_i \in P$ s.t $c \notin P_i$.*

Proof. Consider a Condorcet consistent rule F and a party structure $(N, E, \{P_1, P_2\})$. Observe first that since there are only two parties in the party structure, for every filtration induced by a profile (c_1, c_2) there is exactly one Condorcet winner.

For the forward direction, let us reason by contraposition. Suppose that for every candidate c there is a candidate $c' \notin \mathcal{P}(c)$ such that c' beats c. Further, suppose towards contradiction that there exists a profile (c_1, c_2) which is a NE. W.l.o.g let c_1 beat c_2. Note that given this profile, as F is Condorcet consistent, P_1 is the unique winner from the perspective of F. Observe further that by assumption there is a $c'_2 \in P_2$ such that c'_2 beats c_1. But then P_2 wins under (c_1, c'_2), so (c_1, c_2) is not a NE, which violates the assumptions. Suppose now that there exists a candidate c such that for every candidate $c' \notin \mathcal{P}(c)$, c beats c'. W.l.o.g let $c \in P_1$. Then, consider any strategy profile (c, c_2). Note that as c beats c_2 and F is Condorcet consistent it holds that P_1 is the winner under (c, c_2). Also, as c dominates P_2, P_1 wins under (c, c'_2) for every $c'_2 \in P_2$. Hence, (c, c_2) is a NE.

4 Condorcet Winner Rule

Let us provide an analysis of the Condorcet Winner rule. Let us first observe that if a party contains a Condorcet winner in the initial tournament, then selecting it guarantees victory for that party.

Proposition 3. *For every party structure $T = (N, E, P)$, $P_i \in P$, strategy profile $\mathbf{c}$ and a candidate $c_i \in P_i$ selected in $\mathbf{c}$, if c_i is a Condorcet winner in (N, E), then P_i wins in $T_{\mathbf{c}}$ under CW.*

Proof. Take a party structure $T = (N, E, P)$, strategy profile $\mathbf{c}$ and a candidate $c_i \in P_i$ selected in $\mathbf{c}$, such that c_i is a Condorcet winner in (N, E). Observe that c_i is a Condorcet winner in (N, E), and hence it is a Condorcet winner in $T_{\mathbf{c}}$. So, P_i is a winner in $T_{\mathbf{c}}$ under CW.

Furthermore, checking if a party contains a candidate which might potentially win is tractable.

Proposition 4. CW-POSSIBLE WINNER *is solvable in polynomial time.*

Proof. Take a party structure $T = (N, E, P)$ and a party $P_i \in P$. To check if there exists $c_i \in P_i$ which is a winner from the perspective of CW in $T_{\mathbf{c}}$ for some strategy profile $\mathbf{c}$, it is sufficient to check if it is the case for any of P_i's members. Note that P_i is a winner under some strategy profile in which c_i is selected if and only if for every party P_j there is a $c_j \in P_j$ such that c_i beats c_j. Observe that this condition is verifiable by an algorithm running in $\mathcal{O}(|N|)$ time. So, CW-POSSIBLE WINNER is solvable in $\mathcal{O}(|N|^2)$ time by checking the condition for all members of P_i.

It is worth noting that the algorithm given in the proof allows us to find all possible winners. We show, however, that checking if a NE exists is not tractable by reduction from the 3-SAT problem.

Theorem 1. CW-NE Existence *is NP-complete.*

Intuitively, we construct a party corresponding to each variable in a formula with two candidates each (corresponding to literals), and a party containing a pair of candidates for each clause. We further construct what we call a *base party* with two candidates, such that the beating relation induces the matching pennies game between the base party and each of the pairs in the clause party. Having that a candidate in the clause party is beaten exactly by those candidates in variable gadgets, which correspond to literals in the clause, we obtain that a NE exists in the constructed game if and only if the formula is satisfiable.

Proof. Let us first notice that the problem we consider is in NP. Indeed, given a party structure (N, E, P) and a strategy profile $\mathbf{c}$ we can check whether $\mathbf{c}$ is a NE by examining all potential deviations of all parties, which can be done in polynomial time.

Let us now show the NP-hardness of this problem. Take a formula φ in 3-CNF. Let $X = \{x_0, \ldots, x_n\}$ denote the set of variables in φ, and $C = \{C_0, \ldots, C_m\}$ be the set of clauses in φ. Let us now construct a party structure $T = (N, E, P)$ which we call the *encoding* of φ.

Base, Variable and Clause Parties. First, fix the *base party* $S = \{s_1, s_2\}$. Then, for every variable $x_i \in X$ construct a party $\{x_i, \neg x_i\}$, which we call a *variable party*. Moreover, we say that the party $\{x_i, \neg x_i\}$ *corresponds* to x_i and call its members *literal candidates* corresponding to x_i and $\neg x_i$ respectively. Finally, we construct what we call a *clause party* as follows. For every clause $C_i \in C$, construct a *clause pair* $C'_i = \{C_i^1, C_i^2\}$. We call the members of C'_i *clause candidates.* The clause party is the set $\{C_i^j : i \in [0, m] \text{ and } j \in \{1, 2\}\}$, i.e. is a collection of clause pairs. Note that the construction requires $|X| + 2$ parties and $2|C| + 2|X| + 2$ candidates.

Tournament Relation. Let us now construct the tournament relation. First, for every literal candidate L, let s_1 and s_2 beat L. Furthermore, for every clause pair $C'_i = \{C_i^1, C_i^2\}$, let s_1 beat C_i^1, C_i^1 beat s_2, s_2 beat C_i^2 and C_i^2 beat s_1, creating a cycle. Finally, for every literal candidate L and a clause candidate C_j^k, let L beat C_j^k if literal L is in the clause C_j, and C_j^k beat L, otherwise. Construct all other edges arbitrarily. Observe that, by construction, a variable party is not a winner under any strategy profile, as its representative is always beaten by a member of the base party.

An example of the relation in the encoding of φ is depicted in Fig. 3.

Correctness of the Construction. Let us show that φ is satisfiable if and only if the encoding of φ admits a NE. Suppose that φ is satisfiable. Then take a valuation V over X which makes φ true. Further, take a strategy profile $\mathbf{c}$ such that for every variable party $\{x_i, \neg x_i\}$ we have that candidate x_i is selected whenever x_i is true in V, and the candidate $\neg x_i$ is selected otherwise. Also, let s_1 as well as C_0^1 be selected. Notice that in $T_\mathbf{c}$, s_1 is the Condorcet winner, as

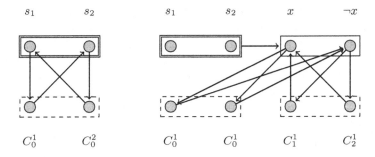

$$s_1 \qquad s_2 \qquad\qquad s_1 \qquad s_2 \qquad\qquad x \qquad \neg x$$

$$C_0^1 \qquad C_0^2 \qquad\qquad C_0^1 \qquad C_0^1 \qquad\qquad C_1^1 \qquad C_2^1$$

Fig. 3. Encoding of the formula $x \wedge \neg x$. The nodes in the double rectangle depict the base pair and the nodes in the single rectangle the variable party corresponding to x. Moreover, in the right figure, the left pair in the dashed rectangle depicts a clause pair such that x is in the corresponding clause, and the right the clause clause pair representing the clause to which $\neg x$ belongs. The left figure shows the relation between the base pair and a clause pair, while the right one shows the remaining relations. It is worth noting at this stage that the tournament restricted to the pair of parties in the left figure has no NE.

it wins against all selected literal candidates and against C_0^1. Furthermore, as V is a model of φ, for every clause candidate C_j^k there is some selected literal candidate L such that L beats C_j^k. Hence, the clause party has no profitable deviation. Finally, as we observed before, all variable parties lose in any strategy profile. Therefore, **c** is a NE. Suppose now that φ is not satisfiable. Then, for every strategy profile there is a pair of clause candidates C_j' such that each of its members beats all selected literal candidates, as otherwise there would exist a valuation over X satisfying φ. Let us now reason by contradiction and suppose now that there is a NE strategy profile **c**. Consider a pair of clause candidates C_j' that beats every literal candidate selected in **c**. Let us show that if there is no Condorcet winner in $T_{\mathbf{c}}$, then there exists a profitable deviation for the clause party. Indeed, if s_1 is selected, let the clause party select C_j^2, and otherwise C_j^1. One can verify that in the modified profile the clause party is the winner. Suppose now that there is a Condorcet winner in $T_{\mathbf{c}}$. If s_1 is the Condorcet winner in $T_{\mathbf{c}}$, let the clause party choose C_j^2, and if it is s_2, let the clause party choose C_j^1. Note that in both of these cases the clause party becomes the winner. Finally, consider the case in which a member of the clause party is the Condorcet winner in $T_{\mathbf{c}}$. In this case the base pair has a profitable deviation by symmetric reasoning. Hence, there is no NE in the encoding of φ.

Furthermore, let us show that it is computationally hard to check if a party has a member who wins in some NE by reduction from 3-SAT.

Theorem 2. CW-WINNER IN NE *is NP-complete.*

Proof. Let us first observe that as verification of whether a profile is a NE can be done in polynomial time, the problem we consider is in NP. Let us show the NP-hardness of this problem. Take a formula φ in 3-CNF. Let $X = \{x_0, \ldots, x_n\}$

be the set of variables in φ and $C = \{C_0, \ldots, C_m\}$ be the set of clauses in φ. Further, consider the encoding of φ as constructed in the proof of Theorem 1. Let us show that the base party a winner in some NE if and only if φ is satisfiable.

Suppose that φ is not satisfiable. Then, by the reasoning used in the proof of Theorem 1 there is no NE in the encoding of φ. So, the base party is not a winner in a NE. Suppose further that φ is satisfiable. Then, a NE in which s_1 is a winner can be constructed as in the proof of Theorem 1.

5   Uncovered Set

Let us now consider the Uncovered Set rule. We will start with providing a few observations showcasing differences between competitions between parties in the context of the Uncovered Set, and Condorcet Winner rules. They in a large part arise due to the fact that the winner under the Uncovered Set always exists but is not unique. One can check that they do not hold for the CW rule. Let us first observe that in the context of *US*, having a member of a party which wins in the initial tournament does not guarantee victory in a filtration induced by a strategy profile in which it is selected.

Proposition 5. *There exists a party structure $T = (N, E, P)$ and a NE profile c such that a winner i in (N, E) is selected in c, but $\mathcal{P}(i)$ loses in T_c.*

Example 2. Consider the party structure (N, E, P) depicted in the Fig. 4. Observe that in the tournament (N, E), the member of the singleton party is a winner from the perspective of *US* as it is the only candidate beating three rightmost candidates in the top tier. Notice, however, that in the filtration induced by a profile c depicted in the right side of Fig. 4, it is beaten by all other chosen candidates and thus does not win under *US*.

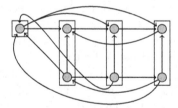 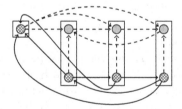

Fig. 4. An example of a party structure (N, E, P) in which a party whose member is winner in (N, E) does not win under some Nash equilibrium. The edges not shown in the Figure point downwards.

Further, it can be the case that replacing a strategy with a member who is a winner in the initial tournament is not profitable.

Proposition 6. *There exists a party structure $T = (N, E, P)$, $P_i \in P$, a winner $c'_i \in P_i$ of (N, E) under US, and a NE profile c such that a P_i wins in T_c, but not in $T_{(c'_i, c_{-i})}$.*

Example 3. Consider the party structure (N, E, P) depicted in the left side of Fig. 5. Observe that the top-left candidate is a winner from the perspective of *US* in the initial tournament, as it is the only player beating the top candidate in the centre. Observe that the top candidate in the centre covers the bottom-left candidate, which hence is not a winner in the initial tournament. Then, consider a strategy profile inducing a filtration in right side of Fig. 5. Observe that then, since all candidates are winners form the perspective of *US*, it is a NE. So, the left party is a winner in a NE. However, replacing its choice with the top-left candidate would result in losing the tournament.

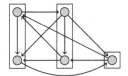 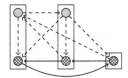

Fig. 5. An example of a party structure in which choosing a weaker player is profitable.

Moreover, it can be the case that none of the candidates selected by some party winning in a NE is a winner in the initial tournament.

Proposition 7. *There exists a party structure $T = (N, E, P)$ and a NE profile c, such that no candidate selected by some party winning in T_c is a winner in (N, E).*

Example 4. Consider a party structure (N, E, P) in the left side of the Fig. 6. Notice that the top-left node there is a Condorcet winner and hence is the only winner from the perspective of Uncovered Set in (N, E). Consider, however, the only strategy profile in which it is not selected, which is depicted on the right side of the Fig. 6. Observe that in this tournament all candidates are winners from the perspective of *US*. Hence, the profile we consider is a NE.

Fig. 6. The left figure depicts a party structure with a candidate (top-left) which is a Condorcet winner. The right shows a filtration in which all teams are winners even though none of their nominees wins in the original tournament.

Let us move to establishing the computational complexity of *US*-POSSIBLE WINNER. We show that this problem is NP-complete by reduction from 3-SAT.

Theorem 3. *US*-POSSIBLE WINNER *is NP-complete.*

Proof. Observe first that the problem is in NP. Indeed, given a party structure and a given party, as well as a strategy profile, checking if it has a possible winner is solvable in polynomial time as winner determination under a given strategy profile is solvable in polynomial time for the Uncovered Set rule. Let us show now the NP-hardness of this problem. Take a formula φ in 3-CNF. Let $X = \{x_0, \ldots, x_n\}$ be the set of variables in φ and $C = \{C_0, \ldots, C_m\}$ the set of clauses in φ. Let us construct the party structure which we will call the *encoding* of φ.

Parties. First, let us fix a *base party* $\{s\}$. We call s the *base candidate*. Further, for every variable $x_i \in X$, we construct a party $\{x_i, \neg x_i\}$. We say that such a party *corresponds* to x_i and call it's members *literal candidates* corresponding to literals x_i and $\neg x_i$ respectively. Finally, for every clause $C_i \in C$ let us construct a party $\{C_i\}$. We call a member of such a party a *clause candidate* corresponding to C_i. Observe that the encoding of φ includes $|X|+|C|+1$ parties with $2|X|+|C|+1$ candidates.

Tournament Relation. Let us construct the tournament relation in the encoding of φ. First, for every literal candidate L, let s beat L. Further, for every clause candidate C_i, let C_i beat s. Finally, for every literal candidate L and every clause candidate C_i, let L beat C_i if the literal L is in the clause C_i, and let C_i beat L otherwise. Let the remaining edges be constructed arbitrarily. Notice that s beats all literal candidates and no other candidates under any strategy profile. It is worth noting that every strategy profile in the encoding of φ corresponds to a valuation V over X such that the party corresponding to a variable x_i selects the candidate x_i if x_i is true in V and $\neg x_i$ otherwise. Then, we say that a clause C_i is *satisfied* in the encoding of φ under a profile $\mathbf{c}$ if the clause candidate C_i is beaten by some literal candidate selected in $\mathbf{c}$. Figure 7 depicts the encoding of the formula $\neg x_1 \vee \neg x_2$.

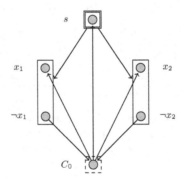

Fig. 7. The encoding of the formula $\neg x_1 \vee \neg x_2$. The node in the double rectangle represents the base party. Nodes in single rectangles are variable parties, and in the dashed rectangle the clause party C_0. Observe that the base party is a winner exactly when $\neg x_1$ or $\neg x_2$ is selected.

Correctness of the Construction. Let us show that $\{s\}$ has a possible winner in the encoding of φ if and only if φ is satisfiable. Suppose first that φ is not satisfiable. Let us show that $\{s\}$ does not have a possible winner. Consider any strategy profile **c**. Notice that as φ is not satisfiable, there is a clause C_i which is not satisfied in the encoding of φ under **c**. This implies that there is a selected clause candidate C_i which beats all selected literal candidates in **c**. Observe further that, as C_i also beats s, s is covered by C_i. So, $\{s\}$ is not a winner under any strategy profile and hence does not have a possible winner. Suppose now that φ is satisfiable. Let us show that $\{s\}$ has a possible winner in the encoding of φ. Consider a valuation V under which φ is true. Also, take the strategy profile **c** in which every party $\{x_i, \neg x_i\}$ corresponding to a variable x_i selects x_i if x_i is true in V, and $\neg x_i$ otherwise. Observe that as φ is true under V, for every clause candidate in **c** there is a literal candidate in **c** that beats it. Hence, s is the only selected candidate which beats all chosen literal candidates. Hence, s is not covered by any selected candidate under some strategy profile. Therefore, $\{s\}$ has a possible winner.

Further, we show that *US*-NE EXISTENCE is NP-complete by reduction from 3-SAT.

Theorem 4. *US*-NE EXISTENCE *is NP-complete.*

Proof. Let us first observe that the problem we consider is in NP. Indeed, for a given strategy profile we can check in polynomial time whether a given party can improve their utility by replacing their representative. Let us then show the NP-hardness of this problem. Take a formula φ in 3-CNF. Let $X = \{x_0, \ldots, x_n\}$ be the set of variables in φ and $C = \{C_0, \ldots, C_m\}$ be the set of clauses in φ. Let us assume for simplicity that $|X| \geq 3$. This is without loss of generality as every formula in 3-CNF can be extended to an equivalent formula in 3-CNF with at least 3 variables. Let us construct the party structure (N, E, P) which we will call the *encoding* of φ.

Parties. First, fix a *base party* $S = \{s_1, s_2\}$. We call the members of this party *base candidates*. Further, for every variable $x_i \in X$ let us construct a *variable party* $\{x_i, \neg x_i\}$. We say that such a party *corresponds* to x_i and call its members *literal candidates* corresponding to x_i and $\neg x_i$ respectively. Then, for every $x_i \in X$ we construct an *auxiliary* party $\{A_{x_i}\}$ and call its member an *auxiliary candidate* corresponding to x_i. Finally, we construct what we call a *clause party* as follows. For every clause $C_i \in C$, construct a *clause pair* $C_i' = \{C_i^1, C_i^2\}$. We call the members of C_i' *clause candidates*. Then, the clause party is the set $\{C_i^j \mid i \in [0, m-1] \text{ and } j \in \{1, 2\}\}$, i.e. the union of all clause pairs. Observe that every strategy profile in the encoding of φ corresponds to the valuation V

over X such that for every variable $x_i \in X$, x_i is true in V if x_i is selected by the corresponding variable party, and false if $\neg x_i$ is selected. Note further that the encoding of φ requires $2|X| + 2$ parties and $2|C| + 3|X| + 2$ candidates.

Tournament Relation. Let us construct the tournament relation in the encoding of φ. First, for a literal candidate L, let s_1 and s_2 beat L. Further, for every clause candidate C_j^k and a literal candidate L, let L beat C_j^k if L is in the clause C_j, and C_j^k beat L otherwise. For a strategy profile $\mathbf{c}$ in which some selected literal candidate L beats C_j^k, we say that C_j is *satisfied* in $\mathbf{c}$. Also, for every auxiliary party $\{A_{x_i}\}$, let A_{x_i} beat all variable, base and clause candidates apart from x_i and $\neg x_i$. Instead, let x_i and $\neg x_i$ beat A_{x_i}. Furthermore, for every clause pair $C_i' = \{C_i^1, C_i^2\}$, let s_1 beat C_i^1, C_i^1 beat s_2, s_2 beat C_i^2 and C_i^2 beat s_1, constructing a cycle. Let the remaining edges be constructed arbitrarily while ensuring that each auxiliary candidate A_{x_i} is beaten by some auxiliary candidate A_{x_j} and for such a pair, members of the party corresponding to x_i are beaten by the members of the party corresponding to x_j. Note that such a relation exists since $|X| \geq 3$, e.g., when there exists a cycle containing all auxiliary candidates, mirrored by variable candidates. The key relation in an encoding of φ is partially depicted in the Fig. 8.

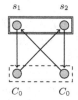 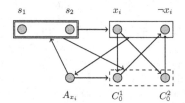

Fig. 8. Key relations in the encoding of φ. Candidates in the double rectangle represent the base party, in the single rectangle a variable party corresponding to x_i, and in the dashed rectangle, a clause pair. In the depicted fragment, x_i belongs to the presented clause, while $\neg x_i$ does not. The remaining candidate is the auxiliary candidate A_{x_i}. The left figure shows the relation between the base pair and the clause pair, while the right one shows the relation between the remaining parties.

Correctness of the Construction. First, we state a few properties of the encoding of φ.

1. Let us show first that no variable party is a winner under any strategy profile. To see that take any variable party $\{x_i, \neg x_i\}$ and an auxiliary candidate A_{x_j} which beats A_{x_i}. We know that such an auxiliary candidate exists by construction of the tournament relation. Observe that under any strategy profile, A_{x_j} beats all candidate beaten by x_i or $\neg x_i$. Namely, it beats all literal candidates apart from x_j and $\neg x_j$, candidates in the base party, all clause candidates and A_{x_i}. Also, by construction of the tournament relation, x_i and $\neg x_i$ are beaten by x_j and $\neg x_j$. So, a nominee of the party corresponding to x_i is covered by A_{x_j} and hence this party is not a winner.

2. We further show that if in a profile in which the clause party chooses a candidate C_j^k some chosen literal candidate L beats C_j^k, then the clause party is not a winner. W.l.o.g let such C_j^k be beaten by a selected candidate x_i. Notice that the candidate A_{x_i} beats all of the candidates that C_j^k does, as it beats all literal candidates apart the members of the party corresponding x_i and the base candidates. Hence the clause party is not a winner under such profile as C_j^k is covered by A_{x_i}.

3. Also, a selected clause candidate C_j^k is not covered by any auxiliary candidate A_{x_i} such that C_j^k beats the candidate selected by $\{x_i, \neg x_i\}$, as it beats A_{x_i}.

We are now ready to show that there exists a NE in the encoding of φ if and only if φ is satisfiable. Suppose that φ is not satisfiable. Let us show that there exists no NE in the encoding of φ. Observe that as φ is not satisfiable, for every strategy profile **c** there is a clause which is not satisfied in **c** and hence there is a pair of clause candidates C'_j, such that both members of C'_j beat every selected literal candidate. Suppose first that the clause party selects a member of such a pair C'_j. By 3., it is in the uncovered set exactly when it is not covered by the selected member of the base party. Similarly, as the chosen member of the base party beats all literal candidates, it is in the uncovered set exactly when it is not covered by the selection of the clause party. Note that if C_j^1 and s_1 are selected, then C_j^1 is covered by s_1. It is not the case, however, if C_j^2 and s_1 are selected, so the clause party has a profitable deviation. Further, if C_j^1 and s_2 are selected, s_2 is covered and the base party has a profitable deviation to s_1. So, there is no NE if C_j^1 is selected. Symmetrically it can be shown that there is no NE in which C_j^2 is chosen. Otherwise, if the clause party selects a candidate which is beaten by some selected literal candidate L, the clause party is not a winner by 2. One can verify, however, that deviating to some player in C'_i is profitable for the clause party. Hence, there is no NE in the encoding of φ if φ is not satisfiable. Suppose now that φ is satisfiable. Let us show that there exists a NE in the encoding of φ. Consider a valuation V over X that makes φ true. We know that it exists since φ is satisfiable. Take also a strategy profile **c** such that, for every party $\{x_i, \neg x_i\}$ corresponding to x_i, we have that x_i is selected whenever x_i is set to true by V, and $\neg x_i$ is selected otherwise. Also, pick s_1 and C_0^1. Notice that as V satisfies φ, for every candidate C_j^k in the clause party there is a selected literal candidate which beats C_j^k. So, by 2., the clause party is not a winner regardless of their choice, and thus has no profitable deviation. Further, as we have observed in 1., variable parties do not win under any strategy profile, and hence have no profitable deviation. Moreover, s_1 is the only selected candidate beating all chosen literal candidates and thus is in the uncovered set. So, the base party has no profitable deviation. Finally, all other parties are singletons and therefore have no profitable deviations. So, **c** is a NE.

Finally, we show the complexity of *US*-WINNER IN NE by reduction from 3-SAT.

Theorem 5. *US*-WINNER IN NE *is NP-complete.*

Proof. Observe first that the problem is in NP as checking if a profile is a NE and winner determination is possible in polynomial time for *US*. We further show the hardness of this problem. Take a formula φ in 3-CNF. Let $X = \{x_0, \ldots, x_n\}$ be the set of variables in φ and $C = \{C_0, \ldots, C_m\}$ be the set of clauses in φ. Let us construct what we call the *encoding* of φ, as in the proof of Theorem 4. Observe that $\{A_{x_0}\}$ is a winner under any strategy profile. Indeed, in any strategy profile A_{x_0} beats the selections of base party and clause parties and hence is not covered by them. Also, it is not covered by selected literal candidates as they do not beat the selected base candidate. Finally, A_{x_0} is not covered by any auxiliary candidate A_{x_j} such that $j \neq 0$, as it beats the selection of $\{x_i, \neg x_i\}$, which by construction beats A_{x_j}. So, A_{x_0} is in the uncovered set in any strategy profile. Let us show now that the party $\{A_{x_0}\}$ is a winner in some profile which is a NE iff φ is satisfiable. Suppose that φ is not satisfiable. Then, by reasoning in the proof of Theorem 4 there is no NE in the encoding of φ. But then $\{A_{x_0}\}$ is not a winner in a NE. Suppose further that φ is satisfiable. Then, by reasoning in the proof of Theorem 4 there exists a NE in the encoding of φ. Also, as we have shown, $\{A_{x_0}\}$ is a winner in this NE.

6   Conclusion

In this paper we provided an algorithmic analysis of nominee selection in the context of tournament solutions. We analysed two methods of selecting the set of winners, namely Condorcet Winner and Uncovered Set rules. As we demonstrated, checking if a pure Nash equilibrium exists for a party structure is NP-complete from the perspective of both of these rules. This result shows a strong difference between the complexity of reasoning about these rules and knockout tournaments, which allow for finding a Nash equilibrium in quasi-polynomial time if it exists as shown in [22]. Furthermore, from the perspective of the Uncovered Set, it is not tractable even to check if a party can win in some strategy profile. Table 1 provides a summary of our contribution.

Table 1. Algorithmic results shown in the paper.

	CW	UC
POSSIBLE WINNER	P	NP-c
WINNER IN NE	NP-c	NP-c
NE EXISTENCE	NP-c	NP-c

Our results provide a vast range of directions for future investigations. Let us discuss a few of them.

- We limited ourselves to two particular tournament rules only. It would be interesting to conduct a symmetric analysis for other rules, such as the Copeland rule. In particular, a natural direction would be to establish computational complexity of finding a NE for all Condorcet-consistent rules.

- We only considered pure Nash equilibrium as a solution concept. It would be of interest to check algorithmic properties of other concepts, such as dominant strategy equilibria, in the setting studied in this paper.
- In our setting we assumed that the beating relation is asymmetric, which in the social choice context corresponds to the assumption that, for a pair of candidates, one of them is preferred to another by the strict majority of voters (or that a tie-breaking rule is applied). This assumption is not applicable in case of many social phenomena, in which accounting for the ties between candidates is important. It would be therefore natural to study the case in which the tournament relation is not asymmetric.
- Even though most of the problems studied in this paper are computationally hard, it can be the case that they are tractable in typical cases. It is therefore interesting to analyse them from the perspective of parametrised complexity. In particular, it is natural to consider the number of parties as a parameter.
- Certain party structures always admit a Nash equilibrium for all Condorcet consistent rules, e.g., when some candidate beats all members of all parties to which it does not belong. Thus, it would be of high interest to identify non-trivial classes of games in which the existence of an equilibrium is guaranteed for meaningful classes of rules.
- In the setting studied in this paper, the tournament relation is deterministic, i.e. it is certain who is the winner of each pairwise contest. Generalisation of this framework in which this is not always the case would be a natural follow-up study.
- A potential avenue for further research involves the strategic behaviour of *voters* in the setting studied in this paper. One could consider agents misrepresenting their preferences over candidates to have a better candidate selected by a winning party.

Acknowledgements. I would like to thank Paul Harrenstein and Paolo Turrini, as well as Jędrzej Kołodziejski, for their helpful comments.

References

1. Altman, A., Procaccia, A.D., Tennenholtz, M.: Nonmanipulable selections from a tournament. In: IJCAI (2009)
2. Aziz, H., Brill, M., Fischer, F., Harrenstein, P., Lang, J., Seedig, H.G.: Possible and necessary winners of partial tournaments. J. Artif. Intell. Res. **54**, 493–534 (2015)
3. Aziz, H., Gaspers, S., Mackenzie, S., Mattei, N., Stursberg, P., Walsh, T.: Fixing balanced knockout and double elimination tournaments. Artif. Intell. **262**, 1–14 (2018)
4. Borodin, A., Lev, O., Shah, N., Strangway, T.: Primarily about primaries. In: Proceedings of the 33rd AAAI Conference on Artificial Intelligence, pp. 1804–1811 (2019)
5. Brandt, F., Brill, M., Harrenstein, B.: Tournament solutions. In: Brandt, F., Conitzer, V., Endriss, U., Lang, J., Procaccia, A.D. (eds.) Handbook of Computational Social Choice, pp. 453–474. Cambridge University Press (2016)

6. Brandt, F., Geist, C., Harrenstein, P.: A note on the McKelvey uncovered set and pareto optimality. Soc. Choice Welfare **46**(1), 81–91 (2016)
7. Brill, M., Conitzer, V.: Strategic voting and strategic candidacy. In: Twenty-Ninth AAAI Conference on Artificial Intelligence, pp. 819–826 (2015)
8. Cross, W.: Democratic norms and party candidate selection: taking contextual factors into account. Party Polit. **14**(5), 596–619 (2008)
9. Cross, W., Blais, A.: Who selects the party leader? Party Polit. **18**(2), 127–150 (2012)
10. Dutta, B., Jackson, M.O., Le Breton, M.: Strategic candidacy and voting procedures. Econometrica **69**(4), 1013–1037 (2001)
11. Eraslan, H., McLennan, A.: Strategic candidacy for multivalued voting procedures. J. Econ. Theory **117**(1), 29–54 (2004)
12. Faliszewski, P., Gourvès, L., Lang, J., Lesca, J., Monnot, J.: How hard is it for a party to nominate an election winner? In: IJCAI (2016)
13. Fishburn, P.C.: Condorcet social choice functions. SIAM J. Appl. Math. **33**(3), 469–489 (1977)
14. Fisher, D., Ryan, J.: Tournament games and positive tournaments. J. Graph Theory **19**(2), 217–236 (1995)
15. Harrenstein, P., Lisowski, G., Sridharan, R., Turrini, P.: A Hotelling-Downs framework for party nominees. In: Twentieth International Conference on Autonomous Agents and Multiagent Systems, pp. 593–601. AAMAS (2021)
16. Harrenstein, P., Turrini, P.: Computing Nash equilibria for district-based nominations. In: International Conference on Autonomous Agents and Multiagent Systems. AAMAS (2022)
17. Hazon, N., Dunne, P., Kraus, S., Wooldridge, M.: How to rig elections and competitions. In: Second International Workshop on Computational Social Choice. COMSOC (2008)
18. Kim, M.P., Suksompong, W., Williams, V.V.: Who can win a single-elimination tournament? SIAM J. Discret. Math. **31**(3), 1751–1764 (2017)
19. Kondratev, A.Y., Mazalov, V.V.: Tournament solutions based on cooperative game theory. Int. J. Game Theory. **49**, 1–27 (2019)
20. Laffond, G., Laslier, J.F., Breton, M.L.: The bipartisan set of a tournament game. Games Econom. Behav. **5**, 182–201 (1993)
21. Laslier, J.F.: Tournament Solutions and Majority Voting. Studies in Economic Theory, vol. 7, 1st Edn. Springer Verlag, Heidelberg (1997). https://link.springer.com/book/9783642645617
22. Lisowski, G., Ramanujan, M., Turrini, P.: Equilibrium computation for knockout tournaments played by groups. In: International Conference on Autonomous Agents and Multiagent Systems. AAMAS (2022)
23. Meir, R.: Strategic Voting. Morgan & Claypool, San Rafael (2018)
24. Miller, N.R.: A new solution set for tournaments and majority voting: further graph- theoretical approaches to the theory of voting. Am. J. Polit. Sci. **24**(1), 68–96 (1980)
25. Moon, J.: Topics on tournaments. Holt, Reinhart and Winston (1968)
26. Obraztsova, S., Elkind, E., Polukarov, M., Rabinovich, Z.: Strategic candidacy games with lazy candidates. In: Twenty-Fourth International Joint Conference on Artificial Intelligence (2015)
27. Vassilevska Williams, V.: Fixing a tournament. In: Twenty-Fourth AAAI Conference on Artificial Intelligence, pp. 895–900. AAAI (2010)
28. Wauters, B.: Explaining participation in intra-party elections: evidence from Belgian political parties. Party Polit. **16**(2), 237–259 (2010)

Sybil-Resilient Social Choice with Low Voter Turnout

Reshef Meir[1]([✉]), Nimrod Talmon[2], Gal Shahaf[3], and Ehud Shapiro[3]

[1] Technion—Israel Institute of Technology, Haifa, Israel
`reshefm@ie.technion.ac.il`
[2] Ben-Gurion University, Beersheba, Israel
`talmonn@bgu.ac.il`
[3] Weizmann Institute, Rehovot, Israel
`{gal.shahaf,ehud.shapiro}@weizmann.ac.il`

Abstract. We address social choice in the presence of sybils (fake or duplicate votes) and low turnout, two behaviors that may each distort the will of the society. To do so we assume the status quo as an ever-present distinguished alternative. We propose a general *Reality Enforcing mechanism*, which can be combined with arbitrary voting rules and operates by adding virtual votes that support the status quo. We measure the tradeoff between *safety* and *liveness* (the ability of non-abstaining non-sybil voters to maintain or to change the status quo, respectively) in a variety of voting domains and show a tight inherent limit to the amount of sybils and abstentions that can be tolerated.

Keywords: Computational social choice · Sybil attacks · Vote abstention

1 Introduction

Voting procedures are a simple and widely used way to aggregate the preferences of multiple individuals. Voting, however, can truly reflect the will of the society only insofar as **all** eligible people in the society—and **only** them—vote.

The problem of partial participation in online voting is particularly acute, as online voting often exhibits very low participation rates [3,12]. Similarly, in participatory budgeting, voter turnout is typically around 2%–4% of the population [11]—extremely low even if taking into account that not all residents can vote. Even in Cambridge MA, one of the most successful participatory budgeting programs, less than 7,500 people (out of a population of more than 100,000) have voted on the allocation of more than $1 million in 2021.[1]

The orthogonal problem of sybil votes has received much attention (see Sect. 1.2). Much of the trouble of dealing with sybils and low participation stems from the common assumption (at least in the Arrovian framework) that all alternatives are a-priori identical, and only differ in the support they get from voters. If these votes are unrepresentative, the outcome cannot be trusted.

---

[1] https://www.cambridgema.gov/news/2021/12/pbvoteresults.

© The Author(s), under exclusive license to Springer Nature Switzerland AG 2022
D. Baumeister and J. Rothe (Eds.): EUMAS 2022, LNAI 13442, pp. 257–274, 2022.
https://doi.org/10.1007/978-3-031-20614-6_15

In almost every voting situation, however, from a Doodle poll on meeting times to organizational elections and a national census, it is rarely the case that all alternatives are completely symmetric. E.g., there is almost always some fallback option (e.g. no meeting), incumbent candidate, or current state of affairs. Indeed, the role of the status quo is extensively discussed in the political science literature, going back to Downs [9] and Grofman [10], although the focus is mainly on how the presence and the position of the status quo affects voters' behavior.

Recently, Shapiro and Talmon [26] argued for the importance of incorporating the status quo (or the 'Reality', in their words) into the design and the analysis of voting schemes, showing how it can resolve several paradoxes and misunderstandings. Shahaf et al. [25] readily applied this agenda as a tool for curbing the power of sybil voters. More specifically, they suggested to use the status quo as an anchor, so that only a supermajority can change it. Then, they formalized the properties of *sybil safety*—the inability of sybils to change the status quo against the will of the honest voters, and *sybil liveness*—the ability of the honest voters to change the status quo despite the existence of sybils. In particular, Shahaf et al. designed specialized sybil-resilient voting rules for: (1) two alternatives; (2) multiple alternatives; and (3) voting on an interval. Two major limitations of their work are the assumption of full participation by the honest (non-sybil) voters, and the lack of a way to quantify partial safety or liveness.

In this paper we suggest a simple and general mechanism that mitigates *both* problems (sybils and partial participation), by adding "virtual votes" to the status quo. This mechanism can be combined with a variety of voting rules in different domains, as well as will other components such as delegation or identity verification.

Note that the role of the status quo in our model (following the work described above) is not just technical, but *normative*: in a sense, the status quo represents what we prefer to do if unsure about voters' true intentions (hence the term 'safety'); this is different than, say, the status quo of the Nash bargaining game [19], which serves the roll of the 'worst-case outcome' we are trying to avoid.

1.1   Contribution and Structure

In Sect. 2 we develop a formal model of social choice that incorporates both sybils and partial participation, and provide general definitions for safety and liveness.

In Sect. 3.1, we define the general Reality-Enforcing (RE) mechanism, which adds fictitious votes in favor of the status quo, and then uses the desired voting rule as a black box. Both our model and our mechanism strictly generalize the domain-specific definitions and results of Shahaf et al. [25].

Then, in Sect. 4, we provide a tight analysis of the safety-liveness tradeoff, extending the results of Shahaf et al. in three directions:

- We quantify the amount of safety and liveness obtained;
- We generalize the results to take into account the amount of abstaining voters;

– We extend the analysis via reductions to other domains including multiple referenda, voting on an interval, and rank aggregation (Sect. 5).

We further show that, when full safety and fairness are required (as in [25]), then no mechanism can do better than RE. From a design perspective, given an estimate of the sybil penetration to a community as well as the fraction of inactive voters, our results allow the community to set the threshold of the RE mechanism to guarantee that the voting rule is safe (i.e., keep the status quo intact if this is the wish of the honest voters) and live (i.e., not be stuck in the status quo more than it is necessary to satisfy safety).

A full version of the paper is available at https://arxiv.org/abs/2001.05271.

1.2 Related Work

Besides the work of Shahaf et al. [25], which we generalize and extend, we mention that, indeed, sybil attacks have been amply studied in the literature of computational social choice [5,6,27], mainly showing impossibility results on the design of *false-name proof* voting rules, i.e., rules where clones cannot affect the outcome. These results do not consider the status quo, hence are not applicable in our safety/liveness model. A related, complementary challenge is keeping the fraction of sybils in online communities low, which may be possible via identification and eradication techniques (see, e.g., [1]).

There is extensive work in the social choice literature on the strategic justification of partial participation/abstention, going back to the "paradox of non-voting" [8,21,24]. Other works consider ways to elicit the preferences of specific voters in order to reduce communication complexity [7]. Yet we are unaware of works that consider resilience to arbitrary partial participation, via the use of the status quo or otherwise.

2 Preliminaries

We consider voting situations with a set A of alternatives, one of which is the current *reality*, or *status quo*, denoted by r; and a set V of n voters (note that we overload notation and treat "voters" and "votes" interchangeably). A voting rule (or mechanism) $\mathcal{R}$ is a sequence of functions $\mathcal{R}^{(n)} : B^n \to A$, for all $n \in \mathbb{N}$, where B is some set of allowed ballots.

Remark 1. Note that, as our goal is to develop a general formalism that can be applied to different social choice settings and to analyse the properties of a broad range of mechanism, under both sybils **and** partial participation, including measures of partial protection. This generality inevitably means that the mathematical exposition and notation is somewhat heavy. However, a reader that wants to avoid some of the complexity can focus on the special case of *full* safety and liveness.

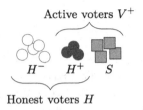

Fig. 1. The general voting population.

2.1   Partial Participation and Sybils

The set of voters V is partitioned into a set of *honest* (i.e., genuine; non-sybil) voters H and a set of *sybil* voters S; so, $V = H \cup S$ with $H \cap S = \emptyset$. We assume that the partition to honest voters and sybils is implicitly included in V, but of course not accessible to the voting rule. Ideally, we would like our voting rules to reflect only the preferences of the honest voters, but without knowing who is honest and who is sybil, and when not all honest voters vote.

Active and Passive Voters. The set of honest voters, H, is further partitioned into $H = H^+ \cup H^-$ (with $H^+ \cap H^- = \emptyset$), where H^+ is the non-empty set of honest voters who did cast a vote, and are thus labeled by their vote, and H^- is the set of honest voters who did not cast a vote. We refer to the voters in H^+ as *active honest voters* and to the voters in H^- as *passive honest voters*, or *passive voters* in short. We assume w.l.o.g that all sybils vote. Thus, both the active honest voters and the sybils are active. Denote $V^+ := H^+ \cup S$. See Fig. 1.

Further Notation. In many places it will be convenient to refer to the *fraction* of some set of voters rather than to their absolute size. For any subset of voters $U \subseteq V$, we denote by the small letter $u := \frac{|U|}{|V|}$ the relative size of this set to the entire population.

For some $U \subseteq V$, we denote by $U_a \subseteq U$ the subset of U who vote for alternative $a \in A$, and by $u_a = \frac{|U_a|}{|V|}$ their relative fraction (this is relevant when the set B of admissible ballots corresponds to picking some subset, possibly a singleton, from a set of alternatives). Lastly, we use a special notation for the fraction of sybils σ and the fraction of inactive voters μ, which have a special use as parameters in our results. Formally, $\sigma := s = \frac{|S|}{|V|}$; and $\mu := h^- = \frac{|H^-|}{|V|}$. Our analysis assumes that μ, σ are known, but our guarantees apply as long as they upper-bound the true fractions of inactive and sybil voters.

2.2   Safety and Liveness

Next we discuss the concepts of safety and liveness. Informally speaking, suppose that we have some preferred voting rule $\mathcal{G}$, for the "standard" setting without sybils and with full participation (this $\mathcal{G}$ will be referred to as a "ground rule").

This may be due to favorable axiomatic properties of $\mathcal{G}$, because of its simplicity, due to legacy, or for any other reason. Ideally, we would like to always get the outcome $\mathcal{G}(H)$, that is, the result of all honest voters voting under $\mathcal{G}$. However, if we use $\mathcal{G}$ in a straight-forward way, then the outcome may be distorted due to the existence of sybil votes and/or partial participation. This is demonstrated by the following simple example.

Example 1 (Running example). Let $V = H \cup S$, where $H = \{x_1, x_2, x_3\}$ are honest voters, $S = \{x_4, x_5\}$ are sybils, and there are two alternatives $A = \{a, b\}$. Suppose that $H_a = \{x_1, x_2\}$ and $H_b = \{x_3\}$, then a is the better outcome under the Majority rule ($\mathcal{G}(H) = a$).

However, if either the two sybils vote for b, *or* the first two honest voters decide to abstain, then the inferior alternative b will win.

Following Reality-Aware Social Choice [26], we assume that a distinguished alternative, the status quo (or *reality*), $r \in A$, always exists. All ties are settled towards the alternative closer to r (the metric defining "closer" will be clear from the context). Recall that r is considered a 'reasonable' outcome, so in case of uncertainty regarding voter intentions, we would prefer to remain as close as possible to r.

Intuitively, safety of a rule $\mathcal{R}$ means that the outcome shall be somewhere "between" the desired outcome $\mathcal{G}(H)$ and the status quo r (so the sybils are not able to enforce undesired outcomes); and liveness means that a sufficient fraction of active honest voters have the power to enforce any outcome in $\mathcal{R}$. (The definition of being in "between" is made concrete for the specific domain considered in Sect. 5; for the binary domain this notion trivializes.) Our formal definitions of safety and liveness apply to arbitrary domains, any aggregation rule, and naturally extend to partial participation and sybils. They may also apply to other notions of vote distortion that are outside the scope of the current work. To achieve our desired generality and mathematical expressive power, we need to formalize two more basic concepts, namely the *outcome range* and the *between set*.

Definition 1 (Outcome Range). *Let $\mathcal{R}$ be an aggregation rule (and consider some voting population $V = H \cup S$). Then, for a parameter $\gamma \geq 0$:*

$$\overline{\mathcal{R}}_\gamma(V) := \{\mathcal{R}(H' \cup S) : \exists H', |H'| \geq |H|, |H' \setminus H| \leq \gamma|H|\}.$$

For $\gamma \in [0, 1]$, this means that $\overline{\mathcal{R}}_\gamma(V)$ contains all outcomes that can be obtained by replacing or adding a fraction of at most γ honest voters by arbitrary votes. Higher values $\gamma > 1$ effectively mean that we may replace all honest voters and, furthermore, add additional $(1 - \gamma)|H|$ voters.

We stress that, following the discussion above, we use γ and the outcome range as a notion of approximation: $\overline{\mathcal{R}}_0(V) = \mathcal{R}(V)$, and the higher γ is, the larger the outcome range becomes. Yet, this approximation is measured not by the similarity of the alternatives, but rather by the amount of voters needed to switch from one to the other.[2]

Recall that $\mathcal{G}$ represents some desired "ground rule", in the sense that we wish to be safe w.r.t $\mathcal{G}$. While in some cases there is an "obvious" ground rule (e.g., majority in the binary domain), this is not always the case and thus we require the ground rule to be specified explicitly.

Safety and Liveness. α-*Safety* informally means that the rule always selects either r; or alternatives that a slightly modified set of honest voters would elect under $\mathcal{G}$; or alternatives "in between" those. We denote the set of all alternatives "between" r and a set S by $\mathcal{B}(r; S)$, but to ease the presentation we defer the general formal definition of this set to Sect. 5. For all of our examples and results that consider only two candidates $A = \{r, p\}$, we use the trivial betweeness notion $\mathcal{B}(r; S) = \{r\} \cup S$ and this will suffice until considering more complicated spaces.

Definition 2 (Safety). *An aggregation rule $\mathcal{R}$ is α-safe w.r.t the ground rule $\mathcal{G}$ and population $V = H \cup S$, if it holds that $\mathcal{R}(V) \in \mathcal{B}(r; \overline{\mathcal{G}}_\alpha(H))$.*

Importantly, *full safety* ($\alpha = 0$) means that an aggregation rule is safe if it always hits between r and the ideal outcome $\mathcal{G}(H)$. For general $\alpha > 0$, indeed α-safety relaxes that notion by using both betweenness and the outcome range as a notion of approximation.

Note that selecting the status quo r is always safe. However a rule that always returns r is also undesired. Our next requirement is *liveness*, which does not depend on a ground rule.

Definition 3 (Liveness). *An aggregation rule $\mathcal{R}$ is β-live w.r.t. population V, if for all $a \in A \setminus \{r\}$, it holds that $a \in \overline{\mathcal{R}}_\beta(V)$.*

I.e., a rule is live w.r.t some population if any outcome can be reached by modifying not-too-many (in particular, β-fraction of) honest voters.

We say that a rule $\mathcal{R}$ is α-safe [β-live], if it is α-safe [resp., β-live] w.r.t. any population V. Crucially, α and β may depend on parameters of the profile V, and in particular on σ and μ.

In particular: *full liveness* (1-liveness) means that the rule is *onto* (sometimes called *citizen sovereignty* [18]), i.e., the honest voters can enforce any outcome. In other words, sybils have no veto power, which is the main liveness requirement we consider.

Remark 2. Our definitions generalize those of Shahaf et al. [25]; under full participation (i.e., $\mu = 0$), their definitions of safety and liveness coincide with our 0-safety and 1-liveness, respectively.

Throughout the following examples, we hold $|V|$, σ, and μ fixed, and all bounds are conditional on these values.

---

[2] This is sometimes called 'input approximation', in contrast to 'output approximation' [15].

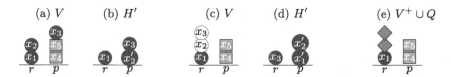

Fig. 2. Red squares are sybils, full/hollow circles are active/passive honest voters, respectively. (a) The population V used in Examples 2 and 3. (b) A set $|H'|$ that demonstrates the $\frac{1}{3}$-safety property in Example 2. (c) The population used in Example 4; note that $MJ(V^+) = p$ whereas $MJ(H) = r$. (d) A set H' that demonstrates the $\frac{2}{3}$-safety property in Example 4. (e) The rule $\frac{2}{3}$-RE-MJ adds $\frac{2}{3}|V^+| = 2$ virtual voters on r (dark diamonds). (Color figure online)

Example 2 (Majority under full participation). As in Example 1, let $H = \{x_1, x_2, x_3\}$ and $S = \{x_4, x_5\}$ be the sets of honest and sybil voters. However, $A = \{p, r\}$, meaning a single proposal p is voted against the status quo r. Note that we have $\sigma = \frac{2}{5}$ (as there are 2 sybils out of 5 voters).

Consider the ground rule $\mathcal{G} = MJ$ which returns p if it has a simple majority, else r. Next, we show that for any $\alpha < \frac{1}{3}$, MJ is not α-safe w.r.t itself even under full participation. To this end, suppose that x_1 and x_2 support r whereas x_3, x_4, x_5 support p (see Fig. 2(a)). As $\alpha|H| < 1$, α-safety does not allow us to change the vote of any voter in $\overline{MJ}_\alpha(H)$. Now, observe that $\overline{MJ}_\alpha(H) = \{r\}$. Then, α-safety requires that the outcome is in $\mathcal{B}(r; \overline{MJ}_\alpha(H)) = \{r\}$; we have, however, that $MJ(V) = p \notin \{r\}$.

Note further, however, that MJ is α-safe w.r.t itself for each $\alpha \geq \frac{1}{3}$: since one of three honest voters is already voting for p, then, by setting $H' := \{p, p, r\}$ (see Fig. 2(b)), we get that $p \in \overline{MJ}_\alpha(H)$. What about liveness? For any 5-voter profile V as above, we can define an alternative profile H' where all $3 = 1 \cdot |H|$ honest voters vote for p, and $MJ(H' \cup S) = p$. Thus $p \in \overline{MJ}_1(V)$, and MJ is 1-live. Also, any lower value $\beta < 1$ means we can change the votes of at most two honest voters in H'. By our tie-breaking rule this means $MJ(H' \cup S) = r$ and thus MJ is not β-live for any $\beta < 1$.

A voting rule may also take the status quo into account [25]:

Definition 4. *Suppose* $A = \{r, p\}$. *Then, the* τ-*Supermajority rule* $(\tau - SMJ)$ *selects* p *if* $v_p > \frac{1}{2} + \tau$ *voters vote for* p *(recall that* v_p *is the fraction of voters voting for* p*); otherwise, it selects* r.

Example 3 (Supermajority under full participation). Consider the same profile of votes from Example 2, but with the supermajority rule $\mathcal{R} = 0.4 - SMJ$. Note that for profiles with five voters this requires a unanimous vote for p to win. For this particular V, $\mathcal{R}$ is 0-safe w.r.t $\mathcal{G} = MJ$. We can also see that letting the two sybils vote r shows a violation of 1-liveness. However $\mathcal{R}$ is $6\frac{1}{3}$-live, since we can construct a set H' of $19 = (6\frac{1}{3})|H|$ voters for p.

2.3   Safety, Liveness, and Partial Participation

Next, we introduce a formal definition that captures the effect of passive voters. Recall that $V = H^+ \cup H^- \cup S$ and $V^+ = H^+ \cup S$. The following definition captures the idea that the voting rule can only see the active votes and cannot distinguish between genuine votes H^+ and sybil votes S.

Definition 5 (Voting with partial participation). *We introduce a notation $\mathcal{R}^+$ for any voting rule $\mathcal{R}$, where $\mathcal{R}^+(V)$ returns $\mathcal{R}(V^+)$ on any input V.*

Therefore, when considering a voting rule $\mathcal{R}$ under partial participation, we care about the safety and liveness properties of $\mathcal{R}^+$. Formally:

- $\mathcal{R}^+$ is α-safe w.r.t. $\mathcal{G}$ if $\mathcal{R}(V^+) \in \mathcal{B}(r; \overline{\mathcal{G}}_\alpha(H))$ for all V.
- $\mathcal{R}^+$ is β-live if $a \in \overline{\mathcal{R}}_\beta(V^+)$ for all V and $a \in A$.[3]

Example 4 (Majority under Partial Participation). We extend Example 2 by partitioning the set of honest voters into one active voter $H^+ = \{x_1\}$ and two passive voters $H^- = \{x_2, x_3\}$. As in Example 2, x_4 and x_5 are sybils, so $\sigma = \frac{2}{5}, \mu = \frac{2}{5}$ (see Fig. 2(c)). The modified rule MJ^+ considers only the active voters. While Example 2 shows that MJ is $\frac{1}{3}$-safe w.r.t MJ, this is not true under partial participation, as it is possible that all three honest voters prefer r but $MJ^+(V) = MJ(\{x_1\} \cup S) = p$. In this case we can only show that MJ^+ is α-safe w.r.t MJ for $\alpha \geq \frac{2}{3}$ (as we need to change two honest voters to include p in the range $\overline{MJ}_\alpha(H)$, see Fig. 2(d)).

The MJ^+ rule is 3-live. To see that $\beta \leq 3$, observe that we can define H' as $3 = 3|H^+|$ voters for p, and then $MJ(H' \cup S) = p$ and $MJ(H' \cup S) \in \overline{MJ}_3(V^+)$. In contrast, the supermajority rule $0.4 - SMJ^+$ is $\frac{1}{3}$-safe which is much better.

3   The General Reality-Enforcing Mechanism

We describe the RE mechanism, which we analyse throughout the paper. We stress that we view its operational simplicity – contrasted with the non-triviality of its analysis – as an advantage, as a simple mechanism may be better understood by voters and may have higher applicability.

Next, for a ground voting rule $\mathcal{G}$, we define a parameterized reality-enforcing version that adds votes to the status quo.

Definition 6 (Reality-enforcing mechanism). *Let $\mathcal{G}$ be a ground rule. Then, we define $\tau\text{-}RE\text{-}\mathcal{G}(V) := \mathcal{G}(V \cup Q)$, where Q is a set of $\tau|V|$ voters voting for r.*[4]

---

[3] Observe that $\overline{\mathcal{R}}_\beta^+(V)$ does not equal $\overline{\mathcal{R}}_\beta(V^+)$. In particular, the former is not well-defined for $\beta > 1$, since we would have to specify which of the honest voters we add to H' are active. Our definition avoids this complication altogether.

[4] Note that ballots need not be a single candidate. As long as the ground rule $\mathcal{G}$ has some notion of candidate score (like Copeland or Borda), the RE mechanism simply increases the score of r.

Intuitively, a higher value of τ increases safety as it makes it harder to leave the status quo; but it may hurt liveness. In Example 4, the $\frac{2}{3}$-RE-MJ^+ mechanism will add $\frac{2}{3}|V^+| = 2$ 'virtual votes' to r (see Fig. 2(e)). Thus $\frac{2}{3}$-RE-$MJ^+(V) = MJ^+(V \cup Q) = MJ(H^+ \cup S \cup Q) = MJ(\{r,p,p,r,r\}) = r$. Note that this entails 0-safety (the maximal safety level).

3.1 The General RE Mechanism vs. Shahaf et al.

Shahaf et al. [25] focused on two domains: a binary vote; and voting on the real line. In each such domain they suggested a designated mechanism to deal with sybils. In this section we show that our RE mechanism coincides with each of these two mechanisms in its respective domain, when all voters participate.

Binary Domain. For this domain Shahaf et al. [25] defined the Reality-aware τ-Supermajority rule (see Definition 4; essentially, it picks the proposal p only if a specific supermajority, and not a mere majority, vote for it).

By applying the RE mechanism to the Majority ground rule $\mathcal{G} = MJ$, we get the $\tau - RE$-MJ rule, which returns the majority opinion after adding $\tau|V|$ votes for the status quo r.

Observation 1. *For $A = \{r,p\}$ and any $\tau \geq 0$, the $2\tau - RE$-MJ rule and the $\tau - SMJ$ rule of Shahaf et al. [25] coincide.*

Proof. Consider the fraction v_p of votes for p. The claim follows since $v_p > v_r + q_r = (1 - v_p) + 2\tau$ (i.e. $\tau - RE$-MJ selects p) iff $v_p > \frac{1}{2} + \tau$ (i.e. p has supermajority). □

The Real Line. In this domain Shahaf et al. [25] defined the τ-Suppress-outer-votes median (τ-SOM) rule: first, compute the population median $m := MD(V)$; now, if $m > r$ ($m < r$), then eliminate the τ-fraction of voters with the highest (resp., lowest) votes; denote the new set V^-; next, compute the new median $m^- := MD(V^-)$; finally, if $sign(m^- - r) = sign(m - r)$ then return m^-, otherwise return r. That is, the $\tau - SOM$ rule first computes the median, then recomputes the median after removing the extreme voters that push the median away from r. The mechanism breaks ties in favor of r. Applying Definition 6 to the median rule MD, we get the *reality enforcing median rule* $\tau - RE$-MD.

Observation 2. *The $\tau - RE$-MD mechanism and the $\tau - SOM$ rule of Shahaf et al. [25] coincide.*

Proof. Sort voters in increasing order, and suppose, w.l.o.g (from symmetry), that $MD(V) > r$. The $\tau - SOM$ rule returns the location of the $\frac{n-\tau|V|}{2}$ voter from V. The $\tau - RE$-MD rule returns the location of the $\frac{n+\tau|V|}{2}$ voter from $V \cup Q$. If $\frac{n-\tau|V|}{2} \leq r$, then both rules return r. Otherwise, note that the $\frac{n+\tau|V|}{2}$ voter in $V \cup Q$ is the $\frac{n+\tau|V|}{2} - \sigma|V| = \frac{n-\tau|V|}{2}$ voter in V. □

For both mechanisms, Shahaf et al. [25] prove that setting $\tau = \sigma$ guarantees both 0-safe and 1-live, as long as $\sigma < \frac{1}{3}$.

In the next sections, we generalize the results of Shahaf at al. in three directions: considering relaxed notions of safety and liveness; allowing partial participation; and extending to additional domains.

4   Binary vote: Status Quo vs. a Single Contender

Equipped with our definitions of safety and liveness and with our general RE mechanism, we are ready to tackle different social choice settings; the first social choice setting we consider is a binary vote: voting on a single proposal p against the status quo r, as in Examples 2-4. Here, it is natural to use Majority as a ground rule; in fact, May's theorem [14] shows that it is the *only* natural voting rule to consider. Denote the proposal by p and the status quo by r, so that $A = \{p, r\}$. Using the Majority rule MJ as the ground rule $\mathcal{G}$, we have that $\mathcal{G}(H) = p$ if there are strictly more honest voters for p and r otherwise (recall that we break ties in favor of the status quo).

We capture the full tradeoff between safety and liveness: In particular, we analyse, for given values of σ, τ, and μ, what values of α and β allow us to obtain α-safety and β-liveness. Intuitively, higher values of α and β are easier to obtain, as in all minimization problems (as α and β are approximation notions). Theorems 1 and 2 are our main results, and most other results are either derived from them, show their tightness, or extend them.

Theorem 1 (Safety). *The* $\tau - RE\text{-}MJ^+$ *voting rule is* α-*safe w.r.t Majority iff* $\alpha > 0.5$ *or* $\alpha \geq \frac{1+\sigma-(1+\tau)(1-\mu)}{2(1-\sigma)}$.

Proof. We show here that the above condition is sufficient for safety. Necessity is shown in the full version by explicitly constructing a violating instance.

Consider a given profile V. Suppose first that $\alpha > 0.5$. In this case we can show that both outcomes $\{r, p\}$ are α-safe. Suppose we move $\alpha(1-\mu)$ honest voters to p, then there are $h'_p > 0.5(1-\mu)$ voters on p, whereas less than $0.5(1-\mu)$ honest voters remain on r, meaning $MJ(H') = p$ and thus $p \in \overline{MJ}_\alpha(H)$.

The main part of the proof deals with the case $\alpha \geq \frac{1+\sigma-(1+\tau)(1-\mu)}{2(1-\sigma)}$.

If $\tau - RE\text{-}MJ^+(V) = r$ or $p \in \overline{MJ}_\alpha(H)$, then there is no violation of α-safety and we are done. Thus, assume that $\tau - RE\text{-}MJ^+(V) = p \neq r$. Recall that h_p^+ denotes the fraction of active honest voters voting for p. W.l.o.g. we may assume that all of S vote for p, since if profile V violates α-safety, we can define a new profile V', by making all S agents who vote for r to vote for p, and we would still have $\tau - RE\text{-}MJ^+(V) = p$ (and $\overline{MJ}_\alpha(H)$ is unaffected) and thus there is still a violation in V' (so, intuitively, profiles in which all sybils vote for p are the hardest case for keeping safety). Similarly, we assume w.l.o.g that all of H^- vote for r, thus $h_r = h^- + h_r^+$, $h_p = h_p^+$ (again, profiles in which all passive voters vote for r are the hardest case for keeping safety, as safety is defined w.r.t all honest voters); so, the fraction of active honest voters voting for r is $h_r^+ = 1 - \sigma - \mu - h_p^+$. Since $\tau - RE\text{-}MJ^+(V) = p$, we have that

$$h_p^+ + \sigma = v_p^+ > v_r^+ + q = h_r^+ + q = h^+ - h_p^+ + q \tag{1}$$
$$= (1 - \mu - \sigma - h_p^+) + \tau(1 - \mu) \tag{2}$$

and thus

$$2h_p^+ > (1 + \tau)(1 - \mu) - 2\sigma . \tag{3}$$

To show that $p \in \overline{MJ}_\alpha(H)$, implying α-safety, we shall show that we can change the votes of $\alpha \cdot h$ honest voters from r to p, to create a new profile H' where p has a strict majority of honest votes. Denote

$$\alpha' = \alpha h = \alpha(1 - \sigma) \geq \frac{1 + \sigma - (1 + \tau)(1 - \mu)}{2} . \tag{4}$$

Indeed, after moving α' votes, r has $h_r' = h_r - \alpha' = h - h_p - \alpha' = 1 - \sigma - h_p^+ - \alpha'$ honest votes, whereas p has $h_p' = h_p^+ + \alpha'$ honest votes. Therefore, we have that

$$
\begin{aligned}
h_p' - h_r' &= (h_p^+ + \alpha') - (1 - \sigma - h_p^+ - \alpha') = 2(h_p^+ + \alpha') - (1 - \sigma) \\
&\geq 2h_p^+ + (1 + \sigma - (1 + \tau)(1 - \mu)) - (1 - \sigma) \qquad \text{(By Eq. (4))} \\
&> (1 - \sigma) - (1 - \sigma) = 0. \qquad\qquad\qquad\qquad \text{(By Eq. (3))}
\end{aligned}
$$

So, there are strictly more honest votes for p than for r. $\qquad\qquad\square$

Theorem 2 (Liveness). *The $\tau - RE\text{-}MJ^+$ voting rule is β-live if and only if $\beta > \frac{(1-\mu)(1+\tau)}{2(1-\sigma-\mu)}$.*

Proof. Since any vote for r reduces liveness, w.l.o.g all voters vote for r. There are $h^+ = 1 - \mu - \sigma$ active honest voters (all vote for r). Suppose we create a new profile $\overline{V}$ by moving a fraction of β votes from r to p, then p has $\overline{v}_p^+ = \overline{h}_p^+ = \beta(1 - \mu - \sigma)$.

In contrast, r has $\overline{h}_r^+ = h^+ - \overline{h}_p^+ = 1 - \mu - \sigma - \overline{h}_p^+$ active honest votes remaining, plus σ sybils. The $\tau - RE\text{-}MJ^+$ mechanism adds $\tau(1 - \mu)$ votes so the total support for r is $\overline{v}_r^+ = (1 - \mu - \sigma - \overline{h}_p^+) + \sigma + \tau(1 - \mu) = (1 + \tau)(1 - \mu) - \overline{h}_p^+$. Since liveness requires $\overline{v}_p^+ > \overline{v}_r^+$, we get a tight bound of $2\overline{h}_p^+ > (1 + \tau)(1 - \mu)$, or, equivalently, $\beta = \frac{\overline{h}_p^+}{1 - \mu - \sigma} > \frac{(1+\tau)(1-\mu)}{2(1-\mu-\sigma)}$, as required. $\qquad\square$

The two theorems confirm and quantify the following observation: as there are more sybils (higher σ) or more abstentions (higher μ), both safety and liveness are jeopardized. We can also see that the effect of sybils is stronger. In particular, in the absence of sybils, partial abstention has no effect on liveness.

As important examples, we consider the special cases of 0-safety and 1-liveness.

Corollary 1. *The following hold:*

- $\tau - RE\text{-}MJ^+$ *is 0-safe w.r.t MJ iff* $\tau \geq \frac{1+\sigma}{1-\mu} - 1$.
- $\tau - RE\text{-}MJ^+$ *is 1-live iff* $\tau < \frac{2(1-\sigma-\mu)}{1-\mu} - 1$.
- *We can get both iff* $3\sigma + 2\mu < 1$.

E.g., with 20% sybils and 20% passives, or with 10% sybils and 35% passives, we can guarantee both 0-safety and 1-liveness by setting τ between the two bounds in the corollary. We emphasize that we do not need to know σ or μ exactly in order to set τ: as long as we have have some upper bound on their real values, $\tau - RE\text{-}MJ$ will have the safety and liveness specified above. A better estimation will allow us to obtain a better tradeoff of safety and liveness.

We complement our analysis with the following lower bound, proving that the last bound in Corollary 1 is tight: no other mechanism can achieve both safety and liveness with this amount of sybils and abstention.

Theorem 3. *There is no mechanism* $\mathcal{R}$ *such that* $\mathcal{R}^+$ *is both 0-safe and 1-live when* $3\sigma + 2\mu \geq 1$.[5]

The proof is by constructing a parametrized class of instances such that no mechanism can perform better on all of them.

Finally, by Observation 1 all of the results in this section apply also to the supermajority mechanism if Shahaf et al. [25], as it coincides with the RE mechanism.

5   Extensions to Other Domains

Our general RE mechanism can clearly be applied in any domain, as long as there is some notion of candidate score (so the mechanism can artificially increase that score by τ). However, it is not a-priori clear how to extend the definition of safety when the space of alternatives has an arbitrary structure (the definition of liveness naturally extends).

It turns out that the our previous definition of safety readily applies without changes, once we consider a general notion of *betweeness*.

Betweeness. Our modeling is such that, generally, we view the alternatives as residing in a metric space (the specific metric space considered in each of our results will be clear from the context), and we require each voter to specify one alternative. Any metric space (A, δ) induces a natural trinary relation of *betweenness*, where b is *between* a and c if $\delta(a,b) + \delta(b,c) = \delta(a,c)$ (first defined by Menger in 1928; see [4,16]).

Definition 7 (Between set). *For* $x, y \in A$, $\mathcal{B}(x,y) \subseteq A$ *is the set of all points that are* between x *and* y, *including* $\{x,y\}$. *We define* $\mathcal{B}(x;Y) := \bigcup_{y \in Y} \mathcal{B}(x,y)$.

---

[5] We assume that there is at least one honest voter, otherwise safety is meaningless.

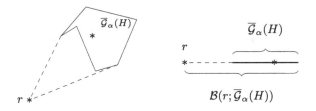

Fig. 3. A demonstration of the α-safety property in some 2-dimensional metric space (left) and in 1-dimensional space (right). The ideal point $\mathcal{G}(H)$ is marked by $*$.

We can now use Definition 2 to measure safety in any domain, with the appropriate between set $\mathcal{B}$. In particular, the following cases are considered in the paper:

- in a discrete unordered set A (including Sect. 4), $\mathcal{B}(x,y) = \{x,y\}$;
- in multiple referenda (with d binary issues and the Hamming distance) $A = \{0,1\}^d$, $\mathcal{B}(x,y)$ is the smallest *box* containing both x and y [20];
- on the real line, $\mathcal{B}(x,y)$ is the smallest *interval* containing both x and y.

Figure 3 demonstrates how betweeness extends the safety definition. The α-safe area $\mathcal{B}(r; \overline{\mathcal{G}}_\alpha(H))$ includes all alternatives enclosed in either dashed or solid lines. Next, we extend our results from the binary domain to other domains, using reductions.

5.1 Multiple Referenda

Suppose that $A = \{0,1\}^d$ (as well as B), where $r = \mathbf{0}$. For a ground rule, we use the issue-wise Majority rule IMJ, which simply selects the majority opinion on each of the d issues (this is a *combinatorial domain* [13]). Note that $IMJ(U)$ minimizes the sum of Hamming distances to all voters in U, thus maximizing the standard definition of the social welfare. It is natural to assume that all the bounds proved above for majority will effortlessly apply for multiple referenda, as the issues are independent. The next example shows that unfortunately this is not the case, and the trivial generalization of Theorem 1 does not hold for arbitrary α.

Example 5. Suppose that $|H| = 60, |S| = 21$ (i.e. $\sigma \cong 1/4$), $\tau = 0, \mu = 0$. Then by Theorem 1 we get 1/6-safety of the $\tau - RE\text{-}MJ$ rule (indeed, if there are 40 honest voters on '0' and 20 on '1', then moving $10 = |H|/6$ to '1' is sufficient).

Now consider $A = \{0,1\}^3$, where honest voters are dispersed as follows: 20 on $(0,0,1)$; 20 on $(0,1,0)$; 20 on $(1,0,0)$ and all of S are on $(1,1,1)$ so the outcome is $IMJ(V) = (1,1,1)$. However it is not possible to get $IMJ(H') = (1,1,1)$ by moving only 10 honest voters, since each voter can only get closer on two of the three dimensions. The best we can do is moving 5 agents from each location to $(1,1,1)$ (so $\alpha = 15/60$). This entails that $\tau - RE\text{-}IMJ$ is only 1/4-safe w.r.t. IMJ.

Yet, a reduction to the single-issue case is possible when considering β-liveness (for any β) or 0-safety.

Theorem 4. *The following hold:*

- *$\tau - IMJ^+$ has the same liveness guarantees as $\tau - RE\text{-}MJ^+$.*
- *$\tau - IMJ^+$ has the same 0-safety guarantees w.r.t. IMJ, as $\tau - RE\text{-}MJ^+$ has w.r.t. MJ.*

Proof (Safety). For an issue $j \leq d$ and voter set U, we denote by $U|_j \in \{0,1\}^{|U|}$ the (projected) opinions of all U voters.

Let $\tau, \mu, \sigma \geq 0$ such that $\tau - RE\text{-}MJ^+$ is 0-safe. Suppose that $\tau - RE\text{-}IMJ^+(V) = p \neq r$ (otherwise 0-safety is trivial). To show 0-safety, we need to prove $p \in \mathcal{B}(r; \overline{IMJ_0}(H)) = \mathcal{B}(r; IMJ(H))$ (note that this is the first nontrivial use of the "betweeness" notion in the paper, see Definition 7). This means showing $p_j \in \{r_j, IMJ(H)_j\}$ for all $j \leq d$.

By 0-safety of $\tau - RE\text{-}MJ^+$, we know that $\tau - RE\text{-}MJ^+(V|_j) \in \{r_j, MJ(H|_j)\}$ for all j. To complete the proof, we observe that $p_j = \tau - RE\text{-}IMJ^+(V)_j = \tau - RE\text{-}MJ^+(V|_j)$ and that $\{r_j, IMJ(H)_j\} = \{r_j, MJ(H|_j)\}$. □

5.2   The Real Line

When voting on a location on the real line (i.e., where B is, say, $[0,1]$), the natural ground rule to consider here is the *Median rule (MD)*, which returns the position of the median voter. The median rule has many desired properties such as Condorcet consistency, strategyproofness, and social optimality [2,17,23] (Fig. 4).

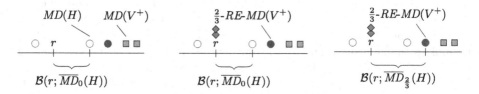

Fig. 4. We use red squares/ full circles/ hollow circles for $S, H^+ \; H^-$ respectively as in Fig. 2. On the left, we see that the median mechanism is not 0-safe, since the median of all active voters is not between $MD(H)$ and r. The middle and right figure show that the $\frac{2}{3} - RE\text{-}MD^+$ mechanism, which adds (in this profile) two virtual voters on r, is still not 0-safe but is α-safe for $\alpha \geq \frac{2}{3}$. (Color figure online)

Example 6 (Median under partial participation). In this example we use exactly the same composition of voter as in Example 4, except that now they are positioned on a line, and thus the betweeness notion is not trivial as in the binary setting. Note that by adding two virtual voters, we get $\frac{2}{3}$-safety, just as in the binary case (since there is an alternative profile with $2 = \frac{2}{3}|V^+|$ additional honest voters that move the outcome further to the right).

Reduction to the Binary Setting. Getting the same safety bound in Examples 4 and 6 was no coincidence.

We consider an arbitrary population $V = H^+ \cup H^- \cup S$ and consider $\tau - RE\text{-}MD^+$. We use the following straightforward connection between the median and majority rules (proof is immediate).

Lemma 1. *Let z be the median of V, and let $x > y \geq z$. Then y has a majority against x.*

The lemma clearly still holds if we modify the set of voters by adding votes for r and/or ignoring passive voters (as long as we apply the same modification). Thus, the lemma still applies if we replace "median" with $\tau - RE\text{-}MD$ or $\tau - RE\text{-}MD^+$, and "majority" with $\tau - RE\text{-}MJ$ or $\tau - RE\text{-}MJ^+$, respectively.

Theorem 5. *The following hold:*

- *$\tau - RE\text{-}MD^+$ has the same liveness guarantees as $\tau - RE\text{-}MJ^+$.*
- *$\tau - RE\text{-}MD^+$ has the same safety guarantees w.r.t. MD, as $\tau - RE\text{-}MJ^+$ has w.r.t. MJ.*

Proof (safety). For a profile U of locations on $\mathbb{R}$ and a pair of locations $x, y \in \mathbb{R}$, we denote by $U|_{xy}$ the projection of U on $A = \{x, y\}$. That is, a binary profile where each voter votes for the closer alternative among x (which is considered as the status quo) and y. In case of a tie, the voter selects x. We show the proof for safety (the liveness's proof is similar, and is in the full version).

Consider any set of parameters $\mu, \sigma, \tau, \alpha \geq 0$ such that $\tau - RE\text{-}MD^+$ is α-safe. Denote $a := \sup(\overline{MD}_\alpha(H))$. If $a = +\infty$ then no violation of safety is possible and we are done. Otherwise, $a = \max(\overline{MD}_\alpha(H))$ since it is obtained as $a = MD(H')$ by placing αh honest voters on a in H'. Denote $z := \tau - RE\text{-}MD^+(V)$. We need to show that $z \in \mathcal{B}(r, a) = [r, a]$. Assume otherwise towards a contradiction, i.e. that $z > a$. By Lemma 1, we have $\tau - RE\text{-}MJ^+(V|_{az}) = z$. On the other hand, for any H' obtained from H by moving $\alpha|H|$ voters, we have $MD(H') \leq a < z$ and thus by the same lemma, $MJ(H'|_{az}) = a$. This entails $\mathcal{B}(a; \overline{MJ}_\alpha(H|_{az})) = \mathcal{B}(a; \{a\}) = \{a\}$, and thus $\tau - RE\text{-}MJ^+(V|_{az}) = z \notin \mathcal{B}(a; \overline{MJ}_\alpha(H|_{az}))$, which is a contradiction to α-safety of $\tau - RE\text{-}MJ^+$. The other direction is trivial. $\quad\square$

The above reduction allows us to transfer all previous results (the bounds in Theorems 1,2 and 3) from the binary domain to the real line domain. By Observation 2, these bounds also apply to the *SOM* mechanism from [25].

5.3   Rankings

Many voting rules are guided or justified by selecting the Condorcet winner, when one exists. These rules typically differ when there is no Condorcet winner, but Talmon and Shapiro [26] suggest a natural way to resolve conflict in a "safe" way; in the current context, this would mean selecting the status quo r whenever there is no Condorcet winner. We call this rule the *Condorcet Conservative* rule

(CC). The τ-Super Condorcet Conservative rule ($\tau - SCC$) is similar but p_i only beats p_j if it has a supermajority of $\frac{1}{2} + \tau$ of the votes.[6]

Theorem 6. *The following hold:*

- τ-SCC^+ *has the same liveness guarantees as* $\tau - SMJ^+$.
- *Let* $\mathcal{G}$ *be any Condorcet consistent rule. Then* τ-SCC^+ *has the same 0-safety guarantees w.r.t.* $\mathcal{G}$, *as* $\tau - SMJ^+$ *has w.r.t. MJ.*

Note that a more general reduction of α-safety fails as in Sect. 5.1, and for similar reasons.

6   Discussion

Motivated by governance and mutual decision mechanisms for online communities, we have considered the common situation in which representation is threatened both by the presence of sybils and by partial participation of the honest voters.

Our takeaway message is simple: adding virtual votes to the status quo is a good (sometimes optimal) way to balance between safety and liveness and to mitigate the negative effects of both sybils and partial participation in a wide range of domains. Moreover, we showed that specific mechanisms suggested earlier in the literature for specific domains, are essentially equivalent to special cases of our general "reality enforcing" mechanism.

In addition, our reductions enable the transfer of results between domains, mainly from the simple binary domain to multi-candidate, multiple referenda, and voting on an interval. In all domains, optimal safety and liveness tradeoff can be guaranteed as long as $3\sigma + 2\mu < 1$, where σ, μ are the fractions of sybils and inactive voters, respectively. Other results included in the full version of this paper show improved safety-liveness tradeoff when absent voters are selected *at random*, and even better bounds where they are allowed to *delegate* their votes to the nearest active voter (that may be a sybil). We conjecture that our adding-virtual-voters-to-the-status quo approach when applied to other metric spaces (with suitable ground rules), would guarantee similar safety/liveness tradeoffs.

Together with mechanisms for identifying and eliminating sybils [1], our results set the foundation for reliable and practical online governance tools.

Remark 3. To set the parameter τ (the bias towards the status quo) effectively, after deciding upon the desired tradeoff of safety and liveness, one has to estimate σ and μ in the population. While μ can be estimated quite accurately (as an election organizer may define the set of eligible voters), this is not the case for σ. The fraction of sybils can be approximated by sampling voters [25, Remark 2] or by techniques that upper bound σ [22]. Note that over-estimating σ or μ always results in a mechanism that is more safe, and thus our bounds still hold. (If an estimate or a bound on μ and σ sounds like a strong requirement, consider that almost all of the results in social choice implicitly assume that μ and σ are zero!)

---

[6] Note that this rule extends the supermajority rule of [25], but this extension no longer coincides with our RE mechanism with more than two candidates.

We believe that many fundamental results— such as axiomatic guarantees and welfare or fairness bounds— should be revisited after relaxing these unrealistic assumptions, and allow for sybils and/or inactive voters in the analysis.

Acknowledgements. We thank the generous support of the Braginsky Center for the Interface between Science and the Humanities.

Nimrod Talmon was supported by the Israel Science Foundation (ISF; Grant No. 630/19). Reshef Meir was supported by the Israel Science Foundation (ISF; Grant No. 2539/20).

References

1. Alvisi, L., Clement, A., Epasto, A., Lattanzi, S., Panconesi, A.: SOK: the evolution of Sybil defense via social networks. In: Proceedings of SP 2013, pp. 382–396 (2013)
2. Black, D.: On the rationale of group decision-making. J. Polit. Econ. **56**(1), 23–34 (1948)
3. Schaupp, L.C., Carter, L.: E-voting: from apathy to adoption. J. Enterprise Inf. Manage. 18(5), 586–601 (2005)
4. Chvátal, V.: Sylvester-Gallai theorem and metric betweenness. Disc. Comput. Geom. **31**(2), 175–195 (2004)
5. Conitzer, V., Immorlica, N., Letchford, J., Munagala, K., Wagman, L.: False-name-proofness in social networks. In: WINE 2010, pp. 209–221 (2010)
6. Conitzer, V., Yokoo, M.: Using mechanism design to prevent false-name manipulations. AI Mag. **31**(4), 65–78 (2010)
7. Conitzer, V., Sandholm, T.: Communication complexity of common voting rules. In: Proceedings of EC 2005, pp. 78–87. ACM (2005)
8. Desmedt, Y., Elkind, E.: Equilibria of plurality voting with abstentions. In: Proceedings of EC 2010, pp. 347–356. ACM (2010)
9. Downs, A., et al.: An Economic Theory of Democracy. Harper, New York (1957)
10. Grofman, B.: The neglected role of the status quo in models of issue voting. J. Polit. **47**(1), 230–237 (1985)
11. Johnson, C., Carlson, H.J., Reynolds, S.: Testing the participation hypothesis: evidence from participatory budgeting. Polit. Behav. 1–30 (2021). https://doi.org/10.1007/s11109-021-09679-w
12. Jönsson, A.M., Örnebring, H.: User-generated content and the news: empowerment of citizens or interactive illusion? J. Pract. **5**(2), 127–144 (2011)
13. Lang, J., Xia, L., Moulin, H.: Voting in combinatorial domains. In: Brandt, F., et al. (eds.) Handbook of Computational Social Choice, pp. 197–222 (2016)
14. May, K.O.: A set of independent necessary and sufficient conditions for simple majority decision. Econometrica. **20**, 680–684 (1952)
15. Meir, R.: Strategic Voting. Synthesis Lectures on Artificial Intelligence and Machine Learning. Morgan & Claypool Publishers, San Rafael (2018)
16. Menger, K.: Untersuchungen über allgemeine metrik. Math. Ann. **100**(1), 75–163 (1928)
17. Moulin, H.: On strategy-proofness and single peakedness. Pub. Choice **35**(4), 437–455 (1980)
18. Moulin, H.: The Strategy of Social Choice. Elsevier, Amsterdam (2014)
19. Nash, J.F.: The bargaining game. Econometrica **18**(2), 155–162 (1950)

20. Nehring, K., Puppe, C.: The structure of strategy-proof social choice-part i: general characterization and possibility results on median spaces. J. Econ. Theory **135**(1), 269–305 (2007)
21. Owen, G., Grofman, B.: To vote or not to vote: the paradox of nonvoting. Pub. Choice **42**(3), 311–325 (1984)
22. Poupko, O., Shahaf, G., Shapiro, E., Talmon, N.: Sybil-resilient conductance-based community growth. In: Proceedings of CSR 2019, pp. 359–371 (2019)
23. Procaccia, A.D., Tennenholtz, M.: Approximate mechanism design without money. In: Proceedings of EC 2009, pp. 177–186. ACM (2009)
24. Riker, W.H., Ordeshook, P.C.: A theory of the calculus of voting. Am. Polit. Sci. Rev. **62**(1), 25–42 (1968)
25. Shahaf, G., Shapiro, E., Talmon, N.: Sybil-resilient reality-aware social choice. In: Proceedings of IJCAI 2019, pp. 572–579 (2019)
26. Shapiro, E., Talmon, N.: Incorporating reality into social choice. In: Proceedings of AAMAS 2018 (2018)
27. Tran, D.N., Min, B., Li, J., Subramanian, L.: Sybil-resilient online content voting. In: Proceedings of NSDI 2009, pp. 15–28 (2009)

A Survey of Ad Hoc Teamwork Research

Reuth Mirsky[1,2], Ignacio Carlucho[3(✉)], Arrasy Rahman[3], Elliot Fosong[3], William Macke[2], Mohan Sridharan[4], Peter Stone[2,5], and Stefano V. Albrecht[3]

[1] Bar Ilan University, Ramat Gan, Israel
mirskyr@cs.biu.ac.il
[2] The University of Texas at Austin, Austin, USA
{wmacke,pstone}@cs.utexas.edu
[3] The University of Edinburgh, Edinburgh, UK
{ignacio.carlucho,arrasy.rahman,e.fosong,s.albrecht}@ed.ac.uk
[4] The University of Birmingham, Birmingham, UK
m.sridharan@bham.ac.uk
[5] Sony AI, Austin, USA

Abstract. Ad hoc teamwork is the research problem of designing agents that can collaborate with new teammates without prior coordination. This survey makes a two-fold contribution: First, it provides a structured description of the different facets of the ad hoc teamwork problem. Second, it discusses the progress that has been made in the field so far, and identifies the immediate and long-term open problems that need to be addressed in ad hoc teamwork.

Keywords: Ad Hoc Teamwork · Collaboration without prior coordination · Agent modelling · Reinforcement learning · Zero-shot coordination

1 Introduction

Ad hoc teamwork (AHT) is defined as the problem of developing agents capable of cooperating on the fly with other agents without prior coordination methods, such a shared task and communication protocols or joint training. Designing an AHT agent is a complex problem, but the underlying capabilities are crucial to enabling agents to take on their designated roles in many practical domains. From service robots and care systems to team sports and surveillance, agents need to reason about the best way to collaborate with other agents and people without prior coordination. Research in AHT has been around for at least 15 years (Bowling and McCracken 2005; Rovatsos and Wolf 2002), and it was proposed as a formal challenge by Stone et al. (2010):

> "To create an autonomous agent that is able to efficiently and robustly collaborate with previously unknown teammates on tasks to which they are all individually capable of contributing as team members."

© The Author(s), under exclusive license to Springer Nature Switzerland AG 2022
D. Baumeister and J. Rothe (Eds.): EUMAS 2022, LNAI 13442, pp. 275–293, 2022.
https://doi.org/10.1007/978-3-031-20614-6_16

Since then, hundreds of papers that include the phrase "ad hoc teamwork" have been published (464 according to Google Scholar at the time of writing this paper) and many more address closely related problems under names such as "zero-shot coordination" (Bullard et al. 2020; Hu et al. 2020). Moreover, much of the work on personalizing agents' interactions with humans can be viewed as instances of AHT (Li et al. 2021).

This survey seeks to make a two-fold contribution. First, it defines the AHT problem by describing the underlying assumptions (Sect. 2.1), key subtasks (Sect. 2.2), and the scope of the problem as considered in this paper (Sect. 3). Second, it surveys the existing work in AHT in terms of the solution methods (Sect. 4) and the evaluation domains that have been developed (Sect. 5), and discusses the open problems in the field of AHT (Sect. 6).

Related Initiatives. Several initiatives over the last decade have contributed to research progress in AHT. In particular, between 2014 and 2017, the Multi-Agent Interaction without Prior Coordination (MIPC) workshop series[1] held at AAAI and AAMAS conferences facilitated discussions and presentations in AHT and related topics. The MIPC workshop series was followed by a special journal issue (Albrecht et al. 2017) which featured a collection of new research works in AHT. Moreover, the RoboCup Drop-in Challenge was introduced to provide a platform to develop and evaluate AHT capabilities in the context of soccer-playing robots (Genter et al. 2017). However, to date there is no comprehensive survey on AHT. We seek to address this gap in the literature and help foster further research in AHT.

2   Background

This section provides a basic formulation of the AHT problem. It takes the original challenge proposed in Stone et al. (2010) and describes it in terms of the inputs and outputs, and the underlying assumptions (Sect. 2.1). It then describes the subtasks of the problem based on issues addressed in relevant papers (Sect. 2.2).

2.1   Problem Formulation

The AHT problem focuses on training an agent to coordinate with an unfamiliar group of teammates without prior coordination. In this work, we refer to the trained agent as the **learner**. The learner's **teammates** are assumed to be capable of contributing to the common teamwork task, meaning that they have a set of skills that are useful for the task at hand. Here we describe the inputs, outputs, and the underlying assumptions of this problem.

Input. The inputs of the AHT problem are the teamwork task to be executed, domain knowledge comprising a description of the domain/environment in which the task is to be executed, a (possibly incomplete) list of attributes characterizing

---

[1] https://mipc.inf.ed.ac.uk.

each agent (e.g., a set of goals, perception, and action capabilities), a description of the learner's abilities, and a list of teammates. The agent attributes' values might differ between each teammate—also see first assumption below—and some teammates might be able to communicate with each other.

Output. The output of the problem is the learner, represented by a policy that determines the action this agent should execute in any given state of the domain. Depending on the agent's sensors, actuators, and the available communication channels, this policy can be deterministic or stochastic, static or adaptable, and might include ontic (physical) actions and epistemic (knowledge-producing) actions, which in turn may contain verbal or non-verbal communication.

Assumptions. Three key assumptions (i.e., claims or postulates) characterize the AHT problem.

1. **No prior coordination.** The learner is expected to cooperate with its teammates when the task begins without any prior opportunities to establish or specify mechanisms for coordination. For example, it is not possible to pre-specify the agents' roles or to have a joint training phase for all agents. The learner might know or assume knowledge of a subset of attributes (e.g., current policies, individual goals) of some subset of its teammates. This knowledge might be acquired from an expert who has had prior interactions with the learner's current teammates, and the assumptions might be the result of generic models or rules based on past interactions in the target domain. The learner's current teammates might or might not be familiar with one another before the current interaction. For example, in drop-in soccer (a spontaneous soccer match where some or all of the team are strangers), a teammate might be perceived to be a good striker because they are fast and the team can work around this assumption even if they have not played with that specific player before.

2. **No control over teammates.** The learner cannot change the properties of the environment, and the teammates' policies and communication protocols; it has to reason and act under the given conditions. We distinguish between *changing the properties* of the environment (e.g. modifying observability level) and *acting in* the environment to change its state (e.g. picking up a box). Similarly, the learner might influence its teammates' actions, but this influence will be in accordance with the pre-defined policy of the teammates. Moreover, teammates' policies may support learning or adaptation, but the learner cannot modify these abilities. Continuing with the soccer example, teammates can learn to work better together with practice, but no teammate can impose their knowledge on the team before the game starts.

3. **Collaborative.** All agents are assumed to have a common objective, but some teammates might have additional, individual objectives, or even completely different rewards. However, these additional objectives do not conflict with the common task (Grosz and Kraus 1999). In the drop-in soccer example, different teammates may have incentives in their contract that encourage them to focus on different skills, e.g., goal-scoring rewards for forwards

or assist rewards for midfielders. The difference in the individual objectives may result in situations in which an individual agent may seem to be acting contrary to the team reward, but each agent in the team is always acting to achieve the common objective. For example, although passing frequently is considered very important to a team's performance in a soccer game, an individual teammate may choose to dribble forward because of a perceived opportunity to score a goal.

2.2   Subtasks in Ad Hoc Teamwork

Based on a survey of the existing literature, we identified four main subtasks that the learner should be able to perform, although much of the existing work only focuses on addressing a subset of these subtasks.

ST1: Knowledge Representation. The learner requires a representation of the domain knowledge. This includes knowledge about the environment (e.g., discrete or continuous, static or dynamic, etc.), its capabilities, and knowledge about potential teammates (e.g., similarity to past teammates, their theory of mind, etc.). These choices influence the solution methods for the other substasks. Most of the attributes characterizing the environment are common to all multi-agent problems. They can be presented in the classical PEAS system (Russell and Norvig 2021) and are not unique to AHT, so we do not elaborate on these here.

ST2: Modeling Teammates. The learner can leverage information about its teammates to improve its decision making. Thus, a key subtask for the learner is to model the information pertaining to teammates' behavior (e.g., classifying teammates by type in order to adapt to different teammates).

ST3: Action Selection. The third subtask is the design of mechanisms used by the learner to select actions once it has an estimate of its teammates' behavior (observed or based on models of teammates). Example methods for this subtask include planning methods and expert policies that are learned or based on expert knowledge.

ST4: Adapting to Changes. During interaction, the learner might receive new information about its teammates, the environment, or task objectives. Based on this information, the learner needs to adapt its behavior to improve coordination. This adaptation also includes merging the models provided by teammates.

3   Boundaries of Ad Hoc Teamwork

Here we further define the scope of the AHT problem by describing factors that can be considered within the basic problem formulation presented above, and by discussing related research problems.

3.1   Variations of the Ad Hoc Teamwork Problem

We first describe additional factors that define the scope of AHT and influence the subtasks described earlier.

Partial Observability. Under conditions of full observability, each agent is aware of the state of the environment, including the location of other agents. Partial observability implies a higher level of complexity in knowledge representation as it introduces uncertainty in certain parts of the domain state. Changing the observability level will affect ST1 and thus the other subtasks described above.

Open Environment. Closed environments assume a fixed number of teammates (Rahman et al. 2021). Relaxing this assumption increases the problem complexity, as the learner will also have to adapt to the changing number of teammates in the environment; this will primarily affect ST2 and ST4.

Communication. Since the exploration of how communication can be leveraged to improve team performance is an important area of research in AHT, we make a distinction based on whether there is any communication channel between agents. When communication exists, it is sometimes presented as predetermined and known protocols, such as the hints allowed in the game of Hanabi (Bard et al. 2020), which affects ST1. If these protocols are unknown in the beginning of the interaction and need to be learned during the task execution, it has an effect on ST3 and ST4.

Adaptive Teammates. We make a distinction between work where the teammates learn alongside the learner, or use policies that stay fixed throughout the learning phase of the learner. Unlike multi-agent reinforcement learning (see Sect. 3.2), which supports joint training for all agents in the team, AHT does not assume that the deployed teammates are the same as those the learner might have trained with. Rather, adaptive teammates learn by reacting to the learner's policy using methods that are not known to the learner, thus affecting ST3 and ST4. An example of such a setup is flocking, where the teammates have a fixed policy, but their actions are directly influenced by the learner (Genter and Stone 2016).

Mixed Objectives. While teammates are assumed to be collaborative, they can have mixed objectives. Two types of scenarios arise depending on the objectives of the learner and its teammates. In the first, the learner and the teammates have a perfectly aligned objective (e.g., the reward functions of all agents are identical). In the second, while all team members have a common goal, each agent might also hold individual goals as long as these are not purely adversarial to the shared one. This factor extends the original formulation in (Stone et al. 2010), is related to the third assumption in Sect. 2.1, and will primarily affect ST2 and ST3.

3.2 Related Problems

In this section, we highlight the main differences between AHT and other related research problems.

Multi-Agent Reinforcement Learning (MARL). It refers to the use of reinforcement learning methods for jointly training multiple agents to maximize their respective cumulative rewards while working with each other (Busoniu et al. 2008; Devlin and Kudenko 2016; Papoudakis et al. 2019). AHT, on the other hand, assumes control over a single agent (the learner) while teammates can have their own learning mechanisms, e.g., a robot interacting with different human. Prior work has shown that the good team performance of MARL methods often comes at the expense of poor performance when interacting with previously unseen teammates (Hu et al. 2020; Rahman et al. 2021; Vezhnevets et al. 2020). MARL methods are thus not particularly well-suited to AHT.

Ad hoc Teaming. The objective is to learn coercive measures that may allow self-interested agents with different skills and preferences to collaborate and solve a task. For example, existing work has trained a manager to assign subtasks to agents based on their skills while also incentivizing agents to complete their tasks (Shu and Tian 2019). In contrast, the learner in AHT might incentivize its teammates to act in a certain way, but cannot dictate the teammates' behavior due to the lack of prior coordination.

Agent Modelling. These methods infer attributes of teammates' behavior such as beliefs, goals, and actions (Albrecht and Stone 2018). Since inferring teammates' behavior is important for decision making in AHT (e.g., ST3 in Sect. 2.2), agent modeling methods are useful for AHT. However, they can be used for a broader class of problems and are not limited to (or necessarily indicative of) AHT.

Human-Agent Interaction. The task of creating agents that interact with previously unseen agents has also been explored in the human-agent/robot interaction community. In human-agent interaction, agents have to achieve their goals in the presence of human decision makers. As in AHT, it is often impossible to jointly train humans and agents to coordinate their behavior; agents must instead find a way to coordinate with previously unseen humans, e.g., by using implicit communication or acting in a legible manner (Breazeal et al. 2005; Dragan et al. 2013).

Zero-Shot Coordination (ZSC). A special case of AHT where teammates' behavior are assumed to arise from a reward function that always provides identical rewards for every agent is known as ZSC (Bullard et al. 2020, 2021; Hu et al. 2021; Lupu et al. 2021). After training different populations of agents under the same fully cooperative setup, a ZSC agent is evaluated by measuring its performance when cooperating with agents from a different population. While ZSC introduced techniques relevant for AHT, there are AHT problems where the controlled agent must interact with teammates whose reward functions are different from its own.

4 Solution Approaches

As stated earlier, while existing methods for AHT often provide a functioning learner, each method's key contribution can often be mapped to one or more of the four subtasks in Sect. 2.2. Here we elaborate on common solution methods for each subtask and refer to representative literature.

4.1 Knowledge Representation

The representation of domain knowledge strongly influences the solution approach used in the other subtasks. This information can be acquired from human experts (or expert knowledge), prior knowledge of past teammates, or using self-play.

To support adaptation based on limited information, it is common to equip agents with preconceptions of the likely behaviors or intentions of previously unseen teammates. These preconceptions are based on prior experience with the task; this can be the agent's own experience or that of a human familiar with the task. *Agent modeling* techniques can be used to represent the teammates (Albrecht and Stone 2018).

Type-Based Methods. The use of type-based methods is common in the AHT literature. These methods represent prior experience with agents (in the target domain) by a set of hypothesized *types*, where each type models an action selection policy. It is assumed that new teammates encountered by the learner have behaviors specified by one of these types.

A range of type representations have been explored. Early work explored a nested representation of agents' beliefs, where agents perform Bayesian updates to maintain beliefs over physical states of the environment and over models of other agents (Gmytrasiewicz and Doshi 2005). It was also common to use hand-coded programs to represent types (Albrecht and Ramamoorthy 2013; Barrett et al. 2011). For approaches that employ a learned type set, learned decision trees were a common representation (Barrett et al. 2017). More recently, latent type methods have been used which learn a neural network-based encoder to map observations of teammates to an embedding of the agent's type (Rabinowitz et al. 2018; Rahman et al. 2021; Xie et al. 2020; Zintgraf et al. 2021).

There are three main approaches to specifying a hypothesized type space: (1) specification by a human expert; (2) learning from data; and (3) using reinforcement learning (RL) methods and access to the environment or an environment model. Barrett et al. (2017) collect diverse behaviors by drawing their types from the output of an assignment presented to a large number of student. Many methods attempt to generate diverse behaviors in a population trained via RL, requiring only access to the target task. They do so using methods such as genetic algorithms (Albrecht et al. 2015a,b; Canaan et al. 2020), regularisation techniques (Lupu et al. 2021), and reward-shaping techniques (Leibo et al. 2021).

Experience Replay. Rather than encoding experience in explicit behavioural models, experience replay methods store transition data in a buffer. Transitions observed during an interaction are compared against the stored transitions to identify the current teammate (Chen et al. 2020).

Task Recognition. In methods based on task recognition, prior experience or information provided by an expert is encoded as a library of tasks referred to as *plays, macro actions,* or *options* (Sutton et al. 1999). Tasks then encode prior experience as applicability conditions, termination conditions, and high-level specifications of a sequence of low-level actions (Wang et al. 2021).

4.2   Identifying Current Teammates

Once a representation is set, estimating the behavior of current teammates allows the learner to determine a suitable behavior.

Type Inference. Methods that represent teammates using types infer beliefs over the hypothesized type space using a history of interactions of the learner with each teammate up to the current timestep. The dominant approach is to use a Bayesian belief update (Albrecht et al. 2016; Barrett et al. 2017). In such methods, prior beliefs about the teammates' types are updated using the history of interactions and a likelihood of the types based on the history. It is also common to assume uniform priors across types and type parameters (Albrecht et al. 2015a).

Experience Recognition. Rather than inferring types, some approaches attempt to measure the similarity of the current observations to that from earlier experience in a more direct manner. PLASTIC-Policy (Barrett et al. 2017) compares the most recently observed state transition to previously stored data. For each team they find the stored transition with the closest state to the current state, and consider the next state observed in that historical transition. They then measure the distance between that state and the observed next state, and use this to compute the likelihood of the team. AATEAM (Chen et al. 2020) takes a more sophisticated approach which uses prior experience buffers to train one attention-based neural network per type, to identify agents from a trajectory rather than a single transition.

Task Recognition. For methods which represent prior knowledge as tasks, the learner attempts to infer the current task being carried out by the teammate under consideration. Wang et al. (2021) achieved this by assuming that the teammate was attempting to complete hypothesized tasks and computing the extent to which the teammate's observed behavior is sub-optimal for that task. Melo and Sardinha 2016 consider a setting in which agents both identify the current task and identify the teammate's strategy, with the teammate's behavior subject to a bounded rationality assumption.

4.3   Action Selection

Given current knowledge about task and teammates, agents must decide which action to take to maximize team return.

Planning. Many AHT approaches use planning methods to select actions. Some, such as Bowling and McCracken (2005) and Ravula et al. (2019), use bespoke planning methods suited to the specific task, and chosen by a human expert. Many approaches use the more general Monte Carlo tree search (MCTS) planning procedure (Albrecht and Stone 2017; Alford et al. 2015; Barrett et al. 2014; Eck et al. 2020; Malik et al. 2018; Sarratt 2015; Wu et al. 2011; Yourdshahi et al. 2018). The upper confidence tree (UCT) algorithm (Kocsis and Szepesvári 2006) for MCTS is often used due to its ability to perform well when the branching factor is large, as is the case when multiple agents are present. These MCTS-based methods require that types are represented by explicit behavioral models to sample teammate actions during rollouts.

Expert Policy Methods. Selecting actions by choosing a policy from a set of expert policies, and then acting according to the chosen policy. There are many ways in which these expert policies can be obtained prior to the ad hoc interaction: they can be provided by an expert, learned offline, using experience data (Chen et al. 2020; Santos et al. 2021), or by online RL training given the task (Albrecht et al. 2015b). One of the advantages of expert policy methods over type-based planning methods is that they can handle large or continuous state and action spaces, where MCTS approaches may struggle (Barrett et al. 2017). However, type-based planning methods are more appropriate when the ad hoc team is likely to have a previously unseen composition, as type-based methods can reason at the level of the types of individual agents. Also, creating expert policies may be impossible when a large variation of situations are encountered. The E-HBA method attempts to achieve the advantages of both type-based reasoning methods and expert policy methods by combining the two (Albrecht et al. 2015b). The GPL method (Rahman et al. 2021), suitable in open AHT problems, uses an action-selection mechanism based on E-HBA .

Leading. Some works explicitly consider adaptive teammates, where a learner's choice of action affects its teammates' behaviors. Works such as Agmon et al. (2014) assume teammates employ a known best response strategy, and that the goal is to lead these teammates to a specific joint coordination strategy. These approaches were addressed in simple games using dynamic programming.Xie et al. (2020) consider cases where the learner does not know the teammate's current behavior, nor how this behavior changes across interactions. Thus, deep learning is used to learn an embedding of the teammate's strategy, and model the teammate's behavioral dynamics and teammates' adaptation process.

Metalearning. Metalearning approaches use action selection policies which are trained to facilitate the entire AHT process. The MeLIBA approach (Zintgraf et al. 2021) trains the policy to carry out interactive Bayesian RL, intentionally taking actions which seek to reveal information about the teammate's type. The action selection policies of metalearning approaches is typically conditioned on the learner's prediction of the teammate's type. In this sense, such methods can be compared to expert policy methods.

4.4 Adapting to Current Teammates

During interaction, the learner receives new information, which can be used to adapt its behavior.

Belief Revision. Most methods employ belief revision protocols to maintain their belief about the identity of other agents across time. For type-based methods, it is typical to assume each teammate's type does not change over time, and that a good representation of the teammate exists in the hypothesized type space (Albrecht et al. 2016). However, if it is assumed that teammates' types change over time, the learner must also adapt. The ConvCPD method (Ravula et al. 2019) considers settings in which the type space is known, but agents can switch types. For these settings, they employ a convolutional neural network (CNN)-based changepoint detection approach, which uses image-like representations of type likelihoods across time to detect changes. An alternative approach is to modify the Bayesian belief revision process to allow beliefs to decay towards the priors over time. This approach is useful when a teammate changes to a type which the learner has assigned low (or zero) probability to. In this case, the learner might struggle (or be unable) to quickly update its belief to reflect the new true teammate (Santos et al. 2021). Sum-based posterior definitions were also proposed to deal with changing types (Albrecht et al. 2016).

Hypothesis Space Revision. Approaches exist for adapting to agents whose behavior may not be adequately represented in the hypothesized space. TwoStageTransfer is a transfer learning method employed by PLASTIC-Model (Barrett et al. 2017) which uses observations of new teammates and prior models to finetune a model for the new teammate.

Metalearning. During the metalearning process, the action selection policy learns its own adaptation procedures, avoiding the need to specify particular adaptation schemes (Xie et al. 2020; Zintgraf et al. 2021).

Zero-Shot Coordination Techniques. The ZSC problem does not allow the learner any behavioral adaptation during ad hoc interactions. For this reason, the focus of these methods is on training agents which robustly coordinate with other agents trained using the same algorithm. One approach is to avoid strategies which are not invariant under symmetries within the underlying tasks (Hu et al. 2020, 2021). Another approach is based on the hypothesis that there are few strategies which perform well with a diverse set of teammates, so ad hoc agents independently trained against diverse teammates (and themselves) are likely arrive at similar pre-coordinated policies (Lupu et al. 2021).

Communication. The learner can quickly adapt to changes is by communicating with its teammates. This communication can either be a query (Macke et al. 2021; Mirsky et al. 2020), transfer knowledge or preferences (Barrett et al. 2014; Mead and Weinberg 2007), or providing an advice (Canaan et al. 2020; Shvo and McIlraith 2020).

5   Evaluation Domains

Many different approaches have been used for evaluating AHT methods. In this section, we categorize them using the identified variations from Subsect. 3.1. Some domains might fit more than one category, but we place them according to the first ad hoc teamwork paper they appeared in. In Table 1, we summarize each of the domains and associated papers.

No Variations. Some evaluation domains do not have any of the variations outlined in Sect. 3.1. Among these AHT domains, some of the simplest are matrix games (Albrecht et al. 2015b; Melo and Sardinha 2016). These games consist of a payoff matrix for two agents who independently choose actions and then receive a payoff based on the actions each agent chose. The game is then repeated with the goal to maximize long term return over repeated trials. Another common domain is predator prey (Barrett et al. 2011; Papoudakis et al. 2021; Ravula et al. 2019). This domain consists of several agents (the predators) attempting to surround and capture other agents (the prey). The predator prey domain requires both recognising a teammate's goal (namely which prey they are pursuing), and also collaborating with other agents to surround the prey. In level-based foraging (Albrecht and Ramamoorthy 2013), the goal of the agent team is to collect food items which are spatially distributed in a grid world. Agents and items have different skill levels which represent different capabilities in agents, requiring that agents decide when and with whom to collaborate in order to collect the items.

Open Environments. There are several instances of open domains presented in AHT. First, open variations of the domains mentioned above exist in Rahman et al. (2021). Another open AHT domain is wildfires, where agents entering and leaving the environment need to work together to contain the spread of wildfires (Chandrasekaran et al. 2016). Finally, ad hoc flocking and swarming domains enable agents to enter and leave the environment freely (Genter and Stone 2016).

Partial or Noisy Observability. Partially observable variants of the domains with no extensions exist in Ribeiro et al. (2022). One domain that has been prevalent in AHT literature is robot soccer. Drop-in soccer where a group of players need to form a team without playing with each other is common among humans in real life, so it has been a frequented challenge by AI as well (Barrett et al. 2017; Genter et al. 2017). The problem typically consists of substituting one member of a team with a learner. The performance is then measured on how robust the learner's performance is regardless of which team it is placed in. This domain presents an additional challenge, as each agent can only observe its local environment. Another partially observable domains are military simulation, which simulate various combat and search tasks using unmmaned autonomous vehicles (Alford et al. 2015), and the collaborative card game Hanabi (Bard et al. 2020). Similar to the RoboCup domain, these domains also present the challenge that agents only have access to their local observations.

Communication. Multiple domains allow communication in some form. The RoboCup domain mentioned above allows limited communication between agents using wireless connections. Others use communication as a more critical part of the domain. The tool fetching domain provides an AHT domain that allows one agent to query another about its goals (Macke et al. 2021). Unlike other domains mentioned so far, the tool fetching domain is specifically focused on evaluating an agent's ability to communicate effectively. The Hanabi domain also presents a structured communication channel. While in the tool fetching domain the learner can query its teammates, in Hanabi the communication channel allows the learner to provide its teammates with information unknown to them (Bard et al. 2020; Canaan et al. 2020). Another domain that focuses on communication is the cops and robbers domain (Sarratt 2015). In this domain, teammates (cops) must work together to capture another, adversarial agent (the robber). Each agent can query the other to gain information about their current plans (Sarratt 2015).

Adaptive Teammates. So far all domains mentioned are focused on evaluating whether a learner can successfully adapt their behavior to collaborate with diverse teammates. Some domains, however, instead try to evaluate how well learner(s) can influence other agents to achieve better performance. While the above domains can be adapted to have learning teammates, several domains exist with this explicit purpose in mind. Some examples of these are domains focused on incentivising the teammate to take a specific course of action (Wang et al. 2021), or on swarming (Genter and Stone 2014), where the learner attempts to move in such a way as to influence the overall behavior of the agents around it.

Mixed Objectives. Works that make the assumption of coupled objectives, such as ZSC (Hu et al. 2020), utilize an environment in which the reward received by all agents is the same. Such environments include the lever environment (Hu et al. 2020) and Hanabi (Bard et al. 2020). Works which do not assume coupled objectives utilize general-sum domains such as level-based foraging (Albrecht and Ramamoorthy 2013), in which the reward changes depending of the contribution of the agent; or the tool fetching domain where each agent has a distinct role in the team (Mirsky et al. 2020).

Table 1. Different environments used for evaluating ad hoc teamwork.

Domain	Paper	Method Description
Matrix games	Albrecht and Ramamoorthy (2012)	Empirically evaluates various multi-agent learning algorithms in ad hoc mixed teams
	Chakraborty and Stone (2013)	Introduces an optimal algorithm to cooperate with a Markovian teammate
	Albrecht et al. (2015b)	Combines type-based reasoning for prediction with expert algorithms for decision making
	Albrecht et al. (2015a; 2016)	Evaluates impact of prior beliefs in type-based reasoning in a range of matrix games
	Melo and Sardinha (2016)	Extends ad hoc teamwork to scenarios where the current task is unknown in addition to the teammates
Predator prey	Barrett et al. (2011)	MCTS (UCT) with type-based reasoning using hand-crafted types in the predator prey domain
	Ravula et al. (2019)	Extends ad hoc teamwork methods to work with teammates which can switch behaviors
	Papoudakis et al. (2021)	Assumes only local observations of ad hoc teamwork agent are available to model other agents
LBF	Albrecht et al. (2013)	Develops type-based reasoning based on game theory model to solve ad hoc teamwork problems
	Liemhetcharat et al. (2017)	Defines the problem of ad hoc team assignment
	Yourdshahi et al. (2018)	Introduces new history-based MCTS
	Rahman et al. (2021)	Uses graph-based learning to handle a dynamic number of agents in the environment
Wildfires	Eck et al. (2020)	Introduces ad hoc teamwork in open environments with large numbers of agents
Flocking swarming	Genter and Stone (2014)	Introduces AHT approaches for influencing a flock's behavior
	Genter et al. (2015)	Determines where to place agents in a flock
	Genter and Stone (2016)	Solves how to force agents to join flock in motion
Robot soccer	Bowling et al. (2005)	Introduces two new approaches for working with ad hoc teams in robot soccer
	Barrett and Stone (2014)	Introduces new method for reusing policies learned from previous teammates to accomplish AHT
	Barrett et al. (2017)	Introduces algorithms for AHT based on previously met teammates, using either policies or models
Military simulation	Alford et al. (2015)	Introduces an algorithm for classifying agent behaviors in air combat simulator
Hanabi	Bard et al. (2020)	Proposes the Hanabi game as a new challenge for AI research, including ad hoc teamwork
	Canaan et al. (2020)	Creates a meta-strategy for solving ad hoc teamwork in Hanabi using a diverse set of possible teammates
	Hu et al. (2020)	An effective algorithm for learning from self-play by attempting to seek out new behaviors
	Hu et al. (2021)	Introduces improved method off-belief learning for learning from self-play in DecPOMDPs
	Lupu et al. (2021)	Creates a new optimisable metric for determining policy diversity in Hanabi self-play
Tool fetching domain	Mirsky et al. (2020)	Introduces SOMALI CAT problem and proposes solution for determining when queries might be useful
	Macke et al. (2021)	Proposes a solution for what to query when multiple possible queries are available
	Suriadinata et al. (2021)	Investigates human behavior in the Tool Fetch Domain

6   Conclusion and Open Problems

In this survey, we presented a review of the AHT literature that has been published over the past decade. This long period of time, along with the abundance of published work, enabled us to draw a big picture view of this topic: setting the boundary on what is, and what is not, AHT; identifying the subtasks that an agent needs to tackle as part of an AHT task; and the various levels of complexity in AHT. Many open problems still need to be addressed to achieve a robust agent that is able to interact with teammates without prior coordination and solve real-world problems. Furthermore, AHT research is currently suffering from a lack of standardised comparison between existing AHT approaches, which increases the difficulty of identifying state-of-the-art methods for solving a certain AHT problem.

Future work could address further extensions of the variations of the ad hoc teamwork problem discussed in Sect. 3.1, or combinations of these variations. For example, considering the presence of teammates with complex adaptive processes, such as teammates which learn via RL while interacting with the learner; or teammates which themselves apply AHT techniques. Current approaches to AHT are not designed to work with adaptive teammates (one notable exception being HBA (Albrecht et al., 2016)), whose presence would mean that the learner needs not only to adapt to teammates' behaviors, but also consider how the teammates adapt to its own behavior. Another extension is the combination of partial observability and open teams, which provides a difficult challenge for the learner, due to this complex dual uncertainty.

In terms of potential solution methods, one of the crucial open problems is improving the generalization to new teammates that have not yet been seen during training. Recent continual learning (Khetarpal et al., 2020) advances showed that training on diverse tasks can result in agents with robust performance in previously unseen tasks (Open-Ended Learning Team et al. 2021). In the same way, training with a diverse set of teammates can improve the learner's ability to collaborate with new teammates. Lupu et al. (2021) proposed a method to generate diverse teammates for ZSC, but it was not evaluated with collaborative teammates with objectives that might not be fully aligned with the learner's. Recently, Rahman et al. (2022) proposed a method for generating a diverse set teammates specifically for ad hoc teamwork applications. However, results were only obtained in a 5 × 5 grid world environment, more work is needed to evaluate how this method performs in more complex environments. These works are a good starting point when designing learners that are robust to different teams, however, they do not specifically address the collaborative aspect of AHT. Additional work is required to properly define the scope of the diverse set of agents a learner should be able to work with. And while generating teammates that display different behaviours and skill levels can improve generalisation during execution time, this is not an easy task, especially in more complex domains.

AHT research could also benefit from the use of more complex or realistic domains in evaluation. Previous works tended to use simple domains (Sect. 5), but these solutions might not perform well in realistic domains. We suggest that future AHT research should consider more realistic testbeds, which can rely on robotics simulators extended to handle multi-agent scenarios (Collins et al. 2021), or on existing scenarios such as the DARPA "Spectrum Collaboration Challenge"[2], which will allow for the evaluation of more complex tasks and algorithms. Social navigation, the problem of a robot navigating through a crowd of people and robots, is another relevant robotics challenge (Mirsky et al. 2021). In this problem, the learner needs to coordinate with previously unmet passerby humans and robots in order to avoid collisions, while allowing each other to get to their destinations. Thus, this challenge poses a series of challenging AHT problems where the learner need to adapt to new incoming teammates based on a highly limited amount of interaction experience.

Another important issue that can be addressed by future work is benchmarking current AHT approaches by providing systematic comparison between them. Existing works in AHT often forgo comparison against other approaches designed to solve the same variation of AHT problems, which makes it hard to identify state-of-the-art approaches in the field. A systematic benchmark between AHT approaches across different environments could therefore be a crucial stepping stone towards further identifying the strengths and weaknesses of different AHT methods.

To conclude, the AHT problem comprises a unique mixture of subtasks that the learner is required to perform, which requires solutions ranging from different fields. In this survey, we identified the existing and open problems in AHT which we hope will contribute to the development of the field, and in turn will advance the multi-agent research community as a whole.

References

Agmon, N., Barrett, S., Stone, P.: Modeling uncertainty in leading ad hoc teams. In: The International Conference on Autonomous Agents and Multi-Agent Systems, AAMAS 2014, pp. 397–404 (2014)

Albrecht, S.V., Ramamoorthy, S.: Comparative evaluation of MAL algorithms in a diverse set of ad hoc team problems. In: The International Conference on Autonomous Agents and Multi-Agent Systems, AAMAS 2012 (2012)

Albrecht, S.V., Ramamoorthy, S.: A game-theoretic model and best-response learning method for ad hoc coordination in multiagent systems. In: Proceedings of the 2013 International Conference on Autonomous Agents and Multi-Agent Systems, AAMAS 2013, pp. 1155–1156, Richland, SC, 2013. International Foundation for Autonomous Agents and Multiagent Systems (2013). ISBN 9781450319935

Albrecht, S.V., Stone, P.: Reasoning about hypothetical agent behaviours and their parameters. In: The International Conference on Autonomous Agents and Multi-Agent Systems, AAMAS 2017, pp. 547–555 (2017)

Albrecht, S.V., Stone, P.: Autonomous agents modelling other agents: a comprehensive survey and open problems. Artif. Intell. **258**, 66–95 (2018)

Albrecht, S.V., Crandall, J.W., Ramamoorthy, S.: An empirical study on the practical impact of prior beliefs over policy types. In: Proceedings of the 29th AAAI Conference on Artificial Intelligence, pp. 1988–1994 (2015a)

---

[2] www.darpa.mil/program/spectrum-collaboration-challenge.

Albrecht, S.V., Crandall, J.W., Ramamoorthy, S.: E-HBA: using action policies for expert advice and agent typification. In: AAAI Workshop on Multiagent Interaction without Prior Coordination, p. 7 (2015b)

Albrecht, S.V., Crandall, J.W., Ramamoorthy, S.: Belief and truth in hypothesised behaviours. Artif. Intell. **235**, 63–94 (2016)

Albrecht, S.V., Liemhetcharat, S., Stone, P.: Special issue on multiagent interaction without prior coordination: guest editorial. Autonom. Agents Multi-Agent Syst. **31**(4), 765–766 (2017). https://doi.org/10.1007/s10458-016-9358-0

Alford, R., Borck, H., Karneeb, J.: Active behavior recognition in beyond visual range air combat. In: Proceedings of the 3rd Annual Conference on Advances in Cognitive Systems. Cognitive Systems Foundation (2015)

Bard, N., et al.: The Hanabi challenge: a new frontier for AI research. Artif. Intell. **280**, 103216 (2020)

Barrett, S., Stone, P.: Cooperating with unknown teammates in robot soccer. In: AAAI Workshop on Multiagent Interaction without Prior Coordination, p. 6 (2014)

Barrett, S., Stone, P., Kraus, S.: Empirical evaluation of ad hoc teamwork in the pursuit domain. In: The International Conference on Autonomous Agents and Multi-Agent Systems, AAMAS 2011, vol. 2, pp. 567–574 (2011)

Barrett, S., Agmon, N., Hazon, N., Kraus, S., Stone, P.: Communicating with unknown teammates. In: The European Conference on Artificial Intelligence, ECAI 2014, volume 263 of Frontiers in Artificial Intelligence and Applications, pp. 45–50. IOS Press (2014). https://doi.org/10.3233/978-1-61499-419-0-45

Barrett, S., Rosenfeld, A., Kraus, S., Stone, P.: Making friends on the fly: cooperating with new teammates. Artif. Intell. **242**, 132–171 (2017). https://doi.org/10.1016/j.artint.2016.10.005

Bowling, M., McCracken, P.: Coordination and adaptation in impromptu teams. In: National Conference on Artificial Intelligence, vol. 1 of AAAI 2005, pp. 53–58 (2005)

Breazeal, C., Kidd, C.D., Thomaz, A.L., Hoffman, G., Berlin, M.: Effects of non-verbal communication on efficiency and robustness in human-robot teamwork. In: IEEE/RSJ International Conference on Intelligent Robots and Systems, pp. 708–713. IEEE (2005)

Bullard, K., Meier, F., Kiela, D., Pineau, J., Foerster, J.: Exploring zero-shot emergent communication in embodied multi-agent populations. arXiv:2010.15896 (2020)

Bullard, K., Kiela, D., Meier, F., Pineau, J., Foerster, J.: Quasi-equivalence discovery for zero-shot emergent communication. arXiv:2103.08067 (2021)

Busoniu, L., Babuska, R., De Schutter, B.: A comprehensive survey of multiagent reinforcement learning. IEEE Trans. Syst. Man Cybern. Part C (App. Rev.) **38**(2), 156–172 (2008). https://doi.org/10.1109/TSMCC.2007.913919

Canaan, R., Gao, X., Togelius, J., Nealen, A., Menzel, S.: Generating and adapting to diverse ad-hoc cooperation agents in Hanabi. arXiv:2004.13710 (2020)

Chakraborty, D., Stone, P.: Cooperating with a Markovian Ad hoc teammate. In: Proceedings of the 12th International Conference on Autonomous Agents and Multiagent Systems, vol. 1, AAMAS 2013, pp. 1085–1092. International Foundation for Autonomous Agents and Multiagent Systems (2013)

Chandrasekaran, M., Eck, A., Doshi, P., Soh, L.: Individual planning in open and typed agent systems. In: Thirty-Second Conference on Uncertainty in Artificial Intelligence, UAI 2016, pp. 82–91 (2016)

Chen, S., Andrejczuk, E., Cao, Z., Zhang, J.: AATEAM: achieving the ad hoc teamwork by employing the attention mechanism. AAAI Conf. Artif. Intell. **34**, 7095–7102 (2020). https://doi.org/10.1609/aaai.v34i05.6196

Collins, J., Chand, S., Vanderkop, A., Howard, D.: A review of physics simulators for robotic applications. IEEE Access (2021)

Devlin, S., Kudenko, D.: Plan-based reward shaping for multi-agent reinforcement learning. Knowl. Eng. Revi. **1**, 44–58 (2016)

Dragan, A.D., Lee, K.C., Srinivasa, S.S.: Legibility and predictability of robot motion. In: ACM/IEEE International Conference on Human-Robot Interaction, pp. 301–308. IEEE (2013)

Eck, A., Shah, M., Doshi, P., Soh, L.-K.: Scalable decision-theoretic planning in open and typed multiagent systems. In: AAAI Conference on Artificial Intelligence, vol. 34, pp. 7127–7134. AAAI Press (2020). https://doi.org/10.1609/aaai.v34i05.6200

Genter, K., Stone, P.: Influencing a Flock via Ad Hoc Teamwork. In: Swarm Intelligence, vol. 8667, pp. 110–121. Springer International Publishing (2014). https://doi.org/10.1007/978-3-319-09952-1_10

Genter, K., Stone, P.: Adding influencing agents to a flock. In: The International Conference on Autonomous Agents and Multi-Agent Systems, AAMAS 2017, pp. 615–623 (2016)

Genter, K., Zhang, S., Stone, P.: Determining placements of influencing agents in a flock. In: Proceedings of the 14th International Conference on Autonomous Agents and Multiagent Systems, pp. 247–255. International Foundation for Autonomous Agents and Multiagent Systems (2015)

Genter, K., Laue, T., Stone, P.: Three years of the RoboCup standard platform league drop-in player competition: creating and maintaining a large scale ad hoc teamwork robotics competition. Autonom. Agents Multi-Agent Syst. **31**(4), 790–820 (2017). https://doi.org/10.1007/s10458-016-9353-5

Gmytrasiewicz, P.J., Doshi, P.: A framework for sequential planning in multi-agent settings. J. Artif. Intell. Res. **24**, 49–79 (2005). https://doi.org/10.1613/jair.1579

Grosz, B.J., Kraus, S.: The evolution of Sharedplans. In: Foundations of Rational Agency, vol. 14, Applied Logic Series, pp. 227–262. Springer, Netherlands (1999).https://doi.org/10.1007/978-94-015-9204-8_10

Hu, H., Lerer, A., Peysakhovich, A., Foerster, J.: "Other-play" for zero-shot coordination. Int. Conf. Mach. Learn. **119**, 4399–4410 (2020)

Hu, H., Lerer, A., Cui, B., Pineda, L., Brown, N., Foerster, J.: Off-belief learning. Int. Conf. Mach. Learn. **139**, 4369–4379 (2021)

Khetarpal, K., Riemer, M., Rish, I., Precup, D.: Towards continual reinforcement learning: a review and perspectives. arXiv:2012.13490 (2020)

Kocsis, L., Szepesvári, C.: Bandit based Monte-Carlo planning. In: Fürnkranz, J., Scheffer, T., Spiliopoulou, M. (eds.) ECML 2006. LNCS (LNAI), vol. 4212, pp. 282–293. Springer, Heidelberg (2006). https://doi.org/10.1007/11871842_29

Leibo, J.Z., et al.: Scalable evaluation of multi-agent reinforcement learning with Melting Pot. In: International Conference on Machine Learning, pp. 6187–6199 (2021)

Li, H., et al.: Individualized mutual adaptation in human-agent teams. IEEE Trans. Human Mach. Syst. **51**, 706–714 (2021)

Liemhetcharat, S., Veloso, M.: Allocating training instances to learning agents for team formation. Autonom. Agents Multi-Agent Syst. **31**(4), 905–940 (2017). https://doi.org/10.1007/s10458-016-9355-3

Lupu, A., Cui, B., Hu, H., Foerster, J.: Trajectory diversity for zero-shot coordination. In: Proceedings of the 38th International Conference on Machine Learning, pp. 7204–7213 (2021)

Macke, W., Mirsky, R., Stone, P.: Expected value of communication for planning in ad hoc teamwork. In: The AAAI Conference on Artificial Intelligence, AAAI, vol. 35, pp. 10 (2021)

Malik, D., Palaniappan, M., Fisac, J.F., Hadfield-Menell, D., Russell, S., Dragan, A.D.: An efficient, generalized Bellman update for cooperative inverse reinforcement learning. arXiv:1806.03820 (2018)

Mead, R., Weinberg, J.B.: Impromptu teams of heterogeneous mobile robots. In: The AAAI Conference on Artificial Intelligence, AAAI (2007)

Melo, F.S., Sardinha, A.: Ad hoc teamwork by learning teammates' task. Autonom. Agents Multi-Agent Syst. 30(2), 175–219 (2016). https://doi.org/10.1007/s10458-015-9280-x

Mirsky, R., Macke, W., Wang, A., Yedidsion, H., Stone, P.: A penny for your thoughts: The value of communication in ad hoc teamwork. In: The International Joint Conference on Artificial Intelligence, IJCAI (2020)

Mirsky, R., Xiao, X., Hart, J., Stone, P.: Prevention and resolution of conflicts in social navigation-a survey. arXiv preprint arXiv:2106.12113 (2021)

Open-Ended Learning Team, Stooke, A., et al.: Open-ended learning leads to generally capable agents. arXiv:2107.12808 (2021)

Papoudakis, G., Christianos, F., Rahman, A., Albrecht, S.V.: Dealing with non-stationarity in multi-agent deep reinforcement learning. arXiv:abs/1906.04737 (2019)

Papoudakis, G., Christianos, F., Albrecht, S.V.: Local information agent modelling in partially-observable environments. arXiv:2006.09447 (2021)

Rabinowitz, N., Perbet, F., Song, F., Zhang, C., Eslami, S.M.A., Botvinick, M.: Machine theory of mind. In: International Conference on Machine Learning, pp. 4218–4227. PMLR (2018)

Rahman, A., Höpner, N., Christianos, F., Albrecht, S.V.: Towards open ad hoc teamwork using graph-based policy learning. In: International Conference on Machine Learning, vol. 139. PMLR (2021)

Rahman, A., Fosong, E., Carlucho, I., Albrecht, S.V.: Towards robust ad hoc teamwork agents by creating diverse training teammates. In: IJCAI Workshop on Ad Hoc Teamwork (2022)

Ravula, M., Alkoby, S., Stone, P.: Ad hoc teamwork with behavior switching agents. In: International Joint Conference on Artificial Intelligence, pp. 550–556 (2019). https://doi.org/10.24963/ijcai.2019/78

Ribeiro, J.G., Martinho, C., Sardinha, A., Melo, F.S.: Assisting Unknown Teammates in Unknown Tasks: Ad Hoc Teamwork under Partial Observability. arXiv:2201.03538 (2022)

Rovatsos, M., Wolf, M.: Towards social complexity reduction in multiagent learning: the ad hoc approach. Technical report SS-02-02, AAAI Press (2002)

Russell, S.J., Norvig, P.: Artificial Intelligence: A Modern Approach. Pearson Series in Artificial Intelligence. Pearson, 4th edition edn. (2021)

Santos, P.M., Ribeiro, J.G., Sardinha, A., Melo, F.S.: Ad hoc teamwork in the presence of non-stationary teammates. In: Progress in Artificial Intelligence (2021)

Sarratt, T.: Tuning belief revision for coordination with inconsistent teammates. In: AAAI Conference on Artificial Intelligence and Interactive Digital Entertainment, pp. 177–183 (2015)

Shu, T., Tian, Y.: M3rl: mind-aware multi-agent management reinforcement learning. In: International Conference on Learning Representations (2019)

Shvo, M., McIlraith, S.A.: Active goal recognition. n: The AAAI Conference on Artificial Intelligence, AAAI 34, pp. 9957–9966 (2020)

Stone, P., Kaminka, G.A., Kraus, S., Rosenschein, J.S.: Ad hoc autonomous agent teams: collaboration without pre-coordination. In: AAAI Conference on Artificial Intelligence, pp. 1504–1509 (2010). https://doi.org/10.5555/2898607.2898847

Suriadinata, J., Macke, W., Mirsky, R., Stone, P.: Reasoning about human behavior in ad hoc teamwork. In: Adaptive and learning Agents Workshop at AAMAS 2021, p. 6 (2021)

Sutton, R.S., Precup, D., Singh, S.: Between MDPs and semi-MDPs: a framework for temporal abstraction in reinforcement learning. Artif. Intell. **112**(1), 181–211 (1999)

Vezhnevets, A., Wu, Y., Eckstein, M., Leblond, R., Leibo, J.Z.: OPtions as REsponses: Grounding behavioural hierarchies in multi-agent reinforcement learning. In: International Conference on Machine Learning, pp. 9733–9742 (2020)

Wang, R.E., Wu, S.A., Evans, J.A., Tenenbaum, J.B., Parkes, D.C., Kleiman-Weiner, M.: Too many cooks: Bayesian inference for coordinating multi-agent collaboration. Top. Cogn. Sci. **13**(2), 414–432 (2021). https://doi.org/10.1111/tops.12525

Wu, F., Zilberstein, S., Chen, X.: Online planning for ad hoc autonomous agent teams. In: International Joint Conference on Artificial Intelligence, pp. 439–445 (2011). https://doi.org/10.5591/978-1-57735-516-8/IJCAI11-081

Xie, A., Losey, D.P., Tolsma, R., Finn, C., Sadigh, D.: Learning latent representations to influence multi-agent interaction. In: Proceedings of the Conference on Robot Learning. PMLR (2020)

Yourdshahi, E.S., Pinder, T., Dhawan, G., Marcolino, L.S., Angelov, P.: Towards large scale ad-hoc teamwork. In: 2018 IEEE International Conference on Agents, pp. 44–49. IEEE (2018). https://doi.org/10.1109/AGENTS.2018.8460136

Zintgraf, L., Devlin, S., Ciosek, K., Whiteson, S., Hofmann, K.: Deep interactive Bayesian reinforcement learning via meta-learning. arXiv:2101.03864 (2021)

Combining Theory of Mind and Abduction for Cooperation Under Imperfect Information

Nieves Montes[(✉)], Nardine Osman, and Carles Sierra

Artificial Intelligence Research Institute (IIIA-CSIC), 08193 Bellaterra, Barcelona, Spain
{nmontes,nardine,sierra}@iiia.csic.es

Abstract. In this paper, we formalise and implement an agent model for cooperation under imperfect information. It is based on Theory of Mind (the cognitive ability to understand the mental state of others) and abductive reasoning (the inference paradigm that computes explanations from observations). The combination of these two techniques allows agents to derive the motives behind the actions of their peers, and incorporate this knowledge into their own decision-making. We have implemented this model in a totally domain-independent fashion and successfully tested it for the cooperative card game Hanabi.

Keywords: Theory of Mind · Abduction · Cooperation · Hanabi · social AI

1 Introduction

The emergent field of social AI deals with the theoretical foundations and practical implementations of autonomous agents that are able to interact with other agents, possibly including humans [7]. In order for autonomous agents to be socially competent, they must take into account not only their own goals and point of view, but also those of their fellow agents. The cognitive ability to put oneself in the shoes of someone else and reason from their perspective is called *Theory of Mind* (ToM). In order to have software agents with ToM capabilities, they must explicitly incorporate some technique for *modelling others*, the preferred term within the AI community [1].

Techniques for modelling others are fairly prevalent within AI, particularly in competitive domains characterised by agents with diverging interests [2,16]. However, endowing agents with ToM faculties has the potential to boost their performance in cooperative tasks too, where agents must collaborate with one another in an efficient manner. In particular, in domains dealing with imperfect information (i.e. where agents do not have access to the complete state of the system but can infer the subset of states that are currently possible), autonomous agents can benefit from observing the actions performed by others, inferring the knowledge their peers were relying upon when selecting their actions, and incorporating this additional information into their own decision-making. This type

D. Baumeister and J. Rothe (Eds.): EUMAS 2022, LNAI 13442, pp. 294–311, 2022.
https://doi.org/10.1007/978-3-031-20614-6_17

of reverse inference, from observations to potential premises, is called *abduction* and is central to the work presented here.

In this paper, we present preliminary work on the formulation and implementation of an agent model combining Theory of Mind and abductive reasoning capabilities in purely cooperative tasks characterised by imperfect information. To cope with this, we propose a framework for agents that observe the actions of their teammates, adopt their perspective (thus utilising Theory of Mind) and generate explanations concerning the knowledge they were relying upon to decide on that action (hence engaging in abductive reasoning). We also review how agents update and incorporate these explanations into their knowledge base for their own decision-making.

Although we provide a tentative decision-making procedure for action selection that takes into account abductive explanations, this is not the main contribution of this work. The focus of this work is the derivation of knowledge using ToM and abductive reasoning. The ways in which agents use such knowledge for strategy selection (the primary concern of the epistemic game theory literature [18]) is a necessary component of the overall agent software, but a thorough examination of it is beyond the scope of this work. Furthermore, it should be noted that our model is completely domain-independent, but works under some broad assumptions that we specify.

Our work can be compared with previous approaches in the plan recognition literature [23], where agents infer the goal and sequence of actions (i.e. the *plan*) that others are pursuing, in order to anticipate and respond to future actions. In this paper, we do not work with plans *per se* that include sequences of actions, but with atomic actions. Consequently, we are not interested in identifying a full sequence of actions under execution, but the circumstances that have led to an action choice. This is analogous to the recognition of the plan *context* in many BDI languages [15].

This paper is organised as follows. First, Sect. 2 provides the necessary background on Theory of Mind and abductive reasoning. Section 2 also presents the cooperative game Hanabi, which we will be using as our running example throughout the exposition of our agent model in Sect. 3. Although the model we provide is totally domain-independent, illustrating it with a running example provides a much clearer picture. Finally, Sect. 4 presents results on the performance of our agent model, and we conclude in Sect. 5.

2   Background

We start by providing an overview of the two techniques that our agent model combines: Theory of Mind (ToM) and abductive reasoning. Both terms are relevant in many fields beyond AI, and hence the precise use we make of them here needs clarification. These introductions are fairly general. The specific way in which we use ToM and abductive reasoning is covered in Sect. 3.

2.1 Theory of Mind

Theory of Mind (ToM) refers to the human cognitive ability to perceive and understand others in terms of their mental attitudes, such as their beliefs, emotions, desires and intentions [14]. Humans routinely interpret the behaviour of others in terms of their mental states, and this capacity is considered essential for successful participation in social life.

From the philosophical and psychological perspectives, there are two disparate views on Theory of Mind: Theory ToM (TT) and Simulation ToM (ST) [20]. Theory ToM argues that the attribution of mental states to others happens according to internally represented knowledge, analogous to a theory of folk psychology. This theory is implicit, and is so pervasive and integral to our lives that it goes unnoticed. In contrast, Simulation ToM takes the view that one uses one's own mind as a model to understand the mind of others, with no theoretical knowledge involved. Instead, one puts oneself in the shoes of others by pretending to be in their circumstances, and performs a sort of mental simulation using one's own mental mechanisms to predict the thoughts and actions of others. In this work, we adhere closer to the ST account than to the TT one, since ST presents a much clearer path to being operational.

Within AI, ToM has been applied in a somewhat fragmented way, with many fields implementing it based on their prevalent techniques. In machine learning, for example, ToM has been conceived as a meta-learning process [19], where a Deep Neural Network model takes as input past agent trajectories and outputs behaviour at the next time-step. ToM approaches have also been investigated from the perspective of game theory. In [24,25], the authors consistently prove that the marginal benefits of employing higher-order ToM (I know that my opponent knows that I know that my opponent knows...) diminish with the recursion level employed. In particular, while first (I know that my opponent knows) and second-order ToM (I know that my opponent knows that I know) present a clear advantage, deeper recursion levels do not.

Finally, purely symbolic approaches to ToM have studied the effect of announcements on the beliefs of others and their ripple-down effects on their subsequent desires and actions. These approaches use modal operators such as K_i, B_i, D_i to designate the knowledge, beliefs and desires, respectively, of agent i. ToM comes into play when such operators are nested within one another, e.g. $K_i K_j \phi$ indicates that i knows that j knows that ϕ holds true, a first-order ToM statement. In [17,21], authors formalise and implement ToM capabilities into symbolic agents for the purposes of deception and manipulation.

2.2 Abductive Reasoning

In the symbolic AI literature, centre stage has traditionally been taken by deductive reasoning, based on the application of the *modus ponens* rule: from knowledge of ϕ and $\phi \rightarrow \psi$, infer ψ. In contrast to deduction, *abductive* reasoning works in the opposite direction: upon knowledge of $\phi \rightarrow \psi$ and the observation of ψ, ϕ is inferred as a potential *explanation* for ψ [10].

At a very high level, abduction takes as input (1) a logical theory representing expert knowledge on the domain of interest; and (2) a query in the form of a logical formula that stands for an observation made in that domain. Then, abductive inference computes an explanation formula that, together with the original logical theory, entails the observation and is logically consistent with it.

Computationally, an Abductive Logic Programming (ALP) theory [9] is a tuple $\langle T, A \rangle$, where T is a logic program and A is a set of ground abducible atoms.[1] Then, an abductive explanation is defined as follows:

Definition 1. *(from [12]) Given an ALP theory $\langle T, A \rangle$ and a query Q, an abductive explanation Δ is a subset of abducible atoms such that $T \cup \Delta \models Q$.*

Often, an ALP theory is extended with a set of integrity constraints (ICs). Then, Definition 1 has to be extended to account for the consistency of Δ with the ICs. One account for this consistency imposes that $T \cup \Delta \cup IC$ must not lead to contradiction. In our agent model, although we do not use ICs in the traditional sense, we adopt a notion analogous to this consistency view. This allows us to work with incomplete explanations, i.e. Δ does not necessarily complement the current knowledge to provide a complete representation of the current state, but nonetheless provides valuable information.

In practice, explanations in ALP are computed by extending Selective Linear Definite (SLD) resolution or its negation as failure version (SLDNF) [8]. The basic idea is that before failing a goal if one subgoal does not unify with a clause, it should be considered as part of a potential explanation, as long as it unifies with an element in A. Hence, goals only fail if they are not provable either by the knowledge base or by matching with the set of abducible atoms. Just as standard SLD(NF) are coupled with backtracking to find all the unifications to a query, so are their abductive counterparts backtracking to find all the possible explanations that render an observation true.

In order for an abductive explanation Δ to be useful, it needs to be assimilated into the agent's knowledge base (KB). Note that this KB does not necessarily correspond to the logic program T in the ALP theory used for computing the abductive explanations in the first place. Several possibilities may arise when integrating Δ into a KB [12]: (1) the explanation may be uninformative ($KB \models \Delta$); (2) the explanation may render a portion of the knowledge base irrelevant ($KB = KB_1 \cup KB_2$, where $KB_1 \cup \Delta \models KB_2$); (3) Δ violates the consistency of KB, $KB \cup \Delta \models \bot$); and (4) Δ is independent of KB. Of these four possibilities, (4) is clearly the most readily actionable, as it provides additional knowledge to the agent without compromising previously acquired information.

2.3   The Hanabi Game

We use the award-winning Hanabi game as the test-bed of our agent model, and we will also use it to exemplify the various components in Sect. 3. Hanabi is a card game where a team of 2 to 5 players work together with the goal of

---

[1] Under the restriction that no predicate in A appears as the head of a clause in T.

achieving the maximum possible team score. Every player is handed four or five cards (depending on the size of the team) such that everyone else can see their cards except the player holding them. Every card has a rank between 1 and 5 and one of five colours.[2]

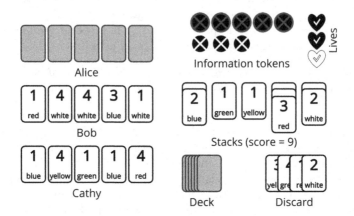

Fig. 1. Hanabi game setting for three players, from the perspective of Alice.

The set-up of a typical Hanabi game from the perspective of player Alice is presented in Fig. 1. To make progress, players take turns to build ordered stacks of cards of the same colour. For example, the red stack is built by playing first a red 1, then a red 2 on top of it, and so on until the red 5. At every turn, players can: (1) play a card on the stacks; (2) discard a card; or (3) give a hint to another player by spending one information token (there are 8 tokens initially available). When playing a card, a participant places it on the stack of the corresponding colour. If the card is not correctly played (e.g. a blue 4 is played when the top of the blue stack has a 2), the whole team lose one life. When a player discards a card, they get rid of it and recover one information token for the team. After playing or discarding a card, players draw a new one from the deck. Finally, players can spend one information token, if available, and give a hint to another player. Players can hint to one another about the rank or the colour of their cards. For example, if Alice hints "white" to Bob in Fig. 1, she must point to the cards on Bob's second, third and fifth slot (starting from the left). Hints are necessarily truthful, as Hanabi is a collaborative game and everyone would lose points by conveying or believing false information. If all information tokens are spent, the player with the turn to move cannot give another hint. The game finishes when the team lose all three lives and get a score of 0, when they manage to finish all of the stacks and get the maximum score of 25, or when they run out of cards to draw from the deck. The final score corresponds to the sum of the top cards in each stack.

---

[2] A detailed description of the rules of the game can be found at https://github.com/Hanabi-Live/hanabi-live/blob/main/docs/RULES.md.

There are three main features of Hanabi that make it an excellent test-bed to assess techniques for modelling others in cooperative domains, and that have led some researchers to point to Hanabi as the next grand challenge to be tackled by the AI community [3]. First, Hanabi is a purely cooperative game. This means that participants can greatly benefit from understanding the mental states of others, e.g. their goals and intentions, in order to align their own actions with those of their teammates.

Second, players in Hanabi must deal with *imperfect* information, as they can see the cards of others but not their own. To cope with this, agents must provide information to one another through hints. There are two facets to this information: the explicit knowledge carried by the hint (i.e. the colour or rank of the cards involved) and the implicit information derived from understanding the player's reasons to make that hint. For example, in Fig. 1, Alice might hint "red" to Cathy, hoping that Cathy will understand that Alice would only provide such a hint if she wanted Cathy to play that card, concluding that, since the card is red, it must be a 4. In our agent model, this implicit information is identified with the abductive explanations that agents compute when they take the perspective of the acting agent and derive additional knowledge from it.

The final interesting feature of Hanabi comes from the fact that information sharing is handled as a collective limited resource. The number of information tokens available must be managed by the whole team, by spending or recovering them, and the total number of tokens is finite.

Previous research on Hanabi-playing agents has, for the most part, adhered to one of two approaches: reinforcement learning (RL) and rule-based agents. In the first case, Hanabi-playing bots are trained using state-of-the-art learning algorithms [3]. In the second case, agents play according to a set of pre-coded rules that indicate what action to take as a function of the game history and the current state [4,6,11]. This is the path that we adhere to in this work, since our agent model relies on the assumption of a pre-coded strategic convention being followed by all teammates. However, we will not go into the details of the particular action selection clauses, since our agent model is agnostic with respect to the specifics of the team strategy.

Interestingly, in a recent survey where software agents were paired with human teammates, RL agents were perceived as more unreliable, difficult to understand and overall worse teammates that rule-based agents [22]. The current state of the art for Hanabi AI combines both RL and pre-coded rules [13]. There, the authors first perform single-agent learning, where they fix the strategy to be followed by all players except one learning agent. All other members of the team act according to the same pre-coded rules. Second, they implement multiagent learning, where all agents perform the same policy update after every action, if feasible (if not they fall back on a set of pre-coded rules), so the learned policy is always maintained as common knowledge.

3   Agent Model

In this section, we present the agent model combining Theory of Mind and abductive reasoning for cooperation under imperfect information. This model applies to all members in a team modelled as a multiagent system (MAS), which we define as follows:

Definition 2. *A multiagent system is a tuple $\langle G, \mathcal{S}, \mathcal{L}, \mathcal{A} \rangle$ where G is a set of agents; $\mathcal{S}$ is a set of global states; $\mathcal{L}$ is a (first-order) logical language used to describe the domain; $\mathcal{A}$ is a set of agent actions.*

We denote the current state of the system by $\mathbf{s}$, formally specified by a set of ground literals composed of the symbols in $\mathcal{L}$. In general, agents do not have access to all of $\mathbf{s}$, but to a partial representation of it. We denote agent i's current view of $\mathbf{s}$ by s^i, also specified by a set of ground literals.

Although Definition 2 is very general, this work is restricted to a particular subclass of problems, which we refer to as *common expertise domains*:

Definition 3. *A* common expertise domain *corresponds to a MAS $\langle G, \mathcal{S}, \mathcal{L}, \mathcal{A} \rangle$ where the following properties hold:*

1. ***Common ontology assumption**: All agents share the same complete ontology about the domain at hand. Agents know about all the features and the possible values that characterise a state. As a consequence, given an arbitrary representation of a state s^i, any agent can deduce the subset of states $\mathcal{S}^i \subseteq \mathcal{S}$ that are compatible with s^i.*
2. ***Common group strategy**: The group strategy is defined as a mapping $\mathsf{Str} : \mathcal{S} \times G \rightarrow \mathcal{A}^{|G|}$ of states to the action that should be performed by every agent. We assume that the group strategy function is known to all members of the team.*
3. ***Non-faulty perception**: The information an agent perceives about the current state $\mathbf{s}$ is true, i.e. $s^i \subseteq \mathbf{s}$. Additionally, at every state $\mathbf{s}$, agents reliably perceive actions performed by all other agents, i.e. the tuples $\langle j, a_j \rangle$, $\forall j \in G$.*

The first feature of common expertise domains reflects the idea that all agents approach the task at hand according to a consensus mainstream theory. For instance, the evolution of species and the theory of continental drift are consensus theories in biology and geology, uncontested in the academic world. Additionally, because the ontology that all team members share is complete, they know the features that states are characterised by, even if they cannot observe their values. Hence, agents have the benefit of *complete* information, although they still have to deal with *imperfect* information. Consequently, agents can infer which states they could be in given their current view of the system.

The second feature entails that all agents can safely assume that everyone else is behaving according to the same set of rules. Necessarily, the team of agents, prior to embarking in the current task, have all agreed on what team strategy to follow. Since we are dealing with cooperative tasks, it is reasonable to assume that agents do not expect any gains from free-riding and deviating from the team strategy, since they benefit from coordinating with one another. Agents extract knowledge from the actions performed by teammates by assuming that they are all following the same strategy. An agent could harm the team if they were to follow a different strategy, thus leading teammates to an erroneous interpretation of their actions. In this paper, we do not investigate how such a strategic convention has come to be selected. We simply assume that such an agreement exists and that it is willingly adopted by all participants. This assumption implies that we are not concerned with synthesising the optimal team strategy. Learning an optimal strategy given the reasoning scheme we present here is a task to be implemented on top of the current agent model, and it is outside the scope of this work.

The third point in Definition 3 makes our approach squarely a *knowledge-based* one, as opposed to a belief-base one, since beliefs are not guaranteed to be true. Beyond the perception of the current state, agents also correctly sense the actions being performed by their teammates. They will need to rely on this knowledge for the abduction task, presented in Sect. 3.1.

The symbols in $\mathcal{L}$ are used to construct the logical program that every agent operates by. For agent i, we denote their program as T_i. T_i is composed of the following components:

- A set of atoms corresponding to i's current view of **s**, i.e. s^i. For example, in the Hanabi game agent Alice can see Bob's cards, and her view would include literals such as `has_card_color(bob,4,blue)` and `has_card_rank(bob,4,3)`, to indicate that Bob has a blue 3 in his 4th slot.
- A set of clauses of the form h :- $b_1, ..., b_n$. We classify the clauses in T_i into the following categories:
  - *Domain-related clauses* provide definitions about the domain. For example:

    ```
    playable(C,R) :- colour(C), rank(R), stack(C,S), S=R-1.
    ```

    expresses that a card can be correctly played if the stack of the corresponding colour is exactly one level below the rank of the card.
  - *Impossibility constraints* are clauses with atom `imp` as their head and whose body contains literals that cannot hold simultaneously true. Together, the domain-related clauses and these constraints encapsulate the ontology of the domain at hand, and are shared among all agents in the team. For example:

    ```
    imp :- has_card_colour(P,S,C1), has_card_colour(P,S,C2), C1\==C2.
    ```

    states that a player cannot simultaneously hold cards of different colours in the same slot **S**.
  - *Theory of Mind clauses*, with head `knows(Agent, Fact)`, express that agent i knows that `Agent` knows that `Fact` holds true. We impose the restriction that the `Fact` argument in the head literal must also appear in the clause body, i.e. `knows(Agent, Fact) :- ..., Fact, ...`. ToM clauses are called upon when agent i switches to the perspective of agent j. However, they play no part when, once i has adopted the perspective

of j, i *reasons* from j's perspective. That is handled by the abductive reasoning process covered in Sect. 3.1. This restriction guarantees that i cannot know that j knows something if i does not know about it in the first place nor has i bothered to reason from j's perspective. In epistemic logic notation, this is expressed by the axiom:

$$\sim K_i\phi \rightarrow \sim K_iK_j\phi \tag{1}$$

For example:

```
knows(Agj, has_card_color(Agk,S,C)) :-
    has_card_color(Agk,S,C), Agj\==Agk.
```

indicates (from i's perspective) that agent `Agj` can see the colour of the cards that any other agent `Agk` has.

- *Abducible clauses*, with head `abducible(Fact)`, express all the information that could potentially be added to i's current perception of the environment s^i to reconstruct the complete state **s**. These clauses are strongly related to point 1 in Definition 3. Again, abducible clauses are shared by all members of the team, since they all must be able to infer $\mathcal{S}^i$ from an arbitrary view s^i. For example:

```
abducible(has_card_colour(P,S,C1)) :-
    player(P), slot(S), colour(C1), colour(C2), C2\==C1,
    not has_card_colour(P,S,C2), not ~has_card_colour(P, S, C1).
```

indicates that a player may have a card of colour `C1` only if it is not known that they have a card of a different colour `C2` at that slot, nor is it explicitly stated that they do not have a card of colour `C1`.[3]

- *Action selection clauses*: a set of clauses with annotated head `action(Agent, Action) [priority(N)]`, where `Agent` is an element in G, `Action` is an element in $\mathcal{A}$ and `N` is a number. Action selection clauses indicate what action to perform given the current observation that i makes of the environment, and hence implement the team strategy function `Str`. Action selection clauses have a particular feature: they are sorted according to the `priority(N)` annotation. When deciding on what action to take, agents consider action selection rules from lowest to highest priority, as detailed in Sect. 3.3. According to the common team strategy assumption in Definition 3, the action selection clauses are shared by all agents. For example:

```
action(P, play_card(S)) [priority(N)] :-
    player_turn(P), has_card_color(P, S, C),
    has_card_rank(P, S, R), playable(C, R).
```

indicates that the agent whose turn it is to move plays a safely playable card.

---

[3] We distinguish strong negation ($\sim$`Fact`) and negation as failure (`not Fact`). In epistemic logic notation, they are expressed as $K_i[\sim \phi]$ and $\sim K_i\phi$, respectively.

- *Abductive impossibility constraints* (AICs) are a set of clauses whose head has the annotated ground atom imp [source(abduction)]. This annotation serves to distinguish it from domain-related constraints, which have the same structure. AICs are used to integrate abductive explanations into the agent's program. Details about the generation and handling of AICs are provided in Sect. 3.2. AICs are not shared across agents, as they are the result of an internal cognitive process. For example, in the example in Sect. 2.3 (where Alice hints "red" to Cathy), Cathy would derive the following clause:

```
imp [source(abduction)]  :- ~has_card_rand(cathy,5,4).
```

Now that we have presented the peculiarities of the domain and the components of the agents' programs, we explain next how agents make use of them when interacting. We split the exposition into three parts: (1) the abduction task that agents are faced with upon perceiving someone's action; (2) the refinement and assimilation of abductive explanations into their own knowledge base; and (3) the action selection process leveraging assimilated abductive explanations.

3.1   The Abduction Task

At the current state $\mathbf{s}$, an *acting agent* denoted by j, operating with logic program T_j, selects and performs action a_j. Denote an *observer* agent by i, operating with logic program T_i. i, upon perceiving j performing a_j, seeks to infer what knowledge j was relying upon to select it. To do so, i must switch to j's perspective and not work with his own program T_i, but with the program that they approximate j is working with at $\mathbf{s}$, which we denote by $T_{i,j}$ and define as:

$$T_{i,j} = \{\phi \mid T_i \models \text{knows}(j, \phi)\} \cup$$
$$\{h :- b_1, ..., b_n \in T_i \mid h \neq \text{imp [source(abduction)]}\} \tag{2}$$

The first part in Eq. (2) states that the observer i substitutes their view of the state s^i by the view that they estimate j has. This view, which we denote by $s^{i,j}$, is derivable from the ToM clauses. Hence, $s^{i,j}$ corresponds to the facts that i knows that j knows (in epistemic logic notation, $K_i K_j \phi$). The second part of Eq. (2) indicates that all the clauses in i's program, with the exception of AICs, are carried over when i adopts the perspective of j. This includes abducible clauses, which are necessary to infer the subset of states that i thinks that j believes to be possible, which we denote by $\mathcal{S}^{i,j}$.

Note that in this work we are assuming that ToM clauses are preserved when i switches over to j's perspective. However, this observation is not consequential to this work, because we only consider first-order Theory of Mind. The observer i only invokes ToM clauses when switching from T_i to $T_{i,j}$. Nonetheless, the switching of perspective can be extended to an arbitrary level of recursion:

$$T_{i,j,...,k,l} = \{\phi \mid T_{i,j,...,k} \models \text{knows}(l, \phi)\} \cup$$
$$\{h :- b_1, ..., b_n \in T_{i,j,...,k} \mid h \neq \text{ic [source(abduction)]}\} \tag{3}$$

For example, i could engage in second-order ToM by simulating the view that they know that j knows that k knows, i.e. $T_{i,j,k}$. In particular, it may be the case that $k = i$ ($T_{i,j,i}$), meaning that i tries to see the world as j thinks that i is perceiving it. To generate $T_{i,j,k}$, then, agent i would need to invoke ToM clauses from $T_{i,j}$, and hence possibly assume that j is operating with the same ToM clauses as they are. Nevertheless, for the scope of this paper, it is not necessary to make such an assumption, as we do not go any further than first-order ToM.

Back to the main track of this work, the switch from program T_i to $T_{i,j}$ corresponds to the observer agent i engaging in first-order Theory of Mind and adopting the perspective of the acting agent j. In our view, this corresponds more closely to ST than to TT (see Sect. 2.1), as i is simulating what the perception of the environment is from the point of view of j. $T_{i,j}$ is the approximation that agent i builds of T_j. In general, $T_{i,j}$ is an incomplete version of T_j, as there are usually some parts of s^j that are inaccessible to i (i.e. the atoms in $s^j \backslash s^i$) and hence, according to Eq. (1), not present in $T_{i,j}$.

$T_{i,j}$, then, is the logic program that i has to work with in order to infer the knowledge that could have led j to select action a_j. In other words, in order to generate abductive explanations for observation $Q = \texttt{action}(j, a_j)$, i has to adopt logic program $T_{i,j}$. However, we are still missing the set of abducible atoms to build a complete ALP theory. The set of abducibles must include all ground literals that could complement the facts in $s^{i,j}$ to reconstruct $\mathbf{s}$. We denote them by $A_{i,j}$ and define them as:

$$A_{i,j} = \{\alpha \mid T_{i,j} \models \texttt{abducible}(\alpha)\} \tag{4}$$

Again, Eq. (4) can be generalised if the observer agent is engaging in higher-order ToM:

$$A_{i,j,...,k,l} = \{\alpha \mid T_{i,j,...,k,l} \models \texttt{abducible}(\alpha)\} \tag{5}$$

In summary, upon getting notice of action a_j, the observer agent i simulates being in the position of the acting agent j and computes abductive explanations for observation $Q = \texttt{action}(j, a_j)$ with ALP theory $\langle T_{i,j}, A_{i,j} \rangle$. Abductive explanations, then, can be computed with the abductive extensions of SLD(NF). The output is a set of explanations $\{\Phi_1, ..., \Phi_m\}$, each corresponding to a subset of ground literals from $A_{i,j}$, $\Phi_l = \{\phi_{l1}, ..., \phi_{ln_l}\}$. Next, we present how such explanations are integrated back into the observer knowledge base, and how they are updated.

3.2 Assimilation of Abductive Explanations

The abductive explanations obtained in the previous step, $\{\Phi_1, ..., \Phi_m\}$ with $\Phi_l = \{\phi_{l1}, ..., \phi_{ln_l}\}$, $\forall l \in [1, m]$, are useful if the observer i can utilise them for their own decision-making. Hence, the abductive explanations have to be integrated into i's original program T_i. For this to happen, some post-processing is necessary. The post-processing of abductive explanations consists of two steps:

1. For every abductive explanation Φ_l, uninformative atoms are removed:

$$\Phi'_l = \{\phi_{li} \mid \phi_{li} \in \Phi_l \text{ and } T_i \not\models \phi_{li}\}$$

Only the informative facts of an explanation are kept, i.e. those that could not be derived from the original knowledge base. If after the removal of uninformative atoms Φ'_l is empty, the explanation is dropped altogether.

2. For every (informative) abductive explanation, check that it is not impossible according to i's current knowledge base:

$$T_i \cup \Phi'_l \not\models \mathtt{imp}$$

Explanations that are found to be impossible are removed. This is the point where our choice to adopt the consistency view of abductive explanations comes across. Here, the impossibility constraints against which consistency is checked include *all* the clauses in T_i with head $\mathtt{imp}$: both domain-related and abductive constraints derived from previous abductive reasoning cycles.

Note that step 1 is not strictly necessary, as (im)possible explanations will remain so even after uninformative facts have been removed. However, it helps to keep explanations less redundant and more compact.

Once the abductive explanations have been refined into $\{\Phi'_1, ..., \Phi'_{m'}\}$, with $\Phi'_l = \{\phi'_{l1}, ..., \phi'_{ln'_l}\}$, $\forall l \in [1, m']$, they are all integrated into a single logical formula in disjunctive normal form (DNF):

$$\bigvee_{l=1}^{m'} \left(\bigwedge_{k=1}^{n'_l} \phi'_{lk} \right) \tag{6}$$

Note that, for this initial proposal of our agent model, all (refined) abductive explanations are considered, i.e. it is not the case that one is selected as the most likely, nor are the various explanations weighed according to some numerical probability. Such extensions are left for future work.

In order to integrate the DNF in Eq. (6) into T_i as a clause, one should consider that, as the DNF must hold, its negation must be false. Hence, the negation of the DNF can be used to construct an additional *abductive impossibility constraint* clause to be appended to T_i:

```
imp [source(abduction)]  :-
     (~φ'₁₁ |  ...  | ~φ'₁ₙ₁') &  ...  & (~φ'ₘ₁ |  ...  | ~φ'ₘₙₘ').
```

The [source(abduction)] annotation indicates that this clause is not domain-related but derived from an internal cognitive process, and hence not shared by other agents. For the time being, the observer agent i does not keep track of what AICs are derived from whose actions. However, a possible extension to this work could, for example, consider the level of trust among agents. The observer i could be willing to integrate an abductive explanation into T_i depending on whether the level of trust on the acting agent j is above some given threshold.

In summary, when i has concluded, through abductive reasoning, that j knows about some fact about the state of the system, i immediately incorporates it (as an annotated AIC clause). In epistemic logic notation, this is expressed by the axiom:

$$K_i K_j \phi \rightarrow K_i \phi \tag{7}$$

Note that this is the logical equivalent to Eq. (1).

Abductive explanations and their corresponding AICs need to be updated as the observer agent gains access to information that was previously hidden. For example, in the Hanabi game, a player learns about the identity of a card they were holding the moment they play or discard it. More generally, denote an incoming piece of information by ψ, and the DNF derived from any previous abduction process by δ, with the structure of Eq. (6). If the addition of ψ to the agent's program T_i makes δ derivable ($T_i \cup \psi \models \delta$), the whole explanation is rendered uninformative. Therefore, the associated AIC clause has to be removed from T_i.

3.3   Action Selection

The whole purpose of the abductive reasoning task outlined in Sects. 3.1 and 3.2 is to provide the observer agent with new information that may be useful during their decision-making; that is, when the observer agent i becomes the acting agent. In this section, we propose a default action selection procedure that takes into account abductive explanations. However, as stated in Sect. 1, this is not the main focus of this work and this default proposal is susceptible of further investigation.

Recall that action selection for any member of the team happens according to the action selection rules, a set of clauses ordered by priority with head action(Agent, Action) and whose body states the conditions that must hold in order for Action to be selected by Agent. Consider the subset of action selection clauses that apply to i, i.e. action(i, Action). Because of imperfect information, it may be the case that the actor does not possess the necessary knowledge to prove the body of an action selection clause true given their current perception of the state s^i. Rather, the agent should evaluate whether the action is to be selected in the set of states $\mathcal{S}^i$ that are compatible with their current view s^i.

Depending on the domain at hand, the size of $\mathcal{S}^i$ may be prohibitively large to store, update, and loop over when evaluating action selection clauses. Instead of explicitly storing $\mathcal{S}^i$ and updating it during the abductive reasoning task, we need to consider only the features of a state that are relevant for selecting an action. The pseudocode for this computation appears in Algorithm 1.

Algorithm 1 loops over the action selection clauses that apply to the now actor i in ascending order of priority. For the clause under examination, all the Skolemised forms of the rule body are generated (line 2). Skolemised forms are computed as follows: whenever a subgoal of the rule body cannot be proven by the current knowledge base, its free variables are substituted by Skolem constants, i.e. constants that have not been previously encountered. This step is

---

Algorithm 1: Action selection query

Data: Set of action selection clauses for i, `action`(i, a) `[priority(n)]` :- β_a
Result: A selected action a_i, or None

1 **foreach** *action selection clause in ascending order of priority* **do**
2 | $\{\beta^{sk}\} \leftarrow$ Skolemised forms of the rule body β_a;
3 | **foreach** *Skolemised form* $\beta_j^{sk} \in \{\beta^{sk}\}$ **do**
4 | | $\{\beta^{tot}\} \leftarrow$ instances of β_j^{sk} that are compatible with the `imp` clauses;
5 | | **if** $T_i \cup \beta_i^{tot} \models action(a_i)$ *for all* $\beta_i^{tot} \in \{\beta^{tot}\}$ **then return** a_i
6 | **end**
7 **end**
8 **return** None

---

analogous to the computation of abductive explanations, where even if a sub-goal cannot be proven, it may be added to the abductive explanation being constructed, as long as some instance of it is in the set of abducible atoms A. In general, for every action selection rule, several Skolemised forms of the rule body are derived.

Then, for every Skolemised form, its possible "total" instances are computed (line 4). This means that in the Skolemised form, Skolem constants have to be removed. Every time a literal is encountered that contains a Skolem constant, it is substituted by an *abducible* atom that matches with it (by treating Skolem constants as free variables). Abducible ground literals derived from A_i, see Eq. (5), are precisely the facts that may complement s^i to build a complete representation of **s**. However, note that we need only complement s^i to the extent that it contains enough information to query the action selection clause under examination. Hence, Algorithm 1 does not generate complete descriptions of the possible states in $\mathcal{S}^i$, but only the strictly necessary portions.

Not all potential instances of a Skolemised form are kept for further querying. Only those that are compatible with the impossibility constraints in T_i, i.e. $T_i \cup \beta_i^{tot} \not\models$ imp. This includes both domain-related and, more importantly, abductive impossibility constraints. It is at this step that the abductive reasoning that the agent has previously engaged in pays off. The expectation is that the set of possible instances of a Skolemised form, $\{\beta^{tot}\}$, is smaller if AICs are considered, compared to the potential instances that would be compatible with domain-related constraints alone.

Finally, if every possible instance of the same Skolemised form leads to the same action being selected, that action is returned (line 5). This approach advocates for a totally safe action selection mechanism, as, for the time being, no quantification of uncertainty nor thresholds over such uncertainty are considered.

Although we only consider the action selection procedure of Algorithm 1 in this paper, further work could extend the possibilities of an agent's action selection procedure based on their personality. For example, an agent may have a preference for action selection clauses that return an action given only their

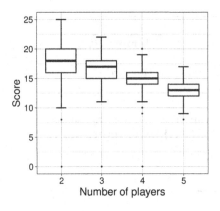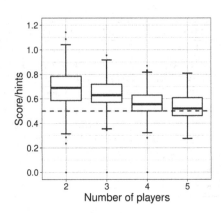

Fig. 2. Results for the score (left) and communication efficiency (right) for our agent model applied to the Hanabi domain, for teams of 2 to 5 players. Every box contains data on 500 runs with different random seeds. The dashed line on the efficiency plot indicates the reference of 2 hints per score point.

current knowledge, before considering additional inaccessible knowledge as in Algorithm 1.

4 Results and Discussion

We have implemented the agent model presented in Sect. 3 for the Hanabi domain in Jason [5], an agent-oriented programming language based on the BDI architecture.[4] Jason allows for literal annotation (such as `imp [source(abduction)]` for AIC clauses) and custom Knowledge Query and Manipulation Language (KQML) performatives for agent communication, which we use to implement a specialised `publicAction` performative for agents to publicly announce their selected actions. The abduction task is performed by a meta-interpreter that does not fail unproven subgoals, but adds them to the abductive explanation under construction as long as they unify with an abducible atom.

As for the strategy being followed by the team, Hanabi has a vibrant community of online players who have gathered a set of "conventions" to follow during game play.[5] We have taken inspiration from these to design our action selection rules. Yet, for this preliminary work we stick to a fairly simple strategy (leaving out special moves such as "prompts" and "finesses").

We present a summary of our results in Fig. 2. We examine the performance of our team of ToM agents in terms of two metrics. The first is the obvious absolute team score (Sect. 4), which is used by researchers involved in Hanabi AI as the standard indicator of performance. Our results do not match to the current state of the art (with average scores of up to 24.6 [13]). However, it should be noted

---

[4] https://github.com/nmontesg/hanabdi.
[5] https://hanabi.github.io/.

that the work we present here is not concerned with the computation of an optimal playing policy, instead our concern is to provide a domain-independent agent model for cooperative domains. Predictably, the strategic conventions we have encoded can be fine-tuned and, potentially, optimised for the cognitive machinery our agents are endowed with.

The second performance metric we use is the *communication efficiency*, which we define as the ratio between the final score obtained and the number of hints provided throughout the game. This metric provides an indication of how effective is the team at converting exchanged information (hints) into utility (score points). To the best of the authors' knowledge, this metric has not been reported in any previous Hanabi AI work. Naively, a lower bound for communication efficiency is $\frac{1}{2}$, as two hints are required to completely learn about a card's identity (colour and rank) to safely play it. Nevertheless, this is a soft bound, due to correlations in colour and rank between different cards, or players being reiterated hints on cards they already have information on to prompt them to play. Still, our results in Sect. 4 show that, for all team sizes, the communication efficiency falls above the $\frac{1}{2}$ mark for over half of the games. Just as the team strategy can be potentially optimised for the absolute score, it can also be automatically fine-tuned for the communication efficiency.

5   Conclusions

In this work, we have presented a innovative agent model combining Theory of Mind and abductive reasoning for cooperation. In our framework, agents are able to understand their peers' motivations and hence enlarge their own imperfect information on the state of the environment. This model has been proven successful for the cooperative game of Hanabi, which offers an excellent test-bed to assess the performance of techniques for modelling others for teamwork.

Future work around this preliminary agent model should look into its generality (how far can the assumptions in Definition 3 be relaxed while keeping the model sound); the optimisation of the team strategy given the proposed reasoning scheme; and its extension for *ad hoc* teamwork, where agents autonomously tune their strategy to coordinate with previously unknown peers. This would require to relax the *common group strategy* assumption of the common expertise domains we have defined in this work, and adapt the agent model accordingly, possibly by incorporating other techniques from the goal and intention recognition literature.

Acknowledgements. This work has been supported by the EU WeNet project (H2020 FET Proactive project #823783), the EU TAILOR project (H2020 #952215), and the RHYMAS project (funded by the Spanish government, project #PID2020-113594RB-100).

References

1. Albrecht, S.V., Stone, P.: Autonomous agents modelling other agents: a comprehensive survey and open problems. Artif. Intell. **258**, 66–95 (2018). https://doi.org/10.1016/j.artint.2018.01.002
2. Baarslag, T., Hendrikx, M.J.C., Hindriks, K.V., Jonker, C.M.: Learning about the opponent in automated bilateral negotiation: a comprehensive survey of opponent modeling techniques. Autonom. Agents Multi-Agent Syst. **30**(5), 849–898 (2015). https://doi.org/10.1007/s10458-015-9309-1
3. Bard, N., et al.: The Hanabi challenge: a new frontier for AI research. Artif. Intell. **280**, 103216 (2020). https://doi.org/10.1016/j.artint.2019.103216
4. van den Bergh, M.J.H., Hommelberg, A., Kosters, W.A., Spieksma, F.M.: Aspects of the cooperative card game Hanabi. In: Bosse, T., Bredeweg, B. (eds.) BNAIC 2016. CCIS, vol. 765, pp. 93–105. Springer, Cham (2017). https://doi.org/10.1007/978-3-319-67468-1_7
5. Bordini, R.H., Hübner, J.F., Wooldridge, M.: Programming Multi-Agent Systems in AgentSpeak Using Jason. Wiley, New York (2007)
6. Cox, C., Silva, J.D., Deorsey, P., Kenter, F.H.J., Retter, T., Tobin, J.: How to make the perfect fireworks display: two strategies for Hanabi. Math. Mag. **88**(5), 323–336 (2015). https://doi.org/10.4169/math.mag.88.5.323
7. Dafoe, A., Bachrach, Y., Hadfield, G., Horvitz, E., Larson, K., Graepel, T.: Cooperative AI: machines must learn to find common ground. Nature. **593**(7857), 33–36 (2021). https://doi.org/10.1038/d41586-021-01170-0
8. Denecker, M., de Schreye, D.: SLDNFA: an abductive procedure for abductive logic programs. J. Log. Program. **34**(2), 111–167 (1998). https://doi.org/10.1016/S0743-1066(97)00074-5, https://www.sciencedirect.com/science/article/pii/S0743106697000745
9. Denecker, M., Kakas, A.: Abduction in logic programming. In: Kakas, A.C., Sadri, F. (eds.) Computational Logic: Logic Programming and Beyond. LNCS (LNAI), vol. 2407, pp. 402–436. Springer, Heidelberg (2002). https://doi.org/10.1007/3-540-45628-7_16
10. Douven, I.: Abduction. In: Zalta, E.N. (ed.) The Stanford Encyclopedia of Philosophy. Metaphysics Research Lab, Stanford University, Summer 2021 edn. (2021)
11. Eger, M., Martens, C., Cordoba, M.A.: An intentional AI for Hanabi. In: 2017 IEEE Conference on Computational Intelligence and Games (CIG). IEEE, August 2017. https://doi.org/10.1109/cig.2017.8080417
12. Kakas, A., Kowalski, R., Toni, F.: Abductive logic programming. J. Log. Comput. **2**, 719–770 (1992). https://doi.org/10.1093/logcom/2.6.719
13. Lerer, A., Hu, H., Foerster, J., Brown, N.: Improving policies via search in cooperative partially observable games. In: Proceedings of the AAAI Conference on Artificial Intelligence, vol. 34, pp. 7187–7194 (2020). https://doi.org/10.1609/aaai.v34i05.6208
14. Malle, B.: Theory of mind. In: Biswas-Diener, R., Diener, E. (eds.) Noba textbook series: Psychology. DEF Publishers (2022). https://noba.to/a8wpytg3
15. Mascardi, V., Demergasso, D., Ancona, D.: Languages for programming BDI-style agents: an overview, pp. 9–15 (2005)
16. Nashed, S., Zilberstein, S.: A survey of opponent modeling in adversarial domains. J. Artif. Intell. Res. **73**, 277–327 (2022). https://doi.org/10.1613/jair.1.12889

17. Panisson, A., Mcburney, P., Parsons, S., Bordini, R., Sarkadi, S.: Lies, bullshit, and deception in agent-oriented programming languages. In: Proceedings of the 20th International Trust Workshop co-located with AAMAS/IJCAI/ECAI/ICML (AAMAS/IJCAI/ECAI/ICML 2018), August 2018
18. Perea, A.: Epistemic Game Theory. Cambridge University Press, Cambridge (2012). https://doi.org/10.1017/cbo9780511844072
19. Rabinowitz, N., Perbet, F., Song, F., Zhang, C., Eslami, S.M.A., Botvinick, M.: Machine theory of mind. In: Dy, J., Krause, A. (eds.) Proceedings of the 35th International Conference on Machine Learning. Proceedings of Machine Learning Research, vol. 80, pp. 4218–4227. PMLR, 10–15 July 2018
20. Röska-Hardy, L.: Theory theory (simulation theory, theory of mind). In: Binder, M.D., Hirokawa, N., Windhorst, U. (eds) Encyclopedia of Neuroscience, pp. 4064–4067. Springer, Heidelberg (2008). https://doi.org/10.1007/978-3-540-29678-2_5984
21. Sarkadi, S., Panisson, A.R., Bordini, R.H., McBurney, P., Parsons, S., Chapman, M.: Modelling deception using theory of mind in multi-agent systems. AI Commun. **32**, 287–302 (2019). https://doi.org/10.3233/AIC-190615
22. Siu, H.C., et al.: Evaluation of human-AI teams for learned and rule-based agents in Hanabi (2021). https://arxiv.org/abs/2107.07630
23. Van-Horenbeke, F.A., Peer, A.: Activity, plan, and goal recognition: a review. Frontiers in Robotics and AI. **8**, 643010 (2021). https://doi.org/10.3389/frobt.2021.643010
24. de Weerd, H., Verbrugge, R., Verheij, B.: Higher-order social cognition in the game of rock-paper-scissors: a simulation study. In: Bonanno, G., Van Ditmarsch, H., Hoek, W. (eds.) Proceedings of the 10th Conference on Logic and the Foundations of Game and Decision Theory (LOFT 2012), pp. 218–232, June 2012
25. de Weerd, H., Verheij, B.: The advantage of higher-order theory of mind in the game of limited bidding. In: Workshop on Reasoning About Other Minds: Logical and Cognitive Perspectives, vol. 751, pp. 149–164, July 2011

A Modular Architecture for Integrating Normative Advisors in MAS

Mostafa Mohajeri Parizi[1], L. Thomas van Binsbergen[1(✉)],
Giovanni Sileno[1], and Tom van Engers[1,2,3]

[1] Informatics Institute, University of Amsterdam, Amsterdam, The Netherlands
{m.mohajeriparizi,vanengers,g.sileno}@uva.nl, ltvanbinsbergen@acm.org
[2] Leibniz Institute, University of Amsterdam, Amsterdam, The Netherlands
[3] TNO, The Hague, The Netherlands

Abstract. This paper introduces a modular architecture for integrating norms in autonomous agents and multi-agent systems. As the interactions between norms and agents can be complex, this architecture utilizes multiple programmable components to model concepts such as adoption of personal and/or collective norms (possibly conflicting), interpretation and qualification as mappings between social and normative contexts, intentionally (non-)compliant behaviors, and resolution of conflicts between norms and desires (or other norms). The architecture revolves around *normative advisors*, that act as the bridge between intentional agents and the institutional reality. As a technical contribution, a running implementation of the architecture is presented based on the ASC2 (AgentScript) BDI framework and eFLINT normative reasoner.

1 Introduction

Norms are widely used to represent ethical, legal and social aspects of multi-agent systems, and normative multi-agent systems are deemed to provide a powerful model for norm-governed complex cyber-infrastructural systems that include social agents (humans, organizations, or other bodies), infrastructural systems, norms and their interactions [11]. At least, designing computational agents that reason with norms—technical instances of *normative agents*—requires having a suitable computational model for reasoning with norms. This is a challenging task because norms are more than a set of formal rules extracted from a legislative text: they emerge from multiple sources with different degrees of priority, require interpretation before being encoded, and qualification to be applied to a social context. Furthermore, they continuously adapt, both in expression and in application [3]. This entails that there are many challenges in modelling the interactions between agents and norms. At *content* level, multiple normative sources may be concurrently relevant, and/or multiple interpretations of the same normative sources may be available (e.g. retrieved from previous cases), and these may be possibly conflicting. Intuitively, enabling to maintain those in a modular fashion is a suitable, and, even necessary precondition for update/adaptation actions, where norms can be changed on the fly, and agents may decide at run-time e.g. to change the relative priority between normative components, requiring some explicit meta-reasoning about those norms. At *method* level, there is still an ongoing debate on what is the most adequate representation model for norms, and on methods for normative reasoning (eg. synthesizing norms [24], managing conflicts [16]). Allowing the recourse to external tools, and supporting programmability of the coordination level, greatly empowers modelers/programmers/designers to test and compare different choices. Finally, at *functional* level, most of the knowledge instilled in norms concerns a whole social system, but only part of the system is contingently relevant to the agent. Enabling the system design so that it distributes and localizes the inferential load at best (and at need) externally from the decision-making seems the most efficient option.

Contribution. Based on these requirements, this work proposes an abstract architecture that encapsulates norms—encoded in terms of normative relationships as in Hohfeld's framework [20]—in a MAS. The architecture centers around *normative advisors* that can be utilized by (other) agents in the MAS as a sort of council about the institutional state of affairs and normative relations between agents, highlighting and enabling the mapping between the social and institutional views of the environment. Agents may resort to personal or to collective advisors, depending on the decentralization constraints set up by the designer. As a technical contribution, we present a practical implementation of this architecture that relies on the AgentScript BDI framework (ASC2) [23] for programming agents, and norm specification framework eFLINT [2] for encoding norms.

Related Work. The B-DOING framework [16] explores logical relations between belief, desire, obligation, intention, norms and goals in agents and their interactions like conflicts and possible approaches to balance them in agent's behavior. Similarly, the BOID architecture [9,25] proposes a belief, obligation, intention and desire architecture with a feedback loop to consider the effects of actions before committing to them. These studies (and many others, e.g., [12,14,32]) propose extensions to the BDI architecture to add (regulative) norms as part of the agents' mind and to solve conflicts via pre-defined rules. The main issue with these works is that putting all relevant normative sources (and logical conflict resolution rules) within the agent is typically not feasible in a real system with complex interactions between norms, actions, and their possible effects on different stakeholders. Consequently, in our approach we propose delegating the normative reasoning to external components, here named *normative advisors*.

In [10], an approach is proposed for ethical reasoning in MAS by programming *ethical governors*. In this approach, when an agent needs ethical advise about certain actions, it will ask dedicated agents named evidential reasoners, providing evidence to an arbiter agent, that in turn picks a suggestion with a predefined strategy, and send it to the requesting agent. The concept of external advisor agents is similar to our proposal. However, while their approach focuses on agents only *querying* for suggestions when they require advise, in our approach the normative advisors keep an explicit institutional state of the environment and are able to notify the agent about different normative events (e.g. new duties

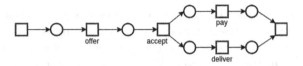

Fig. 1. A sale transaction as a *Petri net* workflow.

or violations). The work in [21] introduces Jiminy advisors that reflect the moral stance of an agent; their approach leans towards using these advisors for coordination purposes specifically when there are multiple agents (stakeholders) that follow different norms and moral dilemmas may arise. Formal argumentation methods are then used to resolve these dilemmas. In the present work, we start from a more neutral stance towards what specific methods/approach needs to be taken to represent norms and resolve conflicts; our aim is to discuss the design of a more general system architecture, whilst presenting a specific implementation of the architecture based on certain implementation decisions.

Structure of the Document. Section 2 gives background on the core components that the proposal uses by providing some detail on the AgentScript/ASC2 and eFLINT frameworks used for the implementation. Section 3 lays out the theoretical framework for the proposed architecture, whereas Sect. 4 describes details of its implementation. Section 5 reflects on the capabilities of our implementation, suggests future directions, and draws connections with related work.

2   Core Components

To illustrate our approach, we will consider as a running example a marketplace environment consisting of buyer and seller agents. This target domain can be seen as an abstract model of many real-world domains, e.g. data market-places and more in general data-sharing infrastructures, electronic trading infrastructures, etc. The process model of a individual sale transaction—prototypical example of bilateral contract—is represented as a workflow through a Petri-net in Fig. 1. A seller offers a buyer an item for a certain price. If the buyer accepts the offer, then the seller is expected to deliver the aforementioned item to the buyer, and the buyer is expected to pay the seller the price agreed upon (in any order). The workflow is a simplified representation of the normative mechanisms in place during an actual sale transaction (cf [29]). Furthermore, it does not consider the intentional aspects on the agents during the transaction, e.g. based on which desires or goals the agents may be willing to engage in the transaction, as these concepts remain external to norms.

2.1   Intentional Agents

Intentional agents are generally approached in the computational realm via the *belief-desire-intention* (BDI) model [27], to specify agents acting in dynamic

```
needed_item("Book1").
fair_price("Book1", 5).
have_money(10).

!init(#sale_advisor.getClass, "sale.eflint", "BuyerAdvisor").

+!init(AgentType,EFFile,Name) => #spawn_advisor(AgentType, EFFile, Name).

+offer(Item ,P) =>
    #achieve("BuyerAdvisor", perform(offer(Source, Self, Item, Price)));
    !consider_buying(Source, Item ,Price).

+!consider_buying(Seller, I, P) :
    needed_item(I) && fair_price(I, FP) && P =< FP && have_money(M) && M >= P =>
    #tell(Seller, accept(I, P));
    +pending(accept(I, P)).

+acknowledge(accept(I, P)) : pending(accept(I, P)) =>
    -pending(accept(I, P));
    #achieve("BuyerAdvisor", perform(accept(Self, Buyer, I, P))).

+duty_to_deliver(Seller,Buyer,I) : Source == "BuyerAdvisor" && Buyer == Self =>
    +expected_delivery(Seller,I).

+delivery(Sender, Item) : expected_delivery(Sender, Item) =>
    -expected_delivery(Sender, Item);
    #achieve("BuyerAdvisor", perform(deliver(Sender, Self, Item))).

+duty_to_pay(Buyer, Seller, P) : Source == "BuyerAdvisor" && Buyer == Self  =>
    !pay(Seller, P).

+!pay(Seller, P) : have_money(M) && M >= P =>
    #pay(Seller, P);
    #achieve("BuyerAdvisor", perform(pay(Self, Seller, P))).

+!pay(Seller, P) => ... ALTERNATE APPROACH TO PAYMENT ...
```

Listing 1: Buyer agent script as an ASC2 program

environments with rational behavior. The BDI model refers to three human mental attitudes [8]: *beliefs* are the factual and inferential knowledge of the agent about itself and its environment; *intentions* are the courses of action the agent has committed to; *desires*, in their simplest form, are objectives the agent wants to accomplish. In practice, BDI agents also include concepts of *goals* and *plans*. Goals are concrete desires, plans are abstract specifications for achieving a goal, and intentions then become commitments towards plans. Multiple programming languages and frameworks have been introduced to operationalize the BDI model, such as AgentSpeak(L)/Jason [7,26], 3APL/2APL [13], Astra [15] and AgentScript/ASC2 [23].

AgentScript/ASC2 Agent Framework. ASC2 is an agent-based programming framework and language with a syntax very close to AgentSpeak(L), consisting of initial beliefs and goals, and plans. Initial beliefs are a set of Prolog-like facts or rules that define the first beliefs the agent has, and, initial goals designate the first intentions to which the agent commits. Plans are potentially non-grounded reactive rules in the form of E : C => A, where E is the head of the plan which consists of a trigger and a predicate, the trigger can be one of +!,-!,+,-,+? respectively used for achievement goals, failure (of) goals, belief-updates (assertion, retraction) and test goals. The expression C is the context condition that can be any valid Prolog expression, and A is the body of the plan that consists of a series of steps that can include belief-updates (+belief,-belief), sub-goal adoption (!goal), primitive actions (#action) which may be any arbitrary callable entity on the class path, variable assignments, and control flow structures (loops and conditionals). It is said that a plan is *relevant* for an event G iff the event-type of G matches with the trigger and the content of G matches with the predicate of E. Furthermore, a relevant plan is *applicable*, iff C is a logical consequence of agent's belief-base. When an agent receives an event, as a reaction, after finding the relevant, and then applicable plans, it will use a selection function to choose a plan to execute as an intention. This process is typically called *planning* in BDI agents.

The communications interface of the agents is based on speech act preformatives and implemented with actions like #achieve which relays an achievement goal event, #tell and #untell which relay belief-update events, and #ask/#respond which can be used between agents as synchronous communication with test goal events. As an example of an AgentScript program and continuing with the example, Listing 1, presents the script of a buyer agent. The initial beliefs (lines 1–3), initial goals (line 5), and plan rules (line 7 and onwards) are the components of the script. The script is further explained in Sect. 4.2.

2.2 Norms and Normative (Multi-agent) Systems

Following Gibbs, norms are "a collective evaluation of behavior in terms of what it ought to be; a collective expectation as to what behavior will be; and/or particular reactions to behavior, including attempts to apply sanctions or otherwise induce a particular kind of conduct" [19]. This definition is relevant to our purposes as it gives primacy to action (rather than to situations). In the context of multi-agent systems, and even more of in MAS, an action-centered approach is intuitively more suitable, as actions are the only means agents have to intervene in the environment, resulting in normative consequences.

Categories of Norms. Norms are traditionally distinguished between *regulative* and *constitutive* norms [5,28,30]. Regulative norms regulate behavior existing independently of norms, and are generally expressed in terms of *permissions*, *obligations* and, *prohibitions* (e.g. traffic regulations). Constitutive norms determine that some entity (e.g. an object, a situation, an agent, a behaviour) "counts as" something else, creating a new institutional entity that does not exist independently of these norms (for example, money as a legal means of payment). The concept of *institutional power* is particularly relevant in the context of constitutive norms, as it is used to ascribe institutional meaning to performances (e.g. raising a hand counts as making a bid during an auction). A conceptual framework that contains both deontic and potestative dimensions is the one proposed by Hohfeld [20], whereas deontic logics, although much more studied in normative multi-agent systems [17,18], by definition focuses on regulative norms.

Normative Systems. The term normative system can be used for a system of norms, as well as for multi-agent system guided by norms. In our work we focus on the latter. We apply the so-called *normchange* definition of normative MAS system by Boella et al. [6]: "a multi-agent system together with normative systems in which agents on the one hand can decide whether to follow the explicitly represented norms, and on the other the normative systems specify how and in which extent the agents can modify the norms". This definition does not assume any particular inner workings of the agents except that they should be able to somehow *decide* whether to follow the norms or not and they should be able to *modify* them. Furthermore, there is no assumption about the representation of the norms, except that they should be *explicit* (i.e. a 'strong' interpretation of the norms [4]) and *modifiable*.

The eFLINT Norm Language. The eFLINT language is a DSL designed to support the specification of (interpretations of) norms from a variety of sources (laws, regulations, contracts, system-level policies such as access control policies, etc.) [1,2]. The language is based on normative relations proposed by Hohfeld [20]. The type declarations introduce types of *facts*, *acts*, *duties* and *events*, that together define a transition system in which states—sets of facts—transition according to the effects of the specified actions and events. The transitions may output violations if triggered by an action with unfulfilled preconditions (e.g. only sellers can make offers) or if any *duties* are violated in the resulting state.[1]

Listing 2 shows an eFLINT specification for our running example. The `Actor` and `Recipient` clauses and `Holder` and `Claimant` clauses of act- and duty-type definitions establish constructs mapping to Hohfeldian power-liability and duty-claim relationships. The `Creates` and `Terminates` clauses describe the effects of actions when performed, enabling reasoning over dynamically unfolding scenarios. An instance of `offer` can be performed without any pre-conditions and it holds when there is a `seller` instance. The act `accept` is only available after an offer: accepting a non-existing offer is considered a violation of the power to accept offers. Acceptance of an offer creates the two act instances `pay` and `deliver` which can be performed in any order. The duties express that the `pay` and `deliver` actions are expected to be performed by their respective holder after they are created as part of the `accept` action. As described in Listing 2, no violation conditions are associated with the duties.

---

[1] In eFLINT, actions capture a permission dimension as well as a power dimension, following from the design choice that a violation is raised when an action with unfulfilled preconditions is performed. Other computational frameworks propose a clear-cut separation between deontic and potestative categories [31].

```
// fact definitions                        Act pay Actor buyer Recipient seller
Fact buyer                                   Related to price
Fact seller                                  Terminates
Fact item                                       duty_to_pay(buyer, seller, price)
Fact price Identified by Int
                                           Act deliver Actor seller Recipient buyer
// act definitions                           Related to item
Act offer Actor seller Recipient buyer       Terminates
  Related to item, price                        duty_to_deliver(seller, buyer, item)
  Holds when seller
  Creates                                  // duty definitions
    accept(buyer, seller, item, price)     Duty duty_to_pay
                                             Holder buyer
                                             Claimant seller
Act accept Actor buyer Recipient seller      Related to price
  Related to item, price
  Creates                                  Duty duty_to_deliver
    pay(buyer, seller, price),               Holder seller
    duty_to_pay(buyer, seller, price),       Claimant buyer
    deliver(seller, buyer, item),            Related to item
    duty_to_deliver(seller, buyer, item)
```

Listing 2: eFLINT Specification for *Sale Transaction* norms

3   Normative MAS via Normative Advisors

Our approach is based on the introduction of *normative advisors* that enable intentional agents to communicate with external norm reasoners. We assume the parent agent is a BDI agent, i.e. it has the capabilities to reason with beliefs, desires and intentions. The tasks of maintaining an institutional perspective (state) and reasoning about specific sets of norms is delegated to the advisors. The advisors are initialized with a particular norm specification and maintain an institutional perspective on the environment, which is continuously updated at run-time. A normative advisor is therefore viewed as maintaining (inferential mechanisms necessary to operationalize) a *norm instance*. Both regulative and constitutive norms are taken into account. The normative (institutional) state of the world is stored in a way that can both be queried and updated at any time. An update can generate normative events that the agent is to be notified about. Through the normative advisors, a social agent acquires various capabilities to interact with norms. As a consequence, norms interactions become programmable parts of the agent, realizing our goal of using norms for behavioural coordination between agents and for specifying qualification processes between social and normative contexts. With such an infrastructure, an agent becomes:

- able to *adopt* or *drop* any number of norm sources as norm instances;
- able to *qualify* observations about their environment as normatively relevant updates, and conversely to *respond* to normative events by acting accordingly in their environment;
- able to *query, update, revert, reset* a normative state of any norm instance;
- able to *receive and process* or *ignore* normative events (e.g. new claims)
- able to *follow* or *violate* normative conclusions (e.g. obligations) or query responses (e.g. permissions and prohibitions)

– able to *modify* any of the above abilities at run-time.

Normative reasoning occurs based on these inputs—triggered by queries or updates— with all conclusions made available as internal events to the advisor. Note that an agent can have multiple advisors for different (instances of) sets of norms. An agent is free to qualify observations about events in the environment, other agents' actions, its own beliefs and actions—or any combinations of these— and report the resulting observations to the relevant normative advisors. In other words, this infrastructure makes possible a rich, recursive interaction between behavioral decision-making and normative reasoning. The proposed model supports a number of programmable concepts applicable to different functions:

1. *Perception*: which internal/external events are received and processed or otherwise ignored;
2. *Reaction and planning*: what are the relevant reactions to an event, which reactions are applicable in the current context and which reaction is the most preferred one to execute;
3. *Norm adoption*: when and how to adopt or drop a set of norms;
4. *Qualification of social context*: how an event or query is qualified, i.e. which is its normative counterpart for each norm instance;
5. *Querying*: when and how the normative state of an instance needs to be queried (e.g. for compliance checking);
6. *Reporting*: what events/updates are reported to which norm instances;
7. *State change*: how a normative event changes a norm instance's state;
8. *Event generation*: what normative events are created as the result of an instance's state update;
9. *Qualification of normative concepts*: which events should be raised as the result of what normative conclusions reported by a norm instance.

To concretize the proposed approach, we will discuss at higher-level why it is feasible to implement a system meeting these requirements by utilizing an AgentSpeak(L)-like BDI framework (AgentScript/ASC2, in particular) and a norm reasoner that can store an updatable and queryable normative state, generating events on updates (eFLINT, in particular). Perception, planning and execution are basic core functions of reactive BDI agents as those specified via AgentSpeak(L), i.e. when an event is received, the agent performs a sequence of actions in reaction. Qualification can be encoded as part of planning: what reaction is selected for an event (or a series of events) in any context signifies how that event is qualified. Norm adoption, querying and reporting intuitively become part of this reaction. Note however that querying can also be part of planning, as a query response may affect what reactions are applicable. State changes happen internally to the norm instance as the result of reporting, and then normative events are generated, which are in turn qualified as events by the agent, creating a full circle. Finally, if both the BDI framework and norm framework allow for run-time changes, as is the case with ASC2 and eFLINT, then all aspects are changeable and dynamic.

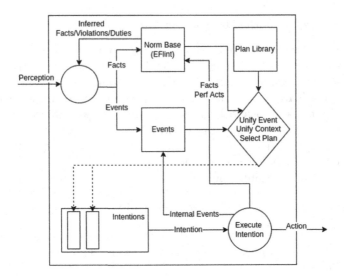

Fig. 2. The architecture of normative advisors.

4   Implementation

This section describes an architecture for advisors and discusses how the ASC2 BDI framework and the eFLINT normative reasoning framework are used to implement the proposed architecture. The eFLINT framework is used to implement the norm base. The advisors as well as the intentional agents that employ them are defined in ASC2. Our implementation benefits from the modularity provided by ASC2, allowing easy replacement of different parts of the agent [23] and the Java API provided by eFLINT.

4.1   Normative Advisor Architecture and Decision-Making Cycle

Figure 2 provides an overview of the architecture of a normative advisor, inspired by the BDI architecture of Jason [7]. A normative advisor can be seen as a BDI agent in which the (typically Prolog-like) belief-base is replaced by the norm reasoner, thus, the reasoning of the agent is replaced with normative reasoning. Apart from the differences between a general-purpose reasoner (e.g. Prolog) and a norm reasoner (e.g. eFLINT), the main architectural differences of an advisor with a typical BDI agents are: (1) the belief-base (in this case, the norm-base) of the agent can generate more than just belief-update (or fact-update) events, it may now also raise duty events, act (enabled/disabled) events, and violation events upon which the agent can react according to its plan library; (2) from the execution context of a plan alongside fact-update actions (+fact and -fact), there can now be act-perform actions (#perform(act)). These differences arise from the fact that unlike a general-purpose reasoner like Prolog that typically uses backward-chaining to infer facts based on queries, the eFLINT framework also produces information in a forward-chaining manner, thus generating more events for the advisor to process. Despite these modifications, the core of the AgentScript DSL, and the capabilities of the framework, like goal adoption, communication, and performing arbitrary primitive actions, remain the same as with 'traditional' intentional agents.

Decision-Making Cycle. When an advisor receives an external or internal event, and if it is a fact-update, then it will be sent to the norm base. If the event is an achievement or test event, it will be sent to the event queue. Events are taken from the event queue by an event-selection function, at which moment the head of the event is matched with the plan library to find all the relevant plans. The context conditions of relevant plans are checked against the normative state of the norm base in order to select only applicable plans. Then, a plan selection function selects one applicable plan and turns the (execution of that) plan into an intention, and, consequently, an intention selection function chooses intentions for execution. If the body of the plan includes any fact-update actions (+fact and -fact) or act performance (#perform(act)), then these are sent to the norm base. Whenever there is any update committed to the norm base, there could be multiple new events or new facts derived by the normative reasoner that are sent back to the advisor as internal events.

These new capabilities are also the result of replacing the Prolog reasoning engine with the eFLINT reasoner. Any Boolean expressions in the DSL can now refer to pre-defined predicates corresponding to eFLINT keywords for querying the norm base: holds is used to check if a fact (or act, duty, etc.) holds, enabled whether the preconditions of an act hold, and violated checks if a duty was violated. A comprehensive list of possible interactions with the eFLINT norm reasoner is given in the next subsection.

4.2   eFLINT Norm Base Implementation

The eFLINT language is implemented in the form of a reference interpreter in Haskell[2]. As discussed in [2], the interpreter can run in a 'server mode' in which it listens to requests on a certain port and produces responses according to some API. A layer has been developed on top of the server to maintain multiple server instances as is need for supporting multiple advisors with a norm base each. An eFLINT server instance can receive the following **requests**:

– *Fact creation/termination/obfuscation.* A created fact (instances of fact-types, act-types, duty-types and event-types are referred to as facts) is set to 'true' in the knowledge base, a terminated fact to 'false' and any existing truth-assignment is removed when a fact is obfuscated.
– *Triggering an action or event.* Instances of act-types and event-types can be *triggered*, resulting in the effects of the action or event manifesting on the knowledge base (#perform in Listing 3). These effects create, terminate,

---

[2] Publicly available online https://gitlab.com/eflint/haskell-implementation.

and/or obfuscate certain facts, as listed in the corresponding (post-condition) clauses of the type declaration of the triggered action/event. Multiple actions/events can be triggered at once because of the synchronization mechanism discussion in Sect. 5.

- *A query in the form of a Boolean expression.* The expression is evaluated in the context of the current knowledge base and can be used to establish whether a certain fact holds true in the current knowledge base, whether an action is enabled (`holds` in Listing 3) or whether a duty is violated, etc.
- *The submission of a new type declaration or the extension of an existing type.* Both have the effect of modifying the norms in the sense that the underlying transition system is modified.

Every request can be associated with additional context information in the form of truth-assignment to facts that override any conflicting assignments in the current knowledge base (e.g. the current UNIX time). This mechanism can also be used to provide truth-assignment for 'open types'—types for which the closed world assumption does not hold. An eFLINT instance generally operates *synchronously*, i.e. will only send out information in **responses** to requests[3], updating the sender upon the following:

- Any created, terminated, and/or obfuscated facts. Note that this includes changes to facts that are (or were previously) derived from other facts and in this sense were indirectly modified by the incoming request
- Any changes to normative positions regarding duties, i.e. whether a duty is no longer held by an actor or whether a duty is now held by an actor (e.g. `-duty` and `+duty` in Listing 3). Violated duties are also reported as such.
- Any changes to normative positions regarding powers, i.e. which actions became (or are no longer) enabled. If the incoming request was triggering one or more actions that were not enabled, the effects of the actions still manifest, but the violations are reported.
- In response to a query, the reasoner responds with the result of the query (state is unchanged).
- If the incoming request requires the evaluation of a fact for which no truth-assignment is given and which is an instance of an open type, then an exception is raised and reported to the sender of the request. Evaluation is interrupted and the state remains unchanged.[4]

All changes to facts' truth-assignment, normative positions and violations register as internal events in the normative advisor (as shown by Listing 3), which will process and possibly report them according to its script.

4.3   Spawning and Interacting with Advisors

Scripts of normative advisors (written in AgentScript, the ASC2 DSL) run on top of the advisor architecture and give the programmer access to the norm

---

[3] A clock event can be used to receive synchronous updates periodically.

[4] The exception can be used by the parent of the advisor to acquire the missing information, e.g. from another agent in the MAS.

```
+?permitted(A) : enabled(A) => #respond(true).
+?permitted(A) => #respond(false).

+!perform(A) : enabled(A) => #perform(A).
+!perform(A) => #tell(Parent, failed(A)).

+duty(D) => #tell(Parent, D).
-duty(D) => #untell(Parent, D).
```

Listing 3: AgentScript specification of a normative advisor.

reasoner, both providing its input in the form of queries and updates and reacting to the normative events the reasoner generates. In such sense, advisors functionally act as "bridges" or chain of transmission between institutional and social realms. Listing 3 shows a basic script for an advisor in our running example. The advisor has four plans related to acts and two related to duties. The synchronous query +?permitted receives an act and responds with true if the given act is "permitted" according to the underlying norm reasoner—in the case of eFLINT "enabled"—and false otherwise. The agent has similar plans to asynchronously submit (or not) the performance of acts (+!perform) to the norm reasoner. The last two plans are triggered when the internal norm reasoner creates (+duty) or terminates (-duty) a duty. The advisor informs their parent of these changes. The fragment demonstrates that observations about created and terminated duties are communicated to the intentional actor (Parent, the agent that spawned the advisor) and that an action A can only be performed when it is enabled according to the norm reasoner (or fails otherwise); however this script does not demonstrate all the features possibly delivered by the architecture such as internal events for violations, enabled/disabled acts, and asserted/retracted facts. Absence of power is mapped here to a prohibitions as, for example, is common in access-control systems. Other solutions may be more suitable in other contexts.

Running Example. To demonstrate spawning and interacting with a normative advisor, consider again Listing 1 in which a script for a buyer agent is given. Together, Listings 1, 2, and 3 show the DSL code for buyer agent in the market-place as presented on the right side of the Figure 3. The buyer agent spawns a normative advisor, which in turn spawns an eFLINT server (norm reasoner). The buyer has its own beliefs and desires: there is a specific item that it needs (needed_item), it has a belief about the fair price (valuation) for that item (fair_price) and it has a belief about how much money it possesses

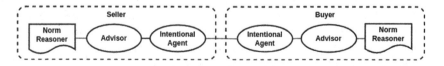

Fig. 3. Market-place model

(have_money). When this agent receives a +offer message about an item and its price, first it interprets it as an offer act and sends it to its advisor. Next, it adopts a goal of consider_buying that item for the price. This goal has one plan associated to it, which checks if the agent actually needs that item, if the price is considered a fair price and finally if the agent has enough money to buy that item. If this is all true, it sends a accept message to the agent that made the initial offer. Unlike before, this alone does not constitute performing the normative accept act. Instead, it waits until it receives a +acknowledge message from the seller before communicating acceptance to the advisor. This extra-institutional step for the buyer to qualify the act of accept, is an example of context-based qualifications in intentional agents.

When the accept act is submitted to the norm reasoner, the two previously mentioned duties of duty_to_pay and duty_to_deliver are generated and sent by the advisor to the intentional part of the Buyer. For the duty_to_deliver the agent is the *claimant* (it holds the expectation of performance); it could be that the agent asks the seller agent at this point to deliver the item, but instead, with the implicit assumption that the Seller agent is also compliant to the same set of norms, this agent simply adds this expectation to its belief-base and only when it has an observation of delivery, it will remove this expectation and send the deliver act to the advisor.

For the duty_to_pay the agent is the duty-holder (it has the obligation to perform) and reacts to this duty by adopting the goal pay (i.e. the agent desires to be compliant). There are two plans for this goal, the first one is straightforward and is applicable if the agent has the required amount of money ; it will simply pay the Seller and submit this act to the advisor. However, the second plan (not implemented) is applicable if the agent does not have enough money, which means it needs to find alternative paths to relieve this duty, e.g. by borrowing from another agent or even asking another agent to pay the seller instead. Specifying these alternatives requires to further encode the models of either the agents, or the norms, or both. Although relevant in practical applications, this level of detail can be overlooked in the present context. Instead, in the next section we will elaborate on various interesting opportunities of extending this straightforward example and reflect on the design of advisors.

5   Discussion

This paper presents an approach to embed (constitutive and regulative) norms into a MAS in a modular and versatile manner, enabling autonomous agents to reason with norms.

Inline with MAS, and distributed computing in general, we consider **consistency as a consequence** of how a system is set up rather than it being ensured by the framework through which the system is built. This allows for a kind of partial consistency that enables freedom for local deviations that are not harmful to the overall system behavior. In our approach, norm adoption and qualification is done by each individual agent, such that their view on the normative state of the world is dependent on both their script and their (bounded) perception.

Particularly desirable for social simulations, we can define agents that adopt and follow the same norms but have different conclusions on the normative state of affairs because they have had different observations. Alternatively, agents do not have to follow the same norms but might still be able to behave in a coordinated fashion. An example of the latter in our sales example is a buyer that believes, on top of the existing norms of our example, that deliveries should be done before payments. The buyer can behave according to their own norms without violating the norms adopted by sellers, even though their norms are different.

As presented in the previous sections, our running example shows how **coordination** between agents is achieved by adopting norms and deciding whether to comply with norms. The example relies on the agents wanting to comply, and therefore exhibiting coordinated behavior. In more adversarial environments, additional *enforcer* agents can be added to provide (positive and negative) incentives to comply. For example, our marketplace can be extended with an agent that acts like a market authority. By responding to violations raised by their advisor(s), the market authority can apply **ex-post enforcement** of norms on the market participants. For example, a buyer refusing to pay can receive a warning or, in the case of continued non-compliance, be banned from the market altogether. This further demonstrates the versatility of our approach: it does not impose *a priori* centralized/decentralized governance or ex-ante/ex-post enforcement. Instead, this approach gives the system designer the flexibility to choose, design and test what their system requires.

Referring to the requirements in Section 3, the notion of **adopting** was illustrated in the simplest form with the buyer agent in Listing 1 with the `#spawn_advisor` to adopt a norm as an initial goal. The agents also have the `#despawn` action to and **drop** an advisor. However, by adding extra mechanisms in the agent's script, more complex archetypes can be modelled, e.g. the agent may be programmed to keep a score for a certain norm's (and advisor's) "utility" to decide if it is an effective norm to keep adopted.

The notion of **qualification**—necessary to fill the gap between computational forms of law and software [3]—can be performed at various stages, thanks to the multitude of programmable layers in our approach. An example of qualification in the sale transaction is how a seller agent perceives a *pay* act from a buyer agent. While represented as an act in the norms, in the social reality many different actions can be perceived as a payment e.g., cash payment or 3rd-party bank transaction (bank transaction) can be qualified as the act of paying. This qualification rule could have been encoded in the script of an agent. For example, a bank agent can update a seller that they have received new funds as part of a completed transaction. The seller can then determine whether these funds constitute a payment by a buyer for a particular item, and inform the corresponding advisor. The same qualification can also be performed purely within norms. In eFLINT, actions and events are synchronized such that preconditions and effects of transitions are effectively 'inherited'. In this way, explicit 'counts as' relations between performed actions (transitions) can be specified. This is useful to a) connect actions from various normative sources which are simultaneously applicable to a system and b) connect agent-behavior to institutional counterparts

```
Fact account
Placeholder sender     For account
Placeholder receiver   For account
Event transaction-completed Related to sender, receiver, price
   Syncs with pay(sender, receiver, price) When buyer(sender) && seller(receiver)
```

Listing 4: An eFLINT fragment connecting a bank transaction to the **pay** action.

with possible normative consequences. For example, through (b) it is possible to connect the concrete actions by (human or software) actors in a system to the rights and obligations laid out in a contract and through (a) to connect actions within the contract to relevant (inter)national law. Listing 4 shows for instance how a transaction event in a banking system is connected with (qualified as) a payment action in our running example. This means the intentional agent only needs to indicate to the advisor that the original event `transaction_completed` was triggered which will automatically be inferred as performance of a **pay** act.

The notions of **query**, **update**, **revert** and **reset** are already afforded by the norm reasoner where query and update are typically provided by most norm frameworks. However, eFLINT can be used to reason about the compliance of historical, hypothetical, and—most relevant here—dynamically developing scenarios: it relies upon a declarative component that lays out the norms in the form of a labelled transition system and an imperative component that describes traces in this system. Similarly to belief queries and revision, the agent is able to query and revise (assert/retract) institutional facts. But, unlike physical state, institutional state is revertible as for example, an agent may notice that its observation about performance of an act was not correct, or even, it wants to infer hypothetical effects of performance of an act before reverting them.

Another important legal/normative requirement is **adaptability** to new (interpretations of) norms. In our approach, such adaptation can be achieved in multiple ways. Apart from spawning new (and despawning old) advisors to start using the new interpretation or encoding of a set of norms, ASC2 agents are able to modify their script at run-time to change the interactions between institutional and social reality, and this is true for both intentional agents and advisors. This type of modifications are also present in other BDI frameworks such as Jason. Secondly, an existing advisor can be instructed to update the norm source of an instance by adding new type declarations or extending existing types. For example, a violation condition can be dynamically added to the payment duty by submitting the fragment `Extend Duty duty_to_pay Violated when <EXPR>` for some Boolean expression, like a parameterized timeout event. These types of modifications are particularly interesting as a future work to explore a principled approach for studying changes in the norms such as issues about consistency between variations of norms and impact of norm changes in social simulations.

The notions of **receive and process/ignore** and **follow/violate** for normative conclusions connect directly to the concept of autonomy in the agent. All of these are already afforded by ASC2 on the language level (or AgentSpeak(L) in a broader sense) as receive and process/ignore, and, follow/violate are simply a matter of implementing the plans in the agent's script that define the reactions to such conclusions. Then, as the intentional agents' language and execution cycle are not modified in this architecture, intuitively, autonomy of the agents is also not demoted by integration of norms, particularly in comparison with any BDI agent that does not integrate norms. As a future work, these concepts—especially follow/violate—should be encoded in a more expressive and transparent manner. This can be done, for example, by utilizing declarative constructs such as preferences on the language level (see [22]) to have an explicit, yet programmable way of ordering between intentional (e.g. desires, goals) and normative (e.g. obligations) dimensions of the agent.

6   Conclusion

In this paper we present a framework for embedding norms in a MAS. It is generally acknowledged that agents in a MAS vastly benefit from utilizing norms for more effective/efficient coordination. Here it was further argued that norms, embodied as institutional views of the state of the environment, need normative advisors to facilitate the bridging between institutional and extra-institutional realms. The proposed architecture included using a BDI framework and a norm reasoning framework for creating normative advisors and was shown to address the main requirements of normative (multi-agent) systems as identified by the community. A practical running implementation of this architecture[5] using mostly off-the-shelf tools was presented via a market example to further illustrate the applicability of the approach.

As autonomous agents, norms, and their interactions deal with notions and constructs that are hard to concretize and on which it may be hard to reach an agreement, they may have different definitions and usages in different scientific communities. Alongside the proposal of the architecture and tools in themselves, this work assumed a high priority for flexibility as a requirement in frameworks utilized in designing normative (multi-agent) systems by proposing multiple programmable components varying from pure context-free and abstract norm specifications to perception/action layer of intentional agents. These components aimed at satisfying the higher level requirements of normative agents and (multi-agent) systems without putting any constraint on the language or logic used in components. In principle, the proposed infrastructure can offer a computational ground to comparing agent embeddings of alternative solutions for normative representation and reasoning.

Acknowledgements. This paper has been partially funded by the 'Data Logistics for Logistics Data' (DL4LD) project, supported by the Dutch Organisation for Scientific Research (NWO), the Dutch Institute for Advanced Logistics 'TKI Dinalog' and the Dutch Commit-to-Data initiative (grant no: 628.009.001) and partially funded by the AMdEX Fieldlab project supported by Kansen Voor West EFRO (KVW00309) and the province of Noord-Holland.

---

[5] Publicly available at: https://github.com/mostafamohajeri/eumas2022-poc.

M. M. Parizi et al.

References

1. van Binsbergen, L.T., Kebede, M.G., Baugh, J., van Engers, T., van Vuurden, D.G.: Dynamic generation of access control policies from social policies. Procedia Comput. Sci. **198**, 140–147 (2022). https://doi.org/10.1016/j.procs.2021.12.221
2. van Binsbergen, L.T., Liu, L.C., van Doesburg, R., van Engers, T.: eFLINT: a domain-specific language for executable norm specifications. In: GPCE 2020 - Proceedings of the 19th ACM SIGPLAN International Conference on Generative Programming: Concepts and Experiences, Co-located with SPLASH 2020, pp. 124–136 (2020). https://doi.org/10.1145/3425898.3426958
3. Boella, G., Humphreys, L., Muthuri, R., Rossi, P., van der Torre, L.: A critical analysis of legal requirements engineering from the perspective of legal practice. In: 2014 IEEE 7th International Workshop on Requirements Engineering and Law, RELAW 2014 - Proceedings, pp. 14–21 (2014). https://doi.org/10.1109/RELAW.2014.6893476
4. Boella, G., Pigozzi, G., van der Torre, L.: Normative systems in computer science-ten guidelines for normative multiagent systems. Dagstuhl Seminar (March), 1–21 (2009)
5. Boella, G., van der Torre, L.: Regulative and constitutive norms in normative multi-agent systems. In: Proceedings of the Ninth International Conference on Principles of Knowledge Representation and Reasoning, KR 2004, pp. 255–265. AAAI Press (2004)
6. Boella, G., van der Torre, L., Verhagen, H.: Introduction to normative multi-agent systems. Comput. Math. Organ. Theory **12**(2–3 SPEC. ISS.), 71–79 (2006). https://doi.org/10.1007/s10588-006-9537-7
7. Bordini, R.H., Hübner, J.F., Vieira, R.: Jason and the Golden Fleece of Agent-Oriented Programming. No. January (2005). https://doi.org/10.1007/0-387-26350-0_1
8. Bratman, M.: Intention, plans, and practical reason (1987)
9. Broersen, J., Dastani, M., Hulstijn, J., Huang, Z., van der Torre, L.: The BOID architecture - conflicts between beliefs, obligations, intentions and desires. In: Proceedings of the Fifth International Conference on Autonomous Agents, pp. 9–16. ACM Press (2001)
10. Cardoso, R.C., Ferrando, A., Dennis, L.A., Fisher, M.: Implementing ethical governors in BDI. In: Alechina, N., Baldoni, M., Logan, B. (eds.) 13190. LNCS, pp. 22–41. Springer, Cham (2022). https://doi.org/10.1007/978-3-030-97457-2_2
11. Chopra, A., van der Torre, L., Verhagen, H.: Handbook of Normative Multiagent Systems. College Publications, Georgia (2018)
12. Criado, N., Argente, E., Noriega, P., Botti, V.: Towards a normative BDI architecture for norm compliance. In: CEUR Workshop Proceedings, vol. 627, pp. 65–81 (2010)
13. Dastani, M., Mol, C., Tinnemeier, N.A.M., Meyer, J. J. C.: 2APL: A practical agent programming language. In: Belgian/Netherlands Artificial Intelligence Conference (March), pp. 427–428 (2007). https://doi.org/10.1007/s10458-008-9036-y
14. Deljoo, A., van Engers, T., van Doesburg, R., Gommans, L., de Laat, C.: A normative agent-based model for sharing data in secure trustworthy digital market places. In: Proceedings of the 10th International Conference on Agents and Artificial Intelligence (April), pp. 290–296 (2018). https://doi.org/10.5220/0006661602900296
15. Dhaon, A., Collier, R.: Multiple inheritance in AgentSpeak(L)-style programming languages. In: AGERE! 2014 - Proceedings of the 2014 ACM SIGPLAN Workshop on Programming Based on Actors, Agents, and Decentralized Control, Part

of SPLASH 2014, pp. 109–120. No. L (2014). https://doi.org/10.1145/2687357. 2687362

16. Dignum, F., Kinny, D., Sonenberg, L.: Motivational attitudes of agents: on desires, obligations, and norms. In: Dunin-Keplicz, B., Nawarecki, E. (eds.) CEEMAS 2001. LNCS (LNAI), vol. 2296, pp. 83–92. Springer, Heidelberg (2002). https://doi.org/10.1007/3-540-45941-3_9

17. Gabbay, D., Horty, J., Parent, X.: The Handbook of Deontic Logic and Normative Systems, vol. 2. College Publications, Georgia (2021)

18. Gabbay, D., Horty, J., Parent, X.: Handbook of Deontic Logic and Normative Systems. College Publications, Georgia (2013)

19. Gibbs, J.P.: Norms: the problem of definition and classification. Am. J. Sociol. 70(5), 586–594 (1965). https://doi.org/10.1086/223933

20. Hohfeld, W.N.: Fundamental legal conceptions as applied in judicial reasoning. Yale Law J. 26(8), 710–770 (1917). https://doi.org/10.2307/786270

21. Liao, B., Slavkovik, M., van der Torre, L.: The Jiminy Advisor: Moral Agreements Among Stakeholders Based on Norms and Argumentation (2018). https://doi.org/10.48550/ARXIV.1812.04741

22. Mohajeri Parizi, M., Sileno, G., van Engers, T.: Preference-based goal refinement in BDI agents. In: Proceedings of the 21st International Conference on Autonomous Agents and Multiagent Systems, AAMAS 2022, pp. 917–925. International Foundation for Autonomous Agents and Multiagent Systems, Richland (2022)

23. Mohajeri Parizi, M., Sileno, G., van Engers, T., Klous, S.: Run, agent, run! architecture and benchmarking of actor-based agents, pp. 11–20 (2020). https://doi.org/10.1145/3427760.3428339

24. Morales, J., López-sánchez, M., Rodriguez-Aguilar, J.A., Vasconcelos, W., Wooldridge, M.: Online automated synthesis of compact normative systems. ACM Trans. Auton. Adapt. Syst. 10(1), 1–33 (2015). https://doi.org/10.1145/2720024

25. Pandžić, S., Broersen, J., Aarts, H.: BOID*: autonomous goal deliberation through abduction. In: Proceedings of the 21st International Conference on Autonomous Agents and Multiagent Systems, AAMAS 2022, pp. 1019–1027. International Foundation for Autonomous Agents and Multiagent Systems, Richland (2022)

26. Rao, A.S.: AgentSpeak(L): BDI agents speak out in a logical computable language. In: Van de Velde, W., Perram, J.W. (eds.) MAAMAW 1996. LNCS, vol. 1038, pp. 42–55. Springer, Heidelberg (1996). https://doi.org/10.1007/BFb0031845

27. Rao, A.S., Georgeff, M.P., et al.: BDI agents: from theory to practice. In: ICMAS, vol. 95, pp. 312–319 (1995). ISBN 0-262-62102-9

28. Searle, J.R.: Speech Acts: An Essay in the Philosophy of Language. Cambridge University Press, Cambridge (1969)

29. Sileno, G., Boer, A., van Engers, T.: On the interactional meaning of fundamental legal concepts. In: Proceedings of JURIX 2014, pp. 39–48 (2014)

30. Sileno, G., Boer, A., van Engers, T.: Revisiting constitutive rules. In: Proceedings of the 6th Workshop on Artificial Intelligence and the Complexity of Legal Systems (AICOL 2015) (2015)

31. Sileno, G., van Binsbergen, L.T., Pascucci, M., van Engers, T.: DPCL: a language template for normative specifications. In: Workshop on Programming Languages and the Law (ProLaLa 2022), co-located with POPL 2022 (2020)

32. Tufis, M., Ganascia, J.G.: Grafting norms onto the BDI agent model. A Construction Manual for Robots' Ethical Systems. Cognitive Technologies (2015)

Participatory Budgeting with Multiple Resources

Nima Motamed[1], Arie Soeteman[2], Simon Rey[2(✉)], and Ulle Endriss[2]

[1] Intelligent Systems, Utrecht University, Utrecht, The Netherlands
[2] Institute for Logic, Language and Computation (ILLC), University of Amsterdam, Amsterdam, The Netherlands
s.j.rey@uva.nl

Abstract. We put forward a formal model of participatory budgeting where projects can incur costs with respect to several different resources, such as money, energy, or emission allowances. We generalise several well-known mechanisms from the usual single-resource setting to this multi-resource setting and analyse their algorithmic efficiency, the extent to which they are immune to strategic manipulation, and the degree of proportional representation they can guarantee. We also prove a general impossibility theorem establishing the incompatibility of proportionality and strategyproofness for this model.

Keywords: Computational social choice · Participatory budgeting

1 Introduction

Participatory budgeting (PB) is an important development in deliberative grass-roots democracy now used in hundreds of cities across the globe [27]. PB allows citizens to vote directly on the funding of projects proposed by their peers. Each project is associated with a cost and the projects selected must not exceed a given budget limit. Both in the theoretical literature and in current practice, such costs are expressed in monetary terms only. In this paper, we argue for and define a richer model of PB that can account for costs with respect to resources other than money—such as energy, spatial demands, or allowances for the emission of certain pollutants.

Such a richer model has several advantages. As noted by Goldfrank [10] and Rose and Omolo [24], governmental officials often need to interfere in the PB process to determine the technical feasibility of projects and to ensure their alignment with public policy, thereby reducing transparency. For example, a proposed water fountain may require significant energy resources or a proposed cultural event might breach noise regulations in a residential neighbourhood. A multi-resource model would allow us to make such costs (in terms of energy or noise) explicit and to take them into account when tallying the votes. As we shall see, allowing for multiple resources also permits us to encode additional constraints of practical interest. For instance, to specify that at most $100k (out

© The Author(s), under exclusive license to Springer Nature Switzerland AG 2022
D. Baumeister and J. Rothe (Eds.): EUMAS 2022, LNAI 13442, pp. 330–347, 2022.
https://doi.org/10.1007/978-3-031-20614-6_19

of a total budget of, say, $500k$) may be spent on cultural projects, we could introduce a new resource ("culture-dollars") with the appropriate budget limit and assign a nonzero cost in terms of this resource to culture-related projects.

Our model is a natural generalisation of the standard single-resource model of PB in which you vote by approving any subset of the projects on the ballot sheet [2]. But now, we require the selected projects not to exceed the budget limit relative to every single one of the resources (rather than just in terms of money). Adopting the methodology of computational social choice [4], we analyse several mechanisms for selecting projects from both an axiomatic and an algorithmic perspective. Regarding the former, we focus on the axioms of proportionality and strategyproofness, and show that no PB mechanism can satisfy both of them, although there are simple mechanisms that perform reasonably well with respect to either one of these desiderata. Regarding algorithmic concerns, we analyse the extent to which the computational complexity of standard mechanisms increases when we move from the single-resource to the multi-resource setting.

Related work. As is well known, PB generalises multiwinner voting [5], a connection we will be using on multiple occasions.

Prior work on PB itself that is of a formal nature has been concerned with the analysis of strategic incentives [9], axioms encoding various fairness requirements [1,21,28], and the computational complexity of PB [6]. Other authors have proposed different extensions of the basic model, e.g., by considering other types of ballots [3,17], allowing for additional constraints [12,13,22], integrating the so-called shortlisting phase—where citizens propose projects—into the basic model [23], modelling several PB exercises running concurrently in districts of the same city [11], and modelling several PB exercises running in consecutive years [16]. Note that Rey et al. [22] also considered multiple resources, although this aspect is not central to their work. We shall discuss specific contributions that are directly relevant to our work in the body of this paper.

We note that the design of PB mechanisms that can account for multidimensional constraints, i.e., budget constraints relative to multiple resources has previously been mentioned as an important challenge by Aziz and Shah [2] in their survey on formal approaches to PB.

Paper outline. The remainder of this paper is organised as follows. We introduce our model of multi-resource PB in Sect. 2, where we also define three mechanisms for this model, formulate suitable axioms of proportionality and strategyproofness, and illustrate the richness of the model by showing how it can accommodate additional constraints on feasible outcomes. We then present our axiomatic results in Sect. 3 and our algorithmic results in Sect. 4.

2   The Model

In this section we define our model of multi-resource PB. We also define three simple mechanisms for selecting projects that are directly inspired by familiar mechanisms for single-resource PB, as well as a number of axioms encoding important normative requirements for such mechanisms. Finally, we briefly discuss how the availability of multiple resources allows us to easily encode various additional constraints directly within our model.

2.1 Scenarios and Profiles

A *PB scenario* with m projects and d resources is a tuple $\langle P, c, b \rangle$, where $P = \{p_1, \ldots, p_m\}$ is a set of *projects*, $c = (c_1, \ldots, c_d)$ is a vector of *cost functions* $c_k : P \to \mathbb{N} \cup \{0\}$, and $b = (b_1, \ldots, b_d)$ is a vector of *budget limits* $b_k \in \mathbb{N}$. Here, c_k maps each project to its cost in terms of the k-th resource, while b_k is the total number of units of that resource we can spend.[1] We extend the definition of each c_k to sets $S \subseteq P$ and write $c_k(S)$ for $\sum_{p \in S} c_k(p)$. Such a set $S \subseteq P$ is *feasible* if $c(S) \leqslant b$, i.e., if $c_k(S) \leqslant b_k$ for all $k \in \{1, \ldots, d\}$, meaning that S does not exceed our budget for any resource. Let $\mathrm{FEAS}(P, c, b) = \{S \subseteq P \mid c(S) \leqslant b\}$ be the set of all feasible sets in this scenario.

W.l.o.g., we shall make two assumptions: (i) every project has a nonzero cost in terms of at least one resource (for all $p \in P$ there exists a k with $c_k(p) > 0$); and (ii) there exists at least one feasible set of projects (i.e., $\mathrm{FEAS}(P, c, b) \neq \varnothing$).

During a PB exercise, we ask a group $N = \{1, \ldots, n\}$ of *voters* to express their preferences by indicating which of the projects in P they approve of. So a *ballot* for a voter i is a set $A_i \subseteq P$. A *profile* is a vector $A = (A_1, \ldots, A_n)$ of such ballots, one for each voter. On the basis of such a profile of approval ballots, we want to select a feasible set of projects to implement.

2.2 Mechanisms

A *mechanism* is a function F that takes as input a scenario $\langle P, c, b \rangle$ and a profile A, and that returns a nonempty set $F(\langle P, c, b \rangle, A) \in \mathrm{FEAS}(P, c, b)$ of projects that is feasible. The scenario is sometimes omitted when clear from context. We now define three mechanisms for multi-resource PB, all of which are simple generalisations of well-known mechanisms for the single-resource case. Together they cover the main types of approaches to the design of mechanisms considered in the PB literature to date.

Two of our mechanisms are defined in terms of so-called *approval scores*. Given a profile $A = (A_1, \ldots, A_n)$, the approval score of a project p is defined as $s_A(p) = |\{i \in N : p \in A_i\}|$. The approval score of a set $S \subseteq P$ is the sum of the approval scores of the projects in S, i.e. $s_A(S) = \sum_{p \in S} s_A(p) = \sum_{i \in N} |S \cap A_i|$.

Greedy-Approval. The *greedy-approval mechanism* F_G goes through all projects in order of their approval scores, with ties being broken by the index of projects in P. Projects are added to the outcome set S one by one, with any project that would render S infeasible being skipped.

For $d = 1$, this is the mechanism most commonly used in practice, though often with certain restrictions on either the size or the cumulative cost of ballots. In case ballots are restricted to feasible sets, the greedy-approval mechanism has been termed *knapsack voting* by Goel et al. [9].

---

[1] Note that *negative costs* can be appropriate as well (e.g., planting trees has "negative environmental cost"). We shall occasionally comment on the effects of doing so.

Max-Approval. The *max-approval mechanism* F_M returns a feasible set that maximises the approval score. In case of a tie, we use *lexicographic tie-breaking* based on the projects' indices to select the final outcome. For $d = 1$, this mechanism and some of its variants have been studied by Talmon and Faliszewski [28].

Sequential Load-Balancing. The *sequential load-balancing mechanism* F_L is parametrised by a set $R \subseteq \{1, \ldots, d\}$ of *relevant resources*. It builds an outcome set S by adding projects one at a time (in a greedy fashion), always picking a project that maintains the feasibility of S and minimises $\max_{k \in R} y_k$, where each y_k is computed by a linear program specific to k and S:

$$\min y_k \text{ where } y_k \geqslant \tfrac{1}{b_k} \cdot \sum_{p \in S} x_{i,k,p} \text{ for all } i \in N \text{ with}$$
$$\sum_{i \in N} \mathbb{1}_{p \in A_i} \cdot x_{i,k,p} = c_k(p) \text{ for all } p \in S \text{ (and } x_{i,k,p} \geqslant 0).$$

Intuitively, for any voter i with $p \in A_i$, the quantity $x_{i,k,p}$ is the part of $c_k(p)$ shouldered by that voter. Only voters approving of p contribute to its realisation, and the loads across projects are balanced so as to minimise the total load carried by the worst-off voter. Then y_k represents the highest proportion of b_k shouldered by any one voter. Ties between projects again are broken by project index.

F_L is inspired by voting rules for committee elections advocated by Phragmén in the 1890s [14] and closely related to the so-called *maximin support method* recently proposed by Sánchez-Férnandez et al. [25]. For PB, a similar mechanism was also proposed by Aziz et al. [1].

2.3 Axioms

In social choice theory, an *axiom* is a formal property of mechanisms that encodes certain normative desiderata. Axioms might relate to the economic efficiency of a mechanism, various notions of fairness, or strategic incentives.

Exhaustiveness. Recall that mechanisms, by definition, return sets that are feasible. But they need not exhaust the budget. This failure to make use of available funds might be considered undesirable. So our first axiom is exhaustiveness. A mechanism F is *exhaustive* if for every scenario $\langle P, c, b \rangle$ and profile A there exists no feasible set $S \in \text{FEAS}(P, c, b)$ with $S \supsetneq F(\langle P, c, b \rangle, A)$.

Proportionality. Intuitively speaking, a mechanism provides proportional representation (or simply: is proportional) if it ensures that sufficiently large groups of voters with sufficiently similar preferences receive adequate representation in the outcome. A range of proportionality axioms has been proposed in the literature, both for PB itself and for the simpler model of approval-based committee elections [1,5]. We define both a strong and weak proportionality axiom. Both are parametrised by a nonempty set R of "relevant" resources (with respect to which we require proportionality).

We call a mechanism F *strongly R-proportional* if, for every scenario $\langle P, c, b \rangle$, profile A, and set $S \subseteq P$, the following two conditions together imply that all of the projects in S get selected, i.e., that $S \subseteq F(\langle P, c, b \rangle, A)$:

(i) $|\{i \in N : A_i = S\}| \geqslant n \cdot \frac{c_k(S)}{b_k}$ for all $k \in R$;

(ii) $c_k(S \cup F(\langle P, \boldsymbol{c}, \boldsymbol{b}\rangle, \boldsymbol{A})) \leqslant b_k$ for all $k \notin R$.

Condition (i) says that there is a coalition of voters approving of precisely S that is large enough to "deserve" the proportion of the budget b_k needed to realise S for every relevant resource k.[2] Condition (ii) expresses that realising S (in situations where it is not yet fully realised) would not exceed the budget for any of the other resources.[3] A mechanism F is *weakly R-proportional* if it satisfies the above conditions for all singleton sets $S = \{p\}$. We stress that the very narrow conditions for the applicability of the axiom make the axiom logically particularly weak and thus normatively particularly appealing.

In the single-resource case (with $d = 1$ and $R = \{1\}$), weak R-proportionality is the natural generalisation of the basic proportionality axiom formulated by Peters [19] for multiwinner voting (except that Peters also restricts the axiom to so-called "party-list profiles"). This proportionality axiom is particularly attractive due to its simplicity and the weak requirements it imposes. We refer the reader to Peters [19] for a discussion of how it relates to some of the myriad of other proportionality axioms found in the literature. Note that for the single-resource case condition (ii) becomes vacuous.

Strategyproofness. We would like voters to vote truthfully. To make this precise, we need to make assumptions about their incentives. We assume that every voter i has a *preference relation* $\succcurlyeq_i$, which is a reflexive and transitive binary relation on feasible sets of projects (i.e. a preorder). We use $\succ_i$ to refer to its strict part. We further assume that $\succcurlyeq_i$ is induced by some set $S_i^\star \subseteq P$ of projects voter i *truthfully* approves of. We consider two types of voters; the manner in which $\succcurlyeq_i$ is induced by $S_i^\star$ depends on the voter's type:

- For a given nonempty set R of relevant resources, voter i has *R-Paretian preferences* in case $S \succcurlyeq_i S'$ holds for two sets $S, S' \in \textsc{Feas}(P, \boldsymbol{c}, \boldsymbol{b})$ if and only if $c_k(S_i^\star \cap S) \geqslant c_k(S_i^\star \cap S')$ for all $k \in R$. That is, such a voter weakly prefers S to S' if the cumulative cost of her truthfully approved projects in S is at least as high as for those in S' with respect to each relevant resource. Thus, $S \succ_i S'$ holds if and only if $c_k(S_i^\star \cap S) \geqslant c_k(S_i^\star \cap S')$ for all $k \in R$ and this inequality is strict in at least one case.
- Voter i has *subset preferences* in case $S \succcurlyeq_i S'$ holds for $S, S' \in \textsc{Feas}(P, \boldsymbol{c}, \boldsymbol{b})$ if and only if $S_i^\star \cap S \supseteq S_i^\star \cap S'$.

---

[2] Observe that for condition (i) it is important to count the number of voters who vote for S exactly rather than those who vote for a (not necessarily proper) superset of S. Indeed, weakening the conditions for the applicability of the axiom in this sense would immediately render it impossible to satisfy in general. To see this, consider a single-resource scenario in which we need to divide a budget of $b = 2$ amongst three projects of cost 1, and in which there are two voters, with approval ballots $A_1 = \{p_1, p_2\}$ and $A_2 = \{p_3\}$. Then each project forms a singleton set S for which $n \cdot \frac{c(S)}{b} = 1$, while $|\{i \in N : A_i \supseteq S\}| = 1$. But we cannot select all three projects.

[3] Note that dropping condition (ii) would render this axiom unsatisfiable in general, since sets satisfying the first condition can exceed the budget for some $k \notin R$.

Let $(\boldsymbol{A}_{-i}, S_i^\star)$ denote the profile $\boldsymbol{A}$ in which the ballot of voter i has been replaced by $S_i^\star$. We can now define strategyproofness in the familiar manner. A mechanism F is *strategyproof* against voters with either R-Paretian or subset preferences if, for every scenario $\langle P, \boldsymbol{c}, \boldsymbol{b} \rangle$ and profile $\boldsymbol{A}$, we get $F(\langle P, \boldsymbol{c}, \boldsymbol{b} \rangle, \boldsymbol{A}) \not\succ_i F(\langle P, \boldsymbol{c}, \boldsymbol{b} \rangle, (\boldsymbol{A}_{-i}, S_i^\star))$ for all voters $i \in N$ with these preferences.

Following Goel et al. [9], we furthermore define F to be *approximately strategyproof* against voters with R-Paretian or subset preferences if, for every $\langle P, \boldsymbol{c}, \boldsymbol{b} \rangle$ and $\boldsymbol{A}$, we get $F(\langle P, \boldsymbol{c}, \boldsymbol{b} \rangle, \boldsymbol{A}) \not\succ_i F(\langle P, \boldsymbol{c}, \boldsymbol{b} \rangle, (\boldsymbol{A}_{-i}, S_i^\star)) \cup \{p\}$ for all $i \in N$ with these preferences and some $p \in P$. This allows for the possibility that a truthful vote might result in a worse outcome—provided the difference is, in some sense, bounded by the value of the most attractive project.

2.4 Modelling Additional Constraints

Recent work on PB has emphasised the importance of enriching the basic model with the possibility of expressing additional constraints the projects selected for funding must satisfy [2,12,13,22]. As we are going to see now, an advantage of working with a multi-resource PB model is that it allows us to encode such constraints directly within the basic framework.

Distributional Constraints. For many real-world PB exercises there are upper bounds on the funding that may be spent on projects belonging to a given category (say, culture or the environment). Suppose $X \subseteq P$ represents a specific category of projects, and that for a certain resource k, we want to limit the part of b_k going to projects in X to $\lfloor \alpha \cdot b_k \rfloor$ for some $\alpha \in [0, 1]$. To achieve this, we can introduce a new resource $k^\star$ with $b_{k^\star} = \lfloor \alpha \cdot b_k \rfloor$ and $c_{k^\star}(p) = \mathbb{1}_{p \in X} \cdot c_k(p)$.

Jain et al. [13] develop a PB model centred around such distributional constraints, and Rey et al. [22] show how to encode them in judgment aggregation. Patel et al. [18] study a different variant of this model, where the distributional constraints relate to the score rather than the costs of the selected projects.

Incompatibility Constraints. Some projects might be incompatible with one another. Suppose we want to express that we cannot realise all of the projects in some nonempty set $X \subseteq P$ together. To do so, we can introduce a new resource $k^\star$ with budget limit $b_{k^\star} = |X| - 1$ and fix $c_{k^\star}(p) = \mathbb{1}_{p \in X}$ for each project p. That is, projects in X cost 1 unit and all others do not cost anything. Then respecting the budget constraint for $k^\star$ implies never accepting all of the projects in X.

In the single-resource setting incompatibility constraints are a special case of distributional constraints. But in general this is not the case, since two incompatible projects might not both have a nonzero cost for the same resource.

Dependency Constraints. Realising a given project might be possible only if certain other projects are implemented as well. If we were to allow for negative costs, we could easily encode such dependency constraints. Suppose we want to express that project $p^\star$ should be selected only if all projects in $X \subseteq P$ are selected as well. We again create a new resource $k^\star$, and set $b_{k^\star} = 1$, $c_{k^\star}(p^\star) =$

$|X| + 1$, $c_{k^*}(p) = -1$ for all $p \in X$, and $c_{k^*}(p) = 0$ for all other projects. Then selecting p^* and thus spending an amount of $|X| + 1$ is possible only if we also select all of the projects in X and thus push the total amount spent down to the budget limit of 1. Rey et al. [22] also discuss modelling such constraints.

The fact that encoding constraints involves introducing some purely technical resources lends additional support to the idea of parametrising mechanisms and axioms by a set of relevant resources R. For example, for F_L we may want to put all "real" resources in R but leave all "technical" resources aside.

3   Axiomatic Analysis

In this section we first analyse the concrete mechanisms defined earlier in view of the axiomatic requirements of proportionality and strategyproofness, and we then show that it is impossible to satisfy both requirements at the same time.

3.1   Proportionality

Unfortunately, neither the greedy-approval mechanism nor the max-approval mechanism can guarantee weak proportionality, and thus certainly not strong proportionality. To see this, consider the following example.

Example 1. Take a single-resource scenario $\langle P, c, b \rangle$ with $P = \{p_1, p_2\}$, $b = 3$, $c(p_1) = 1$, and $c(p_2) = 3$. For profile $\boldsymbol{A} = (\{p_1\}, \{p_2\}, \{p_2\})$ both F_G and F_M return the outcome $\{p_2\}$. However, weak proportionality (with $R = \{1\}$) would require p_1 to be part of that outcome.

This kind of counterexample also works for multi-resource scenarios: simply add any number of dummy resources with budget 1 and cost 0 for both projects (as long as $R \supseteq \{1\}$). On the other hand, the sequential load-balancing mechanism F_L satisfies even our strong proportionality axiom.

Proposition 1. *The sequential load-balancing mechanism F_L is strongly R-proportional for any set R of relevant resources.*

Proof. The proof is similar to that of Proposition 3.13 in the work of Aziz et al. [1]. Suppose F_L is *not* strongly R-proportional, for some R. Then there must be a scenario $\langle P, c, b \rangle$, a profile $\boldsymbol{A}$, and a subset of projects $S^* \subseteq P$ satisfying the requirements of strong R-proportionality but for which there exists a project $p^* \in S^*$ not selected by F_L. Let $N^* \subseteq N$ be the set of voters such that for all $i \in N^*$, we have $A_i = S^*$. Recall that F_L works in iterations. Let ℓ be the first iteration for which selecting p^* would violate the budget constraint of at least one relevant resource which we call $k^* \in R$. Thanks to condition (*ii*) of strong R-proportionality, we know that $\{p^*\} \cup F_L(\langle P, c, b \rangle, \boldsymbol{A})$ cannot exceed the budget of a non-relevant resource. This implies that such an ℓ always exists as otherwise F_L would not have terminated. In the following we will prove a contradiction, namely that F_L should have selected p^* at an iteration before ℓ.

Let S be the set of projects selected by F_{L} at iteration ℓ. Use $x_{i,k,p}$ to represent the part of $c_k(p)$ shouldered by voter i at iteration ℓ (see the definition of F_{L}). Define $x_{i,k} = \sum_{i\in N} \mathbb{1}_{p\in A_i} \times x_{i,k,p}$ to be the total load of voter i for resource k at iteration ℓ. Given that all voters in $N^\star$ approve only of $S^\star$, we see that the cost $c_k(S) - c_k(S\cap S^\star)$ for every relevant resource $k \in R$ should be spread across $n - |N^\star|$ voters. By averaging, there must then be a voter $i \in N \setminus N^\star$ for which:

$$\forall k \in R : x_{i,k} \geqslant \frac{c_k(S) - c_k(S\cap S^\star)}{n - |N^\star|} \times \frac{1}{b_k}.$$

From the definition of ℓ, we know that for $k^\star$ we have $c_{k^\star}(S \cup \{p^\star\}) > b_{k^\star}$. The equation above thus implies for resource $k^\star$ that:

$$x_{i,k^\star} > \frac{b_{k^\star} - c_{k^\star}(p^\star) - c_k(S\cap S^\star)}{n - |N^\star|} \times \frac{1}{b_{k^\star}}.$$

Now from the definition of strong R-proportionality, we know that $\frac{|N^\star|}{n} \times b_{k^\star} \geqslant c_{k^\star}(p^\star) + c_{k^\star}(S \cap S^\star)$. This implies that:

$$x_{i,k^\star} > \frac{b_{k^\star} - \frac{|N^\star|}{n} \times b_{k^\star}}{n - |N^\star|} \times \frac{1}{b_{k^\star}} = \frac{1}{n}. \tag{1}$$

Thus at iteration ℓ, the maximum load of a voter is at least $1/n$.

We now assume that at iteration $\ell-1$, it is project $p^\star$ that is selected, instead of the other project that F_{L} selected. We distinguish between two cases.

First, if all voters have load no more than $1/n$ for all resources $k \in R$ at the "new" iteration ℓ, then we are done: to minimise the maximum load, F_{L} should have selected $p^\star$ at iteration $\ell - 1$ because of Eq. (1).

Suppose now that there is a voter $i \in N$ and a resource $k \in R$ such that i's load for k at the "new" iteration ℓ exceeds $1/n$. Note first that we must have $i \notin N^\star$. Indeed, the costs of projects in $S^\star$ can always be distributed across voters in $N^\star$, keeping their load for every $k \in R$ at most $\frac{|S^\star| \times b_{k^\star}}{n \times |S^\star|} \times \frac{1}{b_{k^\star}} = 1/n$. Then, since $i \notin N^\star$, i's load did not increase by selecting $p^\star$, and so there must then be a smallest iteration $\ell' < \ell$ after which i's load for k exceeded $1/n$. But then, since the maximum load after ℓ' exceeded $1/n$, we find that F_{L} should have selected $p^\star$ at iteration $\ell' - 1$. Indeed, by selecting $p^\star$, all voters in $N \setminus N^\star$ would have a load of less than $1/n$, while the load of voters in $N^\star$ still would not exceed $1/n$.

Overall, by definition of F_{L}, project $p^\star$ should have been selected before iteration ℓ. By contradiction, F_{L} is thus proven to be strongly R-proportional. $\square$

We note that this positive result ceases to hold when we allow for negative costs. Indeed, as the following example demonstrates, in that case satisfying strong proportionality is impossible for any mechanism.

Example 2. Consider a single-resource scenario $\langle P, c, b \rangle$ with $P = \{p_1, p_2, p_3\}$, $b = 2$, $c(p_1) = c(p_2) = 2$, and $c(p_3) = -1$. Then under profile $\mathbf{A} = (A_1, A_2)$ with $A_1 = \{p_1, p_3\}$ and $A_2 = \{p_2, p_3\}$, both voters approve sets with cumulative cost $c(A_1) = c(A_2) = 2 - 1 = 1$, and so strong proportionality requires us to accept both sets. But this would exceed the budget: $c(A_1 \cup A_2) = 2 + 2 - 1 = 3 > b$.

3.2 Strategyproofness

None of our mechanisms are strategyproof against voters with either Paretian or subset preferences (not even for $d = 1$). We again provide an example.

Example 3. Take a scenario with budget $b = 2$ and three projects with $c(p_1) = 1$, $c(p_2) = 2$, and $c(p_3) = 1$. Suppose we receive two ballots, $S_1^\star = \{p_3\}$ and $A_2 = \{p_2\}$. Both F_G and F_M pick p_2 (due to lexicographic tie-breaking). If voter 1 instead (untruthfully) votes $A_1 = \{p_1, p_3\}$, both mechanisms return $\{p_1, p_3\}$. The same applies to F_L if we add a third voter with $A_3 = \{p_2\}$. But $\{p_1, p_3\} \succ_1 \{p_2\}$, for both Paretian and subset preferences.

So let us focus on approximate strategyproofness instead. As we shall see, F_G guarantees approximate strategyproofness for voters with subset preferences, but not (in general) for voters with Paretian preferences. As we shall also see, unfortunately, neither F_M nor F_L can guarantee approximate strategyproofness in either case. For the positive result we first prove a simple lemma.

Lemma 1. *If projects cost 1 unit of one resource and 0 units of all others, then under F_G, voters with R-Paretian preferences weakly prefer the outcome obtained by voting truthfully over any obtained by voting untruthfully (for any R).*

Proof. In this setting, F_G picks, for each $k \in \{1, \dots, d\}$, the b_k most approved projects costing 1 unit of resource k. Now, since every project in $S_i^\star$ is approved at least as often in $(A_{-i}, S_i^\star)$ as in A, we have $F(A_{-i}, S_i^\star) \succcurlyeq_i F(A)$. □

Proposition 2. *F_G is approximately strategyproof against voters with R-Paretian preferences for $R = \{1, \dots, d\}$ and against voters with subset preferences.*

Proof. Let $R = \{1, \dots, d\}$ and consider a scenario $\langle P, \boldsymbol{c}, \boldsymbol{b} \rangle$. Construct a second scenario $\langle P', \boldsymbol{c}', \boldsymbol{b} \rangle$ where all projects in P have been decomposed into smaller projects that cost 1 unit of one resource and 0 units of all other resources, such that the costs of any $p \in P$ equals the sum of costs of the corresponding projects $p' \in P'$. By Lemma 1, no voter with R-Paretian preferences has an incentive to manipulate in the second scenario. F_G accepts, in the first scenario, projects $p \in P$ in the same order as it accepts the corresponding projects $p' \in P'$ in the second scenario, until the first of the d budget limits is reached. For that resource k for which the limit is reached first and that project p that is not accepted, the difference in cost between the two outcomes is at most $c_k(p)$. If we give project p to an R-Paretian voter on top of the outcome of the first scenario, then the amount of resource k spent as she desires is at least as much as in the second scenario, which in turn is at least as much as in any manipulated version of the second scenario, which is at least as much as in any manipulated version of the first scenario. Hence, she will not have any incentive to manipulate in the first scenario either.

Finally, note that strict subset preferences imply strict $\{1, \dots, d\}$-Paretian preferences. Thus, approximate strategyproofness under $\{1, \dots, d\}$-Paretian preferences implies the same under subset preferences, completing the proof. □

In the single-resource setting, F_G has been shown to guarantee approximate strategyproofness against (what we call) Paretian voters using a similar approach [9]. However, as our next example illustrates, for multi-resource PB in which voters might not care about all resources, this is no longer the case.

Example 4. Take a scenario with $P = \{p_1, p_2, p_3, p_4, p_5\}$, three resources, $R = \{1\}$, and the following costs and budget limits:

Cost	p_1	p_2	p_3	p_4	p_5	Budget limit
c_1	0	0	0	1	1	$b_1 = 2$
c_2	2	1	1	0	0	$b_2 = 2$
c_3	1	3	3	4	4	$b_3 = 9$

Let us consider the two-voter profile $(S_1^\star, A_2) = (\{p_2, p_3, p_4, p_5\}, \{p_1, p_2, p_3\})$. Then the greedy-approval mechanism F_G selects the set $\{p_2, p_3\}$. If voter 1 instead votes $A_1 = \{p_1, p_4, p_5\}$, F_G returns $\{p_1, p_4, p_5\}$, which is better for her—in terms of resource 1—than $\{p_2, p_3\} \cup \{p\}$, for every $p \in P$. △

The next two examples demonstrate that neither F_M nor F_L can guarantee approximate strategyproofness against voters with subset preferences (and, thus, certainly not against Paretian voters).

Example 5. Consider the single-resource scenario $\langle P, c, b \rangle$ with projects $P = \{p_1, p_2, p_3, p_4, p_5\}$. Let the first four projects cost 1, while $c(p_5) = 4 = b$. Now let $(S_1^\star, A_2, A_3, A_4) = (\{p_1, p_2\}, \{p_5\}, \{p_5\}, \{p_5\})$. Then F_M returns $\{p_5\}$. However, if voter 1 switches to $A_1 = \{p_1, p_2, p_3, p_4\}$, then F_M returns $\{p_1, p_2, p_3, p_4\}$, increasing the set of accepted projects she truly likes from $\varnothing$ to $\{p_1, p_2\}$.

Example 6. Consider a two-resource scenario with $P = \{p_1, p_2, p_3, p_4, p_5\}$ with these costs and budget limits:

Costs	p_1	p_2	p_3	p_4	p_5	Budget limit
c_1	2	2	0	3	0	$b_1 = 5$
c_2	2	0	2	0	3	$b_2 = 5$

For the profile $(S_1^\star, A_2, A_3) = (\{p_1, p_2, p_3\}, \{p_1, p_4, p_5\}, \{p_1, p_4, p_5\})$, the sequential load-balancing mechanism F_L picks the set $\{p_1, p_4, p_5\}$. However, if voter 1 switches to $A_1 = \{p_2, p_3\}$, then F_L still selects p_1, but also p_2 and p_3, since voter 1 can no longer carry any load for p_1. Thus, by manipulating she can add two projects she cares about to the outcome, without losing any others. △

3.3   An Impossibility Result

We now show it is impossible to guarantee both weak proportionality and strategyproofness together. Our result mirrors (and is inspired by) an impossibility result for multiwinner voting due to Peters [19], although there are subtle differences (meaning that our result is not implied by that of Peters). In particular, Peters requires a (very weak) efficiency axiom (for a discussion of this point, refer to Peters [20]).[4] We are going to prove the following result (for single-resource PB) and then generalise to full multi-resource PB.

Theorem 1. *Let $b \geqslant 3$, $m > b$ and $n = q \cdot b$ for some integer $q \geqslant 1$. Then no mechanism can guarantee both weak proportionality and strategyproofness against voters with Paretian preferences for PB scenarios with a single resource, budget b, m projects, and n voters.*

For ease of reading, let us call a single-resource mechanism F *good* if it satisfies both weak proportionality and strategyproofness against voters with Paretian preferences. We first prove Theorem 1 for the special case of $(b, m, n) = (3, 4, 3)$, and then generalise using induction.

Lemma 2. *No mechanism for $(b, m, n) = (3, 4, 3)$ is good.*

Proof. For the sake of contradiction, suppose F is such a mechanism. Let $\langle P, c, b \rangle$ be a single-resource scenario with $P = \{a, b, c, d\}$, $c(p) = 1$ for all $p \in P$, and $b = 3$. Consider profile $\mathbf{A}^1 = (ab, c, d)$, where we omitted set brackets to improve readability. By weak proportionality, we must have $cd \subseteq F(\mathbf{A}^1)$. Furthermore, by strategyproofness, either a or b must be in the selected project set as well, since otherwise voter 1 can manipulate by removing a single project from her ballot. Thus $F(\mathbf{A}^1)$ is either acd or bcd. W.l.o.g., let us assume the former is the case. Table 1 shows how to derive a contradiction from $F(\mathbf{A}^1) = acd$ by means of a sequence of steps involving 14 different profiles.[5]   □

Next, we prove three inductive lemmas.

Lemma 3. *If there exists a good mechanism for (b, m, n) with $n = q \cdot b$ for some integer $q \geqslant 1$, then a good mechanism also exists for (b, m, b).*

---

[4] We are able to circumvent the need for this additional efficiency requirement because we do not impose exhaustiveness (which in multiwinner voting is an implicit part of the basic model). This gives us more freedom for the inductive lemmas we need to prove. At the same time, our result is weaker than that of Peters in other respects: his proportionality axiom is subtly weaker (as it needs to be imposed only for so-called party-list profiles) and his result applies even under subset preferences.

[5] We found these 14 profiles and the derivation of Table 1 by first encoding the requirements of F as a set of clauses in propositional logic, and then applying a SAT-solver to that set to compute a minimally unsatisfiable set exhibiting the impossibility of finding a mechanism of the required kind. For an introduction to this approach, the reader may wish to consult the expository article of Geist and Peters [8].

Table 1. Derivation for Lemma 2. $M(i, \mathbf{A}, \mathbf{A}')$ means that voter i can successfully manipulate by moving from profile $\mathbf{A}$ to profile $\mathbf{A}'$, while $S \not\cap S'$ signifies that $S \cap S' = \varnothing$.

Profile	Strategyproofness	Proportionality	Outcome
$\mathbf{A}^3 = (b, ac, d)$	$ab \subseteq F(\mathbf{A}^3) \Rightarrow M(1, \mathbf{A}^2, \mathbf{A}^3)$ $ac \not\cap F(\mathbf{A}^3) \Rightarrow M(2, \mathbf{A}^3, (b, a, d))$	$bd \subseteq F(\mathbf{A}^3)$	$F(\mathbf{A}^3) = bcd$
$\mathbf{A}^4 = (b, ac, cd)$	$cd \subsetneq F(\mathbf{A}^4) \Rightarrow M(3, \mathbf{A}^4, \mathbf{A}^3)$	$b \subseteq F(\mathbf{A}^4)$	$F(\mathbf{A}^4) = bcd$
$\mathbf{A}^5 = (b, a, cd)$	$ac \subseteq F(\mathbf{A}^5) \Rightarrow M(2, \mathbf{A}^4, \mathbf{A}^5)$ $cd \not\cap F(\mathbf{A}^5) \Rightarrow M(3, \mathbf{A}^5, (b, a, c))$	$ab \subseteq F(\mathbf{A}^5)$	$F(\mathbf{A}^5) = abd$
$\mathbf{A}^6 = (b, ad, cd)$	$ad \subsetneq F(\mathbf{A}^6) \Rightarrow M(2, \mathbf{A}^6, \mathbf{A}^5)$	$b \subseteq F(\mathbf{A}^6)$	$F(\mathbf{A}^6) = abd$
$\mathbf{A}^7 = (b, ad, c)$	$cd \subseteq F(\mathbf{A}^7) \Rightarrow M(3, \mathbf{A}^6, \mathbf{A}^7)$ $ad \not\cap F(\mathbf{A}^7) \Rightarrow M(2, \mathbf{A}^7, (b, a, c))$	$bc \subseteq F(\mathbf{A}^7)$	$F(\mathbf{A}^7) = abc$
$\mathbf{A}^8 = (b, ad, ac)$	$ac \subsetneq F(\mathbf{A}^8) \Rightarrow M(3, \mathbf{A}^8, \mathbf{A}^7)$	$b \subseteq F(\mathbf{A}^8)$	$F(\mathbf{A}^8) = abc$
$\mathbf{A}^9 = (b, d, ac)$	$ad \subseteq F(\mathbf{A}^9) \Rightarrow M(2, \mathbf{A}^8, \mathbf{A}^9)$ $ac \not\cap F(\mathbf{A}^9) \Rightarrow M(3, \mathbf{A}^9, (b, d, c))$	$bd \subseteq F(\mathbf{A}^9)$	$F(\mathbf{A}^9) = bcd$
$\mathbf{A}^{10} = (b, cd, ac)$	$cd \subsetneq F(\mathbf{A}^{10}) \Rightarrow M(2, \mathbf{A}^{10}, \mathbf{A}^9)$	$b \subseteq F(\mathbf{A}^{10})$	$F(\mathbf{A}^{10}) = bcd$
$\mathbf{A}^{11} = (b, cd, a)$	$ac \subseteq F(\mathbf{A}^{11}) \Rightarrow M(3, \mathbf{A}^{10}, \mathbf{A}^{11})$ $cd \not\cap F(\mathbf{A}^{11}) \Rightarrow M(2, \mathbf{A}^{11}, (b, c, a))$	$ab \subseteq F(\mathbf{A}^{11})$	$F(\mathbf{A}^{11}) = abd$
$\mathbf{A}^{12} = (b, cd, ad)$	$ad \subsetneq F(\mathbf{A}^{12}) \Rightarrow M(3, \mathbf{A}^{12}, \mathbf{A}^{11})$	$b \subseteq F(\mathbf{A}^{12})$	$F(\mathbf{A}^{12}) = abd$
$\mathbf{A}^{13} = (b, c, ad)$	$cd \subseteq F(\mathbf{A}^{13}) \Rightarrow M(2, \mathbf{A}^{12}, \mathbf{A}^{13})$ $ad \not\cap F(\mathbf{A}^{13}) \Rightarrow M(3, \mathbf{A}^{13}, (b, c, a))$	$bc \subseteq F(\mathbf{A}^{13})$	$F(\mathbf{A}^{13}) = abc$
$\mathbf{A}^{14} = (ab, c, ad)$	$ab \subsetneq F(\mathbf{A}^{14}) \Rightarrow M(1, \mathbf{A}^{14}, \mathbf{A}^{13})$ $abc = F(\mathbf{A}^{14}) \Rightarrow M(3, \mathbf{A}^{14}, \mathbf{A}^1)$	$c \subseteq F(\mathbf{A}^{14})$	Contradiction

Proof. Let F be a good mechanism for (b, m, n). We construct F' for (b, m, b) as follows. Given a profile $\mathbf{A}$ with b voters, copy each ballot q times to construct profile $\mathbf{A}^q$, and let $F'(\mathbf{A}) = F(\mathbf{A}^q)$. We show that F' satisfies both axioms, starting with proportionality. Note that, due to $d = 1$, the second proportionality condition is vacuously satisfied. Suppose that for some project p with cost $c(p)$, we have $|\{i \in N : A_i = \{p\}| \geqslant b \cdot \frac{c(p)}{b}$. Then q times as many (i.e., at least $n \cdot \frac{c(p)}{b}$) voters have ballot $\{p\}$ in $\mathbf{A}^q$. Since $p \in F(\mathbf{A}^q)$, also $p \in F'(\mathbf{A})$. For strategyproofness, suppose for the sake of contradiction that $F'(\mathbf{A}) \succ_i F'(\mathbf{A}_{-i}, S_i^\star)$ for some voter i with Paretian preferences. Then $F(\mathbf{A}^q) \succ_i F((\mathbf{A}_{-i}, S_i^\star)^q)$. Now, in $(\mathbf{A}_{-i}, S_i^\star)^q$, let the q voters corresponding to i switch, one by one, to the untruthful ballot A_i. This results in a sequence of q profiles, each of which is not strictly preferred over the former by i, since F is strategyproof. As for $d = 1$ the relation $\not\succ_i$ is transitive, we get $F(\mathbf{A}^q) \not\succ_i F((\mathbf{A}_{-i}, S_i^\star)^q)$, a contradiction. □

Lemma 4. *If there exists a good mechanism for $(b, m+1, n)$, then a good mechanism also exists for (b, m, n).*

Proof. Let F be a good mechanism for $(b, m + 1, n)$. We construct F' for (b, m, n). Add a dummy project $p^\star$ so that $F'(\mathbf{A}, P) = F(\mathbf{A}, P \cup \{p^\star\}) \setminus \{p^\star\}$ for every profile $\mathbf{A}$.[6] To show that F' satisfies proportionality, note that any project

---

[6] Observe that F' might not be exhaustive, with the implications discussed above.

in P satisfying the two conditions is selected by F if and only if it is selected by F'. The strategyproofness of F' follows directly from that of F since no voter approves of $p^\star$ in $\boldsymbol{A}$. □

Lemma 5. *If there exists a good mechanism for* $(b, m, n) = (k + 1, k + 2, k + 1)$, *then a good mechanism also exists for* $(k, k + 1, k)$.

Proof. Let F be a good mechanism for $(k + 1, k + 2, k + 1)$. We construct F' for $(k, k + 1, k)$. Given profile $\boldsymbol{A}^k$ with k voters and $k + 1$ projects in P^{k+1}, add a dummy project $p^\star$ with cost $c(p^\star) = 1$ to form P^{k+2} and a singleton ballot $\{p^\star\}$ to form $\boldsymbol{A}^{k+1}$. Now let $F'(\boldsymbol{A}^k, P^{k+1}) = F(\boldsymbol{A}^{k+1}, P^{k+2}) \setminus \{p^\star\}$. Note that, since F is proportional and $|\{i \in N : A_i = \{p^\star\}\}| = 1 \geqslant \frac{k+1}{k+1} \cdot c(p^\star)$, we always have $p^\star \in F(\boldsymbol{A}^{k+1}, P^{k+2})$, and so F' does not violate the budget constraint (i.e., F' is well-defined). For the proportionality of F', note that if a project $p \in P^{k+1}$ is approved of $\frac{k}{k} \cdot c(p)$ times in $\boldsymbol{A}^k$, it is also approved of $\frac{k+1}{k+1} \cdot c(p)$ times in $\boldsymbol{A}^{k+1}$. Since p is then selected by F, it is also selected by F'. For strategyproofness, again note that a strict preference between two outcomes of F' for a voter $i \in \{1, \ldots, k\}$ implies the same strict preference for the associated outcomes of F, since i does not approve of $\{p^\star\}$. Hence, the strategyproofness of F' follows from the strategyproofness of F. □

We are now ready to prove our theorem.

Proof *(of Theorem 1).* For the sake of contradiction, suppose there exists a good mechanism for some (b, m, n) with $b \geqslant 3$, $m > b$, and $n = q \cdot b$. Then, by Lemma 3, there exists such a mechanism for (b, m, b). Further, by repeated applications of Lemma 4 and Lemma 5, we can get a good mechanism for $(b, b + 1, b)$ and then for $(3, 4, 3)$. But this contradicts Lemma 2. □

Using a straightforward induction over the number of resources, we can generalise to the multi-resource setting and obtain the following corollary.

Corollary 1. *Let* $d \geqslant 1$, $R \subseteq \{1, \ldots, d\}$, $m > b_k \geqslant 3$ *for some* $k \in R$, *and* $n = q \cdot b_k$ *for some* $q \geqslant 1$. *Then no mechanism can guarantee both weak R-proportionality and strategyproofness against voters with R-Paretian preferences for d-resource PB scenarios with relevant resources R, budgets* $\boldsymbol{b} = (b_1, \ldots, b_d)$, m *projects, and* n *voters.*

To what extent this impossibility result can be strengthened further as well as whether relaxing some of our assumptions might allow for the design of attractive mechanisms are interesting open problems. For example, we do not know whether the impossibility persists for voters with subset preferences (the counterexample used for the proof of the base case still works, but some of the arguments used in the inductive lemmas do not). Similarly, we do not have a full picture regarding the impact of the constraints on the numerical parameters involved (such as n being a multiple of one of the budget limits) on the impossibility.[7] Finally, we do

---

[7] The question of whether these constraints can be relaxed is of some technical interest, but arguably less relevant to practice. Indeed, we would want our mechanism to work for *arbitrary* numbers of voters (including those that are multiples of a budget limit).

not know whether there are mechanisms for multi-resource PB that are weakly proportional and approximately strategyproof.[8]

4 Algorithms and Complexity

We now analyse each of the three mechanisms defined in Sect. 2.2 from a computational point of view. We also comment on how allowing for negative costs would affect our results.

4.1 The Greedy-Approval Mechanism

The greedy-approval mechanism F_G clearly can be executed in polynomial time. This remains true when we allow for negative costs. However, as illustrated by the following example, it is questionable whether a greedy mechanism is appropriate in the presence of negative costs.

Example 7. Consider a PB scenario with one resource and three projects, where $b_1 = 5$, $c_1(p_1) = c_1(p_2) = 3$, and $c_1(p_3) = -1$. Suppose p_1 has a higher approval score than p_2, which in turn has a higher score than p_3. Then F_G would first accept p_1 (reducing the budget to $5 - 3 = 2$), then skip p_2 (as it costs more than 2), and finally accept p_3. At this point, the remaining budget is $2 + 1 = 3$, so accepting p_2 would now be feasible. But that would amount to a form of backtracking (given that we now accept a project we previously rejected), which is not allowed under greedy algorithms in general and F_G in particular.

4.2 The Max-Approval Mechanism

For single-resource PB, Talmon and Faliszewski [28] sketch a polynomial-time algorithm implementing the max-approval mechanism F_M. As we shall see next, for multi-resource PB there can be no such algorithm, unless P = NP.

First, let us formally define a decision variant of the problem of maximising the approval score (for a fixed dimension d).[9]

MAXAPPSCORE$_d$

Instance: d-resource scenario $\langle P, c, b \rangle$, profile A, target $K \in \mathbb{N}$

Question: Is there a set $S \in \text{FEAS}(P, c, b)$ with $s_A(S) \geqslant K$?

---

[8] When all resources are relevant (in the single-resource case for instance), there is a trivial mechanism of this kind: simply return the union of all singletons satisfying condition (i) in the definition of proportionality. To see this, recall that condition (ii) is vacuous if there are only relevant resources.

[9] Recall that the approval score of a set S for a given profile A is defined as $s_A(S) = \sum_{i \in N} |S \cap A_i|$, and that F_M seeks to maximise that score.

This problem is closely related to the *d-dimensional knapsack problem* [15]. In particular, in the setting where $d = 2$ and there is just a single voter who approves of all projects, our problem is equivalent to the problem referred to as CARDINALITY (2-KP) by Kellerer et al. [15], which is a weakly NP-hard problem. This insight immediately implies the next result.

Proposition 3. *For any number $d \geqslant 2$ of resources, there exists no polynomial-time algorithm to compute outcomes under the max-approval mechanism F_M, unless* P = NP.

But note that weak NP-hardness still allows for the existence of pseudopolynomial-time algorithms. Indeed, the dynamic programming algorithm of Kellerer et al. [15] for the multidimensional knapsack problem can be applied directly (after translating the input profile into a vector of approvals per project). This yields the following observation.

Proposition 4. *For any fixed number d of resources, outcomes under the max-approval mechanism F_M can be computed in pseudopolynomial time.*

Mapping to a d-dimensional knapsack problem works only when d is a constant. This assumption is often reasonable: we typically have to deal with just a small number of resources (money, space, pollutants). However, we saw in Sect. 2.4 that encoding distributional or incompatibility constraints results in additional "technical" resources, the number of which grows with the number of projects. So it is important to also understand the complexity of F_M relative to d. To this end, we now introduce a variant of the decision problem defined earlier. Instances of this new problem are PB scenarios for arbitrary numbers of resources (rather than for some fixed dimension d).

MAXAPPSCORE

Instance: scenario $\langle P, \boldsymbol{c}, \boldsymbol{b} \rangle$, profile $\boldsymbol{A}$, target $K \in \mathbb{N}$
Question: Is there a set $S \in \text{FEAS}(P, \boldsymbol{c}, \boldsymbol{b})$ with $s_A(S) \geqslant K$?

To analyse the complexity of this problem, we employ a similar construction as the one we used to encode incompatibility constraints in the basic model (see Sect. 2.4). Observe that the following result rules out the possibility of the existence of a pseudopolynomial-time algorithm.

Proposition 5. MAXAPPSCORE *is strongly NP-hard.*

Proof. We proceed by reduction from the INDEPENDENT SET problem, asking whether a given graph $G = \langle V, E \rangle$ has an independent set of size K. This problem is known to be strongly NP-complete [7].

Given $G = \langle V, E \rangle$ and K, construct a d-resource PB scenario $\langle V, \boldsymbol{c}, \boldsymbol{b} \rangle$ with $d = |E|$: $c_k(p) = 1$ if the kth edge contains vertex p (and $c_k(p) = 0$ otherwise) and $b = (1, \ldots, 1)$. So a project set S is feasible if and only if S is an independent set in the original graph. Now consider a profile in which a single voter approves of all projects. Then an approval score of K is attainable if and only if the graph has an independent set of size K. □

Jain et al. [13] use the same kind of reduction to prove hardness for their model of PB with distributional constraints, which they call "project groups". As their model is a special case of ours, this thus entails Proposition 5. We nevertheless included our proof above as it is much easier to follow.

Finally, let us note that, while Propositions 3 and 5 clearly continue to hold when we allow for negative costs, the dynamic programming algorithm of Kellerer et al. [15] does not generalise to this setting.

4.3   The Sequential Load-Balancing Mechanism

Even though the definition of the sequential load-balancing mechanism F_L is rather involved, it is not difficult to show that it is a tractable mechanism.

Proposition 6. *Outcomes under the sequential load-balancing mechanism F_L can be computed in polynomial time.*

Proof. The claim follows immediately from the definition of the mechanism, given that executing F_L boils down to solving a polynomial number of linear programs, each of which is solvable in polynomial time [26]. □

Proposition 6 remains valid when we permit negative costs. But given the "greedy" nature of F_L, it is debatable whether it should be considered appropriate to use F_L in the presence of negative costs (just as it is debatable for F_G). Indeed, conceptually, a core feature of F_L, which arguably makes it a natural mechanism, is the fact that the load of each individual voter never decreases as we accept additional projects. This property is lost once we allow for negative costs.

5   Conclusion

We initiated the systematic study of PB with multiple resources. Our results indicate that—despite the significant increase in expressive power when moving from the single-resource to the multi-resource setting—devising attractive mechanisms does not become insurmountably harder, in either axiomatic or algorithmic terms. We hope that this will encourage others to further develop this approach and to, eventually, field it in real-world PB exercises.

Acknowledgements. This paper grew out of a student project that started in the context of a course on computational social choice at the University of Amsterdam in 2020. We acknowledge the contribution of Gerson Foks during that initial stage. We also would like to thank several anonymous reviewers for their feedback.

References

1. Aziz, H., Lee, B.E., Talmon, N.: Proportionally representative participatory budgeting: axioms and algorithms. In: Proceedings of the 17th International Conference on Autonomous Agents and Multiagent Systems (AAMAS) (2018)
2. Aziz, H., Shah, N.: Participatory budgeting: models and approaches. In: Rudas, T., Péli, G. (eds.) Pathways Between Social Science and Computational Social Science. CSS, pp. 215–236. Springer, Cham (2021). https://doi.org/10.1007/978-3-030-54936-7_10
3. Benade, G., Nath, S., Procaccia, A.D., Shah, N.: Preference elicitation for participatory budgeting. Manage. Sci. **67**(5), 2813–2827 (2021)
4. Brandt, F., Conitzer, V., Endriss, U., Lang, J., Procaccia, A.D. (eds.): Handbook of Computational Social Choice. Cambridge University Press, Cambridge (2016)
5. Faliszewski, P., Skowron, P., Slinko, A., Talmon, N.: Multiwinner voting: a new challenge for social choice theory. In: Endriss, U. (ed.) Trends in Computational Social Choice, chap. 2, pp. 27–47. AI Access (2017)
6. Fluschnik, T., Skowron, P., Triphaus, M., Wilker, K.: Fair knapsack. In: Proceedings of the 33rd AAAI Conference on Artificial Intelligence (AAAI) (2019)
7. Garey, M.R., Johnson, D.S.: Computers and Intractability: A Guide to the Theory of NP-Completeness. W.H, Freeman and Co (1979)
8. Geist, C., Peters, D.: Computer-aided methods for social choice theory. In: Endriss, U. (ed.) Trends in Computational Social Choice, chap. 13, pp. 249–267. AI Access (2017)
9. Goel, A., Krishnaswamy, A.K., Sakshuwong, S., Aitamurto, T.: Knapsack voting: voting mechanisms for participatory budgeting. ACM Trans. Econ. Comput. **7**(2), 8 (2019)
10. Goldfrank, B.: Lessons from Latin America's experience with participatory budgeting. In: Shah, A. (ed.) Participatory Budgeting, chap. 3, pp. 91–126. Public Sector Governance and Accountability Series, The World Bank, Washington, DC (2007)
11. Hershkowitz, D.E., Kahng, A., Peters, D., Procaccia, A.D.: District-fair participatory budgeting. In: Proceedings of the 35th AAAI Conference on Artificial Intelligence (AAAI) (2021)
12. Jain, P., Sornat, K., Talmon, N.: Participatory budgeting with project interactions. In: Proceedings of the 29th International Joint Conference on Artificial Intelligence (IJCAI) (2020)
13. Jain, P., Sornat, K., Talmon, N., Zehavi, M.: Participatory budgeting with project groups. In: Proceedings of the 30th International Joint Conference on Artificial Intelligence (IJCAI) (2021)
14. Janson, S.: Phragmén's and Thiele's election methods. arXiv preprint: arXiv:1611.08826 (2016)
15. Kellerer, H., Pferschy, U., Pisinger, D.: Multidimensional knapsack problems. In: Knapsack Problems, chap. 9, pp. 235–283. Springer, Heidelberg (2004). https://doi.org/10.1007/978-3-540-24777-7_9
16. Lackner, M., Maly, J., Rey, S.: Fairness in long-term participatory budgeting. In: Proceedings of the 30th International Joint Conference on Artificial Intelligence (IJCAI) (2021)
17. Laruelle, A.: Voting to select projects in participatory budgeting. Eur. J. Oper. Res. **288**(2), 598–604 (2021)

18. Patel, D., Khan, A., Louis, A.: Group fairness for knapsack problems. In: Proceedings of the 20th International Conference on Autonomous Agents and Multiagent Systems (AAMAS) (2021)
19. Peters, D.: Proportionality and strategyproofness in multiwinner elections. In: Proceedings of the 17th International Conference on Autonomous Agents and Multiagent Systems (AAMAS) (2018)
20. Peters, D.: Fair Division of the Commons. DPhil thesis, University of Oxford (2019)
21. Peters, D., Pierczynski, G., Skowron, P.: Proportional participatory budgeting with additive utilities. In: Proceedings of the 35th Annual Conference on Neural Information Processing Systems (NeurIPS) (2021)
22. Rey, S., Endriss, U., de Haan, R.: Designing participatory budgeting mechanisms grounded in judgment aggregation. In: Proceedings of the 17th International Conference on Principles of Knowledge Representation and Reasoning (KR) (2020)
23. Rey, S., Endriss, U., de Haan, R.: Shortlisting rules and incentives in an end-to-end model for participatory budgeting. In: Proceedings of the 30th International Joint Conference on Artificial Intelligence (IJCAI) (2021)
24. Rose, J., Omolo, A.: Six Case Studies of Local Participation in Kenya. The World Bank, Washington, DC (2013). http://hdl.handle.net/10986/17556
25. Sánchez-Fernández, L., Fernández-García, N., Fisteus, J.A., Brill, M.: The maximin support method: An extension of the d'Hondt method to approval-based multiwinner elections. Mathematical Programming (2022). (in press)
26. Schrijver, A.: Theory of Linear and Integer Programming. John Wiley & Sons, New York (1998)
27. Shah, A. (ed.): Participatory Budgeting. Public Sector Governance and Accountability Series, The World Bank, Washington, DC (2007)
28. Talmon, N., Faliszewski, P.: A framework for approval-based budgeting methods. In: Proceedings of the 33rd AAAI Conference on Artificial Intelligence (AAAI) (2019)

A Methodology for Formalizing Different Types of Norms

Soheil Roshankish[✉] and Nicoletta Fornara

Università della Svizzera Italiana, via G. Buffi 13, 6900 Lugano, Switzerland
{soheil.roshankish,nicoletta.fornara}@usi.ch

Abstract. In a world where many activities are carried out digitally, it is increasingly urgent to be able to formally represent the rules, norms, and policies that regulate these activities. In multi-agent systems, formalizing policies written in a natural language into a formal model, making them machine-readable, is a demanding task. In this paper, we introduce a methodology to help people to understand the fundamental elements that they should consider for this transformation. In this paper we will focus mainly on a methodology for formalizing norms using the T-Norm norm model, this because it allows us to express a rich set of different types of norms. In any case, the proposed methodology is general enough to also be used, in some of its steps, to formalize norms using other formal languages. This is an important issue because since there is not yet a set of different types of norms that is sufficiently expressive and is recognized as valid by the NorMAS community, papers presenting a given model usually do not explicitly state which types of norms can be expressed with that model and which cannot. Therefore, the second goal of this paper is to propose and discuss a rich set of norm types that could be used to study the expressive power of different formal models of norms and to compare them.

1 Introduction

In a world where many activities are carried out digitally, it is increasingly urgent to be able to formally represent the rules, norms, and policies that regulate these activities. By doing that, it is important to take into account that they are carried out by autonomous subjects who are able to decide to violate these rules. The activities regulated by the norms can be of various types and also include the very important ones related to the use, exchange and manipulation of the enormous amount of digital data that exist nowadays. Since these norms and policies can be violated (for example, it is very difficult to regiment obligations [8]) it is also urgent to propose mechanisms to automatically monitor compliance with these norms.

In the academic literature, there are an interesting number of general models of norms and policies. Some of these are close to being able to be used in real

Funded by the SNSF (Swiss National Science Foundation) grant no. 200021_175759/1.

applications in today's Web as they are expressed with standard Semantic Web Technologies, which is a crucial characteristics for realizing interoperable systems. One of them is the W3C Recommendation ODRL 2.2[1] (the Open Digital Rights Language), which is a policy expression language that provides an information model and a vocabulary for specifying permissions, prohibitions, and obligations about the usage of digital assets and services. Two others are the T-Norm model [10] and the OWL-POLAR model [19]. They are two semantic web based complementary models having an operational semantics for reasoning about norms and policies fulfillments and violations.

The papers that describe these models are mainly focused on the presentation of the model that is exemplified usually with the formalization of some examples of norms, regardless of their type. What is missing, however, is a *methodology* that explains what steps should be followed if one wants to start from a norm written in a natural language (e.g., English) and be able to choose the model for its formalization and use it to arrive at the formal specification of the norm, which can then be used to reason about it and verify its fulfillment or violation. Since there is not a commonly accepted set of *types of norms* in the literature, papers presenting a given model usually do not explicitly state which types of norms can be expressed with that model and which cannot. Thus in this paper we have the following two goals.

Our first goal is to explain the methodology that can be used by people to translate norms written in one natural language into a language specifically designed for the formal specification of norms. The proposed methodology consists in: first understand if the norm can be expressed with a certain model, that means to understand which *type* the norm belongs to and if the type is supported by the model; secondly come to a proper formalization of the norm using the chosen model, this by applying the methodology proposed in this paper. We will focus mainly on formalizing norms using the T-Norm norm model, this because it allows us to express a rich set of different types of norms. However, it is important to emphasize that the proposed methodology is general enough to also be used, in some of its steps, to formalize norms using other formal languages that have some similarities with the T-Norm model, such as at least OWL-POLAR and ODRL.

There are many reasons why it is interesting to specify norms using formal models. First, because norms become machine-readable, therefore it is possible to automatically analyse and query them like for example it is discussed in [15] where the PrivOnto ontology is used for analysing 115 privacy policies. For example, it will be possible to search the set of resources on which it is possible to perform certain actions based on the customers' interests. When a policy is formalized with a machine-readable formal language that has an operational semantics, it is also possible to provide services for compliance checking of policies [9,10,16,19]. This functionality plays an important role especially in domains in which the customers' sensitive data is collected and companies need to monitor the compliance of customers' privacy. This functionality is important

---

[1] https://www.w3.org/TR/odrl-model/.

also to create a trustworthy environment for customers by providing monitoring platform that they can use to see whether their privacy policies (norms) are violated or not. For instance, a customer can attach to one picture the prohibition to publish it on a public platform for advertisement and would like to monitor if the actions which are performed on the picture are compliant with this prohibition.

Another reason why it can be useful to specify norms with formal languages is that it becomes easier for humans to understand their actual meaning, which is not always as immediate as it should be. For example, during the Covid-19 pandemic, it was not always easy to immediately understand what norms are in effect at any given time in a specific location and whether they entail obligations or prohibitions to perform actions. Another example of norms whose meaning and implications are not always immediately clear to the reader are the various privacy policies that regulate the processing of our data when we browse websites and use social networks. Users often accept such policies in order to use online services often without fully understanding what they mean, this is because they are too long or complex.

The second goal of this paper is to propose and discuss a rich set of norm types that could be used to study the expressive power of different formal models of norms and to compare them. Knowing that a certain model of norms is or is not capable of expressing a certain type of norms is fundamental to deciding which model to adopt in a certain application context. For example, if a norm generates a specific obligation that has a deadline, it is necessary to choose a model of norms that allows to express this temporal constraint and to verify its fulfillment. Secondly, once it is clear that a certain type of norm can be expressed in both language A and language B, it will also be possible to translate norms written with the first language into norms written with the second. Thus making systems that use different norm models interoperable, a fundamental aspect in today's world where one software agent must be able to interact with multiple open interaction systems without having to be reprogrammed every time.

This paper is organized as follows: in Sect. 2 the most relevant and recent papers presenting a model for norms and policies specification in which semantic web technologies have been used are discussed. In Sect. 3 the T-Norm model is briefly presented. In Sect. 4 the methodology proposed in this paper is described and the set of different types of norms is discussed. Finally in Sect. 5 we draw some conclusions.

2   Related Works

In the multiagent systems community, over the last twenty years, many models of norms and policies for regulating the behaviour of autonomous agents have been proposed [2,6]. In some of these models semantic web technologies have been used for modeling some components of norms/policies that can be used for expressing obligations, prohibitions, and permissions. The first proposals were the KAoS framework [21], the REI [14] policy language, and the PRovisional

TrUst NEgotiation framework Protune [4]. Those approaches are summarized and compared in [5] where the requirements for a policy framework are discussed and the various approaches are categorized discussing whether the policies are public or not. For example, for the public policies, it is possible to use KAOS and REI frameworks as we need just one step evaluation to see if two policies are compatible. On the other hand, if a policy contains sensitive data, they are required to have *stateful and stateless negotiation* protocols for further security concerns.

An important policy language based on semantic web technologies, which is a W3C Recommendation since 15 February 2018, is the Open Digital Rights Language (ODRL 2.2). It is a policy expression language that can be used to represent permitted, prohibited, and obliged actions over a certain asset. ODRL policies may be limited by constraints (e.g., temporal or spatial constraints). ODRL was originally (in 2001) an XML language for expressing digital rights, that is, digital content usage terms and conditions. In version 2.0 and 2.1 ORDL is a Policy Language formalized in RDF with an abstract model specified by an ontology. It has no formal semantics, so compliance checking of policies written with this language cannot be performed automatically. An interesting attempt to give a formal semantics to ODRL 2.1 policies is presented in [20]. Some extensions of ODRL has been proposed to overcome to some of its limits. In particular, in [9] an extension of the ODRL Information Model has been proposed together with a set of state machines used for describing the evolution in time of the deontic state of obligations, prohibitions, and permissions. Another extension of ODRL is presented in [7] to model both regulatory policies (in the form of nested permissions, prohibitions, obligations and dispnesations), and business policies via discrete permissions. A policy written with that extension of the ODRL language is then translated into an Institutional Action Language (InstAL) policy and thanks to its formal semantics, expressed in Answer Set Programming, it is possible to automatically check compliance and also provide an explanation of the aspects of the policy that brings to the non-compliance. In [13] a specific use case drawn from the social networks field is used to validate the expressiveness of the ODRL 2.0 model.

Other two interesting proposals of a policy/norm model and framework, which are based on semantic web technologies, are OWL-POLAR [19] and T-Norm [10,11] models. Those policies/norms models and their expressivity will be discussed in Sect. 3. An interesting aspect that differentiates the two models is the way in which the two models define mechanisms to reason about policies to test whether agents' behavior satisfies them or not. In the OWL-POLAR a query answering mechanism (DL-safe) has been used to check if any action happened satisfies the policies. In the T-Norm model a rule-based approach is used that brings the generation of several deontic relations used to represent obligations and prohibitions generated by the activations of norms. In addition, the T-Norm model makes it possible to formalize the temporal constraints that exist between the activation of a norm and the class of actions regulated by the norm.

Other interesting models of norms that, like the T-Norm model, are rule-based are: the one proposed by Garcia-Camino et al. [12] where rules are operationalized using the JESS a rule engine for the Java platform; and the one proposed in [1] where reasoning on norms is realized with DROOLS a business rule management system. Another interesting proposal is the OASIS standard LegalRuleML[2], which defines a rule interchange language for the legal domain and is formalized using RuleML.

Logic and Knowledge Engineering Framework and Methodology (LOGIKEY) is another interesting framework which was introduced recently in [3]. The main objective of this framework is to enable and support the practical development of computational tools for normative reasoning based on formal methods. In their approach, they use higher-order logic (HOL) as the formal framework. They also used some GDPR examples to show how their framework supports the ethical and/or legal (ethico-legal) domains theories.

3   The T-Norm Model

The *T-Norm* model can be used to formalize a precise and rich set of *types of norms* that regulate the interactions between autonomous agents. Namely (as we will further discuss in the paper): (i) norms with a activation condition represented by a class of events; (ii) norms without an activation condition; norms that generate (iii) general or (iv) specific obligations or prohibitions to perform (or not to perform) actions that can be constrained to happen before something else happens, (v) exceptions to those norms; (vi) exceptions to obligations and prohibitions (i.e. exemptions and permissions respectively). Once a set of norms is formalized, a specific *framework* has been proposed to automatically check if the agents' behavior conforms or does not conform to the given set of norms. This is done by simulating or monitoring the evolution of the state of those set of norms as time passes, events occur and autonomous agents perform actions. The framework for norms monitoring has been proposed by taking into account the *operational semantics* of the T-Norm model. The model, its operational semantics, and the framework were introduced in [10,11].

The *T-Norm* model captures the following intuitive meaning of norms: whenever a particular *activation condition* is satisfied (i.e. an event that belongs to a particular class of events occurs) a *deontic relation* (general or specific) is created for regulating the performance of a class of actions by certain agents. In turn, every time an action belonging to the *class of the regulated actions* is executed before a certain event happens (for example a certain temporal event representing a deadline) and the deontic relationship represents an obligation it will be *fulfilled*, while if the deontic relation represents a prohibition it will be *violated*. On the contrary, when an action belonging to the class of regulated actions can no longer be performed (for example because the deadline has expired) and the deontic relationship represents an obligation it will be *violated*, while if the deontic relation represents a prohibition it will be *fulfilled*.

In order to formally describe such a dynamic behaviour, the abstract model of a norm cannot consists only of a set of facts (like it is in many models of

---

[2] https://www.oasis-open.org/committees/legalruleml/.

norms and policies, e.g. ODRL[3], OWL-POLAR [19], and the model proposed in
[1]). In all these models the intrinsically dynamic nature of norms is described
in their semantics or is left to their intuitive meaning described in the text.
The T-Norm model allows to specify how the performance of certain actions or
the occurrence of certain events will change the state of the interaction among
agents. Therefore the basic building blocks of the T-Norm abstract norm are
rules of the form ON...THEN...ELSE[4]. The abstract norm has not a pre-defined
deontic type, as discussed in Sect. 4, it is those who formally specify a norm who
will decide whether the norm activation creates obligations or prohibitions. In
the T-Norm model a generic abstract norm has the following form:

```
----------------------------------------------------------------
Abstract Norm
----------------------------------------------------------------
 1:  NORM Norm_n
 2:  [ON ?event1 WHERE conditions on ?event1
 3:   THEN
 4:     COMPUTE]
 5:     CREATE DeonticRelation(?dr);
 6:     ASSERT isGenerated(?dr,Norm_n); [activated(?dr,?event1);]
 7:     ON ?event2 [BEFORE ?event3 WHERE conditions on ?event3]
 8:        WHERE actor(?event2,?agent) AND conditions on ?event2
 9:     THEN ASSERT fulfills(?agent,?dr); fullfilled(?dr,?event2)|
10:                 violates(?agent,?dr); violated(?dr,?event2)
11:  [ELSE ASSERT violates(?agent,?dr); violated(?dr,?event3)|
12:                fulfills(?agent,?dr); fulfilled(?dr,?event3]
```

In the proposed model the first (optional) ON...THEN component (line 2,3)
is used for expressing those norms that have an activation condition. The second ON...THEN component (line 7,9) is used for expressing that when a specific
action, which belongs to the class of actions regulated by the norm, is performed
(before something else occurs) there will be a fulfillment or a violation. In alternative, the ELSE part of the second rule (line 11) will be followed when an action
that belongs to the class of the regulated actions can no longer be performed.

The *formulas* used in the abstract norm are conjunctions (in the WHERE part)
or sequences (in the CREATE and ASSERT part) of *atomic assertions* written using
the classes (unary predicates starting with capital letter) and the properties
(binary predicates starting with a lowercase letter) defined in the *T-Norm Ontology* depicted in Fig. 1[5]. Variables (starting with '?') refers to individuals. Variables used in the WHERE parts of the norm for expressing conditions on events
can be used freely and have to be bound to individuals in the *State Knowledge*

---

[3] https://www.w3.org/TR/odrl-model/.

[4] The ON clause has been chosen instead of the more common IF clause to highlight
that the part after THEN is executed when a particular event or action occurs and
not simply when a condition is satisfied.

[5] The T-Norm ontology in OWL is available at https://raw.githubusercontent.com/
fornaran/T-Norm-Model/main/tnorm.owl.

Base (where the interaction among agents is represented) for the conditions to be met. In the WHERE parts it is also possible to compare the value of a variable with a constant value using any of the symbols $\{<, >, =, \neq, \leq, \geq\}$. A constant is a numerical value or an individual in the ontology. Variables that appear in the ASSERT part of a norm must have been introduced previously in one of its ON or CREATE parts. In the COMPUTE part some values can be calculated (for example the deadlines) using the value of previously introduced variables[6].

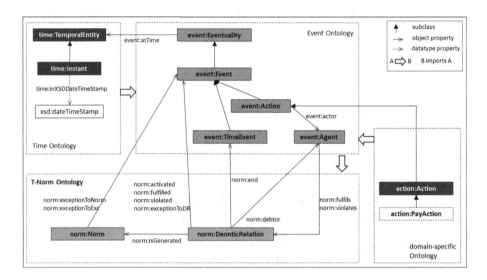

Fig. 1. The T-NORM ontology and its connections with other ontologies.

4   Methodology

In this section, we describe the various steps of the procedure to be followed to transform a norm written in a natural language (for example in English) into a norm written using a formal machine-readable language like the *T-Norm* model. As it will be discussed, some steps of the described procedure can also be used to formalize norms using the OWL-POLAR or the ORDL normative language. Starting from a norm expressed in natural language, following each step of the methodology, the *Abstract Norm*, introduced in the previous section, is made more concrete to the point of being the formalization of the norm from which the process started. In the following, we use two real running examples. We call

---

[6] The choice of using conjunctions or sequences of atomic assertions (analogously to what is proposed in OWL-POLAR to express the various components of their norm model) has the advantage of avoiding requiring the user of the model to learn a specific formal language, once written those expressions can be easily and automatically translated into the conditions or actions of production rules or into SPARQL queries.

the first example Norm1, which is inspired from the law regarding the access to limited traffic area in Milan city such that *"when an agent enters in the limited-traffic area of Milan, between 7:30 and 19:30, they have to pay 5 euros before 24:00 on the day of entry"*[7]. The second example, called Norm2, is the rule that must be followed by libraries in Italy regarding lending of DVDs, it is *"Italian libraries cannot lend DVDs until 2 years are passed from the distribution of the DVD"*[8].

4.1 Using Ontologies for Modeling Norms

In the first step of the procedure, we need to define (or search among the existing ones) one or more formal ontologies to represent the classes of events or actions that are relevant for the norm that we want to formalize. As it is discussed in the previous section, for every norm normally three *classes of events/actions* should be specified:

- The class of events that represent the activation condition of the norm (described using ?event1 in line 2 in the *Abstract Norm*);
- Te class of actions regulated by the norm (described using ?event2 in line 7,8 in the *Abstract Norm*);
- The class of events defined for constraining the performance of the actions regulated by the norm. One action, belonging to the class of the regulated ones, should or should not occur before an event belonging to this constraining class (described using ?event3 in line 7 in the *Abstract Norm*).

Those classes are specified in the WHERE parts of the norm and are represented using the classes and properties defined in formal ontologies. In the *T-Norm* model and in *OWL-POLAR* model, the W3C Web Ontology Language (OWL 2) is used for specifying ontologies. OWL is a Semantic Web language designed to represent knowledge about things, groups of things, and relations between things. An important advantage of using OWL is that it is a well-known standard language, which can make it easier for those who want to formalize their norms. Moreover, the formal semantics of OWL makes it possible to perform automatic reasoning on the state of the world, an operation that has important consequences on the computation of the *deontic force* (it is obliged or it is prohibited) associated to the actions performed by the agents. In ODRL the information model of the language is formalized using an OWL ontology, while the actions, the parties, and the assets involved in one ODRL policy are described using the ODRL Vocabulary[9].

It is possible to use several different ontologies for representing class of actions and their properties inside one T-Norm norm or one OWL-POLAR policy. For compatibility reasons, we suggest to use ontologies that are compatible with OWL ontologies, this because the chosen ontologies (each one referred to as

---

[7] https://www.comune.milano.it/aree-tematiche/mobilita/area-c.
[8] According to Art. 69 c.1 of the Copyright Law (22-4-1941, no. 633).
[9] https://www.w3.org/TR/odrl-vocab/.

domain-specific Ontology in Fig. 1) should be imported into the *Event Ontology* which is written by using the OWL language.

We will now exemplify the formalization of two classes of events necessary for the formalization of `Norm1`. `Norm1` is activated every time a vehicle enters the restricted traffic zone of the city of Milan. We assume that `RestrictedTraffic AreaAccess` is a class of actions, `vehicle` and `owner` are two properties having as domain the `RestrictedTrafficAreaAccess` class, which are defined in an OWL domain-specific Ontology. We can then specify the class of events that activates `Norm1` as (where `?event1` is shortened to `?e1`):

```
ON ?e1 WHERE RestrictedTrafficAreaAccess(?e1) AND vehicle(?e1,?v) AND
owner(?v,?agent) AND atTime(?e1,?inst1) AND inXSDDateTimeStamp(?inst1,?t1)
AND ?t1.time()>07:30:00 AND ?t1.time()<19:30:00
```

In the previous expression the variable `?agent` is introduced because it will be used in the second part of the norm to recognize who fulfills or violates the norm. After representing the activation condition of the norm, we need to formalize the class of actions regulated by the norm. For `Norm1`, the class of actions is the payment of 5 euros before 24:00 on the day of entry. For formalizing it we can for example use the `PayAction` class defined in the *Schema.org* vocabulary, which has an OWL version. *Schema.org* provides a collection of types and properties available at the URL `schema.org`. The major search engine providers use the Schema.org markup to improve the searching and the display of search results. This vocabulary has been designed by and is controlled by these organizations and represents an interesting attempt to realize a lightweight ontology that can be reused in different applications.

As mentioned earlier, the class of events described with the variable `?event3` has the role of constraining the time interval in which the action belonging to the class of actions regulated by the norm (`?event2`) shall or cannot be performed. In `Norm1`, the time interval when the payment action should be performed is constrained by a deadline (referred with the variable `?paymentDeadline`), i.e. the payment action must occur before 24:00 on the day of entry into the limited traffic zone. The formalization of norms where `?event3` is a time event are discussed in Sect. 4.4. To be able to express facts about the topological relationships (ordering) between instants and intervals, along with information about their length, and their value in terms of dates and times, we imported the *W3C Time Ontology*[10] into our *Event Ontology* both written in OWL. However, in the formalization of other norms the time constraint could be expressed with any class of actions (e.g. the payment must be made before leaving the restricted area) and in this case we will need to use another ontology to represent that class. The class of actions regulated by `Norm1` can be specified as (where `?e1` and `?agent` are variables introduced in the previous `ON` clause):

```
ON ?e2 BEFORE ?paymentDeadline
    WHERE PayAction(?e2) AND reason(?e2,?e1) AND recipient(?e2,Milan)
    AND price(?e2,5) AND priceCurrency(?e2,euro) AND actor(?e2,?agent)
```

---

[10] https://www.w3.org/TR/owl-time/.

4.2   Norms with Activation Condition

The goal of this section is to explain how to recognize whether a norm has an *activation condition* or not. In every norms or policy models the activation condition may describe a *class of events/actions* or as a *state of affairs*.

In the T-Norm model, the activation condition is the description of a particular class of events or actions. When an event that belongs to the activation condition class occurs, a new deontic relation is created and some temporal parameters may be computed. In order to recognize the activation condition in the text of a norm, we have to look for the events or actions that induce the model to activate obligations or prohibitions. The temporal relation between an event or action that satisfy the activation condition and the action that should or should not be performed is crucial: the activation condition must be satisfied before the obligation or the prohibition to perform a certain class of actions starts to hold. The instant of time at which the activation condition of a norm is satisfied by an event or action is very important because it can be used to calculate the deadline of obligations generated by the norm or the instant of time at which a prohibition ceases to subsist. For example in Norm1, the activation condition is represented by the class of actions regarding entering the Milan limited traffic zone and it is used for computing the deadline for the payment. In Norm2, the activation condition is given by the class of actions with which a DVD distribution is initiated. It is important to note that in the T-Norm model the activation condition cannot describe *a state of affairs*, although often a state of affairs is the result of an event and therefore the description of the class of events may substitute the description of the state of affairs as activation condition.

The reason why, in a norm model, a class of events and a state of affairs are treated differently is mainly due to their ontological difference: an event when it has happened it can no longer be retracted, a state of affairs can be satisfied at a certain instant of time and it can become unsatisfied subsequently. This is a crucial difference, because in the T-Norm model any satisfaction of the activation condition leads to the permanent creation of deontic relations. This permanent creation is important when the deontic relation regulates a class of actions that should or should not be performed in an interval of time and when the deontic relation itself can generate many violations and fulfillments as it is discussed below when Norm2 will be formalized.

The OWL-POLAR model for policies can be used when the activation condition α describes a state of affairs, like for example "a person is obliged to leave a location when there is a fire risk" or "when a person has a child which is under 18 they have to pay their tuition" [19]. In the OWL-POLAR model a policy is activated for a specific agent when the world state is such that the activation condition holds for that agent and the expiration condition does not hold. Therefore, at the time of activation it is necessary to know the specific agent for whom the policy is being activated, and this is not the case when the activation of a policy leads to the creation of *general deontic relations*, as will be discussed below. In the OWL-POLAR model the time constraint that exists between the initial satisfaction of the activation and the subsequent activation of the policy is not explicitly represented in the norms model, it is expressed in the description of how it is possible to reason about policies, therefore it is not in the model but inside the algorithm proposed for reasoning on policies.

There is another important distinction between an activation condition that describes a class of events and the one that describes a state of affairs. When it describe a state of affairs, it may make sense to ask whether the condition in the text should be formalized as an activation condition or as a set of conditions that restrict the class of actions regulated by the policy. For example in [18] *conditional norms* are discussed and the following example of a norm with a condition is described as: "it is prohibited to litter as long as there is a rubbish bin within x meters from an agent". The condition of being within x meters from a rubbish bin may be modelled as an activation condition in some cases, and it can be considered as a condition that constrains the class of actions regulated by the policy in other cases. In this second case the policy can be modelled with the T-Norm model, and it is a prohibition (without activation condition) to perform the following class of actions: littering when the actor of the action is within x metres from the rubbish bin. If one action belonging to that class is performed then there is a violation of the prohibition.

The choice between the first and the second formalization depends on the type of reasoning that the norm designer[11] wants to be able to perform on the policy. In the first case (with an activation condition) it is possible to compute if the policy is active in a given situation and therefore plan the action for fulfilling or violating it. When computing all the activations may be too costly and the goal of reasoning is monitoring the fulfillment or violation of the policy, the second formalization, without activation condition, is the more efficient because it does not require to compute the activation of many policies.

In the ODRL 2.2 model it is possible to express *constraints* associated to the rules contained in one policy and *refinements* associated to the actions regulated by one rule (a duty, a prohibition, or a permission). Reading the documentation that provides the meaning of a prohibition or duty, the constraint can be used to express the activation condition, but again, like in OWL-POLAR, the temporal constrains between the satisfaction of the activation condition and the performance of the action regulated by the rule is not explicitly expressed in the model. Therefore, when the activation condition is a state of affairs the policy designer has to choose weather it is better to put the conditions in the constraint or in the refinement. Differently, when the activation condition of the norm is represented by a class of events, by using the ODRL 2.2 and OWL-POLAR models it is impossible to specify in the norm formalization the need to compute at run-time the value of the deadline and it is impossible to model those policies that when are activated generates *general* deontic relations.

---

[11] The term "norm designer" refers to the person in charge of formalizing norms with a formal model.

4.3   Representing Obligations and Prohibitions

In this section, we describe how we can distinguish if a norm generates an obligation or prohibition and how to express them using the T-Norm model. In contrary with other approaches such as OWL-POLAR and ODRL, in the T-Norm model there is not a component or a predefined class that may be used to specify if the norm express an obligation or a prohibition. The advantage of this approach is that both obligation and prohibitions can be expressed starting from the same abstract norm and there is not need to formalize the semantics or a state machine (like in [9]) for obligations, another one for prohibitions, and others for other deontic concepts like permission, right, privilege, liability and so on. However, in this Section we focus only on obligation and prohibition.

In the T-Norm model the intuitive meaning of having an obligation or prohibition is that when something happens and certain conditions hold, an agent is obliged or prohibited to do something in a given interval of time. We can use few basic constructs and combine them in different ways to express the obligation to perform an action before a given deadline or the prohibition to perform an action within an interval of time. The main difference in representing a prohibition or an obligation is in the second THEN part of the norm. If the norm designer wants to formalize the obligation to perform an action, performing the regulated action must bring to the specification of the fulfillment of the deontic relation in the THEN part of the norm. The ELSE part have to be used to specify that in case on instance of the class of actions regulated by the policy cannot be performed before than a given event happens the deontic relation, representing the obligation, becomes violated. On the contrary, if the norm designer wants to formalize the prohibition to perform an action (described in the second ON part of the norm) in the specific interval of time, performing the action will bring to the violation of the deontic relation in the second THEN part. Once the prohibited action can no longer be performed (for example, the time interval has expired) the prohibition becomes fulfilled.

As we know from deontic logic literature [22] the expression "it is impermissible (IM) that p" is defined as equivalent to "it is obligatory (OB) that not p" ($IMp = defOB\neg p$). This implies that some norms may be either formalized as an obligation or as a prohibition. When a norm is formalized with the T-Norm model and the activation of the norm brings to the creation of *general deontic relations*, it is very important to evaluate which of the two formalizations would be most cost-effective. That is because, as discussed below, every general deontic relation created by the activation of a norm, may in turn bring to the costly generation of many fulfillments and violations. For example, the norm "when the school bell rings, students should go back to the classrooms in five minutes" can be formalized as a norm that generates obligations or prohibitions. Suppose that the person in charge of formalizing the norm is only interested in computing the violations of the norm. In the first scenario, if we formalize the norm as a generator of obligations, when the activation condition is satisfied because the school bell rings, the norm generates a general deontic relation that will generate fulfillments for all those students who respect the school rule and go back to their classrooms, and violations for those students who did not fulfill the rule before the deadline. In the second scenario, it is possible to formalize such a norm as a generator of prohibitions by reframing it as follows "when five minutes have elapsed since the bell rang, students cannot remain in the court-yard". The formalization of this norm is much easier and cost-effective as we only need to check the violations that are generated for those students who stay in the courtyard.

4.4   Temporal Aspect of Norms

The ability to represent time-constrained norms is one important characteristics of the T-Norm model. Unlike the OWL-POLAR model, in the T-Norm model can be used by the norm designer to easily represent any obligations containing deadlines (that are represented as time events) and prohibitions that holds for an interval of time. A norm governs a class of actions and, as can be seen from the abstract norm in Sect. 3, that class can be temporally constrained by specifying the BEFORE part and another class of events (?event3). The latter class can be specified using the TimeEvent class or the more generic Event class depicted in Fig. 1.

The TimeEvent class is used for specifying a deadline for obligations or the instant at when a time interval for prohibitions ends. In this case the value of the deadline or the end of the time interval can be computed in the COMPUTE part of the norm as exemplified below. For example, in Norm01, an agent is obliged to perform the *paying* action before midnight (the deadline). In Norm02, the time interval in which Italian libraries cannot lend DVDs begins with the release of the DVD and ends after 2 years. Norm2 can be represented with the T-Norm model as follows:

```
------------------------------------------------------------------
Norm2
------------------------------------------------------------------
ON ?e1
 WHERE isReleased(?e1) AND object(?e1,?dvd) AND VideoObject(?dvd) AND
 place(?e1;Italy) AND atTime(?e1,?inst1) AND inXSDDateTimeStamp(?inst1,?t1)
THEN
 COMPUTE ?tend_n=?t1.year+2
 CREATE DeonticRelation(?dr);TimeEvent(?tev_end_n);Instant(?inst_end_n);
 ASSERT isGenerated(?dr,Norm2); activated(?dr,?e1); end(?dr,?tevend_n);
        atTime(?tev_end_n,?inst_end_n);
        inXSDDateTimeStamp(?inst_end_n,?tend_n);
ON ?e2 BEFORE ?tev_end_n
 WHERE LendAction(?e2) AND object(?e2,?dvd) AND actor(?e2,?agent)
 THEN    violates(?agent;?dr); violated(?dr,?e2)
```

The CREATE and ASSERT parts of the norm above, which specify the charac-teristics of the time event used to constrain the class of actions governed by the norm, represent a prototype of what these two parts look like in all such type of norms.

On the other hand, if the temporal constraint (?event3) belongs to a generic Event class (or one of its subclasses), it is not necessary to compute anything. This means that the regulated action is temporally constrained by another generic class of events. For example, in the norm "You should pay the parking ticket before exiting", there exists no deadline for the payment action, but the payment action must be performed before leaving the parking area with one's car. This event should be specified in the WHERE part used to describe ?event3.

In literature there exist approaches, such as [17], in which they used temporal logics such as Linear Temporal Logic (LTL) for representing time-constrained norms. Nevertheless, using these approaches present some difficulties when it comes to the automatic reasoning on the evolution of the normative state from activated to fulfilled or violated.

4.5   Specific and General Deontic Relations

In the T-Norms model, a norm can create several deontic relations when the activation condition of the norm is satisfied. Such deontic relations may belong to one of the following two categories: *specific deontic relations* and *general deontic relations*.

A specific deontic relation is generated, when the regulated action should be performed by a specific agent, e.g. in Norm1, for each vehicle entering into the limited traffic area an obligation to pay for the owner of the vehicle is generated. In the specific deontic relations, the debtor, the owner of the vehicle, is known. Therefore, in case of any violation, the system can recognize who violated the deontic relation. The specific deontic relations generated by Norm1 have a debtor property that connects the deontic relation with the agent that is the owner of the vehicle: ASSERT ... debtor(?dr, ?agent).... This property has to be inserted in the ASSERT part of the norm for all those norms that generate specific deontic relations.

The second type of deontic relations is the general deontic relations. The main difference between general deontic relations and specific deontic relations is that in the first one we do not have any knowledge about the debtor of the class of actions regulated by the norm and the action can be performed by a set of agents, for example in Norm2 by all the people registered in one library. For that reason, we cannot have any predefined estimation about which agent is going to violate or fulfill the deontic relation. It is possible to have many violations and many fulfillments of the same deontic relation. For example Norm2 is activated for every new distribution of a DVD. The general deontic relation created by the activation of Norm2 regulates the actions of lending such a DVD by all the Italian libraries, the debtor is not one specific agent.

Another significant difference between OWL-POLAR and the T-Norm model is in formalizing norms that generates general deontic relations. In OWL-POLAR a policy can only be activated for a specific agent therefore the type of norms that when activated regulate the actions of a set of agents cannot be represented. This is due to the design choice to propose a model for reasoning on policies that does not create deontic relations. In ODRL it not specified the mechanism for reasoning on policies activations.

5 Conclusions

In this paper, we introduced a methodology that explains how a norm designer can formalize norms written in a natural language into a machine-readable format by understanding the types of the norms and choosing the proper model. As it is discussed in the previous section the norm can be: (i) a norm with or without an activation condition; (ii) if there is an activation condition it can be represented by a class of events or by a state of affairs; (iii) a norm can express obligations or a prohibitions; (iv) a norm can regulate a class of actions that is time constrained or not; (v) finally a norm can generate specific or general deontic relations. In our future works we plan to extend the methodology by discussing the formalization of exceptions to norms and in particular of permissions and exemptions and the definition of institutional powers for manipulating norms.

References

1. Alvarez-Napagao, S., Aldewereld, H., Vázquez-Salceda, J., Dignum, F.: Normative monitoring: semantics and implementation. In: De Vos, M., Fornara, N., Pitt, J.V., Vouros, G. (eds.) COIN -2010. LNCS (LNAI), vol. 6541, pp. 321–336. Springer, Heidelberg (2011). https://doi.org/10.1007/978-3-642-21268-0_18
2. Andrighetto, G., Governatori, G., Noriega, P., van der Torre, L.W.N. (eds.) Normative Multi-Agent Systems, vol. 4 of Dagstuhl Follow-Ups. Schloss Dagstuhl - Leibniz-Zentrum für Informatik (2013)
3. Benzmüller, C., Parent, X. van der Torre, L.: Designing normative theories for ethical and legal reasoning: LogiKEy framework, methodology, and tool support. Artif. Intell. **287**, 103348 (2020)
4. Bonatti, P., Olmedilla, D.: Driving and monitoring provisional trust negotiation with metapolicies. In: Sixth IEEE International Workshop on Policies for Distributed Systems and Networks (POLICY 2005), pp. 14–23 (2005)
5. Bonatti, P.A., Olmedilla, D.: Rule-based policy representation and reasoning for the semantic web. In: Antoniou, G., et al. (eds.) Reasoning Web 2007. LNCS, vol. 4636, pp. 240–268. Springer, Heidelberg (2007). https://doi.org/10.1007/978-3-540-74615-7_4
6. Chopra, A., van der Torre, L., Verhagen, H., Villata, S., (eds.) Handbook of Normative Multiagent Systems. College Publications, August 2018
7. De Vos, M., Kirrane, S., Padget, J., Satoh, K.: ODRL policy modelling and compliance checking. In: Fodor, P., Montali, M., Calvanese, D., Roman, D. (eds.) RuleML+RR 2019. LNCS, vol. 11784, pp. 36–51. Springer, Cham (2019). https://doi.org/10.1007/978-3-030-31095-0_3
8. Fornara, N., Colombetti, M.: Specifying and enforcing norms in artificial institutions: a retrospective review. In: Sakama, C., Sardina, S., Vasconcelos, W., Winikoff, M. (eds.) DALT 2011. LNCS (LNAI), vol. 7169, pp. 117–119. Springer, Heidelberg (2012). https://doi.org/10.1007/978-3-642-29113-5_12
9. Fornara, N., Colombetti, M.: Using semantic web technologies and production rules for reasoning on obligations, permissions, and prohibitions. AI Commun. **32**(4), 319–334 (2019)

10. Fornara, N., Roshankish, S., Colombetti, M.: A framework for automatic monitoring of norms that regulate time constrained actions. In: Proceedings of the International Workshop on Coordination, Organizations, Institutions, Norms and Ethics for Governance of Multi-Agent Systems (COINE), co-located with AAMAS 2021, 3rd May 2021, London, UK, 2021 (2021)

11. Fornara, N., Sterpetti, M.: An architecture for monitoring norms that combines OWL reasoning and forward chaining over rules. In: E.M.S. et al. (eds.) Proceedings of the Joint Ontology Workshops 2021 Episode VII: The Bolzano Summer of Knowledge co-located with the 12th International Conference on Formal Ontology in Information Systems (FOIS 2021), and the 12th International Conference on Biomedical Ontologies (ICBO 2021), Bolzano, Italy, 11–18 September 2021, volume 2969 of CEUR Workshop Proceedings. CEUR-WS.org (2021)

12. Garcia-Camino, A., Noriega, P., Rodriguez-Aguilar, J.A.: Implementing norms in electronic institutions. In: Proceedings of the Fourth International Joint Conference on Autonomous Agents and Multiagent Systems, AAMAS 2005, New York, NY, USA, pp. 667–673. ACM (2005)

13. Governatori, G., Iannella, R.: A modelling and reasoning framework for social networks policies. Enterp. Inf. Syst. **5**(1), 145–167 (2011). Feb

14. Kagal, L.: A Policy-Based Approach to Governing Autonomous Behavior in Distributed Environments. Ph.D. thesis, University of Maryland Baltimore County, Baltimore MD 21250, September 2004

15. Oltramari, A., et al.: Privonto: a semantic framework for the analysis of privacy policies. Semant. Web **9**(2), 185–203 (2018)

16. Padget, J., Vos, M.D., Page, C.A.: Deontic sensors. In: Proceedings of the Twenty-Seventh International Joint Conference on Artificial Intelligence, IJCAI-2018, pp. 475–481. International Joint Conferences on Artificial Intelligence Organization, July 2018

17. Panagiotidi, S., Alvarez-Napagao, S., Vázquez-Salceda, J.: Towards the norm-aware agent: bridging the gap between deontic specifications and practical mechanisms for norm monitoring and norm-aware planning. In: Balke, T., Dignum, F., van Riemsdijk, M.B., Chopra, A.K. (eds.) COIN 2013. LNCS (LNAI), vol. 8386, pp. 346–363. Springer, Cham (2014). https://doi.org/10.1007/978-3-319-07314-9_19

18. Savarimuthu, B.T.R., Cranefield, S., Purvis, M.A., Purvis, M.K.: Identifying conditional norms in multi-agent societies. In: De Vos, M., Fornara, N., Pitt, J.V., Vouros, G. (eds.) COIN -2010. LNCS (LNAI), vol. 6541, pp. 285–302. Springer, Heidelberg (2011). https://doi.org/10.1007/978-3-642-21268-0_16

19. Sensoy, M., Norman, T.J., Vasconcelos, W.W., Sycara, K.P.: OWL-POLAR: a framework for semantic policy representation and reasoning. J. Web Semant. **12**, 148–160 (2012)

20. Steyskal, S., Polleres, A.: Towards formal semantics for ODRL policies. In: Bassiliades, N., Gottlob, G., Sadri, F., Paschke, A., Roman, D. (eds.) RuleML 2015. LNCS, vol. 9202, pp. 360–375. Springer, Cham (2015). https://doi.org/10.1007/978-3-319-21542-6_23

21. Uszok, A., et al.: Kaos policy and domain services: toward a description-logic approach to policy representation, deconfliction, and enforcement. In: Proceedings POLICY 2003. IEEE 4th International Workshop on Policies for Distributed Systems and Networks, pp. 93–96 (2003)

22. von Wright, G.H.: Deontic logic. Mind, New Ser. **60**(237), 1–15 (1951)

Explainability in Mechanism Design: Recent Advances and the Road Ahead

Sharadhi Alape Suryanarayana[1,2(✉)], David Sarne[1], and Sarit Kraus[1]

[1] Department of Computer Science, Bar-Ilan University, Ramat Gan, Israel
sharadhi.as@gmail.com, david.sarne@biu.ac.il, sarit@cs.biu.ac.il
[2] Centre for Ubiquitous Computing, University of Oulu, Oulu, Finland

Abstract. Designing and implementing explainable systems is seen as the next step towards increasing user trust in, acceptance of and reliance on Artificial Intelligence (AI) systems. While explaining choices made by black-box algorithms such as machine learning and deep learning has occupied most of the limelight, systems that attempt to explain decisions (even simple ones) in the context of social choice are steadily catching up. In this paper, we provide a comprehensive survey of explainability in mechanism design, a domain characterized by economically motivated agents and often having no single choice that maximizes all individual utility functions. We discuss the main properties and goals of explainability in mechanism design, distinguishing them from those of Explainable AI in general. This discussion is followed by a thorough review of the challenges one may face when working on Explainable Mechanism Design and propose a few solution concepts to those.

Keywords: Explainability · Mechanism design · Justification

1 Introduction

Intelligent systems and automated decision-making are replacing and enhancing human decision-making nowadays to the extent that people are increasingly reliant on them [42]. Despite the increased presence of such systems, people are not often aware that they are interacting with an AI-based system. Recognizing the need for transparency in this evolving policy and technology ecosystem, the ACM U.S. Public Policy Council (USACM) and ACM Europe Council Policy Committee (EUACM) codified a set of principles such as awareness, explainability, accountability, validation and testing to address this [20]. Among which, *Explainability*, which could be understood as a description in some form of the functioning of the system, has gained immense traction in the recent past.

Due to their opacity, domains with black-box algorithms like machine learning and deep learning have been extensively researched in the context of explainability. However, the need for explainability goes far beyond black-box algorithms. For example in various multi-agent systems (MAS), where agents are self-interested, commonly arises a need to aggregate private preferences such as

© The Author(s), under exclusive license to Springer Nature Switzerland AG 2022
D. Baumeister and J. Rothe (Eds.): EUMAS 2022, LNAI 13442, pp. 364–382, 2022.
https://doi.org/10.1007/978-3-031-20614-6_21

availability, budget constraints and geographical location of several agents into a collective decision in a socially desirable way. Mechanism design, an important tool in economics and computer science, is one such research topic which is concerned with the development of a mechanism that takes into consideration the preferences of selfish and intelligent agents exhibiting strategic behavior while adhering to norms such as envy-freeness, budget-balancing and pareto-optimality [57]. The applications of mechanism design can be found in various real-world and, in many cases, high-impact applications such as elections, rent division, resource allocation, and stable matching [28,57].

Regardless of their extensive usage in the real-world, there is a renewed interest in designing and analyzing mechanisms to align with human values. This includes re-designing existing mechanisms to accommodate human preferences [18], viewing existing practices for inclusive housing allocation from a game-theoretic perspective [8], empirical studies on human behavior [66], using the insights from empirical analyses to re-frame a mechanism [52], and devising algorithms to justify the decision of a mechanism [9]. Explaining the results to human participants is a natural and complementary extension to the pursuit of designing mechanisms that are more "understandable" to humans.

Nevertheless, the road to Explainable Mechanism Design systems is replete with its own share of hurdles. One key element in providing an explanation in such domains is the goal of the explanation and the measures of its success— whereas with a single user the system's goal is known, hence the explanation aims to improve her recognition of the optimality of the choice made, in settings of mechanism design, a user does not always know the system's goals since they may depend on other agents' preferences. This focus on preference aggregation of multiple agents, often associated with conflicting goals, may lead to a blatant compromise of the preferences of some of them. The explanations should therefore aim to increase user satisfaction by taking into account the system's decision, the user's and the other agents' preferences, the environment settings, and properties such as fairness, envy and privacy [29]. In addition to the above intricacies, the presence of domains such as voting, scheduling and resource allocation in popular culture, without the necessity to be theoretically aware, has led to people forming their own irrational opinions which the explanations have to uproot [16,38,67].

We also note that even cases where social choice is merely a particular step in a multi-stage decision making process carried out by an agent making decisions on behalf of humans, call for Explainable Mechanism Design. This can hold even when the use of mechanism design is not explicit. Examples of such settings include algorithmic hiring and virtual democracy (an approach to automated decision making) which is used in autonomous vehicles and kidney exchanges to automate moral decisions, and recommendation systems to allocate food donations to recepient organizations [18,36,49,62].

In this survey, we provide a comprehensive summary of the various threads of explainability in mechanism design. We note that while the broad theme of explainability translates to the same meaning with respect to both machine learning and mechanism design, there are a few differences between the premises of the two fields in terms of what leads up to generating explanations. In particular, we first provide a comparison between Explainable Mechanism Design and Explainable AI (XAI) with respect to the taxonomy, the purpose of explanations and who the explainees are. We then outline the methods of generating explanations in mechanism design. Finally, we elaborate on the challenges of conducting laboratory experiments on explainability in mechanism design and shed light on solution concepts combining insights from XAI and behavioral studies.

2 Mechanism Design

Various definitions for mechanism design have been suggested over the years [47,53]. Essentially, a mechanism can be seen as a "communication system" where the participants send messages to each other and/or to a "message center" and every collection of messages is assigned an outcome based on a pre-specified rule [25]. These messages are characterized by private information such as utility from an allocation (in rent division), preference over a set of candidates (in social choice theory), or willingness to pay for a good (in auctions). Thus, the mechanism is analogous to a machine that collects, processes and aggregates the private information of several agents in order to reach a desirable social outcome. In most cases the agents are self-interested and rational, and care only about maximizing their private utility with no guarantee that they will tell the truth. Therefore, a desired property of a mechanism is that the agents have no strategic incentive to deviate from truth-telling [33]. A mechanism satisfying this property is considered *incentive-compatible*, as every participating agent achieves the best outcome by reporting her true preferences [33].

Since incentive-compatibility is a desired feature, most mechanisms are designed to be incentive-compatible. Hence, even though truth-telling might fetch the least utility, say not winning the Vickrey-Clarke-Groves (VCG) auction [33], it is the best response for an agent in most mechanisms. However, as we observe in Sect. 7, due to repeated interactions, humans may be prone to their own biases. Explanations could be a tool to mitigate user biases as well.

The two main branches of designing mechanisms are the axiomatic branch and the Bayesian branch [14]. In the axiomatic branch, the solution is supposed to satisfy a set of desired properties called axioms. Axioms are normative elements designed to conceptualize notions of reason such as fairness, justice and efficiency. Examples of such axioms include envy-freeness and pareto-optimality. In the Bayesian branch the solution achieves an optimal value for a given objective function such as expected revenue or projected loss.

3 Motivations for Explainable Mechanism Design

Consider the example of a rent division problem with 3 housemates, 3 rooms with a total rent of $3. Housemate i values room i at $3 and the other two rooms at $0. One possible solution to this problem is to assign room 1 to housemate 1 at $3 and rooms 2 and 3 to housemates 2 and 3 for free. Even though from an inter-personal perspective, this solution seems blatantly unfair to housemate 1, it is an envy-free solution, hence theoretically acceptable. Housemate 1 is indifferent between the three rooms, given their cost, while housemates 2 and 3 are overjoyed [19]. While this is an overblown depiction of the problem with a rent division setting which has seen an immense improvement in the solutions proposed over the years [19], it is sufficient to illustrate the complexity with respect to devising explanations in mechanism design settings.

As explained in the former section, solutions in mechanism design are obtained by aggregating the preferences of several agents. The nature of the problem necessitates a "social approach" where the solution is expected to aggregate said preferences in some acceptable manner. This can be achieved by mandating the solution to adhere to certain desirable criteria that are egalitarian in nature, maximizing a criterion of social welfare or using any other method that appreciates the social nature of the problem. The need to balance the preferences of several agents, which could be conflicting in nature might result in the solution not being in favor of a few of them. Multi-user Privacy Conflict due to varying privacy preferences of owners of shared content [43], multi-attribute settings such as *team formation* where the solution might not adhere to the preferences of all of the agents with respect to every attribute [21] and settings such as the classical "glove game" where the solution is non-intuitive yet theoretically sound [48] are other real-life examples of mechanism design that necessitate a nuanced approach to obtain the solution as well as to devise explanations.

In addition to the social nature of the problem, solutions in mechanism design face two hurdles. First, the issue of what is socially acceptable can vary according to perception, context and domain which can result in multiple solutions for the same problem. For example, in social choice theory, there are multiple voting rules due to the absence of a unique voting rule that satisfies Arrow's mandatory principles of fairness [5]. The second problem which is a consequence of the first, is that it is easy for the user to challenge the solution. This requires the explanations to not only elaborate on how good the solution is but also how problematic another solution is.

This is in sharp contrast with other domains such as machine learning, planning and recommender systems where a solution, good or bad, results from a definite and often complicated algorithm which needs to be broken down for user understanding [15,42,69]. While solutions in other settings can also rely on metrics such as accuracy, the absence of a unique algorithm in mechanism design settings makes this problem hard as well. Hence, instead of arguing on the theoretical accuracy of the decision or how it results from a particular algorithm which is a common trait in the aforementioned domains, the focus of explanations in mechanism design should be on arguing how the decision is "good" in its social context and how the preferences of the agents have led to the solution.

4   Explainable Mechanism Design Versus XAI

While both Explainable Mechanism Design and XAI aim to explain certain decisions made by the system, in retrospect, there are several factors differentiating the two. Owing to the differences in the domains and the solution concepts, there is an obvious difference in the nature of explanations offered in Explainable Mechanism Design and XAI. One way to reason about the differences in the nature of the explanation to be offered, is by considering the differences in the taxonomy to be used, the explainee and the goals of the explanations. Hence, we focus our comparison in these aspects. Since XAI has become a well established research area, whereas Explainable Mechanism Design is a newly emerging field, we use the first to lead the discussion, mapping and contrasting equivalent notions of Explainability in Mechanism Design accordingly.

4.1 Taxonomy

The common types of Explanations that are found in Explainability Studies are *Explanations*, *Justifications* and *Interpretations*. With respect to mechanism design, the most relevant and consequently most researched capability is Justifiability. *Justifications* deal with explaining the system's decision in terms of acceptable societal norms [32]. These norms (i.e. axioms that formalize desirable social concepts such as fairness, justice and efficiency) are the foundation of many mechanisms. Hence they are natural and, in many cases, effective contenders for explanations [9,48,57].

While there is no consensus on what constitutes an *Explanation* in mechanism design, we adopt the idea proposed by Langley [32], who states that *an intelligent system exhibits explainable agency if it can provide, on request, the reasons for its activities*. Still, the extent of research dedicated to this capability is somehow limited (see Table 1 later on). As for *Interpretability*, this notion is completely absent from Explainable Mechanism Design.

For example, in the domain of fair division, explaining the decision by highlighting how the decision is envy-free is a *Justification* [35]. However, comparing the maximin solution (the solution that maximizes the minimum utility for every player thus resulting in the least disparity) to an arbitrary envy-free solution to demonstrate the superiority of the former solution amounts to an *Explanation* [19].

However, in XAI, the relationship of Explanations and Justifications to the algorithm are reversed. Here, *Explanations* act as an accurate proxy of the model while still being understandable to the human users [4] and *Justifications* defend the decision of the algorithm by explaining why it is a good one without necessarily focusing on how the decision was made [59]. While nearly absent from *Explainable Mechanism Design*, Interpretability which aims to enhance user understanding and comprehension of the model's decision-making process and predictions [42] through *Interpretations* [59] is rigorously researched in XAI. It is also interesting to note that *Justifiability* is the most researched capability in *Explainable Mechanism Design* since there is a need to show how the decision abides by desirable social norms while the need to explain the functioning of black-box nature of the algorithms has led to *Explainability* and *Interpretability* enjoying the most attention from the XAI research community.

4.2   Explanation Purpose

Explanations may be provided for various purposes and goals, with partial equivalences between Explainable Mechanism Design and XAI.

Appreciating System Decision-Making. In Explainable Mechanism Design, an appreciation of the system's decision translates to understanding how the preferences of the different agents are combined to obtain a collective decision [9]. This is akin to understanding how different features contribute to the output in a machine learning model [31], which is the focus of XAI. Still, as explained in Sect. 3, the task of increasing user appreciation of the system's decision making is more challenging in mechanism-design settings, as decisions need to be explained in their wider social context and are often plagued with impossibility theorems [5,60].

Improving User Trust and Reliability. With the decision depending on the preferences of several agents, dissatisfaction is an inevitable evil in mechanism design which might affect the user's trust and reliability. The explanations presented thus need to argue about the legitimacy of the decision and how, even if the decision is unfair to a particular agent, the mechanism as a whole has adhered to mandatory principles of fairness and the dissatisfied agent needs to make peace with it [29]. In fact, as demonstrated in the work of Suryanarayana et al. [65], it is often the explanations provided to those participants for whom the winning candidate is the least preferred that are the most impactful. In XAI, unfavorable situations are also present (e.g., rejection of a loan application), however the prospect of improving the odds of the decision being in her favor through *Counterfactual Explanations* exists [44]. This, unfortunately, cannot be achieved in *Explainable Mechanism Design.*

Ensuring Accuracy of Decision-Making. In mechanism design, explanations can serve as a tool for the verification of results in order to ensure that the decision was made under a set of rules consistently applied in each setting [7]. This somehow resembles the use of XAI as a tool for bias mitigation and fairness assessment [42] in cases where datasets are potentially biased and decision-making might be discriminatory.

4.3   The Explainee

The nature and mode of the explanation to be offered depend on who the explainee is and the purpose of providing explanations to her [59]. One of the main recipients of explanations in *Explainable Mechanism Design* are the end users or participants as they are the ones affected by the decision made.[1] Unlike end users in XAI who are typically passive (as the system is making the decision for them, based on their data) users receiving explanations in mechanism design play an active role in the collective decision process taking place, by reporting their preferences. Examples of such explainees include a researcher whose

---

[1] In many cases the need to provide users with proper explanations is dictated by the regulator, e.g., in the case of GDPR guidelines [29].

grant proposal was rejected [7], one among many roommates who is assigned a particular room and rent based on her actively reported (and hopefully true) preferences [19] or, a user in a hybrid domain like algorithmic hiring where a social choice function is applied in some part of the overall algorithm [62].

Two classes of explainees in Explainable Mechanism Design enjoy some similarity with those of XAI. The first one is the *Decision Maker* who does not need to be an expert in mechanism design but has to have relevant knowledge of the domain in order to make informed decisions. This could include the employees of a refugee resettlement agency who need to be able to override the decision proposed by the algorithm [2] or the members of a committee who cannot decide on a specific voting rule and base the election on a set of desired properties (axioms) [9]. The Decision Makers are similar to *Data Experts* in XAI who use explanations to visualize, inspect, tune and select models [42]. The second class is that of an *External Entity*, similar to its namesake in XAI [59], who is someone not directly interacting with the system, say an auditor who needs to ensure that the decisions made adhere to a set of rules and that there is no violation [7]. In both classes of explainees, the requirements of the explanations to be produced in XAI and Explainable Mechanism Design overlap.

5   Explanation Concepts

As with XAI [42], Explainable AI Planning [15] and Explainable Recommendation [69], we provide a brief overview of the theoretical aspects (natural contenders) and behavioral aspects (necessary for human comprehension) of the explanations available in literature. Table 1 depicts a breakdown of the surveyed papers with respect to the different concepts and the evaluation methods discussed in the next section.

5.1   Norms Versus Attributes

As mentioned earlier, mechanism design has two defining characteristics - the private information (such as preference and cost) of the agents participating in it and the requirement for the solution to recognize its social nature. Both of these can be used to devise explanations. Norms that formalize the desirable social traits are the foundation of solutions in mechanism design and can hence be used to extol its virtues. Attributes, on the other hand, quantify the stake a given agent has in the mechanism. Explanations that relate the solution to an agent's individual stakes can be effective in helping her appreciate the impact of the solution from a selfish perspective and thus convince her. For example, convincing a housemate in a rent division setting that the decision is envy-free amounts to a normatively characterized explanation [35] while the comparison of the maximin (the solution that maximizes the minimum utility for every player thus resulting in the least disparity) solution to an arbitrary envy-free solution to demonstrate the lower disparity achieved by the former solution is an attributive

Table 1. Surveyed literature organized by Explanation Concepts – Normative Characterization (NO), Attributive (AT), Contrastive (CO), Argumentative (AR), Visualization (VI) and Evaluation Methods – Theoretical Properties (TP), Computational Complexity (CC), Empirical Analysis (EA) and User Studies (US).

Work	Setting	NO	AT	CO	AR	VI	TP	CC	EA	US
		Explanation Concepts and Evaluation Methods								
Ahani et al. [2]	Refugee Resettlement	✓	✓			✓				
Belahcene et al. [7]	Approval Sorting	✓		✓	✓		✓			
Boixel and Endriss [9]	Voting	✓					✓		✓	
Boixel et al. [10]	Voting	✓					✓			
Boixel and de Haan [12]	Voting	✓						✓		
Cailloux and Endriss [13]	Voting	✓			✓		✓			
Gal et al. [19]	Rent Division	✓	✓	✓		✓				✓
Georgara et al. [21]	Team Formation		✓	✓					✓	
Kirsten and Cailloux [26]	Voting	✓		✓	✓				✓	
Knapp [27]	Matching Theory	✓					✓		✓	
Lee et al. [35]	Rent Division	✓	✓	✓		✓				✓
Mosca and Such [43]	Multi-User Privacy Conflict	✓	✓	✓	✓					✓
Nardi et al. [46]	Voting	✓					✓		✓	
Nizri et al. [48]	Payoff Allocation	✓								✓
Peters et al. [54]	Voting		✓				✓	✓	✓	
Peters et al. [55]	Voting	✓					✓		✓	
Pozanco et al. [56]	Scheduling		✓	✓						✓
Suryanarayana et al. [65]	Voting	✓		✓		✓			✓	
Zahedi et al. [68]	Task Allocation		✓	✓	✓	✓				✓

explanation [19]. In the following paragraphs, we elaborate on diverse settings where both norms and attributes have been used to devise explanations.

Normative Characterization. Formally in mechanism design, axioms are used to capture the social norms that the solution is expected to adhere to. Procaccia [57] advocates for the use of axioms to not only be used for designing a mechanism but also to justify its solutions with an example of the not-for-profit website *Spliddit* [23]. Justifying an outcome using a set of agreed upon axioms, without having to depend on a particular rule has found a special appeal in the domain of social choice theory, where no unique outcome can be obtained while following fair voting procedures [5].

In social choice theory, given a voting profile, Cailloux and Endriss [13] developed a logic-based language to construct arguments for and against specific outcomes. Using the elements of the proposed language, an algorithm to justify the Borda outcome given a voting profile was developed. Building on said approach, Boixel and Endriss [9] developed a formal notion of justification based on the definition of Langley [32] and an algorithm based on constraint programming to compute the justifications using any set of axioms. To counter the computational complexity of the aforementioned algorithm [12], Nardi et al. [46] used a combination of instance graphs and state-of-the-art SAT solvers to design an algorithm that can provide viable justifications. To enhance the readability of the justifications using the axiomatic approach, Boixel et al. [10] developed a tableau-based calculus. Using a combination of SAT solving and Answer Set Programming to implement the calculus, the authors provide an insight into how the justifications look.

The evolution from Boixel and Endriss [9] to Boixel et al. [10] helps visualize the transformation from a non-automated procedure to an automated procedure, from unstructured justifications to structured justifications and, from manual post processing to obtain the justifications to tableau-based rendering of the justifications for enhanced readability. A demonstration summarizing the application of the aforementioned techniques proposed [9, 10, 45, 46] to find justifications given a normative basis can be found in Boixel et al. [11]. Furthermore, the approach used by Boixel and Endriss [9] has been extended to matching theory [27] where an algorithm is designed to justify outcomes that are of interest to a given agent (local outcomes) instead of the whole outcome.

The axiomatic characterization is also used to derive justifications for the results of approval voting [55] and non-compensatory approval sorting [7]. In the broader sense, non-compensatory approval sorting and voting are concerned with aggregating collective information into a single decision. The reviewed literature on justifying the results of a voting mechanism reveal all of the preference ballots. However, Belahcene et al. [7] show that the classification based on the binary judgements of the participants is compliant with the decision making process by revealing minimal information that is backed by theoretical properties.

One of the key elements used in some of the papers is Automated Reasoning (AR) using SAT or SMT solvers [7, 10, 45]. This combination of AR with social choice theory can be used to identify if a voting rule satisfies a particular axiom (thus arguing against it) [26] as well as verifying the correctness of the system output [12].

User studies to test axiom-based explanations were also successful in increasing satisfaction. Suryanarayana et al. [65] tested explanations based on features constructed from axioms in the domain of ranked-choice voting while Nizri et al. [48] used the axiomatic characterization of Shapley value [64] to come up with explanations in the domain of fair division. The research carried out by Nizri et al. [48] is significant in two ways. First, the solution that is being justified, i.e. Shapley value, satisfies all of the desired properties of fair division [24]. Second, the axiomatic characterization is not only used to justify the solution but also to come up with the algorithm to generate explanations. The authors decompose the coalitional game into sub-games and generate explanations for each of these games based on the additivity axiom which states that the sum of Shapley allocations in each sub-game is equal to the Shapley allocation in the original game. The explanations were successful in convincing the participants that the allocation was fair.

An exception in terms of the norms used can be found in the work of Mosca and Such [43] in the domain of Multiuser Privacy who propose an explainable agent called ELVIRA that collaborates with other ELVIRA agents to identify the optimal sharing policy for shared content. Here, instead of axioms, the authors use a socio-cultural theory of human values by Schwartz [63] known as the *theory of basic values*. The explanations however, are based on both values and individual attributes, i.e. the privacy preferences of the participants.

Attributive Explanation. If norms capture societal acceptance, attributes quantify personal interests. Hence, explanations that relate to the individual attributes of the participants have also been fruitful in increasing participant satisfaction

Zahedi et al. [68] compare the *cost* of a proposed allocation to the cost of the counterfactual allocation proposed by the participant. Ahani et al. [2] depict the change in *employment score* if the refugee allocation proposed by the algorithm needs to be changed. A tangential direction termed *priceability* where voters spend money on buying candidates which forms an intuitive explanation for the committee selected in approval-based committee elections was proposed by Peters et al. [54]. Explaining outcomes based on individual attributes enables the comparison of solutions that are equally good in terms of theoretical requirements. For example, Gal et al. [19] explain their optimal rent division solution by comparing it to another envy-free rent division.

Several explanation generation methods are procedure-agnostic i.e., do not focus on the procedure that leads to the outcome. Here, a framework is developed to encode the different facets of the problems such as explanations, queries and constraints. Notable examples include encoding the Justification Generation Problem for collective decisions into a Constraint Network [9], developing a generic procedure for providing justifications for Team Formation Algorithm (TFA) while keeping the TFA intact [21] and using Mixed-Integer Linear Programming (MILP) to explain why the preferences of a participants were not satisfied [56] while designing a preference-driven schedule. While using such frameworks simplifies the process of finding an explanation, adequate care needs to be taken to convert the explanations provided by the system into a readable form. One solution to this problem is using explanation templates [21,56].

5.2   Catering to the Human Mind

Understanding how human-beings explain and respond to explanations can reveal important insights into how explanations of a system can be presented. Two such behavioral modes of explanations that are considered effective and that have found applications in mechanism design are *Contrastive* explanations and *Argumentative* explanations [41]. Given the fact that mechanism design settings are social in nature, it is imperative that the behavioral nature of the explanations are attended to. Most of the papers that use a behavioral element in their explanations incorporate an element of social-interaction [41], which is necessary for a layman to comprehend the functioning of a complicated AI-based system.

As mentioned earlier, mechanism design settings suffer from the issues of familiarity, non-uniqueness of the solution and the solution not being in favor of the participants. This provides the perfect ground for the participants to challenge the solution. Identifying this, there is a great deal of interest in devising *contrastive* explanations that provide reasons for why a particular event did not occur as opposed to why a particular event did [41]. From Table 1, we can see that in nearly all of the cases where the explanations are based on the individual attributes of the agents, they are contrastive. In these scenarios, contrastive explanations can help the participant compare the difference in her utility across different solutions and thus appreciate the decision better.

In Suryanarayana et al. [65], a contrastive explanation comparing the winning candidate to the participant's most preferred candidate were found to increase user satisfaction and acceptance the most when the winning candidate was the least preferred option of the participant. Similarly, in Mosca and Such [43], contrastive explanations were found to be more appealing than general descriptive explanations when the recommended solution was different from the participant's preference. Contrastive explanations are also especially useful in multi-attribute/multi-preference settings where the outcome may not align with all of the preferences of any participant. Other notable studies that uses the contrastive approach are of Georgara et al. [21] that provide explanations for both collaboration queries (questioning team formation) and assignment queries (challenging the assignment of teams and individuals to tasks) at individual, local and global levels, and the work of Pozanco et al. [56] which provides contrastive explanations regarding the unsatisfied preferences of the participants while ensuring that the explanation is relevant to the participant.

As far as argumentation is concerned, the presence of umpteen conflicting axioms is an encouraging premise to build an argumentation framework. This is demonstrated by Cailloux and Endriss [13] who developed a formal framework for presenting arguments favoring a particular outcome. Zahedi et al. [68] present the case for the a suggested task allocation by demonstrating how a negotiation based on the counterfactual task allocation proposed by the participant can lead to a higher cost. Mosca and Such [43] base their explanation on the argumentation scheme used to obtain the optimal solution. Both in Zahedi et al. [68] and Mosca and Such [43] argumentation is used for devising the optimal solution which was then organically extended to generating explanations in favor of the outcome.

Visualization is a tool that is often viewed as a less technical means of conveying complex theoretical concepts [6]. Human-in-the-loop systems are a natural extension to mechanism design that caters to capturing reality better. Here, the algorithms have the capacity to process large volumes of data while expert insights are required to handle the inherent uncertainty of the real world. Hence, in addition to enabling easier comparisons [19], visual tools can also be used to support human decision-making.

Notable illustrations of visualization can be found in the case of the resettlement agency *HIAS* that is involved in resettlement of refugees into communities in the USA. The matching software *Annie*^{TM} *MOORE* enables the employees to override the proposed allocation by revealing the updated statistics so that no change will have a grievous impact [2].

Explaining the outcome through effective visualizations can aid in enhancing the appreciation of fairness, a theoretical notion that is the bread and butter of mechanism design, as was observed by Gal et al. [19]. While Ahani et al. [2] capture practical elements such as indivisible families of refugees, batching and, an unknown number of refugee arrivals in the context of refugee resettlement, Gal et al. [19] provide the *fairest* division of rent subject to envy-freeness. In both of these cases, the practical relevance and efficacy of the proposed algorithm is demonstrated with the help of explanations. Hence, user studies with explanations can be seen as a complementary extension to establishing the superiority of novel algorithms while comparing them to existing state-of-the-art algorithms. It is also interesting to note that users of the website *Spliddit*, the platform from which data was used by Gal et al. [19], are provided with a detailed explanation on why the proposed rent division is fair, thus signifying the utility of explanations in everyday usage. Lee et al. [35] used visualizations to both provide an elaborate breakdown of the process as well as let the participant experiment with different values in the website *Spliddit*, to observe the changes. When the participants were shown only their outcome, they perceived the results as unfair while when they were shown the preferences and outcomes for all of the participants in the group, the participants perceived the result as fair.

From Table 1 it can be observed that Normative Characterization and Contrastive Explanations are extensively used in comparison to their other theoretical and behavioral counterparts, respectively.

6   Evaluation Methods

There are several dimensions for evaluating methods of Explainable Mechanism Design from theoretical as well as practical perspectives. We provide a description on each of them in the following paragraphs.

Theoretical Properties. Building explanations on the foundation of concepts like Axiomatic Characterization, Logic-based Programming and Automated Reasoning necessitates these methods to be supported by rigid theoretical norms. Examples include proof of an explanation given the problem instance [13,68], uniqueness of the outcome and justification given a voting profile and normative basis [9], the correctness of a tableau-based calculus for generating explanations [10] and an upper bound on the number of steps required to generate justifications to ensure readability [55].

Computational Complexity. Practical feasibility of any explanation-generation method is tantamount to its real-life application. Very few authors have addressed this aspect in their work. Exceptional examples include, Peters et al. [54] that demonstrate the polynomial-time verifiability of their proposed heuristic algorithm. Boixel and de Haan [12] prove the intractability of finding and generating justifications given a normative basis.

Empirical Analysis. Empirical insights act as an intermediate between theoretical guarantees and experimental results. Running the explainability studies on real or synthetic datasets can help compare the running times of several explanation generation methods and pick the fastest one [45], help understand the step-by-step breakdown of the explanation generation method [55], disclose interesting insights about different statistical cultures (e.g., probability distribution of election profiles) that might help in the development of personalized explanations [45], and identify and evaluate metrics for the evaluation of explanation-generation methods before deploying them in real-time studies [21].

User Studies. User studies are an effective means for examining the consequences of explanations on aspects such as reliability, satisfaction, trust and conviction. While it is always desirable to conduct the experiment with the actual participants of a mechanism as in the case of *Spliddit* [19], experiments conducted with synthetic data using platforms such as Amazon Mechanical Turk (AMT) or laboratory settings are a great starting point [48,65].

In addition to the obvious purpose of helping determine the impact of explanations, user studies can also be used to provide insights on curating effective explanations. For example, Suryanarayana et al. [65] hinted at a user bias in favor of plurality voting rule while Mosca and Such [43] used the experimental insights to devise a hybrid explanation framework and improve the wording of the explanations.

From Table 1 we can observe that there is a good mix of all of the evaluation methods in the literature. However, performing *Empirical Evaluation* and *User Studies* to evaluate explanation-generation methods in mechanism design is challenging and we address this issue in detail in the next section.

7 Challenges and Possible Solutions

Despite the rapid increase in interest in explainable systems for mechanism design, the progress made in this field is still far behind compared to XAI. One of the main challenges is that of testing. As far as testing for the efficacy of explanations is considered, the ideal premise would be testing with real users, as in *Spliddit* [19] (where explainees are the actual renters in a rent division setting) or in the work of Pozanco et al. [56] (where a real restrictive *return to office* scenario due to the COVID-19 pandemic was tackled). However, the development of such evaluations is expensive and users of such real-life settings are often inaccessible to the research community. We therefore outline a few challenges in designing nearly realistic experiments that can be conducted in laboratories or platforms like AMT.

User Behavior. Human participants in a mechanism are poles apart from the perfect agents modeled in theory and exhibit short-sighted and downright irrational behavior. Instances of such behavior include reward divisions that adhere to weaker axioms than those that characterize Shapley value [16], playing dominated strategies in cooperative settings such as fair division and bargaining [30], and performing manipulations that can be captured by simple heuristics [40]. Any *social* explanation [41] thus catering to the expected selfish interests, while the participants betray the same, may defeat the purpose of explanations. For example, in an experiment conducted on human behavior in voting, Tal et al. [66] report that the participants exhibit herding by disregarding their most preferred candidate and voting for the candidate with the most first place votes in a predictive poll, even though it is the least optimal choice for them. In this case, framing a contrastive explanation comparing the participant's most preferred candidate and the winning candidate (which might be the candidate the participant voted for) would be counter-productive.

A natural solution to the problem of mismatched behavior is building predictive models using behavioral, game-theoretic and machine learning tools. Examples include models for predicting human decisions in plurality voting [17], approval voting [61] and auctions [50]. The benefits of such models are twofold. First, it might help the explanations to be more *selective* [41] by shedding light on what is important to the explainee. For example, in the game-theoretic model of human behavior in Doodle Polls [52], the concept of *Social Bonus* is proposed in order to reason why voters vote for unpopular slots. Consequently, contrastive explanations comparing the winning candidates to the unpopular ones can be discarded as the latter are insignificant to the voter.

The second and rather consequential utility from such models is that they might help identify the sub-optimal manipulations of the participants which can be contrasted with the optimal choice. In that context, an interesting hypothesis to investigate is if and what kind of explanations can bring irrational humans closer to the rational agents modeled in literature. This will open new avenues for *Interpretability* in mechanism design which has not received as much attention as in the XAI literature [59].

User Biases. The prevelance of mechanisms in society has led to humans forming their own prejudices such as favoritism for plurality voting rule [38,55], altruism towards non-performing participants [16] and a disdain towards algorithmic decisions as being far from reality [34,39,67].

Long before building explainable systems was considered, researchers invested efforts into manually explaining technical jargon to non-expert participants. Notable examples include acquainting participants of a centipede game with backward induction [39] and measuring the frequency of violation of fairness criteria in voting [38]. Coupling these ideas with biases such as *automation bias*, where a user believes that a computing system is more knowledgeable and "intelligent" than it is, is a direction worth exploring [22]. In addition, comparing different modes of presenting explanations such as textual and visual, both of which are extensively used in Explainable Recommender Systems [69], can strengthen the efficacy of explanations. It is also noteworthy that human intelligence can be leveraged to not only rate explanations but also to provide explanations, thus providing valuable insights into human factors that might be useful for generating convincing explanations [56,65].

Lack of Data. A useful tool in bridging the gap between idealized agent behavior and flawed human behavior is empirical analysis and subsequent modeling of human participants in the different mechanism design settings. Also, as mentioned earlier, empirical analysis can act as an intermediate stage between theoretical guarantees and user studies while revealing interesting insights.

However, there are not many datasets in the domains of Computational Social Choice and Preference Reasoning publicly available [37]. Also, while collecting, preserving and presenting data on private preferences, adequate care needs to be taken to ensure that user privacy is preserved [29].

Naturally, the obvious solution to the lack of data is to develop tools for efficient data collection. One such very useful collection of datasets in the domain of Computational Social Choice is *Preflib*[2] which was used by Nardi [45] to examine the practical utility of the proposed algorithm. However the process of data collection is easier said than done. Replicating real-life settings in order to get people to report their preferences, even manipulated ones, is a mammoth task. Anonymizing data is an effective way to protect the privacy of the participants. An alternate technique to preserve privacy was used by Gal et al. [19] where the original valuations for the rooms were perturbed by an acceptable margin and presented to the explainees.

Simulating Synthetic Environments. In order to evaluate the efficacy of explanations, it is vital to have the participant interested in the explanations. In mechanism design, these interests are captured by notions such as preferences, utility and costs which are easy to conceptualize but difficult to replicate and/or induce in lab experiments. XAI, even though tasked with explaining complex algorithms, enjoys relatability with experiments such as image classification [51], review classification [31] and selection of a competent agent [3]. This enables the design of interactive experiments where explanations can be sneaked in without being explicit, hence eliciting an organic response from the participant.

Inspired by the experimental design in XAI, gamification of the problems is a good starting point. Tailoring games such as the centipede game for bargaining [39] and share-the-loot game for resource allocation [16] to accommodate explanations and with the reward tied to the performance of the participant is an idea worth testing. The presence of a monetary reward inadvertently engrosses the participant, thus eliciting a realistic response. Some other tested methods of invoking user interest in synthetic lab experiments were done using the concept of bonus from the winning candidate in ranked choice voting [65] and asking the participant to imagine themselves in the setting and extracting their preferences through meticulously designed questionnaires [43].

Another way to stimulate the interest of participants in explanations might be to leverage the diversity of axioms to build argumentation systems augmented with human input on how convincing the arguments are [58]. The conversion from passive listeners of explanations to active debaters of arguments might trigger a passionate yet honest response from the participants.

In addition to the above ideas, tools used in Social Psychology such as *Experimental Vignette Methodology (EVM)* [1] and online testing methods like A/B testing used in Explainable Recommendation [69] offer valid premises for developing tests for Explainable Mechanism Design.

---

[2] https://www.preflib.org/.

8 Conclusion

In this paper, we survey explainability in mechanism design, provide an overall picture of the various concepts around it and shed light on the challenges faced by researchers in the domain.

While we do propose several workarounds to overcome the aforementioned challenges, we emphasize that implementing each of these is a non-trivial task per se and calls for collaborations between researchers in mechanism design, human-agent interaction, software engineering, and psychology. We hope that both experienced as well as budding researchers find this survey helpful in designing and improving explainability in mechanism design. We also envision a future where designing mechanisms aligned with human values and Explainable Mechanism Design complement each other.

Acknowledgements. This work was supported in part by the Data Science Institute at Bar-Ilan University, the EU Project TAILOR under grant 952215 and the Israeli Ministry of Science & Technology under grant 89583. The research was carried out with the technological support and funding from the HRI Consortium – the Israel Innovation Authority. Sharadhi Alape Suryanarayana is grateful for the President's Scholarship and Erasmus+ Global Mobility Programme that has supported this research.

References

1. Aguinis, H., Bradley, K.J.: Best practice recommendations for designing and implementing experimental vignette methodology studies. Organ. Res. Methods **17**(4), 351–371 (2014)
2. Ahani, N., Gölz, P., Procaccia, A.D., Teytelboym, A., Trapp, A.C.: Dynamic placement in refugee resettlement. arXiv preprint arXiv:2105.14388 (2021)
3. Amir, O., Doshi-Velez, F., Sarne, D.: Summarizing agent strategies. JAAMAS **33**(5), 628–644 (2019)
4. Arrieta, A.B., et al.: Explainable artificial intelligence (XAI): concepts, taxonomies, opportunities and challenges toward responsible AI. Inf. Fusion **58**, 82–115 (2020)
5. Arrow, K.J.: Social Choice and Individual Values. Yale University Press, London (1951)
6. Barwise, J., Etchemendy, J.: Visual information and valid reasoning. In: Logical Reasoning with Diagrams (1991)
7. Belahcene, K., Chevaleyre, Y., Maudet, N., Labreuche, C., Mousseau, V., Ouerdane, W.: Accountable approval sorting. In: IJCAI-ECAI, pp. 70–76 (2018)
8. Benabbou, N., Chakraborty, M., Ho, X.V., Sliwinski, J., Zick, Y.: Diversity constraints in public housing allocation. In: AAMAS, pp. 973–981 (2018)
9. Boixel, A., Endriss, U.: Automated justification of collective decisions via constraint solving. In: AAMAS, pp. 168–176 (2020)
10. Boixel, A., Endriss, U., de Haan, R.: A calculus for computing structured justifications for election outcomes. In: AAAI (2022)
11. Boixel, A., Endriss, U., Nardi, O.: Displaying justifications for collective decisions. In: IJCAI, July 2022. (demo Paper)
12. Boixel, A., de Haan, R.: On the complexity of finding justifications for collective decisions. In: AAAI, pp. 5194–5201 (2021)

13. Cailloux, O., Endriss, U.: Arguing about voting rules. In: AAMAS, pp. 287–295 (2016)
14. Carroll, G.: Design for weakly structured environments. In: Laslier, J.-F., Moulin, H., Sanver, M.R., Zwicker, W.S. (eds.) The Future of Economic Design. SED, pp. 27–33. Springer, Cham (2019). https://doi.org/10.1007/978-3-030-18050-8_5
15. Chakraborti, T., Sreedharan, S., Kambhampati, S.: The emerging landscape of explainable automated planning & decision making. In: IJCAI, pp. 4803–4811 (2020)
16. d'Eon, G., Larson, K.: Testing axioms against human reward divisions in cooperative games. In: AAMAS, pp. 312–320 (2020)
17. Fairstein, R., Lauz, A., Meir, R., Gal, K.: Modeling people's voting behavior with poll information. In: AAMAS, pp. 1422–1430 (2019)
18. Freedman, R., Borg, J.S., Sinnott-Armstrong, W., Dickerson, J.P., Conitzer, V.: Adapting a kidney exchange algorithm to align with human values. In: AAAI, pp. 1636–1645 (2018)
19. Gal, Y., Mash, M., Procaccia, A.D., Zick, Y.: Which is the fairest (rent division) of them all? In: ACM EC, pp. 67–84 (2016)
20. Garfinkel, S., Matthews, J., Shapiro, S.S., Smith, J.M.: Toward algorithmic transparency and accountability. Commun. ACM **60**(9), 5–5 (2017)
21. Georgara, A., Rodriguez-Aguilar, J.A., Sierra, C.: Building contrastive explanations for multi-agent team formation. In: AAMAS (2022)
22. Goddard, K., Roudsari, A., Wyatt, J.C.: Automation bias: a systematic review of frequency, effect mediators, and mitigators. JAMIA. **19**, 121–127 (2012)
23. Goldman, J., Procaccia, A.D.: Spliddit: unleashing fair division algorithms. ACM SIGecom Exchanges. **13**(2), 41–46 (2015)
24. Hart, S.: Shapley value. In: Eatwell, J., Milgate, M., Newman, P. (eds.) Game Theory. The New Palgrave, pp. 210–216. Springer, London (1989). https://doi.org/10.1007/978-1-349-20181-5_25
25. Hurwicz, L.: Optimality and informational efficiency in resource allocation processes. Math. Methods Soc. Sci. (1960)
26. Kirsten, M., Cailloux, O.: Towards automatic argumentation about voting rules. In: APIA (2018)
27. Knapp, D.L.: Justification of matching outcomes. Ph.D. thesis, Master's thesis, ILLC, University of Amsterdam (2022)
28. Kominers, S.D.: Good markets (really do) make good neighbors. ACM SIGecom Exchanges **16**(2), 12–26 (2019)
29. Kraus, S., et al.: AI for explaining decisions in multi-agent environments. In: AAAI, pp. 13534–13538 (2020)
30. Kyropoulou, M., Ortega, J., Segal-Halevi, E.: Fair cake-cutting in practice. In: ACM EC, pp. 547–548 (2019). https://doi.org/10.1145/3328526.3329592
31. Lai, V., Tan, C.: On human predictions with explanations and predictions of machine learning models: a case study on deception detection. In: ACM FACCT, pp. 29–38 (2019)
32. Langley, P.: Explainable, normative, and justified agency. In: AAAI, pp. 9775–9779 (2019)
33. Lavi, R.: Mechanism design. In: Complex Social and Behavioral Systems: Game Theory and Agent-Based Models, pp. 317–333 (2020)
34. Lee, M.K., Baykal, S.: Algorithmic mediation in group decisions: Fairness perceptions of algorithmically mediated vs. discussion-based social division. In: CSCW, pp. 1035–1048 (2017)

35. Lee, M.K., Jain, A., Cha, H.J., Ojha, S., Kusbit, D.: Procedural justice in algorithmic fairness: leveraging transparency and outcome control for fair algorithmic mediation. In: CSCW, pp. 1–26 (2019)
36. Lee, M.K., et al.: Webuildai: Participatory framework for algorithmic governance. In: Proceedings of the ACM on Human-Computer Interaction, vol. 3(CSCW), pp. 1–35 (2019)
37. Mattei, N.: Closing the loop: bringing humans into empirical computational social choice and preference reasoning. In: IJCAI, pp. 5169–5173 (2021)
38. McCune, D., McCune, L.: How can we compare different voting methods? a voting theory project. Primus **29**(5), 487–501 (2019)
39. McKelvey, R.D., Palfrey, T.R.: An experimental study of the centipede game. Econometrica, pp. 803–836 (1992)
40. Mennle, T., Weiss, M., Philipp, B., Seuken, S.: The power of local manipulation strategies in assignment mechanisms. In: IJCAI, pp. 82–89 (2015)
41. Miller, T.: Explanation in artificial intelligence: insights from the social sciences. Artif. Intell. **267**, 1–38 (2019)
42. Mohseni, S., Zarei, N., Ragan, E.D.: A multidisciplinary survey and framework for design and evaluation of explainable AI systems. ACM TIIS **11**(3–4), 1–45 (2021)
43. Mosca, F., Such, J.: An explainable assistant for multiuser privacy. Auton. Agent. Multi-Agent Syst. **36**(1), 1–45 (2022)
44. Mothilal, R.K., Sharma, A., Tan, C.: Explaining machine learning classifiers through diverse counterfactual explanations. In: ACM FACCT, pp. 607–617 (2020)
45. Nardi, O.: A Graph-Based Algorithm for the Automated Justification of Collective Decisions. Master's thesis, ILLC, University of Amsterdam (2021)
46. Nardi, O., Boixel, A., Endriss, U.: A graph-based algorithm for the automated justification of collective decisions. In: AAMAS (2022)
47. Nisan, N., Ronen, A.: Algorithmic mechanism design. Games Econom. Behav. **35**(1–2), 166–196 (2001)
48. Nizri, M., Hazon, N., Azaria, A.: Explainable shapley-based allocation. In: AAAI (2022)
49. Noothigattu, R., Gaikwad, S., Awad, E., Dsouza, S., Rahwan, I., Ravikumar, P., Procaccia, A.: A voting-based system for ethical decision making. In: Proceedings of the AAAI Conference on Artificial Intelligence, vol. 32 (2018)
50. Noti, G., Syrgkanis, V.: Bid prediction in repeated auctions with learning. In: The Web Conference, pp. 3953–3964 (2021)
51. Nourani, M., Kabir, S., Mohseni, S., Ragan, E.D.: The effects of meaningful and meaningless explanations on trust and perceived system accuracy in intelligent systems. In: AAAI, pp. 97–105 (2019)
52. Obraztsova, S., Polukarov, M., Rabinovich, Z., Elkind, E.: Doodle poll games. In: AAMAS, pp. 876–884 (2017)
53. Papadimitriou, C.: Algorithms, games, and the internet. In: STOC, pp. 749–753 (2001)
54. Peters, D., Pierczyski, G., Shah, N., Skowron, P.: Market-based explanations of collective decisions. In: AAAI, pp. 5656–5663 (2021)
55. Peters, D., Procaccia, A.D., Psomas, A., Zhou, Z.: Explainable voting. NeurIPS **33**, 1525–1534 (2020)
56. Pozanco, A., Mosca, F., Zehtabi, P., Magazzeni, D., Kraus, S.: Explaining preference-driven schedules: the expres framework. In: ICAPS (2022). (to appear)
57. Procaccia, A.D.: Axioms should explain solutions. In: Laslier, J.-F., Moulin, H., Sanver, M.R., Zwicker, W.S. (eds.) The Future of Economic Design. SED, pp. 195–199. Springer, Cham (2019). https://doi.org/10.1007/978-3-030-18050-8_27

58. Rosenfeld, A., Kraus, S.: Providing arguments in discussions on the basis of the prediction of human argumentative behavior. ACM TIIS **6**(4), 1–33 (2016)
59. Rosenfeld, A., Richardson, A.: Explainability in human-agent systems. JAAMAS **33**(6), 673–705 (2019)
60. Roth, A.E.: The economics of matching: stability and incentives. Math. Oper. Res. **7**(4), 617–628 (1982)
61. Scheuerman, J., Harman, J., Mattei, N., Venable, K.B.: Modeling voters in multi-winner approval voting. In: AAAI, vol. 35, pp. 5709–5716 (2021)
62. Schumann, C., Foster, J., Mattei, N., Dickerson, J.: We need fairness and explainability in algorithmic hiring. In: AAMAS, pp. 1716–1720 (2020)
63. Schwartz, S.H.: An overview of the Schwartz theory of basic values. Online Read. Psychol. Cult. **2**(1), 1–20 (2012)
64. Shapley, L.S.: A value for n-person games. Contrib. Theory Games **28**(2), 307–317 (1953)
65. Suryanarayana, S.A., Sarne, D., Kraus, S.: Justifying social-choice mechanism outcome for improving participant satisfaction. In: AAMAS (2022)
66. Tal, M., Meir, R., Gal, Y.: A study of human behavior in online voting. In: AAMAS, pp. 665–673 (2015)
67. Uhde, A., Schlicker, N., Wallach, D.P., Hassenzahl, M.: Fairness and decision-making in collaborative shift scheduling systems. In: CHI, pp. 1–13 (2020)
68. Zahedi, Z., Sengupta, S., Kambhampati, S.: Why didn't you allocate this task to them?'negotiation-aware task allocation and contrastive explanation generation. arXiv preprint arXiv:2002.01640 (2020)
69. Zhang, Y., Chen, X., et al.: Explainable recommendation: a survey and new perspectives. Found. Trends Inf. Retr. **14**(1), 1–101 (2020)

Integrating Quantitative and Qualitative Reasoning for Value Alignment

Jazon Szabo[1(✉)], Jose M. Such[1], Natalia Criado[2], and Sanjay Modgil[1]

[1] King's College London, London, UK
{jazon.szabo,jose.such,sanjay.modgil}@kcl.ac.uk
[2] Universitat Politecnica de Valencia, Valencia, Spain
ncriado@upv.es

Abstract. Agents that focus only on achieving their own goals may cause significant harm to society. As a result, when deciding which actions to perform, agents have to consider societal values and how their actions impact these values—the 'value alignment problem'. There is therefore a need to integrate quantitative machine reasoning with an ability to reason about qualitative human values. In this paper, we present a novel framework for value-based reasoning that aims to bridge the gap between these two modes of reasoning. In particular, our framework extends the theory of grading to model how societal values can trade off with each other or with the agent's goals. Furthermore, our framework introduces the use of hyperreal numbers to represent both quantitative and qualitative aspects of reasoning and help address the value alignment problem.

Keywords: Value alignment · Practical reasoning · Value based reasoning

1 Introduction

Context. The creation of autonomous, intelligent and societally beneficial agents is one of the chief aims of artificial intelligence research. To achieve this, we must create agents that can intelligently reason about what they ought to do, i.e. engage in the process of *practical reasoning* [23]. However, it is not enough for such agents to achieve their own goals; agents that ignore their societal impact may inadvertently cause significant societal harm. This problem – ensuring that the actions of autonomous agents are beneficial to society – is called the *value alignment problem* (*VAP*) [6].

What is beneficial to society (what is considered good, bad, etc.) is grounded in the *values* the society upholds. Agents that take into account these values in practical reasoning, are said to engage in *value-based reasoning* [1], wherein encoding information about the relevant values typically requires human input. For example, in a state of the art approach to solving the *VAP* – *cooperative inverse reinforcement learning* (CIRL) [14] – the AI agent gradually learns

This work was supported by UKRI (EP/S023356/1) and EPSRC (EP/R033188/1).

human preferences (i.e. human values) encoded in a utility function, and simultaneously acts so as to respect the thus-far learnt preferences. The learning process not only involves passive observation of human behaviours, but interactive communication, whereby the human teaches and instructs the AI agent, and the AI agent questions the human. The effectiveness of such a strategy requires that the agent be able to represent the human reasoning communicated to them and incorporate it with their own more quantitatively orientated reasoning. On the other hand, in the so-called *debate game* [15] – also proposed to address the *VAP* – two AI agents exchange instrumental arguments for and against performing certain actions, while evaluative judgment of these arguments is provided by a human judge, thus accounting for human values. As a result, the most value-aligned action is chosen as an outcome of human arbitration. For an agent to be optimal in the debate game, they have to be able to anticipate how the human judge evaluates their arguments, and thus need to accommodate value based reasoning in their deliberations. These two approaches to addressing the *VAP* thus point to the need to integrate human and machine reasoning; that is to say, 'to bridge the gap' between the more fine-grained quantitative reasoning employed by machine learning based AI agents, and the coarser-grained, qualitative aspects of value based reasoning employed by humans.

Existing formalisms and frameworks are either predominantly quantitative or qualitative. Regarding the latter, we are interested in qualitative approaches to value based reasoning; the paradigmatic instance being *value-based argumentation* [2,4] and other works that build on [2,4]. In such approaches, actions are judged based on whether they promote or demote a value, from a given set of values that are related by a total order. The main advantage of these qualitative approaches is that they are transparent and understandable. Moreover, qualitative representations are better suited for representing human preferences, especially under uncertainty [22]. However, note that the degree of promotion/demotion, as well as the ordering between the values, is strictly qualitative. As a result, such approaches are too rough-grained and cannot represent quantitative uncertainty or fine-grained trade-offs between various values.

By quantitative approaches, we primarily refer to those assigning each action a utility (e.g. CIRL). Such a representation covers a wide range of approaches, including machine learning, statistical approaches etc. Such methods have historically been very successful and can model fine-grained trade-offs and quantitative uncertainty. However, they are often black-boxes, being difficult to interpret and explain [13]. Moreover, quantitative approaches also cannot accurately represent some ethical values, unlike qualitative approaches [21] (see Sect. 2.2).

Contributions. In this paper, we bridge the gap between qualitative and quantitative approaches by proposing a framework for value-based reasoning, based on the theory of grading [3] and hyperreal numbers [24]. This framework allows agents to represent and reason both with human values and utility functions. Moreover, the agent can flexibly trade off human values and its utility function.

More precisely, our novel contributions are:

- applying the theory of grading to the problem of value-based reasoning;

- applying the use of hyperreal numbers to the problem of value-based reasoning and to the theory of grading;
- extending the theory of grading with the notion of evaluation facts and show how this relates to the problem of evaluation aggregation;
- extending the theory of grading with the notion of weights;
- proposing a novel framework for value-based reasoning that incorporates the above contributions.

1.1 Motivating Example

We now present an example that demonstrates the need for a formalism that bridges the gap between quantitative and qualitative approaches. Moreover, we reuse this example in later sections to showcase how an agent uses our formalism.

In a fictional near future a self-driving boat agent has two aims: 1) to learn to drive at a speed that maximises its task-specific utility 2) to use value-based reasoning to ensure value alignment. The boat can drive at any speed from 0 km/h to 100 km/h. The agent's learnt utility function represents various non explicitly value-based considerations, such as speediness, fuel consumption and comfort. We assume that the expected utility is at a maximum when the speed is 75 km/h and gradually reduces the further the agent deviates from this speed.

Moreover, there are other explicitly value-based considerations distinct from the task utility. At speeds higher than 70 km/h, the ship sends vibrations that affect sea animal behaviour by confusing their senses and thus possibly causing their death. Consider that the fish close to the ship belong to a culturally significant, endangered species. In this case, we expect the agent to first minimise the chance of these animals dying and only optimise the task utility as a secondary consideration.

Now, consider a further complication: the passenger of the boat is stung by a jellyfish. While not in danger, the passenger is in great pain and suffers from a painful fit exactly every sixty minutes. Therefore, to minimise human suffering, the boat needs to carry this passenger to land as fast as possible. However the greater the speed, the more likelihood of causing harm to the fish.

It is not trivial matter to arbitrate as to which is worse: increasing the pain of a human passenger or increasing the probability of killing endangered fish. Moreover, it is not clear how to factor for the qualitative priorities of the different values. Also, how can the agent trade-off these different qualitative priorities with the finer-grained impacts of the actions? And how does the purely quantitative utility function factor? In the remainder of this paper we seek to answer these questions.

2 Requirements

Next we derive specific requirements for bridging the gap between fine-grained quantitative reasoning and the more coarse-grained value-based reasoning.

2.1   Quantitative Reasoning

Utility functions are often the end result of intelligent deliberation by an agent. In particular, in many problem domains, if some reasonable axioms (i.e. the von Neumann-Morgenstern axioms) are satisfied, then the preferences of a rational agent can be represented by a utility function [29]. As a result, machine learning agents and many other kinds of rational AI agents are typically modelled as optimising a utility function. Consequently, we require that 1) the agent be able to use information given in the form of a utility function and 2) the agent use this information in decision making. That is, we require utility compatibility.

2.2   Qualitative Reasoning

In value-based reasoning, the standard assumption is that there are multiple values. There are two justifications for this: 1) values are distinct and cannot be reduced to a single value, 2) values may not be distinct but reducing them to a single value is not feasible in practice [9]. As a result, we require that values are modelled separately and that value-based reasoning is formalised as a multi-criteria decision problem.

Furthermore, in ethical decision making, we humans use a more qualitative value-based reasoning [5]. Human understanding of what is right and what is wrong is often abstract and vague [25]. As a result, ethical reasoning cannot be fully represented by the certainty of a total ordering [12]. Consequently, we require that the end product of value-based reasoning is a partial order over the alternatives[1].

Another characteristic of value-based reasoning is that it can be non-Archimedean; we humans often make such evaluative judgments in our decision making. In this context non-Archimedean means a qualitative relationship between two alternatives, where in *any* situation one alternative is preferred to another, regardless of any quantitative considerations. For example, a commonly held deontological principle is that the loss of a human life is a qualitative order of magnitude worse than the loss of money[2]. In particular, this means that any situation where a human loses their life is always worse than any other situation where a human loses any amount money (but not their life). Such qualitative orders of magnitude can be represented only by non-Archimedean quantities. Therefore, we require that the formalism represent non-Archimedean quantities so that we can represent value-based reasoning fully.

---

[1] Note that this is a generalisation of the standard representation of value-based argumentation, where the total order over values, combined with the strong assumption that each action promotes exactly one value, yields a total order over the actions [2]. By requiring only a partial order over the values, we can relax these underlying strong assumptions.

[2] As is characteristic of many non-consequentialist ethical theories [21].

2.3   Combining Quantitative and Qualitative Reasoning

Inspired by arguments from Bostrom [7] and Peterson [21], we use hyperreal numbers – a non-Archimedean extension of real numbers – in our proposed framework. In particular: 1) hyperreal numbers can represent any arithmetic operation possible on real numbers[3] and hence are compatible with utility functions; 2) hyperreal numbers can represent non-Archimedean aspects of value-based reasoning that real numbers cannot; and 3) hyperreal numbers can represent the interplay between non-Archimedean quantities and real-valued numbers.

Furthermore, we use a grading-based model in our proposed framework. Grades are a way to model preferences with a degree of 'goodness'. This allows us to model the degree of promotion/demotion of values by different actions. Furthermore, in grading, the amount of information that we have is flexible: it may be more qualitative or more quantitative. Finally, grade aggregation – the process of how alternatives are ranked – takes multiple criteria into account and returns a partial order.

3   Preliminaries

3.1   Hyperreal Numbers

Hyperreal numbers [16,24] are an extension of real numbers containing infinite and infinitesimal quantities. The infinite number ω is such that it is greater than any real number, no matter how large the real number may be, i.e. $\omega > 1+...+1$, for any finite number of terms. The infinitesimal number ϵ is defined as $1/\omega$ and is infinitely close to 0 (but does not equal 0). That is, for any positive real number c, $0 < \epsilon < c$.

We can build the hyperreal numbers via the following rules:

- any real number is a hyperreal number;
- ω and ϵ are hyperreal numbers;
- the sum of any hyperreal numbers is a hyperreal number;
- the product of any hyperreal numbers is a hyperreal number;
- the dividend of any hyperreal numbers is a hyperreal number (but division by zero is not allowed).

We denote the set of hyperreal numbers by $\mathbb{R}^*$.

One of the useful properties of the hyperreal numbers is the *transfer principle* that states that any first-order statements about real numbers also apply to the hyperreal numbers[4]. For example, because multiplication is commutative for the real numbers (e.g., for any reals x, y, it is always true that $xy = yx$), multiplication is also commutative for hyperreal numbers (for any hyperreals

---

[3] This is because of the transfer principle. See Sect. 3.

[4] However, second-order statements may not transfer to the hyperreals in the same way. For example, the second order statement that there is no number x such that $1 + 1 + 1... < x$ doesn't carry over to the hyperreals.

x, y, it is always true that $xy = yx$). Because of this, hyperreal numbers behave similarly to real numbers in many ways.

A hyperreal number may be infinitesimal, infinite or finite. A hyperreal number is *infinitesimal* when its absolute value is less than any positive real number. A hyperreal number is *infinite* when its absolute value is greater than any positive real number. Finally, a hyperreal number is *finite* when it is not infinite, that is, when its absolute value is between any two positive real numbers. From this it follows that any infinitesimal number is also finite.

The following properties hold, where c, d are any (non-infinitesimal) finite hyperreals, $\gamma, \delta \neq 0$ are any infinitesimals and N, O are any infinite hyperreals:

- when adding numbers, finite numbers dominate infinitesimal numbers and infinite numbers dominate finite numbers: $\gamma + \delta$ is infinitesimal, $c + \gamma$ is finite, but not infinitesimal, $c + d$ is finite, possibly infinitesimal, and $N + \gamma$, $N + c$ and $N + O$ are both infinite;
- when multiplying numbers, infinitesimal numbers dominate finite numbers and infinite numbers dominate finite numbers: $\gamma \times \delta$ and $\gamma \times c$ are infinitesimal, $c \times d$ is finite but not infinitesimal and $N \times c$ and $N \times O$ are infinite.

In the cases we have not given above, the result is not determined: it may be possibly infinitesimal, finite or infinite.

Finally, denote by $a \ll b$ to mean that $a < b$ and a/b is infinitesimal, to be read a is an order of magnitude smaller than b. For example, $\epsilon \ll 1 \ll \omega \ll \omega^2$. Symmetrically we read $a \gg b$ as a is an order of magnitude larger than b.

3.2   Grades

Grades [3,19] allow to rank alternatives based on their perceived degree of 'goodness'. More precisely, in the theory of grading, different *judges* express their preferences by assigning each alternative a *grade*, where each grade corresponds to a certain standard.

Grades carry some degree of cardinal information. Consequently, grade aggregation can avoid the negative impacts of Arrow's results that affect other preference aggregation methods [3,17]. However, unlike utility functions, grades often do not carry complete cardinal information, i.e. we do not always know how much better one alternative is than another. How much information is lost by grading depends on the context.

We will now formally define the process of *grade aggregation*, the process of how a set of judges decide out of two alternatives, which one is better, based only on the grades they have given. First, we have a set of social alternatives X judged by a set of judges $N = \{1, ..., n\}$. These judges assign each alternative a grade from a set of grades G, where the set of grades G is ordered by the partial order $\preceq_G$.

The opinions of the judges are represented in their appraisals. That is, the *individual appraisal* of a judge i is denoted by $j_i : X \to G$, a function mapping to each social alternative a grade. As a result, the appraisal of alternative x by judge i is denoted by $j_i(x)$. Moreover, the opinions of the judges together is called their appraisal profile. In more technical detail, an *appraisal profile* J is a list $\langle j_1, ..., j_n \rangle$ of individual appraisals of the judges.

Not every combination of grades is possible. The *appraisal domain* $\mathcal{D}$ is the set of appraisal profiles that the judges might produce for a specific grading scenario. When aggregating grades, the grading rules only have to specify what to do for appraisal profiles in the appraisal domain, where a *grading rule* is a function f such that f maps any appraisal profile $J \in \mathcal{D}$ in the grade domain to a partial binary relation $f(J) = \preceq$ on the set of social alternatives X. Intuitively, a grading rule takes the grades assigned to each individual by the different judges and produces a ranking over them.

4   Grade-Based Framework of Value-Based Reasoning

In this section, we introduce a framework that satisfies the previously identified requirements in order to bridge the gap between quantitative and qualitative value-based reasoning. To do this, we base our framework on the theory of grading and extend it with a notion of grade information, judge weights and introduce the use of hyperreal numbers to this context.

In grading, a set of *judges* appraise the *social alternatives* in order to rank them from best to worst. Similarly, in value-based reasoning, a set of *values* evaluate the possible *actions* of the agent in order to rank them from best to worst. Therefore, the judges of value-based reasoning are the values and the social alternatives are the actions.

More precisely, in value-based reasoning, the possible actions A are evaluated by the agent's values V. Various values can be promoted and demoted to different levels; the set of all such levels of evaluation is denoted by L and is ordered by a partial order $\preceq_L$. The levels of evaluation in value-based reasoning correspond to the grades of grading. The *individual evaluation* of an action a with respect to a value v corresponds to what level of value promotion/demotion performing action a brings about.

Definition 1 (Individual evaluation). *Given an agent, a value v that the agent holds and a set of actions A that the agent may perform, the individual evaluation $e_v : A \to L$ is a function that maps any action a to the corresponding level of evaluation.*

Example. Driving at a speed of 55 km/h means that no animals are harmed. This is the status quo, which we denote with the neutral evaluation 0 (zero). Therefore, we denote this individual evaluation as $e_a(drive(55)) = 0$, where $drive(55)$ is the action of driving the boat with a speed of 55 km/h and a is the value of animal welfare.

The *evaluation profile* E of an agent is a list of the individual evaluations of each of the agent's values $E = \langle e_{v_1}, ..., e_{v_{|V|}} \rangle$. The *evaluation domain* D is a set of evaluation profiles that the agent's values may produce for a specific scenario. The agent uses an *evaluation aggregation rule* to order their actions based on the evaluations of the different values.

Definition 2 (Evaluation aggregation rule). *Given an evaluation domain D and a set of actions A, the evaluation aggregation rule is a function $f : D \rightarrow PO(A)$ that maps any evaluation profile $E \in D$ in the evaluation domain to a partial order over the set of actions $f(E) = \preceq_A$, where $PO(A)$ is the set of all partial orders over A.*

Example. An evaluation aggregation rule tells the agent how to trade off the different levels of promotion/demotion for the various values of the agent. Consider a simplified version of the example: there are only two values, animal welfare a and utility u; there are only two actions, $drive(55)$ and $drive(75)$. Furthermore, assume that we know that driving at a speed of 75 km/h is expected to kill precisely one endangered fish. Moreover, assume $u(drive(55)) = \frac{11}{15}$ and $u(drive(75)) = 1$. Hence, for the actions $drive(55)$ and $drive(75)$ we have:

- $e_a(drive(55)) = 0$ and
- $e_u(drive(55)) = \frac{11}{15}$.
- $e_a(drive(75)) = d$ and
- $e_u(drive(75)) = 1$,

where d is the level of demotion $(d < 0)$ that occurs when an endangered fish dies.

Take an evaluation aggregation rule f such that the resulting order $\preceq_A$ contains $drive(75) \prec_A drive(55)$. This rule f implies that increasing the level of promotion of the value of utility from $\frac{11}{15}$ to 1 is strictly worse than demoting the value of animal welfare with a level d. That is, the evaluation aggregation rule f states that the increase in the task utility is not worth the decrease in animal welfare.

Finally, note that the evaluation domain can be used to denote that different values are evaluated differently. For example, by requiring in the evaluation domain that only those evaluation profiles that map every utility function to a real number are permitted, we denote that the value of utility is always evaluated as a real number.

4.1   Evaluation Aggregation Rules

Evaluations by the values correspond to how good the different actions are. That is, they carry some cardinal information, which can be used when comparing the different actions. Therefore, the evaluations cannot be aggregated in arbitrary ways; the evaluations should only be aggregated using evaluation aggregation rules that are compatible with the information they carry. Therefore, we define this notion of *compatibility* and apply it in the context of value-based reasoning.

First, we define the information given by the evaluations of values in the form of equations and inequalities. Such equations and inequalities are called the *evaluation information*. That is, the levels of evaluation correspond to hyperreal variables where the information that we know about them restrict the possible range of hyperreal values they may take.

An *aggregation fact* describes how two different sets of evaluations should be ordered, regardless of what values the evaluations belong to.

Definition 3 (Aggregation fact). *An aggregation fact is a tuple* (L_1, L_2, op) *where* L_1 *and* L_2 *are multisets of levels of evaluation and* $op \in \{<, \leq, =, \ll\}$ *is a comparison operation. Such an aggregation fact is interpreted as the statement* $(\Sigma_{l \in L_1} l) \ op \ (\Sigma_{l' \in L_2} l')$.

Example. We can formalise with an aggregation fact the requirement that increasing the level of promotion of *any* value from $\frac{11}{15}$ to 1 is strictly worse than demoting *any* other value with a level d. This corresponds to the aggregation fact $(\{d, 1\}, \{0, \frac{11}{15}\}, <)$, which we interpret as the inequality $(d + 1) < (0 + \frac{11}{15})$.

The collection of all aggregation facts for a set of values is named *aggregation information*. Formally, the aggregation information I is a set of aggregation facts.

We further require for simplicity's sake, that the partial order $\preceq_L$ over the levels of evaluation be encompassed within the aggregation information. This is to ensure that the aggregation information contains all relevant information about how the different levels of information are related to one another. More precisely, if for some values a and b, $a \preceq_L b$ holds, then the aggregation information has to contain the corresponding aggregation fact, i.e. $(\{a\}, \{b\}, \leq) \in I$.

4.2   Using the Aggregation Information

We now define how the aggregation information can be used to aggregate the evaluations. First, note that a collection of aggregation facts forms a system of equations and inequalities. Here, the variables are the levels of evaluation of the values. Consequently, the evaluation information defines for each level of evaluation a range of possible hyperreal values that is compatible with the information given.

An assignment to each of the level variables is called a *satisfying assignment* if the system of equations and inequalities created by the set of aggregation information is satisfied by the substituted values. Note that for a single variable, there may be a range of different assignments possible that are consistent with the information.

Definition 4 (Assignment (unweighted)). *Given a set of levels of evaluation* L, *a function is an assignment function as* $: L \to \mathbb{R}^*$ *if it maps every level of evaluation* $l \in L$ *to a hyperreal number* $as(l)$.

Note that we sometimes abuse notation and use the same symbols for levels of evaluation and their assignments interchangeably. For example, utility functions' levels of evaluation are denoted by numbers and not as variables. Similarly, we use the number 0 to refer to the level of neutral evaluation and 1 to the level of unit promotion.

We now define the notion of a satisfying assignment by first defining it for an aggregation fact and then for aggregation information.

Definition 5 (Satisfying assignment—fact (unweighted)). *Given a set of levels of evaluation* L, *an aggregation fact* $af = (L_1, L_2, op)$, *an assignment function as* $: L \to \mathbb{R}^*$ *satisfies the aggregation fact* af *if the substituted interpretation* $(\Sigma_{l \in L_1} as(l)) op (\Sigma_{l' \in L_2} as(l'))$ *is true.*

Definition 6 (Satisfying assignment—information (unweighted)).
Given a set of levels of evaluation L, a set of aggregation information I, an assignment function as : L → $\mathbb{R}^*$ satisfies the information I, if for every fact af ∈ I in the information, as satisfies af.

Example. Consider the fact $(\{d, 1\}, \{0, \frac{11}{15}\}, <)$. This fact is satisfied by the function as, where $as(d) = -1$. This is because the interpretation $(as(d) + 1) <$ $(0 + \frac{11}{15})$ is satisfied, as $-1 + 1 = 0 < \frac{11}{15}$. In fact, we can see that any assignment that maps d to a value less than $-\frac{4}{15}$ will be a satisfying assignment.

Aggregation information may have multiple satisfying assignments. The set of all such assignments is called the *solution set* for the information.

Definition 7 *(Solution set (unweighted)). Given aggregation information I, the solution set S_I is the set such that function as is in the solution set as ∈ S_I iff the function as satisfies the information I, i.e. $S_I = \{as : L → \mathbb{R}^* | as \text{ satisfies } I\}$.*

Example. Consider the information $I = \{(\{d, 1\}, \{0, \frac{11}{15}\}, <)\}$. Remember that this is satisfied by any function as such that d is assigned less than $-\frac{4}{15}$, i.e. $as(d) < -\frac{4}{15}$. Therefore, the solution set is given as $S_I = \{as : L → \mathbb{R}^* | as(d) < -\frac{4}{15}\}$.

4.3 Weighing the Values

Recall that the aggregation facts presented in the previous section do not distinguish between different values. This is not always appropriate; the agent may prioritise different values to different degrees. These weighted priorities affect how different values and their respective levels of evaluations are compared.

We model these priorities through a set of weights W, where the weights are hyperreal variables. A *weight profile* maps each value v to a weight $w(v) ∈ W$.

Definition 8 (Weight profile). *Given a set of values V and a set of weights W, a weight profile is a function w : V → W such that w(v) ∈ W denotes the weight of value v.*

Example. The agent has three values: utility u, animal welfare a and human welfare h. Consider that the agent prioritises human welfare over animal welfare and utility in every situation. This can be represented by the weight profile w, that is, $w(u) = 1$, $w(a) = 1$ and $w(h) = \omega$.

Through the use of weights, we can declare how different levels of evaluation of specific values should trade off. We specify such through *weighted aggregation facts* and *weighted aggregation information*, which generalise aggregation facts and aggregation information, respectively.

Definition 9 (Weighted aggregation fact). *Given a set of weights W, levels of evaluation L, a weighted aggregation fact is a tuple (WL_1, WL_2, op) where WL_1 and WL_2 are multisets of pairs (w, l), $w \in W$ and $l \in L$, and $op \in \{<, \leq, =, \ll\}$ is a comparison operation. A weighted aggregation fact is interpreted as the statement $(\Sigma_{(w,l) \in WL_1} wl)$ op $(\Sigma_{(w',l') \in WL_2} w'l')$.*

The collection of all weighted aggregation facts for a set of values is called the *weighted aggregation information*.

Example. Let $w(u)$ represent the weight of the utility function and $w(a)$ represent the weight of animal welfare. We can now formalise with a weighted aggregation fact a requirement from a previous example; namely, that increasing the level of promotion of the value of utility from $\frac{11}{15}$ to 1 is strictly worse than demoting the value of animal welfare to d. This corresponds to the weighted aggregation fact $(\{(w(a), d), (w(u), 1)\}, \{(w(a), 0), (w(u), \frac{11}{15})\}, <)$, which we interpret as the inequality $(w(a)d + w(u)1) < (w(a)0 + w(u)\frac{11}{15})$.

Note. Weighted aggregation facts are strictly more expressive than (unweighted) aggregation facts. This is because unweighted aggregation facts can be understood as uniformly weighted and so can be expressed as weighted aggregation facts. For example, if $1 \in W$, then we can express the (unweighted) aggregation fact (L_1, L_2, op) as weighted aggregation fact (WL_1, WL_2, op), where $WL_1 = \{(1, l) | l \in L_1\}$ and $WL_2 = \{(1, l) | l \in L_2\}$.

Note. We can express a partial order $\preceq_W$ over the weights by a set of facts. In particular, if $1 \in L$ we can express $w_1 \preceq_W w_2$ as the fact $(\{(w_1, 1)\}, \{(w_2, 1)\}, \leq)$. By including all such facts, we can express any partial order $\preceq_W$ in the weighted aggregation information.

Example. If we care about animal welfare a and utility u to the same degree, we can express this as $(\{(w(a), 1)\}, \{(w(u), 1)\}, =)$, that is, $w(a) = w(u)$.

Furthermore, we can extend the definition of a satisfying assignment to apply to weighted aggregation facts and information. Note that to be able to interpret the weighted facts, we have to assign the weights a specific hyperreal value as well.

Definition 10 (Assignment (weighted)). *Given a set of levels of evaluation L and a set of weights, a function is an assignment function $as : (L \cup W) \to \mathbb{R}^*$ if it maps every level of evaluation $l \in L$ to a hyperreal number $as(l)$ and every weight $w \in W$ to a hyperreal number $as(w)$.*

Note that while it is possible to assign a value a non-positive weight[5], we assume that if an agent holds a value v then the agent seeks to achieve that value, i.e. the agent weights the value positively, i.e. for all v $as(w_v) > 0$ holds.

Definition 11 (Satisfying assignment—fact (weighted)). *Given a set of levels of evaluation L, a weighted aggregation fact $waf = (WL_1, WL_2, op)$, an*

---

[5] This can be used to model values the agent is apathetic towards (zero weight) or is even hostile to (negative weight).

assignment function as $: (L \cup W) \to \mathbb{R}^*$ *satisfies the weighted aggregation fact* *waf if the substituted interpretation* $(\Sigma_{(w,l) \in WL_1} as(w)as(l))$ *op* $(\Sigma_{(w',l') \in WL_2} as(w')as(l'))$ *is true.*

Definition 12 (Satisfying assignment—information (weighted)). *Given a set of levels of evaluation L, a set of weights W, a set of weighted aggregation information I, an assignment function as $: (L \cup W) \to \mathbb{R}^*$ satisfies the information I, if for every fact waf $\in I$ in the information, as satisfies waf.*

Example. Consider the previously identified weighted aggregation fact $(\{(w(a), d), (w(u), 1)\}, \{(w(a), 0), (w(u), \frac{11}{15})\}, <)$. This fact is interpreted as $(w(a)d + w(u)1) < (w(a)0 + w(u)\frac{11}{15}) = w(u)\frac{11}{15}$. Therefore, we have $w(a)d < -w(u)\frac{4}{15}$. Let as be an assignment such that $as(w(a)) = 1$, $as(w(u)) = \omega$ and $as(d) = -\omega^2$. In this case, both the left hand side and the right hand side are negative infinities. However, the absolute value of the left hand side is an order of magnitude larger (ω^2 compared to ω) and so the left hand side is less than the right hand side. As a result, as is a satisfying assignment.

Aggregation information may have multiple satisfying assignments. The set of all such assignments is called the solution set for the information.

Definition 13 (Solution set (weighted)). *Given weighted aggregation information I, the solution set S_I is the set such that function as is in the solution set as $\in S_I$ iff the function as satisfies the information I, i.e. $S_I = \{as : (L \cup W) \to \mathbb{R}^* | as$ satisfies $I\}$.*

Example. Consider the previously identified weighted aggregation fact $(\{(w(a), d), (w(u), 1)\}, \{(w(a), 0), (w(u), \frac{11}{15})\}, <)$. This fact is interpreted as $(w(a)d + w(u)1) < (w(a)0 + w(u)\frac{11}{15}) = w(u)\frac{11}{15}$. Therefore, we have $w(a)d < -w(u)\frac{4}{15}$. Also consider that the agent weights these two values equally, i.e. the fact $(\{(w(a), 1)\}, \{(w(u), 1)\}, =)$ holds. As a result, we have $w(a) = w(u)$. From our assumption that every weight is positive, we can then divide by $w(a)$ and conclude that $d < -\frac{4}{15}$. Therefore, the solution set can be defined as $S_I = \{as : (L \cup W) \to \mathbb{R}^* | as(d) < -\frac{4}{15} \wedge as(w(a)) = as(w(u))\}$.

Note. To simplify matters, we assume that the information that the agent is given is consistent, i.e. has always at least one possible solution. In practice, however, if the information is inconsistent, then the solution set will be empty.

4.4   Compatibility

We have thus far defined what assignment of variables are consistent with given information. We now define how an evaluation aggregation rule can be compatible with the information given, based on the possible assignment of variables.

In particular, we are interested in ranking the actions through the evaluation aggregation rule based on the information available and nothing else. That is, if one alternative is better than another under all satisfying assignments, then it must be ordered as the better action. On the other hand, if for different satisfying assignments, we may order the actions differently, then the aggregation rule should consider the two actions to be incomparable.

Definition 14 (Compatibility). *Given weighted evaluation information I, an evaluation profile $E = \langle e_{v_1}, ..., e_{v_{|V|}} \rangle$ in the appraisal domain D, values V, weight profile w and actions A, an evaluation aggregation rule f is compatible with weighted evaluation information I, if for any actions $a, b \in A$ the statement $a \preceq_A b$ holds iff for all satisfying assignments $as \in S_I$ in the solution set it holds that $\Sigma_{v \in V} as(w(v)) as(e_v(a)) \leq \Sigma_{v' \in V} as(w(v')) as(e_{v'}(b))$, where $\preceq_A = f(E)$.*

Note. Since compatibility uniquely determines whether for any actions a, b, $a \preceq_A b$ holds or not, there is at most one compatible evaluation aggregation rule. If the information is consistent, then we also know there is at least one compatible evaluation aggregation rule. Therefore, for consistent weighted aggregation information, we have a unique compatible rule. We denote this rule by f_I.

This means that if in our framework we formalise a value-based reasoning problem fully and appropriately, then there is a unique evaluation aggregation rule that is compatible with the evaluation information. This means that if the agent orders their action based on f_I then any of the maximal elements of the resulting partial order is guaranteed to be a value-aligned action.

Example. Consider the facts $(\{(w(a), 1)\}, \{(w(u), 1)\}, =)$ and $(\{(w(a), d), (w(u), 1)\}, \{(w(a), 0), (w(u), \frac{11}{15})\}, <)$. From these, we derived the solution set $S_I = \{as : (L \cup W) \rightarrow \mathbb{R}^* | as(d) < -\frac{4}{15} \wedge as(w(a)) = as(w(u))\}$.

Now consider the actions $drive(55)$ and $drive(75)$ and their evaluations E by the values utility u and animal welfare a:

- $e_a(drive(55)) = 0$ and
- $e_u(drive(55)) = \frac{11}{15}$.
- $e_a(drive(75)) = d$ and
- $e_u(drive(75)) = 1$,

where d corresponds to the demotion caused by an endangered fish dying.

The weighted sum of evaluations, using any satisfying assignment for driving at a speed of 55 km/h is (which we denote by sum_{55}) $sum_{55} = as(w(u)) as(e_u(drive(55))) + as(w(a)) as(e_a(drive(55)))$. Using the above, we derive that $sum_{55} = as(w(u)) \frac{11}{15}$.

The weighted sum of evaluations for driving at a speed of 75 km/h is $sum_{75} = as(w(u)) as(e_u(drive(75))) + as(w(a)) as(e_a(drive(75))) = as(w(u)) + as(w(a)) as(d)$. Since for all as, $as(w(u)) = as(w(a))$, we have $sum_{75} = as(w(u))(1 + as(d))$.

We also know that $as(d) < -\frac{4}{15}$ and so $sum_{75} < as(w(u))(\frac{11}{15})) = sum_{55}$.

Therefore, for all as, $sum_{75} < sum_{55}$, so the unique compatible aggregation evaluation rule f_I aggregates the evaluations E such that $drive(75) \prec_A drive(55)$, where $\preceq_A = f_I(E)$.

4.5   Applying Formalism to Example

We now showcase how an agent could utilise our proposed formalism, using our motivating example from Sect. 1.1. We assume that the agent has three distinct values: the task utility (u), animal welfare (a) and human welfare (h). We also assume that the agent prioritises human welfare over animal welfare and utility. That is, the partial order over the weights of the values is given as $w(u), w(a) \ll w(h)$.

This agent chooses the action that maximises the total level of evaluation of the different values. To handle uncertainty, the agent uses expectations to calculate the sum of the evaluations. For the 'value' of utility, it's simply the expected utility, which is given by the function $u(x)$. For simplicity's sake, we assume that the utility function u is given by the following equation:

$$u(x) = \begin{cases} x/75 & x \leq 75 \\ (100 - x)/25 & x > 75 \end{cases}$$

where x is the speed of the boat in km/h. We can see that the expected utility is maximal when the speed is 75 km/h and gradually reduces the further the speed deviates from 75.

For animal welfare a, we assume the expectation is:

$$e_a(drive(x)) = \begin{cases} 0 & 70 \geq x \\ 1d & 80 \geq x > 70 \\ 2d & 90 \geq x > 80 \\ 3d & 100 \geq x > 90 \end{cases}$$

Here, d is the level of demotion associated with the death of a single endangered fish. Furthermore, assume that $d \ll 0$; that is, the death of a single fish is a level of magnitude worse than the status quo. Consequently, this value is maximally promoted when the agent maintains the status quo by driving slower than 70 km/h.

For human welfare, recall that the passenger is in pain after being stung by a jellyfish. This pain is not distributed evenly: the passenger gets painful fits after exactly sixty minutes of completed journey. Therefore, the amount of pain depends on the length of the journey. Assume that the journey is 210 km. Thus, the expectation is:

$$e_h(drive(x)) = p\lfloor 210/x \rfloor$$

Here $p < 0$ corresponds to the level of demotion from the pain of a fit. Therefore, this value is maximally promoted when the agent minimises human pain by minimising the number of fits, which happens in the range $(70, 100]$.

We represent the agent's objective, i.e. the sum of the weighed expectations, by the function $V(x)$. More precisely, $V(x) = w(u)u(x) + w(a)e_a(drive(x)) + w(h)e_h(drive(x))$.

We can see that the agent's different values evaluate the range of possible velocities differently. We can use the weights of the values to find the optimal speed, that is, the speed x which maximises $V(x)$.

Let us start with a simpler case, where $w(a) = 0$ and $w(u) = 1$; that is, the agent is indifferent towards animal welfare but values the learnt utility. In this case, we can see that the agent prioritises maximising human welfare first, and then the learnt utility. This is because $w(u) \ll w(h)$. The agent maximises human welfare by only accepting speeds within the range $(70, 100]$ and then maximises the utility by picking a value from within this range that maximises the utility. This local maximum of the utility function is the global maximum, which is when $x = 75$. Therefore, in this simpler case, the agent would choose to drive at a speed of 75 km/h.

Now, consider the more complex case where $w(a) = w(u) = 1$. First, we see that for speeds $x \in (90, 100]$ we have $V(x) = u(x) + 3d + w(h)2p$. For speeds $x \in (80, 90]$ we have $V(x) = u(x) + 2d + w(h)2p$. We can see that this range is better than the previous one, as $d \ll 0$. For speeds $x \in (70, 80]$, we have $V(x) = u(x) + d + w(h)2p$. This is similarly better than the latter range. Therefore, in the range $(70, 100]$, the range $(70, 80]$ is optimal; within this range, the exact speed of 75 km/h maximises the utility. Therefore, $x = 75$ is optimal in this range.

For speeds $x \in (52.5, 70]$, we have $V(x) = u(x) + w(h)3p$. For speeds $x \in (0, 52.5]$, we have $V(x) < u(x) + w(h)4p$, which is worse than the latter range, as $w(h)p \ll 0$. Therefore, in the range $(0, 70]$, the optimal range of speed is in the range $(52.5, 70]$. In this range, the exact speed of 70 km/h maximimises the utility. Therefore, $x = 70$ is optimal in this range.

To derive whether $x = 75$ or $x = 70$ is better, we have to compare $V(75) = u(75) + d + w(h)2p$ and $V(70) = u(70) + w(h)3p$. We can do this by evaluating $V(70) - V(75) = u(70) - u(75) + w(h)p - d$.

Note that $u(70) - u(75) = -1/15$. Moreover, we know that $w(h)p \ll 0$ as $w(h) \gg 0$ and $p < 0$. Further, we also know that $d \ll 0$. From the properties of hyperreal numbers, we know that the sum of a (positive) infinity $-d$ and a (negative) infinity $w(h)p$ may be infinitesimal, finite or infinite. Therefore, based on the information we have, we cannot decide which of the options is better. As a result, there are two maximal elements of the partial order of the possible actions, $drive(75)$ and $drive(70)$.

When there is a tie, it may be because the agent does not have enough information. In such cases, the agent may ask for information from a human. Imagine that the agent learns from communication the weighted evaluation information $(\{1\}, \{d\}, \{w(h)\}, \{p\}, <)$. This is interpreted as $d < w(h)p$. That is, the death of an endangered fish is worse than one fit of pain for one person. Note that this is still not enough to decide between the two alternatives, however, because of the utility. That is, even though we know that $0 < w(h) - d$, we do not know whether $0 < -1/15 + w(h)p - d$.

Now consider instead that the agent learns the information $(\{1\}, \{d\}, \{w(h)\}, \{p\}, \ll)$, that is, $d \ll w(h)p$. Then by the properties of the hyperreal numbers, we would also know that $0 \ll -1/15 + w(h) - d$ and hence that 70 is an optimal speed. In other words, if the agent prioritised the survival of animal species over the lessening of human suffering, the agent would prefer to drive at 70 km/h.

Finally, consider the agent has the information $(\{w(h)\}, \{p\}, \{1\}, \{d\}, \leq)$, which is interpreted as $w(h)p \leq d$. That is, one painful fit is not better than the death of an endangered fish. In this case, this information is enough to decide, because $0 \leq d - w(h)p$ and so it must also be that $0 \leq w(h)p - d$ and, moreover, that $0 > -1/15 + w(h)p - d$ holds. That is, if the agent believes that the painful fit is at least as bad as the death of an endangered fish, the agent would prefer to drive at 75 km/h.

5   Related Work

In this section, we divide the related work into two broad categories: whether the values are represented in a more qualitative or a more quantitative way.

5.1   Related Qualitative Approaches

Argumentation emerged as an alternative approach to classical utility-based decision theory, where argument and logic-based representations are the basis for decision making [31]. Which argument is accepted is subjective and depends on the *audience* (effectively a total ordering on values). As a result, subjective human preferences, i.e. values, can model which argument succeeds and so what decision should be made, based on a specific audience [2]. This is modelled in *value-based argumentation* [2,4], where agents propose arguments in favour of different actions. Note that each argument promotes exactly one value and there is a total order over the values (i.e. the audience's preferences). The different arguments may attack one another; an attack is successful if the defending argument's value does not promote a more important value than the attacking argument's value. However, value-based argumentation is limited in expressiveness: each argument can promote only one value and no other level of evaluation is possible, (i.e. no demotion, no magnitude of promotion etc.). Moreover, arguments are decided solely based on the total ordering of values, i.e. no fine-grained trade-offs between the different arguments are possible.

To remedy this, many subsequent models have used more expressive representations of evaluations. For example, Serramia et al. [26] allow values to label alternatives with a degree of promotion or demotion. Then, the alternatives are ordered based on which values promote and demote different alternatives and to what levels. This approach also considers how many values of the same importance are promoted and this is traded-off against how many values are demoted. Therefore, some basic quantitative considerations can be represented in this approach. However, values are only counted against other values from the same rank (i.e. importance) and are all uniformly weighed within the same rank. Furthermore, the rank of a value and the level of evaluation are rigid and cannot be flexibly traded-off.

Zurek and Mokkas propose a framework [30,31], which allows for a more flexible trade-off between the various values and their different levels of promotion/demotion. They do this by prescribing only some basic properties of how individual evaluations should be aggregated. Similarly to our framework, their approach also permits the input of agent knowledge about how different levels of evaluation and value importance are related. However, their framework does not allow for the representation of anti-Archimedean priorities over the importance of different values or levels of evaluation.

5.2   Related Quantitative Approaches

Similarly to the qualitative methods, many quantitative methods associate with alternatives a degree of promotion/demotion; such approaches then use the weighted sum of values and their degrees of promotion and demotion [11,18,27,28]. The advantage of this is the flexible and fine-grained trade-off of values and their levels of promotion and demotion. For example Serramia et al. [27] use the sum of the promoted values's weights and compare it against the relative cost. On the other hand, Szabo et al. [28] use the weighted sum of evaluations to filter out desires and intentions of a BDI agent that would cause the agent to violate their own values. However, these approaches cannot represent qualitative priorities between different values.

Values are also often represented through utility functions [8,14,20,29]. For example, human preferences may be learned through cooperative inverse reinforcement learning [14] or other machine learning methods. An agent that acts based on an appropriate utility function would behave in a value-aligned way [20]. However, while utility-based frameworks allow for a more fine-grained trade-off between various values, they do not allow for more qualitative, anti-Archimedean trade-offs between them.

6   Conclusion and Future Work

Computational agents need to reason as to how to accomplish their goals while accounting for the values of the society in which they are embedded. As a result, there is a need to integrate the primarily quantitative based reasoning distinctive of machine learning based AI with qualitative human values. To address this problem, we have identified various requirements and presented a novel formalism that can integrate various properties of quantitative and qualitative reasoning for value alignment. To do so, our framework uses a combination of hyperreal numbers and a grading-based model.

Moreover, we conjecture that our framework *generalises* quantitative and qualitative reasoning in the context of *VAP*. We further conjecture that generalising the two requires the use of a non-Archimedean extension of real numbers[6], such as the hyperreal numbers. This is because of the utility compatibility and non-Archimedean requirements. Finally, we also argue that evaluations carry different amounts of information (sometimes finer-grained, sometimes rougher-grained) and a grading-based model can capture these features.

We have described how to represent the problem of value-based reasoning through our formalism. While we have described an informal example of how an agent may use this formalism, future work should propose an agent framework that makes use of this formalism, and will require: (i) an algorithm that can efficiently reason about the aggregation information and derive the value aligned evaluation aggregation rule; (ii) an algorithm for learning aggregation facts from observation and communication.

References

1. Atkinson, K., Bench-Capon, T.J.M.: Taking account of the actions of others in value-based reasoning. Artif. Intell. **254**, 1–20 (2018) https://doi.org/10.1016/j.artint.2017.09.002, https://doi.org/doi.org/10.1016/j.artint.2017.09.002
2. Atkinson, K., Bench-Capon, T.J.M.: Value-based argumentation. FLAP. **8**(6), 1543–1588 (2021). https://collegepublications.co.uk/ifcolog/?00048
3. Balinski, M., Laraki, R.: A theory of measuring, electing, and ranking. Proc. Natl. Acad. Sci. **104**(21), 8720–8725 (2007)
4. Bench-Capon, T.J.M.: Value-based argumentation frameworks. In: Benferhat, S., Giunchiglia, E. (eds.) Proceedings of 9th International Workshop on Non-Monotonic Reasoning (NMR 2002), 19–21 April Toulouse, France, pp. 443–454 (2002)
5. Bench-Capon, T.J.M., Modgil, S.: Norms and value based reasoning: justifying compliance and violation. Artif. Intell. Law **25**(1), 29–64 (2017). https://doi.org/10.1007/s10506-017-9194-9
6. Bostrom, N.: Superintelligence: Paths, Dangers, 1st edn. Strategies. Oxford University Press Inc, USA (2014)
7. Bostrom, N., et al.: Infinite ethics. Anal. Metaphys. **10**, 9–59 (2011)
8. Brown, D.S., Schneider, J., Dragan, A.D., Niekum, S.: Value alignment verification. In: Meila, M., Zhang, T. (eds.) Proceedings of the 38th International Conference on Machine Learning, ICML 2021, 18–24 July 2021, Virtual Event. Proceedings of Machine Learning Research, vol. 139, pp. 1105–1115. PMLR (2021). http://proceedings.mlr.press/v139/brown21a.html
9. Chang, R.: Value pluralism. In: Wright, J. (ed.) International Encyclopedia of the Social and Behavioral Sciences (Second Edition), pp. 21–26. Elsevier (2015)
10. Conway, J.H.: On Numbers and Games. AK Peters/CRC Press, Boca Raton (2000)
11. Cranefield, S., Winikoff, M., Dignum, V., Dignum, F.: No pizza for you: Value-based plan selection in BDI agents. In: Sierra, C. (ed.) Proceedings of the Twenty-Sixth International Joint Conference on Artificial Intelligence, IJCAI 2017, Melbourne, Australia, 19–25 August 2017, pp. 178–184. ijcai.org (2017). https://doi.org/10.24963/ijcai.2017/26, https://doi.org/10.24963/ijcai.2017/26

---

[6] Hyperreal numbers are not the only such number system; for example, surreal numbers [10] are also a non-Archimedean extension of real numbers. We have decided to use hyperreal numbers because of the transfer principle.

12. Eckersley, P.: Impossibility and uncertainty theorems in AI value alignment (or why your AGI should not have a utility function). In: Espinoza, H., hÉigeartaigh, S.Ó., Huang, X., Hernández-Orallo, J., Castillo-Effen, M. (eds.) Workshop on Artificial Intelligence Safety 2019 co-located with the Thirty-Third AAAI Conference on Artificial Intelligence 2019 (AAAI-19), Honolulu, Hawaii, 27 January 2019. CEUR Workshop Proceedings, vol. 2301. CEUR-WS.org (2019). http://ceur-ws.org/Vol-2301/paper_7.pdf
13. Geffner, H.: Model-free, model-based, and general intelligence. In: Lang, J. (ed.) Proceedings of the Twenty-Seventh International Joint Conference on Artificial Intelligence, IJCAI 2018, July 13–19, 2018, Stockholm, Sweden. pp. 10–17. ijcai.org (2018). https://doi.org/10.24963/ijcai.2018/2, https://doi.org/10.24963/ijcai.2018/2
14. Hadfield-Menell, D., Russell, S.J., Abbeel, P., Dragan, A.D.: Cooperative inverse reinforcement learning. In: Lee, D.D., Sugiyama, M., von Luxburg, U., Guyon, I., Garnett, R. (eds.) Advances in Neural Information Processing Systems 29: Annual Conference on Neural Information Processing Systems 2016, December 5–10, 2016, Barcelona, Spain. pp. 3909–3917 (2016), https://proceedings.neurips.cc/paper/2016/hash/c3395dd46c34fa7fd8d729d8cf88b7a8-Abstract.html
15. Irving, G., Christiano, P.F., Amodei, D.: AI safety via debate. CoRR abs/1805.00899 (2018). http://arxiv.org/abs/1805.00899
16. Keisler, H.J.: The hyperreal line. In: Ehrlich, P. (eds.) Real Numbers, Generalizations of the Reals, and Theories of Continua. Synthese Library, vol. 242, pp. 207–237. Springer, Dordrecht (1994). https://doi.org/10.1007/978-94-015-8248-3_8
17. Little, I.M.: Social choice and individual values. J. Polit. Econ. **60**(5), 422–432 (1952)
18. Mercuur, R., Dignum, V., Jonker, C.M.: The value of values and norms in social simulation. J. Artif. Soc. Soc. Simul. 22(1), 9 (2019). https://doi.org/10.18564/jasss.3929
19. Morreau, M.: Grading in groups. Econ. Philos. **32**(2), 323–352 (2016)
20. Noothigattu, R., et al.: Teaching AI agents ethical values using reinforcement learning and policy orchestration. IBM J. Res. Dev. **63**(4/5), 2:1–2:9 (2019). https://doi.org/10.1147/JRD.2019.2940428
21. Peterson, M.: A royal road to consequentialism? Ethical Theory Moral Pract. **13**(2), 153–169 (2010)
22. Popova, A., Regenwetter, M., Mattei, N.: A behavioral perspective on social choice. Ann. Math. Artif. Intell. **68**(1), 5–30 (2013)
23. Raz, J.: Practical Reasoning. Oxford University Press, Oxford (1978)
24. Robinson, A.: Non-standard Analysis. Princeton University Press, Princeton (2016)
25. Schwartz, S.H.: An overview of the Schwartz theory of basic values. Online Read. Psychol. Cult. **2**(1), 1–20 (2012)
26. Serramia, M., López-Sánchez, M., Moretti, S., Rodríguez-Aguilar, J.A.: On the dominant set selection problem and its application to value alignment. Auton. Agents Multi Agent Syst. **35**(2), 42 (2021). https://doi.org/10.1007/s10458-021-09519-5
27. Serramia, M., et al.: Exploiting moral values to choose the right norms. In: Furman, J., Marchant, G.E., Price, H., Rossi, F. (eds.) Proceedings of the 2018 AAAI/ACM Conference on AI, Ethics, and Society, AIES 2018, New Orleans, LA, USA, 02–03 February 2018, pp. 264–270. ACM (2018). https://doi.org/10.1145/3278721.3278735

28. Szabo, J., Such, J.M., Criado, N.: Understanding the role of values and norms in practical reasoning. In: Bassiliades, N., Chalkiadakis, G., de Jonge, D. (eds.) EUMAS/AT -2020. LNCS (LNAI), vol. 12520, pp. 431–439. Springer, Cham (2020). https://doi.org/10.1007/978-3-030-66412-1_27

29. Von Neumann, J., Morgenstern, O.: Theory of Games and Economic Behavior. Princeton University Press, Princeton (2007)

30. Zurek, T.: Goals, values, and reasoning. Expert Syst. Appl. **71**, 442–456 (2017) https://doi.org/10.1016/j.eswa.2016.11.008

31. Zurek, T., Mokkas, M.: Value-based reasoning in autonomous agents. Int. J. Comput. Intell. Syst. **14**(1), 896–921 (2021). https://doi.org/10.2991/ijcis.d.210203.001

Resource Allocation to Agents with Restrictions: Maximizing Likelihood with Minimum Compromise

Yohai Trabelsi[1(✉)], Abhijin Adiga[2], Sarit Kraus[1], and S. S. Ravi[2,3]

[1] Department of Computer Science, Bar-Ilan University, Ramat Gan, Israel
yohai.trabelsi@gmail.com, sarit@cs.biu.ac.il
[2] Biocomplexity Institute and Initiative, University of Virginia,
Charlottesville, VA, USA
abhijin@virginia.edu, ssravi0@gmail.com
[3] Department of Computer Science, University at Albany – SUNY,
Albany, NY, USA

Abstract. Many scenarios where agents with restrictions compete for resources can be cast as maximum matching problems on bipartite graphs. Our focus is on resource allocation problems where agents may have restrictions that make them incompatible with some resources. We assume that a PRINCIPAL chooses a maximum matching randomly so that each agent is matched to a resource with some probability. Agents would like to improve their chances of being matched by modifying their restrictions within certain limits. The PRINCIPAL's goal is to advise an unsatisfied agent to relax its restrictions so that the total cost of relaxation is within a budget (chosen by the agent) and the increase in the probability of being assigned a resource is maximized. We establish hardness results for some variants of this budget-constrained maximization problem and present algorithmic results for other variants. We experimentally evaluate our methods on synthetic datasets as well as on two novel real-world datasets: a vacation activities dataset and a classrooms dataset.

Keywords: Matching advice · Bipartite matching · Resource allocation · Submodular function

1 Introduction

There are many practical contexts where a set of **agents** must be suitably matched with a set of **resources**. Examples of such contexts include matching classes with classrooms [24], medical students with hospitals [27], matching buyers with products [19], matching customers with taxicabs [12], matching agricultural equipment with farms [13,26], etc. We assume that the matching process assigns at most one resource to each agent and that each resource is assigned to at most one agent. It is possible that some agents are not assigned resources and some resources are unused.

Agents have **restrictions** (or preferences) while resources have **constraints**. We assume that agents' restrictions are *soft*; that is, agents are willing to *relax* their restrictions so that they can get a resource. An agent who is unwilling to compromise may not get any resource. However, the constraints associated with resources are *hard*; they *cannot* be relaxed.

Example: An instructor who indicates her restriction for the classroom capacity as "Capacity ≥ 70" may be willing to relax this restriction to "Capacity ≥ 60" to improve her chances of obtaining a classroom. However, a classroom of size 50 imposes the hard constraint "Capacity ≤ 50".

An agent is **compatible** with a resource (i.e., the agent can be matched with the resource) only when the (hard) constraints of the resource are satisfied by the agent's restrictions. The problem of assigning resources to agents can be modeled as a matching problem on the following bipartite graph, which we refer to as the **compatibility graph**: the graph has two disjoint sets of nodes corresponding to the agents and resources respectively; each edge $\{u, v\}$ in the graph indicates that the agent represented by u is compatible with the resource represented by v. A PRINCIPAL (who is not one of the agents) chooses a maximum matching in the graph to maximize the number of agents who are assigned resources. Usually, there are many such maximum matchings, each one allocating resources to a (possibly) different set of agents. For fairness, the PRINCIPAL chooses a maximum matching randomly out of a given distribution. The PRINCIPAL may use, for example, an algorithm for fair matching [10] or a straight-forward process that randomly orders the agents and uses a deterministic matching algorithm like the Hopcroft-Karp algorithm [15] to generate a maximum matching.

It is natural for an agent, who is concerned that she will not be matched in the randomly generated matching, to seek advice from the PRINCIPAL in the form of changes to her restrictions in order to increase the likelihood of getting matched. We assume a nonnegative cost associated with relaxing each restriction. Agents are desperate to get such advice when there are several rounds of matching and they failed in previous ones; such a situation arises, for example, in the case of medical students who were not matched during the first round of the residency matching process [17]. Developing such recommendations can be modeled as the following budget-constrained optimization problem: find a set of modifications to an unmatched agent's restrictions under a budget constraint so that the likelihood of the agent being matched to a resource is maximized, given the resource compatibility information for the other agents.

Several recommendation systems in environments where agents compete for resources are similar to our notion of a PRINCIPAL. As an example, many route planning and satellite navigation apps provide advice to a given agent (driver) without taking into account possible changes in the behaviors of other agents due to similar recommendations. These recommendations often lead to undesirable consequences that are referred to as the price of anarchy [31]. The study of how to decrease the price of anarchy is beyond the scope of this paper.

Summary of Contributions

1. The matching advice problem. We develop a formal framework for advising agents in a resource allocation setting viewed as a matching problem on an agent-resource bipartite graph. We formulate a budget-constrained optimization

problem to generate suitable relaxations of an unmatched agent's restrictions so as to maximally increase the probability that the agent will be matched. We identify and study different forms of restrictions arising from agent restrictions and resource properties in real-world applications.

2. Complexity of improving the likelihood of matching. We show that, in general, the budget-constrained optimization problem is **NP**-hard.

3. Algorithms for improving the likelihood of matching. Under uniform costs for relaxing restrictions and uniform random selection of maximum matchings, we present algorithmic results for some classes of restrictions (which will be defined in Sect. 2.3). Specifically, we present an efficient approximation algorithm (with a performance guarantee of $(1 - 1/e)$) for the Multi-Choice Single-Restriction case. This result relies on the submodularity of the objective function. For another class called *threshold-like* restrictions, we develop a fixed parameter tractable algorithm, assuming that the budget and the cost of removing each restriction are non-negative integers.

4. Experimental Study. We study the performance of our recommendation algorithms on both synthetic data sets as well as two real-world data sets. The latter data sets arise in the contexts of assigning classrooms to courses and matching children with activities. We evaluate our algorithms under different cost schemes. The insights gained from this study can inform the PRINCIPAL (e.g., university administration) on issues such as adding, removing or modifying resources to cater to the needs of agents.

Related Work. Resource allocation in multi-agent systems has been studied by a number of researchers (e.g., [3,5,14]). The general focus of this work is on topics such as how agents express their resource requirements, algorithms for allocating resources to satisfy those requirements and evaluating the quality of the resulting allocations. Nguyen et al. [21] discuss some complexity and approximability in this context [21]. Zahedi et al. [32] study the problem of allocating tasks to agents in such a way that the task allocator can respond to queries dealing with counterfactual allocations.

Motivated by e-commerce applications, Zanker et al. [33] discuss the design and evaluation of constraint-based recommendation systems that allow users to specify soft constraints regarding products of interest. These constraints are in the form of rank ordering of desired products. Both algorithms for the problem and a system which includes implementations of those algorithms are discussed in [33]. Felfernig et al. [9] provide a discussion on the design of constraint-based recommendation systems and the technologies that are useful in developing such systems. Parameswaran et al. [23] discuss the development of a recommendation system that allows university students to choose courses; the system has the capability to handle complex constraints specified by students as well as those imposed by courses. Zhou and Han [34] propose an approach for a graph-based recommendation system that groups together agents with similar restrictions to allocate resources. To our knowledge, the problem studied in our paper, namely advising agents to modify their restrictions to improve their chances of obtaining resources, has not been addressed in the literature.

Note: For space reasons, most of the proofs do not appear in this version; they can be found in [28].

2 The Matching Advice Framework

2.1 Graph Representation and Problem Formulation

Agents, Resources, and Compatibility. We consider scenarios consisting of a set of *agents* (denoted by $\mathbb{X}$) and a set of *resources* (denoted by $\mathbb{Y}$). Every agent would like to be matched to a resource. However, agents may have *restrictions* that prevent them from being matched to certain resources. Such agent-resource pairs are said to be *incompatible*. We represent this agent-resource relationship using an $\mathbb{X}\mathbb{Y}$-bipartite graph called the *compatibility graph* $G(\mathbb{X}, \mathbb{Y}, E)$, where the edge $\{x, y\} \in E(G)$ iff the agent $x \in \mathbb{X}$ is compatible with $y \in \mathbb{Y}$. A PRINCIPAL assigns resources to agents. To maximize resource usage, the PRINCIPAL picks a *maximum matching* [4] from the compatibility graph.

The Advice Seeking Agent and Its Restrictions. The special agent who seeks advice will henceforth be denoted by x^*. Let $\mathbb{Y}_I \subseteq \mathbb{Y}$ be the set of resources that are incompatible with x^*. Let $R = \{r_1, r_2, \ldots, r_\ell\}$ be the set of restrictions of x^*. A *resource–restrictions* pair (y, R') consists of a resource y and a restriction set $R' \subseteq R$ such that (i) y is incompatible with x^* and (ii) R' is a minimal set of restrictions to remove so that y becomes compatible with x^*. A resource-restriction pair describes precisely why resource y is currently incompatible with x^* (i.e., the edge $\{x^*, y\}$ is not in the compatibility graph), and how it can be made compatible. Suppose a set A of restrictions is removed. Then, a previously incompatible resource y becomes compatible iff there exists $(y, R') \in \Gamma$ such that $R' \subseteq A$. We then add the new edge $\{x^*, y\}$ to the compatibility graph. Let $\Gamma = \{(y, R') \mid y \in \mathbb{Y}, R' \subseteq R\}$ be the set of such resource–restrictions pairs. We refer to Γ as the *incompatibility set* of x^*. Note that there could be more than one resource–restrictions pair with the same resource when there are multiple choices for removing restrictions to make the resource compatible with x^*. For a restriction $r \in R$, let $\rho(r)$ be a positive real number denoting the cost incurred by x^* for relaxing r. For any $A \subseteq R$, the cost of relaxing all the restrictions in A is $\rho(A) = \sum_{r \in A} \rho(r)$.

Resource Allocation Using Bipartite Maximum Matching. To maximize resource usage and ensure fairness for all agents, we assume that the PRINCIPAL picks a maximum matching from the set of all possible maximum matchings. There are two components to this part of the framework: (i) generating a random maximum matching of the compatibility graph and (ii) computing the probability that x^* is picked in a random maximum matching. Firstly, we note that a maximum matching of a bipartite graph can be obtained in polynomial time [15]. Given any deterministic algorithm for maximum matching, one can permute the set of agents or resources (or both) randomly and obtain a random matching or one could use approaches such as the fair matching algorithm [10]. In any case, the first part can be computed in polynomial time. The second part however is computationally harder. The distribution from which the matching is sampled depends on the algorithm used by the PRINCIPAL. In order to provide advice to an agent, the PRINCIPAL must find the probability that a maximum matching chosen from this distribution includes that agent. This problem is closely related to a computationally intractable (technically, #**P**-hard) problem, namely counting the number of maximum matchings in bipartite graphs (or sampling them uniformly) [18,29].

One way to estimate this probability is as follows: given an algorithm that generates a random maximum matching, sample a large number of maximum matchings and compute the ratio of the number of matchings in which x^* was matched to the total number of samples.

The Advice Framework. The following are the steps in the maximum matching advice framework, given the set of agents $\mathbb{X}$ and the set of resources $\mathbb{Y}$.

1. An agent x^* approaches the PRINCIPAL seeking advice. The inputs to the framework are a compatibility graph G, the restrictions set R of x^*, and its incompatibility set Γ.
2. The PRINCIPAL computes (or estimates) the probability that x^* is matched to a resource and provides this information to x^*.
3. If x^* is not satisfied with the probability, then it specifies the cost $\rho(\cdot)$ of relaxing its restrictions and a budget β as an upper bound for the cost it is willing to pay.
4. The PRINCIPAL suggests a relaxation solution (if one exists) that results in an *augmented compatibility graph* G' for which the improvement in probability of the agent being matched is maximized under the budget constraint.

The Probability Gain. Let us denote G as the original compatibility graph and G' as the new compatibility graph obtained by adding edges after relaxing the restrictions R^* chosen by the special agent x^*. Denote by $p(G)$ and $p(G')$ the probability that x^* is matched in a maximum matching of G and G' respectively. The probability gain $g(R^*)$ is defined as $p(G') - p(G)$. Since $p(G)$ does not change when x^* relaxes some restrictions, maximizing $g(R^*)$ is equivalent to maximizing $p(G')$. Now, we define the MATCHINGADVICE problem formally.

Problem MatchingAdvice

<u>Given:</u> A bipartite compatibility graph $G(\mathbb{X}, \mathbb{Y}, E)$, an agent $x^* \in \mathbb{X}$ seeking advice, its set of restrictions R, the cost of removing each restriction, incompatibility set Γ, and a budget β.

<u>Requirement:</u> A set of restrictions R^* with $\rho(R^*) \le \beta$ such that removal of R^* maximizes the gain in probability g(R^*).

2.2   An Example

We use the following example of matching courses to classrooms (see Fig. 1). Each classroom is a resource and each course (or instructor) is an agent. Each classroom has two attributes: capacity and region where it is located. Each course has restrictions such as the required minimum capacity and desired regions. Agent x^* prefers a classroom of size at least 40 and regions in the order $r_1 > r_2 > r_3$. In the example of Fig. 1, x^* is incompatible with all resources to begin with. To model the capacity restrictions, we discretize the relaxation: we will assume that x^* relaxes the capacity constraint in steps of 10. Accordingly, we have labels c_{10}^i, where c denotes the capacity and i denotes the step. For example, the capacity labels associated with edge $\{x^*, y_1\}$ are c_{10}^1 and c_{10}^2 as x^* must relax its capacity constraint by 20 for it to be compatible with y_1 with respect to capacity. There is an option to increase the capacity by adding more seats (for a fee). Again, we assume that the seating capacity can be increased in steps of 10. This is represented by labels s_{10}^i. Relaxing capacity constraint by 10 is same as increasing seating capacity by 10. Hence, as seen in Fig. 1, there are three ways for y_1 to become compatible with x^*: reduce capacity requirement by 20 (remove labels c_{10}^1 and c_{10}^2), increase seating capacity by 20 (remove labels s_{10}^1 and s_{10}^2), or reduce capacity requirement by 10 and increase seating capacity by 10 (remove labels c_{10}^1 and s_{10}^1). For the region constraint, we have one label r_i for every region i. For y_3 to be compatible with x^*, both r_1 and r_2 must be removed. This is equivalent to saying that the restriction that the classroom be located in regions 1 or 2 is relaxed.

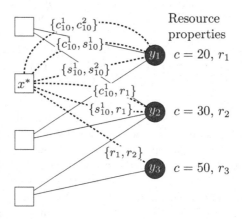

Fig. 1. A course-classroom example of matching advice framework. The agent x^* requires that the classroom capacity be at least 40 and located in region 1.

2.3   Incompatibility Types

In this work, we consider advice frameworks with different forms of incompatibility relationships.

Single-Choice-Multi-Restriction Incompatibility. In an incompatibility set with this property, there is exactly one choice for relaxing restrictions for each incompatible resource. This means that in the incompatibility set Γ, for every incompatible resource $y \in \mathbb{Y}_I$, there exists exactly one resource–restrictions pair (y, R'). Note however that $|R'|$ may be ≥ 1; i.e., more than one restriction may need to be removed to make y compatible with the agent.

Multi-Choice-Single-Restriction Incompatibility. In an incompatibility set with this property, for each resource–restriction pair $(y, R') \in \Gamma$, $|R'| = 1$. This means that only one restriction needs to be removed in order to make any resource compatible. However, it is possible that there are multiple choices of restrictions to remove.

We also consider **Single-Choice-Single-Restriction** incompatibility where for a resource, there is exactly one choice of one restriction to be removed to make it compatible. Similarly, we have **Multi-Choice-Multi-Restriction** incompatibility, a special case of which is the threshold-like incompatibility described below.

Threshold-Like Incompatibility. This type of incompatibility is motivated by capacity and region restrictions (as in Example 1). In this case, the restrictions set R can be partitioned into α blocks or *attributes* R_ℓ, $\ell = 1, 2, \ldots, \alpha$. In each $R_\ell = \{r_{\ell,1}, r_{\ell,2}, \ldots, r_{\ell,t(\ell)}\}$, the restrictions can be ordered $r_{\ell,1} < r_{\ell,2} < \ldots < r_{\ell,t(\ell)}$, where $t(\ell) = |R_\ell|$. The incompatibility set Γ satisfies the following property: $\forall (y, R') \in \Gamma$, if $r_{\ell,s} \in R'$, then, it implies that $r_{\ell,s+1} \in R'$ (if $r_{\ell,s+1}$ exists). In other words, if a restrictions set R' includes $r_{l,s}$, then it also includes all higher elements $r_{l,s+1}, r_{l,s+2}, \ldots$ (provided they exist). Let $r_{\ell,s}$ be the minimum element in $R_\ell \cap R'$. It can be considered as the *threshold* corresponding to the ℓth attribute induced by the agent's restrictions. If a resource is incompatible with regard to the ℓth attribute, it means that the value of the resource with respect to that attribute is less than $r_{l,s}$. In the above example, the threshold for capacity is 40. Any classroom with capacity less than 30 is below the threshold and hence is incompatible.

We also use abbreviated forms when necessary. For example, the short form for Single-Choice-Multi-Restriction is Single-C-Multi-R.

3 Preliminaries

Here, we present some preliminary results regarding maximum matching size and matching probability computation.

Lemma 1. *Let G denote the original compatibility graph and $G' \neq G$ denote the compatibility graph obtained after some restrictions of agent x^* are removed.*

1. *Any maximum matching in G' that is not a maximum matching in G matches agent x^*. In addition, the edge from x^* to the matched resource is not in G.*
2. *The size of a maximum matching in G' is at most one more than that of G.*

Proof (Idea): We use the simple fact that each new edge added to G' is incident on x^*. For details, see [28]. $\qquad \Box$

Definition 1. *Scenarios: Let G and G' denote respectively the original compatibility graph and the one that results after some restrictions of agent x^* are removed. There are two possible scenarios depending on the sizes of maximum matchings of G and G'.*

1. **Scenario 1.** *Maximum matching size in G' is one more than that of G. In this case, x^* is matched in all maximum matchings in G'. Thus, in this scenario, the probability that x^* is matched has the maximum possible value of 1.*
2. **Scenario 2.** *Maximum matching size in G' is the same as that of G. In this case, all maximum matchings of G' which are not maximum matchings in G will have x^* matched to a resource.*

4   Hardness Results

In this section, we present computational intractability results for MATCHIN-GADVICE. To do this, we first define the decision version of MATCHINGADVICE, which we denote by D-MATADV, as follows.

Decision Version of MatchingAdvice (D-MATADV) :

Given: A compatibility graph $G(\mathbb{X}, \mathbb{Y}, E)$, a special agent $x^* \in \mathbb{X}$ seeking advice, its set of restrictions R, the cost of removing each restriction, the incompatibility set Γ, a budget β, and a required benefit ψ.

Question: Is there a set of restrictions R^* with $\rho(R^*) \leq \beta$ such that the gain in probability g(R^*) is at least ψ?

The following result establishes the complexity of D-MATADV for the Multi-C-Single-R advice framework.

Theorem 1. D-MATADV *is **NP**-hard for the Multi-C-Single-R advice framework.*

Proof (Idea): Our reduction is from the MAX-COVERAGE problem which is known to be **NP**-complete [11]. For details, see [28].   □

Since the Multi-C-Single-R incompatibility is a special case of threshold-like incompatibility, the following holds.

Corollary 1. D-MATADV *is **NP**-hard for the threshold-like advice framework.*

5   Algorithms for Advice Frameworks

5.1   Notation

Let G denote the compatibility graph before any restriction of the special agent x^* is removed. For a subset of restrictions $A \subseteq R$, let G_A denote the compatibility graph obtained by removing/relaxing A and let $f(A)$ denote the number of new maximum matchings in G_A. By Part (1) of Lemma 1, x^* is matched in all these matchings. We call $f(\cdot)$ the *new matchings count* function. Using this notation, G corresponds to $G_\varnothing$ and $f(\varnothing)$ equals to 0, where $\varnothing$ is the empty set. Note that the probability that x^* is matched in G, $p(G)$ (defined in Sect. 2) increases with $f(\cdot)$. We will use the standard definitions of monotone, submodular and supermodular functions [1]. For simplicity, we use "monotone" to mean "monotone non-decreasing".

5.2   Scenario Identification

We recall from Lemma 1 and Definition 1 that two scenarios are possible when edges incident with x^* (meeting budget constraint) are added to the compatibility graph. Further, in the case of Scenario 1, the probability of matching x^* is 1; therefore, the probability that x^* is matched needs to be estimated only for Scenario 2. In this section, we will show an efficient method to (i) determine whether Scenario 1 exists, and if so, (ii) find the set of restrictions to relax. If the situation corresponds to Scenario 2, the algorithm returns the new incompatibility set Γ' of x^*.

Our method crucially uses the Dulmage-Mendelsohn (DM) decomposition of the node set of G [6,25]. Under this decomposition, any maximum matching M in a bipartite graph $G(\mathbb{X}, \mathbb{Y}, E)$ defines a partition of $\mathbb{X} \cup \mathbb{Y}$ into three sets: odd ($\mathcal{O}$), even ($\mathcal{E}$) and unreachable ($\mathcal{U}$). A node $u \in \mathcal{E}$ (respectively, $\mathcal{O}$) if there is an even (odd) length *alternating path*[1] in G from an unmatched node to u. A node $u \in \mathcal{U}$, that is, it is unreachable, if there is no alternating path in G from an unmatched node to u. We will use the following well-known results.

Lemma 2 (Irving et al. [16]). *Consider a bipartite graph $G(\mathbb{X}, \mathbb{Y}, E)$ and let $\mathcal{E}$, $\mathcal{O}$ and $\mathcal{U}$ be defined as above with respect to a maximum matching M of G.*

1. *The sets $\mathcal{E}$, $\mathcal{O}$ and $\mathcal{U}$ form a partition of $\mathbb{X} \cup \mathbb{Y}$, and this partition is independent of the maximum matching.*
2. *In any maximum matching M of G the following hold.*
   (a) M contains only $\mathcal{U}\mathcal{U}$ and $\mathcal{O}\mathcal{E}$ edges.
   (b) Every vertex in $\mathcal{O}$ and every vertex in $\mathcal{U}$ is matched by M.
   (c) $|M| = |\mathcal{O}| + |\mathcal{U}|/2$.
3. *There is no $\mathcal{E}\mathcal{U}$ edge or $\mathcal{E}\mathcal{E}$ edge in G.*

Lemma 3. *Let M be a maximum matching and $x \in \mathbb{X} \cap \mathcal{E}$. Adding edge $\{x, y\}$, where $y \in \mathbb{Y}$ is an incompatible resource, increases the matching size iff $y \in \mathcal{E}$.*

A proof of this lemma appears in [28]. The method to identify Scenario 1 is described in Algorithm 1.

Correctness of Algorithm 1. We will now show that the algorithm detects Matching Scenario 1, if it exists. We note that this scenario can happen if and only if the following two conditions are met: (i) there exists a resource $y \in \mathcal{E}$ and (ii) there exists a resource-restrictions pair (y, R') such that $\rho(R') \leq \beta$. The first condition is due to Lemma 3, while the second follows from the budget constraint. The algorithm checks for precisely these conditions. Hence, it detects Scenario 1 if it exists. Also, note that the algorithm filters out resource-restrictions pairs that do not meet the budget constraint.

Lemma 4. *Algorithm 1 runs in time $O(m\sqrt{n} + |\Gamma|))$, where n and m are the number of nodes and edges in G and Γ is the incompatibility set of x^*.*

---

[1] Given a matching M, an alternating path between two nodes is a path in which edges in M and edges not in M alternate [25]. The length of such a path is the number of edges in the path.

Algorithm 1: Detecting Matching Scenario 1 and updating the incompatibility set

---

    Input : Agents $\mathbb{X}$, Resources $\mathbb{Y}$, compatibility graph G, special agent x^*, its incompatibility set Γ and budget β.

    Output: Decide if Matching Scenario 1 has occurred or not. If not, output the new incompatibility set Γ' that accounts for the budget.

1 Set $\Gamma' = \emptyset$
2 Compute the DM-decomposition of $\mathbb{X} \cup \mathbb{Y}$ into $\mathcal{O}$, $\mathcal{U}$, and $\mathcal{E}$
3 **for** *each* $(y, R') \in \Gamma$ **do**
4   **if** $\rho(R') \leq \beta$ **then**
5   **if** $y \in \mathcal{E}$ **then**
6   **return** "Matching Scenario 1 detected" and R'
7   **else**
8             $\Gamma' \leftarrow \Gamma' \cup \{(y, R')\}$.
9 **return** "Matching Scenario 2 detected" and Γ'

Algorithm 2: Greedy algorithm for Multi-C-Single-R corresponding to Matching Scenario 2 with uniform probability of choosing a maximum matching and uniform cost for relaxing restrictions

---

    Input : Agents $\mathbb{X}$, Resources $\mathbb{Y}$, compatibility graph G, special agent x^*, its incompatibility set Γ, budget β and an oracle for the probability $p(G)$ that x^* is matched in the compatibility graph G.

    Output: Set of restrictions $A^* \subseteq R$, $|A^*| \leq \beta$

1 $A^* = \varnothing$.
2 **while** $|A^*| < \beta$ **do**
3     $r^* = \arg\max_{r \in R} p(G_{A^* \cup \{r\}})$.
4     $A^* \leftarrow A^* \cup \{r^*\}$ and $R \leftarrow R \setminus \{r^*\}$.
5 **return** A^*

Proof: To compute the DM-decomposition, we need to first compute a maximum matching M. This takes $O(m\sqrt{n})$ time using the Hopcroft-Karp algorithm [4]. Given M, computing the DM-decomposition can be done in $O(m)$ time [16,25]. Using this decomposition, checking whether a node y is in $\mathcal{E}$ can be done in $O(1)$ time. Since for each $(y, R') \in \Gamma$, the value $\rho(R')$ can be precomputed, checking whether $\rho(R') \leq \beta$ can also be done in $O(1)$ time. Thus, each iteration of the for loop in Line 3 uses $O(1)$ time. Hence, the total time used by the loop is $O(|\Gamma|)$. Therefore, the running time of the algorithm is $O(m\sqrt{n} + |\Gamma|)$. ∎

5.3 Multi-Choice-Single-Restriction

Here, we consider the Multi-Choice-Single-Restriction incompatibility framework where any resource can be made compatible with the removal of exactly one restriction. We will assume throughout that the cost of removing any restriction is 1 and that the maximum matching algorithm samples matchings uniformly from the space of all maximum matchings. We note that for the latter case, the probability of x^* being matched is the fraction of the maximum matchings of the given compatibility graph in which x^* is matched.

Lemma 5. *Consider the Multi-C-Single-R incompatibility. Then, for Matching Scenario 2, the new matching count function $f(\cdot)$ is monotone submodular.*

For a proof of the above lemma, see [28]. Since f is monotone submodular, we can use the greedy algorithm that iteratively picks a restriction with the highest benefit-to-cost ratio to relax [20]. Since each addition has the same cost (namely, 1), the highest benefit-to-cost ratio is achieved by a restriction that has the highest benefit. The resulting algorithm, which provides an approximation for the Multi-C-Single-R case, is shown as Algorithm 2. Note again that in the algorithm, we are using the fact that $p(\cdot)$ increases with $f(\cdot)$. The following result is again due to the fact that f is a monotone submodular function; see [28] for a proof of the following result.

Theorem 2. *Consider the Multi-C-Single-R incompatibility. Suppose each restriction has the same removal cost and the maximum matchings of the compatibility graph G are chosen from the uniform distribution. Then, given an oracle for computing the probability $p(\cdot)$, Algorithm 2 provides a solution to the* MATCHINGADVICE *problem with cost at most β and benefit at least $(1 - 1/e)$ of the optimal solution.*

Suppose the incompatibility set satisfies single restriction and single choice properties. Then, it can be shown that f is monotone and modular, in which case, the greedy algorithm is optimal [8].

Corollary 2. *Consider the* MATCHINGADVICE *problem under single restriction and single choice incompatibility. Suppose each restriction has the same removal cost and the maximum matchings of the compatibility graph G are chosen from the uniform distribution. Then, Algorithm 2 is optimal.*

Proof (Idea): We show that the function f is modular, that is, it is both submodular and supermodular (see [28]). Hence, the greedy strategy in Algorithm 2 gives an optimal solution [8]. □

5.4   Threshold-Like Incompatibility

We now describe an algorithm for finding an optimal solution to the MATCHINGADVICE problem for threshold-like incompatibility. We assume that the budget β and cost of removing each restriction are non-negative integers. Let $R = \biguplus_{1 \le \ell \le \alpha} R_\ell$ be a partition of variables where each part contains variables corresponding to values of an attribute. We say that an α-tuple $(\beta_1, \beta_2, \ldots, \beta_\alpha)$ of non-negative integers is an α-partition of the budget β if $\sum_{\ell=1}^{\alpha} \beta_\ell = \beta$. Let Π_β^α denote all the α-partitions of β. Algorithm 3 exhaustively explores all possible budget allocations to the attributes. Once the budget is allocated, the best solution among the restrictions in each R_ℓ can be computed using a binary search.

We identify the least restriction r_ℓ^* in R_ℓ such that the sum of costs of all $r \geq r_\ell^*$ in R_ℓ are removed. Unlike the previous cases, this algorithm does not assume uniform cost or uniform probability of picking a maximum matching.

Algorithm 3: Algorithm for threshold-like incompatibility corresponding to Matching Scenario 2

Input : Resources $\mathbb{Y}$, agents $\mathbb{X}$, compatibility graph G, special agent x^*, its incompatibility set Γ, budget β and a probability oracle $p(\cdot)$.
Output: Set of restrictions $A \subseteq R$ with $\rho(A) \leq \beta$

1 $p^* = p(G)$ and $A^* = \varnothing$
2 **for** *each* $(\beta_1, \beta_2, \ldots, \beta_\alpha) \in \Pi_\beta^\alpha$ **do**
3   **for** $\ell = 1, 2, \ldots, \alpha$ **do**
4          $r_\ell^* = \arg\min_{r \in R_\ell} \sum_{r' \geq r} \rho(r') \leq \beta_\ell$.
5   Let $A_\ell = \{r \mid r \in R_\ell, r \geq r_\ell^*\}$.
6   Let $A = \bigcup_\ell A_\ell$.
7   **if** $p(G_A) > p^*$ **then** $A^* = A$, $p^* = p(G_A)$
8 **return** A^*

Theorem 3. *For* MATCHINGADVICE *with threshold-like incompatibility where the budget β and the cost of removing each restriction are non-negative integers, given an oracle for probability $p(\cdot)$, Algorithm 3 provides an optimal solution in $O(\beta^\alpha \log |R|)$ calls to the probability $p(\cdot)$ computing oracle, where R is the restrictions set of special agent x^*, and α is the number of blocks in $\mathbb{Y}$.*

Our proof of the above result appears in [28].

6 Computing Matching Probability

A crucial component of the advice framework is to estimate the probability that a maximum matching chosen uniformly randomly from the set of all maximum matchings includes x^*. This problem is closely related to a computationally intractable (technically, #P-hard) problem, namely counting the number of maximum matchings in bipartite graphs [18,29]. In our case, this probability computation must be repeatedly performed each time a possible solution is to be evaluated. Our goal here is to reduce the number of such computations. We will show that under certain independent sampling of matchings, one can precompute a relatively small number of probabilities that can be used to find the probability of x^* being matched after relaxing any set of restrictions.

Suppose the set $\mathbb{Y}$ of resources can be partitioned into η blocks $\mathbb{Y} = \mathbb{Y}_1 \uplus \mathbb{Y}_2 \uplus \cdots \uplus \mathbb{Y}_\eta$ such that for any set of restrictions $A \subseteq R$ and any block $\mathbb{Y}_\ell$, relaxing A either makes all resources in $\mathbb{Y}_\ell$ compatible or none of its resources compatible with x^*. Let G_A denote the compatibility graph after the restrictions in A are

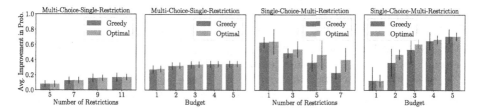

Fig. 2. The results for Multi-C-Single-R and Single-C-Multi-R on random bipartite graphs for varying number of restrictions and budget. The range of values on the y-axis of all plots are the same.

removed. Under the assumption that the matchings are sampled independently of one another from G_A, to compute the probability after relaxing A, it is enough to know the probability value p_ℓ that x^* is matched to a resource in $\mathbb{Y}_\ell$, $1 \leq \ell \leq \eta$ when sampled from all possible maximum matchings. Let p_0 denote the probability that x^* is not matched. Let $\mathcal{R}(A)$ denote the set of blocks whose resources become compatible with x^* after relaxing A. Then, probability that x^* appears in a maximum matching after relaxing A is given by $\frac{\sum_{\mathbb{Y}_\ell \in \mathcal{R}(A)} p_\ell}{p_0 + \sum_{\mathbb{Y}_\ell \in \mathcal{R}(A)} p_\ell}$. The justification for the summation used here is that every maximum matching containing x^* has exactly one resource matched to it. Therefore, the events that x^* is matched to a resource in $\mathbb{Y}_\ell$, $1 \leq \ell \leq \eta$ are disjoint.

We note that the number of resources m is a trivial upper bound for η, the number of blocks. In the case of threshold-like incompatibility, another upper bound can be specified. For budget β and number of attributes α, the number of optimal solutions is bounded by β^α (Algorithm 3). This serves as an upper bound for η.

7   Experimental Results

We experimented extensively on real-world and synthetic datasets to evaluate our algorithms for the advice frameworks considered.

Datasets. We considered a family of synthetic graphs and real-world datasets. We used Erdös-Renyi random bipartite graphs [7] $G(n, p)$ for experiments to evaluate the greedy algorithms for the Multi-C-Single-R and Single-C-Multi-R incompatibility frameworks. For the threshold-like incompatibility, we considered two real-world datasets. The first dataset is the *Course-Classroom* (COCL) dataset. This comes from a university[2] for the year 2018–2019[3]. In the experiments we focused on a two-hour slot on a specific day of the week (Tuesday), and used all the courses that are scheduled in this time slot and all available rooms. There are 144 classrooms and 154 courses. Each classroom has four attributes: its *capacity*, the *region* to which it belongs, whether it allows students with physical disability and whether it allows students with hearing disability. Following

---

[2] Bar-Ilan University, Ramat Gan, Israel.

[3] Dataset is available at https://github.com/yohayt/RAR_EUMAS2022.

the COVID-19 epidemic, additional features were added to the classes such as whether the class has facility for remote learning (https://zoom.us/ in this case). If the classroom has no feature for remote learning, then the teacher must bring the required equipment. Another feature was flexibility to add chairs to a class to increase its capacity. So, we have the attribute-augmented dataset CoCL-zc with the following extra features compared to CoCL: (i) adding chairs as an alternative to reducing capacity, (ii) remote learning in the classroom, and (iii) portable Zoom equipment as an alternative to (ii). Note that CoCL corresponds to Single-C-Multi-R threshold-like incompatibility, while CoCL-zc corresponds to Multi-C-Multi-R threshold-like incompatibility. Even though assigning classrooms to courses is well-studied [24] we did not find any publicly available dataset. The *Children Summer Vacation Activities* or *Passeport Vacances* (PassVac) [30] corresponds to online registration for assigning holiday activities to children. There are three attributes – minimum and maximum permissible age for participation with ranges. In addition, each child has restrictions as to which activity they would like to participate in. The minimum and maximum age restrictions each correspond to a threshold function. Note that the activity might be either too trivial for the child if the minimum age is relaxed, or the child may not fully understand the activity if the maximum age is relaxed. The numbers of children and activities are 634 and 533, respectively. We focused on one of the vacations in the dataset. In this vacation, there were 249 activities.

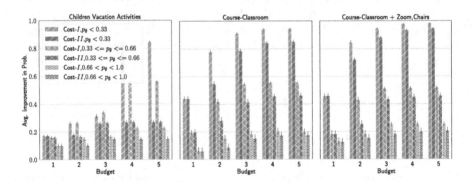

Fig. 3. The benefit obtained by removing restrictions for the threshold-like incompatibility on (i) PassVac, (ii) CoCL, and (iii) CoCL-zc. For analysis, we have partitioned the agents based on their original estimated probability of matching $p_\emptyset$.

Probability Computation. In all the experiments, the probability that the special agent x^* is matched was estimated in the following manner. A random maximum matching was generated by first randomly permuting the set of agents and using the resulting compatibility graph as input to the Hopcroft-Karp algorithm [15]. Each time, 1000 such maximum matchings were generated. The probability of x^* being matched is simply the ratio of total number of matchings in which x^* is matched to 1000.

Multi-C-Single-R with Synthetic Graphs. We generated 100 random bipartite graphs, each with 40 agents and 20 resources. Each edge has the probability of 0.2 to be matched. Then an additional agent was generated as x^*. A subset of restrictions was generated randomly for each resource. If the generated set is empty, then that resource would be made compatible with the agent. We experimented extensively on synthetic graphs to evaluate the greedy approach of Algorithm 2 by varying the size of the restrictions set and budget size. We used exhaustive search to obtain a pseudo-optimal solution (since the probabilities are only estimates) and compared it with the greedy solution. For each instance, we ran 100 experiments of finding sets of restrictions to be removed. The results are in the first two parts of Fig. 2. We varied the maximum number of restrictions allotted per resource from 2 to 4. In the top left plot, we fixed the budget β to 2 and varied the number of restrictions from 5 to 11. In the bottom left plot, we fixed the number of restrictions to 19 and varied the budget β from 1 to 5. We observe that in each case, the greedy algorithm closely matched the performance of the pseudo-optimal solution. We note the gain is high for small budgets as only one restriction per resource needs to be removed to make it compatible. Therefore, increasing the budget only increases the gain marginally. Increasing the number of restrictions does not have much effect on the benefit.

Single-C-Multi-R Incompatibility with Synthetic Graphs. Here, we apply the greedy algorithm (Algorithm 2). It is known to have performance guarantee of γ times the best solution given the budget, where γ is the submodularity ratio [2]. Again, we used exhaustive search to obtain a pseudo-optimal solution and compared it with the greedy solution. The experiment design is similar to that of the Multi-C-Single-R case. In the third and fourth parts of Fig. 2, the results are presented for varying sizes of restrictions and budget. The number of restrictions per resource is at most 4. We note that unlike the Multi-C-Single-R case, the probability of being matched decreases with increase in the number of restrictions; this is because all the restrictions corresponding to a resource must be removed for it to become compatible. Also, increasing the budget provides significant benefit in this case as many more restrictions must be removed for resources to become compatible compared to the Multi-C-Single-R case.

Threshold-Like Incompatibility with Real Data Sets. For CoCL dataset, we used 140 courses out of the 154 available and for each agent, each cost function, and each budget value, we have 100 replicates. For PassVac, we used 603 children out of the 634 children. For each agent, each cost function, and each budget value, we have 30 replicates. For both PassVac and CoCL datasets, we used two cost schemes: Cost-I is the uniform cost function where all attribute values have cost 1 and Cost-II is a linear cost function, where, for a given attribute, the cost of removing the first restriction is 1, the second is 2, and so on. Therefore, if t labels corresponding to an attribute are removed, the cost incurred is $t(t+1)/2$ (the more the PRINCIPAL deviates from the threshold set by the agent, the higher the regret or penalty). Here, we considered multiple agents, one at a time in our analysis. These agents were categorized based on their initial probability of being matched, $p_\varnothing$: (i) $[0, 1/3)$, (ii) $[1/3, 2/3)$, and (iii) $[2/3, 1)$. The results shown in Fig. 3 are discussed below.

Application specific observations. For COCL, hearing disability feature is typically the first to be relaxed. This seems to suggest that for the number of students with hearing disability, the number of classrooms which can accommodate their needs is not adequate. In the PASSVAC case, the abrupt increase in probability was due to a large number of activities being ranked as low preference by multiple agents (children). These are a few observations that can help the PRINCIPAL to better cater to the needs of the agents.

Single-C-Multi-R vs. Multi-C-Multi-R in the COCL dataset. We recall that the COCL dataset has two scenarios: with Zoom and chairs and without these facilities. We note that there is not much difference in the benefits. In particular, we can see that there is no significant decrease in the improvement compared to the case when not having these facilities. This seems to indicate that the university is well prepared to the COVID-19 special needs.

Increase in benefit with budget. We observe that as the budget increases, in the case of COCL, the probability of being matched increases gradually under both cost schemes. Also, the benefits for both cost schemes are comparable. However, in the case of PASSVAC, we observe an interesting threshold effect in the case of Cost-I. For example, when $p_\varnothing < 0.33$, until a budget of 4, there is no appreciable increase in the probability. However, for $\beta = 4$, the probability is almost 1. We observed a similar phenomenon in the case of Cost-II for budget 6, which is not presented in the plot. This knowledge of the required budget can help us to give agents an indication of the budget needed to achieve a reasonable improvement in probability.

8   Limitations and Future Work

A natural direction for future work is to extend the framework to allow changes to the restrictions of multiple agents. In such cases, an optimal allocation solution (e.g., Nash equilibrium [22]) can be considered. Our work assumes that each agent is matched to a single resource. So, another direction is to extend the advice framework by allowing agents to specify the number of resources needed. In such a case, when an agent does not receive the requested number of resources, the agent may be advised to either change her restrictions or reduce the number of requested resources. We note that our framework can be extended to many scenarios where resources can be shared. In such cases, for a shared resource, one can simply create copies of resources with identical properties.

Acknowledgments. We are grateful to the reviewers of EUMAS 2022 for carefully reading the manuscript and providing valuable suggestions. This work was supported by Israel Science Foundation under grant 1958/20, the EU Project TAILOR under grant 952215, Agricultural AI for Transforming Workforce and Decision Support (AgAID) grant no. 2021-67021-35344 from the USDA National Institute of Food and Agriculture, and the US National Science Foundation grant OAC-1916805 (CINES).

References

1. Bach, F., et al.: Learning with submodular functions: a convex optimization perspective. Found. Trends® Mach. Learn. **6**(2–3), 145–373 (2013). https://doi.org/10.1561/2200000039
2. Bian, A.A., Buhmann, J.M., Krause, A., Tschiatschek, S.: Guarantees for greedy maximization of non-submodular functions with applications. In: Proceedings of the 34th ICML, vol. 70, pp. 498–507. PMLR (2017)
3. Chevaleyre, Y., et al.: Issues in multiagent resource allocation. Informatica **30**(1), 3–31 (2006)
4. Cormen, T.H., Leiserson, C.E., Rivest, R.L., Stein, C.: Introduction to Algorithms. MIT Press, Cambridge (2009)
5. Dolgov, D.A., Durfee, E.H.: Resource allocation among agents with MDP-induced preferences. J. Artif. Intell. Res. **27**, 505–549 (2006)
6. Dulmage, A.L., Mendelsohn, N.S.: Coverings of bipartite graphs. Can. J. Math. **10**, 517–534 (1958)
7. Easley, D., Kleinberg, J.: Networks, Crowds and Markets: Reasoning About a Highly Connected World. Cambridge University Press, New York (2010)
8. Edmonds, J.: Matroids and the greedy algorithm. Math. Program. **1**(1), 127–136 (1971). https://doi.org/10.1007/BF01584082
9. Felfernig, A., Friedrich, G., Jannach, D., Zanker, M.: Developing constraint-based recommenders. In: Ricci, F., Rokach, L., Shapira, B., Kantor, P.B. (eds.) Recommender Systems Handbook, pp. 187–215. Springer, Boston (2011). https://doi.org/10.1007/978-0-387-85820-3_6
10. García-Soriano, D., Bonchi, F.: Fair-by-design matching. Data Min. Knowl. Disc. **34**(5), 1291–1335 (2020). https://doi.org/10.1007/s10618-020-00675-y
11. Garey, M.R., Johnson, D.S.: Computers and Intractability: A Guide to the Theory of NP-Completeness. W. H. Freeman and Co., San Francisco (1979)
12. Ghoseiri, K., Haghani, A., Hamed, M., et al.: Real-time rideshare matching problem. Technical report, Mid-Atlantic Universities Transportation Center (2010)
13. Gilbert, F.: A guide to sharing farm equipment (2018). https://projects.sare.org/wp-content/uploads/Sharing-Guide-2018-_-Web.pdf
14. Gorodetski, V., Karsaev, O., Konushy, V.: Multi-agent system for resource allocation and scheduling. In: Mařík, V., Pěchouček, M., Müller, J. (eds.) CEEMAS 2003. LNCS (LNAI), vol. 2691, pp. 236–246. Springer, Heidelberg (2003). https://doi.org/10.1007/3-540-45023-8_23
15. Hopcroft, J.E., Karp, R.M.: An $n^{5/2}$ algorithm for maximum matchings in bipartite graphs. SIAM J. Comput. **2**(4), 225–231 (1973)
16. Irving, R.W., Kavitha, T., Mehlhorn, K., Michail, D., Paluch, K.E.: Rank-maximal matchings. ACM Trans. Algorithms (TALG) **2**(4), 602–610 (2006)
17. Izenberg, D., Marwaha, S., Tepper, J.: Medical students who don't match through CaRMS: "it's like a scarlet letter" (2018). Healthy Debate: https://healthydebate.ca/2018/03/topic/medical-students-carms/
18. Jerrum, M.: Two-dimensional Monomer-Dimer systems are computationally intractable. J. Stat. Phys. **48**(1–2), 121–134 (1987). https://doi.org/10.1007/BF01010403
19. Lü, L., Medo, M., Zhang, Y.C.: The role of a matchmaker in buyer-vendor interactions. Eur. Phys. J. B **71**(4), 565–571 (2009). https://doi.org/10.1140/epjb/e2009-00315-0

20. Nemhauser, G.L., Wolsey, L.A., Fisher, M.L.: An analysis of approximations for maximizing submodular set functions-I. Math. Program. **14**(1), 265–294 (1978). https://doi.org/10.1007/BF01588971

21. Nguyen, T.T., Roos, M., Rothe, J.: A survey of approximability and inapproximability results for social welfare optimization in multiagent resource allocation. Ann. Math. Artif. Intell. **68**(1–3), 65–90 (2013). https://doi.org/10.1007/s10472-012-9328-4

22. Osborne, M.J., Rubinstein, A.: A Course in Game Theory. The MIT Press, Cambridge (1994)

23. Parameswaran, A.G., Venetis, P., Garcia-Molina, H.: Recommendation systems with complex constraints: a course recommendation perspective. ACM Trans. Inf. Syst. **29**(4), 1–33 (2011)

24. Phillips, A.E., Waterer, H., Ehrgott, M., Ryan, D.M.: Integer programming methods for large-scale practical classroom assignment problems. Comput. Oper. Res. **53**, 42–53 (2015)

25. Pulleyblank, W.R.: Matchings and extensions. In: Handbook of Combinatorics, vol. 1, pp. 179–232 (1995)

26. Rakhra, M., Singh, R.: Internet based resource sharing platform development for agriculture machinery and tools in Punjab, India. In: Proceedings of the 8th International Conference on Reliability, Infocom Technologies and Optimization (Trends and Future Directions) (ICRITO), pp. 636–642 (2020)

27. Roth, A.E.: On the allocation of residents to rural hospitals: a general property of two-sided matching markets. Econom.: J. Econom. Soc. **54**(2), 425–427 (1986)

28. Trabelsi, Y., Adiga, A., Kraus, S., Ravi, S.S.: Resource allocation to agents with restrictions: maximizing likelihood with minimum compromise. arXiv Report, August 2022

29. Valiant, L.G.: The complexity of enumeration and reliability problems. SIAM J. Comput. **8**(3), 410–421 (1979)

30. Varone, S., Beffa, C.: Dataset on a problem of assigning activities to children, with various optimization constraints. Data Brief **25**, 104168 (2019)

31. Wapner, L.M.: GPS navigation apps and the price of anarchy. Math. Gaz. **104**(560), 235–240 (2020)

32. Zahedi, Z., Sengupta, S., Kambhampati, S.: Why not give this work to them? Explaining AI-moderated task-allocation outcomes using negotiation trees. arXiv: 2002.01640 (2020)

33. Zanker, M., Jessenitschnig, M., Schmid, W.: Preference reasoning with soft constraints in constraint-based recommender systems. Constraints Int. J. **15**(4), 574–595 (2010). https://doi.org/10.1007/s10601-010-9098-8

34. Zhou, W., Han, W.: Personalized recommendation via user preference matching. Inf. Process. Manag. **56**(3), 955–968 (2019)

PhD Day Short Papers

Proactivity in Intelligent Personal Assistants: A Simulation-Based Approach

Awais Akbar[(✉)] [iD]

ADAPT Centre, Dublin, Ireland
awais.akbar@adaptcentre.ie

Abstract. Intelligent personal assistants (IPAs) are playing an increasingly significant role in our everyday lives. However, their reactive behaviour limits their assistance to a user's explicit requests. Integrating proactivity in these assistants would allow them to perform tasks on behalf of users without an explicit request and, in turn, improve the user experience. To explore this goal, this work presents MAIS (Multi Agent Interactions Simulator) which is capable of generating simulations of proactive agents. MAIS allows us to study the behaviour of agents, their interactions with each other in a multi-agent environment, and the importance of different agent features to accomplish a particular task. This paper presents the results from my experiments for a use case based on meeting scheduling in an organisational setting and the potential opportunities and challenges related to the adoption of IPAs. Human-in-the-loop control is introduced as a key component and the challenges arising with varying levels of autonomy in agents are also studied.

Keywords: Intelligent personal assistants · Proactivity · Multi-agent systems · Simulation · Personalisation

1 Introduction

Intelligent personal assistants, digital personal assistants, and virtual assistants are the synonyms for the representation of personalised systems that are fueled by artificial intelligence [2]. When requested to perform a task, these assistants collect the required information from their user, evaluate it, and generate a relevant response [3]. Aiming to assist users from different walks of life, the IPAs of today are becoming an integral part of our lives, helping us in day-to-day tasks ranging from information search to making restaurant reservations, setting alarms and reminders, and controlling home automation devices etc. [7,12]. These assistants, however, have certain limitations because of their reactive behaviour achieved by a request-response approach through conversational input [10]. While this behaviour is still helpful for the users to some extent, it increases both the number of actions necessary to perform a particular task and the cognitive load in managing them, potentially leading to the users exerting a great amount of effort to achieve those tasks. Furthermore, the user's goals are not sufficiently modeled in these systems and, as a result, a reference model of IPAs proactively acting on

D. Baumeister and J. Rothe (Eds.): EUMAS 2022, LNAI 13442, pp. 423–426, 2022.
https://doi.org/10.1007/978-3-031-20614-6_24

user's behalf can be found missing. A high degree of proactivity and personalisation should be the essence of the next generation of IPAs [1,5,6]. Detecting and considering user's goals or intentions will help these IPAs in goal-based decision making and delivering intervention or providing the support proactively [6,10]. My work aims to take IPAs research to the next level by integrating proactive behaviour to accomplish users' goals. To achieve this, I propose a simulation-based approach to study agent-to-agent interaction in a multi-agent environment. I design and implement a use case of meeting scheduling on my simulation system (MAIS) to understand some of the challenges that may arise with the adoption of proactive agents in an organisational setting. My motivation for a simulation-based study is that it provides significant control over key variables that can yield initial insights for the design of a more expansive user-based study [13]. Furthermore, a multi-agent simulation makes it possible to model the interactions between agents with different behaviours to achieve a common goal which would otherwise be beyond an individual agent's capabilities.

2   Related Work

A significant amount of research has been conducted on IPAs in the last two decades, however, integrating proactivity in these systems is rarely researched [2,7]. In addition to commercial IPAs, e.g. Amazon Alexa and Apple Siri, several other IPAs have also been developed by the researchers, but most of them follow a reactive approach to assist the users [2,7,16]. For example, the CALO agent [9,11] was developed to assist the workers with routine office tasks such as online form filling, meeting scheduling, office supply purchasing, and conference travel arrangements, but did not include any proactive support. Another example of reactive IPAs is Electric Elves project [15] in which a dozen IPAs were deployed in an office environment for a period of 7 days to undertake the routine office tasks, for example, tracking the status of activities, gathering information, and communicating the information with other agents in the organisation. There are two pieces of research that incorporate proactivity. Meurisch et al. [10] present a model of IPAs that integrates users' goals and proactive behaviour. To act on users' behalf, the model relies on different processing stages from sensing of information to goal and context modelling and goal based decision making. This model has not been implemented yet by the authors and the model itself is very minimalist with a lack of details which hinders the researchers from reusing or complementing it. Similarly, Neil et al. [16] proposed a framework to operationalise proactive behaviour within IPAs by extending the BDI model of agency [4] with a meta-level layer that identifies potentially helpful actions and determines when to perform them. This work focuses only on assisting a busy worker in an office desktop setting, which limits it to a single application. My research, on the other hand, potentially has a wider scope and focuses on proactive behaviour in a multi-user context where different users may exert different levels of control over their agents. Both the related works on proactive IPAs [10,16] have a different focus compared to my work and do not involve any simulations to study multi-agent interactions.

3   Methodology and Results

To run the simulation experiments, I develop a Python based tool that uses mediator pattern of object oriented programming to allow the agents to interact with each other. The configuration for the controlled experiments includes different parameters such as the number of users, number of meetings, users' schedule (n days × m slots), users' busyness level on a scale of 0–10, and human-in-the loop control. The baseline configuration contains 20 users, each having their own agent and 25 slots which can be mapped to a week schedule (5 days × 5 slots). Initially, all the users have blank schedules, which are then randomly filled based on the assigned busyness level. A busyness level of 6 would mean that the users' schedule is 60% busy which would lead to 15 out of 25 slots getting filled. When human-in-the loop (HITL) control is set (parameter value is set to 1), it induces a delay of 0–15 s as this time would be required by the user to respond to a notification. Each experiment is run 3 times to avoid any statistically imbalanced data. In **Experiment 1A**, a uniform low busyness level of 2 is set with no HITL control. The experiment is run with three configurations each with a varying number of meetings (20, 40, and 60). For n meetings, n pairs of agents are randomly selected and the meetings are scheduled between them. **Experiment 1B** has the same experiment design as 1A except the busyness level is increased to 7, 8, and 9 for any of three users. **Experiment 1C** follows the same setup as that of 1B. However, the random selection of agents is skewed towards the busy people. **Experiment 2** has the same three variants as that of experiment 1, but with HITL control being introduced for 20% of the users. **Experiment 3** uses the same configuration as that of experiment 2, but the 20% HITL control is assigned only to the busy people. Overall, results from the above experiments show that when one of the two users is busy, the number of interactions required to schedule the meeting increases significantly ranging from 7 to 20. Consequently, the time duration required for meeting scheduling also increases. On the other hand, a low busyness level leads to a reduced number of interactions (1–2) and a low time duration. Introducing the HITL control results in a lag, which further increases when a user is more busy.

4   Conclusion and Future Work

I have briefly introduced a multi-agent simulation approach, implemented in my MAIS tool, to study the efficiency of proactive IPAs with varying degrees of HITL control. The meeting scheduling use case is chosen and realised for a range of different experiments, thereby, providing us with the statistical significant data. The future work aims to design a set of diverse use cases which would then be implemented and tested on MAIS. Furthermore, as IPAs require negotiations in many cases be it meeting scheduling, restaurant reservations, buying or selling products etc., I would be interested in investigating whether the theory of negotiation [8] could empower IPAs to negotiate more effectively in complex situations. I further want to investigate how an extended version of the BDI model [16] can be used to support proactivity in IPAs. Lastly, I would be also be interested in modelling different contextual signals and tracking user's intent to measure their impact on proactive goal generation [14].

Acknowledgements. This research was conducted with the financial support of Science Foundation Ireland [13/RC/2106_P2] at ADAPT, the SFI Research Centre for AI-Driven Digital Content Technology at Trinity College Dublin, The University of Dublin.

References

1. Meneguzzi, F., Oh, J.: Proactive Assistant Agents, Papers from the 2010 AAAI Fall Symposium, Arlington, Virginia, USA, 11–13 November 2010, AAAI Technical Report, vol. FS-10-07 (2010)
2. de Barcelos Silva, A., et al.: Intelligent personal assistants: a systematic literature review. Expert Syst. Appl. **147**(C), 113–193 (2020)
3. Enge, E.: The rise of personal assistants (2017)
4. Georgeff, M., Pell, B., Pollack, M., Tambe, M., Wooldridge, M.: The Belief-Desire-Intention Model of Agency. In: Müller, J.P., Rao, A.S., Singh, M.P. (eds.) ATAL 1998. LNCS, vol. 1555, pp. 1–10. Springer, Heidelberg (1999). https://doi.org/10.1007/3-540-49057-4_1
5. Islas-Cota, E., Gutierrez-Garcia, J.O., Acosta, C.O., Rodríguez, L.F.: A systematic review of intelligent assistants. Fut. Gener. Comput. Syst. **128**(C) (2022)
6. Jeromela, J.: Scrutability of intelligent personal assistants. In: Proceedings of the 30th ACM Conference on User Modeling, Adaptation and Personalization, UMAP 2022, pp. 335–340. ACM, New York, NY, USA (2022)
7. Lopatovska, I.: Overview of the intelligent personal assistants. Ukr. J. Lib. Inf. Sci. 72–79 (2019)
8. Lopes, F., Coelho, H.: Negotiation and Argumentation in Multi-agent Systems: Fundamentals, Theories, Systems and Applications, Bentham Science Publisher, December 2014
9. Mark, W.G., Perrault, R.: Calo: Cognitive assistant that learns and organizes
10. Meurisch, C., Ionescu, M.D., Schmidt, B., Mühlhäuser, M.: Reference model of next-generation digital personal assistant: Integrating proactive behavior. In: Conference: the 2017 ACM International Joint Conference on Pervasive and Ubiquitous Computing and the 2017 ACM International Symposium on Wearable Computers, UbiComp 2017, ACM (2017)
11. Myers, K., et al.: An intelligent personal assistant for task and time management. AI Mag. **28**(2), 47 (2007). Jun
12. O'Leary, D.E.: Google's duplex: pretending to be human. Int. J. Intell. Syst. Acc. Financ. Manage. **26**(1), 46–53 (2019)
13. Siebers, P.O., Aickelin, U.: Introduction to multi-agent simulation, March 2008
14. Sun, Y., Yuan, N.J., Wang, Y., Xie, X., McDonald, K., Zhang, R.: Contextual intent tracking for personal assistants. In: Proceedings of the 22nd ACM SIGKDD International Conference on Knowledge Discovery and Data Mining (2016)
15. Tambe, M.: Electric elves: what went wrong and why. AI Mag. **29**(2) (2008)
16. Yorke-Smith, N., Saadati, S., Myers, K.L., Morley, D.N.: The design of a proactive personal agent for task management. Int. J. Artif. Intell. Tools **21** (2012)

Stability, Fairness, and Altruism in Coalition Formation

Anna Maria Kerkmann$^{(\boxtimes)}$ [ID]

Heinrich-Heine-Universität Düsseldorf, Düsseldorf, Germany
`anna.kerkmann@hhu.de`

Abstract. In coalition formation games, agents form partitions based on their preferences. Common questions concerning these games are how to represent the agents' preferences efficiently, what are desirable properties of the partitions, and how to find or verify such partitions. This article answers some such questions for special cases of coalition formation games, summarizing the three main topics of my PhD thesis: FEN-hedonic games, local fairness in hedonic games, and altruism in coalition formation games.

Keywords: Coalition formation · Hedonic games · Cooperative game theory · Stability · Fairness · Altruism

1 Introduction

Coalition formation is a vibrant topic of cooperative game theory. These games model situations where players form partitions based on their preferences. The research on hedonic games, a class of coalition formation games where players only care about those coalitions that they are part of, has been initiated by Drèze and Greenberg [5] and popularized by Banerjee et al. [2] and Bogomolnaia and Jackson [3]. Since general hedonic preferences can have exponential size (in the number of agents), the literature has proposed several succinct, yet reasonably expressive preference representation formats. Among those are cardinal representations where the agents assign individual utility values to each other. These single-agent utilities can be lifted to preferences over coalitions in different ways. In *additively separable* hedonic games, agents value coalitions by the sum of the valuations that they assign to its members [3]. In *fractional* and *modified fractional* hedonic games, the average is used instead of the sum [1,12]. The *friends-and-enemies* encoding by Dimitrov et al. [4] constitutes a subclass of additively separable hedonic games where the agents only distinguish between friends and enemies, assigning only one of two values to each other.

Given some hedonic game, it is natural to ask which partitions might form and whether a given partition will be accepted by the agents. There are several notions of stability, optimality, and fairness that measure the quality of a given partition. For example, a partition is *core stable* if there is no set of agents that would prefer to leave their current coalitions and form a new one.

© The Author(s), under exclusive license to Springer Nature Switzerland AG 2022
D. Baumeister and J. Rothe (Eds.): EUMAS 2022, LNAI 13442, pp. 427–430, 2022.
https://doi.org/10.1007/978-3-031-20614-6_25

In the scope of my dissertation, I introduced further preference representation formats, studied stability, optimality, and fairness in the resulting games, and enhanced a branch of research that deals with the consideration of altruism in coalition formation. After providing some foundations in Sect. 2, I will give an overview of my dissertation topics. Specifically, Sect. 3 gives an insight in FEN-hedonic games and the underlying preference representation. In Sect. 4, I elaborate on notions of local fairness and their relations to other solution concepts. Afterwards, several models of altruism in coalition formation games are summarized in Sect. 5.

2   Background

In coalition formation, we consider a set of *agents* $N = \{1, \ldots, n\}$ where each subset of N is called *coalition*. The set of all coalitions containing an agent i is denoted by $\mathcal{N}^i = \{C \subseteq N \mid i \in C\}$. A partition of the agents is also called *coalition structure* and the set of all partitions of N is denoted by $\mathcal{C}_N$. For a given partition $\pi \in \mathcal{C}_N$, the unique coalition containing agent i is denoted by $\pi(i)$. A *coalition formation game* $(N, \succeq)$ consists of a set of agents and a preference profile $\succeq$ with $\succeq_i \subseteq \mathcal{C}_N \times \mathcal{C}_N$ for each $i \in N$. A coalition formation game is *hedonic* if the preferences of the agents only depend on those coalitions that they are part of. We can also represent a hedonic game by a tuple $(N, \succeq)$ where, for each agent $i \in N$, $\succeq_i \subseteq \mathcal{N}^i \times \mathcal{N}^i$ is a weak ranking over all coalitions containing i.

The preferences in a hedonic game can be represented efficiently by using cardinal single-agent utilities. A hedonic game $(N, \succeq)$ is *additively separable* [3] if there exists a value function $v_i : N \to \mathbb{Q}$ for each agent $i \in N$ such that for any two coalitions $A, B \in \mathcal{N}^i$ we have $A \succeq_i B \iff \sum_{j \in A} v_i(j) \geq \sum_{j \in B} v_i(j)$.

In the friends-and-enemies encoding [4], each agent i specifies a set of friends F_i (and a set of enemies $E_i = N \setminus F_i$). Under the *friend-oriented* extension, i then prefers a coalition with more friends to a coalition with less friends and prefers the smaller coalition whenever the numbers of friends are the same. This extension can be represented via additively separable preferences where each agent assigns value n to each of her friends and value -1 to each of her enemies. This leads to the a utility of $v_i(C) = n|C \cap F_i| - |C \cap E_i|$ for any agent $i \in N$ and coalition $C \in \mathcal{N}^i$.

3   FEN-Hedonic Games

In this section, I summarize a work about *FEN-hedonic games* [6]. The idea of these games is that the preferences of the agents are represented via *weak rankings with double thresholds*. To provide such a ranking, each agent partitions the other agents into friends, neutral agents, and enemies; and specifies a weak ranking over the friends and enemies, respectively.

For example, consider a FEN-hedonic game with six agents $N = \{1, \ldots, 6\}$ where agent 1 has agents 2 and 3 as friends, preferring 2 over 3, is neutral towards agent 4, and has agents 5 and 6 as enemies while being indifferent between them. Then agent 1's preferences could be represented as $\unrhd_1^{+0-} = (2 \rhd_1 3 \mid \{4\} \mid 5 \sim_1 6)$.

We then used the *responsive extension* to lift these rankings to preferences over coalitions. Intuitively speaking, this extension leads to preferences where an agent prefers friends being added to her coalition, enemies being removed from her coalition, friends being replaced by better friends, and enemies being replaced by better enemies, while she does not care about neutral agents being added to her coalition. Note that the resulting preferences are not complete, e.g., the coalitions $\{1\}$ and $\{1, 2, 5\}$ are incomparable concerning agent 1's ranking given above. Therefore, when studying stability in FEN-hedonic games, we considered *possible* and *necessary* stability and provided several complexity bounds for the verification and existence problems of several common stability notions.

4 Local Fairness in Hedonic Games

In another paper [7], we introduced three notions of *local fairness* for hedonic games that are based on individual threshold coalitions. Based on these thresholds, it can be decided whether a given coalition is fair for an agent by comparing this coalition to the agent's threshold coalition. In particular, we define *min-max, grand-coalition*, and *max-min fairness*. For example, the *grand coalition threshold* of agent i is defined by $GC_i = N$ if i prefers N to $\{i\}$, and $GC_i = \{i\}$ otherwise. Hence, a coalition structure π is *grand coalition fair* for agent i if her coalition in π is at least as good as N and $\{i\}$.

After introducing the three local fairness notions, we study their relations to other commonly studied stability notions: While all three notions lie between perfectness and individual rationality, min-max fairness (the weakest of the three fairness notions) is also implied by Nash stability. Moreover, we determine the computational complexity of computing threshold coalitions and of deciding the existence of fair partitions in additively separable hedonic games. Finally, we also study the price of local fairness.

5 Altruism in Coalition Formation Games

Another line of research investigates aspects of *altruism in coalition formation* [8–11]. The idea of these games is that agents not only care about their own well-being but also about the well-being of their friends. The relations among the agents are given by a network of (mutual) friendship which is a simple graph where two agents are connected exactly if they are friends of each other. To obtain an agent's altruistic preference, we consider her own and her friends' friend-oriented valuations and distinguish three degrees of altruism: *selfish first, equal treatment*, and *altruistic treatment*. These degrees differ in how the friends' valuations are integrated into an agent's utility function. Also, the altruistic models differ in whether only the friends in an agent's current coalition or all her friends are considered. The works cited above study the various altruistic models with respect to axiomatic properties and present results concerning the complexity of the associated stability problems.

References

1. Aziz, H., Brandl, F., Brandt, F., Harrenstein, P., Olsen, M., Peters, D.: Fractional hedonic games. ACM Trans. Econ. Comput. **7**(2), 6:1–6:29, 6 (2019)
2. Banerjee, S., Konishi, H., Sönmez, T.: Core in a simple coalition formation game. Soc. Choice Welfare **18**(1), 135–153 (2001)
3. Bogomolnaia, A., Jackson, M.: The stability of hedonic coalition structures. Games Econom. Behav. **38**(2), 201–230 (2002)
4. Dimitrov, D., Borm, P., Hendrickx, R., Sung, S.: Simple priorities and core stability in hedonic games. Soc. Choice Welfare **26**(2), 421–433 (2006)
5. Drèze, J., Greenberg, J.: Hedonic coalitions: optimality and stability. Econometrica **48**(4), 987–1003 (1980)
6. Kerkmann, A., Lang, J., Rey, A., Rothe, J., Schadrack, H., Schend, L.: Hedonic games with ordinal preferences and thresholds. J. Artif. Intell. Res. **67**, 705–756 (2020)
7. Kerkmann, A., Nguyen, N., Rothe, J.: Local fairness in hedonic games via individual threshold coalitions. Theoret. Comput. Sci. **877**, 1–17 (2021)
8. Kerkmann, A., Rothe, J.: Altruism in coalition formation games. In: Proceedings of the 29th International Joint Conference on Artificial Intelligence, pp. 347–353 (2020)
9. Kerkmann, A., Rothe, J.: Four faces of altruistic hedonic games. In: Nonarchival Website Proceedings of the 8th International Workshop on Computational Social Choice (2021)
10. Kerkmann, A., Rothe, J.: Popularity and strict popularity in altruistic hedonic games and minimum-based altruistic hedonic games (extended abstract). In: Proceedings of the 21th International Conference on Autonomous Agents and Multiagent Systems, pp. 1657–1659. IFAAMAS (2022)
11. Nguyen, N., Rey, A., Rey, L., Rothe, J., Schend, L.: Altruistic hedonic games. In: Proceedings of the 15th International Conference on Autonomous Agents and Multiagent Systems, pp. 251–259. IFAAMAS (2016)
12. Olsen. M.: On defining and computing communities. In: Proceedings of the 18th Computing: The Australasian Theory Symposium, vol. 128, pp. 97–102 (2012)

Engineering Pro-social Values in Autonomous Agents – Collective and Individual Perspectives

Nieves Montes[(✉)]

Artificial Intelligence Research Institute (IIIA-CSIC), Barcelona, Spain
nmontes@iiia.csic.es

Abstract. This doctoral thesis is concerned with the engineering of values with an explicit *pro-social* (as opposed to a personal) focus. To do so, two approaches are explored, each dealing with a different level at which interactions are studied and engineered in a multi-agent system. The first, referred to as the *collective* approach, leverages *prescriptive norms* as the promoting mechanisms of pro-social values. The second, referred to as the *individual* approach, deals with the internal reasoning scheme of agents and endows them with the ability to reason about others. This results in empathetic autonomous agents, who are able to take the perspective of a peer and understand the motivations behind their behaviour.

Keywords: Values in AI · Normative MAS · Social AI

1 Introduction

The focus of this thesis is the development of complementary approaches to engineer moral values with an explicit *pro-social focus* in autonomous agents and multi-agent systems (MAS). This includes values that seek to promote the greater good of the community, such as universalism, benevolence, and tradition. To achieve this goal, two components are explored as potential avenues to embed such pro-social values: the *prescriptive norms* that apply to a MAS as a whole, and the *individual cognitive machinery* that is triggered in direct agent-to-agent interactions. I refer to the former as the *collective approach*, and to the latter as the *individual approach*.

2 The Collective Approach

The collective approach leverages societal level constructs, in particular *prescriptive norms*, to engineer pro-social values into societies of autonomous agents. In

---

This work is funded by the EU TAILOR project (H2020 #952215).

D. Baumeister and J. Rothe (Eds.): EUMAS 2022, LNAI 13442, pp. 431–434, 2022.
https://doi.org/10.1007/978-3-031-20614-6_26

this line of research, we have first proposed a general methodology for the automated synthesis of prescriptive norms based on their degree of alignment with respect to some value [7,8]. There, norms are tied to optimisable parameters. This enables us to use off-the-shelf meta-heuristic techniques to find the set of norms that most successfully promote some value. Moreover, we also provide an analytic toolkit to examine the resulting optimal normative systems: the Shapley values of individual norms (which quantify the contribution of a single norm towards the alignment), and the compatibility among values (which quantifies to what degree the aggressive promotion of value v_i may hinder the achievement of a different value v_j).

Despite the progress made in [7], it has one major limitation: its rigid representation of norms requires to define the space of normative systems from scratch every time the methodology is to be used in a new scenario. To tackle this limitation, we have defined the Action Situation Language (ASL) [5,6], inspired by Elinor Ostrom's Institutional Analysis and Development framework [10].

The ASL is a logical language, implemented in Prolog, that allows communities of agents to represent a wide variety of norms in a machine-readable and syntactically-friendly way (as `if-then-where` statements). The ASL is complemented by a game engine, which takes as input a rule configuration description and automatically builds its formal semantics as an extensive-form game. This model, then, can be analysed using standard game-theoretical tools.

Overall, ASL and its complementary game engine provide a complete connection from the set of norms and regulations in place to the outcomes most incentivised by them and, consequently, the values that are being promoted by these outcomes. After this computation has been performed, the community of agents can decide whether the most likely outcomes are aligned with respect to the values most important for them. Using ASL, we have been able to model several benchmark social scenarios from the policy analysis literature. For example, we have been able to demonstrate the eradication of violent outcomes once announcement rules are introduced in a fisher community.

The ASL follows in the footsteps of previous languages for the systematic definition of extensive-form games [4,11]. However, the main feature that sets ASL apart is the fact that ASL descriptions are meant to be *extensible*. Its full power is leveraged when the effects of adding, retracting, or changing the priorities of rules (which indicate the precedence of rule statements when conflicts arise) are assessed in an automated fashion.

3   The Individual Approach

In contrast to the collective approach, the individual approach focuses on the cognitive machinery that individual agents must possess in order to abide by socially-focused values. In particular, we are interested with the values of *cooperation* and *empathy*.

To embed empathetic attitudes into autonomous agents, we are developing an agent model that combines two techniques (or families of techniques): Theory of Mind and abductive reasoning. Theory of Mind (ToM) refers to the human cognitive ability to put oneself in the shoes of someone else and reason from their perspective. Within AI, ToM approaches are often referred to as *modelling others* and they are most prevalent in competitive domains [9]. Meanwhile, abduction refers to the logic reasoning scheme that derives, given an input observation, the best explanation for it.

The basic model consists of an observer agent i, operating with logic program T_i, and an acting agent j, operating with logic program T_j. The interaction begins when i is notified that j has selected some action a_j to perform. Then, the observer i engages in ToM by simulating the perspective that the actor j has of the state of the system at the point where they concluded that a_j was the action to perform. This means that i substitutes their program T_i by the program they estimate that j is working with, which we denote by $T_{i,j}$. In general, $T_{i,j}$ is incomplete, as i can, in general, only construct an approximation of the view that j has of the state of the system. Next, the observer i computes, using abductive reasoning, the explanations that would justify j selecting a_j. These explanations contain additional knowledge that the observer i incorporates back into their own knowledge base, to make use of them for later decision-making.

We have developed this model in Jason [2], an agent-oriented programming language. We provide a complete domain-independent implementation. Furthermore, we have tested it successfully for the cooperative card game of Hanabi. Hanabi is an award-winning card game where agents must collaborate to build stacks of cards with identical colour, however they can only see the cards of others and not their own. Players can share information with one another through hints, however doing so will spend one information token, which can later be recovered.

There are several features of Hanabi that make it an excellent benchmark to test techniques for modelling others in collaborative settings. First, Hanabi is a purely cooperative game where agents all share a common goal and need to coordinate as a team to achieve it. Second, agents have to deal with imperfect information, as they do not have access to their own cards. Therefore, there is additional information to be gained by deriving and incorporating the knowledge that peers were relying upon to select their actions. Third, information itself is collectively managed by the team as a collective resource. All of these features have led some researches to propose Hanabi as the next major challenge to be undertaken by the AI community [1], especially as interest on social and cooperative AI grows [3].

4   Conclusion

In summary, my research deals with approaches to embed socially-oriented values (i.e. those related to the greater good of the community) into autonomous agents. Two avenues are being explored to this end, which correspond to the two levels at which interactions in a multi-agent system take place: the collective level (through prescriptive norms that make up the institutional environment where are group of agents are embedded), and the individual level (that engineers the cognitive machinery of individual agents).

Work in cooperative aspects of AI is gathering increasingly more attention, as researchers realize that AI systems are deployed in communities including other software agents and humans, and should be designed with this realization in mind [3]. The multi-agent systems community is uniquely well-positioned as this shift in focus takes place. Therefore, I believe that work seeking to embed pro-social values and mutually beneficial behaviour is highly relevant, important, and timely.

Acknowledgements. The author would like to thank her supervisors, Dr Nardine Osman and Dr Carles Sierra, for their continued guidance and support.

References

1. Bard, N., et al.: The Hanabi challenge: a new frontier for AI research. Artif. Intell. **280**, 103216 (2020). https://doi.org/10.1016/j.artint.2019.103216
2. Bordini, R.H., Hübner, J.F., Wooldridge, M.: Programming Multi-Agent Systems in AgentSpeak using Jason. Wiley, Hoboken (2007)
3. Dafoe, A., Bachrach, Y., Hadfield, G., Horvitz, E., Larson, K., Graepel, T.: Cooperative AI: machines must learn to find common ground. Nature **593**(7857), 33–36 (2021). https://doi.org/10.1038/d41586-021-01170-0
4. Koller, D., Pfeffer, A.: Representations and solutions for game-theoretic problems. Artif. Intell. **94**(1–2), 167–215 (1997). https://doi.org/10.1016/S0004-3702(97)00023-4
5. Montes, N., Nardine, O., Sierra, C.: A computational model of Ostrom's institutional analysis and development framework. Artif. Intell. 103756 (2022). https://doi.org/10.1016/j.artint.2022.103756
6. Montes, N., Osman, N., Sierra, C.: Enabling game-theoretical analysis of social rules. In: Frontiers in Artificial Intelligence and Applications, vol. 339, pp. 90–99. IOS Press (2021). https://doi.org/10.3233/FAIA210120
7. Montes, N., Sierra, C.: Value-guided synthesis of parametric normative systems. In: Proceedings of the 20th International Conference on Autonomous Agents and Multiagent Systems, pp. 907–915. AAMAS 2021, International Foundation for Autonomous Agents and Multiagent Systems, Richland, SC (2021). https://dl.acm.org/doi/10.5555/3463952.3464060. (Best paper award finalist)
8. Montes, N., Sierra, C.: Synthesis and properties of optimally value-aligned normative systems. J. Artif. Intell Res. (2022)
9. Nashed, S., Zilberstein, S.: A survey of opponent modeling in adversarial domains. J. Artif. Intell. Res. **73**, 277–327 (2022). https://doi.org/10.1613/jair.1.12889
10. Ostrom, E.: Understanding Institutional Diversity. Princeton University Press (2005)
11. Schiffel, S., Thielscher, M.: Representing and reasoning about the rules of general games with imperfect information. J. Artif. Intell. Res. **49**, 171–206 (2014). https://doi.org/10.1613/jair.4115

Axiomatic and Algorithmic Study on Different Areas of Collective Decision Making

Tessa Seeger[(✉)][iD]

Heinrich -Heine -Universität Düsseldorf, Düsseldorf, Germany
`tessa.seeger@hhu.de`

Abstract. Our research investigates axiomatic and algorithmic properties in various areas of collective decision making. Studied areas include participatory budgeting, multiwinner voting and opinion diffusion. The goals of our research are to define or adapt appropriate frameworks in order to represent reality in the best possible way. Further, we want to adapt axioms or define new desirable properties and study, which procedures, rules or methods satisfy them in a given framework. In particular, we study budgeting methods from an irresolute point of view, strategic campaigns in apportionment elections and the impacts of social networks underlying collective decision processes.

Keywords: Participatory budgeting · Voting · Opinion diffusion

1 Research Areas

Our research focuses on collective decision making specifically in the area of *computational social choice*. Such areas include participatory budgeting, voting and opinion diffusion. Additionally, frameworks, axioms and other means from different research areas such as judgment aggregation may be used to make models more general, express relationships, represent reality more accurately and possibly achieve better results. In the following, the concepts are presented segregated from each other by giving an introduction, a way of formalization, impact, possibly already obtained results and future work to each of these research areas.

1.1 Participatory Budgeting

Participatory budgeting (short: PB) deals with the distribution of public funds in local communities or cities. It is a relatively new and emerging democratic model, that allows members of a community to participate directly in the allocation of a certain public budget. The agents can give their preferences on a set of items each of which has fixed costs. The items describe the possible projects for the municipality and can be a wide variety of options, e.g. renovating a school.

Specifically, in our work [2] we consider approval-based preferences, i.e. agents express their preferences by identifying the set of projects which they approve of.

D. Baumeister and J. Rothe (Eds.): EUMAS 2022, LNAI 13442, pp. 435–438, 2022.
https://doi.org/10.1007/978-3-031-20614-6_27

The remaining projects are considered rejected. Given a budget limit, the task is to select a set of items that will meet this bound while aiming to achieve the highest possible satisfaction of the agents. Building on Talmon and Faliszewski [11] we study axiomatic properties of introduced methods from an irresolute point of view, i.e. allowing more than one winning bundle. For a mathematical analysis, we formalize PB by adopting the framework introduced by Talmon and Faliszewski [11]. A budgeting scenario is defined as $E = (A, V, c, \ell)$ with a set of items $A = \{a_1, .., a_m\}$, a set of voters $V = \{v_1, ..., v_n\}$, a cost function $c : A \to \mathbb{N}$, that assigns an integer cost to every item, and a budget limit $\ell \in \mathbb{N}$. The ballots are defined as sets of approved items $A_v \subseteq A$ for every voter $v \in V$. B_v denotes the set of items in a budget $B \subseteq A$ approved by voter v $(B_v = A_v \cap B)$. We interpret the budgeting methods introduced in [11] as irresolute, i.e. given a budgeting scenario E, a method $\mathcal{R}_f^r$ returns a set of winning budgets $\mathcal{R}_f^r(E) \subseteq 2^A \setminus \{\emptyset\}$ by using a budgeting rule r with respect to a satisfaction function $f : 2^A \times 2^A \to \mathbb{N}$. Next to the satisfaction functions and rules defined in [11], we introduce an additional type of rules, specifically *hybrid greedy rules*. We define irresoluteness in greedy, i.e. iteratively designed, rules by making every bundle, that can result from breaking ties in each iteration, a winning one. In our work [2] we show that irrespective of the used tie-breaking two of the considered methods are equivalent. Thus, also in the framework of Talmon and Faliszewski [11] those budgeting methods coincide. When analysing the axiomatic properties of the irresolute variants, we found that our results are consistent with the results in [11] for resolute budgeting methods. Unfortunately, axiomatic results for the additional budgeting methods, composed of the newly introduced rules, are poor. Nevertheless, some negative results stem from the fact that tie-breaking is undetermined, hence, they could be addressed by introducing reasonable mechanisms for tie-breaking.

For future work, we want to consider other satisfaction functions, rules and axioms to identify procedures with the best possible properties. Additionally, we want to find methods to allow an easy application of those theoretical results to real-world problems.

1.2 Voting

Voting is a field of research whose applications we encounter everywhere. We find voting in social contexts, such as political elections or even in groups of friends, but also in multiagent systems in the field of artificial intelligence. An election is defined as a pair (C, V) with a set of candidates $C = \{c_1, ..., c_m\}$ and a list of voters $V = \{v_1, ..., v_n\}$ giving preferences over C. An election system $\mathcal{E}$ takes an election (C, V) as input and returns a single candidate (*single-winner rules*) or a set of candidates (*multiwinner rules*) as winners. [3] Since voting is enormously widespread, running strategic campaigns on elections, i.e. attempting to influence the outcome, is a problem, that has to be addressed in research.

One type of *multiwinner elections* are *apportionment elections*, which are used for parliamentary elections in many countries such as Spain, Germany, Austria, Switzerland and Israel. In apportionment elections, there is a fixed number of seats in the parliament, which is to be distributed among the parties according to the vote distribution. Bredereck et al. [4] study constructive bribery in apportionment elections in a single-district and multi-district case. Formally, there is a set of *parties* $\mathcal{P} = \{P_1, ..., P_m\}$ and a *vote allocation* $\hat{p} = (p_1, ..., p_m) \in \mathbb{N}^m$. A *seat allocation* $\hat{a} = (a_1, ..., a_m)$ is determined by an *apportionment method* $\mathcal{R} : \mathbb{N}^m \rightarrow \mathbb{N}^m$, which distributes how many seats each party P_i is assigned given a vote allocation $\hat{p}$. Since Bredereck et al. [4] focus on constructive bribery, the study of additional forms of strategic campaigns in apportionment elections remains open and is part of our future research.

1.3   Opinion Diffusion

Decisions, preferences and judgments of agents are not always static. Especially, if the decision-making entities are connected via a (social) network, voters may be influenced by other voters' opinions and in turn influence other voters themselves. This results in a dynamic process of expressions of opinions and decision making. The research area of *opinion diffusion* deals with the study of such models and related issues, formalizing the evolution of opinion distribution and conditions, under which opinions converge in a social network. [8] Opinion diffusion is mainly driven by social influence, i.e. opinion formation based on opinion expressions of other members of society (see e.g. [1,6]). A major motivation for studying opinion diffusion is the impact that social networks have on social processes such as collective decision making, since in a society, decisions are usually not made without observing and considering other agents' opinions. Hence, social networks have an enormous influence on individual opinions and decisions. Known examples include phenomena such as polarization, majority illusion and the echo chamber effect (see [5,7,9]) for more information on these phenomena). Depending on what neighbouring and thus influential agents do within the social network, agents are exposed to different impressions that contribute to opinion formation and expression. However, social networks and related processes not only affect individual opinions but also influence the next step, i.e. when a collective decision is to be made on a global level based on individual opinions.

Formally, such an *influence network* can be defined as a directed graph $G = (\mathcal{N}, E)$, where $\mathcal{N} = \{1, ..., n\}$ is a set of agents and there is an edge $(i, j) \in E$ if and only if agent i influences agent j. Loops are allowed, showing that agent i also takes her own opinion into account. [8] The iterative process of opinion diffusion forms by agents observing the opinions of their neighbours and using an aggregation procedure to update their individual opinions.

The field of opinion diffusion is of great relevance due to its enormously broad applicability. Among other things, the combination of opinion diffusion with other research areas such as voting and judgment aggregation is of great interest to investigate the effects of social networks on known problems.

2   Further Future Work

A big area of interest for future work is the combination of different fields of computational social choice and graph theory. Similar research has for example been done by Rey et al. [10] and Grandi et al. [8]. Rey et al. [10] designed PB methods grounded in judgment aggregation, while Grandi et al. [8] defined a model for opinion diffusion by combining social network analysis with judgment aggregation in order to create the possibility of expressing correlations and dependencies between individual opinions on multiple connected topics. Firstly, naturally combining different research areas, e.g. through interdisciplinary work, can create new perspectives and insights on complex topics and problems. More specifically, a combination can be used to model scenarios, processes, and situations more accurately and realistically. Furthermore, using different, expressive frameworks like judgment aggregation or even designing new ones can contribute to a better analysis of the underlying characteristics of processes modelled in computational social choice. For example, desirable properties can be defined and studied. Also, existing methods, rules and procedures can be adapted, used in another context or new ones can be designed, possibly improving axiomatic and algorithmic properties. In the best case, this leads to higher satisfaction and a more accurate representation among the agents as well as better transparency.

References

1. Asch, S.E.: Studies of independence and conformity: I. A minority of one against a unanimous majority. Psychol. Monogr. Gen. Appl. **70**(9), 1 (1956)
2. Baumeister, D., Boes, L., Seeger, T.: Irresolute approval-based budgeting. In: Proceedings of the 19th International Conference on Autonomous Agents and Multi-Agent Systems, pp. 1774–1776 (2020)
3. Baumeister, D., Rothe, J.: Preference aggregation by voting. In: Rothe, J. (ed.) Economics and Computation. STBE, pp. 197–325. Springer, Heidelberg (2016). https://doi.org/10.1007/978-3-662-47904-9_4
4. Bredereck, R., Faliszewski, P., Furdyna, M., Kaczmarczyk, A., Lackner, M.: Strategic campaign management in apportionment elections. In: Proceedings of the Twenty-Ninth International Conference on International Joint Conferences on Artificial Intelligence, pp. 103–109 (2021)
5. Cota, W., Ferreira, S.C., Pastor-Satorras, R., Starnini, M.: Quantifying echo chamber effects in information spreading over political communication networks. EPJ Data Sci. **8**(1), 1–13 (2019)
6. Festinger, L.: Informal social communication. Psychol. Rev. **57**(5), 271 (1950)
7. Grandi, U.: Social choice and social networks. In: Endriss, U. (ed.) Trends in Computational Social Choice, pp. 169–184. AI Access (2017)
8. Grandi, U., Lorini, E., Perrussel, L.: Propositional opinion diffusion (2015)
9. Kleiner, T.M.: Public opinion polarisation and protest behaviour. Eur. J. Polit. Res. **57**(4), 941–962 (2018)
10. Rey, S., Endriss, U., de Haan, R.: Designing participatory budgeting mechanisms grounded in judgment aggregation. In: Proceedings of the International Conference on Principles of Knowledge Representation and Reasoning, vol. 17, pp. 692–702 (2020)
11. Talmon, N., Faliszewski, P.: A framework for approval-based budgeting methods. In: Proceedings of the AAAI Conference on Artificial Intelligence, vol. 33, pp. 2181–2188 (2019)

Participatory Budgeting: Fairness and Welfare Maximization

Gogulapati Sreedurga[(✉)]

Indian Institute of Science, Bengaluru, India
gogulapatis@iisc.ac.in

Abstract. Participatory Budgeting (PB) is a democratic paradigm used to allocate a divisible resource (budget) to multiple alternatives (projects). PB is broadly classified into indivisible PB and divisible PB. In indivisible PB, each project is atomic and has a cost. A project must receive an amount equal to its cost or none at all. In divisible PB, projects are fractionally implementable and any amount can be allocated to a project. Our work looks at both these models and studies PB rules that guarantee fairness or maximize the welfare of the voters in different frameworks.

Keywords: Participatory Budgeting · Fairness · Welfare Maximization

1 Introduction

Participatory Budgeting (PB) is the process of dividing a budget among a set of alternatives, also referred to as projects. The problem is to aggregate the preferences of agents (or voters) and propose a desirable budget allocation.

Divisible and Indivisible PB. In divisible PB, projects are fractionally implementable and any amount can be allocated to each project. Hence, it is analogous to random single-winner voting where each entry in the outcome probability distribution is interpreted as the fraction of budget allocated to that project. In indivisible PB, each project is atomic and has an associated cost. If selected, a project must be allocated its entire cost. This model can be viewed as a generalization of a multi-winner voting where the cardinality constraint is replaced by the knapsack constraint. If all the projects are of unit cost and the budget is k, indivisible PB reduces to multi-winner voting.

Approval Votes and Rankings. As in any social choice setting, approval votes and rankings are natural methods of preference elicitation for PB due to their real-world applicability. In approval votes, every voter reports a subset of projects she likes. Rankings are of mainly two kinds: strict and weak. Weak rankings allow voters to have ties between projects, while strict rankings do not.

Our results are primarily in three directions: (i) indivisible PB with approval votes [15] (ii) indivisible PB with weak rankings [14] and (iii) divisible PB with single-peaked rankings (a special case of strict rankings) [16]. Our work on indivisible PB with approval votes looks at egalitarian welfare (maximizing the utility of worse-off voter), the work on divisible PB with strict rankings looks at

D. Baumeister and J. Rothe (Eds.): EUMAS 2022, LNAI 13442, pp. 439–443, 2022.
https://doi.org/10.1007/978-3-031-20614-6_28

fairness, while the work on indivisible PB with weak rankings looks at fairness as well as utilitarian welfare (maximizing the sum of utilities of all the voters).

2   Divisible PB

In the divisible PB literature, several individual fairness notions have been studied for approval votes [2,7], strict rankings [1] and weak rankings [5,6]. Also, group-fairness has been looked at [2,5,8]. However, all the group fairness notions, when applied to strict rankings, reduce to trivial random dictatorship rule, which could lead to less desirable outcomes in many situations [16]. Thus, imposing a fairness constraint on every subset of voters is a strong and avoidable requirement. Often, in the real-world, we can find a natural partition of voters into groups based on factors such as gender, race, economic status, and location. It will be sensible and adequate to guarantee fairness, both within and across these existing groups. Hence, in our work [16], we assume a natural partition of voters into groups. Each group q has an associated function ψ_q that selects some (κ_q) alternatives to represent the preferences of voters in the group. Every group also has a quota, η_q, which is a lower bound on the budget that its representatives together deserve. The social planner gets to choose three parameters: (1) the number of representatives to be selected for each group; (2) a method of selecting them; and (3) the quota of each group. We propose weak and strong fairness notions to ensure that representatives of each group receive at least the budget the group is entitled to. We completely characterize divisible PB rules that are group-fair in this sense under the single-peaked domain.

3   Indivisible PB

3.1   Approval Votes

For divisible PB with approval votes, several goals including the optimization of utilitarian welfare and egalitarian welfare have been studied in the literature. In addition to them, several fairness notions have been proposed and studied in depth. On the other hand, most work in indivisible PB with approval votes is focused on utilitarian welfare [10,11,17] or the fairness notion of proportionality [3,4,9,13] which ensures that every cohesive group of voters are given a right on the fraction of budget proportional to the group size. However, surprisingly, the egalitarian welfare remained to be studied in indivisible PB with approval votes, barring a case-study by Laruelle [12] that experimentally evaluates a sub-optimal greedy algorithm. Egalitarian objective is important for PB, especially in the situations where the designer wants to cater to all the voters. For example, if the government wants to construct schools, it would want to cover as many counties as possible to promote universal literacy instead of building multiple schools in populous counties. This motivates us to introduce and study an egalitarian PB rule, *maxmin participatory budgeting (MPB)* [15].

Throughout this section, we use function c to output the cost of a set of projects and b to denote the budget. We define the utility of a voter i from a set S, $u_i(S)$, as the cost of projects included in S that are approved by i. MPB rule outputs all the feasible subsets of projects that maximizes the utility of the voter with least utility. That is, it outputs all S such that $S \in arg\,max_{S:c(S)\leq b}\min_i u_i(S)$. We prove that MPB is strongly NP-Hard. We then look at its parameterized tractability considering parameters like the number of projects and the number of distinct approval votes. We also study a new parameter scalable limit that refers to cost of the most expensive project after we scale down the budget and all the costs to as low values as possible. We propose a greedy approximation algorithm for MPB and empirically show its optimal performance. Finally, we axiomatically analyse MPB rule and in the process, introduce two new axioms respectively to capture exhaustiveness of the outcome and the fairness notion of diversity.

3.2   Rankings

The study of indivisible PB with rankings, unlike divisible PB, is very sparse. An example in this direction is the paper by Aziz and Lee [3] which introduced proportionality axioms for this setting. Rather surprisingly, there is, as yet, no known class of indivisible PB rules with rankings that has been studied. We fill this gap by proposing three major classes of PB rules: (1) Greedy-truncation rules; (2) Cost-worthy rules; and (3) Need-based rules [14]. We study the computational and axiomatic aspects of each of these classes of rules in depth.

Utilitarian Welfare. Unlike indivisible PB with approval votes, the utility notion for PB with rankings is not straight-forward, because of the additional attribute 'rank' for each project w.r.t. each voter. Our first two classes of rules, greedy-truncation rules and cost-worthy rules, come under a family of rules, which we call *layered approval votes*. They use a *layer* which carefully exploits the weak rankings of the voters to deduce critical information and uses this information to further translate the weak rankings into approval votes. After this translation, we apply the well studied utility notions in the approval-based PB literature [17] to the resultant instance with approval votes and determine an outcome that maximizes the utilitarian welfare.

To give an intuition into the functioning of a layer, we explain the information captured and used by the layers in both our classes of rules. The layer in greedy-truncation rules captures, for each voter, all the projects present in her most desired feasible outcomes. This can be viewed as an extension of knapsack voting [11] for weak rankings and is motivated by the fact that knapsack voting does not fare well in the presence of ties between the projects [14]. The idea of the layer in the cost-worthy rules is to capture whether or not a project is worth its cost based on the *degree of preference* voters have for it. That is, these rules help to express the desire for less expensive projects in many PB contexts.

Fairness. Our third class of rules, need-based rules, enable the key issue of fairness to be captured in PB. While the existing fairness notions in indivisible PB literature mostly deal with proportionality [3,4,9,13], fairness in divisible PB is based on guarantees for each voter at individual level (or in other words, *need-based*). In many real-world scenarios, a voter will be happy if a certain minimum fraction of the budget is spent on projects favorable to her. This is captured in divisible PB by *fair share* [1,2,5-7]. Need-based rules capture such a requirement for indivisible PB using a parameter $\eta \in (0, b]$, called *need*, that denotes the amount needed to make a voter happy.

4   Summary

The broad spectrum of the PB literature can be classified on two axes: (i) divisible PB and indivisible PB; (ii) preference elicitation method (e.g., approval votes and rankings). While divisible PB with approval votes is well studied both in terms of welfare and fairness, indivisible PB with approval votes lacks the study of egalitarian welfare and fairness. If we look at the PB with rankings, the study of group-fairness for divisible PB is in a primitive stage, whereas a systematic framework for indivisible PB is almost non-existent. We close all these gaps with our works. Notably, the study of fairness in PB at large is still in its inception. There is a lot more to achieve, especially taking the relations between the projects and voters into account. We preserve such problems for future work.

References

1. Airiau, S., Aziz, H., Caragiannis, I., Kruger, J., Lang, J., Peters, D.: Portioning using ordinal preferences: fairness and efficiency. In: IJCAI 2019, pp. 11–17 (2019)
2. Aziz, H., Bogomolnaia, A., Moulin, H.: Fair mixing: the case of dichotomous preferences. In: Proceedings of the 2019 ACM Conference on Economics and Computation, pp. 753–781 (2019)
3. Aziz, H., Lee, B.E.: Proportionally representative participatory budgeting with ordinal preferences. In: AAAI, vol. 35, no. 6, pp. 5110–5118 (2021)
4. Aziz, H., Lee, B.E., Talmon, N.: Proportionally representative participatory budgeting: axioms and algorithms. In: AAMAS, pp. 23–31 (2018)
5. Aziz, H., Luo, P., Rizkallah, C.: Rank maximal equal contribution: a probabilistic social choice function. In: AAAI 2018, pp. 910–916 (2018)
6. Aziz, H., Stursberg, P.: A generalization of probabilistic serial to randomized social choice. In: AAAI 2014, pp. 559–565 (2014)
7. Bogomolnaia, A., Moulin, H., Stong, R.: Collective choice under dichotomous preferences. J. Econ. Theory **122**(2), 165–184 (2005)
8. Fain, B., Goel, A., Munagala, K.: The core of the participatory budgeting problem. In: Cai, Y., Vetta, A. (eds.) WINE 2016. LNCS, vol. 10123, pp. 384–399. Springer, Heidelberg (2016). https://doi.org/10.1007/978-3-662-54110-4_27
9. Fairstein, R., Meir, R., Gal, K.: Proportional participatory budgeting with substitute projects. arXiv preprint arXiv:2106.05360 (2021)
10. Freeman, R., Pennock, D.M., Peters, D., Vaughan, J.W.: Truthful aggregation of budget proposals. J. Econ. Theory **193**, 105234 (2021)
11. Goel, A., Krishnaswamy, A.K., Sakshuwong, S., Aitamurto, T.: Knapsack voting for participatory budgeting. ACM TEAC **7**(2), 1–27 (2019)

12. Laruelle, A.: Voting to select projects in participatory budgeting. Eur. J. Oper. Res. **288**(2), 598–604 (2021)
13. Pierczyński, G., Skowron, P., Peters, D.: Proportional participatory budgeting with additive utilities. In: Advances in Neural Information Processing Systems, vol. 34 (2021)
14. Sreedurga, G., Narahari, Y.: Indivisible participatory budgeting under weak rankings. arXiv preprint arXiv:2207.07981 (2022)
15. Sreedurga, G., Ratan Bhardwaj, M., Narahari, Y.: Maxmin participatory budgeting. arXiv preprint arXiv:2204.13923 (2022)
16. Sreedurga, G., Sadhukhan, S., Roy, S., Narahari, Y.: Characterization of group-fair social choice rules under single-peaked preferences. arXiv preprint arXiv:2207.07984 (2022)
17. Talmon, N., Faliszewski, P.: A framework for approval-based budgeting methods. In: AAAI, vol. 33, pp. 2181–2188 (2019)

Human Consideration in Analysis and Algorithms for Mechanism Design

Sharadhi Alape Suryanarayana$^{(\boxtimes)}$ [iD]

Bar-Ilan University, Ramat-Gan, Israel
sharadhi.as@gmail.com

Abstract. Mechanism Design, a domain characterized by economically motivated agents, is an important tool in computer science and economics. Despite being extremely pervasive and applied across diverse settings, there is a renewed interest in incorporating human factors within the design and implementation of classic mechanisms. In this thesis, we cater to the aforementioned interest wherein we align the development and analysis of mechanisms with human consideration. We focus on two problems, Information Design in Affiliate Marketing and Explainability in Mechanism Design, both of which are inspired by human interactions with algorithmic systems. The research is based on a thorough literature review, theoretical analysis, and experimental validation of the solutions proposed. The methods proposed are also proven to be economically beneficial, in terms of increased profits and reduced costs, thus abiding by another key aspect of mechanism design.

Keywords: Mechanism design · Human factors · Information design · Explainability

1 Introduction

Mechanism Design is a classic yet increasingly relevant domain with a significant impact on areas such as school choice programs and kidney exchange [4]. Characterized by economically-motivated and selfish agents that are privy to some private information such as preferences, costs, and utility, mechanism design in its general approach is tasked with collecting, processing, and aggregating the private information of said agents in order to reach a desirable social outcome [2].

Due to its applications in presumably mundane yet highly consequential day-to-day applications such as elections, auctions, scheduling, and resource allocation, there is an omnipresent need for mechanism design to be able to adapt to the evolving dynamics to remain practical. Notable examples of such improved models can be found in the context of medical residency matching mechanism [5] and refugee resettlement algorithms [1].

In this thesis, we focus on the challenges induced by human interaction with algorithmic systems and address them accordingly. We consider the following two domains which bring with them unique complexities due to the sophisticated nature of the present world.

D. Baumeister and J. Rothe (Eds.): EUMAS 2022, LNAI 13442, pp. 444–447, 2022.
https://doi.org/10.1007/978-3-031-20614-6_29

1. *Information Design in Affiliate Marketing*: Modern-day marketing mechanisms carried out over social networks bring with them complexities in the form of the interconnectedness of the networks and the costs involved. This calls for developing new models to represent the agents and their strategies and leveraging the role of information to devise better reward mechanisms.
2. *Explainability in Mechanism Design*: With the increase in the usage of AI-based decision-making, there is an increased focus on explaining the decision to the end user. In this thesis, we focus exclusively on Explainability in Mechanism Design.

The research carried out uses varied domains such as game theory, social choice theory, human factors for the development of the solutions and, both theoretical as well as experimental methods to establish the superiority of the solutions. The study on *Affiliate Marketing* models the mechanism game-theoretically with two types of agents, the affiliate marketing platform and the affiliates. The issues revealed as the analysis progressed were subsequently addressed. For the *Explainability Studies*, a thorough survey, and the development of two explanation-generation methods were carried out. The explanation-generation methods were tested using an interactive experiment with human participants. The investigation of both domains has resulted in cost-efficient solutions with the solutions for Affiliate Marketing leading to higher profits while the algorithm for generating explanations leads to lower costs.

2 Information Design in Affiliate Marketing

Affiliate Marketing is a highly lucrative yet under-researched marketing strategy used by content creators in order to monetize their content and generate revenue. Here, said content creators, called partners henceforth, promote a product or service to their audience (followers) and are remunerated for their efforts in the form of a set commission. The fact that the followers can be connected to multiple partners, a common feature in present-day social media, calls for a nuanced approach both in terms of the partner's decision to promote a product and the commission structure are offered. This was modeled as a mechanism with two distinct types of agents, the platform that advertises the deal to the partners and the partners. The key decision for the platform is to decide on the commission to be offered while the partners need to decide on whether or not to promote the product given the expenses they incur, the social network of followers, and their earnings from commissions. The profit of the platform depends on the specific equilibrium reached by the partners.

The game-theoretical analysis revealed that affiliate marketing, as it is done today, suffers from a multi-equilibrium problem. Hence, there is no way for the platform to determine the profit-maximizing commission to be offered to the partners. To overcome this, a revised mechanism called Sequential Mechanism was proposed. Here, to every partner that considers promoting the product, the number of partners that have already been acquainted with the opportunity is revealed. Even though the Sequential Mechanism helps overcome the multi-equilibrium problem, it does not offer any significant advantage in terms of profit as it is weakly dominated by the legacy mechanism. The Sequential mechanism was then augmented with a dynamic commission structure which not only solved the multi-equilibrium problem but also resulted in the highest possible profit for the platform. Our full results are reported in Suryanarayana et al. [6,7].

3   Explainability in Mechanism Design

Solutions in mechanism design settings are obtained by aggregating the preferences, often conflicting, of several agents in a socially acceptable manner which might end up in the solution being undesired by a few of them. For example, in an election the candidate that is the first preference of a voter might not win, in a rent division setting a housemate may not get her most preferred room and in task allocation, a participant might not be allotted the tasks she is very skilled in. Thus explanations in mechanism design need to focus on subtly reducing the dissatisfaction of the agents by highlighting the social merits of the decision. The research on Explainability in Mechanism Design is split into two parts as explained below.

3.1   Recent Advances and the Road Ahead

In the first part, we carried out a survey on said topic. The survey is split into three parts. In the first part, a comparative analysis between XAI and Explainable Mechanism Design was carried out with respect to the taxonomy, the goal of explanations and the recipient of explanations. In the second part, the existing literature was reviewed in terms of the concepts used for generating explanations as well as evaluating explanations. Both of these reviews had a theoretical and behavioral component to them.

In the third section, we also shed light on the unique challenges one may face while testing the explanation-generation methods. The motivation for this primarily comes from the fact that the receiver of explanations is an imperfect and in some cases, irrational human being. Hence, adequate care needs to be taken to devise explanations that consider these human factors [3]. In order to overcome the challenges, we have also proposed several workarounds with inspiration from XAI, behavioral studies, and Human-Computer Interaction. Our full results are reported in Suryanarayana et al. [8].

3.2   Justifying Social-Choice Mechanism Outcome for Improving Participant Satisfaction

In the next part, we designed two explanation-generation methods, crowdsourced and feature-based. A two-step approach was proposed to obtain crowdsourced explanations of the highest quality. For the feature-based explanations, theoretical properties in mechanism design literature were converted into possible explanations by quantifying them into features, and an algorithm to pick the best among them was developed.

These explanation-generation methods were tested on the popular domain, ranked-choice voting, which was implemented as an election to determine the best cereal in a distant country. A web-based application was developed to mimic the setting of ranked-choice voting in a synthetic experiment. This experiment incorporated human factors such as reciprocity bias and motivation to read explanations that would elicit organic responses from human participants. The results of the experiment, carried out on Amazon Mechanical Turk, revealed that explanations were indeed effective in improving user satisfaction and acceptance. Also, the feature-based explanations were on par with and in some cases even better than the crowdsourced explanations, thus eliminating the need to keep humans in the loop. Our full results are reported in Suryanarayana et al. [9].

Acknowledgments. Sharadhi Alape Suryanarayana was supported by the President's Scholarship (Milgat Nasi) of Bar-Ilan University to carry out the above research as a part of her doctoral program (PhD).

References

1. Ahani, N., Gölz, P., Procaccia, A.D., Teytelboym, A., Trapp, A.C.: Dynamic placement in refugee resettlement. arXiv preprint arXiv:2105.14388 (2021)
2. Lavi, R.: Mechanism design. Complex Social and Behavioral Systems: Game Theory and Agent-Based Models, pp. 317–333 (2020)
3. Miller, T.: Explanation in artificial intelligence: insights from the social sciences. Artif. Intell. **267**, 1–38 (2019)
4. Papai, S.: On the future of economic design-the personal ruminations of a matching theorist. In: The Future of Economic Design, pp. 3–8. Springer (2019)
5. Roth, A.E., Peranson, E.: The redesign of the matching market for American physicians: some engineering aspects of economic design. Am. Econ. Rev. **89**(4), 748–780 (1999)
6. Suryanarayana, S.A., Sarne, D., Kraus, S.: Information disclosure and partner management in affiliate marketing. In: DAI, pp. 1–8 (2019)
7. Suryanarayana, S.A., Sarne, D., Kraus, S.: Information design in affiliate marketing. Auton. Agent. Multi-Agent Syst. **35**(2), 1–28 (2021)
8. Suryanarayana, S.A., Sarne, D., Kraus, S.: Explainability in mechanism design: recent advances and the road ahead. In: EUMAS (2022). (to appear)
9. Suryanarayana, S.A., Sarne, D., Kraus, S.: Justifying social-choice mechanism outcome for improving participant satisfaction. In: AAMAS, pp. 1246–1255 (2022)

Author Index

A. Rodríguez-Aguilar, Juan   152
Ade, Leyla   3
Adiga, Abhijin   403
Akbar, Awais   423
Albrecht, Stefano V.   275
Ancona, Davide   22
Assefa, Samuel   41
Aviv, Aviram   41

Berceanu, Cristian   60
Bielous, Gili   79
Borrajo, Daniel   41

Carlucho, Ignacio   275
Chalkiadakis, Georgios   171
Colley, Rachael   96
Criado, Natalia   383

Endriss, Ulle   330

Faliszewski, Piotr   116, 134
Ferrando, Angelo   22
Fornara, Nicoletta   348
Fosong, Elliot   275

Gawron, Grzegorz   116, 134
Georgara, Athina   152
Geronymakis, Pavlos   171
Grandi, Umberto   96

Hetland, Magnus Lie   188
Hummel, Halvard   188

Ianovski, Egor   207

Jain, Pallavi   221

Kerkmann, Anna Maria   427
Kraus, Sarit   41, 364, 403
Kuka, Valeriia   207
Kusek, Bartosz   116

Lisowski, Grzegorz   239

Macke, William   275
Mascardi, Viviana   22
Meir, Reshef   79, 257
Mirsky, Reuth   275
Modgil, Sanjay   383
Montes, Nieves   294, 431
Motamed, Nima   330
Mustapha, Toby   41

Novaro, Arianna   3

Oshrat, Yaniv   41
Osman, Nardine   294

Papageorgiou, Markos   171
Parizi, Mostafa Mohajeri   312
Patrascu, Monica   60

Rahman, Arrasy   275
Ravi, S. S.   403
Rey, Simon   330
Roshankish, Soheil   348

Sarne, David   364
Seeger, Tessa   435
Shahaf, Gal   257
Shapiro, Ehud   257
Sierra, Carles   152, 294
Sileno, Giovanni   312
Soeteman, Arie   330
Sornat, Krzysztof   221
Sreedurga, Gogulapati   439
Sridharan, Mohan   275
Stone, Peter   275
Such, Jose M.   383
Suryanarayana, Sharadhi Alape   364, 444
Szabo, Jazon   383

Talmon, Nimrod   221, 257
Teplova, Daria   207
Trabelsi, Yohai   403
Troullinos, Dimitrios   171

van Binsbergen, L. Thomas   312
van Engers, Tom   312
Veloso, Manuela   41

Printed in the United States
by Baker & Taylor Publisher Services